SIR ROBERT COTTON
AS COLLECTOR

*Essays on an Early Stuart Courtier
and his Legacy*

Sir Robert Cotton, by Cornelius Janssen. *Reproduced by kind permission of the Rt. Hon. Lord Clinton, D.L., Devon*

SIR ROBERT COTTON AS COLLECTOR

Essays on an Early Stuart Courtier and his Legacy

Edited by

C. J. WRIGHT

THE BRITISH LIBRARY
1997

© 1997 THE BRITISH LIBRARY BOARD
ISBN 0 7123 0358 8
PUBLISHED BY THE BRITISH LIBRARY
GREAT RUSSELL STREET
LONDON WC1B 3DG

SET IN MONOPHOTO EHRHARDT
PRINTED IN GREAT BRITAIN BY
THE UNIVERSITY PRESS, CAMBRIDGE

CONTENTS

EDITOR'S FOREWORD

The Library of Sir Robert Cotton (1571–1631) is arguably the most important collection of manuscripts ever assembled in Britain by a private individual. Amongst its many treasures are the Lindisfarne Gospels, two of the contemporary exemplifications of Magna Carta and the only surviving manuscript of 'Beowulf'. Early on in his career, Cotton had advocated the foundation of a national library of which his collection would form a part and, however rapacious he might have been in his pursuit of manuscripts, he was always generous in the loans he made to other scholars. His son and grandson, Sir Thomas and Sir John, as far as the troubles of the times allowed, maintained this tradition of scholarly accessibility and at the beginning of the eighteenth century Sir John Cotton bequeathed the collection to the nation.

Despite the fame and universally acknowledged importance of his manuscripts, Sir Robert Cotton himself has remained until lately a curiously neglected figure. In this he resembles that other great collector and national benefactor, Sir Hans Sloane. However, in recent decades, interest both in their lives and the manner in which they assembled their collections has revived, and in the case of Cotton, at least, it has become clear that the manner in which he treated his manuscripts and the vicissitudes they have suffered since his death are of the greatest relevance to the way modern scholars should approach them.

The object of this book is threefold. It attempts to touch on as many facets of Cotton's life as possible, setting his career as an antiquary, for example, in the wider context of his activities as a statesman and country landowner. It also aims to draw attention to the multifarious nature of his acquisitions. In his lifetime he was famous not only for his manuscripts but also for his coins and Roman inscriptions. Finally, it seeks to cast a penetrating new light on the subsequent fates of his various collections.

Versions of eight of the papers in this present volume, those by Backhouse, Carley, Howarth, Manning, Parry, Teviotdale, Tite ('Lost or stolen or strayed') and Van Houts, were first published in Volume XVIII of the *British Library Journal* (1992), which was devoted to Sir Robert Cotton. Colin Tite's article, 'A Catalogue of Sir Robert Cotton's printed books?', had already appeared in Volume XVII (1991). The eight other papers have been written especially for this volume. Gay van der Meer's article has also appeared in *Jaarboek voor Munt- en Penningkunde*, LXXXI (1994). The remainder are published here for the first time.

C. J. Wright

NOTES ON CONTRIBUTORS

JANET BACKHOUSE: Curator, Department of Manuscripts, British Library.

JAMES P. CARLEY: Professor, Department of English, York University, Toronto.

GLENYS DAVIES: Senior Lecturer, Department of Classics, University of Edinburgh.

ELIZABETH HALLAM: author of books and articles on Domesday Book and the history of record keeping; Director of Public Services, Public Record Office.

DAVID HOWARTH: Senior Lecturer, Department of Fine Art, University of Edinburgh.

HILTON KELLIHER: Curator, Department of Manuscripts, British Library.

DAVID MCKITTERICK: Librarian and Fellow of Trinity College, Cambridge.

ROGER B. MANNING: Professor, Department of History, Cleveland State University.

GRAHAM PARRY: Professor of English, University of York.

ANDREW PRESCOTT: Curator, Department of Manuscripts, British Library.

NIGEL RAMSAY: Research Officer, Cotton Manuscripts Trust, British Library.

KEVIN SHARPE: Professor of Early Modern History, School of Research, University of Southampton.

E. C. TEVIOTDALE: Assistant Curator, Department of Manuscripts, J. Paul Getty Museum, Los Angeles.

COLIN G. C. TITE: historian; author of *The Manuscript Library of Sir Robert Cotton*, The Panizzi Lectures 1993 (London, 1994).

GAY VAN DER MEER: Former Curator of Medals, Rijksmuseum Het Koninklijk Penningkabinet, Leiden.

ELISABETH M. C. VAN HOUTS: Fellow of Newnham College, Cambridge.

INTRODUCTION:

REWRITING SIR ROBERT COTTON

KEVIN SHARPE

WHEN I first encountered him over twenty years ago, Sir Robert Cotton proved as useful to me as he had to many of his contemporaries. I was interested in exploring the interrelationship of scholarship and politics in early modern England, and in particular in investigating how study of the past and political experience shaped each other in an age that venerated custom and antiquity. For the twentieth-century historian, as for the Jacobean and Caroline antiquary and politician, all roads led to Sir Robert Cotton's library, the unique repository of precedents used by scholars, English and continental, and, as much, by men of affairs. Cotton and his library became for me the focus of a study which was intended to illuminate what were then (and in some senses remain) dark corners of the history of early Stuart England: historical scholarship and its relationship to continental humanism, circles of patronage, court and parliamentary politics, attitudes and ideological tensions and differences.[1]

Some reviewers, quite justifiably, commented that as a consequence Cotton himself remained in the shadows and criticized my study for neglecting key aspects of Sir Robert's life or for eschewing a more straightforward biographical approach.[2] Some (curiously in one or two cases the same reviewers) doubted whether Cotton was of any particular importance as a historian, political figure or thinker and wondered whether my claims for him to be taken more seriously did not surpass the evidence to sustain them.[3] Certainly there is a tendency natural among scholars (and especially enthusiastic young scholars) to exaggerate the importance of their subject. In this case, however, I would rather plead guilty to failing to do Cotton justice than concur with the view that he did not, or does not, merit study. For Cotton proved to be of the first importance to early modern history and historiography. In my own case (and perhaps others') he led to the fundamental questioning of prevailing orthodoxies about, and towards a reconfiguration of, early seventeenth-century politics – a development that came to be known as 'revisionism'.[4] And, beyond, he and his circle pointed me to other investigations of the politics of scholarship and the broader culture of politics, which I am continuing, and to a more nuanced understanding of the political valence of all literary and historical texts in Renaissance England.[5]

Indeed since 1979 the whole landscape of the political and intellectual (I would now prefer the term cultural) history of early modern England has been redrawn – both by

I

theory and by empirical research. The revisionists' emphasis on court faction and consensus over crown-parliament conflict and ideological fissure has itself been revised;[6] New Historicism has elucidated the interrelationship of all writing and structures of authority and power;[7] and reader-response criticism and the history of the book have helpfully complicated, historicized and so politicized the very acts of reading and writing which we used to take as 'natural' activities unchanging through the centuries.[8] But, if our understanding of the broader context of early Stuart scholarship and politics has been revolutionized, Cotton, who was a central figure in those worlds, has largely been left behind. Though Professor Fritz Levy quite appropriately commented in 1980 that the 'absence of a full biography [of Cotton] is astonishing', no scholar has come forward to attempt it, or even to take up the many loose threads left dangling from my own study.[9]

Of course, the notable, and excellent exception, is Dr Colin Tite, who was embarking on a thorough re-examination of the Cotton manuscripts even as my Sir Robert went to press.[10] In a series of important articles and now in his Panizzi Lectures he has added immensely to our knowledge of the collection, its creation, development and history.[11] And his work has not only served as the basis of a major exhibition of Cotton manuscripts in the British Library; it has stimulated a whole series of studies on Cotton's collections, and (to a lesser extent) writings and life.[12] The publication of such new research prompts us again to take stock of Sir Robert Cotton and his library and to re-evaluate their importance in the (newly reconfigured) context of early modern scholarship and politics.

II

One of the most important scholarly advances has been the beginnings of a historical reconstitution of the Cottonian collection. For all too long, though its deficiencies were glaringly obvious to librarians and manuscript scholars, the catalogue of the Cotton manuscripts has been treated as though it were a reasonably reliable guide to the manuscripts collected by Sir Robert Cotton. Further research has demonstrated in a number of ways just how far that is from the truth. Colin Tite has calculated that as a result of Cotton's generous lending and careless recording of loans, as many as one tenth of his manuscripts strayed in his lifetime. He has found manuscripts with marks of Cotton's ownership in the Bodleian, the Royal Library (now the Royal MSS. in the British Library) and Archbishop Ussher's manuscripts in Dublin.[13] Several Harleian Manuscripts (105, 513, 525, 547) have Cotton's name on the first folio; a catalogue of charters in Add. MS. 5161 bears his hand and other manuscripts written by him and now in other repositories (his notes on Chancery, for example) were likely to have once resided, in some copy, in his own collection.[14]

Yet, if the current Cottonian collection is missing large numbers of manuscripts once owned by Sir Robert, it undoubtedly includes many which came into the library after his death. Sir William Dugdale contributed books to the collection while he was its custodian during the Civil War and Commonwealth period.[15] Cotton's and Sir Simonds

D'Ewes's charters were confused when the two libraries shared a home in the early eighteenth century; some manuscripts from the Royal Library strayed into the Cotton collection when both were housed in Ashburnham House; forty-four volumes of Thomas Rymer's manuscripts were placed in the Cottonian library in 1715.[16] Other manuscripts appear to have entered the library after the end of the seventeenth century from unknown sources: Caligula A. XVII, XVIII and E. XIII, for example, do not appear in Thomas Smith's catalogue of 1696, nor do Claudius C. XII, Nero E. VIII, Galba A. XX-XXI, E. XIII, Otho E. XIV, Vespasian A. XXIV, Vespasian D. XXIII-XXVIII, Titus F. XIV or Faustina A. X.[17] Examination of these manuscripts shows they bear no marks of Cotton's ownership; others listed in Smith's catalogue which bear no traces of Cotton's ownership (Otho C. XV, D. X, Vitellius F. XVII, Titus C. XI, for instance), but do have Thomas Cotton's inscription (Julius D. IX, Tiberius C. XII, D. XXII) suggest at least that they may have been acquired later.

Fortunately, we do not have to depend solely upon the printed catalogues of Cotton's library. Scholars have drawn valuable attention to the manuscript listings drawn up in, and shortly after, Cotton's lifetime, which add much to our knowledge of the development of the collection and which deserve to be edited and better known. Unfortunately, the exact status of these listings, even after Colin Tite's thorough examination, remains unclear.[18] In the case of the only list drawn up in Cotton's lifetime, the so-called catalogue of 1621 (Harleian MS. 6018), there are many reasons for thinking that it was never completed, and may not even have been intended as a full inventory of the collection. Harleian 6018 lists only 413 manuscripts, well less than half the 958 manuscripts in the Cottonian collection in 1731, at the time of the fire at Ashburnham House; even allowing for Sir Robert's later acquisitions and gifts to or strays from the library after his death, we are left with the strong suspicion that Harleian 6018 was far from complete. It is confirmed by Cotton's own promise to Bishop Ussher in 1622 that he would send him a catalogue of his manuscripts when it was drawn up.[19] This was not ready by 1626 when Dr Bainbridge told Ussher that Cotton's books were 'not yet ordered in a catalogue' and evidently remained unfinished at his death when the Privy Council required a catalogue.[20]

Just as important as the deficiencies in any contemporary lists, there is more than the 'possibility' (as it is considered by Colin Tite) that 'there were manuscripts in the library that were not incorporated into it'.[21] Faustina C. I, for example, has notes in Sir Robert's hand but does not appear in the lists of 1621, 1635, 1654 nor any catalogue before 1696; Nero C. VIII, a wardrobe book collated by Cotton, does not appear in a list until 1696; Titus F. IV, which I suggested may have been Cotton's own parliamentary diary, is listed neither in 1621 nor 1635 but appears on Cotton's loan list in the same manuscript as the 1621 catalogue.[22] In general it would appear that Cotton's estate and financial papers were not incorporated into his library, and may even have remained in his house at Conington.[23] And in London, it may well be that loose papers in the process of arrangement and binding may not have been fully incorporated into the library, or given any classification or call mark.

In 1638 Sir William Dugdale informed his friend Nathaniel Johnstone: 'Sir Thomas [Cotton] told me he had two large bales of ancient papers of state and other things ... which had never been opened since they were so packed by his father'.[24] These may have been included among the volumes of manuscripts on England's relations with Rome (Vitellius B.), with Spain (Vespasian C. I-XII), with Flanders (Galba B.) and the Netherlands (Galba) which Dugdale compiled from Cotton papers, which did not appear in the lists of 1621 or 1635. According to W. Hamper, his biographer, Dugdale sorted papers of Wolsey, Cromwell, Burleigh, and Walsingham, letters of Mary Queen of Scots and the Duke of Norfolk 'methodically both as to time and otherwise and caused them to be bound up with clasps and Sir Thomas Cotton's arms'.[25] Though almost certainly in Sir Robert Cotton's possession before his death, these more than eighty volumes may have entered the library proper only after a process of compilation and editing by another. If there are other such instances, we not only begin to see how the library apparently 'grew' between Cotton's death and Smith's Catalogue; we also begin to appreciate how complex is the question of what constituted the Cottonian collection during Cotton's lifetime.

The later history of the library only compounds the problem. We know very little of what happened to the collection during the 1640s and 1650s, though there is evidence of gifts enhancing it: Titus C. XVI and XVII, for example, were given by Sir Edward Walker after 1645. In 1650 the library was evacuated to Stratton, Bedfordshire, but it is not clear when it returned to Cotton House. John Selden, a parliamentarian friend of the Cottons, protected the collection from plunder and he, Dugdale, Dodsworth, and other scholars continued to work there. Figures of importance in the affairs of the Commonwealth, the Earl of Manchester and Bulstrode Whitelocke, borrowed from the collection, but there are no very substantial loan lists for this period, nor do we know the circumstances that led to the compilation of two more catalogues of the manuscripts in the 1650s.[26] Because we lack this information and because there has been no systematic comparison between the lists of 1621, *circa* 1635 and 1656/7, we have little sense of what manuscripts were lost or lent and not returned during these crucial decades or where to look for them among the collections of borrowers.[27]

If the library was less used during the troubled years of civil war, the Restoration and the revival of a political culture in which disputes were solved by precedent rather than violence placed the Cottonian library again at the centre of the overlapping circles of scholarship and politics. Elizabeth Teviotdale's inventory of the large numbers and arrangement of catalogues of Cotton's manuscripts in private hands, and in the hands of men like Samuel Pepys, Thomas Gale, High Master of St Paul's, William Petyt, Edward Stillingfleet, Bishop of Worcester, and William Sancroft, underlines the need for a thorough investigation of the use made of the Cottonian manuscripts in the scholarly and political polemics of the Augustan age.[28] Not least such an investigation, starting with the collections of those who had catalogues of the Cottonian library, might well unearth items that went missing between the 1650s and Smith's Catalogue of 1696 (such as Nero

E. VIII, Tiberius B. VII, and Vitellius B. I which were recorded in 1654, but had disappeared by 1656/7).

If the fate of the Cotton manuscripts during the period from Sir Robert's death to the issue of the first published catalogue remains vague and uncertain, we might be tempted to think their subsequent history has been a straightforward, albeit a tragic, one. We know that in 1700 Cotton's grandson bequeathed the collection to the nation and that in 1731 a fire at Ashburnham House consumed a large number of the treasures of the Cotton (and Royal) collection. But, as we now see, the events and their consequences are far from straightforward and add yet a further set of complications to our attempts at a reconstitution of the Cottonian manuscripts. From the very beginning there was significant disagreement about the nature and extent of the damage. A report was prepared for the parliamentary committee investigating the fire by Rev. William Whiston, Clerk of the Records in the Chapter House, Westminster, and by David Casley, deputy librarian of the Cotton library. According to a schedule dated 29 January 1732 in the Antrobus Papers, of the 958 manuscripts in the library 120 were deemed to have been entirely burnt, and 114 were listed as defective.[29] Whiston, however, gave the figures slightly more optimistically – as 114 and 98 respectively; by 1777 those lost had been reduced to 114 in a catalogue of that year.[30]

Andrew Prescott's essay now makes startlingly clear what lay behind these seemingly trivial discrepancies. For, as he shows, where manuscripts were concerned, 'destruction' is a matter of judgement and of history and technology. Emergency conservation and subsequent restoration work have ultimately reduced the list of manuscripts destroyed to only thirteen; but the history of these processes also revolutionized the nature and organization of Sir Robert Cotton's library.

Working under the constraints of time – not least to prevent mould further damaging manuscripts soaked in the water used to douse the fire – Whiston broke up many manuscripts and had them rebound. As Prescott warns us, it has become almost routine to assume that, where the leaves of a particular manuscript are out of sequence, this is due to interference by Sir Robert Cotton. In fact, it is just as likely that disordered collations of this sort are the result of the efforts of Whiston and his colleagues to preserve what they could of Cotton's collection.[31] Whiston and his assistants placed 'a very great gulf between the modern user of the Cotton library and the library as it existed before the fire'.[32] Later efforts only widened this gulf. The survival of loose sheets, the movement of items for restoration work and new experiments led to future confusions – reordering, reconstruction – and indeed to losses as well as gains. Whilst scholars are greatly indebted to Sir Frederic Madden for his indefatigable labours in indentifying, flattening and binding thousands of loose leaves, there is no doubt that in some cases his interpretations and reconstructions bore no relation to the original Cottonian compilation.[33] Albeit in the name of scholarship, the rearrangements of Sir Robert's manuscripts have been on a scale greater than his own separations and compilations of the medieval documents that came into his hands.

What all these complications point to is the urgent need now for a full and thorough re-examination of the Cottonian library: an edition and careful comparison of the various 'catalogues' or lists of the collection from 1621 to 1696; a search of the archives (where they still exist) of those listed as borrowing from the collection for manuscripts with marks of Cotton ownership; a reinvestigation of volumes we know to have been restored either by Whiston or Madden, using ultra-violet light and other techniques not available to them; a search for transcripts of burnt Cotton manuscripts made by Cotton's contemporaries (such as Ralph Starkey who copied many) and later users of the library (like Selden and Dugdale) as was recommended after the fire at Ashburnham House;[34] in fine, a study of each individual manuscript (in conjunction with loan lists and catalogues) for evidence of provenance, ownership marks, fire damage, and compilation. The results would not only lead to the catalogue raisonné, the need for which was identified in 1732, and so provide a proper entrée to the collection for scholars;[35] they would also add invaluable chapters to the history of scholarship and politics in Cotton's day and beyond.

III

The Cottonian collection, as we have always known, was never the manuscripts alone.[36] But it is only recent work that is enabling us to evaluate the importance of Cotton's books, and more particularly his stones and monuments, coins and medals and seals in the collection, for the historical scholarship of his contemporaries and of our own age. In 1979, after some investigation, I was forced to conclude that Cotton's printed books remained a mystery.[37] Colin Tite now offers the fascinating hypothesis that the list of 575 titles in Add. MS. 35213 may be a list of an earlier collector's books acquired by Cotton; and whilst the case is by no means concluded, it certainly provides a list of items to be searched for evidence of Cotton's ownership when they are found in the collections of his known contemporaries.[38]

Most welcome is the attention now being paid to the stones, medals and coins. Cotton probably attributed almost as much importance to physical artefacts as to manuscripts. Though Camden made famous the fruits of his and Cotton's tour of Hadrian's Wall and the stones and objects found and excavated, it is not often enough noted that Cotton continued to seek out such artefacts throughout his lifetime: in 1622 he was still actually tracking down stones;[39] in 1629 John Barkham was endeavouring to obtain statues on his behalf.[40] Other agents sent Cotton medals from Paris and Roman coins from Dublin;[41] he evidently gathered the coins of all the Roman emperors from Pompey to Mauritius, the coins of all kings of England from the Saxons to Charles I, and the seals of monarchs from Edward the Confessor to Richard II as well as 'divers medals' of the Asians and Egyptians.[42] Like the manuscripts, these were intended for *use*. Cotton drew diagrams of artefacts as well as copying inscriptions.[43] As well as Camden and Speed, Cotton and his co-author of the 'Topographical Description of England' referred to the stones and coins for elucidation of the history of the realm.[44] When in *Nero Cæsar*, Cotton's friend

6

and fellow antiquary Edmund Bolton pleaded for greater study and use of coins in recalling the great deeds of the past, it is most likely that his sense of their value derived from Cotton's finds and collection.[45]

Glenys Davies, David McKitterick and Gay van der Meer have greatly helped us to see how important the stones and coins were. Davies's descriptive catalogue of Cotton's stones vividly underlines the unique contribution they made to an appreciation of British antiquity and may suggest a vital link, even if one not pursued by the antiquaries themselves, between such scholarship and the beginning of an aesthetic interest in collecting Roman statuary.[46] We are left to ponder whether the location of Cotton's stones – at his Huntingdonshire seat in Conington, rather than London – did not limit their effecting an historical and aesthetic revolution. McKitterick has no doubt that the results of Cotton's finds, especially along Hadrian's Wall, 'were as dramatic as any in the history of British archaeology' and fascinatingly suggests how Cotton's stones may even have come to inform Ben Jonson and Inigo Jones's court masques.[47] Van der Meer's discovery of an inventory by Nicolas Claude Fabri de Peiresc of Cotton's Anglo-Saxon coins not only gives a sense of what has gone missing from the collections in material artefacts as well as manuscripts (how many coins Cotton had that were unknown to Speed), but opens the exciting prospect of further research enabling a reconstitution of the original collection – not least through identifying lists in Cotton's manuscripts as catalogues of his own holdings.[48] As more becomes known about Cotton's cabinet, his rarities (we should not forget his excitement about the excavation of a fossilized fish),[49] and his monuments, we may understand better how the various elements of the Cottonian collection complemented – and even were acquired to complement – each other, to provide a new range of material for the study of the British past.

IV

The contents of the collection, however, are only one part of the story. The other is Cotton's treatment of, we might even more generally say his relationship to, his collection. And here, I would argue, work on the Cottonian collection has yet to ask the most interesting questions raised by library scholars and historians of the book. Though some work has been done on listing the various catalogues of Cotton's manuscripts, there has been no satisfactory analysis of them: of what they show about how Cotton described (or remembered) his books, why he first listed them in numerical sequence, then adopted the famous imperial pressmarks, and how the latter related to the former.[50] Similarly, although the loan lists have been cited as evidence of who consulted the collection (and to a limited extent how they used the manuscripts they borrowed), scholars have not seen their importance for Sir Robert Cotton himself. How he described and remembered books he loaned (perhaps especially when he could not recall the name of the borrower) may tell us much about how he viewed the importance of particular manuscripts – and items within bound volumes – as well as how he acquired them. 'The book of St Albans having the history in pictures' not only reminds us that we each have individual mental

7

devices for recalling items, it may indicate Cotton's sense of the importance of the illustrations.[51] His large thick book of precedents in ecclesiastical courts, Cotton remembered particularly as 'of good use'.[52] Though he did not remember the name of the borrower of a volume on the history of religious orders, he did recall that 'it had at the end of it the prophecy of John of Bridlington and somebody borrowed it of me for this prophecy, I remember'.[53] Some books Cotton identified in terms of their source rather than subject – a book he had of 'Mr Whitt the scrivener', a volume that 'was the Earl of Salisbury's book'; a book given by Mr Griffith, parson of Hinckley.[54] Interestingly Cotton described several of his books in terms of their bindings. Evidently he himself deployed a variety of different materials and colours – and it would be worth pursuing how the choice of cloth, leather, vellum or velvet might speak to his valuation of a manuscript, or whether the colour related in any way to manuscripts that he arranged or intended to consult together.[55] If there is any consistency to the loan lists, we may also deduce that Cotton bound only some of his manuscripts with clasps and/or with his arms; and regarded some loose papers as obviously fit for binding in a collection at the time of lending them.[56] Examination of a number of the manuscripts in the light of Cotton's brief descriptions of content, condition and binding might well open further avenues into his priorities and values as a collector. One obvious area for fruitful study is the little known engravings that form the title-pages of some volumes: Nero B. II and Galba B. IV (by William Hole), Cleopatra E. I-III (by Richard Elstrack), Cleopatra F. I-II (by K. Sichen), Vespasian C. II, Julius C. V, Tiberius B. I (anonymous). (There is also an anonymous drawing in Vespasian C. XII.)[57] Why did Cotton privilege these manuscripts with the charge of engraved title plates? Did he intend to publish them? What may we learn from Colin Tite's observation that in binding Cotton made no effort to preserve recently written marginalia?[58] Twentieth-century scholars have fortunately abandoned the anachronistic judgements of earlier bibliographers who condemned Cotton (and his contemporaries) for their treatment of manuscripts: dividing originals, disrespecting provenance, rebinding separates, writing on documents. But as yet they have made little study of how we might use such physical practices as evidence of attitudes to the manuscripts – and indeed to affairs outside the world of books. For in some cases it seems obvious that a volume Sir Robert compiled can be traced to a particular moment, patron or need. The collection on heralds and arms (Titus C. I), for example, may well be related to Cotton's advising the Earl of Northampton when the latter was appointed a commissioner for the office of Earl Marshal;[59] Cotton's sense that his papers on England's relations with Spain might make 'a great book' may well have been prompted by his own role in the negotiations for a Spanish marriage.[60] More research might fruitfully tie other Cotton collections, their organization, condition and his description of them, to particular moments.

Most surprisingly, there has been no systematic investigation of Cotton's marks of ownership (permanent or temporary) or reading in the manuscripts in his library, or those once owned by him but now elsewhere. We are just beginning to realize how serious is this neglect. Historians of the book have not only drawn our attention to the need to situate historically the activity of 'reading' - aloud or silent, in public or private, as 'reader' or listener; they are also beginning to study marks such as marginalia, interlinings, even casual scribblings and ephemera of a domestic or personal nature in books as evidence of engagement with the text: by agreement, dispute, emphasis, degree of interest.[61] In cases where the documentation is rich, as with Gabriel Harvey's copy of Livy, brilliant exegesis has enabled historians to show us how 'Livy's early Rome change[d] contours, shadows and colours as Harvey inspected [it]...on successive occasions', and how readings were determined by the needs of patrons and moments.[62] The Cottonian collection offers a rich opportunity for the application of these approaches to early modern manuscripts as well as printed books. Careful study of hand, ink and annotations in the context of what we know about the manuscript, Cotton's acquisition and/or compilation, his description (or lending) of the item, and of his scholarly and political activities might offer invaluable insights into Cotton's readings and possibly rereadings and their relationship to his activities and values. Like divisions, compilations and bindings, marks are evidence that the acquisition, ownership and reading of books or manuscripts expressed values; that they were, it is not too much to say, ideological practices.

So was lending itself. Cotton's generosity in lending his books of manuscripts is of course well known. Yet it has largely been studied in the context of losses from the library rather than in terms of Cotton's and his contemporaries' attitudes to manuscripts – or ideas. It is not too simple a question to ask why Sir Robert was willing to lend the manuscripts that he had so painstakingly, and expensively, garnered – especially to men whom, as in some cases, he did not know.[63] After a time it must have been apparent to him that as a consequence of his openness, losses were incurred but the loan lists indicate no diminution in the ranks of those permitted to borrow.[64] Even some of Cotton's contemporaries appeared to be surprised at the freedom with which he lent, surprised – as Bolton puts it – at his not exploiting the monopoly that he had.[65] Did Cotton see himself as providing a service, supplying privately a resource nowhere else available when his and others' petition for a public library came to naught?[66] Was the collection compiled as his own research base – not for the 'pure' pursuit of scholarship but to equip him to rise to the ranks of adviser to magnate and M.P., minister and monarch – and as a stock he could also lend, the interest being his advancement?

The answer to such questions, and to the larger issue of the importance of Cotton's library to his age, awaits the large study, never even attempted in miniature, of how borrowers *used* the manuscripts for their own purposes: scholarly, personal and political. Why, for example, did John Selden borrow, as well as medieval and legal manuscripts, the *Sententiae* of Guicciardini and how did his reading of that inform his own writings?[67] What might Arundel have read in the book on the Earl Marshal's office while he was in the Tower?[68] How did Dudley's book of accounts of Henry VII's reign affect Treasurer Cranfield's practices or reforms?[69] For what entertainments did Inigo Jones use the books of triumphs he borrowed?[70] A re-examination of the works, both written and performed, of Cotton's contemporaries (and successors) in the light of what they

9

borrowed from him, and when, and how they deployed it, would not only add in general invaluable chapters to the history of Renaissance reading practices. It would enable us to see how Cotton's manuscripts performed and were deployed differently in a myriad of contexts, how scholarly research and politics interacted in the number of careers and moments.[71]

For this moment, it is time for us to reconsider how they interacted in Sir Robert Cotton himself.

V

In 1979, I made a number of claims for Cotton's importance in the historical scholarship of his day, some of which have proved to be contentious. One was the argument that Sir Robert Cotton arrived at an understanding of the nature of the knight's fee and of the feudal system before Sir Henry Spelman 'discovered' feudalism and published his findings in his *Archaeologus* of 1626. The argument had broader implications: if Cotton and his fellow antiquaries arrived at an understanding of feudal tenures and the changes effected by the Norman Conquest, then we must question J. G. A. Pocock's thesis that early Stuart historical and legal thought was restricted by ignorance of such historical developments, and characterized by an insular belief in the unbroken continuity of immemorial English customs, as asserted by Sir Edward Coke.[72] If Cotton and others were aware of what English legal developments owed to the French, then Coke becomes less the paradigm of a universally held view, rather the forceful spokesman for a selective view of the past, a polemical argument that owed more to contemporary Stuart political debate than historical knowledge of the medieval past.[73]

Not least because the implications of these suggestions were wide-reaching, the debate about the antiquaries' understanding of feudalism has continued. In 1979, quite independently in a study of natural rights theories, Richard Tuck questioned *The Ancient Constitution* and, observing that practising lawyers and members of the Society of Antiquaries were quite able to contemplate historical change in English law, argued that 'the real puzzle is why men like Sir Edward Coke did not…'.[74] Others, notably Hans Pawlisch, published studies that raised doubts about the Pocock thesis.[75]

In 1986, Professor Pocock himself returned to the theme, to what he regarded as the efforts of his critics 'to transform a mentalité [of the ancient constitution] into a series of "moves"'.[76] Pocock acknowledged that early Stuart scholars knew of law outside their realm, including Roman civil law, and accepted too that in the light of Hans Pawlisch's findings he had exaggerated the insularity of Sir John Davies, Attorney General for Ireland. What he continued to doubt was the willingness of the English to apply this knowledge comparatively, to place indigenous customs and law in a broader historical and legal context: 'as a key to their past, the English knew of one law alone'.[77] And Pocock took the newly printed debates on the Petition of Right to sustain his point that Englishmen in 1628 still debated using the insular language of custom and common-law.[78] 'Defenders of the view that royal authority operated according to a plurality of leges terrae had no counter history to offer';[79] 'the common law still furnished the only historic past which could be visualized by those engaged in English government ... '.[80]

This, however, – possibly a recurring weakness of Pocock's methodology – is to take language at face value and out of context.[81] In 1628 all participants in debate were anxious to find a form of agreement. Charles I, no less than the proponents of the Petition of Right, believed in custom and common law. But he did not necessarily mean the same as all of them by it. He appears to have believed that prerogative actions outside the law had come to be part of the common law, obviating any need for a counter history or discourse to support his position. His father had clearly enunciated such a view. In the context, as he acknowledged, of fears that he intended to elevate civil law and alter the nature of government, James reasserted the divine origin of royal authority, comparing the king's prerogative to God's power of miracle. As God seldom intervened directly, preferring to govern through natural law, so in a settled state kings governed in accordance with the established forms and laws. Those who did not rule according to law, in such settled circumstances, were to be deemed tyrants. But, like God's power of miracle, the prerogative was a divinely given power that remained to kings for them to discharge their 'accompt to God'. As such James regarded it as a power that did not contest with common law but completed and fulfilled it; nevertheless his view had the potential to clash with the Cokeian doctrine of immemorial custom.[82]

The complexities of these positions have recently been clarified by Glenn Burgess's re-examination of the ancient constitution.[83] Burgess enables us to understand how, whilst James's speech expressed a tension or ambiguity in contemporary thought, it did not conflict with most ideas of English law, except as they were enunciated by Coke.[84] (And he suggests too that even in 1628 it was not Charles I's theory, but his articulation of it in an inappropriate time and context, that was chiefly at issue.)[85] For the most part, the languages of common law and civil law were held together in the 'Jacobean consensus', which only later circumstances fractured.[86] Such a nuanced analysis may provide a helpful context for studying the developing ideas and politics of a number of early Stuart lawyers and antiquaries – including Cotton. What it is important to note here is that, revising Pocock, Burgess posits Coke as the exceptional figure of his age and identifies several lawyers – notably John Dodderidge – who saw the law as mutable, and a product of history as well as reason.[87] Dodderidge was a member of the Society of Antiquaries and with Cotton one of the joint petitioners to Queen Elizabeth for the erection of a public library.[88] His scholarly development, like Spelman's, may have owed much to the Society's discussions and debates. For, as Burgess reminds us, the Society of Antiquaries had come to an understanding of the historical fact of conquest in English society, and 'indeed it can be said that it was the growth of antiquarianism that led to the writing of recognizable histories of the law'.[89] In the intellectual world of those antiquarian debates and the facilities in Cotton's library, the insularity of Coke was not only exceptional; it was, rather than a *mentalité*, a choice – or 'carefully developed principle'.[90] Like the Brutus legend, the myth of the ancient constitution was articulated out of polemical strategy rather than scholarly ignorance.

Cotton's and other antiquaries' understanding of the Conquest and the *feudum* derived from their familiarity with the etymological scholarship of the continental humanists. In *Sir Robert Cotton*, I suggested that Cotton continued to be an important link between continental and English scholars, perhaps even after Camden's retirement from London to Chislehurst, and death in 1623. At least one reviewer countered that this was to overestimate Sir Robert who was only introduced to European circles by Camden and who always remained in the shadow of the older man.[91] This is not an unreasonable criticism. Cotton never published, like Camden, works that secured him an international audience. But here, as in English scholarship (and politics), his role as a facilitator should not be negated. Clearly Cotton's library was essential to European scholars such as Peiresc, De Thou, Fronto du Duc, André Duchesne, Pierre Dupuy, Lucas Holstenius, Janus Gruter, Franciscus Sweertius, and others. Not least because the library was the hub where so many European and English scholarly roads intersected, Cotton may well have effected introductions that bequeathed continental connections to the younger generation of scholars. Here much new research is needed in continental archives, but there are already hints that when it is done Cotton's stature is more likely to increase than diminish. Van der Meer's discovery in The Hague of Peiresc's inventory of Cotton's Saxon coins indicates at least that Cotton's collections may have been known in detail on the Continent, and other than just by scholarly hearsay.[92] If Colin Tite's identification is correct, we also begin to obtain a sense of the high profile of continental scholarship in Cotton's library of printed books as early as 1595. Under almost all the headed sheets on which book titles were pasted, we find books published in Antwerp, Cologne, Frankfurt, Paris and Venice.[93] In addition, we know that Peiresc and other continental scholars sent Cotton books, including the *Historiae Normanorum Scriptores Antiqui*.[94] The list of printed books Cotton lent to Selden in 1622 includes works in French, Dutch, Italian and Portuguese, as well as Latin works published on the Continent.[95] Further research may well reveal Cotton's collection to be of importance for printed continental works as for manuscripts. If, as Daniel Woolf maintains, in early Stuart England 'many less well known historians were indebted to earlier and contemporary continental authors', it was also to the scholarship of the Society of Antiquaries and Cotton's library that they were indebted.[96]

Cotton may have contributed more than the loan of manuscripts to his continental contemporaries. There is the odd reference to his being asked to write for a project, and it may be that pages by him or based on his notes are contained within the works of Duchesne or Peiresc, as they are in Speed or Ussher.[97] In one particular case, against the long-established tradition, I argued that Cotton rather than Camden wrote the history of Mary of Scots' reign which was forwarded to De Thou for incorporation in his *Historia Sui Temporis*. It is rather surprising that no one either challenged or developed the suggestion. I would now add Thomas Leke's letter to Northampton, informing him that James was anxious Cotton progress with the history to be sent to De Thou, which adds a point of confirmation.[98] Recently, however, Daniel Woolf has filled out the story, using Peiresc's and De Thou's correspondence from the Bibliothèque Nationale. Whilst he confirms my story in outline, he is able to add the valuable information that Francis Bacon believed Cotton to be the author not only of the material sent to De Thou but also of the *Annales*, and that James ordered Cotton to correct the second part for publication, after Camden's death in 1625.[99] Below David McKitterick cites the royal warrant to publish the first part in 1615 issued to both 'our wellbeloved servants Sir Robert Cotton Knight and Baronett and William Camden Clarenceux one of our Kings of Arms'.[100] And Nigel Ramsay's discovery of Cotton's list of services to the crown, among which he includes compiling memoirs to be sent to De Thou, clinches the case.[101] So if what I thought a strong suggestion has become a certainty, we must not only wonder how much of what scholars persist in calling Camden's *Annales* was in fact written, drafted, or corrected by Cotton, but also reread the text with that possibility in mind.

The memoirs he sent to De Thou *may* have been Cotton's greatest written contribution to European scholarship. That they emerged from a royal need and directive sharply reminds us of a truism that still discomforts many scholars: that in early modern England at all points historical scholarship inhabited a world of authority, power and politics.[102]

VI

'The personal ownership of the past', writes Sir John Plumb, 'has always been a vital strand in the ideology of all ruling classes.'[103] It was especially so in early modern England when precedents were looked to both to reinforce and resolve novel problems. Men studied history primarily for its use and application for contemporary affairs rather than, as we still often wish, to advance historical understanding. When Cotton and Dodderidge petitioned Queen Elizabeth to establish a library, they stressed the utility of history – and not merely as a rhetorical point. Edward I, they reminded the Queen, had made use of historical records in establishing his claim to rule Scotland, as had Henry VIII in freeing the realm from the usurped authority of the Roman pontiff.[104] Later Cotton himself was to readvise Prince Charles about the rights of English kings to France not, as he boasted, 'by way of pleasing discourse as in these days is in use but by sound ground and substantial arguments' from history.[105]

Historians of the arts, drama and court festivals of the Renaissance write naturally of the driving force of patronage and politics on artistic production.[106] In a system of personal monarchy, monarchs did much to shape an intellectual culture, even when they did not directly commission works. The shift in cultural style from the reign of Elizabeth to that of James, or from James to his son, is manifest in changes in portraiture and architecture, poetry and plays, masques and music. We still need to see historical writing in this context: to study the changes in genre from chronicle to antiquarian treatise to 'politic history' as an expression of, as well as influence on, these broader changes, as a political as well as intellectual history.[107] Daniel Woolf has incisively observed that the type of narrative history that flourished under Elizabeth and James entered the doldrums under Charles I; and, significantly, the same has been argued about the drama.[108]

13

Histories in verse too appear to have had their heyday in the late years of Elizabeth's reign and James's when, for all Sidney's distinctions, historians and poets (among them King James himself) often wrote to the same ends. The issues of early modern politics informed historical, as all other, scholarship, even when historians were not directly employed by the state. Camden's *Britannia* cannot be separated from the threats to England in the 1580s; John Speed's *Theatre of the empire of Great Britain*, with its engraved frontispiece of a Roman, Saxon, Dane and Norman, flanked by an ancient Britain, clearly speaks to James I's self-styling as King of Great Britain and royal plans for union. It may even be that Cotton's and Camden's excavation of Hadrian's Wall in 1600 was stimulated by their perceived expectation that the two old hostile kingdoms might soon share one sovereign.[109] Ben Jonson for one used one of the stones they found for his court masque celebrating union.[110]

History, like the law, the Bible, the classics, was a validating text. Yet like all those other texts, as well as sustaining authority, it could be deployed, appropriated and interpreted by others. James VI had seen clear evidence of this as King of Scotland, when the Presbyterians' reading of the Scottish past formed the basis of their contractual theory of politics. In the *Basilikon Doron*, he advised his son Prince Henry to read histories, but not those of John Knox or George Buchanan.[111] In Jacobean England, the Earl of Arundel was to accuse Sir Edward Coke and his precedents of stirring up subjects against their sovereign.[112] Woolf is right to maintain that before the Civil War there were no fundamental historical controversies expressing rival and antagonistic views of the past, but he goes too far in writing of a 'monochromatic image' of the national past.[113] Like the law, history was still a shared language; but men – often to their consternation – did read it differently, or at least with different emphases. Historical scholarship, therefore, was not only in general shaped by political conditions and questions, it was coloured by political tensions and differences.[114]

As the past became a disputed text, the custody of records became a political question too. Given her famous sensitivity to unflattering historical parallels, it is surprising that Queen Elizabeth did not accept Cotton's offer to pool his books with the royal collection to form a national library. As yet, the attitude to public records remained somewhat cavalier: state papers were allowed to drift; Burleigh gave to Camden official correspondence which was never returned; Secretaries of State kept their papers as private possessions.[115] Behind Cotton's petition may have been a political sense that there was a need to safeguard the records of state. Later, in urging that commissions to ambassadors be enrolled in Chancery and delivered into the Exchequer, he recalled that in Elizabeth's time, the King of Denmark had insisted on a clause in a past negotiation and the English could not discover whether they were bound to it or not![116] Papers were in private hands, Cotton advised, that ought to be kept safe in the public records. Given what we know of how many he 'acquired', Cotton's advice may sound like blatant hypocrisy. It may be, however, that he regarded his own library, open to all, as a safe repository, a supplement to the official records in the Tower. Others, however, who began to share his concern about the public records, did not concur that he was the right custodian. Thomas Wilson, Keeper of the Records in the Tower, issued warnings about Cotton's acquisitions of state papers and even advised that papers bequeathed to Cotton should be retained by the Crown.[117] Clearly attitudes were changing and the factional rivalries and political tensions of the 1620s focused attention on the custody of the records of precedents that all looked to for support and ammunition. In 1621, Francis Bacon was evidently prevented from access to official records and to Cotton's library, at the time of judicial proceedings against him.[118] In 1626, when he himself was facing impeachment, the Duke of Buckingham recommended that Cotton's library be closed.[119]

The debates on the Petition of Right, centred on precedent in general and on Magna Carta (of which Cotton had copies) in particular, exacerbated the concern about ownership of the records of state. In 1629, Attorney General Heath, who, we now know, was not averse to altering official documents to sustain a claim,[120] observed: 'There are found in Sir Robert Cotton's study not copies or transcripts but the very originals of records... which indeed are not fit for a subject to keep.'[121] Interestingly, however, one of the leading protagonists of the Petition of Right in the Lords had come to quite a different view: the Earl of Bedford had supported the search for precedents to bolster the liberty of the subject: 'The records as he thought were the subjects... he judged it no offence if out of them he desired to know the utmost both of his right and duty.'[122] Never one to share his father's love of debate, and dismayed at some of the arguments promulgated in 1628, Charles I moved quickly to establish control over archives of state: he impounded Sir Edward Coke's papers, and ordered his Attorney to purge his reports of dangerous matter; he perused Attorney William Noy's and Secretary Dorchester's papers on their deaths, removing 'such as the state may have any use of'. Charles required his Keeper of the Records to recover documents that had been (as he now saw it) 'embezzled'. He forbad prisoners access to Tower records.[123]

And, most importantly for us, he closed Sir Robert Cotton's library. The King's concern to restrict and control access to records expressed not only his authoritarian personality, and desire for order. Historical records and historical scholarship were becoming increasingly not just political, but politically contentious, objects and pursuits. Historians and antiquaries were embroiled in political disputes. Rubens may have regretted his friend Selden's involvement in a political controversy that led to his confinement and wished that he had restricted himself to scholarship, but – as the Ambassador Rubens of all people knew – it was something of a false distinction.[124] Even Sir Henry Spelman, who appeared to remain most aloof from the political fray, was reading Oliver St John's treatise against benevolences in 1625. For his part, Cotton was in the thick of it. To better understand his importance for early modern scholarship we have further to examine his political activities and attitudes.

VII

Just as we can only truly elucidate Cotton's collecting and scholarship in the broader context of the politics of culture, so his political career needs to be studied in the culture

15

of politics in early modern England. Since I began work on Sir Robert Cotton in 1971 that broader landscape has been transformed. In 1975, my study of Cotton's career graphically demonstrated what was wrong with the prevailing Whig interpretation. At a time when, it was argued, conflict between crown and parliament, court and country was inevitable and escalating, Cotton resisted categorization or placement on either 'side'. A Huntingdonshire gentleman and baronet with (as we shall see) pride in his ancestry and locality, he was also connected to powerful magnates and monarchs; he advised princes as well as M.P.s; his criticisms of royal policies and favourites never transmuted into 'opposition' to the King or royal government; rather he offered counsel to reinvigorate royal government. Like others, Cotton remained devoted to the idea of the commonweal and exemplified the shared values and languages that, I then argued, characterized the political culture.

Since then, further research and debate have refined and developed our canvas, with implications for Cotton's place in it. For one, Dr David Starkey has directed historical attention away from the major officeholders of state and towards lesser figures, bedchamber men and the like, who enjoyed intimacy with the king and could act as channels of communication for others.[125] Though Starkey did not have figures like Cotton in mind, it is helpful to reconsider him in this light, as a figure who served and had direct contact with favourites, princes and monarchs and who was seen by others as able to advance suits and suggestions to the government. More importantly, critics have questioned or rejected some of the revisions that Conrad Russell and I offered towards a remapping of the Stuart terrain. The 'post revisionists' argue that we exaggerated the importance of court faction, underplayed ideological commitments and differences and underestimated the importance of parliaments and of conflict between king and parliament.[126] Rereading Sir Robert Cotton (as Harvey reread his Livy) we can see how he can certainly lend support to some of those criticisms. Though undoubtedly attached to Howard patrons, Cotton, on the evidence we have, questions an undue emphasis upon faction. He served Somerset, but may have deserted him; he worked for Arundel but advised Arundel's enemy the Duke of Buckingham – even when the Earl Marshal was confined.

In other respects, however, rereading Cotton suggests that post revisionist premises themselves require re-examination. Even as I attempt it again in 1994, I find it difficult to place Cotton on any 'side'. Clearly – and I would now wish to emphasize it – Sir Robert exhibited real concern about the course of politics in the 1620s, and even fears for the liberty of the subject. But, as we now know, his concerns were shared by Privy Councillors as well as M.P.s. Indeed, the commissioning of Cotton to advise on the state of the realm before the calling of the 1628 parliament to me seriously questions Richard Cust's argument that by 1626 lines were hardening and the King's hostility to such counsels was manifest.[127] Cotton too gives the lie to all those scholars who persist in perpetuating the myth of widespread censorship in early Stuart England.[128] Amidst much heat, light has been shed by scholars like Blair Worden and Sheila Lambert who have demonstrated that censorship of literature was seldom effective and rarely attempted.[129] Middleton, Massinger and Jonson were punished and jailed, but continued to perform regularly at court. Similarly Cotton was twice confined, yet also appointed to a number of offices and commissions and considered as a candidate for Secretary of State. Even in 1630, when his library was closed, he was appointed as one of the 'persons of trust and quality' who made up the royal commission on fees.[130]

What Cotton's career undoubtedly underpins is the post revisionists' injunction to give more emphasis to ideology. With that I would never have disagreed: in 1979 I wrote that it would be essential for the historian of politics 'to investigate intellectual interests and values'.[131] Here the leading revisionist, Conrad Russell, has signally failed. The way forward is not to be found, however, in a retreat to the old model of ideological conflict, but to a more richly complicated reconfiguration of the meaning and performance of ideology in the political culture generally and in individuals like Cotton in particular.[132] Already new questions pose themselves. Did Cotton's interests in stones and coins commend him to an Arundel whose own collecting of marbles and medals expressed wider values and beliefs?[133] Did Franciscus Junius, author of *The Painting of the Ancients*, come to work in Arundel House through his link with Janus Gruter, one of Cotton's continental correspondents?[134] What did Henry Peacham learn as a Huntingtonshire schoolmaster from his antiquarian neighbour that led him to dedicate his *Art of Drawing* to Cotton in 1606?[135] Did he owe his place as tutor to Arundel's son to his link with Cotton? Were, as Blair Worden has powerfully argued, Ben Jonson's values formed amidst the circles of historians in which he moved: notably Selden, Camden, his schoolmaster, and Cotton, a fellow student, who incidentally hung Jonson's picture in his library?[136] Did shared concerns about the course of politics underlay the writings of dramatists, poets and historians who dedicated works to each other and many of whom borrowed from Cotton's library? Were those values and ideas more shaped by reading or political experience – or is the distinction itself unhelpful when both activities involved processes of interpretation and application? Did James I as scholar and poet, as well as king, himself encourage a culture in which history and poetry were favoured discourses of political participation and counsel?[137] And did his more taciturn son's succession effect a change in this broader political culture, with consequences we have yet to explore? A full biography of Cotton (or of Camden, Selden, or Jonson[138] for that matter) would have to consider such large questions and would undoubtedly contribute towards answering them. In the space that remains we can only return to a few episodes that may take on a renewed importance in the light of recent research.

Since *Sir Robert Cotton* was published in 1979, historians have focused much more attention on a subject to which Cotton made an early contribution: the succession of James VI and the union of England and Scotland. Bruce Galloway and Brian Levack have studied the vast pamphlet literature that the debates on union produced, and the obstacles to James's scheme.[139] Questions about the extent of union (full incorporation, federal union, or mere dynastic union), about the union of law, about the uniformity of religion and church government, about trading rights and commercial union, and about the adoption of the name of Great Britain preoccupied lawyers, poets, historians and antiquaries such as Sir John Dodderidge, John Hayward, Sir Henry Spelman and Sir Francis Bacon. James himself, under all heads, favoured complete union, which did not secure widespread support. Cotton, however, was wholeheartedly behind the scheme. In the tract he penned within two days of Elizabeth's death, Cotton wrote of 'both kingdoms being of one descent in blood, of one language ... the religion all the same ... their municipal laws near alike ... ', their estates of 'self name and nature'.[140] Reading in the *Basilikon Doron* of James's intent to 'reduce these two potent kingdoms to that earlier state wherein it stood of old', Cotton recommended 'Britain' as the name most fit: 'for the first these kingdoms of England and Scotland were received under that name about 2000 years ago ... for a second as a title sovereign it is the far oldest and so most honourable ... After Caesar his invasion that name this kingdom held and our kings that title.'[141] The antiquary rapidly surveyed the history of the name, citing ancient and medieval authorities before concluding: 'Sithence then so many regards of peace and safety, the affinity of language, law and religion, the former domestic precedents, foreign example and modern intentions do bring such a confluence of convenience to rebuild entire up this glorious empire it may pass happily with all acclamation by the name of Great Britain.'[142]

It was a powerful support for union before James had even arrived in London. With his patron Henry Howard, Earl of Northampton, Cotton continued to back the scheme in parliament where most M.P.s expressed fears of constitutional change or of Scottish competition for trade and patronage. Sir Robert (was his title a reward for his service?) continued to argue for the antiquity of the name where others objected that 'we should lose the ancient name of England' or feared 'the precedency of England in danger';[143] he tried to resolve the dispute and arguments against naturalization;[144] he laboured to promote the bill to abolish hostile laws;[145] he supported free trade, arguing that it enhanced wealth and shipping; he insisted that the Scots were not aliens but 'the offspring of an English root'.[146] Few went so far in their support of James's plans for full union, for 'one kingdom entirely governed, one uniformity in laws'.[147] Recent historiography has suggested how perceptive he may have been. Conrad Russell has argued that the problems of ruling multiple kingdoms, bequeathed by the failure of full union, were a force for political instability that contributed significantly to civil war. In particular, he contends, religious differences between the kingdoms created a problem of 'explosive force', which detonated in 1637.[148] Historians and antiquaries who defended the union concurred in this diagnosis. 'Where there is no unity of religion', John Dodderidge wrote in his *Brief Consideration of the Union*, 'there can be no hearty love'; the two realms, he thought, should embrace the episcopal form of government to strengthen church and state.[149] Cotton clearly felt religious uniformity should be restored, recalling that Scottish bishops 'from their first erection a long time were under the see of York in all spiritual causes, thence all receiving their consecrations.'[150] One is left wondering whether, had more in parliament shared these views, James I might have effected a full conformity of church government and so left a far more stable legacy to his son.

18

Cotton's service to the Earl of Northampton and advocacy of administrative reform may also now profitably be placed in a broader context. After the publication of *Sir Robert Cotton*, Professor Linda Peck developed my and her earlier arguments for Henry Howard to be re-evaluated as a leading proponent of reform in Jacobean government.[151] In an important chapter of *Northampton* she shows how the Earl fought for reform of household expenditures, purveyance, the ecclesiastical courts, the Navy, the Earl Marshal's office and of the practice of duelling. In every part of his campaign it would appear that Cotton was his leading adviser, not merely lending manuscripts or compiling lists of precedents, but drafting speeches, position papers and reports. Sir Robert presented evidence of the punishments suffered by duellers in the past; he drew up notes on purveyance; he prepared a volume of papers in connection with Northampton's endeavour as a commissioner to reform the College of Arms; most importantly he was Northampton's full partner in the investigation into abuses in the Navy; in 'The Manner and Means how the Kings of England Have from time to time Supported and Repaired their Estates', he counselled the end of waste in the royal household and economy, to 'reduce' it again 'to the best, first and most magnificent order'.[152] More than Northampton's amanuensis, Cotton and his patron shared the same values and spoke the same language to the point where it is impossible (and inappropriate) to determine who most influenced whom. Northampton wrote passionately to Somerset about the need for reform: 'without some care to pull up those suckers that draw the very moisture radical from the root it is no more possible for this exhausted monarchy to subsist...'.[153] Cotton, deploying the same metaphor, recommended immediate action against corruption because 'these privy stealths are the petites fleaux... that by silent progressions and augmentations eat daily into the very marrow and consume the radical moisture of this state.'[154]

Sir Robert endeavoured to promote the campaign for reform after his Howard patron's death in 1614. He advised Somerset on the reformation of the Heralds' office; he sat on the commission to inquire into fees charged in courts. The war years halted reforming initiatives, but in 1628 Cotton urged the Duke of Buckingham to champion the cause; and he counselled reduction of expenses and waste and the eradication of corruption. It was not long before another minister took up Northampton's and Cotton's programme, advocating a thorough reformation of the administration and state. We know little of Cotton's relationship with Thomas Wentworth who came to prominence towards the end of the antiquary's life. But it may be, as we shall suggest, that Cotton provided an important bridge between the Jacobean and Caroline movements for reform.

The broader historical context in which we must study Cotton's political activities in the 1620s has been radically rewritten since 1979. Conrad Russell has constructed a famous new narrative countering the thesis that the decade was one of crisis in relations between king and parliament, and arguing that war was the principal cause of political tension.[155] Roger Lockyer has published a revisionist biography of Buckingham, offering a more positive evaluation of the Duke's abilities, aims and policies.[156] Tom Cogswell has restudied the parliament of 1624 and the onset of war with Spain, Richard Cust the forced loan which was an expedient of war finance, and John Reeve the origin of Charles I's decision to rule without parliament that initiated the eleven years Personal Rule.[157] Though they by no means concur, and this is not the place to review their respective contributions, all these publications do cast valuable light on the shadows and inconsistencies in Cotton's career.

In the first place, Russell's analysis not only exonerates us from an obligation to place Cotton in the court or parliamentary camp, it enables us to make sense of Cotton's aiding the government with wartime fiscal expedients, whilst expressing concern at the perceived threat to liberties of unusual exactions and courses and his desire for a parliament. As Richard Cust demonstrates the concern over the illegality of the loan was shared by some Privy Councillors as well as M.P.s; a figure like Sir John Coke could deplore and yet appreciate the necessity that had dictated new courses.[158] Lockyer's *Buckingham* makes it easier to understand Cotton's initial support for the Duke and his reluctance until the end to give up on his being rewon for the public service. For, more than any, Buckingham sponsored reform of the Navy, a new commission for which was issued in 1626.[159] Cotton may also in 1624 have been one of those (elucidated by Professor Cogswell) who ardently advocated a war with Spain after the chicanery and assaults to national honour over a decade of marriage negotiations, in which Cotton had himself played a role, and so supported the Duke as a new found champion of the cause; certainly his relation of the Spanish 'disguises' was well publicized. If the war was a cause dear to him, we can also better understand how Cotton, like other frustrated 'patriots', came to be despondent at the disastrous military outcome and to despair of Buckingham in whom so much hope had been placed. Sir Robert's seeming volte-face from serving to attacking the Duke needs no factional explanation: Buckingham had failed the nation.[160]

Because he wished to continue the war – he opposed those who counselled peace[161] – Cotton was willing to continue to help with means, even dubious means, of raising money.[162] But he feared that ineptitude and waste made the country less inclined to pay and doubted the effectiveness of extra-parliamentary courses.[163] Whatever his reservations about the Duke, Cotton did not advocate his impeachment. He urged a thorough ongoing reform as a prelude to another parliament, which he hoped would restore normal courses and see the more successful prosecution of the war. Somewhat surprisingly Cotton was not prominent in the 1628 parliament: he clearly understood the fears of M.P.s about arbitrary courses; he and his patron Arundel had been on the receiving end of Buckingham's vindictiveness; yet Cotton could also understand the plight of the government and saw nothing fundamentally wrong that vigorous good counsel would not put right. Recent scholarship enables us to reread Cotton as a more explicable, less inconsistent figure, who, like so many, experienced heightened political tensions in the period 1626–8, but as yet felt no harsh alternative between serving king and country.

Nigel Ramsay's important discovery of Cotton's own list of his services to the crown also refines and develops our understanding of the antiquary's position during the 1620s.[164] Most important here, the dating of some Cotton tracts places them and their author in a different light and perspective. First, that Sir Robert was asked for advice on ways of raising money and men 'in the distress of the Pallatinat' suggests that as early as 1620 or 1621, the antiquary was consulted about a war, even though his patron, Arundel, was against belligerent courses.[165] It may be this service that brought Cotton to Prince Charles's attention and so helps explain the rôle he played in 1624. Secondly, we must, in the light of Ramsay's document, redate Cotton's tract arguing 'That the Sovereign's Person is Required in Great Councils'. Where I ascribed this to 1621 and the judicial proceedings against Bacon, it now appears that the treatise relates to the impeachment of Buckingham in 1626. This not only indicates that Charles I was considering permitting the judicial proceedings to continue, but with himself present; importantly it also suggests that Cotton was not yet regarded as an implacable enemy of the Duke, even after the 1625 parliament.[166] If this is the case, it would add to my argument that by 1626 the lines were not yet drawn and Charles was not yet bent on unparliamentary courses.

How then are we to explain Cotton's last years and the events that led to his confinement and the closure of his library? Was Cotton punished, on a spurious pretext, by clients of Buckingham for his support of the liberties of the subject in 1628? Or was Sir Robert prosecuted for the alleged dissemination of Dudley's tract which advocated non-parliamentary government and, if need be, the use of force? If the tract were the central issue, was Cotton behind it and, if so, did it express views he had come to hold in 1629, or tendencies he perceived and felt compelled to publicize and possibly answer? Even after the recent work on 1629 by Reeve and David Berkowitz, it is not easy to give a straightforward answer to these questions.[167] Factional politics is clearly not a sufficient explanation: those named as informants against Cotton and others in 1629 include Wentworth who was no friend to Buckingham, Arundel who had long been at odds with the Duke and a patron of Cotton, and Manchester, Cotton's kinsman who had sought his advice and who in 1630 was to plead for his pardon and restoration to favour.[168] Similarly the names of Wentworth, the leading proponent of the Petition of Right, and Arundel, a supporter in the Lords, question whether divisions over the issues of 1628 are central to the story. Reeve is right to argue in general that 'there is a wider political and ideological significance to the Cotton case'; and he reminds us that contemporaries associated it with the trial of Sir John Eliot and others after the parliamentary session of 1629; but he remains uncertain as to what use Cotton intended to make of the pamphlet – whether to discredit the government or prompt a debate about recent political developments.[169] The evidence suggests that the whole episode may have been based on a series of misunderstandings. When the tract came into his hands, Cotton, possibly suspecting that it represented extreme and unpalatable advice to Charles I, apparently set out to *answer* the treatise. When a search of his study revealed 'drafts for an answer to [the] proposition' the Council exonerated Cotton from the charge of authorizing the pamphlet.[170] Further investigation revealed it as an old document, sent from Florence by Sir Robert Dudley in 1614, to the Earl of Somerset, from whose papers it had entered Cotton's library. Sir Robert was still not entirely free of the suspicion that he might have deliberately published it in 1629 to foster fears of innovation in government, but the government began to relax as it became apparent that there had been no conspiracy; and the prisoners were first released and then discharged when the birth of the Prince offered an occasion to show mercy. Sure enough, both Cotton and his co-defendants and the government had exhibited distrust and edginess: Sir Robert may have genuinely feared the courses the Dudley pamphlet outlined, the Privy Council a conspiracy to paint the government in the colours of tyranny. But the distrust was not irreparable in 1630, not least because Charles I – as Wentworth's elevation manifests – was himself still capable of distinguishing between criticism and sedition. Despite his criticism of some courses Sir Robert evidently believed it still possible, by recounting his past services, to reassure the King of his 'uprightness and loyalty'.[171] Cotton's library remained closed, pending the completion of a catalogue. But where Sir John Eliot and other M.P.s festered in the Tower, Cotton was free; he reappeared in court circles and again sat on the commission on fees. In November 1630 the Councillors examining Cotton's library praised his readiness to serve the King and newsletters reported the reopening of the library and his restoration to royal favour. Had he lived longer, Cotton may have embarked on a whole new political career as an adviser, like William Noy, during the Personal Rule.[172]

VIII

During the proceedings against Cotton, the Earl of Manchester informed Sir Edward Montagu that the business 'makes a great noise in the country'.[173] We are beginning to learn more about Cotton's own country, his relationship to his seat in Huntingdonshire and their importance for understanding his intellectual and political activities. Firstly, it seems that Conington Castle may have been a second major repository for the Cottonian collection. We know that Sir Robert kept his stones there and built a special summer-house for them, though it is not clear whether this was for practical reasons – ease of transport, space – or to make a local impression, or indeed what it suggests about how the antiquary regarded his collection as a whole.[174] Camden refers to Cotton's 'cabinet' at Huntingdon, a term which implies rarities other than stones.[175] He evidently kept estate papers and documents at Conington, and may have had books there: Sidney Montagu promised to return borrowed books to Conington and a loan list in Cambridgeshire may have drifted from Cotton family papers.[176] Scholars too visited Conington as well as Cotton's London residence; many who saw his stones, for instance, must have viewed them there.[177] Huntingdonshire also featured more than has been noted in Cotton's scholarly activities: he searched for books there; he excavated and found there a fossilized fish; and he collected material for a history of the county.[178]

It is also becoming clearer that Cotton's scholarly activities were as much related to local as they were to national politics. David Howarth poses the crucial question why

22

Cotton erected cenotaphs to Scottish princes in the middle of the Fens and is surely right to answer that Cotton was keen to vaunt his ancestry and relationship to Robert the Bruce, not least against his rival Sir Simeon Steward.[179] Scholarship was also put to more practical, some might say, sinister uses. Professor Manning shows how when the copyholders of the manor of Glatton filed in Chancery a complaint against Cotton, his uncle John and son Thomas, Sir Robert responded with a carefully supported cross bill which 'illustrates the application by Sir Robert Cotton of antiquarian research to the task of estate administration'.[180] Cotton was indeed embroiled in local politics – in boundary disputes, also with the tenants of Glatton, and in quarrels about drainage schemes;[181] he was threatened with proceedings for failing to repair a highway in Conington.[182] And, though he spent little time in his house and county, both remained important to him, as to other county gentlemen whose careers took them to London or to court.[183] He continued to oversee his rental accounts; he was involved in purchases of more land and of advowsons; he continued to build and improve Conington Castle up to his death.[184] Sir Robert also held local office – as sheriff, as one of the commissioners to raise an aid for the marriage of James I's daughter Elizabeth, as a surveyor of a royal manor, and as a member of the commission for sewers.[185] It is worth remembering that Cotton wished to be buried not in London, but in the south chapel of the parish church in his native Conington, the name of which often featured as part of his inscription in books and manuscripts.[186] Though he became a J. P. for Westminster in the 1620s, Cotton remained a country squire: we may need to think further about the importance of that for Cotton's attitude to his collection and still more to his perception of politics.

Further research on Huntingdonshire may throw light on the facets of Cotton not illuminated by the glare of London and court politics. Yet there are shadowy corners of the personality which will pose a challenge to the biographer who sets out to paint Cotton – not only in the flesh but warts and all. Historians of the early modern period tend to write the biographies of political and administrative figures, perhaps too of scholars, as though they had no life outside the office or study. It greatly changes our view of him, even as Secretary of State, to read of Sir John Coke in his seventies discussing the latest fashions with his tailor.[187] Certainly it would seem Cotton had a colourful side. He gathered and may have written verse; he enjoyed the company of poets and was obviously the host to lively gatherings of a social and scholarly nature.[188] Passion was certainly not unknown to him. The young man who bemoaned to his commonplace book the shortage of faithful and trustworthy women proved to be a philanderer and adulterer.[189] At some early point, probably by 1603, Cotton left his wife and lived at Lady Hunsdon's residence, possibly as her lover. And while D'Ewes tells us Cotton was reconciled to his wife after the fall of Somerset, the evidence suggests other instances of infidelity.[190] It was said that Sir Robert employed as an assistant *one* of his bastard sons;[191] and the conspiracy to set up the antiquary in a compromising position with a woman so as to blackmail him makes far more sense if Cotton had a reputation for extramarital affairs.[192] Cotton took aphrodisiacs in his fifties.[193] Such a side to an otherwise serious character may help to explain how Cotton befriended men like Ben

Jonson, who was also given to overindulgence, and the other wits who met at the Mermaid, as well as more sober figures. Unless, however, we are able to find out more, we can only imagine how the several passions in his life, sexual and scholarly, integrated in the man. Cotton is still 'in danger of being lost amidst the many volumes of manuscripts which he collected'.[194] But if we cannot find him, we should at least remember that he is there.

IX

A full evaluation of Cotton's writings demands a greater knowledge of the circumstances that produced each piece, and of the personality of the man himself – knowledge that we may never have. But Graham Parry makes an invaluable contribution to directing our attention back to the pieces collected in *Cottoni Posthuma* and Cotton's 'counsels'.[195] *Cottoni Posthuma* by no means contains all Cotton wrote. We have already remarked on sections by Sir Robert folded in the work of others: in Camden's *Annales*, in *Britannia*, in Speed's *History*; in addition he helped Ben Jonson pen a history of Henry V which burned in the fire at Jonson's house; he started with John Hayward a history of the House of Norfolk; and he wrote on arms and seals.[196] On the more obviously political side, Cotton considered the question of jurisdiction in ecclesiastical affairs; he drew, according to D'Ewes, a full declaration outlining the breach with Spain in 1624 (that was never published); fragments and allusions in correspondence suggest other works undertaken and either unfinished or lost.[197] Moreover, as with other antiquarian and historical works, Cotton may have been the ghost writer behind official speeches and declarations: like 'reading', 'authoring', as we are beginning to appreciate, is not a straightforward matter.[198] The volume *Cottoni Posthuma* itself wrongly attributes a treatise to Cotton and includes under its title two essays which are acknowledged as written by others. But *Cottoni Posthuma*, if only a selection of Cotton's œuvre (chosen as we shall see for its editor's purposes in 1651), offers an opportunity to analyse some of the texts for which, albeit they were not all then published, Cotton was known in his day.

What strikes the reader immediately is how few of the pieces are works of history as we understand them. Though several draw on knowledge of precedent, others offer straightforward political analysis, and all feel written at some distance from the rich manuscript holdings and massive erudition of Cotton's library. Even the most obviously historical piece, *The Life and Reign of Henry the Third*, reads, according to Parry, 'like the precis of an Elizabethan play of the 1590s in which the action is historic but the relevance contemporary'.[199] Parry's acute observation alerts us to the artificial barrier scholars have erected (and still police) between literature and history; and makes apparent what still discomforts us: that Cotton's purposes as a historian were political. Another commentator shows how little regard Cotton had in fulfilling his political purposes for what we would call scholarly integrity. The portraits of Simon de Montfort and Henry himself are one-sided and wooden. *Henry III*, writes Daniel Woolf, 'is perhaps the most extreme Jacobean example of the deliberate distortion and compression

24

of historical fact for the sake of offering counsel.'[200] Cotton had important general advice to give: the need for economy, for the reinvigoration of the Privy Council, for the court to set an example of reform to the country, for a monarch who would lead and govern 'in his own person'.[201] Yet the genre in which he gave this advice was important to him. Cotton expressed undisguised contempt for those who devised 'imaginary and fantastic forms of Commonwealths', as for those who 'flatter their own belief and ability that they can mould any state to these general rules which in particular application will prove idle.'[202] Historical example and parallel was for Cotton the best medium for conveying counsel. By corollary, the basis of the best political advice was knowledge of precedent circumstances which might cast light on present occasions.

In each of his political commissions therefore Cotton surveyed the past, not primarily out of a legalistic attachment to precedents, but for the best courses in similar circumstances. Tracts that read at first as mere catalogues of precedents always contain advice – and sometimes warnings. In his 'Manner and Means how the Kings of England Have from time to time Supported and Repaired their Estates', Cotton lists a number of past courses for raising money. But he warns against waste and extravagant expenditure on favourites, strongly counsels reform and cautions the King about expedients which, though lucrative, are impolitic.[203] Impositions, for example, he describes boldly as 'of late so stretched as it is feared it will prove the overthrow of trade, neither do I find this course at any other time…'.[204] In a piece written for James I to counter the arguments for war emanating from Prince Henry's circle, Cotton staunchly backs the King's policy of neutrality and flatters his standing, but issues another reminder of the need for the monarch not to dissipate his estate: 'as well by reason of state as rules of best government the revenues and profits quae ad sacrum patrimonum principis pertinent, which belong to the sacred patrimony of the crown, should remain firm and unbroken.'[205] In histories as well as masques and other literary panegyrics, criticism could be combined with compliment.[206]

Because Cotton always read the past for its direct applicability to the present moment, it is not surprising that his use and interpretation of the past altered with changed circumstances. Graham Parry confirms my sense that increasingly Cotton's writings 'emphasized the need for the full participation of Parliament in government', as experience again demonstrated the dangers of bad counsel.[207] In the 1625 speech he wrote or drafted, Cotton comes to quite a different view of his own Jacobean past and so of the most suitable precedents from which to learn. In his tract 'That the Sovereign's Person is Required in Great Councils', Sir Robert collects the precedents which support James's right to be involved in impeachment proceedings but concludes: 'He dares not say precedents are warrants to direct; the success … as the knowledge of them sometimes have made ill example by extension of regal power through ill counsels with ill success.'[208] The counsel to moderation owes more to contemporary circumstances than the precedents themselves.

Cotton's most widely distributed pamphlet, which he published under his own name in 1628, was his least historical piece. 'The Danger wherein The Kingdom now Standeth and the Remedy' was written in January 1628, probably in response to a request by the Privy Council.[209] Though it drew on medieval precedents – Cotton evoked the fates of Edward II and Richard II – the past that most shaped it was the recent past, of Cotton's own memory (or idealization), of Queen Elizabeth's reign and early James. And, more than any other work, it was focused on the present. Cotton catalogued his contemporaries' (and his own?) fears for the liberty of the subject threatened by loans, conscription and arbitrary arrest; the dangers of invasion from Spain; and concern for the safety of Protestantism. Most of all he pointed to the failure of counsel and distrust of the Duke of Buckingham. By way of remedy he counselled a return to more moderate courses and a parliament to win back hearts and purses.

It was just such counsel that drew James Howell to an edition of Cotton's writings in 1651. A Royalist who had written a political allegory to support the King's cause on the eve of civil war, Howell spent much of the 1640s in prison. During his confinement, he looked back on, and may have written his familiar letters to reconstruct, a past in which sensible men had advocated moderate courses. Howell must have known Cotton, as he knew Selden and Jonson. He cited the great historical scholars – Camden, Ralegh, Selden (and Coke) – and, like Cotton, collected proverbs and axioms. In 1651, at a time of uncertainty for the future of government, he turned, like so many, to the best of Elizabethan practice, which Howell saw encapsulated in Cotton's life and writings.[210] As he explained in his preface: 'what a great Zelot he was to his Countrey ... in all Parlements, where he served so often, his main endeavours were to assert the public Liberty, and that *Prerogative* and Privilege might run in their due Channels ... '.[211] A recent sketch of Howell's career goes a long way to explain his edition of *Cottoni Posthuma* in 1651. Evidently, however, the volume was more than a book for that moment. The whole collection was reissued in 1657, 1672 and 1679; individual pieces were separately republished in 1641, 1642, 1651, 1655, 1657, 1659, 1661, 1665, 1675, 1679, 1681, 1689 and beyond.[212] As Cotton reinterpreted the past with changing circumstances, so generations reread his writings and applied them to new conditions: 'The usefulness of such works depended as much on the response of the reader, on his ability to draw connections with a current situation as it did on the wit of the author.'[213] There is a whole history to be written of such readings. But do they echo the spirit of Sir Robert Cotton? Howell had no doubt that they did. Cotton, he felt sure, shared his belief that one studied and read to make 'useful application of it' and that Cotton wrote in the same spirit that he read – for use and application.[214]

As we begin to reconstruct the reading habits of the Renaissance, we come to understand how typical such views were and how they operated in general and in particular. Whether at the theatre, or reading the classics or the fables, contemporaries read to derive morals for their own time, the commonplace book being often the site of the readers' mediations between old text and modern circumstances.[215] Authors wrote in and for a culture in which readers not only applied a text, but searched between its lines and decoded meanings.[216] Histories were no exception; they may even have replaced the drama as a principal medium of contemporary comment; they were seldom read for their 'contribution to scholarship', our own academic benchmark of worth. When that quintessential antiquary Simonds D'Ewes, who pored over charters and rolls, picked up Hayward's history of Henry IV, he was 'the rather drawn to read further because his reign came somewhat near our hard times'.[217] Amongst the ivory towers of Oxford, the Queen's College scholar Thomas Crosfield was no less alert to present concerns. In 1627 he noted: 'There is a little book published comprising several passages of state historically related as they were carried in the long reign of King Henry III, with some observations or applications to our state at this present which by reason of favourites and discontented peers resembles in many things that ancient government.'[218] Cotton's readers do not appear to have doubted that he wrote to impart counsel and to convey values – or that he had something important to say.

X

That sense of importance has not been shared by modern commentators. Blair Worden did not think Cotton's ideas very impressive; Clive Holmes was harsher still about Sir Robert's 'rambling and platitudinous sentiments'.[219] As with Cotton's historical activities, such judgements rest on anachronistic criteria of importance – and once again perhaps on the issue of originality. As Blair Worden observed, much of what Cotton believed and counselled was part of the general currency of the age, even platitudinous. But the rearticulation of commonplace and traditional values at a time when they appear to be in danger gives particular force to the familiar, and reinvests old paradigms with powerful contemporary endorsement. As Richard Cust observes of Cotton's arguments in 1628: 'There was ... nothing unusual in such views. What is interesting is the fact that they then were presented at all, that someone felt that it was necessary to restate the principles which had normally been taken as read ... '.[220]

What were those principles and how did Cotton restate them? One, as I have argued, was balance and moderation in government. We have seen Cotton warn against the straining of the prerogative to excessive heights, but he had a greater horror of populism and disobedience. What was needed, he noted in passing in a treatise on Chancery, was to sustain a mean between the extremes of majesty and common law.[221] In his discussion of 'Other Descriptions ... of the Parliament', his metaphors became as platitudinous as the ideas expressed. The relations of King, Lords and Commons were an imitation of the natural corpus of man, head, breast and body, 'and harmonical because so well turned a bass, mean and treble, there proceedeth an exquisite consert and delicious harmony'.[222] The point is that, at a time when experience was beginning to suggest their redundancy, Cotton not only restated these ideals *for* his age, he tried to demonstrate how they could be maintained in practice. The principles were not at fault, only the way in which they were applied. Before the Petition of Right rendered contentious the issue of imprisonment without due process, Cotton observed that before and after Magna Carta 'the kings of this realm ... did exercise their kingly authority in that behalf which was so far from offending the subject for a long time ... '.[223] The

27

question was not one of fundamental conflict between government and liberty. Subjects needed to obey, but a monarch 'should consider that nothing is more worth his apprehension than to see his subjects well satisfied of his actions.'[224] And nothing satisfied men more than a sense of the king's commitment to customary courses and values.

Such was also Cotton's solution to the mounting tensions within the church which have recently been the subject of much historiographical debate. Cotton had no time for popery; in 1624 he and D'Ewes discussed 'the danger and detestableness of popery since the Council of Trent'; and he advised James on how to check the influx of Jesuit priests.[225] But the antiquary was no fanatic. Not least because his maternal grandfather and uncle had been recusants, Cotton appreciated (as did James I) that Catholics could be loyal Englishmen, as they had proved in 1588.[226] The solution to the Catholic challenge lay not in making martyrs but in reinvigorating the Church of England, and restoring the old and best times of Elizabeth: 'In those days there was an emulation between the clergy and the laity; and a strife arose whether of them should show themselves most affectionate to the gospel. Ministers haunted the houses of the worthiest men, where Jesuits now build their tabernacles, and poor country churches were frequented with the best of the shire. The word of God was precious, Prayer and Preaching went hand in hand together.'[227] Prayer and Preaching: the two words seem intended to conjoin what increasingly religious quarrels were putting asunder. Cotton made no direct comment on the quarrels between the Arminians and Puritans.[228] When Sir John Eliot asked his assistance in 1629 to deal with the Arminian question, Cotton, to bring about 'a happy conclusion of your dispute of religion', advised firm adherence to the Elizabethan settlement, to 'the Catholic body of the church of England'.[229] Similarly the authors of the 'Topographical Description of England' praised an Elizabethan church whose doctrine was proved out of the Scriptures, Church Councils and the Fathers and rejected as factious the names of Lutheran and Calvinist.[230] 'How', Cotton asked in urging all to subscribe to one faith and church, 'can we draw others to our church, if we cannot agree where and how to lay on our foundation?'[231]

These traditional ideals for church and state informed Cotton's personal political ideology and morality – a belief above all in one's duty to serve the commonweal. When he described his own activities, scholarly and political, Sir Robert most often used the language of public duty and service. In the books he donated to Sir Thomas Bodley's library he inscribed his gift as 'for the public good';[232] his great library of manuscripts he collected, he claimed, 'out of my duty to the public'; his collections and learning, 'the labours of my life', he was 'most ready to offer to all public service'.[233] Men's self-description is not always the best key to their principles. But in Cotton's case his contemporaries spoke of his employment for the public good and his love of his country 'which yourself seek first to adorn'.[234] For his part his editor often heard Cotton say 'that he himself had the least share in himself but his country … had the greatest interest in him', and as a good Stoic, Howell commended a man 'in a perpetual pursuit after Vertu and knowledge … '.[235]

28

Cotton saw his service performed in the very advice that historians have scorned as platitudinous. It was, we might say, *deliberately* not original advice. But neither was it the tired repetition and evocation of outmoded values that had no relevance to the needs of the day. Clive Holmes is right to observe that Cotton's conservative ideals of moderation, harmony and public service need to be discussed as part of the ideology of the 'country'. Yet Cotton regarded them no less as the best values for the court – and indeed served ministers whom he believed embodied them.[236] Sir Robert expressed some concern that the government might be becoming out of touch with the mood in the localities, but while the Huntingdonshire baronet was still called upon to give counsel in 1628, there was no need for him to conclude that those beliefs divided the country from the court, or parliament from the crown. Advice in the form of the politic history was advice for court *and* country.[237]

The politic history is a genre that belongs to the revival of interest in the classics, particularly Tacitus, and of commentaries on the classics in the late sixteenth century.[238] The influence of 'Taciteanism', more notoriously of Machiavellianism, produced an ambivalent response in early modern England.[239] On the one hand, the ideals of a Christian commonweal, of government as an ethical activity and of the need to subordinate private interest to the public good, remained the prevailing paradigm. On the other, experience showed all too clearly that *realpolitik*, intrigue and ambition characterized human and public behaviour, that Machiavelli and his disciples described accurately what men did, if not what they ought to do. Historians were particularly prone to reveal the ambivalence towards Machiavellian doctrines that characterized late Elizabethan and Jacobean culture. As Daniel Woolf puts it well, 'Ralegh's ambivalence to the *realpolitik* of Tacitus and Machiavelli represents a conflict in early Stuart historiography between the duty to recommend effective worldly policy and the desire to advocate moral behaviour, a conflict which Ralegh (who was not alone) never resolved.'[240] Reviewers were sceptical about my claims for the influence of these ideas on Sir Robert Cotton. In some instances they were right to point out that such influence – of Giovanni Botero, for example – cannot be conclusively demonstrated. But there are notes on Guicciardini among Cotton's manuscripts, and *pace* Blair Worden, there is evidence that Cotton read Machiavelli who is cited in his treatise on the Jesuits.[241] Rereading Cotton's maxims, I can hear him struggling with the conflict that Ralegh never resolved, even, more than Ralegh, endeavouring to resist acknowledging the force of Machiavellian observations. Yet whilst rejecting Machiavellian morality, Cotton adopted a central message of the Florentine: that success in public affairs depended upon acting in a manner appropriate to time and circumstance. For Sir Robert this meant no new amoral or radical courses. English history taught that the strongest regimes and best times were those in which the best examples and courses were followed and enacted. Accordingly, his advice to act on the moment was reiterated in the traditional language of statesmen behaving as skilful musicians, 'qui artem musices non mutant sed musices modum'.[242] Following the Taciteans, Cotton drew up axioms for the conduct of politics, but when it came to conveying advice he enfolded them in a history – a history not of

29

classical times but of a medieval English king who had applied traditional remedies to the problems of his day.[243] Cotton's scholarship was always directed to 'useful application' in public life.[244] No less his public counsels, whatever they owed to new Italian influences, were presented as the lessons of English tradition and history.

XI

What then of Cotton's importance for and reputation in early Stuart English scholarship and politics? None has ever questioned the centrality of his library and Colin Tite's researches are adding to our appreciation of just how important it was; Edmund Bolton's claims for its standing in Europe as well as England may soon appear description rather than hyperbole.[245] Similarly, few have doubted the role Cotton played in helping fellow scholars, not only with books, but with suggestions, contacts and notes. Again we are gaining a fuller picture of how widespread and sometimes how deep that assistance was, how far Cotton was a facilitator for a generation of scholars. He was asked to be an unpaid research assistant, an adviser on what to include in books, and sometimes a partial or co-author, often not acknowledged in the manner that our own standards would require.

That said, few modern commentators have had much to say for him as a scholar. To John Kenyon, he was a 'dilettante ... in love with abstruse and curious learning which he assembled without the least discrimination'.[246] Fritz Levy dismissed him as 'an intellectual satellite of Camden'.[247] Though more favourable, the latest historian of early Stuart historical writing was forced to conclude that 'as neither historian nor antiquary ... was Cotton himself especially outstanding'.[248] By the twentieth-century historian's criteria of scholarly judgement, such evaluations are not unreasonable. Lurking behind them, however, is an anachronistic disdain for a figure who, for all his resources, never made a major original contribution to scholarship and who (here one might have expected more sympathy) failed to finish books. Moreover, such judgements smack of the academic's continuing contempt for the scholar involved in the world of affairs, the figure who left the pure groves of academe for the corrupting influences of the public sphere. Even Colin Tite dismisses Cotton's political pieces as 'more ephemeral achievements'.[249] Cotton himself, however, would have demanded to be judged in the round – as a public figure *and* scholar – because the two spheres were not separate for him.

Unfortunately, as a politician, he has not enjoyed a much better press: Holmes thinks him 'pompous'; Kenyon considered him 'entirely without political sense'. These read as strange verdicts on a man who was weekly called upon to advise M.P.s, ministers and monarchs, and whose advice was often taken – both at the time and later. The calling of the 1628 parliament, for instance, may have been due to his 'Danger and Remedy'; and there is much to suggest that during the 1630s Charles I carried out the programmes of reform at court and fiscal expedients outlined in Cotton's 'Henry the Third' and 'Manner and Means'. It was Cotton's 'cousin' Sir John Borough who, following the precedents outlined by the antiquary in 1610, drew Charles I's attention to knighthood

30

fines, and other prerogative rights exploitable for fiscal gain.[250] But it was Charles I himself who appears to have directly taken up Cotton's advice: in his endeavour to reform the court, economize on the household, reinvigorate the Privy Council and, dispensing with favourites, 'dispose of affairs of most weight in his own person'.[251] Certainly, like Sir Robert, the King never doubted that 'Princes' Manners, though a mute law, have more of life and vigour than those of letters.'[252]

Cotton too was held in great esteem by those who, like him, stressed the utility of historical study, and the need for governors to be learned in its lessons. In the extraordinary collection of Sir William Drake's papers (in the Ogden bequest at University College, London) that esteem is made abundantly clear.[253] Sir William Drake was the son of Sir Francis Drake of Esher and Joan Tottel, who inherited his considerable estate, Shardeloes in Buckinghamshire, from his maternal grandfather in 1626. Drake attended Christ Church, Oxford, and the Middle Temple, where he was bound with Sir Simonds D'Ewes.[254] He was a man of voracious appetite for learning, and especially for reading histories and antiquities, in manuscript and printed works, English and continental. In his quest for manuscripts on English law and parliament, Drake, like most of his contemporaries, was directed to the library of Sir Robert Cotton and, after 1631, to Sir Thomas Cotton.[255] He borrowed from Cotton as he did from D'Ewes, who may have introduced him to Sir Robert.[256] But Drake does more than add another name to the list of those borrowing from the Cottonian library. For Drake was, like Cotton, a man of affairs. He sought and obtained the reversion of an office;[257] in 1640 he sat as M.P. for Amersham; and throughout the 1630s, whilst he was in England and travelling on the Continent, he kept diaries and notebooks – of public events, and of his reading.[258] Drake read and annotated the classical histories and humanist commentators on them: Xenophon and Plutarch, Tacitus and Cicero. But most of all, he read and constantly reread the works of Lipsius, Cardanus, Bodin, and especially Machiavelli, Guicciardini and – the man Drake saw as their English disciple – Francis Bacon. And there was a method to Drake's reading: he distilled from his studies a collection of maxims and rules for the conduct of his personal and public life, believing that 'when a man is deliberate and governed by order, rules and principles, no difficulty he meets with faints or abates his courage.'[259] Drake had little time for study as contemplation. To enable a man for action he thought nothing more important than the constant study and application of histories to the times: 'He that is well read in history seems to be of every country, to have lived in all ages and to have assisted at all councils.'[260]

Such a philosophy as well as a quest for manuscripts drew Sir William Drake to Sir Robert Cotton. Evidently, one of Drake's friends, 'Mr Pots' (Sir John Pots of Norfolk?) thought Cotton made such little use of his books, that – he told Sir William – he was like a man that had many weapons and never fought.[261] Drake clearly did not agree. His notes reveal that he read and annotated Cotton's writings more often than he borrowed from the antiquary's library. He laboured to obtain Cotton's account 'of the house of Austria practice', presumably the speech delivered in the 1624 parliament.[262] He reminded himself to see 'Sir Robert Cotton's advice to help the King without aid of parliament

...'[263] and it evidently impressed him: 'read often' Cotton's project, he counselled himself, and 'let my fancy work upon the reading.'[264] Indeed Cotton became one of Drake's English models for his own development as a rhetorician and a writer. Significantly, after all his vast reading, he had decided to take Queen Elizabeth's and James I's chief minister, Lord Salisbury, as his pattern; but noted: 'to supply his defect of writing many things read much Lord Bacon and Sir Robert Cotton's writings.'[265] The pairing of Bacon and Cotton was no mere whim of the occasion. Elsewhere, Drake instructed himself to 'read often Sir Francis Bacon's, Sir Robert Cotton's works'.[266]

It is not clear whether Drake knew Cotton personally, though it would seem quite likely. Certainly he noted that the Duke of Buckingham laboured to secure a match for Cotton's son, and, while he was overseas, he was informed of the search of Cotton's study following the discovery of the Dudley project (which Drake read).[267] Whether he knew him or not, however, Drake regarded Cotton as a man of affairs and valued his writings, as his collections, for their use, rather than their 'scholarship' in our sense of the word. He regarded Cotton's library as an 'arsenal' rather than repository for disinterested scholarly research.[268] He read Cotton, as he read Machiavelli, Guicciardini, and Bacon, for his advice for the present, as much as his comments on the past. Sir William Drake's papers offer rich evidence of how a highly educated Englishman read his histories in the Renaissance, and how, at every point, historical learning was applied to present circumstances.[269] They remind us that, for all that subsequent generations of scholars have praised Cotton for assembling one of the greatest repositories for the academic study of the medieval past, Cotton's contemporaries perceived him, and valued him, differently: as a collector, writer and historian always engaged with his seventeenth-century present – with its political values, problems and disputes.

1 K. Sharpe, *Sir Robert Cotton 1586–1631: History and Politics in Early Modern England* (Oxford, 1979).

2 B. Worden, 'Unmatched Antiquary', *London Review of Books* (21 Feb. 1980), p. 22; J. P. Kenyon, 'Antiquarian at Court', *Times Literary Supplement* (16 May 1980), p. 563; F. Levy, *American Historical Review*, lxxxvi (1981), p. 127.

3 Kenyon, art. cit.; C. Holmes, *Historical Journal*, xxiv (1981), p. 1026; see below p. 27.

4 See K. Sharpe (ed.), *Faction and Parliament: Essays on Early Stuart History* (Oxford, 1978) and 'Revisionism Revisited' (2nd edn 1985); also see C. Russell, *Parliaments and English Politics 1621–1629* (Oxford, 1979), p. 8, n. 1.

5 K. Sharpe, *Politics and Ideas* (London, 1989); K. Sharpe and S. Zwicker (eds.), *Politics of Discourse* (Berkeley and London, 1987); K. Sharpe and P. Lake (eds.), *Culture and Politics in Early Stuart England* (Basingstoke, 1994).

6 See most importantly R. Cust and A. Hughes (eds.), *Conflict in Early Stuart England* (Harlow, 1989), and D. Hirst, 'The Place of Principle', *Past and Present*, xcii (1981), pp. 79–99.

7 The most obvious examples are Stephen Greenblatt, *Renaissance Self-Fashioning* (Chicago, 1980); idem (ed.), *The Power of Forms in the English Renaissance* (Norman, Oklahoma, 1982); L. Montrose, 'A Poetics of Renaissance Culture', *Criticism*, xxiii (1981), pp. 349–59; J. Goldberg, *James I and the Politics of Literature* (Baltimore and London, 1983).

8 See E. Freund, *The Return of the Reader: Reader-Response Criticism* (New York, 1987); R. Darnton, 'What is the History of Books?', *Daedalus*, cxi (1982), pp. 65–83; R. Chartier, *The Cultural Uses of Print in Early Modern*

Europe (Princeton, 1987); A. Grafton and L. Jardine, '"Studied for Action": How Gabriel Harvey read his Livy', *Past and Present*, cxxix (1990), pp. 30–78.

9 *Am. Hist. Rev.*, lxxxvi (1981), p. 127.

10 C. G. C. Tite, 'The Early Catalogues of the Cottonian Library', *British Library Journal*, vi (1980), pp. 144–57.

11 See C. G. C. Tite, '"Lost or stolen or strayed": a survey of manuscripts formerly in the Cotton library', *British Library Journal*, xviii (1992), pp. 107–47, reprinted below, pp. 262–306, and *The Manuscript Library of Sir Robert Cotton*, 9th Panizzi Lectures, 1993 (London, 1994). I am grateful to Colin Tite for his generosity in allowing me to read these important lectures in advance of publication and for other advice.

12 *British Library Journal*, xviii (1992), *passim*.

13 C. G. C. Tite, '"Lost or Stolen or Strayed"', below pp. 268–70; idem, *The Manuscript Library of Sir Robert Cotton*, pp. 1–39, esp. p. 15.

14 BL, Add. MSS. 5161, ff. 1–8; 36106; Harl. MS. 6018, f. 150.

15 Tite, '"Lost or Stolen or Strayed"', below p. 276.

16 Ibid., p. 283; *Cal. Treas. Books*, vol. xix (1957), p. 642.

17 I would like to thank Godfrey Davis for sharing with me his research on Cotton manuscripts.

18 Tite, 'Early Catalogues'; Sharpe, *Cotton*, pp. 68–73.

19 R. Parr, *The Life of James Ussher...with a Collection of 300 Letters* (London, 1686), p. 79.

20 Ibid., p. 230; P.R.O., PC 2/41, p. 91.

21 Tite, '"Lost or Stolen or Strayed"', p. 281.

22 Sharpe, *Cotton*, appendix, pp. 251–2; BL, Harl. MS. 6018, ff. 159, 164v.

23 Some are now in Huntingdonshire R.O., Conington Papers, 2B Steeple Gidding Papers, Conington Papers Rental Estate books, Charters Box 14, Conington Lincoln diocese papers. See below pp. 22–3.

24 *H.M.C. 6th Report App.*, p. 453.

25 W. Hamper, *The Life, Diary and Correspondence of Sir William Dugdale* (London, 1827), p. 9.

26 BL, Harl. MS. 6018, ff. 178, 182, 190; Cotton MS. App. XLV, art. 13.

27 To add examples, Claudius C. VII is found in no catalogue before 1654, Otho B. VI appears in the 1621 list but not 1654, Otho A. XVIII is on a 1635 list but has disappeared by 1654; Vitellius B. I disappears from view in the 1656 catalogue.

28 That it remained a controversial collection is evident from the remark of Cotton's grandson in 1687, that the time was not appropriate for a catalogue because the Library contained much 'very cross to the Romish interest': Tite, *The Manuscript Library of Sir Robert Cotton*, p. 71.

29 Cambridgeshire Record Office, Antrobus MSS.

30 A. Prescott, '"Their present miserable state of cremation": The Restoration of the Cotton Library', below p. 392; *A Catalogue of the Manuscripts in the Cottonian Library* (London, 1777).

31 Prescott, below pp. 393–5.

32 Ibid., p. 395.

33 Ibid., p. 429.

34 Cambs. R.O., Antrobus MSS., Memo on Cotton Library. For Starkey, see C. E. Wright, *Fontes Harleiani* (London, 1972), q.v. See too H. Love, *Scribal Publication in Seventeenth-Century England* (Oxford, 1993), pp. 86–7. Harold Love's study has much to contribute to an understanding of Cotton's library and the importance of Cotton's writings. Colin Tite is planning an edition of the loans lists.

35 Antrobus MSS., Memo.

36 Cf. Sharpe, *Cotton*, pp. 56–7, 66–8.

37 Ibid., p. 57.

38 C. G. C. Tite, 'A Catalogue of Sir Robert Cotton's printed books?', *British Library Journal*, xvii (1991), pp. 1–11, reprinted below pp. 183–93.

39 BL, Cotton MS. Julius F. VI, f. 314: Roger Dodsworth to Cotton.

40 BL, Cotton MS. Julius C. III, ff. 15, 16.

41 Ibid., f. 26 (William Bold); f. 388 (James Ware).

42 BL, Add. MS. 35213, f. 42.

43 See BL, Cotton MS. Julius C. IX, f. 101.

44 BL, Sloane MS. 241, ff. 27v, 68v; W. Camden, *Britannia* (London, 1610), p. 88; J. Speed, *History of Great Britaine* (London, 1614), pp. 322, 593; Sharpe, *Cotton*, p. 38.

45 E. Bolton, *Nero Cæsar, or Monarchie Depraued* (London, 1627), pp. 14–15. See too Bodl. MS. Ashmole 1149, f. 113.

46 Arundel provides an obvious link; see below pp. 17–21.

47 D. McKitterick, 'From Camden to Cambridge: Sir Robert Cotton's Roman inscriptions, and their subsequent history', below pp. 105–28.

48 G. van der Meer, 'An Early Seventeenth-century Inventory of Cotton's Anglo-Saxon coins', below pp. 168–82.

49 G. Keynes (ed.), *The Letters of Sir Thomas Browne* (London, 1941), p. 337; Sir W. Dugdale, *The History of Imbanking and Drayning* (London, 1772), pp. 172–3.

50 Though Tite's suggestion that the imperial pressmarks followed Charles I's purchase of Titian's Caesars is an interesting one: *The Manuscript Library of Sir Robert Cotton*, p. 86.

51 BL, Harl. MS. 6018, f. 154.

52 Ibid., f. 159.

53 Ibid., f. 174; cf. f. 160, 'Books lent, I know not to who'.

54 Ibid., ff. 148v, 158v; cf. ff. 154, 156, 162, 174, 176. On Griffith, see now R. Ovenden, 'Jaspar Gryffyth and his books', *British Library Journal*, xx (1994), pp. 107–39, which appeared after my essay was written.

55 See, for example, Harl. MS. 6018, ff. 157, 170, 174. When he lists a book as 'new bound', Cotton seldom mentions its colour.

56 Harl. MS. 6018, ff. 152v, 174v; ff. 148, 150, 153, 154v, 159, 161, 162, (arms) 148, 163, 176 (clasps).

57 I owe my knowledge of these engravings to Godfrey Davis.

58 Tite, *The Manuscript Library of Sir Robert Cotton*, p. 48.

59 BL, Cotton MS. Titus C. I, f. 140 and *passim*; Sharpe, *Cotton*, p. 26; BL, Add. MS. 25247, f. 46.

60 Harl. MS. 6018, f. 174v; Cotton loaned these to Secretary Sir Ralph Winwood who held the office from 1614 to 1617. For Cotton's role in negotiations with Spain, see Sharpe, *Cotton*, pp. 131–3.

61 Prof. Steve Zwicker is currently writing a book on reading practices in early modern England. I am enormously grateful to him for stimulating discussions on this subject as I am also to Heidi Brayman, who is completing an important and impressive Ph.D. thesis on Renaissance reading, and Bill Sherman who is soon publishing his case study of John Dee's marginalia.

62 Grafton and Jardine, '"Studied for Action"', p. 66.

63 E.g., BL, Cotton MS. Julius C. III, ff. 3 (Simon Archer), 5 (Edmond Ashfield), 171 (John Everard).

64 Ibid., f. 30.

65 And the number of signed receipts for books borrowed does not increase over time.

66 Sharpe, *Cotton*, pp. 27–8.

67 Harl. MS. 6018, f. 147, '2 February 1622'.

68 Ibid., ff. 149–149v.

69 Ibid., f. 150.

70 Ibid., f. 179v.

71 For instance, the King's goldsmith, Mr Williams, borrowed volumes on Welsh law and the life of St Dunstan; the parson of Conington, Mr Williamson, had Sir Henry Cobham's letters (ibid., ff. 158v, 160).

72 J. G. A. Pocock, *The Ancient Constitution and the Feudal Law: English Historical Thought in the Seventeenth Century* (Cambridge, 1957); cf. D. Kelley, 'History, English Law and the Renaissance', *Past and Present*, lxv (1974), pp. 24–59.

73 Sharpe, *Cotton*, pp. 22–5; C. Brooks and K. Sharpe, 'History, English Law and the Renaissance', *Past and Present*, lxxii (1976), pp. 133–42; Kelley's reply, ibid., pp. 143–6.

74 R. Tuck, *Natural Rights Theories* (Cambridge, 1979), p. 83.

75 H. S. Pawlisch, 'Sir John Davies, the Ancient Constitution and Civil Law', *Historical Journal*, xxiii (1980), pp. 689–702; idem, *Sir John Davies and the Conquest of Ireland* (Cambridge, 1985).

76 J. G. A. Pocock, *The Ancient Constitution and the Feudal Law: A Reissue with a Retrospect* (Cambridge, 1986), p. 262.

77 Ibid., pp. 282, 30.

78 Ibid., pp. 299–301; R. C. Jonson, M. Cole *et al.* (eds.), *Commons Debates 1628*, 4 vols. (New Haven, 1977).

79 Pocock, *Ancient Constitution* (1986), p. 303.

80 Ibid., p. 304.

81 Cf. Sharpe, *Politics and Ideas*, pp. 32–4.

82 See James I's speech in J. P. Kenyon (ed.), *The Stuart Constitution* (Cambridge, 1966), p. 12; cf. F. Oakley, 'Jacobean Political Theology: The Absolute and Ordinary Powers of the King', *Journal of the History of Ideas*, xix (1968), pp. 323–46.

83 G. Burgess, *The Politics of the Ancient Constitution: An Introduction to English Political Thought 1603–1642* (Basingstoke, 1992).

84 Ibid., pp. 155, 158, 168.

85 Ibid., p. 201.

86 Ibid., p. 199.

87 Ibid., pp. 40–2, 51 and ch. 2 *passim*.

88 BL, Cotton MS. Faustina E. V, ff. 89–90.

89 Burgess, *Politics of the Ancient Constitution*, pp. 83, 59.

90 Ibid., p. 81.

91 F. Levy, *Am. Hist. Rev.*, lxxxvi (1981), p. 127. See the caveats in Sharpe, *Cotton*, p. 102.

92 See Van der Meer below, pp. 168–82; Peiresc advised Dupuy to secure a list of Cotton's manuscripts, J. P. Tamizey de Laroque (ed.), *Lettres de Peiresc*, 7 vols. (Paris, 1888–98), vol. i., p. 57.

93 C. G. C. Tite, 'A Catalogue of Sir Robert Cotton's printed books?'.

94 Sharpe, *Cotton*, pp. 58, 103. Duplicates were sent from France to Camden and Cotton: for those sent to Camden, see Bodl. MS. Smith 89, f. 1.

95 BL, Harl. MS. 6018, f. 147.

96 D. Woolf, *The Idea of History in Early Stuart England* (Toronto and London, 1990), p. xii.

97 See, e.g., Sharpe, *Cotton*, p. 97.

98 BL, Cotton MS. Titus C. VI, f. 189; cf. Julius C. III, f. 59.

99 Woolf, *Idea of History*, pp. 117–23.

100 D. McKitterick, 'Sir Robert Cotton's Roman inscriptions', below p. 115.

101 N. Ramsay, 'Sir Robert Cotton's Services to the Crown', below pp. 71–2.

102 Here a New Historicist approach to literary texts would pay dividends in the historicizing of works of history.

103 J. H. Plumb, *The Death of the Past* (Harmondsworth, 1973), p. 26.

104 BL, Cotton MS. Faustina E. V, ff. 89–90.

105 BL, Lansdowne MS. 223, f. 7.

106 See, for example, G. F. Lytle and S. Orgel (eds.), *Patronage in the Renaissance* (Princeton, 1981).

107 See Sharpe and Lake, *Culture and Politics*, passim.

108 Woolf, *Idea of History*, p. 243; A. Harbage, *Cavalier Drama* (New York, 1964).

109 Cf. Sharpe, *Cotton*, pp. 199–202.

110 McKitterick, 'Sir Robert Cotton's Roman inscriptions', below pp. 116–17. On the masque *Hymenaei* celebrating political union, as well as the marriage of Essex and Frances Howard, see D. J. Gordon, '*Hymenaei*: Ben Jonson's Masque of Union' in his *The Renaissance Imagination*, ed. S. Orgel (Berkeley and London, 1975), pp. 157–84.

111 J. Craigie (ed.), *The Basilicon Doron of King James VI*, Scottish Text Society, 2 vols. (Edinburgh, 1844), vol. i, p. 149; for the context, see J. Wormald, 'James VI and I, *Basilikon Doron* and *The Trew Law of free Monarchies*: The Scottish Context and the English Translation', in L. Peck (ed.), *The Mental World of the Jacobean Court* (Cambridge, 1991), pp. 36–54.

112 BL, Harl. MS. 389, f. 133.

113 Woolf, *Idea of History*, p. xiii.

114 Sharpe, *Politics and Ideas*, pp. 41–2. We await a study of the politics of historical writing and of the readings of history in early modern England.

115 Woolf, *Idea of History*, p. 120; R. B. Wernham, 'The Public Records in the Sixteenth and Seventeenth Centuries' in L. Fox (ed.), *English Historical Scholarship in the Sixteenth and Seventeenth Centuries*, Dugdale Soc. (Oxford, 1956). See too *H. M. C. Cowper*, vol. ii, p. 234.

116 BL, Cotton MS. Titus B. V, f. 3.

117 *Calendar of State Papers Domestic 1611–18*, p. 305; *C.S.P.D. 1623–5*, p. 548.

118 Tite, *The Manuscript Library of Sir Robert Cotton*, p. 21.

119 T. Birch, *The Court and Times of Charles I*, ed. R. F. Williams, 2 vols. (London, 1848), vol. i, p. 98.

120 See J. A. Guy, 'The Origins of the Petition of Right Reconsidered', *Historical Journal*, xxv (1982), pp. 289–312.

121 Bodl. MS. Rawlinson C 839, f. 7v.

122 Bodl. MS. Rawlinson D 1104, f. 17.

123 P.R.O., C 115/M36/8432; K. Sharpe, *The Personal Rule of Charles I* (New Haven and London, 1992), pp. 655–8.

124 M. F. S. Hervey, *The Life, Correspondence and Collections of Thomas Howard, Earl of Arundel* (Cambridge, 1921), p. 284; Sharpe, *Cotton*, p. 110.

125 See D. Starkey (ed.), *The English Court from the Wars of the Roses to the Civil War* (London, 1987); idem, 'Representation through intimacy' in I. Lewis (ed.), *Symbols and Sentiments* (London, 1977).

126 Some of these criticisms are gathered in Cust and Hughes, *Conflict in Early Stuart England*.

127 R. Cust, *The Forced Loan and English Politics 1626–28* (Oxford, 1987), passim.

128 Notably C. Hill, 'Censorship and English Literature', in his *Collected Essays I: Writing and Revolution in 17th Century England* (Brighton, 1985), pp. 32–71.

129 B. Worden, 'Literature and political censorship in early modern England', in A. C. Duke and C. Tamse (eds.), *Too Mighty to be Free* (Zutphen, 1988), pp. 45–62; S. Lambert, 'The

Printers and the Government, 1604–37', in R. Myers and M. Harris (eds.), *Aspects of Printing from 1600* (Oxford, 1987), pp. 1–29.

130 Sharpe, *Cotton*, p. 145.

131 Ibid., p. 220.

132 Cf. my critique of J. P. Sommerville's *Politics and Ideology in England 1603–40* (London, 1986) in *Politics and Ideas*, pp. 283–8; and see Sharpe and Lake, *Culture and Politics*, introduction.

133 Hervey, *Life of Arundel*, p. 267.

134 Sharpe, *Cotton*, p. 100.

135 Cf. McKitterick, 'Sir Robert Cotton's Roman inscriptions', below p. 118.

136 B. Worden, 'Ben Jonson among the Historians', in Sharpe and Lake (eds.), *Culture and Politics*, pp. 67–90, 336–41.

137 See Sharpe, 'The King's Writ: Royal Authors and Royal authority in early modern England', in ibid., pp. 117–38, 343–7.

138 There are helpful suggestions in D. Riggs, *Ben Jonson: A Life* (Cambridge, Mass., and London, 1989).

139 B. Galloway, *The Union of England and Scotland* (Edinburgh, 1986); B. Galloway and B. Levack, *The Jacobean Union: Six Tracts of 1604*, Scottish Hist Soc. (Edinburgh, 1985); B. Levack, *The Formation of the British State* (Oxford, 1987).

140 P.R.O., SP 14/1/3: 'A Discourse of the descent of the King's majesty from the Saxons'.

141 Ibid.

142 Ibid.

143 *Commons Journals*, i, p. 176, 19 Apr. 1604.

144 *Ibid.*, i, p. 339; BL, Harl. MS. 293, f. 179.

145 P.R.O., SP 14/27/44; L. Peck, *Northampton: Patronage and Policy at the Court of James I* (London, 1982), pp. 191–2.

146 BL, Lansdowne MS. 486, f. 86v; Peck, *Northampton*, pp. 190–1; Levack, *British State*, ch. 5.

147 Levack, *British State*, p. 72; Galloway, *Union of England and Scotland*, pp. 97, 99.

148 C. Russell, *The Causes of the English Civil War* (Oxford, 1990), ch. 2 and *passim*, quotation on p. 214. Russell makes too much of an interesting perspective.

149 Dodderidge, 'Brief Consideration' in Galloway and Levack, *Jacobean Union*, p. 9; Levack, *British State*, p. 150.

150 P.R.O., SP 14/1/3.

151 Peck, *Northampton*; eadem, 'Problems in Jaco-

bean Administration: Was Henry Howard, Earl of Northampton, a reformer?', *Historical Journal*, xix (1976), pp. 831–58.

152 Sharpe, *Cotton*, ch. iv *passim*; Peck, *Northampton*, ch. 8; James Howell (ed.), *Cottoni Posthuma* (London, 1651), pp. 168–9.

153 BL, Cotton MS. Titus C. VI, f. 123.

154 BL, Egerton MS. 2975, f. 83v.

155 C. Russell, *Parliaments and English Politics 1621–1629* (Oxford, 1979).

156 R. Lockyer, *Buckingham: The Life and Political Career of George Villiers, First Duke of Buckingham, 1592–1628* (London, 1981).

157 T. Cogswell, *The Blessed Revolution: English Politics and the Coming of War, 1621–1624* (Cambridge, 1989): Cust, *Forced Loan*; J. Reeve, *Charles I and the Road to Personal Rule* (Cambridge, 1989).

158 Cust, *Forced Loan*, ch. 3.

159 P.R.O., SP 16/42/17; Lockyer, *Buckingham*, pp. 341–4.

160 Cogswell, *Blessed Revolution*, ch. 5 and *passim*; Sharpe, *Cotton*, pp. 131–4, 171–5.

161 D'Ewes to Mede, 10 Dec. 1628; BL, Harl. MS. 383, f. 76.

162 BL, Cotton MS. Julius C. III, ff. 192, 236, 269–70; Lansdowne MS. 209, ff. 176–234; Harl. MS. 383, f. 92; Birch, *Court and Times of Charles I*, vol. i, p. 327.

163 Birch, *Court and Times of Charles I*, vol. i, pp. 155–7; Cotton, 'The Danger Wherein The Kingdom now Standeth and the Remedy', *Cottoni Posthuma*, pp. 316ff.

164 Ramsay, 'Sir Robert Cotton's Services to the Crown', below pp. 68–80.

165 Ibid., p. 74.

166 Sharpe, *Cotton*, pp. 177–82.

167 Reeve, *Charles I*, pp. 158–64; D. Berkowitz, *John Selden's Formative Years* (Washington D.C., 1988), pp. 268–76.

168 Reeve, *Charles I*, p. 158 and n. 184.

169 Ibid., pp. 159–61.

170 *Acts of Privy Council May 1629–1630*, p. 176; Berkowitz, *John Selden*, p. 272; Ramsay, 'Sir Robert Cotton's Services', below pp. 78–9.

171 Ramsay, below p. 78.

172 Sharpe, *Cotton*, pp. 145–6.

173 *H.M C. Buccleuch–Whitehall*, vol. i, p. 269.

174 D. Howarth, 'Sir Robert Cotton and the Commemoration of Famous Men', below pp. 42–4. It is worth remembering that Cotton had a substantial garden in Westminster.

175 D. McKitterick, 'Cotton's Roman inscriptions', below pp. 114–15.

176 BL, Harl. MS. 7002, f. 65; Cambs. R.O., Antrobus MSS.; Hunts. R.O., Estate papers.

177 Antrobus MSS., Cotton's Commonplace Book; Camden's and Jonson's residence at Conington during the plague is well known.

178 Parr, *Life of Ussher*, p. 338; above p. 7; Cambs. R.O., Antrobus MSS.: Commonplace Book; notebook on history of Huntingdonshire and Cambridgeshire; Hunts. R.O. dd M 20/A/10, Cotton's notebook on the parishes of Huntingdonshire; BL, Cotton MS. Julius F. VI, f. 395.

179 D. Howarth, below pp. 45–6.

180 R. B. Manning, 'Sir Robert Cotton, antiquarianism and estate administration: a Chancery Decree of 1627', below p. 96; see also idem, 'Antiquarianism and the Seigneurial Reaction: Sir Robert and Sir Thomas Cotton and their Tenants', *Historical Research*, lxiii (1990), pp. 277–88.

181 Hunts. R.O., Heathcote collection 12/1596, Inspeximus: Qu. Elizabeth to Cotton *et al.*, 1596; *V.C.H.*, *Huntingdonshire*, 3 vols. (1926–36), vol. iii, p. 268.

182 BL, Cotton MS. Julius C. III, f. 20.

183 Thomas Cotton said his father spent not four years residing there in forty. Howarth, below p. 44.

184 Hunts. R.O., Heathcote collection, dd Con II/Cl-110; Conington Papers 2A, 2B; Charters box 14; Steeple Gidding boxes; bundles 5/1–5; *V.C.H.*, *Hunts.*, vol. iii, p. 144.

185 BL, Cotton MS. Julius C. III, ff. 408, 321–322, 119, 131; Harl. MS. 298, f. 14; Add. MS. 33466, ff. 56, 174ff, 201.

186 P.R.O., Prob. 11 1 St John 159/68 (67).

187 Sharpe, *Personal Rule*, p. 154.

188 W. H. Kelliher, 'British post-mediaeval verse in the Cotton collection', below pp. 307–90; Sharpe, *Cotton*, pp. 202–3, 226–7; BL, Add. MS. 4712.

189 Antrobus MSS., Commonplace Book: 'Ah me poor wretch that never yet could find / Ne faith ne trust in fruitless woman kind'.

190 J. O. Halliwell (ed.), *The Autobiography and Correspondence of Sir Simonds D'Ewes*, 2 vols. (London, 1845), vol. i, p. 80.

191 BL, Harl. MS. 7002, f. 218.

192 *Autobiography ... of Sir Simonds D'Ewes*, vol. ii, p. 42.

193 BL, Add. MS. 14049: 'An Abstract and all the proofs of the conspiracy of Stevenson and others against Sir Robert Cotton'.

194 Sharpe, *Cotton*, p. ix.

195 G. Parry, 'Cotton's counsels: the contexts of *Cottoni Posthuma*' below pp. 81–95; it is interesting that a literary scholar has turned to a historicized reading of this text. See also H. Love, *Scribal Publication*, pp. 49, 83–9, for the wide circulation of these tracts.

196 BL, Cotton MS. Julius C. III, ff. 70, 191; C. H. Herford and P. Simpson, *The Works of Ben Jonson*, 11 vols. (Oxford, 1925–52), vol. viii, p. 207.

197 Cotton MS. Julius C. III, f. 28; E. Bourcier (ed.), *The Diary of Sir Simonds D'Ewes 1622–4* (Paris, 1974), p. 188.

198 See BL, Sloane MS. 241, f. 20.

199 Parry, 'Cotton's counsels', below p. 83.

200 D. Woolf, *Idea of History*, pp. 160–2.

201 Cotton, 'A Short View of the Long Life and Reign of Henry III' in *Cottoni Posthuma*, pp. 1–27, p. 26. The dating of this remains a problem. Rereading it, I feel sure that as published, it applied to 1627, rather than 1614, when Cotton claimed he wrote it (Cf. Camb. U.L. MS. Gg.II.28).

202 Cotton, 'Henry III', p. 3.

203 Cotton, 'The Manner and Means how the Kings of England Have from time to time Supported and Repaired their Estates', *Cottoni Posthuma* (London, 1672 edn), pp. 168–9.

204 Ibid., p. 188.

205 Cotton, *Wars with Foreign Princes Dangerous to Our Commonwealth* (London, 1657), p. 57.

206 See K. Sharpe, *Criticism and Compliment* (Cambridge, 1987) *pace* M. Butler, 'Reform or Reverence? The Politics of the Caroline Masque' in J. R. Mulryne and M. Shewring (eds.), *Theatre and Government under the Early Stuarts* (Cambridge, 1993), pp. 118–56.

207 Parry, 'Cotton's counsels', below p. 90.

208 *Cottoni Posthuma* (1651), p. 55.

209 Sharpe, *Cotton*, pp. 182–3; Cust, *Forced Loan*, pp. 81–4; Cotton, *The Danger Wherein The Kingdom Now Standeth and the Remedy* (London, 1628. STC 5863). See Love, *Scribal Publication*, p. 313.

210 On Howell, see D. Woolf, 'Conscience, Constancy and Ambition in the Career and Writings of James Howell', in J. Morrill, P. Slack and D. Woolf (eds.), *Public Duty and Private Conscience*

in Seventeenth-Century England (Oxford, 1993), pp. 244–78.

211 Howell, *Cottoni Posthuma* (1651), sig. A3ᵛ.

212 A sample provides some idea of the reapplication of Cotton's writings to other moments: his 'Henry III' was published in 1641, 1651 and 1681, his 'Treatise Showing the Sovereign's Person is required in Great Councils' in 1641, and his 'Wars with Foreign Princes' (under other titles) in 1655, 1665, and 1675.

213 Woolf, *Idea of History*, p. 168.

214 Woolf, 'Conscience, Constancy', p. 242.

215 For one example see Annabel M. Patterson, *Fables of Power* (Durham, N.C., and London, 1991).

216 See Annabel M. Patterson, *Censorship and Interpretation* (Madison, Wisconsin, 1984).

217 Bourcier (ed.), *Diary of D'Ewes*, p. 138.

218 Quoted in F. J. Levy, *Tudor Historical Thought* (San Marino, California, 1967), p. 270.

219 Holmes, *Historical Journal*, xxiv (1981), p. 1026.

220 Cust, *Forced Loan*, p. 82; cf. Sharpe and Lake (eds.), *Culture and Politics*, introduction.

221 BL, Add. MS. 36016, f. 38v.

222 BL, Egerton MS. 2975, f. 32.

223 Add. MS. 36016, f. 37v; Sir Edward Coke had also accepted the royal power of imprisonment without cause: Sharpe, *Faction and Parliament* (1985 edn), p. xiii.

224 Bodl. MS. Tanner 103, f. 198.

225 Bourcier (ed.), *Diary of D'Ewes*, p. 190; 'Twenty Four Arguments Whether it be more expedient to suppress Popish Practises … By the Strict Execution touching *Jesuits* …' in *Cottoni Posthuma*, pp. 111–59.

226 *V. C. H.*, *Hunts.*, vol. i, p. 365: Sir Francis and Sir Henry Shirley. 'Twenty Four Arguments', p. 146.

227 Cotton, 'Twenty Four Arguments', pp. 149–50.

228 For a guide to the current state of historiography, see K. Fincham (ed.), *The Early Stuart Church, 1603–42* (Basingstoke, 1993).

229 Sharpe, *Cotton*, pp. 108–9, 181, 186; Port Eliot, MS. X, f. 37.

230 Sloane MS. 241, f. 22v and ch. 2 *passim*.

231 'Twenty Four Arguments', p. 144.

232 Tite, '"Lost or Stolen or Strayed"', below p. 263.

233 Inner Temple Library, Petyt MS. 537/18/50: Cotton to Speaker of House of Commons, 16 May 1614.

234 BL, Cotton MS. Julius C. III, ff. 358–359.

235 *Cottoni Posthuma*, sig. A3ᵛ.

236 Holmes, *Historical Journal*, xxiv (1981), p. 1027; on the need to reconfigure 'Court' and 'Country', see *Culture and Politics*, pp. 7–8.

237 Cf. M. Smuts, 'Court Centred Politics and the Uses of Roman Historians c. 1590–1630' in Sharpe and Lake (eds.), *Culture and Politics*, pp. 21–43, 325–31.

238 Ibid.; see also P. Burke, 'A Survey of the Popularity of Ancient Historians, 1450–1700', *History and Theory*, v (1966), pp. 135–52.

239 F. Raab, *The English Face of Machiavelli* (London, 1964); Sharpe, *Politics and Ideas*, pp. 25–8.

240 Woolf, *Idea of History*, p. 48.

241 BL, Cotton MS. Titus B. I, ff. 6–53v; 'Twenty Four Arguments', p. 123 (Machiavelli cited); Worden, 'Unmatched Antiquary'.

242 *Cottoni Posthuma*, p. 131; 'Wisdom perfecteth her rules and ordinances by observation of time', Egerton MS. 2975, f. 93.

243 Sharpe, *Cotton*, pp. 235–40.

244 J. Howell, *Epistolae Ho-elianae*, ed. J. Jacobs (London, 1890), p. 526.

245 BL, Cotton MS. Julius C. III, f. 29. Bolton said it made Paulus Jovius's library look like a charnel house.

246 *Times Literary Supplement* (16 May 1980), p. 561.

247 *Am. Hist. Rev.*, lxxxvi (1981), p. 127.

248 Woolf, *Idea of History*, p. 159.

249 Tite, *The Manuscript Library of Sir Robert Cotton*, p. 3.

250 Cotton, 'Manner and Means'; BL, Add. MS. 34234, f. 169: extracts from Tower records by Borough (on whom see Harl. MS. 6018, f. 149).

251 Cotton, 'Henry III', pp. 23–4, 25 (reform of waste), 26.

252 Ibid., p. 25.

253 For a guide to this collection, see S. Clark, 'Wisdom Literature of the Seventeenth Century: A Guide to the Contents of the "Bacon–Tottel" Commonplace Books', *Trans. Camb. Bib. Soc.*, vi (1976), pp. 291–305; vii (1977), pp. 46–73. Volumes 7, 8, 11, 23, 26, 29, 33–6, 38, 45, 48, 51–2 are in Drake's own hand. Recently the Huntington Library purchased another of Drake's notebooks, containing his political diary for the 1630s and Long Parliament (HM

55603). Harold Love also points to the very large number of Cotton's tracts in circulation, *Scribal Publication*, pp. 87–9.

254 M. Jansson, *Two Diaries of The Long Parliament* (Gloucester, 1984), pp. xiii-xx; Phillips Sale Catalogue, 18 Mar. 1993; *V.C.H., Buckinghamshire*, vol. iii, pp. 141, 145–8, 153.

255 Hunt. Lib. MS. HM 55603, ff. 1 and *1 (Drake annotated his notebooks from each end; the Huntington Library has asterisked folios running from the back); University College, London, Ogden MS. 7/7, f. [74v].

256 Hunt. Lib. MS. HM 55603, f. 1.

257 Drake's negotiations for various offices are found in HM 55603. He purchased the reversion of a post in the Fine Office in the Court of Common Pleas; see G. E. Aylmer, *The King's Servants: the Civil Service of Charles I, 1625–1642* (London and New York, 1961), pp. 97–8.

258 Drake sat for Amersham in the Short and Long Parliaments. Jansson prints his parliamentary notebook from Ogden MS. 7/51, but this now needs to be supplemented by his notes for his speech and other parliamentary proceedings in HM 55603.

259 Ogden MS. 7/8, f. 91.

260 Ogden MSS. 7/7 unfoliated – my foliation [f. 50]; 7/23, f. 23.

261 HM 55603, f. *4.

262 Ogden MS. 7/7, [f. 94v].

263 Ibid., [f. 61v].

264 Ibid., [ff. 4v, 62v].

265 Ibid., [f. *25v on the Huntington principle of asterisks from back].

266 Ibid., [f. 73v].

267 Ibid., [ff. 18v, 61v].

268 HM 55603, f. *4.

269 I am preparing two articles on 'The mental world of Sir William Drake' and 'Sir William Drake and the Origins of The English Civil War'.

39

SIR ROBERT COTTON AND THE
COMMEMORATION OF FAMOUS MEN

DAVID HOWARTH

THIS article is concerned with the interest Sir Robert Cotton took in the funerary monument as shown by a group of tombs and epitaphs which he had erected in All Saints, Conington, Huntingdonshire, probably *circa* 1613–15. The appearance and placing of these were influenced by Cotton's views on the use of the *stele* and *cippus* in antiquity. It will be suggested that Sir Robert has a distinguished if modest place in developing the repertoire of Jacobean sculptors, whilst his close involvement with the Conington monuments, encourages the view that he had wider concerns than has been appreciated. The article ends with a consideration of a monument to Sir Robert himself, also in All Saints, erected by his son, Sir Thomas Cotton.

One of Sir Robert's abiding interests was the culture of the antique world, something he shared with his teacher William Camden. Camden was the greatest of the Elizabethan antiquaries whose *Britannia* (1586) was the first attempt at a systematic account of early Britain. In 1599 Cotton and Camden travelled in search of inscriptions to the Roman Wall, or as it was then considered the Picts Wall, and so began Cotton's collection of Roman antiquities. Thereafter, the northern antiquaries Reginald Bainbridge and Lord William Howard offered him stones on separate occasions,[1] while within two years of Cotton's death in May 1631, the Essex antiquary John Barkham arranged to send him some Roman relics: a bronze dish from an altar found at Bocking in Essex and a brick of 'ancient cemented work' which Barkham asked Cotton to pass on to John Tradescant in Lambeth.[2]

Barkham's letter suggests that Sir Robert's interest in the artefacts of the ancient world may have extended beyond the antiquary's fascination for archaeological remains, to include a virtuoso's interest in free-standing sculpture, a view encouraged from a reading of other letters to Cotton. After writing about the 'ancient cemented work' referred to above, Barkham concluded by asking Cotton to let him know whether Cotton wanted him to acquire some statues on Cotton's behalf which, it appears from another letter from Barkham to Cotton, had belonged to a certain Mr Herlakenden to whom Barkham had sent his minister 'to know his mynde for parting with them'.[3] We glean nothing more about these statues but the possibility remains that besides the well-known sarcophagi and inscriptions, the remnant of which can still be seen in the Museum of Archaeology at Cambridge,[4] and in addition to the cabinet of curiosities, Cotton also had

40

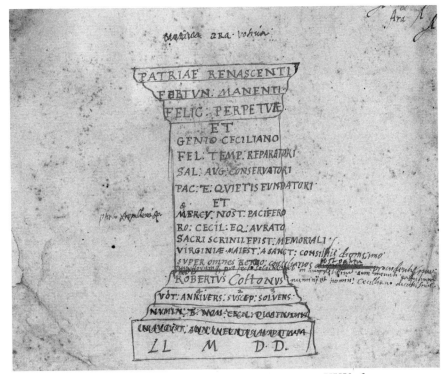

Fig. 1. The Cecil Altar. Cotton MS. Fragments XXV, f. 25v

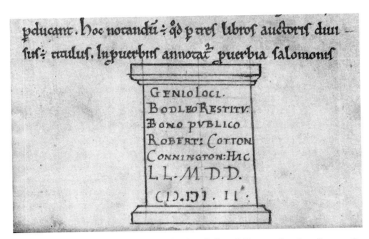

Fig. 2. Cotton's donation inscription to the Bodleian Library in the form of a votive altar.
BL, Harl. MS. 988, f. 1 (detail)

41

a collection of free-standing statuary. What is certain, however, is that Sir Robert sustained an interest in sculpture, as well as epigraphy and numismatics. One of the earliest letters from his son, the future Sir Thomas, is dated 1621 and in it he promises to send some heads from Conington to his father in London: 'Sr my humble duty remembred I have sent up the three marble heads you writt for and packd them up as carfully as I could.'[5]

The meetings of the Society of Antiquaries in the Summer and Autumn of 1600 were taken up with discussions of burial customs perhaps because Camden and Cotton, by then its leading luminaries, had just returned to London from the Picts Wall. There is amongst Cotton's manuscripts a free-hand sketch of a Roman altar, with a long inscription in Cotton's hand, dedicated to the 'Genio Ceciliano', that is to say, to the genius of Robert, first Earl of Salisbury (fig. 1; cf. fig. 2).[6] There is no record of the erection of this 'altar', nor can it be dated precisely, but, since it refers to Salisbury as Sir Robert, it must date before 13 May 1603, when he was created Baron Cecil of Essendine. It is most likely that the design relates to Cotton's journey to the Picts Wall of 1599–1600, in which case it was probably executed after Cotton returned to London in 1600.

In order to understand the local context of the Conington funerary monuments which will constitute the main focus of this article, it will be useful to begin with a brief survey of the family estate and the various building works which Sir Robert and his son undertook there in the first half of the seventeenth century. Conington Castle, the ancestral home of the Cotton family, lay deep in the fens of Huntingdonshire, eight miles south-east of Peterborough. The estate was substantial enough to provide the means to enable Sir Robert to acquire his house in Westminster and pursue his cultural interests, as well as to keep the Cottons on a footing with other leading Huntingdonshire families: the Cromwells, Montagus, Wingfields and St Johns. It appears from an agreement dated 23 April 1632 between Sir Robert Naunton, Master of the Court of Wards, and Cotton's son Sir Thomas, whereby auditors should be appointed to value all manors, lands and other holdings at Conington, following Sir Robert's death the previous May, that Sir Robert's agricultural wealth had comprised:

3 messauges: 200 acres land, 100 acres meadow, 100 acres pasture and a free fishery in Whittlesmere formerly purchased of Sir Richard Williams alias Cromwell and of John Parris by Thos. Cotton Esq., Grandfather of the aforesaid Robt. Cotton. And 10 messauges, 6 tofts, 200 acres land, 40 acres meadow, and 40 acres pasture with apps. in Conington which were formerly purchased of the Master, Fellows and Scholars of Trinity College, Cambridge by the aforesaid Thos Cotton, the Grandfather, And 1 windmill, 2 dovecotes, 8 gardens, 500 acres meadow, 1500 acres pasture, 1100 acres marsh with apps. in Connington Yearly value £15 16s. 8d.[7]

Doubtless Sir Thomas was to add to this since, like his father before him, he became an energetic commissioner for the draining of the Fens.[8]

Despite its financial value, Conington had drawbacks. It was remote from London where Sir Robert was at the centre of intellectual life and, even on those rare occasions when the family lived at Conington, it was considered a melancholy place. As will be seen, however, when we come to discuss the Cotton monuments in the church, it exercised a powerful sentimental influence on the family and both Sir Robert and his son Thomas undertook extensive improvements there.

At the Castle, Sir Robert constructed a long gallery, and a terrace with octagonal summer houses at either end to accommodate his collection of inscriptions. There is a tradition that for the building of the long gallery, Sir Robert bought panelling from the hall at Fotheringhay Castle in which Mary Queen of Scots had been executed and stone from the same source.[9] The evidence suggests, however, that this is unlikely since there is no reference to stone or panelling from Fotheringhay in two detailed rental and disbursement books which cover work at Conington Castle from 1603 until 1612 and from 1617 until the death of Sir Robert in 1631.[10] However, the account book which includes the period from Sir Robert's death until the Civil War, does show that Fotheringhay stone was indeed acquired for Conington but not until 1638, when Sir Thomas undertook an extensive programme of embellishments to the church: battlements, oculi and buttresses for the tower.[11] Since the purchase of the Fotheringhay stone was accounted for at Michaelmas 1638, and Sir Thomas's steward paid out £12 for battlementing the church at the same time, it would appear that the '200 load of ston from fodringhay' was for church and not castle as has been assumed.[12] But although there would appear to be more romance than truth in the supposed connection between Sir Robert and Fotheringhay Castle, he did indeed use stone from Maxey Castle, Northamptonshire.[13]

At first glance, it might appear that Sir Robert was a conventional enough patron.[14] His long gallery seems to have been decidedly old-fashioned. Here he followed a practice which had become prevalent among builders since the Reformation, the recycling of stone from a disused or demolished structure; in this case, probably for the building of an arcade beneath the long gallery. However it may be that Cotton was not merely driven by reasons of economy in adapting parts of an earlier structure for incorporation into his new building. It is possible that he thought that the arches from Maxey represented twelfth-century architecture; that is to say, the style of the period when his Scottish ancestors first became lords of Conington. If that was Sir Robert's thinking, his purchase of the Maxey stone would have been undertaken in a revivalist, even romantic spirit, and should not therefore be viewed simply as evidence of good housekeeping. Such a gesture on his part would have been entirely in keeping with attitudes prevalent amongst the antiquarian circle in which he moved. For example, Sir Robert's close friend, Lord William Howard, with whom he had visited Roman sites in 1599–1600, certainly promoted a revival of Gothic architecture. After Lord William had been restored to favour by James I, he took up residence at Naworth Castle in Cumberland which 'he restored in a conservative Gothic style introducing genuine carved and painted medieval ceilings from nearby Kirkoswald Castle.'[15] As for Sir Robert's octagonal buildings in the environs of Conington Castle, they had more in common with a chapter house than a temple. There was nothing classical about them even though they were created to house inscriptions and altars.[16] Sir Thomas finished what his father had left incomplete by building a staircase at the western end of the long gallery where it adjoined the main body of an earlier house. At Lady Day 1633, £64 13s. 4d. was disbursed for 'the new fine windowes for the gallery stayres' followed by a payment at Michaelmas 1633 of £69 7s. 5d. for 'building up the stayrecase the 2 dormant windows and a third part of the east end of the house and slating the n. side'.[17] Thereafter Sir Thomas spent significant amounts on repairing delapidations to a building which had been added to over the years, a process of accretion which might account for the considerable outlay at Conington Castle during the 1630s.

This, of course, had been before the Civil War. Sir Thomas, as a Royalist, was to be forced to loan money to the Parliamentary cause in 1643 and thereafter to appear at the Parliamentary Committee for Sequestrations, as a result of which he would be assessed at £4,000 per annum and fined £800. Once Sir Thomas was before the committee, it may be supposed that he would have been anxious to play down the significance of Conington to the family in order to reduce his fine; nevertheless his testimony reinforces the view that Conington had remained shut up for years amidst the empty Fens. In a draft of a letter, probably sent to his acquaintance the Earl of Manchester, Sir Thomas wrote: '...my Lord knowes how unholsome that place is, and I never used to live ther but for some small times, I dare say lesse ther in in [sic] any house I have for [in?] 13 [?] yeares that I have had it I have not lived ther 3 and my father in 40 yeares lived not ther 4.'[18] Sir Thomas must have contemplated Conington with still less relish once the fighting had begun. At that point, ungallantly, he had abandoned a wife in an advanced stage of pregnancy, to decamp with the rest of his household to a property at Eyworth in Bedfordshire. He explained to the committee that he had found the Conington air 'fenney', while telling them that Lady Cotton had been left to deal with marauders.[19] However, the true value which the family placed on Conington in the seventeenth century can perhaps be assessed when we turn to consider the work which Sir Robert and Sir Thomas commissioned in the interior of their local church.

THE CONINGTON MONUMENTS

All Saints, Conington, contains five pre-Restoration wall monuments which are of particular interest: the first, a cenotaph, commemorates Prince David of Scotland, Earl of Huntingdon, while the second may be described as the Double Cotton monument since it commemorates Sir Robert's grandfather and father, both Thomas Cottons (d. 1574 and 1592) and their respective wives, Lucy Harvey and, in the case of the second Thomas Cotton, his first wife, Elizabeth Shirley. The Prince David and the Double Cotton monuments are conceived as a pair and hang opposite each other just outside the chancel. The third monument, also a cenotaph, is to Prince David's father, Prince Henry of Scotland (d. 1152), and this is paired with the fourth monument which carries the names of Sir Robert's great-grandfather Thomas Cotton (d. 1519) and his wife Joanna Paris or Parys.[20] These are suspended opposite each other on the aisle walls. The fifth

44

monument is to Sir Robert himself (d. 1631), which was to be paired eventually with a very similar wall tablet erected to the memory of Sir Thomas (d. 1662), both attributed to Joshua Marshall.[21]

But why did Cotton want to erect cenotaphs to medieval Scottish princes in the middle of the English Fens? Cotton claimed descent from the Scottish royal line and from the Bruce family: his ancestors, the Bruces of Conington, being collaterally descended from Robert the Bruce whose great-grandfather, Robert Bruce, Lord of Annandale, had married Isabella, daughter of Prince David, Earl of Huntingdon. Before then, the Scottish royal line had become English barons by virtue of the marriage of King David I (d. 1153), to Maud, daughter and heir of Waltheof, Earl of Northampton, through whom the Earldom of Huntingdon and Lordship of Conington came to the line of Scotland. What David I had been accorded by way of territorial honours in England, had then been augmented by the English king, Stephen, who had granted David I's son Henry, Prince of Scotland (d. 1152), (whose monument we shall consider), the Earldom of Huntingdon. Thereafter it was through Prince Henry's third son David, Earl of Huntingdon (the second of the Scottish princes commemorated by Sir Robert Cotton in Conington church), that the houses of Bruce and Balliol had inherited in the female line their claims to the crown of Scotland. It was thus by descent through Prince Henry of Scotland, and his son Prince David, that Cotton had been able to claim kinship with his sovereign James Stuart. Such a claim was no mere affectation on Cotton's part, but a gesture calculated to attract the attention of James I who had depended so heavily on Cotton's patron the Earl of Northampton in the delicate business of the accession of the Stuarts in 1603. It is surely not without relevance to Cotton's considerable political aspirations that he took to signing himself 'Robert Cotton Bruceus' in the year of James's accession, and began to initial his books and manuscripts 'RCB', books and manuscripts handled by so many Jacobean policy-makers rummaging for precedent and argument in the promotion of policy.[22] In addition to signing his library thus, either Sir Robert or his son Sir Thomas, had the Cotton pedigree painted on the wall of the great hall at Conington.[23] There was then a degree of shrewd calculation about Cotton's absorption with family history with regard to national and local perspectives alike. Before Cotton commissioned the cenotaphs for Conington, he was enjoying frequent access to King James.[24] James had taken to addressing him as 'cousin' after they had met, probably at Sir Oliver Cromwell's great house at Hinchingbrooke, as James travelled south in March 1603 for his coronation. Thereafter James may well have learned of Cotton's shrine in Conington which perhaps had been erected in something of the same spirit as Elizabeth I's rehabilitation in 1573 of her Yorkist ancestors at St Peter's, Fotheringhay, ten miles from Conington.[25]

King David had been the first Scottish monarch to acquire hereditary territorial honours within England. When Stephen, Count of Blois, broke his oath to Henry I of England that Henry's daughter Matilda should succeed him, and seized the throne instead, King David invaded England in support of Matilda, his niece. Hopes of reinstating Matilda and giving the Scottish crown decisive sway over English affairs had, however, to be abandoned after David was routed by King Stephen at the Battle of the Standard in 1138. Yet David's descendant James had achieved more by peaceful means than David had managed to gain by force; James VI of Scotland had become James I of England. Thus, by erecting cenotaphs to King David's son and grandson, Cotton was not only commemorating the achievement of a Scottish regal ambition but, by implication, may have been suggesting the superiority of James, the wise and pacific monarch, over David the defeated war lord. James I and Cotton were powerful advocates of a policy of peace: Peace and Wisdom were the two attributes which James came to prize above all others,[26] while Cotton composed an address to James I's son Henry, Prince of Wales, on why it was more politic to pursue a policy of peace rather than war with Spain.[27]

Cotton was anxious to commemorate the kings of Scotland in their own fiefdom but fenland rivalries may also have come into the story. At an unknown date, but after 1603, Sir Simeon Steward, a member of a leading family in the Isle of Ely, had erected a monument in the Cathedral to his father, Sir Mark Steward (d. 1603), with whom Cotton had sat on Fenland drainage commissions. Sir Simeon, also well known to Cotton, had inscribed his father's descent as running back to the Royal House of Stuart, an exercise in local self-advertisement which must surely have aroused Cotton's competitive instincts.[28]

Cotton's interest in commemorating the sovereigns of Scotland may also have extended to an act of piety performed by James VI and I for his dead mother. On 19 April 1606 a contract had been signed for James I by Salisbury and Cotton's patron, the Earl of Northampton, between the King and the sculptor Cornelius Cure.[29] For payment of £825 10s. Cure was to build a tomb for Mary, who had been executed in 1587 at Fotheringhay Castle. Thus James began his attempts at expunging that tragedy; attempts which then continued with the recruitment of Cotton in his capacity not only as an historian but also perhaps as epigraphist. James commissioned the great French historian De Thou to write a new life of his mother which would counter 'the vituperative prose of George Buchanan's history'.[30] As has been demonstrated, De Thou relied on the advice and manuscripts of Cotton.[31] Within the Cotton Manuscripts are drafts for the epitaph to Mary Queen of Scots on her tomb in Westminster Abbey in the hand of Henry Howard, Earl of Northampton, who had played such a central role in ensuring the accession of the Stuart dynasty. Northampton was the intimate and patron of Sir Robert and the existence of Northampton's drafts within Cotton's papers suggests that Cotton may have been involved in the composition of the epitaph.[32]

It is not known when Cotton embarked on the Conington epitaphs. Nevertheless, there is evidence to suggest that it is unlikely that he would have done so before 1608 at the earliest and probably not until the Spring of 1614. On 20 April 1608 John, Lord Harington of Exton, sold his half of the advowson of Conington to Cotton.[33] An advowson gave the right of presentation to a benefice or living, and it is doubtful whether Cotton would have embarked upon changes to the appearance of the interior of the church unless he had full control of its patronage. 1608 was also the year in which Cotton

46

bought out the final quit-claims on Conington of his various relations.[34] The net effect of these legal agreements was to clear the ground and it seems unlikely that Cotton could have considered embarking on an expensive programme of refurbishment at Conington until he was sure that he was master of all that he surveyed.

It was probably Cotton who in 1611 suggested to James I that a new order of baronets should be created to help sustain the ailing finances of the Exchequer.[35] There was of course a central paradox in creating an order of chivalry on the basis of selling titles, but that was something Cotton manœuvred around by arguing that the baronet would merely represent a revival of the vestigial medieval order of knights banneret. During the debates as to the propriety of this policy, Cotton was actually living at Conington and thinking about the putative medieval origins of his new order. Cotton's proposal was adopted, though not without considerable opposition, and he himself obtained a baronet's patent on 29 June 1611. Thus, in the Spring and Summer of 1611 he had a mind cast back into the Middle Ages whilst contemplating the church in which he would shortly place his epitaphs. In the light of the controversy which surrounded the establishment of baronets, and the conferment of the honour upon himself, Cotton might well have wished to advertise his newly elevated status by giving three dimensional expression to his family's long and distinguished line. But there were other factors which made these the years when Cotton might well have felt it appropriate to emphasize his distinguished ancestry and connections: in 1611 he had been talked of as a likely candidate for one of the two Secretaryships of State and it was now, in the period 1611–14, that he had greater influence than at any other point of his career; surely, he must have felt he was set to achieve great office himself.

One problem remained, however, and that was to ensure that the ambitious heraldic claims which were to be set out, barnacle-like, on the Conington monuments were correct. Could it be, therefore, that it was Cotton himself who persuaded his closest friend William Camden, in his capacity as Garter King of Arms, to order the visitation of Huntingdonshire, which was undertaken by Nicholas Charles, Lancaster Herald, in the Summer of 1613? In his notes of the Visitation, Charles writes about heraldic glass relating to the Cottons in Conington church, but there are no references to monuments: and there surely would have been had they been *in situ*. Corroborative evidence that work had not been begun on the monuments before Charles's visitation is forthcoming in a letter sent to Cotton by Charles shortly after he had completed field work in Huntingdonshire. Charles refers to issues of the correct armorial bearings of Cotton's Tudor ancestors. Thus it would appear that Cotton used Charles's visitation as a builder would work to a surveyor's specification:

since I Come home I have found a little note in my owne collections of your family of Harvy w[ch] I have here sent enclosed unto you ... As for the Cote of the Cheveron betwene the Eagles I thinke it was no match wth Wesenham but rather wth the Folviles fo[r] I have Looked in my booke of Church notes of Leicester Shire where I finde in the Churches of Reresby and Ashby that Cote hath very often and sometymes quartred with Folvile and nothing of Wesenham there at all

Fig. 3. Anon.: The Prince David Monument, All Saints, Conington, *c.* 1613

48

Fig. 4. Reverse of coin of Constantine the Great. W. Camden, *Britannia* (1610), p. 94 (detail)

Whereby I gather it was rather a match wth Folvile then Wesenham as I said before. So much for that.[36]

The Prince David monument in All Saints (fig. 3) is a cenotaph incorporating elements from what Cotton had learned about ancient funerary monuments on his visit of 1599 to the Picts Wall. It consists of three tiers: a long thin chest with shields and inscription proclaiming Prince David descended from 'Imperator Rex, Franciae, Anglo Saxonvm, Angliae, Scotiae'. Above, three columns carry a lintel sustaining an arch flanked by two seated unicorns facing outwards, surmounted by a coat of arms and crown.[37] However, it is the second tier which is of particular interest because its design appears to have been taken from the description of cenotaphs and ash chests on Imperial Roman coins of which Cotton himself had the finest collection in England at that time.[38] The unicorns on the Prince David monument are intended as an allusion to the two which supported the arms of the kings of Scotland. But, instead of functioning as such, they face away from the arms which are themselves on the tier above. Camden illustrates a coin of Constantine the Great (fig. 4) which belonged to Cotton, showing two eagles flanking the portal of a funerary chest but facing outwards as do our unicorns on the Prince David monument.[39] This coin may well have given Cotton the idea. Certainly there are no other examples of armorial bearings on Elizabethan or Jacobean monuments being treated in this way. The triumphal arch against which the unicorns rest their backs is a well proportioned and striking aspect of the monument. The arch, or portal, as a symbol of entry into a celestial realm, was a specific point that had been raised in a paper delivered to the Antiquaries and its deployment here is another attempt to commemorate Prince David *al antica*.[40] In that anonymous discourse of 1600 – a discourse which might very well have been delivered by Cotton himself – it was argued that: 'The shape of a great gate or house intimateth that the decesed are recieved into houses by the great gate of death, there perpetually to remain in happiness'.[41]

Three of the remaining monuments need to be discussed: the Cotton–Paris (fig. 5) with its pair dedicated to Prince Henry of Scotland (fig. 6), and the wall monument to Sir Robert himself (see fig. 10). The two monuments which make up the second of our

Fig. 5. Inigo Jones (?): The Cotton–Paris Monument, All Saints, Conington, *c.* 1615

50

Fig. 6. Inigo Jones (?): The Prince Henry Monument, All Saints, Conington, *c.* 1615

51

Fig. 7. Inigo Jones: Design for the Tomb of Lady Cotton, *c.* 1608.
R.I.B.A. Drawings Collection, Shelf L5/1

pairs are the same size and they have attached corinthian columns supporting a salient architrave and frieze surmounted by a heavy cornice. The cornices support coats of arms set in cartouches and each monument is placed against a pillar on a ledge between opposite aisle windows. There are functional and formal differences between them: the Cotton–Paris monument is a grave altar because the people commemorated lie beneath, whereas the Prince Henry monument is a cenotaph; the coat of arms on the Cotton–Paris monument is larger in proportion to the whole; the central panel between the columns of the Cotton–Paris monument is less recessed; the stone behind the attached columns is plain where there is strap-work patterning on the Prince Henry monument; the columns of the Cotton–Paris are plain, whereas they are fluted and have fillets on the Prince Henry monument. Whatever the differences between them, however, taken together, they can be seen to be far superior artistically to the pair of the Prince David and the Double Cotton. With the Cotton–Paris and Prince Henry pair, the designer rises above the additive approach to composition of the typical Elizabethan sculptor, an additive approach which is very much in evidence with the Double Cotton and Prince David pair. By contrast, the Cotton–Paris and Prince Henry monuments reveal a mastery of proportion, an integrity, and a simplicity of design which make them stand out amongst early Jacobean examples. Who then could design as well as this at the turn of the seventeenth century?

Inigo Jones's design (fig. 7) for the tomb of Lady Cotton (no relation) at Norton in Hales, Shropshire, which dates to *circa* 1608, shows striking similarities with the Cotton–Paris and Prince Henry monuments, both as regards appearance and proportional relationships.[42] Both the Jones sketch for Lady Cotton's tomb and the tomb itself have come under further scrutiny in a recently published *catalogue raisonné* of Jones's architectural drawings.[43] There it is demonstrated how carefully Jones sustained harmonic proportions: the sill of the sarcophagus in which Lady Cotton is interred relates in simple proportions of $1:1$ and $1:2$ to other features of the design. But careful measurement of the total height of the Lady Cotton tomb in relation to its total width, and the same measurement taken on the Conington monuments, reveal that the proportion of height to breadth is the same in all three: that is to say $1:1\frac{3}{4}$.

The case for an attribution of the Cotton–Paris and Prince Henry monuments to Inigo Jones rests in part on the congruity between the proportional relationships within each and the Norton in Hales design. But the architectural framework for the tomb of Lady Cotton is strikingly similar to the Cotton–Paris and Prince Henry monuments: each has an altar framed by corinthian columns with an inscription suspended on the altar front, a heavy entablature above, with a coat of arms contained within a strap-work frame resting on the cornice. Jones would certainly have had every opportunity to work for Sir Robert because they were well known to each other. Jones was indebted to Cotton for the loan of manuscripts and folios,[44] and both were members of the 'Fraternity of Sirenaical Gentlemen',[45] a club of wits and intellectuals which met once a month at The Mermaid Tavern in Bread Street in London during the early years of the seventeenth century.

Fig. 8. Francesco Villamena: Engraving of Inigo Jones

Furthermore, if our supposition is correct that Cotton began the process of embellishing Conington church not earlier than the Spring of 1613, then the startling qualitative difference between the Prince David and Double Cotton monuments on the one hand, and the Prince Henry and Cotton–Paris on the other, could be accounted for by supposing the earlier pair to be the work of a sculptor Cotton had employed in Jones's absence on the Continent where he was travelling with the Earl of Arundel between April 1613 and Christmas 1614, a sculptor who, unlike Jones, was content to follow convention as it had been established in the Elizabethan church monument. By contrast, the second pair at Conington was perhaps the work of Jones after he had returned from Italy in the Winter of 1614. When in Italy, Jones had shown himself deeply interested in the antique funerary monument since he had had his portrait (fig. 8) engraved by Francesco Villamena in which he appears as a bust within an oval, framed by an altar, with swags and rams heads on the corners, and a short Latin inscription cut in antique lettering below, very much in the spirit of antique funerary monuments such as Jones had then been observing on the Appian Way whilst Cotton enjoyed his own at Conington.

The attribution to Inigo Jones must remain mere speculation, but it would appear from a reading of the 1610 edition of Camden's *Britannia* that the basic conception for the design of the Conington monuments was Cotton's. That edition provided an

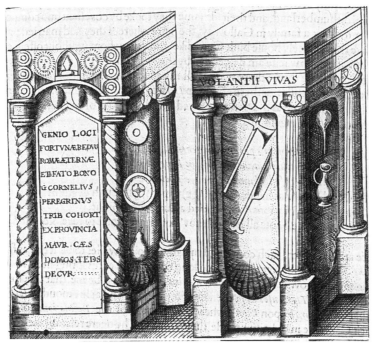

Fig. 9. The Alauna Altar. W. Camden, *Britannia* (1610), p. 770 (detail)

opportunity to incorporate 'discoveries' which Cotton and Camden had made on their
northern tour in 1599–1600. One such find, to which I believe Cotton perhaps directed
his designer's attention, was a military altar (fig. 9) of the type set up by officers
commanding the garrisons along the wall, one of which Cotton and Camden had
examined together at Alauna in 1599.[46] In the 1610 English edition of the *Britannia*
Camden not only provided an unusually long description of that Alauna military altar,
now on loan to the British Museum, but also thought it important enough to illustrate:

The ancient vaults stand open, and many altars, stones with inscriptions, and Statues are heere
gotten out of the ground. Which, I. *Sinhous* a very honest man, in whose grounds they are digged
up, keepeth charily, and hath placed orderly about his house. It the mids of his yard their
standeth erected a most beautifull foure square Altar of a reddish stone right artificially in antique
worke engraven five foote or there abouts high, with an inscription therein of an excellent good
letter: But loe the thing it selfe all whole, and every side thereof, as the draught was most lively
taken out by the hand of Sir *Robert Cotton* of *Connington*, Knight, a singular lover of antiquity...[47]

The Cotton–Paris monument is in better condition than the Prince Henry cenotaph.
The main body of the Cotton–Paris altar contains three inscriptions. The principal,
within a cursive scrolled frame, is an account of virtues in this world and hopes for the
next, while above and below, are two short inscriptions imitating the practice of the

55

Fig. 10. Joshua Marshall: Monument to Sir Robert Cotton, All Saints, Conington, 1655

ancients in addressing the passer-by: one asks him to pause while the other instructs him to go on his way.[48] The altar front of the Prince Henry cenotaph has crumbled away leaving faint traces of an indigo blue pigment but no evidence of any inscriptions. However, below the altar itself, between consoles supporting the attached columns, is a short inscription which reads: 'Prince Henry of Scotland Lorde of Connington'.

We come now to the last of the Conington monuments to be discussed, the grey marble wall tablet to Sir Robert (fig. 10), suspended above his grave in the south aisle. Here the sculptor has created what has been defined as a 'scholar monument'. This consists of a bust-length figure above a tablet or altar, usually depicted, as in this case, with a mixture of contemporary and antique dress and eyeballs blank rather than incised as was the norm with the realistic polychrome Tudor tombs. The type of the 'scholar monument' was a formula, dependent on the antique *cippus* which had had a long pedigree in English sculpture. Thus its adoption for the monument to Sir Robert was something of a cliché. However, it was singularly appropriate since it is very likely that Sir Robert had helped to give the type its most sophisticated expression. The 'scholar monument' had been perfected in the memorial to William Camden (d. 1623) in Westminster Abbey, attributed to Nicholas Stone.[49] Almost certainly this had been overseen by Sir Robert himself who was not only the chief beneficiary of Camden's will, but had been the recipient of a shipment of grave altars just before Camden's monument came to be discussed. The Lancashire antiquary Roger Dodsworth had written to Cotton in February 1622/3 about finds for which he wanted instructions:

Honble S^r,
wth my due acknowledgement of your multiplied favors presupposed, I thought good to adver-tise you that, since I saw you, I have used such meanes, as my health would permitt, to enquire after such things as you desired. I have beene att Cattericke wher I was informed of 2 Romaine monuments wch were found in a° 1620 and are now in my lo: of Arundells keeping. I have found, a peece of a round piller, att Ribblecester, being almost half a yeard thick, and half an ell in height, wth such letters, on the one side thereof, as I have figured in this paper inclosed. I saw, ther, a little table of free stone, not half a yeard square, wth the portraitures of 3 armed men cutt therin, but no inscription att all theron. I saw likewise 2 other stones of the nature of slate, or thicke flaggs some yeard square, wth fretted antique workes engraven on them, without any letters. I shalbe very gladd that my uttmost endeavors, might availe to requite the least of many respects you have done unto me. And do desire you to signify your pleasure, what you would have mee to doo touching the premisses, and I shall not faile to do my best in effecting thereof...
                    Yours faythfully faythfully
                    Roger Dodsworth
Hutton grange 16 Feb 1622.[50]

The monument to Sir Robert was conceived shortly after his death but probably not executed until the Interregnum. The story begins with the King's Master-mason Nicholas Stone and seems to end with the sculptor Joshua Marshall. Nicholas Stone wrote to Sir Thomas Cotton on 31 July 1638:

This wold be most Antick and
best befetting the work's

Fig. 11. Sketch attributed to Nicholas Stone

58

Right wor[shipfu]ll

Yo^r Servant hase bine wth me and showed me a letter which came from me [you] signifiinge yor pleasure conceringe your fathers moneum^t and that you desire to have the stone a foote thicke which is to thicke by 4 ynches 8 beinge Enought and then that block woold make 2 for it is 16 ynches thicke if it most be a foote thicke I cannot aford it under 45:^{li} for that peece of 4 ynches thicke the length and breadth of all that stone is woorth 10^l for any mans occasion, the whole Blocke as now it is Stands me in above 20:^l for Stones of that Breadth and length are sildome had unlese they are sent for a purpose so if It be yor pleasure that I shall cut out my Marble for it and begine the woorke you will also be pleased to appointe money for I have alwaies appon such aworke as that half my money in hand and the rest when It is donne Thus Expecktinge your answer I rest

Yo^r humble Servant

London this 31th of Julij 1638   Nicho: Stone[51]

Sir Thomas appears to have been negotiating for some time and it may be that a recently discovered free-hand sketch (fig. 11), identified as being by Stone, represents a preliminary but rejected idea for this monument.[52] There is a similarity between Cotton's bust as it appears in the monument and the bearded head in Stone's sketch. In addition, the comment, 'This wold be most Anteik and best befeting his works', written by Stone under his sketch, seems appropriate to Sir Robert, an international authority on the Roman world.

However, it is doubtful whether negotiations ever went beyond Stone's letter. In the first place, the monument is not up to Stone's standards, variable though these were. For example, Sir Robert's head is bland and has none of the crispness of the bust of Sir William Peyto in Chesterton Church, Warwickshire, executed in 1639. Secondly, a further document, which may very well be connected with a monument to Sir Robert, points in the direction of the Marshall family of sculptors and probably to Joshua, an attribution supported by the evidence of the monument itself. The document records a payment of twenty pounds made by Sir Thomas Cotton in 1655 'Per water to Mr Marshall 6d For ye monument to Mr Marshall £20'.[53] Twenty pounds may not seem a large enough amount for a project of this nature, but then times were disrupted and it was difficult for a sculptor to find work during the Interregnum. The Marshalls were much influenced by Stone and this would explain why the Conington monument is based on a formula developed so successfully by Stone in the pre-Civil War period. Furthermore, the head of Sir Robert is similar to the male heads in Joshua Marshall's grandiose monument to the Crispe family of about 1651 at Birchington in Kent.

Beneath Sir Robert's bust is a tablet containing a long inscription, conventionally pious except for the last line which reads: 'communis mundo superest rogus'.[54] A letter of 1695 tells us that the line was added by Sir John Cotton who took the phrase from Lucan's *Bellum Civile* where Lucan is describing Caesar gloating over the unburied corpses of Pompey's army after the battle of Pharsalus.[55] The literal meaning of the line is 'there remains for the world a communal funeral pyre'. But although it is easy enough to identify the source of Sir John's quotation, it is not at all clear why a line was chosen from one of the least attractive passages in Roman literature. Perhaps the choice was dictated by Sir John's understanding of his grandfather's life.

As we have seen, in the early years of James's reign Sir Robert had had a promising career but with the deaths of his first patrons Northampton and Somerset, and the eclipse of their successor Arundel by the Duke of Buckingham, Sir Robert's fortunes gradually declined as he became increasingly alienated from the King's party at court by whom he came to be perceived as a factious opponent. Sir Robert Cotton died in disgrace in 1631 and although Charles I sent Cotton's Huntingdonshire neighbour, the Earl of Manchester, to his death-bed with a message of comfort as a gesture of reconciliation, underlying tensions between the Court and the world of early Stuart scholarship did not allow Sir Robert the grand public funeral in London such as had been accorded to his mentor William Camden, which would have been his in easier times. All that was possible was burial at Conington. Given the unremarked passing of an authority on the funerary monument, the lines in the *Bellum Civile* which follow that added by Sir John Cotton may have had a certain irony and may hold the key to explaining why that single line was added by Sir John Cotton:

Dead men are free from the vicissitudes of Fortune, Mother Earth has room for every one of her children, and a corpse to whom an urn is denied has the whole sky to cover it.[56]

Sir John Cotton may have felt that negative sentiments were appropriate as he looked back from the end of the century on his grandfather's blighted career. Also, it might have been thought Lucan was suitable in the light of England's own Civil War. Perhaps Sir John believed that the closing of Sir Robert's library on the orders of Charles I in 1629 had broken his grandfather's spirit and brought on his death, while the fighting itself had destroyed a golden age of scholarship over which Sir Robert had presided.

APPENDIX

TWO LETTERS OF JOHN BARKHAM TO SIR ROBERT COTTON

1. Letter of Barkham to Sir Robert Cotton, n.d. (BL, Cotton MS. Julius C. III, f. 15).

Worthy and dearest S^r. It was not any forgetfulnes of my promise, which was the cause of my not sending unto you, since my retourne into Essex; but onely want of opportunity; wch now I gladly embraced by occasion of this bearers iourney to Lond; whom I have desyred to see you, and to acquaint you with the full state of those Monuments at Hemingham, whereof y^u desyred me to enforme y^u. I requested this bearer (being my Minister, and one acquainted wth Mr Herlakenden) to goe to viewe the statues, and to know his mynde for parting with them, and I hope they shalbe procured without any charge of plate or Coachehorses. He desyres onely to have some likeing and leave from the Earle of Oxford, wch I think you can easily procure, (for the Earle (I know) will not meddle with them, his land there being made from him:) But if y^r self have not so much interest in the Earle (as I think you have or easily may) I suppose I know how to work it, by a frend of mine: for I would doe any service wch might be any way acceptable to you; And when the Statues are to bee caryed, I will see it [d   ?] my self, for the more salf convayance by water. Of other Circu*m*stances, this my honest frend (a learned and true harted yong Man) will acquaint y^u at full, and I pray impart y^r pleasure to him, that we may doe o^r endevo^rs suteable to y^r desyres. On thursday or fryday you shall receave the Romane reliques wch were found here in Bocking viz, a large Brick wch covered the Glasse, wherein perchance there was Ignis Perpetuus; for there was oyle olive wch smelled as fresh as if newly poured in. And also the dish with <u>Coccilli</u> written in it; whence I suspect the name of <u>Coccill</u> (now called Cocksall) might be given to the Towne neer adioyning; and the high way fast by the place where they were taken up, is called <u>Cocksall way</u>. I have sent y^u also a pott taken up therwth. I trust you are (ere now) a free man; for wee, qui Musis litamus; have thought the Muses themselves confined in the restraynt of their Apollo: if this bearer see y^r Library the Arschenall of Learning; he will esteem it an obligation to doe y^u all possible service. And so I assure you, shall you ever finde me also

Y^r most faythfull frend to be com*m*anded,
John Barkham.

[Bo]cking [th]is Sunday night

2. Letter of Barkham to Sir Robert Cotton, n.d. (BL, Cotton MS. Julius C. III, f. 16).

Honoured S^r. Great Jewells are hardly purchased and long exspected, as it may seeme by those precious stones I now at length send you: for our wonted Caryars having intermitted their iourneys to London, this is the first day of their setting forth againe. I fear nothing but the meaneness of them, otherwise had they been of more value, they should have been sent with the better will. I have sent you a peece of the bone and one of the coales taken up wth the rest. I need not tell you, that the <u>M</u> after <u>Coccilli</u> is, <u>Manibus</u>, and with those kinde of dishes, they used to <u>libare</u>. I haue sent you also a peece of another stone digged up in another place 2 miles off from hence, it is ancient cemented work, but not worth your sight; yet such as it is Mr Tredescan (now y^r Neighbour at Lambeth) did ernestly write to me to send it to him; and therfore, if, when any of y^r servants cross the River, y^u please to send it to him, he will accept it thankfully. I desyre to heare from you concerning y^r pleasure and purpose about the statues, for I long to doe y^u any service in that or any thing els. I thank you for y^r kinde respect to my Minister at his being wth you; but I was sory that he could bring no newes of the opening of Helicons Fou*n*tayne yet, (y^r renowned Library:) My interest in y^r Love, emboldens me to relye on y^r memory for some Coynes, wch y^u can spare; and any that I have (wch you want) are yours; but I cannot beleeve my poore store, hath any thing nere y^r choice. Thus in the syncerity of a faithfull Heart, wch hath a combat in it self, whether it doth love you more, or honour you: I leave you to the hapines of y^r noblest thoughts and desyers, and rest.

Bocking in Essex Jan. 5°.

Y^r frend ever ready to serve
you, as you shall dispose of me =
John Barkham.

S^r I pray y^u, suffer not y^r Serva*n*t to pay either Caryar, or Porter, for I have taken order for it, already.

61

I would like to thank the following for help with aspects of this article: Brian Ashmore, Michael Bury, William Drummond, Roland Somervell, and Adam White.

1 For Bainbridge, see F. Haverfield, 'Cotton Julius F VI. Notes on Reginald Bainbridge of Appleby, on William Camden and some Roman Inscriptions', *Transactions of the Cumberland and Westmorland Antiquarian and Archaeological Society*, ii (1911), pp. 343–78. For Howard's dealings with Cotton, see BL, Cotton MSS. Julius C. III, ff. 210 and 211, and Vespasian F. XIII, f. 322.

2 Barkham is one of the most interesting Jacobean antiquarians, though little is known about him. However, John Speed makes reference to him in 'A summary conclusion of the whole', an epilogue to *The History of Great Britaine*. After acknowledging his predecessors, the Tudor map-makers, 'learned *Cambden*', and 'learned *Sir Robert Cotten*', Speed continues: 'The like most acceptable helpes, both of Bookes and Collections, (especially in matters remoter from our times) I continually receiued from that worthy *Divine, Master John Barkham*, a gentleman composed of *Learning, Vertue* and *Curtesie*, as being no lesse ingenuously willing, then learnedly able, to aduance and forward all vertuous endeuours'. For transcripts of two letters from Barkham to Cotton, see the Appendix to this article, pp. 60–1.

3 Cotton MS. Julius C. III, f. 15; for a transcript of the whole letter, see above pp. 60–1.

4 The remnant of Cotton's collection of altars was presented to Trinity College, Cambridge, by the last Sir John Cotton in 1750. After Sir John's death without male issue in 1752, the Conington estate was bought in 1753 by the Heathcote family. Trinity has deposited the Cotton altars at the Museum of Archaeology. See below, D. McKitterick, 'From Camden to Cambridge: Sir Robert Cotton's Roman inscriptions, and their subsequent treatment', pp. 105–28, and G. Davies, 'Sir Robert Cotton's collection of Roman stones: a catalogue with commentary', pp. 129–67.

5 Cotton MS. Julius C. III, f. 119, dated '23rd 1621'. Sir Robert also owned some notable pictures including Robert Peake's masterpiece, the equestrian portrait of Henry, Prince of Wales, now at Parham Park, Sussex. This Cotton acquired in 1613 after the death of his patron Henry Howard, Earl of Northampton. The picture is listed in an inventory of Northampton's effects. It was noted as hanging in the Lower House at Greenwich: 'S^r Ro. Cotton. Item a picture at large of Prince Henry on horsebacke in armes'; 'An Inventory of the Effects of Henry Howard, K. G., Earl of Northampton', *Archaeologia*, xlii (1869), p. 372. Cotton also owned part of the cranium of Thomas à Becket, or at least thought he did. In May 1635 Sir Thomas Cotton gave the papal envoy Gregorio Panzani a conducted tour of the cabinet and library. Besides the cranium, Panzani noticed two gospels bound together which had been given by St Gregory to St Augustine, a Greek Genesis which had belonged to Origen, letters relating to Henry VIII's divorce, a bull written in Clement VII's hand instructing the Curia what to do in the event of Clement dying a prisoner during the Sack of Rome, Martin V's attack on Marsilio of Padua, and a MS. on Roman ecclesiastical law which had been stolen from the Vatican Library and which Sir Thomas offered to let Panzani have copied, along with anything else of interest. Gregorio Panzani to Cardinal Francesco Barberini, 25 May 1635, Vatican Library, Barberini Latina MS. 8634, f. 99.

6 BL, Cotton MS. Fragments XXV, f. 25v. It is interesting to note the similarity between the format of the 'altar' to Robert Cecil, and the inscription in the form of a *votiva ara* with which Cotton's donations to Bodley's library were embellished. These donations were made at the same time as, it is suggested above, he dedicated the 'altar' to Cecil. See C. G. C. Tite, '"Lost or stolen or strayed": A Survey of Manuscripts formerly in the Cotton Library', *B.L.J.*, xviii (1992), pp. 108–11, and below, pp. 263–6.

7 County Record Office Huntingdon [hereafter C.R.O.H.], CON3/1/1/15.

8 *V.C.H., Huntingdon*, vol. iii, p. 144: 'the systematic drainage was begun by Sir Thomas Cotton in 1639, and in the following year the first pump was erected.' Sir William Dugdale in *The History of Imbanking and Draining* (London, 1772), p. 379, makes it clear that Sir Robert had been actively involved in draining and agricultural improvements since the last years of the Elizabethan era. Dugdale transcribes a document to which Sir Robert put his signature, dated Huntingdon, 19 May 1605, in which the

commissioners opined that: 'this work of draining was...the most noble work...and most beneficial to the countries interested, to have good by, that ever was taken in hand of that kind in those days.' Cotton's fellow subscribers included Sir Oliver Cromwell and the Cambridge bibliophile and antiquarian, Sir Henry Spelman. It would appear that Cotton's pecuniary interests had complemented his antiquarian studies. Dugdale explains how the Fens originally became water-logged by reference to a discovery made by Sir Robert at Conington at an unspecified date: 'I am now to demonstrate by what means it came to pass, that the ocean, at first, brake into it with such violence, as that the woods then standing throughout the same, became turned up by the roots; and so great a proportion of silt brought in, as not only for divers miles, next towards the sea, did cover the ground to an extraordinary depth (as I shall plainly shew anon) but even to the remotest parts on the verge of the highlands, as is apparent from that discovery made of late years, at the skirt of Conington down in Huntingdonshire; where, upon making of a pool, by the famous Sir Robert Cotton baronet, he found the skeleton of a large sea-fish (near XX feet long, as was then conjectured) lying in perfect silt, above six feet below the superficies of the ground, and as much above the present level of the fen; which, by so long a continuance in that kind of earth, was petrified, as is evident from divers of the bones, both of the back and other parts, which are still preserved by Sir Thomas Cotton baronet, his worthy son, amongst other rarities that were collected by that learned person.' Ibid., p. 172.

9 J. M. Heathcote in his *Reminiscences of Fen and Mere* (London, 1876), p. 28, wrote: 'Sir Robert removed from Fotheringhay Castle to this mansion the room in which Mary Queen of Scots was beheaded. The colonnade was likewise removed, and was placed in a situation similar to that in which it stood at Fotheringhay.' The 6th annual excursion of the Cambridgeshire and Huntingdonshire Archaeological Society, on 30 May 1905, consisted of a visit to Conington, Gatton and Little Gidding. *Trans. of Cambs. and Hunts. Archaeological Society*, ii, 1905–8 (Ely, 1908), pp. 240–1: 'Sir Robert Cotton, the celebrated antiquary, is said to have built the first house on the present site – the home of Waltheof and the Bruces [Bruce's Castle] being some distance off – and having purchased in 1626, eleven of the arches of the hall of Fotheringhay Castle, built them into the house. The house and gardens were demolished in 1722, by the then baronet, who preferred an estate in Bedfordshire, but in 1753 Conington was purchased by Sir John Heathcote, since which time the house has been restored and enlarged. The eleven arches of the front, the porch and the lodge gates are said to have come from Fotheringhay Castle; this is probably true of the eleven arches, which are of coarse Perpendicular design and may well have formed the arcades of the Castle Hall, but as regards the porch and gates it is more doubtful, the former being good Renaissance design of such a late date that one is tempted to doubt it.' I have been unable to find any reference to a purchase of Fotheringhay stone by Sir Robert in 1626 among the Conington papers at the Cambs R. O., but the Archaeological Society may have had access to manuscripts which have since disappeared.

10 C.R.O.H., CON4/2/1/1, 'Conington Rental and payments, 1603–12' and CON4/2/1/2, 'Conington Rental and payments, 1617–32'.

11 C.R.O.H., CON4/2/1/3, 'Conington Rental and payments, 1632–62'.

12 Ibid.

13 C.R.O.H., CON4/2/1/2. Under the date 'the 16th daie of March 1630 [1631]', the account reads: 'To Henry Thorpe of Mket deeping for 60 loade of free stone at Maxey Castle'. William of Thorpe obtained a royal licence to embattle the manor-house at Maxey in 1274–5. Otherwise nothing further is known about this castle.

14 It is worth remarking, however, that at a later stage, and at his house at Westminster, Cotton may have shown a rather more sophisticated aspect as a patron. For his garden, he employed Thomas Styles to make a balustrade resting on cartouches over the water. Thereafter Styles became principal mason employed in giving the medieval nave of Old St Paul's a classical casing. Styles was one of the most skilled artisans in the London building trade.

15 John Martin Robinson, *The Dukes of Norfolk* (Oxford, 1982), p. 95.

16 For Conington Castle and its octagonal summer houses, see *V.C.H., Hunts.*, vol. iii (London, 1936), p. 145 and opposite, for a drawing of the

grounds of Conington Castle from BL, Add. MS. 29936, f. 40. See also below, D. McKitterick, p. 119, fig. 2. I would suggest that the erection of the summer houses may date from *c.* 1608. Among the Cotton MSS. are letters from Lord William Howard to Cotton about shipping stones from the Picts Wall to Cotton in the south, dated Summer 1608: BL, Cotton MSS. Julius C. III, ff. 210–211, and Vespasian F. XIII, f. 322.

17 C.R.O.H., CON4/2/1/3.

18 BL, Cotton MS. Appendix XLIX, f. 35.

19 Ibid., f. 71, where Sir Thomas wrote: 'my wife only staying to dispose of things att Connington whether Colonell Cromwell came to see hir, and advised hir not to stay ther but to goe into Bedfordshire because that howse standing neare the rode wouldbe dayly troubled with Soldiers in the passage from Cambrigg into Linconshire, and while she stayed she was 26 times plundred lost hir coach horses most of hir other horses, and had the house riffled hir gowne, bible, and other things taken away, for which she complaynd to Sergeant maior whalye, who did beat the soldiers and restord hir the goods taken out of the house, but advisd hir not to stay ther for the soldiers passing that way wouldbe unruly, captaine mason likewise comming that way searched hir trunks and tooke 85 [pounds] from hir, which col: cromwell told hir should be allowed in the 5 and 20 part when it came to be assessed, after this 20 soldiers were billited ther and when they were removed more [sent?] so that she was compelled to remove and dispose of what she could there for security.'

Cromwell may have been well disposed to Sir Thomas, and to Conington, since his uncle, Sir Oliver Cromwell, and Sir Robert Cotton had been elected M.P.s for Huntingdonshire on 18 Feb. 1604; 'sergeant maior whalye', or Edward Whalley, was Oliver Cromwell's first cousin and became one of the most redoubtable parliamentary commanders of the English Civil War. When he visited Conington he had already distinguished himself at the battle of Gainsborough in nearby Lincolnshire where his conduct caused Cromwell to write that 'Major Whalley did in this carry himself with all gallantry becoming a gentleman and a Christian.' In 1645 Cromwell divided the command of the New Model Army with Whalley who then led his regiment at the battle of Naseby. He was entrusted with the safe-keeping of Charles I after the King was taken at Holdenby and the King left Whalley a letter thanking him for his courtesy when he fled Hampton Court. Whalley signed Charles's death warrant and fought alongside Cromwell at Dunbar. He became one of Cromwell's Major-Generals. He was excluded from the Act of Indemnity at the Restoration, fled to America, where unsuccessful attempts were made by Royalist spies to hunt him down, and died in 1675.

Sir Thomas was right about the insalubrious air of Conington. Although Cotton, Camden and Jonson had spent an agreeable Summer there in 1603 when escaping the London plague, Edmund Gibson in his revision of Camden's *Britannia* (London, 1695), p. 423, wrote: 'By reason these parts lye so low, are under water some months, and some so hollow that they seem to float, they are much troubled with the noisome smells of Lakes, and a thick foggy air.'

20 Sir Henry Ellis (ed.), *The Visitation of the County of Huntingdon by Nicholas Charles A.D. 1613*, Camden Soc., 1st Series, xliii (1849), pp. 26–8.

21 K. A. Esdaile, *English Church Monuments, 1510–1840* (London, 1946), p. 88.

22 Kevin Sharpe, *Sir Robert Cotton 1586–1631* (Oxford, 1979), p. 115.

23 C.R.O.H., CON8/1.

24 Sharpe, op. cit., ch. IV *passim.*

25 The identical monuments are memorials to Edward, 2nd Duke of York (d. 1415) and his nephew, Richard, 3rd Duke of York (d. 1460), erected in 1573 by Elizabeth I. They are opposite each other like the Conington monuments and, like them too, are without figures. For the tombs, see H. M. Colvin *et al.*, *The History of the King's Works*, vol. iii, 1485–1660, (Part 1) (London, 1975), p. 251.

26 Most conspicuously in Rubens's allegorical paintings for the Whitehall Banqueting House.

27 Sharpe, op. cit., p. 120.

28 For the Steward tomb, see Nigel Llewellyn, 'Claims to Status through Visual Codes: Heraldry on post-Reformation Funeral Monuments', in Sydney Anglo (ed.), *Chivalry in The Renaissance* (Woodbridge, 1990), pp. 145–61. Llewellyn regards Sir Simeon's action as: 'a piece of blatant politicing at a critical moment in English history', describing the Stewards' claim as 'bogus'. Here Llewellyn is following nineteenth century antiquaries who believed the

Steward claims to be erroneous. However, Sir Henry Steward proved that Sir Mark, and indeed James VI and I, were collateral descendants of Alexander Stuart of Dundervale. This was in an article, which may have been unknown to Llewellyn, entitled 'Cromwell's Stuart Descent', *Proceedings of the Cambridge Antiquarian Society*, xxvii (1926), pp. 86–122. The reason for the title of Sir Henry's article was that the Stewards and Cromwells were intermarried. Sir Henry made the point that the Jacobean world in general would certainly have believed the Stewards' claim to be authentic: 'It is however a fact that the pedigree was on divers occasions ratified and confirmed by the proper authorities at the College of Arms.' For a splendid engraving of the Steward tomb, see James Bentham, *The History of Ely* (Cambridge, 1771), pl. xxxix.

29 Cecil Papers (Marquess of Salisbury, Hatfield House), vol. 121, f. 1, and vol. 206, f. 1.

30 Sharpe, op. cit., p. 89.

31 Ibid., p. 90.

32 Cotton MS. Titus C. VI, ff. 206r–211v.

33 *V.C.H.*, *Hunts.*, vol. iii, p. 151.

34 C.R.O.H., CON2/4/1/21. This was made by Sir Robert's half-brother, John, and witnessed in Chancery by Sir Matthew Carew on 7 Feb. 1608.

35 Sharpe, op. cit., pp. 123–6.

36 Nicholas Charles to Sir Robert Cotton, 'London this first day of october 1613'; Cotton MS. Julius C. III, f. 88. The Cottons descended from Robert the Bruce through the Wesenhams.

37 The base of the monument contains five shields which denote Prince David's descent from: Henry the Fowler, Emperor of Germany; the kings of France; the Anglo-Saxon kings; William the Conqueror; and the crown of Scotland itself. For further light on the armorial bearings of this monument, see *V.C.H.*, *Hunts*, vol. iii, p. 150.

38 John Speed, the famous cartographer, paid tribute to Cotton's collection which remained the best coin cabinet in Britain until the purchase of the Gorleus cabinet for Henry, Prince of Wales, shortly before the Prince's death in 1612. In *The History of Great Britaine* (London, 1611), p. 169, Speed wrote: 'Many of these [coins] are amongst vs remaining, whereof I haue inserted some few, as in their due places shall follow, which I receiued from the liberall hand of that most learned Knight, and worthy storer of

Antiquities Sir Robert Cotten of Cunington.' (See below, Gay van der Meer, 'An early seventeenth-century inventory of Cotton's Anglo-Saxon coins', pp. 168–82). There are five letters from Speed to Cotton, Julius C. III, ff. 354–358, which demonstrate how Cotton was in effect editor of Speed's *History*. Speed sent Cotton proof sheets for Cotton to scrutinize, and he asks Cotton to send his comments on separate sheets to make it easier for the printer to read his emendations. In a postscript to f. 358, Speed adds: 'Remember to Signify the forms of yoᵣ Altars.'

Further public acknowledgement of Cotton's role was provided in the same passage in which Speed had thanked John Barkham (see n. 3 above). In Speed's 'A summary conclusion of the whole' appended to his *Historie*, the author writes: 'For the body of the Historie, many were the manuscripts, notes, and Records, wherewith my honored and learned friends supplied me; but none more (or so many) as did the worthy repairer of eating times ruines, the learned *Sir Robert Cotten* Knight Baronet, another *Philadelphus* in preseruing old Monuments, and ancient Records: whose Cabinets were vnlocked, and Library continually set open to my free accesse; and from whence the chiefest garnishments of this worke haue beene enlarged and brought; such as are the antique altars, and Trophies in Stone, by him preserued from perishing oblivion; The Coines of gold, siluer, alcumy, and copper, of the *Britaines*, *Romans*, *Saxons*, *Danes*, and *English*, with the Broade Seales of those Kings since the same were in vse: all of them so followed from the originall moddles, and moneyes, by the most exquisit and curious hand [in margin: Christ. Swister] of our age, as any eye may witnes they are the true prints from those stamps.'

An important point which has been overlooked in connection with Cotton's interest in numismatics is that Cotton MS. Julius C. III, f. 375, is a letter from Abraham Gorleaus in which the writer offers to sell a collection of coins. Gorleaus had been Councillor of the Count of Nieuwenaar and Meurs in Utrecht and from 1595 lived in Delft in easy retirement where he amassed what became the most celebrated cabinet of seals, gems and coins in northern Europe. The existence of the letter amongst Cotton's correspondence, suggests that Cotton was instrumental in acquiring the Gorleus cabinet for the Prince of Wales to whom it passed in 1611. If that is right, then the letter should be dated 1611; not 1600 as in the index to Cotton MS. Julius C. III. For the contents of the Gorleus cabinet, see A. Gorleaus, *Dactyliotheca* (Delft, 1601).

39 Camden, *Britannia* (1610), p. 94.

40 Many of the Society's papers are printed in Thomas Hearne, *A Collection of Curious Discourses*, ed. J. Ayloffe (London, 1771), vol. i, pp. 228–60.

41 Ibid, p. 235.

42 J. Newman, 'An early drawing by Inigo Jones and a monument in Shropshire', *Burlington Magazine*, cxv (1973), pp. 360–7, 558.

43 John Harris and Gordon Higgott, *Inigo Jones: Complete Architectural Drawings* (London, 1989), pp. 42–4.

44 BL, Harl. MS. 6018, ff. 152–180, esp. 179v and 180r.

45 For friendships among artists and antiquaries at this club in the early years of James I's reign, see M. Strachan, *The Life and Adventures of Thomas Coryat* (Oxford, 1962).

46 Camden thought the spot where he and Cotton examined this find was Volantium. Since then, however, there has been much further debate: the settlements of Olenacum, Virosidum and Uxellodunum have all been suggested. Recent work has, however, established that Senhouse's property was at Alauna. The remnant of John Senhouse's collection went on public view with the opening of the Senhouse Roman Museum at Maryport in April 1990.

47 Philemon Holland (trans.), *Britain or a Chorographicall Description of the Most flourishing Kingdomes England, Scotland and Ireland* (London, 1610), p. 769. 'I Sinhous' was John Senhouse (d. 1606) whose importance in the Jacobean antiquarian movement has been somewhat overlooked. He was Camden's age and had thus begun excavations a whole generation before the likes of Cotton. Camden in another part of *Britannia* refers to him as a man who had 'a great veneration for Antiquities (wherein he is well skilled) with great diligence preserves such inscriptions'. The reference to at least ten inscriptions having been dug up on Senhouse's land is unparalleled elsewhere in *Britannia*. Senhouse lived at Alneburgh Hall, later known as Netherhall, near Ellenborough. Ellenborough is close to Maryport which formed one of the westernmost defences behind the line of Hadrian's Wall. For the Alneburgh Hall (Netherhall) collection, see J. B. Bailey and Professor Haverfield, 'Catalogue of Roman Inscribed and Sculptured Stones, Coins, Earthenware, etc., discovered in and near the Roman Fort at Maryport, and preserved at Netherhall', *Transactions of the Cumberland and Westmorland Antiquarian and Archaeological Society*, n.s., xv (1915), pp. 135–72.

48 The short inscriptions read: 'Asta Te Amabo Lege' and 'Et Abi in Rem Tuam'.

49 It is difficult to see who else could have designed the Camden monument though, as John Newman has pointed out to me, it is curious that Stone makes no mention of such a celebrated work in his notebook which contains an (incomplete) list of works. Adam White coined the term 'the scholar monument' in his analysis of Nicholas Stone's funerary monuments. In his 'Classical Learning and the Early Stuart Renaissance', *Journal of the Church Monuments Society*, i, pt. i (1985), pp. 20–33, he describes Jones's design of a monument to the poet George Chapman (d. 1634), as based on a Roman grave altar probably from Arundel House, adding that it was a 'direct imitation of the Antique... without precedent in the history of English monuments'. However, the Double Cotton and Prince Henry monuments, and indeed Cotton's design for a votive altar to the Earl of Salisbury, suggest that a sophisticated grasp of the antique funerary monument existed some twenty years earlier. I see the scholar monument as evolving over a longer period than White. He believes it to be the creation of Jacobean sculptors, stemming from the impetus given to antiquarian studies by the publication in 1586 of Camden's *Britannia*. However, the basic essentials of the type were present in the monument to John Colet (d. 1519) erected sixty years earlier in Old St Paul's.

50 Roger Dodsworth to Sir Robert Cotton, Hutton, 16 Feb. 1622/3, Cotton MS. Julius F. VI, f. 314.

51 Nicholas Stone to Sir Thomas Cotton, 'London this 31 Julij 1638', Cotton Appendix LVIII, f. 10.

52 For a discussion of the Stone drawing, see Adam White, 'Inigo Jones and the spread of classicism' in *The Georgian Group Symposium 1986* (Leeds,

1987), pp. 49–60. White suggests that Stone's drawing may be a preparatory study for the monument of 1634 to Isaac Casaubon in Westminster Abbey. However, as White is aware, the physiognomy of the head in the drawing is not very like Casaubon. I would suggest, however, that the rather prominent nose, the beard, and sweep of hair over the shoulders, resemble these features as they are to be observed in Cotton's monument in All Saints, Conington.

53 BL, Add. MS. 8128, f. 51. Quoted without reference by K. A. Esdaile, *English Church Monuments* (London, 1946), p. 88. Esdaile points out that Sir Thomas Cotton's steward took a boat to Temple Stairs, the river approach to the Marshall's yard in Fleet Street. I am grateful to Adam White for bringing this manuscript to my attention and for suggesting that the monument was probably executed by one of the Marshalls and not by Stone himself.

54 Lucan, *Bellum Civile*, VII, l. 814.

55 'Sr,... For the inscription upon my Grandfathers monument it was writ by my father; I only added out of Lucan Communis mundo superest Rogus.' Sir John Cotton to Thomas Smith, [between July and Nov. 1695], Bodleian Library, MS. Smith 48, f. 291r + v.

56 Lucan, op. cit., ll. 818–19.

67

SIR ROBERT COTTON'S SERVICES TO THE CROWN: A PAPER WRITTEN IN SELF-DEFENCE

NIGEL RAMSAY

I T is difficult to assess the character or personality of Sir Robert Cotton. Very few of his letters survive, and his personal papers seem largely to have perished. His library of printed books has been scattered, and it is notorious that his collection of manuscripts and charters has come down to us bereft of the accompanying documentation that might reveal the sources from which it was formed. The short treatises and the speeches that Cotton wrote in such quantity still await an overall investigation, and only a few of them have been looked at in detail; each poses its own problems – of dating, establishment of text, and even of authorial identity.[1]

The papers of two of the librarians of the Cotton collection, Richard James (d. 1638) and Dr Thomas Smith (d. 1710), have long been in the Bodleian Library, Oxford: they offer some of the clearest evidence about the texts and the history of the collection. The transcripts by James have quite frequently been found of value in this connection, but the papers of Smith are still valued less than they deserve. The volume now shelved as MS. Smith 28 is stated in the Bodleian Library's *Summary Catalogue, s.v.* no. 15635, to contain at p. 33 'Part of the original draft of sir Robert Cotton's defence of himself and of his services done to the crown' (fig. 1); this follows Smith's own description (on a small piece of paper affixed to p. 34, and now termed p. 34c), 'Sir Robert Cottons paper in defense of himselfe, & of his Services done the Crowne.' Given that this description is perfectly accurate, it might seem strange that the document has so far escaped scholarly attention.

There are perhaps two principal reasons for this neglect: in the first place, the document is of uncertain date and purpose, and, secondly, it is in places extremely hard to read. It is in Cotton's own hand, and it gives signs of having been written when he felt under pressure. Its script deteriorates in clarity, and its form breaks down; towards the end, its paragraphs cease to be numbered, and the lines become longer, while Cotton finished by writing along the sheet's margin. The document is a single sheet, and has been torn across as well as being folded and unfolded many times. It was bound up by Smith or the legatee of his papers, Thomas Hearne (d. 1735), but it is impossible to say how much older than this time the tear and folds may be. The text begins *in medias res* with a paragraph that is numbered 4, and there was clearly originally a preliminary sheet;

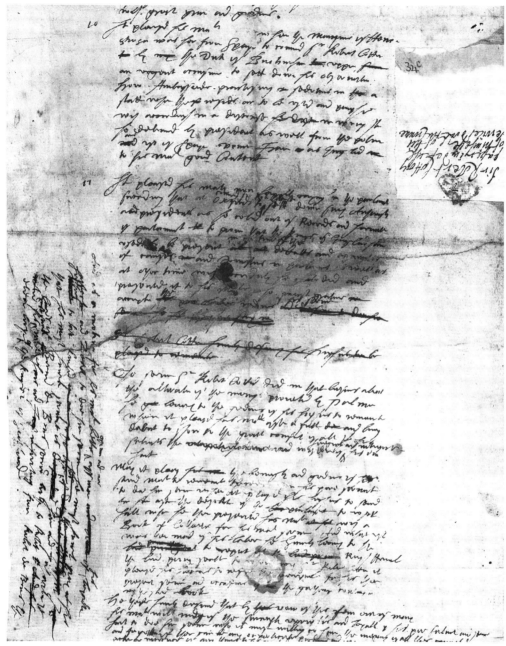

Fig. 1. Oxford, Bodleian Library, MS. Smith 28, f. 34a (detail). *By kind permission of the Bodleian Library, Oxford*

69

to judge from the length of the paragraphs on the surviving sheet, the lost sheet was much smaller than the present one (which measures 12 × 7 in., 303 × 195 mm.).

It appears that Smith heard of the document only after his *Catalogue* of the Cotton manuscripts had been printed: on 3 December 1695 he wrote to Philip Cotton, younger brother of Sir John Cotton: 'I wish you had found the entire list of the Services done to the Crown by your Grandfather, wch hee put into the hands of K. Charles I. – however the fragment you mention, is & will bee very usefull & acceptable, for most of the particulars of wch I have accompted at large in the life, wch is undoubtedly printed off at Oxon. by this time.'[2] Smith seems first to have heard of the document in November 1695.[3] On 30 June 1696 he had it in his own custody in London, when he wrote to Philip Cotton seeking a fair copy of it, the original being 'illegible in several places'.[4] It is impossible to say why Smith never returned the document; it may simply have been because he found it so hard to transcribe. Philip Cotton died a bachelor in 1710.[5] Smith came to possess other Cotton materials including Sir Robert's copy of the 1607 edition of Camden's *Britannia* with notes in William Camden's own hand (now Bodleian Library, MS. Smith 1; *Summary Cat.*, no. 15608). MS. Smith 19 has the note 'These papers I designe to print; & then to give them to the Cottonian Library. Tho: Smith.' Smith, as a Nonjuror, was a man with a tender conscience, and there is no reason to think that his retention of the paper that now forms part of MS. Smith 28 was in any way unjustified or unwarranted.

THE TEXT OF COTTON'S DRAFT

EDITORIAL NOTE: To a large extent, Sir Robert Cotton's paper must be taken as it stands and is to that extent self-explanatory. Comments have, however, been added on individual paragraphs; the numbering of paragraphs 12 to 14 is an editorial intervention. The line-beginnings of the original have been followed, any carry-over being indented. Deletions are enclosed within square brackets and insertions within angle brackets. Square or angle brackets that enclose blank spaces indicate words that proved illegible; there would have been many more of these had it not been for the kind assistance of Carl Berkhout, Ian Doyle, Arnold Hunt, Glyn Redworth and Andrew Watson. I have also benefited enormously from the guidance of Simon Adams, Ken Fincham and Richard Cust.

4.   The Proiect of the Baronetts was first deuysed [?]
and framed by Sir Robert Cotton and from him
by the Earl of Salisbury presented to Kinge James [what *deleted*]
whas raysed by [*word deleted*] it to his Ma^ti and his seruice as [*reading of last two words uncertain*]
apperith by record.

Credit for inventing baronetcies has been claimed by or for a variety of people, including Sir Thomas Shirley and Henry Howard, Earl of Northampton. That Cotton first devised the scheme was surmised by K. Sharpe, *Sir Robert Cotton, 1586–1631: History and Politics in*

Early Modern England (Oxford, 1979) [hereafter: Sharpe, *Cotton*], p. 123; Salisbury's role as its promoter was mentioned by Sir Walter Cope. The idea was perhaps in Cotton's mind as early as 1606, although it came to fruition only in 1611. In its first three years, the device yielded £90,885 to the Crown: L. L. Peck, *Northampton: Patronage and Policy at the Court of James I* (London, 1982) [hereafter: Peck, *Northampton*], p. 115.

See further: J. G. Nichols, 'The Institution and Early History of the Dignity of Baronet', *Herald and Genealogist*, iii (1866), pp. 193–212, 341–52, 449–58; K. S. van Eerde, 'The Creation of the Baronetage in England', *Huntington Library Quarterly*, xxii (1958–9), pp. 313–22; eadem, 'The Jacobean Baronets: An Issue between King and Parliament', *Journal of Modern History*, xxxiii (1961), pp. 137–47; Lawrence Stone, *The Crisis of the Aristocracy, 1558–1641* (Oxford, 1965), pp. 78, 82–97; Sharpe, *Cotton*, pp. 123–6; Peck, *Northampton*, pp. 51–5, 115–16; G. D. Squibb, *Precedence in England and Wales* (Oxford, 1981), pp. 36–8.

5. Thuanus [   ] publysed in his History by Fals
Informations [of *deleted*] som scandalus passages concerning
the Quen of Scotts of holy memory His ma^{ti} being
therwith mouid sent for Sir Robert Cotton who
informed his highnes that he had preserved from the
fier in Q. Eliz. time most of the Originall letters
of the Quen of Scott together with many of the
protestations Answers [and of *deleted*] < and Iustific[...]es [not mad *deleted*] [   ]
  inserted > hir M. subiects and
[seruants *deleted*] Commissions sent into England against
the vntruths and falshoods of hir rebellus subiects
in Scotland all which he had preserued and bound vp
in seuerall volumes for [Justification of hir Ma^{ti} *deleted*; *reading of first word uncertain*]
[   ] of hir Ma^{ti} Honor [what *deleted*; *reading uncertain*] wher time
might serue Out of [wich *reading uncertain*] by his [Ma *deleted*] highnes Command
he [m *deleted*] coulected abstracts wich wer sent ouer to
Thuanus to insert into his Annalls All wich wer
after [*reading uncertain*] by express order and warrant vnder the Kings
own hand wich [he hath *deleted*] Sr Robert Cotton hath compyled
into a story of Q Eliz time by m^r Camden and
published in print

The French courtier and scholar, Jacques Auguste de Thou, gave offence to James I by some passages about Mary, Queen of Scots, in his *Historiarum Sui Temporis* (books 1–18, 1604; reprinted with a further eight books, 19–26, 1606; books 27–80, coming down to 1585, 1606–9). The Cotton collection still contains many letters of and about Mary, principally in the volumes Caligula B. VIII–X and C. I–IX. Sir Robert Cotton evidently worked his way through these, and sent abstracts to de Thou in France, before the publication of the later volumes that covered the years after 1587. In the last sentence, Cotton seems to be indicating that the same material was used for the first part of *Annales Rerum Anglicarum et Hibernicarum* published as by Camden in 1615. James I undoubtedly valued Cotton's efforts in favour of his mother's reputation and of his own actions in the 1580s, for in 1624 he wanted Cotton to review further books that concerned her, making one of them 'more authentic': *Cal.S.P.Dom., 1623–5*, p. 283.

See further H. R. Trevor-Roper, *Queen Elizabeth's first Historian: William Camden and the Beginnings of English History*, Neale Lecture (London, 1971), reprinted in idem, *Renaissance Essays* (London, 1985), pp. 121–48; Sharpe, *Cotton*, pp. 89–95 (rightly surmising Cotton's leading role in advising de Thou); D. R. Woolf, 'Two Elizabeths? James I and the late Queen's Memory', *Canadian Journal of History*, xx (1985), pp. 167–91; and idem, *The Idea of History in Early Stuart England ...* (Toronto, 1990), pp. 115–19 (suggesting a greater share for Cotton in the writing of the *Annales*); and K. Sharpe, 'Rewriting Sir Robert Cotton', prefacing this volume.

[6.]   His Ma^{ty} [16 *rest of date illegible; deleted*] <1607 *inserted*> commnd. Sr Robert
   Cotton to mak a
Collections of suche courses as the King of England had
formerly vsed for reparyng [of *deleted*] and increasing ther
Reuenues uery accurately out of Record and on the lik
warrant he performed and deliuered to his Ma^{ti} The
Copy of wich is in the hands of many lords of his
Ma^t Councell and than was mad som espetiall
wyth it.

This collection must be identifiable as the paper printed as the eighth item in *Cottoni Posthuma*, at pp. 161–202 of the 1672 edition: 'The Manner and Means how the Kings of England have from time to time supported and repaired their estates.'

A considerable range of sources, partly drawn from his own collection, is cited, although it is noticeable that few of these authorities are from later than the reign of Henry VI. The Rolls of Parliament and the Council proceedings are most frequently cited (the former possibly from his own set, in Titus E. II–XIV and F. I–II; the latter perhaps from Cleopatra F. III–V), while early sources include Gervase of Canterbury, John Eversden, William Rishanger and Ralph of Coggeshall. One set of accounts of Lord Burghley as Treasurer, 1569–70, is drawn on, and Cotton refers to an estimate of the King's household expenditure of 1 May 1604. Cotton himself was clearly a little unsure of the date of the tract's compilation, since 1607 was not the first date that he wrote. In *Cottoni Posthuma* it is dated on its title-page 1609, as also in a manuscript copy mentioned in H.M.C., *2nd Report*, Appx., p. 90; this is stated to be erroneous, and a date of 1610–11 or 1611–12 seems to be preferred, by Sharpe, *Cotton*, p. 122, n. 49. R. W. Hoyle has suggested that the work was perhaps derivative from one of 1612? that is attributed to Francis Bacon: '"Shearing the Hog": The Reform of the Estates, *c.* 1598–1640', in R. W. Hoyle (ed.), *The Estates of the English Crown, 1558–1640* (Cambridge, 1992), pp. 204–62, at 223, n. 112, and cf. p. 243, and yet cf. also p. 363. A copy in Cotton MS. Cleopatra F. VI, ff. 41–51r, is headed in a hand that is possibly that of Cotton himself 'An°. 10: Jacobi Regis. Means to repayr the Kings Estate 1612 Jacob: Rex | collected by Sr Robert Cotton for the Earl of Northampton.' It is signed at the end, very probably in Cotton's own hand, 'Ro: Cotton. 1612: Sept. 25'; it also has marginal notes on ff. 41–43v that are in the hand of Henry Howard, Earl of Northampton.

See also Sharpe, *Cotton*, pp. 121–3.

[7.]   The Kings Ma^t in the year 1608 vppon especiall trus[t]
reposed in the Earl of Northampton for serching out the
great abuses and deceipt done to his highnes by the
officers [*reading uncertain*] and Ministers of his nauy royall granted his
Commission vnder the great seall who [*reading doubtful*] amongst other th[ings?]
pleased his highness to nam Sir Robert Cotton who
together with Capley [*reading uncertain*] & Norris wer designed to
confer with such persons as could best discouer thes
deceipt which accordingly [*letter deleted*] as may apper both of time [*reading doubtful*]
and < mony *inserted*; *reading doubtful* > by the same Sr Robert Cotton the Names of
    thes peop[le]
were deliuered in [*reading doubtful*] being 144 and ther examinations [*reading doubtful*]
    taken
[ ].
[And *deleted*] The report of all wich seruice was apoynted to
be drawn up [and pr *deleted*] by Sr Robert Cotton and presented
to his Ma^{ti} wich accordingly was by him done with great
diligence and Integrity don. as may apere by the [record *deleted*]
[in *deleted*] book wich he hath still in his hand hauing vsed in the
wholl discours no other [*word deleted*] phrais [*reading doubtful*] but the letter of
the depositions. yett composed it a confused busines into
an easy and orderly conception.

Henry Howard, Earl of Northampton, Robert Cotton and others were granted a commission to investigate abuses, deceits and frauds in the Royal Navy, 30 April 1608 (H.M.C., *Report on the Laing Manuscripts preserved in The University of Edinburgh*, vol. i, pp. 110–11). Cotton took a leading role in the investigation, which lasted until June 1609; he was assisted by John Clyfton, purser, and Captain Thomas Norris. (The uncertain reading 'Capley' in MS. Smith 28 cannot be 'Clyfton', although it is possibly 'Capton'.) The resultant depositions and examinations, which actually total rather more than 144, form Cotton MS. Julius F. III; this has been edited by A. P. McGowan as *The Jacobean Commissions of Enquiry, 1608 and 1618*, Navy Records Soc., cxvi (1971).

There are two versions in the Department of Manuscripts of Cotton's report, 'Considerations of the present state of the Navy, and by what means it may be reduced to a better order': Add. MS. 9334, ff. 20–84v (with Cotton's own signature on f. 82), and Egerton MS. 2975, ff. 34–97v. The version presented to James I is presumably that in the Public Record Office, SP 14/41.

See further Sharpe, *Cotton*, pp. 117–18; L. L. Peck, 'Problems in Jacobean Administration: Was Henry Howard, Earl of Northampton, a Reformer?', *Historical Journal*, xix (1976), pp. 831–58, at 835–40; Peck, *Northampton*, pp. 152–4; A. P. McGowan, 'Further Documents from the Commission of Enquiry, 1608', in *Navy Miscellany*, V, Navy Records Soc., cxxv (1984), pp. 1–14.

8.   In the distress of the Pallatinat it pleased his M^at to
command Sr Robert Cotton to collect such ways as the Kings of
this realm had formerly vppon vrgent necesity vsed In
the raysing of Men Munitions [*reading doubtful*] and Money wich Discourse all
    gathered out of record
he presented to the Lords in Councill at [whitt *deleted*] whitt Hall [uppon *deleted*]
[*six words deleted*] < the well [ ] *inserted* > it he reserued [*reading doubtful*] to the
    [*word deleted*] [ ] of ther
Lordships to report.

It is not certain when in the 1620s Cotton prepared this collection of ways used for the collection of troops and money. A possibility is the time of the forced loan discussions, 1626–7, and it is worth noting that in March 1627 Cotton was asked by the Attorney-General, Heath, for precedents for the duty of all men to serve by their person or their purse in the King's wars (P. E. Kopperman, *Sir Robert Heath, 1575–1649: Window on an Age* (London, 1989), p. 79). However, the reference to the Palatinate does not fit; the levy in 1627 was for the King of Denmark; Cotton's undoubted contribution at this time took form as *The Danger wherein the Kingdom now Standeth, and the Remedy thereof* (Jan. 1628), which argues a different case (see R. Cust, *The Forced Loan and English Politics, 1626–1628* (Oxford, 1987), pp. 81–4); and the monarch is not designated 'his majesty now reigning' as in paragraph 11 below.

    The date must therefore be either the autumn of 1620, directly after the invasion of the Palatinate, when James proposed raising money via a benevolence (attempted in October, but then superseded by the proclamation summoning parliament on 6 November; a collection was made by the Elector Palatine's envoy, however), or else about January 1622, when there was a fresh decision to raise a benevolence for the Palatinate's defence.

[*p. 34a*]
9.   It pleased his Matie 1614 to intrust Sr Robert
Cotton [with *deleted*] to attend that O[ ] of
Mariadg [*reading of last three letters doubtful*] begun
in december by the Duk of Lerma with the lord Digby
in Spain and [J *deleted*] in January following [for *deleted*] by [*reading doubtful*]
    Gondomer
the [A *deleted*] Spanish Embass[*rest of word illegible*] in England. The payns [he
    deleted]
[toke the *deleted*] and Car he toke then he rerfers [*reading doubtful*] to the
gratious remembrance of his now [*reading uncertain*] Ma^ti [before *deleted*] to whom
and at whos apoyntment he mad a full report in the
paynted Chamber before the Lords and Commons in parliament
when [hi *deleted*] it pleased then his highnes to receave
with great grace [*reading uncertain*] and goodnes [*reading uncertain*].

Negotiations for a Spanish match for Prince Charles began in Spain in December 1614, between Sir John Digby (later Earl of Bristol) and Francisco Gómez de Sandoval, Duke of Lerma; Cotton himself began negotiating in England with Diego Sarmiento de Acuña, later Conde de Gondomar, in January 1615, and continued to do so for most of the year. No copy of Cotton's report has been located.

See further Sharpe, *Cotton*, pp. 131–3, 172–3.

10.　　It pleased his Ma^{ti} [*blank*] when the Marquis of Hene
strosa [*reading doubtful*] was her from Spayn to command Sr Robert Cotton
[to *deleted*] by [my *deleted*] the Duk of Buckingham [to *deleted*] vppon [*word deleted*]
an vrgent occasion to sett down his observations
How Ambassadors practising [a *deleted*] seditions in [the *deleted*] a
statt where they reside are to be vsed and punyshed
wich acordingly in a discourse [he *and another word deleted*] in wrighting [*reading uncertain*]
he deliuered by president as well from the policie [*reading uncertain*]
[word *deleted*] < and *inserted* > use of Spayn Venice France [*letter deleted*] as England
　　[*word deleted*]
to his Ma^{tis} good Content.

Don Carlos Coloma succeeded the Conde de Gondemar as the Spanish ambassador to England, and was subsequently joined, in the summer of 1623, by Juan Hurtado de Mendoza, Marqués de Hinojosa. Cotton's collection of precedents was put together, at the Duke of Buckingham's request, as a warning to Coloma and Hinojosa, for their breach of diplomatic protocol. The collection, which is commonly entitled either 'Relation' or 'Declaration of the proceedings against ambassadors who have miscarried themselves and exceeded their commission', survives in numerous copies: some are dated 27 April 1624 (see Sharpe, *Cotton*, p. 174, n. 124; also e.g. Harl. MS. 830, ff. 211–217v, and a manuscript that was formerly Lord Mostyn's, sold at Sotheby, 13 July 1920, lot 127). Hinojosa was forced to leave England two months later, on 26 June; for the Spanish plot against Buckingham, see R. E. Ruigh, *The Parliament of 1624: Politics and Foreign Policy* (Cambridge, Mass., 1971), ch. 5. From a reading of this paragraph by itself, it might seem that it was Charles I who is referred to in the first line; on the other hand, the reference in paragraph 11 to 'his Majestie now rayning' would suggest that in the present paragraph it is the monarch then reigning, i.e. James I, who is referred to.

Cotton's discourse is printed as the first item in *Cottoni Posthuma*; in the 1672 edn. it is at pp. 1–10.

11.　　It pleased his Matie now happily rayning in the parlement
succeeding that at Oxford to < command Sr Rob Cotton to *inserted* > sett down such
　　Authorities [*reading uncertain*]
and presidents as he could [*reading uncertain*] out of Records and Jornalls
of parliament [to *deleted*] to prove that the Kings of England haue
vsed to be present [at all *deleted*] < in the time of the inserted > debatts and examples
　　[*reading uncertain*]

75

of causes [in *deleted*] and Questions in parliament as well as
at other time wich accordingly he [*word deleted*] did and
presented it to his Matie who most gratious [w *deleted*]
accepted [his poor *and another word deleted*] < the *inserted* > [   ] [*four words deleted*]
    < of his service *inserted* >
[*whole line deleted*]

The parliament at Oxford was in 1625; it must have been at the time of the parliament of 1626,
therefore, that Cotton prepared this collection of precedents. He was not a member of this
parliament.

    The paper is usually known by the title under which it is printed in *Cottoni Posthuma*, as the
third item (in the 1672 edn., pp. 41–57): 'That the Sovereign's Person is Required in the Great
Councells or Assemblies of the State.' He makes rather better use than usual of the manuscripts
in his own collection, and there are, for instance, references to the Chronicle of Henry
Knighton (in either Claudius E. III or Tiberius C. VII), the Burton Annals (Vespasian E. III),
the journal and papers of Edward VI (Nero C. X) and the Rolls of Parliament. Of the latter,
he notes that 'The Raigne of Henry the seventh affords us upon the Rolls no one example [of
the sovereign's presence]. The journall Bookes are lost, except so much as preserves the
passages of eight dayes in the twelfth year of his Reigne; in which the King was some dayes
present at all debates, and with his owne hand the one and thirtieth day of the Parliament,
delivered in a bill of Trade then read.'

    This last observation, which seems so carefully considered, is now thought to be a
misapprehension on Cotton's part: as W. H. Dunham pointed out, the Fane Fragment of 1461
(Add. MS. 34218, ff. 100–103v) answers so well to Cotton's description – there are eight
parliamentary days in it, and on 9 December, the thirty-first day of the Parliament, Edward
IV is recorded as putting in a bill remedying grievances of merchandise – that it must have
been this that Cotton had seen and misdated. Cf. G. R. Elton, 'The Early Journals of the
House of Lords', *English Historical Review*, lxxxix (1974), pp. 481–512, at 485–6 (reprinted in
idem, *Studies in Tudor and Stuart Politics and Government*, 4 vols. (Cambridge, 1974–92), vol.
iii, pp. 58–92, at 63–4).

[Sr Robert Cotton formerly desiring his highnes to be
pleased to remember *deleted*]

[12.]   The service Sr Robert Cotton did in that busines about
    the alteration of the moneys prouided [*reading of last five letters doubtful*] by
        Parliament
    he [*word deleted*] leaveth [*reading doubtful*] to the goodnes of his highnes to remember
    when it pleased his Matie after [*reading uncertain*] a full [de *deleted*] and busy
    debat to show to the great [*reading doubtful*] counsil if [*or of*] all [the *deleted*] his
    subiects the [*about three words deleted*] wrightings < Journalls and interpret [*reading
        uncertain*] *inserted* > his [   ]
    sent [*reading doubtful*]

This paragraph is particularly hard to interpret, not least because of the possible mention of

76

money as 'provided by parliament' (which it had not been since 1625). From the reference to 'alteration of the moneys' it seems likeliest that Cotton is referring to his part in the debate about the debasement of the coinage in 1626: on 3 September he made a speech at the Council Table opposing any alteration of the coin (reprinted in W. A. Shaw (ed.), *Select Tracts and Documents Illustrative of English Monetary History, 1626–1730* (London, 1896), pp. 23–9). He was regarded as an authority on monetary matters, having been a member of the 1622 commission on currency and the exchanges. On the other hand, Charles I might not have been expected to be grateful to be reminded of Cotton's successful intervention on behalf of the City's mercantile interests against the proposals put forward by officials of the Mint and supported by the Duke of Buckingham.

See further T. Birch (ed.), *The Court and Times of Charles the First*, 2 vols. (London, 1848), vol. i, pp. 145–6; B. E. Supple, *Commercial Crisis and Change in England, 1600–1642. A Study in the Instability of a Mercantile Economy* (Cambridge, 1959), p. 190; Sharpe, *Cotton*, pp. 141, 148–9; R. Cust, *The Forced Loan and English Politics, 1626–1628* (Oxford, 1987), p. 36.

[13.]   May it please [his M *deleted*] the benignity and goodnes of his
said Ma^{ti} to remember the redines in his pore seruant
to do him seruice when it pleased his highnes to send
for him after the despatch of the [*word deleted*] parlament to whitt
hall when he then presented his ma^{ti} [at his *deleted*] with a
Book of Collections [*reading uncertain*] for his ma^{ti} service. And what vse
was then mad of his labor he humbly leaues to the
[lord privy seal *deleted*; *readings uncertain*] < *two? words inserted and deleted* > to
    report of the [lord priu *deleted*] Royal [*reading uncertain*] [   ]
the lord privy seall to whom with Sr Robert Cotton it
pleased his highnes to refer [*reading doubtful*] the perusal [*reading uncertain*] for his
    then
present [*reading doubtful*] service [*reading doubtful*] and occasions of [*word deleted*] the
    gathering [*reading uncertain*] contained [*reading doubtful*]
[   ] the said book

This paragraph may also be concerned with events of the summer of 1626: Cotton's fourth line may refer to the dissolution of parliament (15 June). Henry Montagu, Earl of Manchester, was President of the Council and a key figure in its deliberations over the summer (cf. the paragraph's latter part), as the Crown cast about for new financial expedients. But the mention of a 'Book of Collections' (if correctly read) is tantalizingly obscure, unless it is taken to mean some such volume of papers as Cotton MS. Cleopatra F. VI, entitled in Cotton's own hand 'A Collection mad by Sr Robert Cotton for his Maties Seruice in time of Extremytie', and containing papers gathered at various dates from 1609 onwards (including at ff. 41–51r the paper on 'The Manner and Means how the Kings of England have from time to time supported and repaired their Estates', discussed above in the notes to paragraph 6).

[14.]   He therfor humbly desires that by [that *deleted*; *reading uncertain*] warr [*reading doubtful*] of this, them [*reading doubtful*] [   ] of many [*reading doubtful*]

77

his Ma^ti will iudg of the sincerity uprightnes [*reading uncertain*] and loyalti [*reading uncertain*] of his pore subiect and seruant [*reading doubtful*]
sent to doe him [*reading doubtful*] seruice who is most willing to [ ] the means [*reading doubtful*] in all thes coun[*rest of word and line illegible*]
and Inquestes [*reading doubtful*] if ther can be any opportunitie [ ] and proceed [*reading doubtful*] wherein he hath been either [*reading uncertain*]
[ ] or interest [*reading doubtful*] of any thing to his Ma^ti [ ]
[*continued in the left margin*:]
And as a motive for his ma^ti better < opinion and mor *inserted* > assurance [*reading uncertain*] [and *and another word deleted*] of < his *inserted* > loyalte
affection and Zeall to doe him seruice he most humbly prays [at *deleted*] his
[Ma^ti *deleted*] < highnes inserted > to tak [ ] [if on further [*reading uncertain*] < *word inserted* > of duty < then *and another word inserted* > [ ] his highnes In *deleted*]
that his most humble seruant is [descended *deleted*] heir [*reading uncertain*] and Inheritor [*reading uncertain*] of [*reading doubtful*]
the [ ] Baron De Brus second birth to Robert [*letter deleted*; And his *deleted*]
And his < most *and another word inserted* > Ma^ti [ ] and [ ] inheriting from Robert de Brus the
elder birth < of *inserted* > the kingdom of Scotland.

CONCLUSION

Taken as a whole, the ten paragraphs form a sequence that builds up to Cotton's plea of his own consanguinity with Charles I.[6] With the exception of paragraphs 8 and 9 (which would need to be inverted), the sequence appears to be in chronological order. If paragraph 12 refers to the parliament of 1628, then clearly the document postdates that, and if paragraph 13 refers to the parliament of 1629, then it must be later than March 1629. The uncertainty as to the dates of the services rendered, the suggestion of desperation in the way the handwriting deteriorates and the general sense of Cotton's throwing himself on Charles I's mercy – all this suggests that he was writing after November 1629, when his library was locked up and he himself brought before the Council. Cotton's plight was not at first as serious as is sometimes implied: on 15 November he was told that he could still enter his 'studies' or library rooms, 'provided that he did it in the presence of a Clerke of the Counsell, and that whereas the Clerke attending hath the keyes of twoe of his studies, he might put a second lock on either of them, so that neither dores might be opened, but by him and the saide Clerke both together.'[7] In January 1630 he was named as a member of an intended new Commission of Inquiry into Exacted Fees, and he was named on the actual commission on 17 April 1630.[8] His position gradually weakened over the next few months. In July, and again in October, a search was ordered to see what records in his library properly belonged to the Crown, and in about September he and his son Thomas petitioned to the Council, to be allowed access to the library – which (save when in the company of a Clerk of the Council), they had not enjoyed since the previous November, so that 'manie of the bookes are almost vtterlie lost and rotted for want of ayreinge', while the petitioners were also deprived of the use of the best rooms in the house.[9] A petition of Cotton to Charles I, which in the *Calendar of State Papers Domestic* is dated to 'May? 1630', is not dissimilar in tone to the tenor of the statement in MS. Smith 28: it is an apology for having given offence and also a reminder of his past services to the Crown.[10] The petition 'Most humbly sheweth: that your Majesty's displeasure is the greatest vnhappines which cane befall a loyall harte, And though all livinge men haue imperfeccons, and none more errors than my selfe, yet yt hartilie greives me to haue given any occasion of offence to so gratious a Kinge. But I am nowe an old man, and if any acceptable services haue bin done in my age past I was willing to haue done more. And to a Prince that vouchsafeth his favour & grace, with all humilitie doe most humbly offer my life and future seruices...'. Very tentatively, it may be suggested that the document in MS. Smith 28 is of the same date as this petition; it is not impossible that it even represents a draft that Cotton subsequently rejected in favour of the petition's terser message.

Whatever the document's precise date may be, however, its interest lies not so much in what it shows about Cotton's plight after his downfall as in the light it has to shed in how he perceived – or at least, portrayed – his actions over the previous thirty-odd years. He had served on a number of royal commissions, and it is of interest that he chose not to refer to some of these or to other actions of his that might have been portrayable as services to the Crown, such as his membership of the commission on the exchanges, in 1622.

Was he conscious of the folly of exaggerating the value of his past services? If so, it might explain why the statement perhaps never went beyond the draft stage. In the reference in paragraph 5 to his saving from the fire in Elizabeth's reign some of the letters of Mary Queen of Scots, there is surely to be detected a defence of his possession of state papers, such as was certainly liable to be held against him at about this time. Equally, however, it would have done him no good to exaggerate unduly his part in, say, the invention of the baronetcy: Charles will have known what truth lay in such an assertion. Nor is it likely that Cotton was taking advantage of the death of Camden to overstate his own part in what might otherwise be taken for purely Camdenian writings: Cotton and the herald, his erstwhile schoolmaster, undoubtedly did collaborate closely on a variety of projects. Camden's *Britannia* itself was in a sense adopted by Cotton and enlarged by him, and in 1614–15 it was to Cotton and Camden together that was granted the royal licence to print it.[11]

Cotton fairly certainly lacked the depth of knowledge to write a full-length work on any aspect of English medieval or Tudor history. Temperamentally, however, he was as well suited as he was also capable of producing short papers that collected together historical precedents for a particular course of action. His first such paper may have been that on the question of precedence between England and Spain, which he compiled in about May 1600, at Queen Elizabeth's command.[12] The stream of tractates that followed, mostly written either for the Crown or for Henry Howard, Earl of Northampton, gave him a focus for his interests and enabled him to feel that he, too, was able to profit from the library that he was assembling and to which he granted access to so many other scholars. His known readiness to write the papers ensured a stream of commissions and requests, from the Commons as well as the Crown, and kept him close to the centre of political life. It would have been a bitter blow if, near the end of his life, he felt on reflection that the statement of his services to the Crown would not assist him in regaining the freedom of his library, that his various little treatises would after all count for nothing, and that the statement had better remain merely a draft.

1 See the comments of Harold Love, *Scribal Publication in Seventeenth-Century England* (Oxford, 1993), pp. 87–8, 313; he describes the two 1628 editions (one of which was set from the other) of Cotton's *The Danger wherein the Kingdom now standeth, and the Remedy* as an 'incredibly corrupt' text, 'so corrupt as to be little better than gibberish in places'.

2 Bodl., MS. Smith 59 (*S. C.* 15666), p. 277.

3 Ibid., p. 275.

4 Bodl., MS. Smith 59 (*S. C.* 15666), p. 256. He was still seeking 'the faire transcript' in a letter to Philip Cotton of 7 Sept. 1697, MS. Smith 59 (*S. C.* 15666), p. 279.

5 Public Record Office, PROB 6/68, f. 191 (stamped 124).

6 Cotton believed that he was descended from Bernard de Bruce, of Conington, co. Hunt., second son of Robert de Bruce V (d. 1245); cf. H. Ellis (ed.), *Visitation of the County of Huntingdon, under the Authority of William Camden, Clarenceux King of Arms, by his Deputy, Nicholas Charles, Lancaster Herald, A.D. MDCXIII*, Camden Soc., O.S. xliii (1849), p. 26.

7 *Acts of the Privy Council, 1629–30*, p. 177, no. 570.

8 Ibid., pp. 179, 236–7.

9 P.R.O., SP 16/173, art. 95; cal. in *Acts of the Privy Council, 1629–31*, p. 352, where dated Sept. 1630.

10 *Cal. S.P. Domestic, 1629–31*, p. 271, from P.R.O., SP 16/167, art. 65.

11 A copy of the licence is in Cambridge, Trinity College, MS R.5.20; cf. M. R. James, *Western Manuscripts in the Library of Trinity College, Cambridge: A Descriptive Catalogue*, 4 vols. (Cambridge, 1900–4), vol. ii, p. 426, no. 715.

12 Printed as the 5th item in *Cottoni Posthuma*; in the 1672 edition it is at pp. 73–89; summarized in H.M.C., *Cal. of the MSS. of the Marquis of Salisbury*, pt. x (1904), pp. 166–7.

COTTON'S COUNSELS: THE CONTEXTS OF
COTTONI POSTHUMA

GRAHAM PARRY

COTTON'S name is constantly alluded to in books on antiquarianism, history, genealogy, topography and law published in the first three decades of the seventeenth century. Invariably these references to 'my worthy friend', the honoured, the learned, the worshipful Sir Robert Cotton, are accompanied by expressions of gratitude for his generosity in granting access to his library, his cabinet of coins and medals, or for his advice on procedure. The sense we have of Cotton as a universal facilitator among men of learning is overwhelming. Yet, although he was always willing to contribute to other men's works, and though books were his life and authors his friends, he made but a slender appearance in print himself. In fact, he published only one short tract under his own name.[1] It was not until 1651 that a volume of his writings appeared, with the title *Cottoni Posthuma*. Then, twenty years after his death, the world could form some estimate of his political judgement, and understand why Cotton's incomparable knowledge of the parliamentary records was so valued by his contemporaries. Cotton's own reluctance to publish meant that he left his literary character to be formed by other men, by selective editing of his writings, and his first editor presented him almost exclusively as a patriotic political adviser who had anatomized the ills of the Stuart kings, and had done his best to offer remedies. In retrospect, his writings could be seen as describing the inward decay of Stuart kingship, and explain why the monarchy had collapsed within two generations of Queen Elizabeth's death. It is my intention in this article to provide some context for the various items in *Cottoni Posthuma*, and to read them as a critical commentary on the political developments of the second and third decades of the century.

The brief discourses that make up *Cottoni Posthuma* were put together by James Howell, a minor littérateur and quondam royalist. Howell had probably come into contact with Cotton when they were both part of Ben Jonson's circle in the 1620s. He had been a notable traveller, and was especially well acquainted with Venice and Madrid. Whilst in Spain in 1623, trying to obtain the release of an impounded English merchant vessel, he had met up with Prince Charles and his party on their ill-starred visit to arrange a marriage with the Infanta. Thereafter he had tried, and failed, to get a post on the Duke of Buckingham's staff. He spent some years as secretary to the President of the Council of the North, before returning to London, where he developed into one of those self-conscious 'gentlemen of parts' who hung around the fringes of the Caroline court. Well-travelled, urbane, ever ready with opinion and advice, he attempted to make a living by writing. Perhaps his most inventive and successful production was the prolix allegory on the international political scene entitled *Dendrologia, or The Vocall Forrest* (1641), in which all the characters are trees. A vociferous supporter of King Charles, he was imprisoned by order of Parliament in 1643, ostensibly for debt. He remained in jail until 1651, conducting an active literary life from a secure if unwelcome base. During these years he published *Familiar Letters*, which profess to be his correspondence with his numerous well-connected friends up and down the country, though, since none of his letters has been found, they were probably sent only in the imagination. After the King's death, he found it possible to revise his loyalties, and in 1651 he dedicated his *Survey of the Signorie of Venice* to the Long Parliament. He appears to have compiled *Cottoni Posthuma* just after his release from prison. He must have had access to some of Cotton's papers, and recognized that they cast an intermittent light on early Stuart politics. Collected together, they demonstrated how the crisis of the monarchy had unfolded. They also put before the public a man whom Howell obviously admired, and who had filled a role close to the centre of events in the 1610s and 20s, as an informal adviser to the King and major political figures. Cotton had tried to maintain a balance between King and Parliament, and his moderation and judgement made him a man who could readily be respected in the confused beginnings of the Commonwealth. Howell evidently learned from his subject, for during the 1650s he too tried to offer politic advice to Cromwell on state affairs by means of pamphlets. The publication of his volume of Cotton's writings formed part of a larger upsurge of interest in Jacobean politics in the early 1650s, caused, one imagines, by the desire to trace the origins of the recent conflicts.[2]

The last item that Howell included in his collection was Cotton's most sustained piece of writing, *The Life and Reign of Henry the Third*. Since this was a thinly disguised parallel with the reign of James I, full of Cotton's shrewd judgements on political conduct, judgements that by 1651 had been fulfilled more terribly than he could have imagined, it provides a useful starting-point to study Cotton's method as a historical commentator and to identify the values he held most desirable for the maintenance of good government. This history of Henry III had been first published in 1627, anonymously and apparently without Cotton's permission. It was immediately held to be critical of King Charles; Cotton was suspected as the author, and examined by the authorities, but released when he persuaded them that he had not approved publication, and that he had written the work in 1614.[3] Certainly, the manuscript of the history in Cambridge University Library carries the note 'Written by Sir Robert Cotton Knight Baronett in anno 1614 and by him presented to his Majestie the same year.' Given that the *Life and Reign* contains much about the pernicious influence of favourites, which seems to bear specifically upon Buckingham, whose rise began in 1616, it is possible that Cotton either wrote it later than he claimed, or revised it to take account of Buckingham's career. I assume that Cotton did present a manuscript copy to King James, for almost everything he wrote had a specific audience in mind, and he would have regarded it as a piece of wise counsel that applied the lessons of history to contemporary problems. One needed to be hardy to offer even veiled criticism to the King, but Cotton no doubt took courage from his distant kinship to James, which both men acknowledged, for both traced their descent from Robert the Bruce.

The history is an outline of events in Henry III's reign, interspersed with reflections on the art of government and precepts concerning effective rule. It is written in the sparse economical style that Cotton usually employed, and reads like a precis of an Elizabethan play of the 1590s in which the action is historic but the relevance contemporary. (No playwright chose the reign of Henry III for dramatization, in fact.) It is a cautionary tale. The King ascends the throne when there are few distempers in the state, only the familiar tension between the Commons greedy of liberty and the Nobility of rule. The King's principal adviser is the well-established Earl of Kent, but the young nobles of the realm come to resent him, chafing to get their hands on power, a situation not dissimilar to that around the Earl of Salisbury in James's reign. The sovereign after some years reveals the great weakness of his rule, a penchant for a favourite, the Frenchman Simon de Montfort. De Montfort is rapidly made Earl of Leicester, the King lavishes money on him, and the business of state begins to run through his hands. The English nobility 'began to grieve' at this deflection of power from them, and Cotton intervenes to comment on the risks of adopting a favourite: 'Great is the Sovereign's error when the hope of subjects must recognise itself beholden to the servant.' The favourite's position is unstable, dependent on the whim of the King's fancy. As the favourite begins to restrict access to the sovereign, and draws bishops to his support, his unpopularity grows, yet he controls more business than ever. 'Thus is the incapacity of government in a King, when it falls to be prey to such lawless ministers, the ground of infinite corruption in all the members of the State.' Alienated peers begin to form a party against the favourite, and hope to persuade the King to a better judgement of state affairs.

The circumstances would fit 1614, when Cotton claimed to have written it, for James had then begun to turn away from the advice of his Privy Councillors and Parliament towards a dependence on his favourite Robert Carr, a foreigner in that he was a Scot. At the end of 1613 he was created Earl of Somerset, to the outrage of the older nobility. The King was heavily in debt, and paying little attention to business.[4] The Howard faction supported the favourite, the Pembroke faction was deeply critical; the Howards were resisting calling a Parliament to resolve the King's financial difficulties, their opponents pressed for one. Parliament was summoned in April 1614.

At a corresponding time in Henry III's reign, a Parliament was called, reluctantly, by the sovereign. Cotton observes that kings who have alienated their subjects never like Parliaments, for their critics then can confront them. So they did: they denounced Henry for choosing his principal officers privately, without the aid of Common Council, for favouring foreigners above Englishmen, and for delegating power to the favourite. Using language that would be familiar to Stuart readers, Cotton records how Henry's

Parliament complained about the granting to favourites of monopolies which alienated the merchants of the realm and depressed trade. Significantly too there were complaints that great lords were exacting money from subjects by activating little used laws relating to forests. The upshot was that a disgruntled Parliament voted only a pittance by way of supply to the King, and its members departed full of resentment. Cotton's choric voice intervenes: 'Thus Parliaments that before were ever a medicine to heal up any rupture in Princes' fortunes, were now grown worse than the malady, sith from thence more malignant humours began to reign in them, than well composed tempers.'[5]

The Parliament of 1614 refused to vote supply to James. Instead, the members investigated the corruption of offices, and attacked the King's way of raising money by arbitrary impositions. The King defended this right to exact impositions as 'one of the flowers of his prerogative'. Parliament was rapidly dissolved, not to meet again until 1621.

In Henry III's case, when deprived of parliamentary support, he started to sell royal lands and some of his possessions. He even pawned the jewels from Edward the Confessor's shrine to alleviate his poverty. James in 1615 began to sell titles of nobility, a move even more desperate than the sale of knighthoods earlier in his reign, and he also sold the Cautionary Towns in Holland to the Dutch. Thereafter, easy parallels between King Henry and King James were more difficult to make. A date then of 1614–15 would be quite apt for this history, but since the vices and the problems of the Stuarts were of a recurring nature, the history of Henry III, which is so full of warnings of the disastrous consequences that follow from wasteful spending, from surrender of power to favourites, and from reluctance to work with parliaments, also had an uncomfortable relevance to James's position in 1621, on the eve of a new Parliament, when Buckingham was fully in the ascendant and debts were worse than ever. It was equally applicable to the circumstances of 1627, when it was published at the height of the Commons' hostility to Buckingham, and when King Charles was already well enmeshed in the familiar Stuart problems.

Cotton narrates the remainder of Henry's long reign, past the crises of debt, favouritism and parliamentary opposition that make such a telling parallelism with Stuart politics. It is a tale of disaster followed by reform and recovery. What this history lesson teaches above all is the near-fatal damage done to the Crown by favouritism: 'Favours past are not accompted, we love no bounty but what is merely future. The more that a Prince weakeneth himself in giving, the poorer he is of friends. For such prodigality in a Sovereign, ever ends in the rapine and spoil of his subjects.'[6] When Henry is finally forced to call another parliament, he is so necessitous and so friendless that he is obliged to render up his royal power to a committee of government, and is reduced to a cypher. England slides into confusion as De Montfort and his allies try to wrest power from the governors, and then their opponents 'invited her ancient enemy to the funeral of her liberty' by calling in the French for assistance. After a military dénouement in which De Montfort is killed and the King restored, Henry attempts to understand why his reign has been so disastrous, 'why that virtue and fortune that had so long settled and maintained under his ancestors the glory of his Empire' had deserted him. Here is history teaching by example in characteristic Renaissance fashion. Henry realizes that 'his wasteful hand' has impoverished him and alienated his people, that by his 'neglect of grace', 'by making merchandize of peace...by giving himself over to a sensual security and referring all to base, greedy and unworthy ministers whose counsels were ever more subtle than substantial...he had thrown down those pillars of sovereignty and safety: Reputation abroad and Reverence at home.'[7] For Cotton, history is a mirror for princes, and King James would have no difficulty in recognizing himself.

Henry III's response was reform. 'In himself he reformed his natural errors, [for] Princes' manners through a mute law have more of life and vigour than those of letters, and though he did sometimes touch upon the verge of vice, he forebore ever after to enter the circle.' He reformed his court so that it might again be a theatre of honour: where previously 'the faults of great men did not only by approbation but by imitation receive true comfort and authority, now he purged them, for from the Court proceeds either the regular or irregular condition of the State.'[8] He curbed his immoderate liberality, recognizing that 'this bounty bestowed without respect, was taken without grace, discredited the receiver and detracteth from the judgement of the giver, and blunteth the appetites of such as carried their hopes out of virtue and service. Thus at last he learned that reward and reprehension justly laid do balance government.' He begins for the first time to live within his means: 'expense of house he measureth by the just rule of his proper revenue.' Equally important is the change of his manner of governing. He dismisses tainted and unworthy ministers, and fills 'the seats of Judgement and Council with men nobly born, (for such attract less offense).' He sits in Council daily, 'and disposeth of affairs of most weight in his own person.' As Cotton frequently emphasized, the Prince must rule: his counsellors 'must have ability to advise, not authority to resolve.'

The mood of the nation changed as the people felt the benefits of Henry's reform, and Cotton notes that a Prince should 'lay the foundations of Greatness upon popular Love' and that the people 'measure the bond of their obedience by the good they always receive.' Nor did Henry neglect the future of the kingdom, for he attended to the political education of his successor, Edward, 'to make him partner of his own experience and authority. He (the first of his name since the Conquest) became capable to command not the realm but the whole world.'[8]

It is not difficult to read these signals. The need for the Crown to be free of debt, the Prince to be the source of honour sustaining and sustained by an authentic nobility, and protected by the love of his people, the duty of the King to rule and not be ruled, all these observations point up Cotton's dismay at the course and character of King James's reign. This dismay is coupled with a belief that the kingdom can be saved by the application of known remedies culled from history. Whether the time was 1614, or later in the reign, whether the favourite was Somerset or Buckingham, the pattern of politics remains the same. Such was the fundamental conviction of Cotton, always a conservative thinker. The detail of the education of the heir to the throne is a pointed admonition to the King.

Prince Charles was the first of his name since the Conquest, as Edward had been in the time of Henry III. King James had taken an idealistic view of the education of his heir in his younger days when still King of Scotland, for he had written *Basilikon Doron* to instruct Prince Henry in the art and mystery of kingship; (one should not forget that James himself had aspired to the role of philosopher-king in the first years of his reign in England). Prince Henry had realized his father's dream of an educated, judicious, pious prince, apt for the studies of peace as for the camps of war, and had been allowed to establish his own independent court at an early age, a court which stood in notable contrast to the increasingly louche court of King James. Once Henry was dead, however, the King took little care for the education of Prince Charles, and after the rise of Buckingham, the favourite effectively moulded the political development of the heir. Cotton surely disapproved the King's negligence in securing the future of England.

The directness of the analogies makes it highly unlikely that *The Life and Reign of Henry III* was intended for publication. Offered to the Sovereign privately as a respectful admonition, it could be understood as timely counsel, with the authority of the historical record giving it a power beyond the personal concerns of a subject. Published in 1627, it must have seemed quite derogatory to King James, and unpleasantly critical of King Charles and the current political situation, with the King dominated by the Duke of Buckingham, who was no wise adviser with the well-being of England in mind, but an initiator of reckless and wasteful policies of war against Spain and attacks on France. No wonder Cotton was taken in for questioning. The history was reprinted in 1642, evidently to discredit the Stuart regime. Howell's inclusion of it in *Cottoni Posthuma* would seem to have been in the spirit of a post-mortem, and to vindicate Cotton's historical judgement.

Many of the other tracts in *Cottoni Posthuma* bear on issues raised in the history of Henry III. They show an author who was deeply patriotic, and devoted to the monarchy, but also a man 'whose main endeavours', as Howell wrote in his Preface to the Reader, 'were to assert the publick Liberty, and that Prerogative and Priviledge might run in their due Channels.' That is to say, he desired that the royal prerogative and the privileges of Parliament should co-exist in mutual respect so that there was neither undue oppression from above nor excessive power assumed by the Commons. For Cotton, the reign of Elizabeth was always the model of good government.

The tracts, in fact, offer a short view of Cotton's own political career and values. The earliest piece with a definite political bearing is the discourse concerning the legality of duels, a piece he wrote about 1608 for his patron Henry Howard, Earl of Northampton, who, as one of the Commissioners for the Earl Marshalship, was anxious to ban duelling in England in accordance with the wishes of the King. The rapid growth of this practice from the 1590s has been documented by Laurence Stone, who pointed out that the introduction of the rapier brought with it a great increase in fatalities, and, of course, these fatalities tended to occur in the higher echelons of society, and were detrimental not only to good order but to aristocratic succession.[9] Cotton supplies details of the history of combats fought in the presence of the King or the Earl Marshal or Constable, with the rules governing them, and he outlines the measures taken by these figures to suppress duels in England, noting the punishments imposed over the centuries since the time of Edward I. He believes there are occasions when combat is lawful, in cases of treason for example, but in cases touching personal honour, the cause of almost all Jacobean quarrels, he finds these have long been banned by the Sovereign. The tract provides a brisk legal brief for suppression in the national interest. Presumably it was intended to help the Earl of Northampton's plans to gain the office of the Earl Marshal, which had been hereditary in the Howard family for generations. (In this, Northampton did not succeed, but the King re-established the office and conferred it on Thomas Howard, Earl of Arundel, in 1621.)

Cotton undertook a far more important task for Northampton, and by extension for the King, when he compiled, 'The Manner and Means how the Kings of England have from time to time supported and repaired their Estates' in 1610 or 11. These suggestions were put forward after the failure of the Great Contract, which the Earl of Salisbury had tried to broker between Parliament and the King in order to resolve the perennial problem of the royal finances. Salisbury proposed that Parliament should pay off the King's debt and grant him a regular income raised from taxation, in return for the King's restraining his expenditure and relinquishing certain rights of imposition and some of the much-disliked feudal dues, especially those relating to tenure and wardship. When both parties were close to agreement in July 1610, the Contract broke down because Parliament was dissatisfied with James's response to several of their grievances presented to him in conjunction with the financial bargain. Salisbury died in May 1612 with the crisis of the King's finances still unresolved. He had held the position of Treasurer as well as Secretary, but James did not appoint an individual to succeed him as Treasurer, but a commission, of which Northampton was First Lord. Cotton applied his antiquarian skills to the business of providing his patron with serviceable ways for the King to raise money, based on ancient practice. He emphasizes equally the possibility of the King's improving his income with the help and advice of Parliament or the Privy Council, and by the exercise of his prerogative. He recommends, too, better management of royal estates, and above all, retrenchment of household expenses. The state archives reveal various kinds of loans and benevolences that Parliament might make and had made to the Sovereign, special payments to relaunch him after a shipwreck. Invariably, however, a *quid pro quo* is required, and the King must reform his household, cut back on pensions, get rid of 'strangers' and shake off favourites. He should 'reduce the household to the best, first and most magnificent order...so all things being spent in public will be to the King's honour.' 'The secret waste by Chamber, diet and purloining [must be] prevented to the King's benefit. For there is never a back-door in Court that costs not the King 2000 l. yearly, and few mean houses in Westminster that are not maintained with food and firing, by the stealth of their Court-Instruments.'[10] The tightly regulated court that Prince Henry maintained at St James's Palace was a standing reproach to Whitehall in the matter of discipline, decorousness and economy.[11]

Many of Cotton's ideas foresee the monarchy transformed from an inert state to an active economic empire. As the greatest landowner in Britain, James should take a more purposeful view of his possessions. Cotton recommends that the Crown should rent much more of its land and raise existing rents. More importantly, the Crown must modernize its affairs; it should improve the management and productivity of its estates, and enter the market by selling commodities raised on its lands. It could even rent ships, and thus enjoy the profits of trade.

Although a Member of Parliament himself, Cotton was not one of the majority who wanted to restrict the King's prerogative. In 'The Manner and Means' he surveys the many options the King possesses to improve his revenue, by the familiar ways of raising customs dues, farming out the customs more lucratively, and also by more tendentious means. Cotton searches the records for precedents that might justify the King's use of prerogative rights that have long been in abeyance. He suggests reviving the practice of calling in the charters and liberties of corporations and other bodies for renewal at a price. Intervention could be made in legal suits 'for mitigation or despatch of justice' by transferring cases to the King's Council, with the parties concerned paying a fee. Offices of state, with the exception of the Judicature, might be sold. (King John provides an unseemly precedent here with his sale of the Chancellorship for 5000 marks.) Then there is the great profit to be made from the sale of honours. Far from being shocked by the sale of knighthoods at the beginning of James's reign, Cotton proposes the institution of a new title of honour, the Baronet; recipients would rank next under Barons, and would pay £1000 for the privilege of joining the order. By 'judicious election', this title would 'be a means to content those worthy persons in the Common-Wealth' who were discontented with the indiscriminate recruitment to the class of Knights that occurred at the beginning of the reign. King James adopted this suggestion, and the new rank was established; Cotton himself became a Baronet. Cotton also recommends that the King should continue to fine men who have the qualifications to be made a Knight and decline the honour. Bishoprics might also be sold, and the bishops be moved around regularly to ensure a steady profit from entrance fees into a See.

Whilst willing to approve honours sold for money, Cotton was not willing to damage the honour of money itself. He warned against any debasement of the coinage (a project which was in the air), showing by example that such a move always marked the beginning of economic decline. He also disapproved of the King's issuing monopolies, as a restraint of trade with damaging consequences to the nation.

Cotton's loyalty to King James was unwavering. Though James had many imprudent habits, he had to be supported because he was the indispensable centre of power. At worst, his reign had to be endured because God in His wisdom sends good and bad kings to rule over men. 'Religion bindeth a good subject to desire a good Sovereign and to bear with a bad,' Cotton noted in a list of political maxims he drew up round about 1613.[12] Throughout his career there was a tendency for his historical research to result in readily applicable precepts. Foremost among them was the duty of experienced men to offer good counsel to the monarch. Parliament, as the supreme body of experienced men, had as its primary duty to advise the sovereign, but not to contest power. Such a view would always keep Cotton among the moderates, even among the conservatives in Parliament, and makes all the more ironic his eventual arrest in 1629 on the orders of King Charles's ministers.

A fine example of Cotton's direct advice to the King is his tract of 1613 on policy towards Jesuit priests who were entering England in some numbers and who appeared to be attempting to subvert the allegiance of Catholics to the King. Should they be executed, or imprisoned for life? He offers twelve arguments on either side, leaving no doubt that imprisonment is the better course. Partly this is because history has taught him the danger of making martyrs, partly because he believes that the wiser course lies through mercy rather than justice. However, he recognizes the strength of Catholicism's attraction, and is reluctant to be severe against recusants and their ministers, because he admires the tenacity of their faith. Most recusants are in any case patriotic Englishmen, he believes: there was no rising when the Armada came. Such reflections cause Cotton to break into a plea more heartfelt than anything I have encountered elsewhere in his writings. Catholicism retains its hold because the Church of England does not bring the true faith to the people with sufficient zeal. There is not enough instruction given to parishioners; children are not adequately catechized; prayer and preaching are lukewarm in the Church. Clergy and bishops should share the blame for this failure to bring the gospel to life in every parish. If the faith is not actively maintained at all levels of society, men and women will understandably revert to the old religion, which has generations of belief behind it. The Reformation began with such conviction, and now it slackens. 'Many times I have stood amazed to behold the Magnificence of our Ancestors' buildings, which their Successors at this day are not able to keep up; but when I cast mine eyes upon this excellent Foundation laid by the Fathers of the Church, and perceive their Children neglect to build thereupon, with exceeding marvel, I rest almost beside myself, for never was there better ground-plot laid, which hath been seconded with less success.'[13] As so often for Cotton, the best times were those of Elizabeth: 'In those days there was an emulation between the Clergy and the Laity: and a strife arose whether of them should show themselves most affectionate to the Gospel. Ministers haunted the Houses of the worthiest men, where Jesuits now build their Tabernacles, and poor country Churches were frequented with the best of the Shire. The Word of God was precious, Prayer and Preaching went hand in hand together.'[14] King James, as head of the Church, was given plenty to think over in Cotton's submission.

Several of the pieces in *Cottoni Posthuma* preserve the counsels that Cotton gave on state affairs in the latter years of James's reign. Two items relate to the Parliament of 1621, in which he was exceptionally active as an ally of Arundel. In the earlier part of the year, Parliament had begun the impeachment of Francis Bacon, the Lord Chancellor. The Privy Council sent to Cotton to know what Parliament might do by itself without the presence of the King, and what were the powers of the House of Lords as a court.[15] The King himself seems to have asked Cotton to define his role. Cotton's answer was most helpful in clarifying Parliament's scope as a judicial body on the basis of ancient practice. His paper 'That the Sovereign's Person is required in the Great Councils, or

Assemblies of the State, as well at the Consultations as at the Conclusions' gave the Commons the right to hear evidence and the Lords to pronounce judgement, but the King's presence was required at all stages, and he must approve the verdict. About the same time, Cotton also prepared his 'Brief Discourse Concerning the Power of Peers and Commons of Parliament in Point of Judicature', in which he justifies the right of the Commons to sit in judgement over a person who is not a member of the House. The case in question concerned a Catholic barrister who had slandered the Elector Palatine and the Princess Elizabeth. Cotton's opinions, as Kevin Sharpe has remarked, lacked weight for once, and the assertion of the Commons' position may perhaps be taken as a sign of his growing concern to strengthen the powers of the Commons against the Lords and against the malignant influence of Buckingham which dominated the Privy Council and was beginning to infiltrate the Lords.[16]

The 1621 Parliament was also complicated by foreign issues. The Palatinate had been lost, and the Spanish match for Prince Charles was being refloated, now with the thought that the Palatinate might be retrieved for Frederick and Elizabeth as part of the deal. The Commons wished to discuss these developments, but convention decreed that foreign policy and marriage schemes were the business of the King, part of the *arcana imperii*, which should not be open to debate. Parliament launched a challenge to this convention, and Cotton was asked for an opinion by one of the Lords, probably Arundel or Buckingham.[17] 'That the Kings of England have been pleased, usually, to consult with their Peers in the Great Council and Commons in Parliament of Marriage, Peace and War' argued that precedent did not justify the convention by tracing the growth of a process of consultation throughout the Middle Ages over both state marriages and the making of war. He closes his presentation with a detailed account of a period of Henry VIII's reign when the King was entangled by both Spain and the Empire, who used the bait of marriage to lure Henry into conflict with France in order to serve their own territorial ambitions. Cotton sees a clear parallel here to contemporary circumstances and, whilst asserting the right of Parliament to discuss the King's business, warns against the designs of Spain and doubts 'the princely sincerity of the Catholique'.

Increasingly, Cotton's writings emphasized the need for the full participation of Parliament in government, in conjunction with the King. The King was becoming excessively dominated by Buckingham, and the Privy Council was also falling under his control. The national interest was best served by the debates of Parliament, though their aim in deliberation should always be to advise the King. James did finally seek the advice of Parliament about the wisdom of proceeding with the Spanish match in February 1624, the occasion of Cotton's thoughts on 'The Treaties of Amity and Marriage' with Austria and Spain, which he delivered to the King on behalf of both Houses. Once again he went over the misfortunes endured by Henry VIII through his marriage with Catherine of Aragon, and the international misadventures contrived by Spain and the Empire. Then Queen Mary's marriage to Philip II had brought a succession of dangers to English sovereignty, throughout Elizabeth's reign, and Spain still harboured ill will against

England, as could be seen by the enemies of the state that she pensioned. By no means should Parliament recommend a further engagement with Spain.

Relations with Spain also provoked the 'Relation against Ambassadors who have miscarried themselves', which was written as advice to Buckingham in 1624 on the occasion when the Spanish ambassadors in London, who were treating for the marriage of the Prince of Wales, denounced Buckingham, the main opponent, to King James, accusing him of plotting to overthrow the King. This extraordinary move, in which foreign representatives interfered in domestic politics and made accusations directly to the King, left Buckingham in a very awkward position. Buckingham had persuaded James to break off negotiations with Spain after the failure of the escapade in Madrid in which Prince Charles and the Duke had been duped, as they felt, and humiliated. The Duke's next move was to persuade the King and Parliament to declare war on Spain. At this point, in April 1624, the Spanish ambassadors, in desperation, approached James and warned him that Buckingham was plotting a coup, and was engaged in a design to marry his daughter to Princess Elizabeth's son, thus putting his family in the line of succession. James was perturbed. Buckingham turned to Cotton for advice on how to outmanœuvre the Spaniards. His request was unexpected, since Cotton was a client of Arundel, and Arundel was hostile to Buckingham, but the urgency of the threat must have sent Buckingham to the best source of advice on procedure, and that was Cotton. Since Cotton at this stage was strongly anti-Spanish, and believed that national interests were not served by any alliance with Spain, his patriotic instincts must have overcome his dislike of the favourite and caused him to offer Buckingham help. Prefacing his response with a brief history of ambassadors who have gone beyond the limits of diplomatic privilege, Cotton advised the Duke to complain against their behaviour in Parliament, 'and leaving it so to their advice and justice, to depart the House' while the Lords conferred with the Commons. Parliament would demand proof, and would send a delegation to the ambassadors' lodgings to show how seriously Parliament viewed the incident. If no proofs were given, then Parliament would complain to the King of Spain about their conduct, and if the King did not apologize, war would be declared.

In fact, Buckingham got out of his predicament by an emotional confession of loyalty and love to the King, followed by a breakdown in health that aroused all the King's old affections for him.[18] James also interrogated under oath all his Privy Councillors to find out if there was any substance to the ambassadors' charges. Buckingham revived. Cotton's counsel, however, showed once again how much faith he placed in the Lords and Commons acting together, 'the great Council of the Kingdom, to the which, by the fundamental Law of the State, the chief care of the King's safety and public quiet is committed.'[19] Parliament can act as a judicial body, and is increasingly looked to as the guide and guardian of the nation in times when Kings and favourites veer into irresponsible actions.

With King Charles's accession in 1625, Cotton found himself in a chillier climate. The kinship he enjoyed with James, which cemented his loyalty to the Crown and ensured that his advice was always offered with the best interests of the King in mind, was not readily acknowledged by Charles. Buckingham, now dominant as the royal policy-maker, soon forgot whatever gratitude he had felt towards Cotton over the affair of the Spanish ambassadors. When the first Parliament of the reign met in August 1625 in Christ Church hall in Oxford (escaping from the plague in London), Cotton sat as M.P. for Thetford, a seat in the Earl of Arundel's control. Buckingham gave an account of the preparations to send a fleet against Spain under his command, and relayed the King's request for subsidy. The Commons were recalcitrant, doubtful of Buckingham's competence, alarmed at his lack of consultation in the planning of the expedition, and suspicious of his agreement with France, then actively persecuting Protestants, for help against Spain. *Cottoni Posthuma* includes a speech that Sir Robert was supposed to have made on this occasion, although there is no mention of it in the Parliamentary record. Gardiner believed that Cotton wrote the speech for Sir John Eliot; Sharpe believes that it was for Sir Robert Phelips who led the attack on Buckingham.[20] It certainly reads like Cotton's work, with its laying out of precedents and its several glances at the problems of Henry III's reign.

In its preliminaries, the speech brings up, non-specifically, the question of impeachment, and then proceeds to analyse the frail condition of the Crown and the disorders that have crept into government. By 1625, the early years of James's reign seemed assured and competent in contrast to the present. As long as Elizabeth's officers had continued to serve James, things went well: debt was kept in check, pensions were restrained, trade flourished. 'All things of moment were carried by public debate at the Council-table; no Honour set to sale...Laws against Priests and Recusants were executed.' The King wrote vigorously against Catholicism. In government, there was 'no transcendant power in any one Minister. For matters of state, the Council-table held up the fit and ancient dignity.'[21] Cotton then passes to the praise of Somerset as a man of integrity, whose main care was the well-being of the state. All this is a very rosy retrospect, and quite at odds with the view of the state assumed in *The Life and Reign of Henry III*. For once, political opportunism seems to have made Cotton change his recollection of recent history quite markedly. Now he dates the troubles of James's reign from his inclination to arrange a Spanish match for Prince Charles. The King was thereafter indulgent towards England's chief enemy, and reluctant to enforce the laws against Catholics. Once Gondomar had come to London as Spanish ambassador, James was never again his own master. The King allowed favourites (unnamed) to exercise and abuse his power; (the unsavoury name of Piers Gaveston, Edward II's homosexual favourite, is invoked). The King's honour was tarnished by the sale of titles; his reputation abroad declined; his role as Protestant champion no longer convinced. The Privy Council was no longer a source of advice, for free debate had ceased there. The speech ends with a plea to the King to develop his policy with advice from a broadly based Privy Council, if he wishes to prevent 'disasters in State', and to avoid 'young and single Counsel'. Buckingham's name is never mentioned, but the target of the speech is clear. Cotton creates a mood and exploits it, maintaining all the while the air of giving an objective, historical account of the nation's difficulties. He is preparing the ground for impeachment.

Even though the speech appears not to have been delivered, Buckingham was well aware of Cotton's antagonism. He gained revenge of a sort the next year when he prevented King Charles from landing at Cotton's garden at Westminster, as appointed, on his way to his coronation. So public a snub must have galled Cotton exceedingly. The unexplained circumstances of the publication of *Henry III* in 1627 may have inconvenienced Cotton, but the event cannot altogether have displeased him, for the history expressed very plainly his views about favourites who usurp power.

The last item, chronologically, in *Cottoni Posthuma* was also provoked by Buckingham and the national and international mess he had contrived. 'The Danger wherein the Kingdom now standeth and the Remedy' was a pamphlet Cotton actually published under his own name in 1628, an exceptional move and a measure of his alarm. The gravity of events was pushing him to a more direct expression of his beliefs than was natural to him. By this time, Buckingham had incurred the enmity of France by attempting to relieve the Protestants of La Rochelle, and was also trying to fight a war against Spain. Cotton spells out the historical lessons of England's disadvantage when the alliance with France breaks down and Spain is also hostile. England risks precipitating another invasion attempt from Spain, yet has neither men nor money to defend herself adequately. Even worse, popular affection for the monarch is so low that the nation will not rally in a crisis, as it did so remarkably in Elizabethan times. Rumour growls that Buckingham inclines to Catholicism, and English Protestants feel their religion is not safe while Buckingham dominates the national scene. His abilities as a leader are gravely suspect. A parliament must be called to vote subsidy for the King, and take order for the defence of the nation. Surprisingly, Cotton does not call for Buckingham to be stripped of power or publicly disavowed by the King. The Duke should take his place among the other leading peers in the Privy Council, and he should communicate in some fashion the King's patriotic and Protestant intentions to the nation. Cotton wishes 'to remove away a personal distaste of my Lord of Buckingham amongst the People', and to change the image of the King to that of 'a zealous Patriot'.

Cotton was swayed by no love of Buckingham but by the enduring principle of his career: loyalty to the monarch as the legitimate centre of power and ultimate guarantor of the nation's stability. History instructs him that if there arises a popular passion to sacrifice any of his Majesty's servants, 'I have ever found it ... no less fatal to the Master, than the Minister in the end.'[22] He reminds his readers of the fate of Edward II, Richard II and Henry VI. Moderate policies should prevail, in Cotton's view. But though Charles reluctantly agreed to the calling of a new parliament, and though Buckingham was removed by assassination later in 1628, moderation and mutual assistance did not prevail. Parliament grew more angry with the King as it fought to assert its rights and liberties. In 1629 Charles ordered Cotton's library to be closed, for it was the arsenal from which so many parliamentary arguments drew their strength. It was a bitter punishment to visit on a man who had always wished to maintain the primacy of the King, whilst ensuring that he enjoyed honest advice from the Privy Council and Parliament. All his precedents had not prepared him for a monarch as fractious and hostile to parliamentary opinion as Charles.

The publication of these tracts in 1651 was an attempt to revive the memory of Cotton's service to the state. The volume showed him as a royalist who believed that the best support for the monarch was a strong Parliament. The individual tracts illustrate a career as an active politician, firm Protestant and shrewd adviser across nearly thirty years. As a bonus, the editor, James Howell, included two extraneous pieces which he had presumably found among Cotton's papers: 'Valour anatomized in a Fancy', attributed here to Sir Philip Sidney, and Sir Francis Walsingham's essays on Honesty, Ambition and Fortitude.[23] These serve to remind us of the forthright Elizabethan values that Cotton admired all his life. Their presence here, with their clear and witty praise of virtue, leads one to feel that Cotton lived on into a period when politics and behaviour were becoming too complex and devious for a man who 'lived by old Ethicks and the classical rules of Honesty'. Cotton's love of precedent and his fondness for reducing political experience to a maxim revealed him as one who loved ordered and principled procedure. He would have been utterly bewildered by the Civil War. But his political methods had strength and clearmindedness, and they retained their power to win admiration. *Cottoni Posthuma* was republished in 1674 and again in 1679, when Parliament and the King were once more falling into conflict, over the Exclusion crisis. Cotton liked to say that he had little personal stake in the issues he addressed, and that he lived for his country and his friends; he continued to gather friends after his death, and his concern for his country's well-being has kept his reputation fresh, and still honoured today.

1 This was *The Danger wherein the Kingdom now standeth and the Remedy* (1628).
2 Kevin Sharpe notes this revival of interest in the reigns of Elizabeth and James at this time, citing two works about Raleigh, Fulke Greville's Life of Sidney, and Anthony Weldon's *Court and Character of King James*. To this list one should add Arthur Wilson's *The History of Great Britain* (1653), the first history of the reign of King James. See Kevin Sharpe, *Sir Robert Cotton, 1586–1631* (Oxford, 1979), p. 246. Sharpe's book is indispensable to the study of Cotton, and I have found its account of his political career most valuable in preparing this paper.
3 See Sharpe, p. 142.
4 The King's debts were estimated at £680,000 early in 1614. See D. H. Willson, *King James I & VI* (1956), p. 344.
5 'The Life and Reign of Henry the Third', in *Cottoni Posthuma* (1651), p. 25.
6 Ibid., p. 26.
7 Ibid., pp. 43–4.
8 Ibid., p. 49.
9 Laurence Stone, *The Crisis of the Aristocracy* (Oxford, 1965), pp. 242–50.
10 *Cottoni Posthuma*, p. 169.
11 The household regulations laid down for Prince Henry's court are a model of fiscal prudence. They are printed as an appendix to Thomas Birch, *The Life of Henry, Prince of Wales* (1760).
12 See Sharpe, pp. 235–7. These maxims distilled Cotton's experience of politics. Sharpe wonders if they were put together for the benefit of the King. They are preserved in Bodleian Library, MS. Tanner 103, ff. 196–198.
13 'Twenty-four Arguments concerning Popish Practices', in *Cottoni Posthuma*, p. 147.
14 Ibid., p. 148.
15 See Sharpe, p. 166.
16 Ibid., pp. 167–9.
17 Sharpe prefers to think that Buckingham was the

most likely begetter, being most anxious to break off relations with Spain.

18 Roger Lockyer, *Buckingham* (1981), pp. 192–7.
19 *Cottoni Posthuma*, p. 7.
20 S. Gardiner, *History of England, 1603–42*, 1891 ed., vol. v, pp. 425–7, notes; Sharpe, *Cotton*, pp. 177–80.
21 *Cottoni Posthuma*, pp. 274–5.
22 Ibid., p. 322.
23 The piece attributed to Sidney is, in fact, a reworking of one of Donne's Paradoxes.

SIR ROBERT COTTON, ANTIQUARIANISM AND ESTATE ADMINISTRATION: A CHANCERY DECREE OF 1627

ROGER B. MANNING

THE Chancery Decree of 5 November 1627, found on Public Record Office, Chancery Decree Roll, C. 78/300/1, is a lengthy, but very interesting document, consisting of eleven membranes of a parchment roll. It illustrates an aspect of Sir Robert Cotton's antiquarian researches, which has been but little investigated.

The document consists of a bill of complaint filed in the Court of Chancery in Trinity term 1618 by Marsilian Sampson and seven other copyholders of the Manor of Glatton and Holme, Huntingdonshire, on behalf of the whole body of tenants, alleging an attempt by Sir Robert Cotton, John Cotton, his uncle, and Sir Thomas Cotton, his son and heir, defendants, to overthrow the tenants' copyhold estates of inheritance and to increase the entry fines and rents contrary to manorial custom.[1] Sir Robert Cotton and the other defendants responded by exhibiting a crossbill in Michaelmas term 1626 alleging various corrupt practices contrary to ancient manorial custom by the tenants in collusion with the stewards of the manorial court in the century or so before Sir Robert and the other defendants purchased the manor of Glatton and Holme from the Duchy of Lancaster in 1611. The crossbill is especially interesting because it illustrates the application by Sir Robert Cotton of antiquarian research to the task of estate administration and demonstrates that Sir Robert's investigations, whether applied to antiquarian endeavours in parliamentary politics, heraldry or estate management, were always of a practical nature, and, in this instance, were intended to yield a profit.

The third part of the document consists of the chancery decree itself, dated 5 November 1627. Despite a heavy investment of time and effort in searching through court rolls and other manorial records in order to document ancient manorial custom reaching back to the reign of Edward I, the Cottons achieved considerably less than a full victory and many of the tenants' claims were upheld by the decree of the Lord Keeper, Sir Thomas Coventry. It seems that the tenants, led by Robert Castle, who possessed legal training and experience as a steward presiding over manorial courts elsewhere, and later by his son and heir, John Castle, had acquired enough expertise in deciphering old muniments to hold their own against the Cottons.

Although both the complainants and defendants accepted the Chancery decree of 1627, its very complexity gave rise to a number of differences of interpretation and application of the decree. The Court found it necessary to amend the original decree in

96

Trinity term 1628 with regard to a number of particulars. None of these emendations substantially altered the original decree, and that portion of the document is omitted altogether.

Aside from the rich documentation of Sir Robert Cotton's practice of fiscal seigneurialism,[2] the Chancery Decree of 1627 also provides a useful exemplification of Chancery procedure, the role of lawyers in Chancery practice, the attempts by the court to achieve a settlement by arbitration, and the application by the Lord Keeper of the principles of equity to his judgments.[3]

The edited version of PRO, C. 78/300/1 which is printed here reproduces about forty per cent of the full text. The original spelling has been retained, but modern punctuation has been added. The dates are old style except for the year which is given in new style.

PRO, Chancery Decree Rolls, C. 78/300/1, *Marsilian Sampson* et al. [copyholders of the manor of Glatton and Holme] vs. *Sir Robert Cotton, bt.* et al.[4]

Where before this tyme, that is to saie in the Tearme of the Holie Trinitie, one thousand, six hundred and eighteene, Marsilian Sampson, Thomas Kingston, Gilbert Abbott, Thomas Joyce, Henry Barton, William Barton, Henry Lea and Edward Norwood, eight of the coppiehoulders of the lordshipp or manor of Glatton and Holme in the County of Huntington, in the name and behalfe of themselves and all the residue of the coppiehoulders of the said lordship or manor, being aboue a hundred, which number exhibited theire bill of complaint into this most honourable Courte of Chancery against Sir Robert Cotton, knight and Baronett, John Cotton, Thomas Cotton, Esquires, and Raphe Hartley, gentleman, declaring thereby: That Whereas the late Queene...Queene Elizabeth was lawfully seised in her demeasne of ffee in the right of her highnes' Dutchie of Lancaster of and in the said lordshippe or mannor of Glatton and Holme...in the said county of Huntington; And whereas the same coppiehould tenants of the said manor had vsually paied vnto the said late Queene...one yeare's coppiehould or customary rent...for a ffyne for theire admittance vppon the death, alienacon[5] or chaunge of any the said tenants holding by coppie of Courte Rolle according to the custome of the said manor. And yet neuertheles aswell for the reducing of the said ffynes of the said mannor...of Glatton and Holme to a perpetuall certainty...And for the strengthininge and confirmacon of the coppiehould estates of all the then coppiehoulders...the said complainants and others the then coppiehoulders lawfully had a decree...obteyned in the Tearme of Saint Michaell in the three and thirtieth yeare of the Raigne of the late Queen Elizabeth [1591] in her highnes' Courte of Dutchie Chamber[6] vppon the peticon of said coppiehould tenaunts...Whereby it was ordered, decreed and adiudged that all manner of estates before that tyme graunted to any tenaunte or coppiehoulder within the said mannor by coppie of Courte Rolle, Whether for life, yeares or inheritaunce according to the custome of the said mannor should continue and be enjoyed for and during estate or estates...And it was thereby further ordered and decreed that for a better increase of her Maiestie's Revenewes every coppiehoulder of the said mannor respectively should vppon everye admittance after deathe, Surrender or other chaunge of tenante paie such ffyne...[of] ffower yeares rent and noe lesse of the ould and accustomed rent....It was alsoe provided that the coppiehould estates of the said mannor should not be questioned or impeached. ...And whereas the said late king's maiestie,[7] in or about the nynth yeare of his highnes' Raigne, …did make or graunt a commission to certaine lords and others…for sale of divers lordshippes, mannors and other lands, and amongst the rest, the said lordshippe or mannor of Glatton and Holme, Wherein his maiestie's pleasure…was that the complainants and other the tenants of the said mannor should have the first offer for the purchase of the said coppiehould tenements and of the manor. And…the tenants of the said manor…did become humble suitors to the said lords in commission for the purchase of the said manor. The which being perceaved by Sir Robert Cotton, knight and Baronett, whoe did much desire to obteyne the purchase of the said mannor, being neare vnto his cheife house of Conington in the saide Countie of Huntingdon, he the said Sir Robert Cotton did first gett fourth a particuler of the said mannor of Glatton and Holme…to make the complainants and other the tenants of the said lordshipp or mannor to desist in going on with the purchase of the said lordshipp or mannor. And the said Sir Robert Cotton, perceaving that the…said tenaunts…would not be beaten of[f] from the said purchase, he the said Sir Robert Cotton did deale in direct tearmes with the plaintiffs…and did earnestlie perswade them to relinquishe theire suit for the said purchase of the said mannor of Glatton and Holme, alledging vnto them that they…would not be [able to] vndergoe and compasse the said purchase. And that the estates of the complainants and other the coppiehoulders of the said mannor were as goode as the lords in commission[8] could make them. And if that they would desist theire said suits and give way, that the said Sir Robert Cotton might purchase the same, he faithfully promised and protested that then…the coppiehoulders of the said mannor should quietlie and peceablie haue and houlde theire said coppiehould estates to them and theire heires…And should paie a ffyne certaine of four years of the ould rent.…Wherevppon the said…coppiehoulders of the said mannor, giving over their said suite for the said purchase of the said mannor, …Sir Robert Cotton did treate with the said lords in commission for buying of the said lordshipp or mannor and did affirme…that the… coppiehoulders of the said mannor should be well vsed and that they and theire heires should quietlie enioye the same as they had formerlie enioyed the same vnder the King's maiestie that then was. Wherevppon at length he the said Sir Robert Cotton did procure a warrant…for the buying of the said mannor of Glatton and Holme, …the said mannor being a great and populus mannor, in length, fower miles, and in circuite, fower and twentie miles, conteyning, by auncient survey, tenn thousand acres of land of all sorts, that vsing greate demeasnes and coppiehoulds and free rents of Assise thereof amounting to ffowerscore twoe poundes by the yeare…besides the fishing of Whittlesey meare, the greatest ffreshwater in this Kingdome, having five other mannors holden of the same; yett he the said Robert Cotton was onelie for to paie the sume of eight and twentie hundred pounds…And…procured…the graunt thereof of the King's maiestie…vnto him the said Sir Robert Cotton, John Cotton, his vncle, Thomas Cotton, his sonne, and to theire heires and assignes for ever. …And the said complainants…by theire said bill of complainte further shewed that the said Sir Robert Cotton, John Cotton and Thomas Cotton, haveing thus obteyned soe greate a mannor in Royaltie, rente, services and demeasnes at soe lowe a valewe, intending and ayminge (as it seemed) the ruine and vndoeing of the poore complainants…did…endeavor to make the ffines of the said coppiehould estats of the said mannor to be incertaine, And to overthrowe the coppiehould estats…being coppiehould estats of inheritance; And did expressly denie to make any admittance of the complainants and other coppiehoulders of the said mannor to the messuages, lands and tenements they did severally and respectivelie hould by coppie of Court Rolle. …Soe as the poore complainants and other the

98

tenants of the said manor, holding lands and tenements of the said mannor to them and theire heires by coppie of the Court Rolle according to the custome of the said mannor, ... by reason of the said deniall of their admittances and questioning of theire said coppiehould estates were not able to make any disposicon thereof, but were like to be disinherited by the said Sir Robert Cotton, John Cotton and Thomas Cotton, And theire families, being a thousand persons in the leaste, like to be vtterlie undone and impoverished. ... And forasmuch also as it was against equity and conscience ... that the said defendants should question the coppiehould estates of inheritance of the said ... coppiehoulders of the said mannor, and denied to make admittaunce vnto them ... and had no remedie at lawe to compell the said defendant to admitt the said complainants, ... they the said complainants praied the aide of this courte and that proces of subpena might be awarded against ... the said defendants. Which being graunted and they therewithall served the defendants, appeared accordinglie and made theire severall Aunsweres vnto the said bill. Wherevnto the said complaynaunts replied, and the sayd partyes being at yssue, Wittnesses were examined in the cause aswell by commyssion in the Country as also in Court, which was retorned and published accordingly, as by the sayd pleadings remayning of record in this Court appeareth. But before the sayd cause came to be heard, Thomas Cotton, Esquire, Sonne and heire of the sayd Sir Robert Cotton, exhibited in Michaelmas secundo Caroli[9] his crosse bill[10] vnto this Court against John Kastell, Esquire, Robert Castell, parson of the sayd parrish of Glatton and Holme, Willyam ffuller, William Warrener, Richard Berridg, Willyam Clarke, Robert Maken, Henry Key, Michaell Wells, Marsilian Sampson, Alice Curtis, Thomas Kyngston, for and in the name ... of all other tennants of the sayd mannor of Glatton and Holme. ... And the said complainant ... shewed That the said mannors of Glatton and Holme had, tyme out of memory of man, beene Twoe severall and distinct mannors and twoe mannor houses and twoe severall courts, and severall customes vnto them belonging; And that the Custome of the said mannor of Holme warranting coppiehold of Inheritance, paying vncertaine ffynes at the lord's will for Admittance vpon deathes, surrender or forfeitures; And the tenants of the said mannor of Holme from tyme to tyme for many hundred yeares past did vse to pay besides theire auncient rents twoe pence yearlie for every tenante in leiwe[11] of satisfacon, and for theire Workes auncientlie due to the lorde, and double theire auncient rent yearlie in leiwe for theire aides auncientlie due to the lorde of the said mannor, and ffynes arbitrary [and] vncertaine vppon deathe or change of every tenure; All of which rents and promisses the tenants of the said mannor of Holme continually before and at the tyme of the graunt and suite had from tyme to tyme paid the same vnto the said Sir Robert Cotton, John Cotton and the complainant. ... And whereas tyme out of memory of man, the said mannor of Glatton was divided or did consist of demeasnes in the possession or hands of the lord of the said mannor or theire lessees or ffarmors and of thirty-six yard lands and an halfe in the occupacon and tenure of severall customary and other tenants of the said mannor, And whereas auncientlie, vntil about the tyme of King Edward the ffirst, as might appeare by the Records and other evidences of the said mannor, That all the said yard lands in the said mannor of Glatton except ffreehold were held by the tenants in villainage tenure, and the tenants thereof doing and paying to the lord of the said mannor besides theire rents divers works, servics and herriotts and ffynes for every yard land more or lesse at the will of the lord, about which tyme of King Edward the first or soone after, the lord of the mannor taking compassion on the miserable estate of the Inhabitants, thereof afflicted with a great plague, reduced the said yard land to a certainty, that out of every yard land should be yearlie paid to the lord four and twenty

99

shillings, seaven pence for the rent, and fower shillings, one penny for the work, and five shillings and sixpence for the aydes of every of the said yard lands, reserving to the lords theire herriotts and other ffynes for dwellilng from theire said yard lands, Which said rent and somes for workes and aydes, herriotts and ffynes as aforesaid all the tenants of the said yard lands continually, from tyme to tyme, payed to the Earles and Dukes of Lancaster, and to all other his Maiestie's Progenitors, lords of the said mannor, vntill about the tyme of King Henry the Sixt vppon a greate murraine of cattell and decay of the tenants of the said mannor, by authoritie of the King and Councell of the Dutchie of Lancaster, When anie of the said yard lands fell into the lord's hands, they were some tymes demised for yeares or, at will, an abated or lesser rent…vntil it might againe be ymproved to the auncient rent aforesaid. …And since that tyme by the corrupcon or ignorance of the stewards of the said mannors the said yard landes had at severall tymes beene graunted at farre lesser rents, and without the said somes for works and ayds as aforesaid. Butt, in all the Bayliffs' accompts from the said tyme of the purchase aforesaid, there was yearely deliuered vnto the King's Auditor, And there a power reserved to the lord of the mannor, to rayse, improve and reduce the said yard lands to the said auntient and accustomed somes for workes and ayds aforesaid by a clause conteyned in theire severall accompts. …And whereas after the chaunge of the tenancies of the said mannor of Glatton from tenancies at will by Villainage tenure as aforesaid into coppiehoulders, which beganne to be first altered and chaunged about the tyme of King Richard the second, and not before, All the said yard lands were constantlie and vniformely graunted for the tearme of life by coppie of Courte Rolle according to the custome of the said mannor, and never any coppie graunted otherwise then for lives, and never to any man and his heires, from the said first graunt by coppie about Richard the second's tyme vntill by corrupcon or ignorance of the vnderstewards of the said mannor, contrary to theire iust power and the auncient custome of the said mannor, about the end of King Henry the eight's raigne some fewe graunts were made by coppie of lands, Which were at that tyme butt tenures at will. …And, in name, one John Castell, in the one and twenty yeare of King Henry the eight, procured an estate by coppie of Court Rolle to be made to him and his heires, not according but contrary to the custome of the said mannor, of one of the said messuages and yard lands, part of the demeasnes of the mannor, Which parte of the demeasnes was at this tyme holden by lease and not by coppie. And, afterwards, in the tyme of Queene Mary and in the beginning of the Raigne of Queene Elizabeth, there were five and twentie yardlands of the said six and thirtieth and halfe from coppiehoulds of life and tenures at will, taken by coppies of Inheritance contrary to the custome of the said mannor and at lesse then halfe the Rent aforesaid, besides the somes for works and aydes aforesaid. …And the most parte of the residue of the said thirtie-six yard lands and a halfe in the said mannor of Glatton were, by coullor of the like, voide coppies of Inheritance graunted by the corrupcon of the vndersteward within fewe yeares last past and for farre lesse rent and without the said somes due for workes and ayds as aforesaid the complainant could manifestlie prove vnto this honourable court. And the better to conceale and detayne the same ffrom the complainant, one Robert Castell, Esquier, one of the pretended coppiehoulders of the said mannor, deteyned divers Court Rolls, Rentalls, Accompts and Surveys and other Evidencs of the said mannor from the said complainant vntill they were recovered from him by suits in lawe. And all the said were estates of Inheritance soe granted by coppie as aforesaid, beinge voide in lawe without warrant of the custome of the said manor. …And the tenants of the mannor of Glatton were knoweing and perceaving such theire said estates to be voide in lawe and in deceipt and

100

disinheritance of the then Queene. ...Wherevppon the pretended coppiehoulders of the said mannor in the twoe and thirtieth yeare of the Raigue of the Queene's maiestie petitioned the then Chaunceller and councel of the said Dutchie to prevent the graunting of such leases and to confirme theire coppiehould estates. ...And therevppon the said Chancellor and Councell of the said Dutchie being misinformed by the said peticon by the generaltie and confusion thereof, not expressinge in their peticon Whether they claymed estats of Inheritance or what estates in certaine, nor what rents they were to pay yearelie for the same. And not being trulie informed that the said mannor of Glatton and Holme were twoe distinct mannors and had severall customes, and that the auncient rents of Holme were then dulie paid and the custome thereof warranting coppieholds of Inheritance; and that rents of the said mannor of Glatton were abated and not trulie aunswered, and that the custome thereof did not warrant any coppiehoulds of Inheritance; Vnder pretence of benefitting the Queene by theire said offer gott a decree of the said Court without hearing any proofes of the premisses in such generall words as were in theire peticon as aforesaid for the confirmacon of theire coppiehould estates...and by coullor of the said decree so desceiptfully gotten...did challenge and claime to hould the said messuages and yard lands as coppiehoulds of Inheritance...and by coullor thereof, had ever since the said purchase made by the said Sir Robert Cotton, John Cotton and the complainante held and kept them out of possession of the same and deteyned the same from the complainante; And had alsoe, ever since the said purchase, refused to pay the auncient and accustomed rent of ffower and twentie shillings, seven pence and the said ffower shillings and a penny yearelie for works and five shillings for ayds...for every yard land. ...The tenants of the said mannors, or some of them, having before the said purchase taken out the same particulers from the auditor and perused the same, and one Robert Castell, Esquier, ffather to John Castell, being a councellor at lawe and a pretended coppiehoulder and Bayliffe of the said mannor delivering the accompt of the same things conteyned in the particulers to the Auditor to make his particulers by, with the Intent with the rest of the Tenants to purchase the said mannor, butt finding the price thereof too high and to exceede theire abilities, they directlie refused to purchase it. Wherevppon the said tenants desired the said Sir Robert Cotton he would confirme their estates and make theire ffynes certaine, which he directlie denied to doe, butt then offered that every coppiehoulder should have bought his owne coppiehould at the same rate they were purchased att within twoe yeares, which they refused to doe, And combyned themselves in respect of theire multitudes to keepe the said lands from the said complainante...and most vnconscionablie refused and denied to pay the said auncient rent and somes due for workes and aydes as aforesaid. By which theire iniurious and vnconscionable courses the said Robert Cotton, John Cotton and the complainante since the said purchase had never made nor receaved threescore and tenn pounds by the yeare of the said mannors, having bought all liberties and powers to increase the same to the auncient and true value as appeareth by theire graunt aforesaid. ...And lastlie shewed that whereas tyme out of minde severall parcels of the demeasne lands of the said mannors had beene vsually in the lord's possession or demised for yeares, and there had beene kept vppon the same greate fflocks of sheepe and beasts to pasture, and tyme out of minde had beene severall all the yeare, and none of the Tenants of the said mannors ought to have had any common at any tyme of the yeare in the same respect that there was noe common allotted to the said demeasne lands in the great commons of the said mannors belonging to the tenants. And the said John Castell, Robert Castle, parson of the Towne, William ffuller, Edward Abbott, William Warriner, Richard Berridge,

William Clarke, Robert Makin, Henry Key and Michaell Wells, and manie other of the tenants of the said mannors having had severall leases of the said severall demeasnes before specified ever since the seaventeenth yeare of the said late Queene Elizabeth by coullor thereof suffered the said demeasnes to lye and to be vsed as common for all the Tenants of the said mannors most parte of the yeare that by that meanes and coullor of such longe vsage...they might clayme or pretend as they alredy did clayme and pretend to have had common in the same. ...And that proces of subpena might be awarded against the said John Castell [et al.]...for and in the name of all other the tenants of the said mannors of Glatton and Holme, Aswell ffreehoulders as coppiehoulders. Which being graunted, the said John Castell, Esquiere, Michael Wells, Henry Key and Henry Barton, by the especiall Order of the right honourable lord Keeper[12] aswell for in the behalfes of themselves as the rest of the said Tenants, both ffreeholders and coppiehoulders, made theire Aunsweares thereto, as by the said pleadings remayning alsoe of Record in this Courte appeareth. Wherevppon, and without any further proceeding had in this Cause, the Matter in question vppon both the said bills came to be heard on Satterday the tenth daie of ffebruary in the second yeare of the king's maiestie's Raigne[13] that nowe is in the presence of the councell learned on both sides for and touchinge the certainty of ffynes vppon Admittance, vppon deathe or alienacon and estates of Inheritaunce in the said mannor of Glatton as the tenants pretend and for which they prayed releife by theire Bill. ...And for and touching divers other particulers in the proceedings comprehended, this courte therefore conceaving that this cause might very well be determined by way [of] mediacon did order that maister serieant Hetley and the Maister Taylor, Whoe were of councell with the said parties, should fforthwith consider of the matters whatsoever in difference betweene them, and end the same if they could. If not, then to certifie theire difference vnto Maister Justice Dodderidge, whoe was desired by this Court to vmpire the same. ...And for the better discovering of the truth of the customes of the said mannors, the said Sir Robert Cotton and Thomas Cotton, as alsoe the said tenants should bring vnto the said Referr[ee]s all such Court Rolls and coppies as they had in Towne, Which concerned any of the said mannors vppon oath, And vppon sight thereof the said Referrees should not be satisfied therewith, and that the said tenants had anie other coppies in the country that would give them better satisfaction, And the said Referrees should be desirous to see the same, Then they maye give vnto the said tenants further tyme for the bringing vpp thereof, if they should soe thinke fitt. ...But all they could doe was only to sett downe the true estate of the matter and reduce the differences betweene the said parties to certaine heades. Wherevppon aswell the said complaymant, Marsilian Sampson and others the tennants of the mannors, as Sir Robert Cotton, John Cotton and Thomas Cotton, defendants, did the five and twentith day of the monthe of October last past ioyntlie petition the lord Keeper to end and vmpire the same differences according to the said Order. Vppon hearing in open Courte, the which being graunted by his lordshipp the said Matters in difference came to be hearde before his lordshipp in the Tearme of St. Michaell the fifte daie of November in the thirde yeare of the Raigne of our said Soveraigne lord, king Charles,[14] in the presence of the said Referrees and of maister Serieant Crewe of Councell with the said Tenants of the said mannor of Glatton, and of Maister Noy and Maister Ball of Councel with the said defendants, and alsoe in presence of the said John Castell, esquier, Michaell Welles, gentleman, and Robert Goode, in the name and behalfe of the said tenants, and Sir Robert Cotton and Thomas Cotton, Esquier. When, vppon opening and debating matters in difference betweene the said parties, his lordship did by and with the assent and consent of the said parties and theire councell, order and awarde in manner and forme following: ffirst, that the complainants and other coppiehoulders of the said mannor of Glatton and Holme, theire heires and assignes, should enioye theire severall coppiehoulds as coppiehoulds of inheritance according to the custome of the said mannor; And that the said defendants, theire heires and assignes, lords of the said mannor of Glatton and Holme, should not at any tyme or tymes then after question or impeach anie of the said coppiehoulders of the said mannors, theire heires or assignes for or in respect that they had not a customary Inheritance in the said severall coppiehoulds, butt should and would vppon deathes and surrenders of anie coppiehoulders of the said mannor graunt admittance to the heire of every coppiehoulder soe dyinge and to anie person to whose vse such surrender should be made vppon payment of such ffyne as is hereafter menconed. Secondlie, that the said Defendants, theire heires and assignes should and might, from and after the end, determinacon for yeares yet to come of the demeasnes of the said mannors of Glatton and Holme, conteyning by estimacon fower or five hundred acres or soe, soone as the said demeasne lands or anie part thereof should come into theire hands, have, hould and enioy the same demeasnes which should soe come to theire hands, Withall the balkes and highewayes nowe held as common intermixed with the demeasne lands of the said mannors in severalty without lett or interrupcon of anie Coppiehoulder, ffreeholder or other person or persons clayming anie manner of common or other proffitt in the same. ... And to the intent that the defendants maye the better inclose the said demeasnes, his lordshipp did order, with the consent of the said John Castle, Michaell Wells and Robert Good, the Tennants present for and in the names of all the rest, That whereas certaine of the Tenants of the said mannor have some acres of arrable intermixed in divers parts of the said demeasnes, That such persons shall either exchaunge or sell and convey the said parcells of ground to the Defendants, theire heires and assignes for other lands of like yearlie value or such sommes of money as the same are nowe worth to be sould. ... And his lordshipp did also order that the said Sir Robert Cotton, John Cotton and Thomas Cotton and theire heires and assignes should not in respect of the said lordshipp or mannor or demeasne lands intercommon with theire or any of theire cattell in anie other of the commonable ffields other then the ffenns within the said lordshipp or mannor of Glatton cum Holme; And that the tennants of the said demeasne grounds should not during the tyme of the said lease plowe vpp anie of the sward grounds that had not beene plowed within the tyme of thirtie yeares nowe last past. Thirdly, Whereas ... the complainant Marsilian Sampson and the rest of the Tennants vsed to paie for some of the said yard lands fowerteene shillings [and] for some of the said yard lands sixteene shillings by the yeare, And the said Sir Robert Cotton, John Cotton and Thomas Cotton did pretend by Accompts of Bayliffs in the tyme of Henry the sixt that the rent of the said yard lands oughte to be fower and twentie shillings, seaven pence, his lordshipp did order and award that every of the said thirtie six yard lands should paye yearlie fower shillings, six pence of increase over and aboue the coppiehoulds' rent vnjustly paid at such tyme as the coppiehould abated rent was vsed to be paied ... and every other parcell of land not being knowne or reputed as a yard land ... should paye proporconably after the most common rate of a yard land, accompting fower and twenty acres to a yard land. ... ffourthlie, Itt was ordered by his lordshipp that the ffyne be paied for every coppiehoulder thentofore to have been admitted and then after to be admitted vppon death or surrender should be after the rate of fower yeares of the coppiehould rent of late tyme vsually paied with the addicon of ffower shillings, six pence for every yard land hereby ordered and awarded, and according to that rate and proporcon. ... And it was then lastlie ordered that the end and award aforesaid should be ratified and established by the decree of the Court of Chancery; And either party did agree that theire equall chardge to endeavor to procure that an Act of Parli[a]ment might passe for the confirminge of the end and award aforesaid.

1 The manor of Glatton and Holme, consisting of 10,000 acres, was adjacent to Sir Robert Cotton's manor and seat of Conington, Hunts.

2 A full account of the troubled relations between Sir Robert Cotton and his son Sir Thomas, on the one hand, and the tenants of their various manors may be found in R. B. Manning, 'Antiquarianism and the Seigneurial Reaction: Sir Robert and Sir Thomas Cotton and their Tenants', *Historical Research*, lxiii (Oct. 1990), pp. 277–88. For a more extensive discussion of the seigneurial reaction and 'fiscal seigneurialism', cf. my *Village Revolts: Social Protest and Popular Disturbances in England, 1509–1640* (Oxford, 1988), pp. 4, 34–37, 61, 63–66, 117–30, 132–54. Readers will also wish to consult K. Sharpe, *Sir Robert Cotton, 1586–1631: History and Politics in Early Modern England* (Oxford, 1979).

3 The standard introduction to the history of this court in early-modern times is W. J. Jones, *The Elizabethan Court of Chancery* (Oxford, 1967).

4 Unpublished crown copyright material, printed by kind permission of the Controller of H.M. Stationery Office.

5 I.e., alienation.

6 The Court of Duchy Chamber of the Duchy of Lancaster was an equity court, which had a jurisdiction over duchy tenants and heard causes similar to those that arose in the Courts of Chancery and Star Chamber.

7 King James I and VI.

8 The Duchy of Lancaster commissioners who were authorized to sell off Crown lands in 1611.

9 Autumn 1626.

10 A bill filed in Chancery or other equity court by the defendant in the original suit against the complainant or plaintiff requiring the plaintiff to make written answer and be examined under oath.

11 I.e., in lieu.

12 Sir Thomas Coventry.

13 1627.

14 1627.

FROM CAMDEN TO CAMBRIDGE: SIR ROBERT COTTON'S ROMAN INSCRIPTIONS, AND THEIR SUBSEQUENT TREATMENT

DAVID McKITTERICK

The value of Roman inscriptions as historical material is immense. They are contemporary and authoritative documents, whose text is a first-hand record, free from subsequent corruption by copyists. They are the most important single source for the history and organization of the Roman Empire; and their cumulative and comparative value, in the hands of judicious scholars, trained to handle them in the mass, is astonishingly great.[1]

MOST of the Roman inscriptions collected by Sir Robert Cotton survive today in the Museum of Archaeology and Anthropology at Cambridge. They have been much published since they were collected, although those that have thus converted stone into print have not always done so without introducing corruptions. For some, we depend on contemporary transcriptions, of more or less authority. But the fame and the continuing importance of Cotton's manuscript collection, celebrated and used ever since he first assembled it in the last years of the sixteenth and the beginning of the seventeenth centuries, have distracted most observers from his other activities as a collector. While, for his contemporaries just as to modern scholars, the manuscripts offered a range of interests in which history, politics and literature all figure prominently, for a smaller number of his contemporaries his collections of coins and of Roman inscriptions were of scarcely less concern.

They reflected a crucial assumption as to the nature of his library. In forming collections of coins and of inscriptions, to accompany his manuscripts and printed books, he was assembling a library in which each of these various forms was expected to complement the others. The inscriptions on stone, and the portraits and legends on the coins, recorded the past in different materials; but their evidence was also to be read, in a literal sense. The whole manifested some of the interests that made him a prominent member of the Elizabethan Society of Antiquaries that flourished for a few years until its politics and history clashed, and it disappeared in the reign of James I.[2] Amongst Cotton's contemporaries, collections of coins were kept as parts of libraries both by institutions, such as Cambridge University, and by private individuals, such as Andrew Perne in Cambridge or Sir Thomas Knyvett in Norfolk.[3] Collections of inscriptions on stone were less usual in England, where Cotton was in several respects a pioneer. But, again, it was not a new association. In ancient Rome, and to take but one example, Trajan's Column had been placed between two libraries, the stone images and inscriptions thus accompanying those on papyrus, membrane and clay.[4]

It is important to recognize the interrelated nature of Cotton's interests in this respect. His purposes were essentially those connected with his library; apart from coins, he was not collecting other antique artefacts with similar discipline. Unlike the Earl of Arundel a generation later, he made no collection of antique marbles, or even of antique sculpture from Roman Britain. So far as is known, he had little of the connoisseur's more general interest. It also seems that, for the most part, he took a close interest in Romano-British inscriptions only for a very few years, a period that coincides with William Camden's fundamental revisions to his *Britannia*.[5]

The influence of Camden was paramount, though in the end it was Cotton, not Camden, who acted as the preserver – of Roman inscriptions as he did of coins and later manuscripts. In due course, Camden was to pay Cotton ample compliments in his *Britannia*; but Cotton was his pupil and protégé. They were born twenty years apart, Camden in 1551 and Cotton in 1571; and at Westminster School, where the two met perhaps for the first time, it was as master and schoolboy. Thus by the time that Cotton graduated from Jesus College, Cambridge, in 1586, Camden was already well embarked on the succession of excursions to different parts of England undertaken as preparation for writing his *Britannia*, of which the first edition, a plain small and all but unillustrated octavo, appeared in 1586.[6] In 1578 Camden was in East Anglia, searching out Roman antiquities on the coast at Caister, north of Great Yarmouth, and considering the history and nomenclature of Colchester and Maldon in Essex.[7] In 1582 he journeyed to Yorkshire, returning via Lancashire. In 1590 he went to Wales; in 1596 to Salisbury and Wells.[8] Then in 1597 he fell seriously ill. By that year, four editions of *Britannia* had appeared in London, and one in Frankfurt, the most recent edition in a quarto format rather than octavo. In each, he incorporated his most recent observations and so increased each succeeding edition. The edition of 1594, the first in quarto rather than octavo, marked a departure in setting out the various inscriptions assembled by Camden within simple typographical frames. A further edition appeared in 1600, dedicated now to Queen Elizabeth rather than William Cecil. This edition introduced an ornamental title-page (engraved by William Rogers)[9] and a group of further engravings including Roman coins and a view of Stonehenge. It also depicted a Roman altar, the first in an English printed book and the most obvious first fruit of a site visit.

In 1599, Camden and Cotton had travelled to the north of England, where they spent much of the second part of the year investigating the Roman Wall and its associated sites. The results were as dramatic as any in the history of British archaeology. Between them, the two men set out for the first time the materials for an ordered account of the Roman occupation of northern Britain, based not simply on literary evidence but, now, on surviving archaeological remains. In Cumberland, the two came across an altar in the possession of John Senhouse. Camden had first recorded it, by report, in 1587, in the second edition of *Britannia*: but now he and Cotton had been able to see it. What previously he had recorded simply as a transcription was transformed in 1600 into an engraving (after a drawing by Cotton) displaying in views from two angles not only the inscriptions, but also the distinctive decoration on each side of this exceptional survival:

Their standeth erected a most beautifull foure square Altar of a reddish stone right artificially in antique worke engraven five foote or there abouts high, with an inscription therein of an excellent good letter: But loe the thing it selfe all whole, and every side thereof, as the draught was most lively taken out by the hand of Sir *Robert Cotton of Connington*, Knight, a singular lover of antiquity, what time as he and I together, of an affectionate love to illustrate our native country, made a survey of these coasts in the yeare of our redemption 1599. not without the sweet food and contentment of our mindes.[10]

The next edition of *Britannia*, published in 1607, broke with several of the conventions hitherto followed by Camden. The new edition, in folio, was greatly increased in content as well as in bulk. County maps, by Saxton and Norden, established a tradition for Britain that had already been explored overseas by Ortelius and Mercator. And whereas earlier editions had recorded a few inscriptions from Roman Britain, the journey to the north enabled Camden now to record dozens, many of them illustrated as woodcuts, while also repeating the Senhouse engraving. An English version by the indefatigable translator Philemon Holland (he had already translated Livy, the younger Pliny, Plutarch, Suetonius and Ammianus Marcellinus) followed in 1610.

In 1586, Camden made it clear to his readers that his book owed much of its origin to the challenge issued by Abraham Ortelius, whose *Theatrum orbis terrarum*, with its large and detailed maps, had first appeared in 1570. Ortelius's encouragement of those willing to investigate the geography and place-names of early Britain dated at least from his first meeting with Camden, probably on a visit to London in 1577.[11] As a result, though Camden dedicated the first edition of *Britannia* to Sir William Cecil, he attributed to Ortelius the inspiration and established this fact in his first sentence. Ortelius's own brief account, with Johannes Vivian, of an *Itinerarium per nonnullas Galliae Belgicae partes* had been published in 1584, just two years before the first edition of *Britannia*, and he gave a copy to Camden.[12] His own interests in inscriptions and early marbles were well known.[13] But as each succeeding edition of *Britannia* appeared, the extent of Camden's sense of collaborating in a loosely organized international project became ever more prominent. Their literary predecessors were works such as Mazzochi's *Epigrammata antiquae urbis* (Rome, 1521), or Petrus Apianus and Bartholomaeus Amantius's *Inscriptiones sacrosanctae vetustatis* (Ingoldstadt, 1534). Judging by the number of surviving or recorded copies, the latter was better known in late Elizabethan England.[14] Slightly more recently, there was Fulvius Ursinus's *Imagines et elogia virorum illustrium* (Rome and Venice, 1570), whose postscript, with its allusions to the libraries of ancient Rome and its stress on portraiture as an accompaniment to reading, spoke directly to Cotton's later organization of his own library. Above all, there was Smetius and Lipsius's *Inscriptionum antiquarum, quae passim per Europam, liber* (Leiden, 1588),[15] to whose design the modern *Corpus Inscriptionum Latinarum* owes its appearance.

The search for antique inscriptions in the last two decades of the sixteenth century reached across Europe in the wake of the *Inscriptionum antiquarum liber*, itself the product of the pursuit of classical antiquities by scholars such as Justus Lipsius or (especially for coins) Hubert Goltzius. Within two years, Marcus Welser had produced an account of inscriptions at Augsburg, *Inscriptiones antiquae Augustae Vindelicorum*, published by the Aldine press at Venice in 1590; and within four, Adolphus Occo saw published at Heidelberg his *Inscriptiones in Hispania repertae* (1592). Above all, the appearance at Amsterdam in 1602–3 of Janus Gruterus's *Inscriptiones antiquae totius orbis Romani*, fruit of collaboration with Lipsius and Welser and dedicated to the Emperor Rudolf II, proffered the discipline a direction that has been broadly followed ever since. By the publication of the new edition of *Britannia* in 1607, many of the comparative and international characteristics of epigraphy had been thoroughly established. In an earlier version, *Britannia* had been published at Frankfurt in 1590. However, for much Continental scholarship, as for Britain, the crucial edition was that of 1607, in which so many inscriptions were recorded in print for the first time. *Britannia* retained much of its original character; but it also offered materials to modern Europe, and for a much wider tradition of classical learning. In its systematic mapping it took on something of the character of an atlas; and in its details of inscriptions it became in this respect (as it was to remain for many years) the best record of Roman Britain. Both in the manner of presenting its several different kinds of contents, as well as in the nature of the contents themselves, it took on an international air.

The journey undertaken by Cotton and Camden in 1599 followed the spirit of like-minded antiquaries in the fifteenth and earlier sixteenth centuries. In Italy, Flavio Biondo had similarly sought out classical antiquities, in the itinerary that provided the shape for his *Italia illustrata* in 1474. The brief excursion made in 1464 round the southern shores of Lake Garda by Felice Feliciano, Andrea Mantegna and two of their friends pursued a comparable goal.[16] In England, Camden and Cotton's most celebrated predecessor was John Leland, whose more comprehensive but less organized investigations, usually on behalf of Henry VIII, were recorded in part in the *Laboryouse journey & serche ... for Englandes antiquitees, geuen of hym as a newe yeares gyfte to Kynge Henry the viij* (1549). Leland's example will have been familiar to Camden, others' less so. But whatever the literary predecessors or the more pressing practical reasons for undertaking such a journey at this point, Camden was following an established tradition, if not a very well-worn path, as he recorded their itinerary in the 1607 edition of his *Britannia*, working in the notes of his various correspondents as he did so.

Camden's reflections on his expedition in 1599 did not mark the first time he had thought of such study as 'sweet food' for the mind. In his preface 'To the reader', he explained that while there were some who would condemn and 'avile' the study of antiquity, as a 'backe-looking curiosity', his purpose was rather to address those who appreciated the appropriateness of understanding the history of one's country: 'well bread and well meaning men, which tender the glory of their native Country: and moreover could give them to understand that in the studies of Antiquity, (which is alwaies accompanied with dignity, and hath a certain resemblance with eternity) there is a sweet food of the minde well befiting such as are of honest and noble disposition.'[17]

For Camden, this meant in particular a proper understanding of Roman Britain, the *Britannia* of his title. With the departure of the Romans came the 'down-fall or destruction of Britain', 'this most lamentable ruine & down fall of Britain' (p. 107). But while much might be gathered out of Tacitus, Suetonius and Bede, the principal evidence lay in the material survivals visible on the landscape, whether roads, ruined remains, coins or sculpture. As he returned to revise each succeeding edition of his book, so his strong sense of place became ever more frequently demonstrated. In particular, as he recorded his journeying and observations so *Britannia* acquired some of the qualities of a travel book rather than an historical monograph. It was also a chorography of Elizabethan England, of rivers from which antiquities had to be fished, of castles and hovels, of robbers and generous hospitality. While much of his time, naturally, was addressed to local landowners, at Carvoran, in Northumberland, he was helped by 'a poore old woman that dwelt in a little poore cottage'.[18] Camden and Cotton's visit to Busy Gap, near Housesteads, had to be cut short because of the dangers they were risking: 'a place infamous for theeving and robbing; where stood some castles, Chesters they call them, as I have heard (but I could not with safety take the full survey of it, for the ranke robbers there about).'[19] In its way, it was as lively an account of discoveries on land as those written by voyagers to countries overseas.

In the sixteenth century, most of the visible Roman remains were in the north of the country. Although towns such as Silchester were known (and to some extent investigated), many of the major sites that are now familiar in the southern half of the country were not discovered, or their nature or extent appreciated, until the eighteenth century and later. By far the most celebrated was the Roman Wall, its date uncertain but its interest none the less for the division that still separated England and Scotland until 1603, even if that division now lay somewhat farther to the north. Lying in a thinly populated region, it had been little quarried for building stone, unlike the fate of Roman sites in southern England. In these circumstances, and given its recognized importance, it seems surprising that Camden did not attempt to visit it until his journey with Cotton in 1599. Until then, he relied on correspondents.

On this journey, Cotton saw for the first time many of the inscriptions that he was gradually to assemble at Conington, his country residence just off the Great North Road between Huntingdon and Peterborough. An altar at Old Carlisle (*RIB* 897; Davies 11)[20] had been long known, and had featured in the first edition of *Britannia*. Others were either more recent discoveries, or were now found for the first time; but as many of the stones concerned were easily visible, 'discovery' meant more perhaps to Camden and Cotton than to the local inhabitants who acted as their guides. The recording of such stones was another matter entirely, to which both men, and several of their correspondents, devoted considerable energy. The worn and folded scraps of paper, and the longer, more formal, reports among Cotton's manuscripts, bear witness to a process that took those concerned on constant field trips.

Eventually Cotton was to possess stones from old Carlisle in Cumberland and from Risingham, High Rochester, Halton Chesters and (probably) Housesteads in Northumberland. The last two were both sites on the Wall itself, and each yielded a single object for Cotton's collection. But numerically, and sometimes massively, most of the stones came from Risingham, or *Habitancum*, a fort beside Dere Street near where it crossed the River Rede at the foot of Redesdale, fifteen miles and more north-west of Corbridge on the modern road to Jedburgh. High Rochester, or *Bremenium*, from which Cotton obtained an inscribed altar, was yet further north. Much earlier in the century Leland had also explored the North Tyne valley and Redesdale, though not in pursuit of specifically Roman antiquities. His remarks on the subject were concerned instead with numbers of parishes and churches, though he noted also the 'witriding men othar wvyse theues of that Englishe marche'.[21] Camden's interests, pursued with the enthusiastic and knowledgeable help of Reginald Bainbrigg, the headmaster of Appleby School, reached well beyond the Roman Wall, into country still unfamiliar to and remote from the ordinary circles of London and Continental scholarship. It is difficult now to ascertain exactly how much Camden and Cotton saw on their visit to the north in 1599, and how much Camden relied on Bainbrigg (whom he did not meet in 1599) for his account later published in *Britannia*. Following his first visit to the wall in 1599, Camden pursued his interest with vigour. 'I can not find wordes, to expresse my Love towardes you,' wrote Bainbrigg, 'who take suche paines, that our countrie maie Lyve for eu*er*.'[22] Meanwhile Oswald Dykes, a friend of Bainbrigg, was arranging for stones to be shipped south to Cotton: 'I returned home through Bowes from Carlile, and if I cold either for mony or gould haue had ye Stone yt shold haue bene brought yow to Newcastle er yow remoued from thence.'[23] Perhaps this was the altar (*RIB* 730; Davies 12) from Bowes that eventually found its way to Conington and Cambridge.[24] As for other sites, where Cotton enjoyed considerable success, Bainbrigg himself seems only to have visited the upper Tyne and Redesdale in 1601; but as he saw and recorded most of the stones that Cotton obtained from these sites, some at least of the stones cannot have been removed until after August that year.[25] The absence of a description by Bainbrigg is probably an unreliable guide. But it is worth noting that he omitted both a large altar (*RIB* 1215; Davies 4) and a much smaller fragment of another (*RIB* 1237; Davies 3): it is conceivable that by the time he surveyed Risingham the stones had already been removed. Cotton himself seems to have made a separate expedition after 1599 to this area in particular, if Camden is to be read literally: 'Moreover, these inscriptions also were here found: for which with others, we are to thanke the right worshipfull *Sir Robert Cotton of Connington* Knight, who very lately both saw them copied them, out and most kindly imparted them to this work.'[26]

Cotton's skills as a draughtsman were those of a practical amateur. Certainly they were thought sufficient not only to be acknowledged by Camden on various occasions, but also to figure obliquely in the dedication to Henry Peacham's first book, *The Art of Drawing* (1606). Peacham was then still a Huntingdonshire schoolmaster, and a compliment was clearly expected for the occasion; but it had the ring of truth: 'How necessarie a skill drawing or painting is; & how manie waies the use thereof is required, none knoweth better than your selfe.'

Meanwhile among his other helpers in forming his collection, Cotton also engaged the interest of William Howard, of Naworth Castle (between Carlisle and Haltwhistle), who in 1608 was still working to remove stones despite the wet weather of that summer, and trying to persuade him to take another northern tour.[27]

The river bed at Risingham produced two altars, one of which recorded the name perhaps of a German soldier on his first tour of duty at the fort; each was transcribed for *Britannia* (*RIB* 1225, Davies 5; *RIB* 1226), though the second (and less interesting) is now lost. Principal among the half-dozen stones that Cotton obtained from the site was a large dedication slab, erected by a cohort from Gaul and depicting Mars and Victory (*RIB* 1227; Davies 1). To Camden, this 'far surmounteth all the rest for curious workmanship, a long table ... artificially engraven, set up by the fourth Cohort of the Gauls Horsmen, and dedicated to the sacred Maiestie of the Emperours'. Bainbrigg gave it pride of place in his account of the site, the inscription 'worth the sight for fyne and cunning workmanship', though he mistranscribed the first line. Others since have echoed his and Camden's enthusiasm, and it has remained the most reproduced of Cotton's inscriptions. It is now split down the middle, as it was by the time it was depicted in Horsley's *Britannia Romana* (1732), though the 1607 woodcut and the engraving in Speed's *Theatre* in 1611 (fig. 1) both show it as a single piece.

From Housesteads, where dangers from thieves cut short Bainbrigg's investigations ('Est in Locus infestus excursionibus, et frequentioribus Latrociniis expositus ad praedandum'),[28] Cotton obtained only one stone, an altar over three feet tall and clearly recording the name of a prefect stationed there, with the date of its erection (*RIB* 1589; Davies 9).

Bainbrigg's notes, preserved mostly among Cotton's papers, formed a principal source for Camden; but they were to be set beside the stones that Cotton caused to be removed south. Cotton's acquisition of some at least of his collection from the Roman frontier can thus be dated between the late summer of 1601 (when Bainbrigg undertook his tour) and 1607, the date of the first revision of *Britannia* to incorporate all these various elements: Camden and Cotton's own tour of 1599, Cotton's drawings, Bainbrigg's notes of a little later, and remarks about the several stones now in their new home at Conington.

Although most of Cotton's collection came from the vicinity of the Roman Wall in Cumberland and Northumberland, and it has been valued principally for the sake of this by most later generations, his net also drew in some examples from elsewhere. Close to hand in London, Sir William Cecil had in his garden a tombstone found at Silchester:[29] it passed into Cotton's possession probably after 1600, if the slight change to Camden's wording at this point of his text is any guide. But of Roman London itself no inscription is known to have been discovered before 1669, when a limestone tombstone almost seven

Fig. 1. A group of Cotton' stones, including (centre) a dedication slab from Risingham, and two altars from (bottom left) Housesteads and (bottom right) Carvoran. From Anne of Denmark's copy of John Speed, *The Theatre of the Empire of Great Britaine* (London, 1611): the original is coloured. *By kind permission of Trinity College, Cambridge*

feet tall was dug up in the course of rebuilding St Martin's church, Ludgate Hill.[30] Two stones in Cotton's collection came from Yorkshire – an altar from Bowes (*RIB* 730; Davies 12), commemorating the restoration of a bath-house following a fire at the end of the second century, and a slightly smaller altar (*RIB* 627; Davies 13) from Greetland, just south of Halifax. Both were recorded in time for the second edition of *Britannia* in 1600, and were then still in their native county: Cotton acquired them soon afterwards.[31] Finally among the stones that have survived, the Cotton collection included a milestone from near Conington itself, probably from Ermine Street (*RIB* 2239; Davies 15).

By comparison with the inscriptions to be found in other parts of the Roman Empire, these stones were unsophisticated – their lettering often cut roughly with a pick, rather than properly chiselled, while the soft local stone has meant that even reasonably competent work has been poorly preserved. In Yorkshire, Lancashire, Cumberland and Northumberland there was little marble to hand; it was an area where, in the words of Collingwood and Richmond, 'the many excellent monumental stones are largely swamped by small and crude dedications or tombstones cut by poorly trained masons for half-barbarian soldiers'.[32]

But crude or no, these inscribed stones provided documentation about Roman Britain of a quality unmatched by any other kind. Although the stones that Camden and Cotton concerned themselves with were easily, if not conveniently, visible without major excavation, few of them had been recorded before the first edition of *Britannia* in 1586. It was not from difficulty, but simply because few people had taken an interest. British antiquarian curiosity lagged over a century behind Italy in this respect, and it needed Camden both to prompt a search and to introduce this aspect of a remote province in the Roman Empire to the Continent. By the time that the much revised edition of his book came out in 1607, over seventy inscriptions had been recorded, mostly in the north but also in Bath and Caerleon. No contemporary catalogue of Cotton's collection survives (there is little reason why there should ever have been so formal a document), and the collection was damaged before it came to Cambridge in 1750; but even in this surviving portion, and in what can be reconstructed, Cotton possessed almost a quarter of all the inscriptions then recorded in Britain.

The inscribed stones from northern England offered an evocative accompaniment to the maps in Speed's *Theatre of the Empire of Great Britaine* (1611), with its engraved title-page depicting a flamboyantly dressed Roman, Saxon, Dane and Norman, dominated by an ancient Briton. Speed's text was heavily dependent on *Britannia*, though he also drew on local knowledge to extend his accounts of many parts of the country. Cotton's library provided a crucial resource for the project, providing the originals for the town maps of Carlisle and Berwick. But to the margins of the maps of Cumberland and Northumberland were added depictions of Roman antiquities. For Cumberland these included Senhouse's unusually decorated altar (*RIB* 812), that had appeared as engraved illustrations to *Britannia* in 1600 and again in 1607. And in the margin of Northumberland were Cotton's perhaps most valued stones, including the large dedication slab from Risingham and altars from Carvoran and Housesteads (fig. 1).

Cotton's close interest in Speed's project is to be seen in the proofs of the maps, a few sets of which seem to have been circulated before publication. For the final edition, the map of Huntingdonshire, Cotton's own county, was much altered. The engraving and printing of the long series of maps, quite apart from the time needed to print a long text, seem to have occupied Speed from perhaps as early as 1607, though the date when he was occupied with the Roman portions (of the text and engravings) is not clear. He also depended on Cotton for the woodcuts of the Roman coins. 'This day,' he wrote to Cotton at one point, 'not only I, but the printers prese doth expect the returne of my last sent leaves. I well hope they are come though not so early delivered the daye beinge yonge. I have sent you all the coppy of the Romane storye, desyring your corrections and augmentations both matter and monuments of your altars so farr as to your wisdome shall seme mett.'[33] In postscript to another letter, Speed reminded Cotton, 'Remember to signify the formes of your Altars.'[34] The proof of the map of Northumberland does not include inscriptions on his stones: they were only added once Cotton had had an opportunity to amend any readings, or even (as in the case of the altar from Carvoran, *RIB* 1792; Davies 10) compose what had been lost.[35] In the case of at least this last inscription, the publication of Speed provided an opportunity for Cotton to reconsider the texts that had been published in 1607.[36]

Britannia was the work of Camden, not of Cotton, though without the latter it would not have assumed many of the features of a *corpus inscriptionum* that characterized the editions of 1607 and later. The fashion by which Cotton, already important to Camden, had by that year become the custodian of inscriptions as well as of manuscripts, was often revealed in the revisions made to the 1607 edition. Not only had the notes taken in 1599 been set in order, and collated with information received from others; but Cotton had also followed up many of these records, and succeeded in gathering in a substantial proportion of the inscriptions for his own collection. In the light of the several changes of ownership recorded between the editions of 1600 and 1607, it sometimes seems almost as if the archaeological and historical research report became the collector's list of desiderata. In the edition of 1600, published soon after their return from the north, Cotton was amicably alluded to as 'priscae antiquitatis admirator, & indagator studiosissimus'.[37] By 1607, many if not most of the inscriptions gathered as a result of their itinerary had been set up at Conington. The stones' presence here provided Camden with an opportunity to acknowledge – not in a preface, but hidden in the body of the book – the help given by their owner:

qui praeter caeteras virtutes bonarum artium admirator & indagator summus, conquisitis undique monumentis venerandae Antiquitatis hic instituit armarium, e quo mihi in his tenebris lumen pro singulari humanitate saepenumero praetulit.[38]

Or, in Philemon Holland's translation:

who over and beside other vertues, being a singular lover and searcher of antiquities, having gathered with great charges from all places the monuments of venerable antiquitie, hath heere [i.e.

at Conington] begunne a famous Cabinet, whence of his singular courtesie, he hath often times given me great light in these darksome obscurities.[39]

Camden's remark about 'great charges' was not made wantonly, for the expense of bringing these cumbersome and heavy stones to Conington must have been considerable: one altar from Risingham was almost four feet tall, while the dedication stone erected by the Gaulish cohort was almost six feet long and over two feet high. In Northumberland, the North Tyne offered the beginning of a route by water – a route busy with colliers that offered a ready passage down the east coast.[40] It was fortunate that Coningon lay on the edge of the Fens, and was therefore then accessible via Wisbech and the River Nene from the North Sea. In 1768, Richard Gough recorded a tradition that 'a boat or two' of such stones had been lost at sea *en route* to Conington.[41]

The collaborative nature of Cotton and Camden's work, alluded to by the latter in his last few words, was acknowledged in print on more than one occasion. More fulsomely, when in 1605 Camden issued (anonymously) his *Remaines … concerning Britaine* he dedicated it to Cotton. Their collaboration seems to have continued subsequently, for when in 1615 Camden saw published his *Annales Rerum Anglicarum, et Hibernicarum, Regnante Elizabetha*, taking the narrative down to 1589, the royal warrant to publish was issued to both men, 'our wellbeloued servants Sr Robert Cotton Knight and Baronett, and William Camden Clarenceux one of oure Kings of Armes':

Oure pleasure is that you cause forthw[th] according to our direction to you so much of the historie of England in Latin as we haue perused to be printed and published that is from the yeare of our Lord 1558. vntill the end of the yeare a thousand fiue hundred eighty-eight. And this our commaund shalbe your warrant.[42]

Only Camden's name appeared on the title-page as author; but the drafts and the preparatory materials survive in the Cotton library. While the two men may not have collaborated as authors, Cotton certainly seems, on this evidence, to have had a role as consultant – as he had for the 1607 edition of *Britannia*. But in the spring of 1615 he was at the centre of royal policy,[43] and the authority to the two men jointly may perhaps have been more political than reflective of authorship.

The work of Camden and Cotton on Roman Britain, encouraged by Ortelius, was inspired by historical, linguistic and perhaps political curiosity. They were studying in two related disciplines, each designed to explore the records of the past. One was comprehensive, the tradition that reaches down to the *Corpus Inscriptionum Latinarum*, and which has been already mentioned. The other discipline was related, but more restricted. In 1600 Camden published, anonymously, the first survey to be printed of the inscriptions in Westminster Abbey, its title-page graced with quotations from Euripides and St Augustine, of which the latter read, 'Sepulchrorum memoria magis vivorum est consolatio, quam defunctorum utilitas' – justification that might be taken to apply also more widely to some historical research.[44] This manifestation in print of interest in national epitaphs, shared also amongst his fellow antiquaries, was further encouraged by

Camden's return to the subject in a more general way in his *Remaines* in 1605. In turn, it led to work by others, not least on St Paul's Cathedral; but most of all in John Weever's ambitious *Ancient Funerall Monuments*, published in 1631 and offering a survey of modern equivalents of one small aspect of Cotton's collection. Like Camden and Cotton, Weever looked over his shoulder to overseas: 'Having seen ... how carefully in other Kingdomes, the Monuments of the dead are preserved, and their Inscriptions or Epitaphs registred'. Neither Camden nor Cotton had been able to pay substantial attention to epitaphs in 1599. Thanks to the nature of their material, they had had no dealings at all with Christian inscriptions. But Weever, having seen the work of antiquaries such as Lorenz Schrader, Nathan Chytraeus and Franz Sweerts (all published within a few years round the turn of the century), set out 'to collect such memorials of the deceased, as were remaining as yet undefaced; as also to revive the memories of eminent worthy persons entombed or interred, either in Parish, or in Abbey Churches; howsoever some of their Sepulchres are at this day no where to be discerned; neither their bones and ashie remaines in any place to bee gathered. Whereupon with painefull expences (which might have beene well spared perhaps you will say) I travailed over the most parts of all England, and some part of Scotland.'[45] He never completed his ambitious project to cover the entire country, embarked on with the substantial folio published in 1631 – shortly after Cotton's death. Through Augustine Vincent, Keeper of Records in the Tower of London, Weever met Cotton, who made his library available to this project comparable, if restricted to Christian inscriptions, to what he had pursued with Camden, and of which he had examples to show at Conington. It was Weever who paid posthumous tribute to Cotton in the phrases that have been so much quoted since: 'this worthy repairer of eating-times ruines, this *Philadelphus*, in preserving old Monuments, and ancient records: this Magazin, this Treasurie, this Store-house of Antiquities'.

It is perhaps foolhardy to attempt to suggest subjects other than history in which the influence of Cotton's collection may be discerned. As we have seen, there were already published collections of inscriptions, albeit not in much substance (until the 1607 edition of *Britannia*) for Roman Britain. But the example of Ben Jonson offers circumstances in which a direct influence is at least possible. In 1603, in order to escape the plague that made London too dangerous, Jonson spent part of the year at Conington, in the company also of Camden.[46] Cotton had by then acquired many of his stones; he may even that very year have been erecting or altering the summer-house in which to set them. The three men had a common background in Westminster School, and Jonson made occasional use of Cotton's library. It was a friendship of shared interests. Jonson has left no direct comment on the Roman inscriptions and altars; but in January 1606 he and Inigo Jones presented the masque *Hymenaei* at Whitehall to mark the wedding of the Earl of Essex and Frances Howard, daughter of the Earl of Suffolk, with a cast including the Earl of Arundel. The occasion was heavy with potential, marking an alliance of considerable political importance in an entertainment of literary, musical and visual splendour – the first masque of its kind. The action revolved round the inscription on a Roman altar:

> *On the night of the masques (which were two, one of men, the other of women) the scene being drawn,*
> *there was first discovered an altar, upon which was inscribed in letters of gold,*
>
> IONI. OIMAE. MIMAE.
> UNIONI
> SACR.[47]

Jonson himself emphasized the mythological and historical allusions in his text. But the centrepiece, the inscription on the altar (which seems to have been an invention), he left unattributed to any archaeological or literary inspiration. For the altar at least, we may reasonably look to Cotton's collection at Conington. Cotton certainly took an interest in the production, for there survives an account of it, of unusual value because it is so detailed, sent to him by John Pory.[48]

Jonson's inscription was inspired by Rome, although the political and dynastic implications in the circumstances of this production were vastly removed from the stones set up by soldiers from a foreign country, facing barbarians and deep in the countryside on the Scottish border. But the detail of the colouring in gold is of some interest. Insofar that Roman inscriptions in Britain were coloured at all, it was in red.[49] For gold, one must look rather to the gaudy decoration on sculpture contemporary with Cotton himself, and particularly on monuments to the dead. In this manner, contemporary practice was conflated with archaeological inspiration. The 1607 edition of *Britannia* was to prove a popular book to be coloured for special readers, albeit not usually with gold. In a royal environment (if not, on the occasion of *Hymenaei*, for a specifically royal masque), gold was an obvious addition. It was to reappear as decoration for Roman sculpture a few years later, in the special copy of Speed's *Theatre of the Empire of Great Britaine* (1611) prepared for Anne of Denmark – the copy that, above all others, acknowledged the supreme importance and influence of the Queen and her court as patrons of the arts.[50]

Cotton continued his pursuit of Roman inscriptions and antiquities for several years after 1599, though he had accumulated most of his collection within less than a decade after that. In 1622 he was still enquiring after stones in Yorkshire, and heard from Roger Dodsworth:

I thought good to aduertise you that, since I saw you, I haue vsed such means, as my health would permitt, to enquire after such things as you desired, I haue been att Cattericke when I was informed of 2 Romaine monumentes wch were found in a°. 1620. and are now in my lo: of Arundells keeping. I haue found, a peece of a round piller, att Ribblecester, being almost half a yeard thick, & half an ell in height, wth such letters, on the one side thereof, as I haue figured in this pap*er* inclosed. I saw, ther, a little table of free stone, not half a yeard square, wth the portraitures of 3 armed men cutt therin, but no inscription att all theron. I saw likewise 2 other stones of the nature of slate, or thicke flaggs some yeard square, wth fretted antique workes engrauen on them, wthout any letters. I shalbe very gladd that my uttmost indeauors, might availe

117

to requite the least of many respects you have done vnto me. And do desire you to signify your pleasure what you would haue mee to doo touching the promisses, and I shall not faile to do my best in effecting thereof.[51]

Cotton continued to make notes, both in his copy of the 1607 edition of *Britannia* and independently;[52] but by the mid-1620s his collecting of the stones themselves was over.

Throughout the time that he had concerned himself with inscriptions from Roman Britain, Cotton seems never to have been tempted to enlarge his interests to encompass either inscriptions or stone sculpture from other countries. In this he was quite unlike the most celebrated of those who, during his lifetime, began to turn their attention to antique sculpture from the Continent.[53] For although (as Dodsworth mentioned) the Earl of Arundel took some interest in inscriptions from Roman Britain, he took much greater interest in sculpture from overseas. In his chaplain, William Petty, Arundel found an ideal agent, unscrupulous and wonderfully successful in collecting antiquities from Greece.[54] But in Petty also there was a link between Cotton the antiquary and Arundel the connoisseur. For Petty had been born in Soulby, a village between Appleby and Kirkby Stephen; and his early interest in such matters had been fostered by Bainbrigg himself. Thus the Roman antiquities of Westmorland became the training ground for the more alluring south of Europe. British connoisseurship of the later seventeenth and eighteenth centuries was to look back to Arundel. It might have looked back with gratitude also to the influence of Cotton and his circle. But by the eighteenth century Bainbrigg's part in the history of collecting had been temporarily forgotten by most people. There was also a further relevant link between the circles of Cotton and Arundel. Not surprisingly, when Henry Peacham, another of Arundel's protégés, addressed the question of antiquities in *The Compleat Gentleman*, he paid especial deference to his patron's collection, and placed much greater emphasis on the collecting of sculpture than he did on inscriptions – excusing his few lines with a reference to the work of Lipsius. By the time he wrote, Peacham was no longer a schoolmaster in Huntingdonshire, near enough to Cotton to dedicate to him *The Art of Drawing* (1606). Instead, he was in London.[55]

At Conington, Cotton devoted considerable energy to improving the main dwelling house, including the addition of a long gallery. He arranged his stones in an octagonal summer-house in the garden just to the north (fig. 2).[56] It proved to be a place of safety for only a relatively short period; for whereas his descendants took a keen interest in the fate of his manuscripts, until ownership passed to the nation in 1700, the stones were kept in a building that was neglected. The main house having become ruinous, the fourth baronet, Sir John Cotton (d. 1731) pulled most of it down, and converted the remainder into a farmhouse.[57] William Stukeley, making a pilgrimage to the estate, found himself 'concern'd to see a stately old house of hewn stone large and handsom ly in dismal ruin, the deserted *lares* and genius of the place fled'.[58] In 1731, James West found the house desolate, but much worse, the Roman stones broken and trodden under foot.[59] It is impossible now to tell how much was lost in this period. A little later, John Horsley

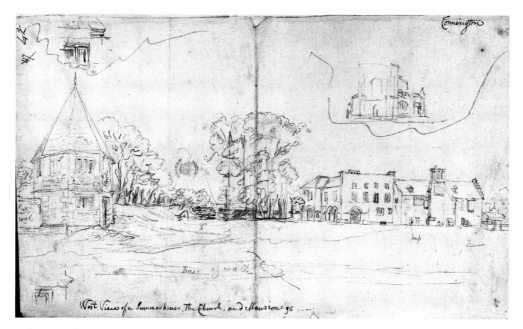

Fig. 2. The summer-house, church and mansion at Conington, drawn by J. Carter, 1798.
Add. MS. 29936, f. 40

visited the place in preparation for his *Britannia Romana*, and found a similar state of ruin, made the more poignant because he himself came from Morpeth in Northumberland. Unlike Stukeley, he remarked on the inscriptions in particular:

When I looked round me in that summer-house, and observed particularly the inscriptions which had been removed from our own county and neighbourhood, it gave me for some time a great deal of pleasure; tho' it was afterward much abated, by reflecting on the ruinous state both of the house and inscriptions.[60]

In this condition they remained until the middle of the century. They had always been separated from the manuscripts in London, and they formed no part of the settlement of the manuscripts on the nation in 1700. As the family preferred to live three miles away at Denton, there was little to encourage active interest other than among antiquaries. But it remained for the sixth baronet, also Sir John, who succeeded to the title in 1749, to set the seal on the collection. When he succeeded to the title he had no male heirs, and he died three years later. Thus the line ended with him, and there was much sense in his arranging for the collection to be sent elsewhere. It is ironic that he presented it to Trinity College, Cambridge, only three years before the British Museum Act of 1753 brought together the Cotton, Harleian and Sloane collections of manuscripts – and of Sloane much else besides.

It seems not to be recorded who it was that persuaded Sir John Cotton to present the collection to Trinity College. At that date, as for many years afterwards, it was still thought that Sir Robert Cotton had been at the College: this erroneous belief reached at least as far back as Thomas Fuller, and it had been repeated by Thomas Smith in his introduction to the catalogue of the Cotton library published in 1696.[61] More recently, Sir Robert Cotton, fifth baronet (d. 1749), had been at Trinity. But if Sir John, sixth baronet, had sought advice, the name of the college would soon have emerged independently. In 1738 Roger Gale, editor of Antoninus's *Iter Britanniarum* (1709) had presented to Trinity the great collection of manuscripts assembled by himself and his father Thomas Gale, Dean of York. In 1745 Beaupré Bell of Narford Hall, in the west of Norfolk, and one of the most knowledgeable antiquaries in the locality, whose interests in the Fens and in Roman coinage were well known, left his collection of coins to the College. That he did so was due in no small part to his close friend the Vice-Master of Trinity, Richard Walker. Ever since it had been erected, Wren's great library had invited donations, and under the Master, Robert Smith, the College was encouraging gifts of objects besides books. The first of the busts by Roubiliac – of Newton, Bacon, John Ray and Francis Willoughby – were placed in the Wren in the mid-century.

Far too heavy for the inside of the library room itself, on the first floor, the stones were instead placed at the foot of the staircase. Although Horsley had included engravings in his *Britannia Romana*, the College soon commissioned the local engraver P. S. Lamborn to prepare a special engraving, conveniently showing the collection on a single sheet (fig. 3): he arranged the stones in conformity to contemporary taste, suggesting the shape of a ruined building. This was presented to the Society of Antiquaries in May 1759, though it was never included in the series for which it was perhaps designed, the *Vetusta Monumenta*.[62] It shows the slabs and altars as if they were all set into the wall, as was never the case at Trinity and as cannot (in view of the size of some of the altars) have been the case at Conington. Though he conveyed a much better impression of the stones as damaged antiquities, Lamborn generally followed his predecessors in ignoring the three-dimensional bulk of most of the stones, and thereby diminished their material interest as vehicles for the inscriptions that they bore. Most importantly, he recorded the condition of the stones as he saw them, and was content to record damage rather than what had been seen (or even imagined by Cotton) in the past. He was not always correct in his readings, but some measure of the damage of which sundry eighteenth-century witnesses at Conington spoke can here be estimated.[63] Quite aside from this attempt at a suitably balanced composition of antiquity, the plate is of some independent importance for institutional reasons. For the College, and for the first time, the stones were gathered together for publication as a collection in their own right. Both Camden and Horsley had divided them up (as the *Corpus Inscriptionum Latinarum* was to do in the nineteenth century) according to what they believed to be their original localities. In 1588, Lipsius had divided his corpus according to topic or group of people; but now, in eighteenth-century Cambridge, a clear statement was being made as a curatorial matter.

The stones quickly became a feature to be noticed by tourists; and both tourists and

Fig. 3. Engraving by P. S. Lamborn depicting Cotton's Roman inscriptions soon after their arrival at Trinity College, Cambridge, in 1750. The arrangement is Lamborn's fancy. *By kind permission of Trinity College, Cambridge*

121

members of the College were reminded of the history of the collection by a stone tablet affixed to the wall:

Haec Romanorum Monumenta a Cl. Viro Rob. Cotton Bart. in Angliae Partibus Boreis undique conquisita, & in Villam suam de Cunnington in Agro Hunting. comportata; huc tandem anno 1750 suis Sumptibus transferenda curavit Joh. Cotton de Stratton Baronettus.[64]

Apart from the engraving prepared by Lamborn, the stones continued to attract other artists. Horsley had been the last to illustrate them all, even if he was not always clear in his own mind as to what his illustrations were intended to represent. Of the largest and most celebrated (it will be recalled that it graced Speed's map of Northumberland, heightened in gold in the copy of Anne of Denmark), he remarked:

Much of the sculpture here perhaps is without any farther design, than to please the fancy of the sculptor. A friend imagines the two birds to be a heron and a cock, and conjectures that it may denote the *Roman* victory by sea and land. The stork sometimes appears on medals at the foot of *Piety*, but neither of these birds seem to resemble a stork. Possibly the birds, little fish, and flower-pot, signify only in the general, abundance both of provisions and pleasures. EQ (with a single Q) in this and some other inscriptions seems to be *equestris* rather than *equitum*, and it is *cohors equestris* in *Pliny*. But since *cohors equitum* and *cohors equestris* are equally good, as well as *tribunus militum* and *tribunus militaris*; I have yielded so far to custom, as to retain the word *equitum* in the reading...[65]

So, in confusing what are now thought to be a crane and a goose for a heron and a cock, his friend failed to identify the figures of Victory and of Mars with his associated bird – not so much general abundance as, more convincingly, gods of specifically military significance.

In the 1590s there had been only a few collections of this kind. In the north of England, John Senhouse of Netherhall was exceptional; pieces from his collection were the first to be illustrated in *Britannia*. At Appleby, Bainbrigg possessed a collection, though much of it seems to have been in the form of copies, and some was pure invention.[66] In the south, the stone resting in Sir William Cecil's London garden was, as we have seen, eventually acquired by Cotton. By the early eighteenth century, interest in Roman Britain had been maintained not least by successive editions and revisions of *Britannia*, first by Camden himself, and in 1695 by Edmund Gibson, whose new and expanded version was further extended in 1722. This remained the standard until Richard Gough brought out an even further annotated version, now spread over three folio volumes, in 1789. But nonetheless, in 1732 Horsley still remarked that in Northumberland there were no very large collections, even at Housesteads, where altars and inscriptions lay exposed to the weather: Horsley's own collection, drawn mostly from Northumberland, was modest. And although John Warburton (whose map of the county appeared in 1716, and who in 1753 was to produce *Vallum Romanum*, a shamelessly derivative account of more modest dimensions than Horsley's folio, for the use of visitors to the Wall) had possessed the largest collection of all, he had not acted responsibly. Horsley claimed that 'he unhappily broke many of them in order to make them more portable, and so carried off only that part of the stone which had the inscription. By this means it has happened that many of the stones collected by him are only faces of altars, and in several instances the inscriptions themselves have suffered damage by this unhappy frugality.'[67] We may recall Camden's acknowledgement of the expense to which Cotton had been put in assembling his own collection, in which whole stones had been removed, rather than merely in part. By the date Horsley wrote, Warburton's collection had already passed, with that of Christopher Hunter, to the cathedral library at Durham. In the north-west, there were substantial collections at Naworth and Ellenborough, and smaller ones elsewhere. In Horsley's view some of the 'most curious' had been removed to Conington, where he thought that these in particular had suffered by the neglect of which he and others wrote. In Yorkshire, there were small collections in several places, 'two or three fine ones' at Rokeby and Mortham near Greta Bridge, and Thoresby's collection remained at Leeds. But for Yorkshire also, Horsley again alluded to Conington. Elsewhere in the country, and apart from a few scattered stones in Monmouthshire, Horsley could think only of Bath, where the inscriptions were 'in a great measure defaced'.[68] More importantly, there were also two collections in particular in Scotland, one belonging to Sir John Clerk (1684–1755), friend of Roger Gale, and the other to the University of Glasgow.

In other words, it was clear from this survey that Cotton's collection still remained, a century after his death, not only the most important for Northumberland, but also one of the finest assembled anywhere in the country. To set the collection in the College library was thus in several respects satisfactory. It ensured that they would no longer be victims of the weather, falling masonry, or casual neglect. It also introduced a collection – the first such in a British university other than Glasgow – into an environment that offered literary support, a context in which they could be both valued and further compared with other forms of evidence. Just as the British Museum was founded (within three years of the arrival of these stones in Cambridge) on a combination of libraries and other artefacts, so the Wren Library was perceived as an appropriate complement to these stones. Museum and library combined, as an extension of the familiar concept of a library that consisted of not only manuscripts and printed books, but of coins and portrait sculpture as well. The stones were soon to prove but the first collection to depart from books and the other media already represented in the Library. Sixteen years later, the Countess of Bute presented the celebrated inscription from fourth-century Athens, discovered by the Earl of Sandwich in a lumber yard in Athens, brought to England in 1739, and the subject of an illustrated memoir in 1743.[69] In very different vein, and of crucial importance for their documented detail, a selection of the ethnographical specimens gathered during Captain Cook's first voyage was presented by the Earl of Sandwich in 1771. In the second half of the eighteenth century the Wren Library began to assume the appearance of a museum, a tendency that developed into a profuse flowering by the end of the nineteenth century. At first it did so in the absence

Fig. 4. The stones on display in 1969, at the foot of the staircase in the Wren Library. The portrait busts are not part of the collection. *By kind permission of Donald W. Insall and Associates*

of any museum in Cambridge, for the Fitzwilliam Museum was not founded until the nineteenth century.

It was not alone in such diversity. When in 1803 Edward Daniel Clarke, Professor of Mineralogy, brought back from the eastern Mediterranean a collection of antique sculptures, these were set up in the most obvious space available, the vestibule of the then University Library, in the Old Schools.[70] With the opening of the Fitzwilliam Museum in 1848 there was an opportunity to improve the arrangements for Clarke's and other gifts, and the collection was removed there in 1865. But the Cotton collection, a group of very different character and collected for very different purposes, remained with various later gifts of sculpture from the Mediterranean in their eighteenth-century home, much to the disapproval of Adolf Michaelis, who remarked of them, 'It is much to be wished that the latter should be deposited in the first-mentioned locality, all the more as their present place of preservation is utterly unworthy of them.'[71] Roman altars and inscriptions, already dealt with in the *Corpus Inscriptionum Latinarum* were not Michaelis's principal concern, though he alluded to them; instead, his descriptions concentrated on the assortment of Greek marbles that had by then joined the so-called Sandwich marble. In 1880, the local guidebook briefly described the attractions before the visitor to one of the finest libraries in the world sighted any book at all: not only the Cotton altars and other stones but, also on the ground floor, the stone from Athens, some Babylonian bricks and an Egyptian mummy. Further up the stairs was a case displaying

124

the dried body from a cave in Tenerife; and at the top was another containing the collection from Cook's voyage. Only then might the visitor enter the Library itself, and see the books.[72]

Cotton's collection remained in this position until 1969, when it was agreed as a part of the restoration of the Wren Library that they should be removed from a corner that was perilously crowded (fig. 4), and offered to the University's Museum of Archaeology and Anthropology. There they remain today, as a part of a more general display of Roman Britain. At no time in their history had they formed a physical part of Cotton's library. Their great weight would have meant more adjustments to his buildings than he was perhaps prepared to countenance. It would have been easier to transport the stones to Cotton House, by the Thames in Westminster, than to Conington, on the extreme edge of the Fens. But whatever Cotton's reasons for keeping these two elements of his collections apart, it is clear that he thought of the stones primarily as inscriptions, and therefore as literary evidence. As such, they were an intellectual, albeit not a physical, partner of his library.

1 R. G. Collingwood, *The Archaeology of Roman Britain*, rev. by Sir Ian Richmond (London, 1969), p. 193.

2 Joan Evans, *A History of the Society of Antiquaries* (Oxford, 1956), pp. 1–13; May McKisack, *Medieval History in the Tudor Age* (Oxford, 1971), pp. 155–69; Kevin Sharpe, *Sir Robert Cotton, 1586–1631: history and politics in early modern England* (Oxford, 1979), pp. 28–32.

3 J. C. T. Oates, *Cambridge University Library: a history. From the beginnings to the Copyright Act of Queen Anne* (Cambridge, 1986), pp. 139–41; David McKitterick, *The Library of Sir Thomas Knyvett of Ashwellthorpe, c. 1539–1618* (Cambridge, 1978), pp. 15–16.

4 Samuel Ball Platner and Thomas Ashby, *A Topographical Dictionary of Ancient Rome* (Oxford, 1929), pp. 242–5; Ernest Nash, *Bildlexikon zur Topographie des antiken Rom*, 2 vols. (Tübingen, 1961–2), vol. i, pp. 283–6, 450–55; Donald Strong, *Roman Art* (rev. ed.; Harmondsworth, 1980), p. 144.

5 In 1621, long after Cotton had ceased to take an active interest in collecting Roman inscriptions in Britain, he received a letter from William Bolde, in Florence: 'Heare I finde daily by the death of one of other good antiquityies (both for medalls and statues) to be sould; but dare not venter on any, my abilitie beinge to weake, and to by them for you ...' (BL, Cotton MS. Julius C. III, f. 27).

6 Sir Thomas Kendrick, *British Antiquity* (London, 1950), p. 151, has claimed the depiction of a medieval inscription in Lewes to be 'the first archaeological illustration in England'.

7 Camden to Ortelius, 24 Oct. 1578: A. Ortelius, *Epistulae, Ecclesiae Londino-Batavae Archivum*, vol. i (Cambridge, 1887), ed. J. H. Hessels, pp. 181–3. On Camden, see especially the biography prefaced to his *Epistolae*, ed. T. Smith (Oxford, 1691); Sir T. Kendrick, *British Antiquity*, pp. 143–56; and Stuart Piggott, 'William Camden and the *Britannia*', *Proceedings of the British Academy*, xxxvii (1957), repr. in his *Ruins in a Landscape* (Edinburgh, 1976), pp. 33–53.

8 Trinity College, Cambridge, MS. R.5.20, f. 2r; William Camden, *Epistolae*, appendix, p. 85.

9 For Rogers as an engraver, see A. M. Hind, *Engraving in England in the Sixteenth & Seventeenth Centuries. I. The Tudor Period* (Cambridge, 1952), pp. 258–80.

10 William Camden, *Britain*, trans. Philemon Holland (London, 1610), p. 769. Notwithstanding the criticisms of Holland's translation that have been made by Edmund Gibson, among others, all translations from Camden are from this edition.

11 F. J. Levy, 'The Making of Camden's *Britannia*', *Bibliothèque d'Humanisme et Renaissance*, xxvi (1964), pp. 70–97.

12 The copy given by Ortelius to Camden is now in the Beinecke Library, Yale University: see

Richard L. DeMolen, 'The Library of William Camden', *Proceedings of the American Philosophical Soc.*, cxxviii (1984), pp. 327–409, at p. 391.

13 See for example Carolus Brooman to Ortelius, written from Brussels, 11 Sept. and 12 Oct. 1590, the first forwarding a docket from Phillippus Winghe. Winghe's first surviving letter to Ortelius is dated from Rome, 24 Dec. 1589: Hessels, pp. 450–3.

14 I have not attempted a census, but the Arundel-Lumley-Prince Henry copy of the latter is now in Trinity College, Cambridge (see Sears Jayne and Francis Johnson (eds.), *The Lumley Library; the Catalogue of* 1609 (London, 1956), p. 153), and the copy belonging to Andrew Perne, Master of Peterhouse (d. 1589), is still in his own college library: see Elisabeth Leedham-Green, *Books in Cambridge Inventories*, 2 vols. (Cambridge, 1986) and David McKitterick (ed.), *Andrew Perne: Quatercentenary Studies* (Cambridge Bibliographical Soc., 1991). One copy in the University Library (M*.3.27(C)) has a Cambridge provenance, dated 1587, though the name of the owner is now cut off. By contrast, only one copy of Mazzochi's book survives in Cambridge, at Gonville and Caius College, given to the College by William Barker, former fellow and friend of Caius, in 1579: none is to be found in the Lumley library or in the Cambridge inventories. If Camden owned either book, they do not seem to have survived: see Richard L. DeMolen, 'The Library of William Camden', pp. 327–409. The question of whether the list of books in BL, Add. MS. 35213 represents Cotton's library, or part of it, is addressed in Colin G. C. Tite, 'A Catalogue of Sir Robert Cotton's printed books?', *British Library Journal*, xvii (1991), pp. 1–11, and reprinted below, pp. 183–93. The general literary background is discussed in John Sparrow, *Visible Words: a Study of Inscriptions in and as Books and Works of Art* (Cambridge, 1969) and more widely in Roberto Weiss, *The Renaissance Discovery of Classical Antiquity* (Oxford, 1969), especially ch. 11, 'The Rise of Classical Epigraphy'.

15 Among the Cambridge copies, that at Peterhouse belonged to Andrew Perne.

16 Giovanni Mardersteig, *Felice Feliciano Veronese. Alphabetum Romanum* (Verona, 1960). The activities of early Italian epigraphists are surveyed in Weiss, *The Renaissance Discovery of Classical Antiquity*.

17 Camden, *Britain*, f. *1v.

18 Ibid., p. 800. The transcription in *RIB* 1801 relies on this episode. References to *RIB* are to R. G. Collingwood and R. P. Wright, *The Roman Inscriptions of Britain. I. Inscriptions on Stone* (Oxford, 1965).

19 Camden, *Britain*, p. 800.

20 References to Davies are to Glenys Davies, 'Sir Robert Cotton's Collection of Roman Stones: a catalogue with commentary', in the present volume, pp. 129–67.

21 John Leland, *Itinerary*, ed. Lucy Toulmin Smith, 5 vols. (London, 1906–10), vol. v, p. 62. Smith explains that 'witriding' = 'outriding'.

22 Bainbrigg to Cotton, 27 Mar. 1600: BL, Cotton MS. Julius F. VI, f. 337r.

23 Dykes to Cotton, 9 Jan. 1599/1600: BL, Cotton MS. Julius C. III, f. 162r.

24 *Britannia* (1600), p. 658 (still in Yorkshire); (1607), p. 595 (in Conington).

25 F. Haverfield, 'Cotton Julius F. VI. Notes on Reginald Bainbrigg of Appleby, on William Camden and on some Roman inscriptions', *Transactions of the Cumberland & Westmorland Antiquarian & Archaeological Soc.*, n.s., xi (1911), pp. 343–78, reprints most of Bainbrigg's notes.

26 *Britain*, trans. Holland, pp. 803–4.

27 Howard to Cotton, 13 Aug. 1608: BL, Cotton MS. Julius C. III, f. 210. This proved a prolonged affair: see Peter Riddell to Cotton, ibid., f. 314.

28 BL, Julius MS. F. VI, f. 330.

29 *RIB* 87; *Britannia* (1586), p. 135.

30 *RIB* 17, now in the Ashmolean Museum.

31 *Britannia* (1600), pp. 613, 658; (1607), pp. 563, 595.

32 Collingwood and Richmond, *The Archaeology of Roman Britain*, p. 195.

33 Speed to Cotton, 5 Sept. 16[ ]: BL, Cotton MS. Julius C. III, f. 355.

34 Speed to Cotton, n.d.: ibid., f. 358.

35 I have used the proof copy of Speed's *Theatre* (1611) in Cambridge University Library, Atlas 2.61.1. For Speed, see especially A. M. Hind, *Engraving in England in the Sixteenth & Seventeenth Centuries. II. The Reign of James I* (Cambridge, 1955), pp. 67–90, and R. A. Skelton, *County Atlases of the British Isles, 1579–1850* (London, 1970), pp. 30–44. Neither

records the proof copy at Cambridge University Library or the coloured copy at Trinity College prepared specially for Anne of Denmark.

36 Cotton's deliberations on the text of the inscription from Carvoran (*RIB* 1792) are to be seen in the marginalia to his annotated and corrected copy of the 1607 edition of *Britannia*, now Bodleian MS. Smith 1 (SC 15608).

37 *Britannia* (1600), p. 446.

38 *Britannia* (1607), p. 368.

39 *Britain*, p. 500.

40 Oswald Dykes to Cotton, 9 Jan. 1599/1600: BL, Cotton MS. Julius C. III, f. 162.

41 [Richard Gough], *Anecdotes of British Topography* (London, 1768), p. 8.

42 Trinity College, Cambridge, MS. R.5.20, f. 112v, dated 25 Feb. 1614/15. The book was entered in the Stationers' register on 21 March, 'licensed to be printed by the Kinges Maiesties letter vnder the Signett Directed to Sir Robert Cotton knight and Master William Camden, Clarenceux'.

43 Sharpe, *Sir Robert Cotton*, pp. 131–2. The background to Camden's *Annales* is summarized by E. Maunde Thompson in the *D.N.B.*, s.v. Camden.

44 [William Camden], *Reges, Reginæ, Nobiles & alii in Ecclesia Collegiata B. Petri Westmonasterii Sepulti* (London, 1600). In 1600, the Elizabethan antiquaries heard several papers on epitaphs: see Thomas Hearne (ed.), *A Collection of Curious Discourses*, 2 vols. (London, 1771), vol. i, pp. 228–60.

45 John Weever, *Ancient Funerall Monuments* (London, 1631), 'The author to the reader'.

46 Ben Jonson, *Works*, ed. C. H. Herford and Percy Simpson (Oxford, 1925–52), vol. i, p. 139.

47 Stephen Orgel and Roy Strong (eds.), *Inigo Jones. The Theatre of the Stuart Court*, 2 vols. (London, 1973), vol. i, pp. 105–6. See also D. J. Gordon, '*Hymenaei*: Ben Jonson's Masque of Union', *Journal of the Warburg and Courtauld Institutes*, viii (1945), pp. 107–45.

48 Cory to Cotton, 7 Jan. 1606: BL, Cotton MS. Julius C. III, ff. 301–2, printed in Jonson, *Works*, vol. x, pp. 465–6, and (slightly truncated) in Strong and Orgel, *Inigo Jones*.

49 See, for example, *RIB* 321, from Caerleon.

50 This copy, bound by John Bateman, who did much work for the royal library, is now in Trinity College, Cambridge, among a substantial

group of books deriving from the household of Prince Henry. Its survival, in these circumstances, lends support to the thesis by Leeds Barroll, 'The Court of the First Stuart Queen' in Linda Levy Peck (ed.), *The Mental World of the Jacobean Court* (Cambridge, 1991), pp. 191–208, respecting the cohesion of the circles of the Queen and Prince Henry. For Bateman, see M. M. Foot, *The Henry Davis Gift: a collection of bookbindings*, 2 vols. (London, 1978–83), vol. i, pp. 35–49.

51 Roger Dodsworth to Cotton, 16 Feb. 1622, BL, Cotton MS. Julius F. VI, f. 314r. The two stones from Catterick were perhaps *RIB* 725 and 727, both now lost.

52 Bodleian Library, MSS. Smith 1 (*Britannia*) and 84 (notebook of inscriptions).

53 The first edition of John Selden's *Marmora Arundelliana* was published in 1628.

54 D. E. L. Haynes, *The Arundel Marbles* (Oxford, 1975); David Howarth, *Lord Arundel and his Circle* (New Haven, 1975), pp. 127–48; Michael Vickers, 'Greek and Roman Antiquities in the Seventeenth Century', in Oliver Impey and Arthur MacGregor (eds.), *The Origins of Museums. The Cabinet of Curiosities in Sixteenth- and Seventeenth-Century Europe* (Oxford, 1985), pp. 223–31.

55 Alan R. Young, 'A biographical note on Henry Peacham', *Notes and Queries*, May–June 1977, pp. 214–7.

56 *V.C.H., Hunts.*, vol. iii, p. 145, with reproductions of a map of *c.* 1595 and a drawing by J. Carter, 1798, depicting the summer-house, church and much altered mansion, BL, Add. MS. 29936, f. 40.

57 *V.C.H., Hunts.*, vol. iii, p. 145.

58 William Stukeley, *Itinerarium Curiosum. Centuria I* (London, 1724), p. 77.

59 Thomas Hearne, *Remarks and Collections*, ed. C. E. Doble, etc. 11 vols. (Oxford Historical Soc., 1885–1921), vol. xi, pp. 10–11.

60 John Horsley, *Britannia Romana* (London, 1732), p. 182.

61 Thomas Fuller, *The History of the Worthies of England* (London, 1662), Huntingdonshire, p. 52. In fact he had been at Jesus College: see Robert Sinker, 'Sir Robert Cotton', *Notes and Queries*, 6th ser., vi (1882), p. 533.

62 Trinity College, Muniments, Junior Bursar's accounts, 1758–9; William Stukeley, *Family*

Memoirs, 3 vols., Surtees Soc. (Durham, 1882–7), vol. ii, p. 52. Two hundred copies were printed. Stukeley records that the stones had been kept in a 'gallery' at Conington, but he can hardly have meant the gallery erected in the seventeenth century, and there is no reason to suppose that he meant anything more than the summer-house.

63 A contemporary manuscript catalogue, including remarks on condition compared with that in Camden's time, is in the college library, MS. Add.aa.7, accompanying a copy of the engraving.

64 *Cantabrigia Depicta* (Cambridge, [1763]), p. 86.

65 Horsley, *Britannia Romana*, p. xv.

66 *Britannia* (1610), p. 761; Haverfield, 'Cotton Julius F. VI', p. 349. For examples of Bainbrigg's inventions, see *RIB* 2356, 2357.

67 Horsley, *Britannia Romana*, p. 182.

68 Ibid.; [Richard Gough], *Anecdotes of British Topography*, pp. 8–9 follows Horsley in his details in this respect.

69 John Taylor, *Marmor Sandvicense* (Cambridge, 1743).

70 Edward Daniel Clarke, *Greek Marbles brought from the Shores of the Euxine, Archipelago, and Mediterranean, and deposited in the vestibule of the Public Library of the University of Cambridge* (Cambridge, 1809).

71 Adolf Michaelis, *Ancient Marbles in Great Britain* (Cambridge, 1882), p. 241.

72 *The Railway Traveller's Walk through Cambridge*, 6th ed. (Cambridge, 1880), pp. 70–1. These cases were slightly rearranged a few years later, but all remained in the staircase pavilion.

SIR ROBERT COTTON'S COLLECTION OF ROMAN STONES: A CATALOGUE WITH COMMENTARY

GLENYS DAVIES

FIFTEEN stones collected by Sir Robert Cotton, originally housed at Conington, then at Trinity College, Cambridge, are now kept by the Cambridge University Museum of Archaeology and Anthropology. The extent of the original collection is not certain, but there is no evidence to suggest that any significant part of it has been lost, although it may well have suffered some damage, and Horsley laments the poor conditions the stones were kept in when he visited Conington (some time before 1732). Most of the stones came from Roman sites in the north of England: six from Risingham and one from High Rochester north of Hadrian's Wall, three from sites on or close to Hadrian's Wall, and one each from Old Carlisle, Bowes and Greetland (fig. 1). It is likely that most of these were seen by Camden and Cotton in 1599 when they made their visit to the Wall, and no doubt Cotton's desire to collect the stones and his choice of the stones to be collected date to that period. In addition, a tombstone from Silchester (no. 14 below) was acquired from Lord Burghley, and the one milestone in the collection (no. 15) appears to have been found somewhere close to Cotton's estate at Conington near Peterborough.

Cotton has left no explanation of why he chose these particular pieces: clearly there were others known in his day and seen by him which he did not collect. The task must have been considerable: most of the stones are bulky and heavy, and the distances to be covered great, suggesting some enthusiasm on Cotton's part for the project. The trip to the North was evidently also of great importance to Camden, providing him with a substantial body of new information: it is significant that most (nine) of Cotton's stones were not included in previous editions of Camden's *Britannia*, but appear for the first time in the 1607 edition.[1] Camden's commentary makes it clear that for him the main interest of such stones was the inscription: there is little indication of the form the stones took, or interest in the decoration, even in the case of the highly ornate building slab from Risingham (no. 1). It was Horsley (in his *Britannia Romana* of 1732) who first attempted to represent the monuments as objects and not just as inscriptions, including illustrations showing the inscription in position on the stone, and drawings of decorative features. (Compare Camden's illustration of the altar to Hercules, no. 4 below, with that of Horsley – figs. 8 and 9, and see fig. 16.) The inscriptions, however, have continued to be

Fig. 1. Sketch map showing approximate find-spots of the Cotton stones. The numbers are those used in the text: 1–6 Risingham; 7 High Rochester; 8 Halton Chesters; 9 Housesteads; 10 Melkridge/Carvoran; 11 Old Carlisle; 12 Bowes; 13 Greetland near Halifax; 14 Silchester; 15 Conington/Peterborough

the main focus of interest for scholars in these stones, and many of them have played a valuable if small part in the reconstruction of the history of Roman Britain.

The stones have all been published before, some to a greater extent than others, and all appear in Collingwood and Wright's collected *Roman Inscriptions in Britain*, vol. i (*RIB*). So why publish them again? Clearly one intention is to reassemble his collection of stones in a volume devoted to various aspects of Cotton's life. I am not an epigraphist, and will not be offering new readings, or new interpretations, of the inscriptions, as these have been mulled over by others far more competent in this field. More attention will be paid to the physical aspects of the stones, something which has tended to be neglected in earlier works (partly because until quite recently the stones have been embedded in walls at Trinity College with only their front surfaces showing). E. J. Phillips made an excellent start on this for the few pieces included in his volume of the *Corpus Signorum Imperii Romani* series. My intention is also to put the stones in context, both that of the Roman world in which they were made, and that of antiquarian study and scholarship: because these stones were known from the time of Camden onwards we can see in their study by Camden, Horsley and twentieth-century scholars the evolution of ideas and knowledge about Roman Britain.

Risingham

Six of Sir Robert Cotton's Roman stones come from Risingham, a fort built in the area north of Hadrian's Wall, at the point where Dere Street crosses the River Rede. It appears to have been built under Lollius Urbicus in the mid second century A.D. after Hadrian's Wall was built, to act as an outpost. At this stage its garrison was a cavalry unit of Gauls: they erected the dedication slab that is now part of the Cotton collection (no. 1 below). At the end of the second century the fort appears to have been abandoned or destroyed, but it was rebuilt in the early third century with more massive defences: at this stage in its history its garrison was the first cohort of Vangiones, which appears in inscriptions 2 and 4 below. The fort's Roman name was 'Habitancum', as is shown by inscription no. 5. Although this has not been excavated, it clearly had a civilian settlement (*vicus*), as numerous civilian tombstones have been found: one of these is in Cotton's collection (no. 6). It is not certain why Cotton collected so many stones from this particular site: it seems from Camden's words that Cotton had both seen and copied the inscriptions at some time (presumably on the tour of 1599) before he had them removed to Conington. However, *RIB* lists several other stones from the site known to Bainbrigg and Camden that were presumably not removed by Cotton, and which have subsequently been lost, which raises the question of why Cotton took some but not others. Certainly, the only three stones decorated with figures in his collection came from here, and he may have made a deliberate choice from what was available: on the other hand, there may have been practical constraints. Camden appears to have found the area interesting not just because of its antiquities, but also for its folklore traditions: he comments on the meaning of the name of the town, and the folk memory of the god

Fig. 2. Dedication slab (no. 1)

Mogons (see under no. 5). It is worth quoting the beginning of his entry on Risingham (as it appears in the 1695 English version, col. 850):

A little lower the river *Rhead* washes (or rather has almost wash'd away) another Town of venerable antiquity, now call'd *Risingham*; which, in the old-English and high Dutch languages, signifies as much as *Giants-Town*, as *Risingberg* in *Germany* is *Giants-Hill*. There are here many remains of antiquity.

1. *Dedication slab to the divine spirits of the emperors* (figs. 2–4)

From Risingham, where it was seen in 1601 by Bainbrigg, and probably by Cotton and Camden in 1599.[2] Horsley says that when he visited Conington (before 1732) the slab was placed above the summer-house door. Now on display in the Cambridge University Museum of Archaeology and Anthropology, inv. D 1970.5. Of local buff sandstone.
Ht. 72.5 cm.; w. 145 cm.; d. 14 cm.

A large rectangular slab designed to be set in a wall (original position not known). It is now split into two diagonally down the centre, cutting across the inscription, but this does not appear in early drawings of the stone (compare Camden's with Horsley's – see figs. 3 and 4). A triangular piece of stone is missing at the top of the break, and there is also a piece missing at the bottom left corner. The stone is generally chipped at the edges and corners, and there is some weathering, particularly noticeable on the figures. The front only is worked: the sides and back were left rough.

The decoration can be divided into three basic sections: a central framed inscription flanked by figures in niches. The inscription is in an octagonal frame which itself is inside

132

Fig. 3. Woodcut of dedication slab (no. 1) as it appears in the 1695 edition of Camden's *Britannia*. This illustration first appeared in the 1607 edition.

Fig. 4. Drawing of dedication slab (no. 1) by Horsley, reproduced in his *Britannia Romana* p. 192 N.29

a square frame with flanking pelta (i.e. half-moon shaped) shields. The square frame has plain mouldings: the octagonal frame is arranged so that four of its points overlap the centre of each side of the square frame. Each side of the octagonal frame is decorated with a stylized vegetable/floral motif, arranged so that sections lying opposite one another have the same design. Proceeding anticlockwise from the top centre, sides *a* and *e* have a scale-like design of laurel leaves and berries pointing toward the centre; *b* and *f* have a rinceau with rosettes in the four circular fields created by the tendrils; *c* and *g* have long leaves arranged in threes pointing into the centre, with berries in the spaces between the leaves; *d* and *h* have jagged-edged leaves with central ribs (possibly meant to be oak, but if so rather elongated), also pointing towards the centre. In the four corners between the octagonal and square frames is a single rosette: earlier in this century Richmond noticed that although the other three are five-petalled, the one in the bottom left-hand corner has only four petals.

Flanking the square frame are pelta-shaped designs: these act as linking motifs between the central panel and the side niches, as the points of the shields overlap the nearer pilasters of the niches. Below the pelta on both sides are knot designs (a *nodus Herculeus*). Above are heads: on the left a three-faced unbearded male head with two eyes and three noses and mouths, on the right a single male head, balding with a full curly beard, possibly the head of Hercules according to Phillips. Rope-like cable designs separate the peltae from the fields above and below.

To the left is an arch supported by pilasters: the capitals are decorated with roundels, and the arch has a series of parallel grooves running round it. Inside the arch is a Victory. She stands hovering with her right foot on a globe and her left foot in the air. She wears a garment that appears to be a chiton with a long overfall: the skirt billows around her legs and the drapery slips down under her right breast, so it is exposed. In her right hand she holds out a wreath, and in the crook of her left arm she has a palm branch. She is winged and her hair is arranged in a bun. She stands in a frontal pose, but with her head turned slightly towards the centre of the relief. The Victory stands on a base (which is also contained within the archway): this is decorated with a band of a geometric design (squares) along the top. Below in the main field of the base is a long-legged, long-necked bird facing towards the left. This has been identified as a crane, and it may, as Camden says, be moving towards a fish, but this feature is no longer distinguishable. Behind it is a design of three incised circles, said to be a 'conventional fruit tree' by Richmond, but this identification does not seem very likely.

To the right of the inscription panel is a niche, again with an arched top and flanking pilasters, but this time the back of the niche is concave, like an apse. The pilaster capitals are decorated with a series of mouldings which continue as a cornice round the inside of the niche, behind the figure of Mars. He again stands on a base decorated with a similar upper border and a bird: this faces to the right but is more squat than the bird on the other base, and it may be a goose. In front is a cantharos-shaped vase containing fruits or flowers. Mars stands in a frontal pose, with his weight on his right leg and the other slightly bent. He wears a tunic and boots with a modelled cuirass and a military cloak fastened on his right shoulder, a baldric and a sword, and on his head a helmet with a plume. His right hand is raised to lean on a spear, while his left is lowered to rest on the rim of a round shield resting at his left side: the inside of the shield is visible, decorated with radiating strigillations. He too faces to the right, away from the inscription. The inscription reads:

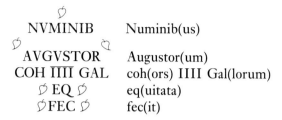

NVMINIB	Numinib(us)
AVGVSTOR	Augustor(um)
COH IIII GAL	coh(ors) IIII Gal(lorum)
EQ	eq(uitata)
FEC	fec(it)

To the Deities of the Emperors: the fourth cohort of Gauls, part-mounted, set this up.

The fourth cohort of Gauls was a part-mounted unit of 500 men: it was stationed at Castlehill on the Antonine Wall under Antoninus Pius, but was at Risingham later in the Antonine period, after the withdrawal from the Antonine Wall, and in the third century was at Chesterholm (Vindolanda).[3] The inscription alludes to a period of joint imperial rule, presumably therefore the rule of Marcus Aurelius with either Lucius Verus or Commodus (A.D. 161–9 or 176–80). The dedication is to the 'Numen' of the emperor, a subtle concept which allowed the people of Rome to honour their emperors while stopping short of actual deification of a living man. Deification of an emperor after his death was quite common, but openly worshipping a living emperor was not acceptable, at least in the Western provinces. Worship of the Numen, the guiding spirit or deity of the emperor, was allowed, though more commonly in conjunction with other deities: the appearance of the Numina of the reigning emperors on their own here is unusual.[4]

This slab is by far the most elaborately decorated of Sir Robert Cotton's stones, and the iconography and style have been variously interpreted. Bainbrigg, who failed to understand the inscription commented:

This inscription was worth the sight for fyne and cunning workmanship, Numinius was engraven in stone in his cote armure with his shield and target ...[5]

Camden, however, did not attempt to identify the motifs, and it is Horsley who provides the first analysis. In his own person he suggests that the two heads were 'probably designed for those of the emperors referred to by the inscription', and he recognizes Mars and Victory as such: 'The Victory treads on a globe, and no doubt the general meaning is, that the emperor had warred successfully, and gained the victory over the whole world.' However, he also ascribes some more imaginative interpretations to 'a friend', who

imagines the two birds to be a heron and a cock, and conjectures that it may denote the Roman victory by sea and land ... Possibly the birds, little fish, and flower-pot, signify only in the general, abundance both of provisions and pleasures.[6]

135

As for the rest, 'The other ornaments seem only to be such as pleased the fancy of the sculptor.'

The figures of Mars and Victory are standard in the military repertoire, and appear again on a later building slab from Risingham (*RIB* 1234) where they may be copied from this earlier stone. The other motifs are more unusual. Richmond pointed to the association of Victory and Mars with the birds represented beneath them: the goose was the sacred bird of Mars, and he sees the crane as a 'bringer of good luck', and its association with Victory as specifically Gallic, citing shields represented on the arch at Orange. Phillips takes this further, pointing out that the crane is sometimes associated with the Gallic deity, Esus, who was equated with Mars, and suggesting it may have been an emblem of the cohort. The fish he sees as a reference to water and therefore Mars's healing powers, and the bowl of fruit possibly as alluding to his function as a god of fertility. The triple form of the head on the left is a Celtic feature, and presumably relates to the Gallic origin of the unit: Phillips suggests it may represent a Gallic version of Hercules. In fact Phillips sums the iconographic repertoire up as follows: 'Thus the slab reflects the native religious beliefs of the Cohors IV Gallorum and provides a remarkable example of Celtic religious symbolism on an official military dedication.'[7]

Richmond and Phillips are less in accord over the style of the carving: Phillips comments that 'Despite the Celtic symbolism, the style of the sculpture is wholeheartedly classical', while Richmond states that 'the style of the decoration is thoroughly Gallic. It exhibits the same horror vacui, and the same jumble of by no means clearly related motifs, as Gallic Samian ware'. In fact, such a method of composition, juxtaposing individual motifs represented in different scales, is every bit as Roman as it is Gallic, and can be seen on many monuments of funerary art in Italy itself. The individual motifs would be chosen from a pattern book, and the finished sculpture would derive its individuality and its meaning from the sculptor's choice and combination of standardized motifs. Phillips also points to the fact that the carving at the right end of the relief is better than that on the left, and surmises that either two sculptors worked on the stone, or that a single sculptor began work at the right end but ran out of time, and had to rush the left end.

Bibliography: *RIB* 1227; *CIL* VII 1001; Camden, *Britannia* (1607), p. 664; Horsley, pp. xv and 237, Northumberland no. LXXXVIII, ill'd on p. 192 N. 29; Richmond, *HN* XV, pp. 134–5, no. 18, pl. opp. p. 80; Phillips, *CSIR*, pp. 72–4, no. 215, pl. 55; M. Henig, *Religion in Roman Britain* (London, 1984) p. 70, fig. 24.

2. *Building stone* (fig. 5)

From Risingham, where it was seen by Bainbrigg in 1601, and possibly by Camden and Cotton in 1599.[8] Now in the store of the Cambridge University Museum of Archaeology and Anthropology, inv. D 1970.7.
Ht. 65 cm.; w. 76.5 cm.; d. 24.5 cm.

136

Fig. 5. Building stone (no. 2)

The stone appears to be broken at the top and has large chips missing down the right side, but is reasonably intact along the bottom and left edges. The back and sides have been left roughly worked. The worked area on the front consists of an inscription in a plain moulded frame: this is surrounded on three sides (sides and bottom) with a crude but effective design of parallel grooves carved into the stone, arranged vertically below and horizontally at the sides. The surface of the stone above the inscription panel is now weathered, but appears to have been left plain and smooth. The top edge of the stone may originally have been curved, but it is no longer possible to be sure of this. Despite the damage to other parts of the stone the surface of the inscription is good, and tool marks are still visible. The letters are well cut and spaced, and the inscription is easy to read.

COH Ī VANG	Coh(ors) I Vang(ionum)
FECIT CVRANTE	fecit curante
IVL PAVLLO TRIB	Iul(io) Paullo trib(uno)

The first cohort of Vangiones made this under the direction of the tribune Iulius Paullus.

It is not now known which building this stone came from, or what exactly it was that the first cohort of Vangiones built under Iulius Paullus. The Vangiones were a cavalry unit, one thousand strong, originally raised in the upper Rhineland:[9] they were stationed at

Fig. 6. Altar (no. 3)

Risingham in the early third century when the fort was rebuilt with massive defences, and are mentioned in a number of inscriptions from the site. Another building inscription from the South Gate of the fort (*RIB* 1234) names them as the unit responsible for the restoration of the gate and can be dated precisely to A.D. 205–7 from the names of the emperors provided. The man named as the commander (tribune) of the unit, Iulius Paullus, also appears on another inscription from Risingham (*RIB* 1213) as the dedicator of an altar to Hercules.

Bibliography: *RIB* 1241; *CIL* VII 1007; Camden, *Britannia* (1607), p. 662; Horsley, p. 236, Northumberland no. LXXXII, ill'd on p. 192 N. 28; Richmond, *HN* XV, p. 131, no. 3.

3. *Lower part of an altar mentioning the Emperor Caracalla* (?) (fig. 6)

From Risingham (seen there in 1599?).[10] Now in the store of the Cambridge University Museum of Archaeology and Anthropology, inv. D 1970.16. Local buff sandstone.
Ht. 61 cm.; w. 50 cm. at base; d. 19 cm. at the top, 22.5 cm. at the base.

The upper part of the altar is missing, and the back of the altar has been cut away so that only the front now remains (it is not known whether this happened in earlier times or was done when the altar was removed to Conington). The surviving parts are quite badly damaged, with signs of burning on the front. The altar has a deep base with a series of plain mouldings at the top. Above is an inscription in a frame, although most of the frame on the sides has been chipped away. The base with its complex set of mouldings also appears on the sides of the altar: above this there is a vertical moulded frame at the front edge, and the rest of the surviving field is roughly pecked. There appears to have been a wreath carved in relief on the left side: this was cut in half when the back of the altar was removed. Despite its present dilapidated state the altar appears to have been a high quality piece, and would have been quite large when complete.

Only the lower four lines of the inscription are really legible now, though the line above is partly visible. This is indicated in the drawing in *RIB*, although the text records six lines as follows:

IMP CAES M	imp(eratoris) Caes(aris) M(arci)
AVR ANTON	Aur(eli) Anton[i]-
NI PII AVG M	ni Pii Aug(usti) M(arcus)
MESSORIVS	Messorius
DILIGENS TRI	Diligens tri-
BVNVS SACRVM	bunus sacrum.

... (*for the welfare?*) *of the Emperor Caesar Marcus Aurelius Antoninus Pius Augustus. The tribune Marcus Messorius Diligens* (*set up*) *this sacred offering.*

The emperor named in the inscription is probably Caracalla, who ruled from A.D. 211 to 217, but it could refer to Marcus Aurelius.

Bibliography: *RIB* 1237; *CIL* VII 1005; Camden, *Britannia* (1607), p. 663; Horsley, p. 237, Northumberland LXXXVII; Richmond, *HN* XV, p. 136, no. 20; Phillips, *CSIR*, p. 112, no. 308, pl. 84.

4. *Altar to Hercules* (figs. 7–9)

Found in or before 1590 at Risingham, now on display in the Cambridge University Museum of Archaeology and Anthropology, inv. D 1970.8. Local buff sandstone.
Ht. 123 cm.; w. 65 cm.; d. 44.5 cm.

This is a large altar which would have looked very impressive before it was damaged: Horsley describes it as 'I think, one of the largest altars I have seen, that are so beautiful'. The top in particular is now very weathered and battered, though the edges generally have suffered and the monument appears to have been heavily burnt at some point in its history. The top of the altar clearly has bolsters on either side with a hollow space in between for making offerings (the *focus*). Any decoration there may have been in the front pediment is now quite indecipherable. One detail that is visible however is the representation of ropes as if tying down the centre of the bolsters. The inscription on the front of the middle section of the altar is framed with a plain fascia at the sides but more complex mouldings at the top and bottom, and below there is a deep base with a series

Fig. 7. Altar to Hercules (no. 4)

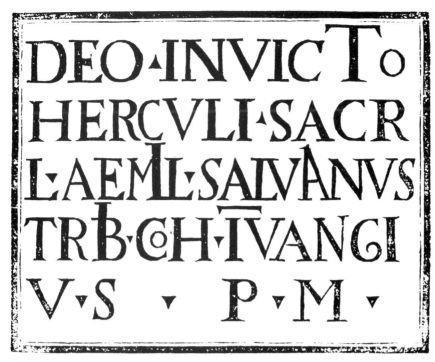

Fig. 8. Inscription of altar (no. 4) as recorded by Camden: from the 1695 edition of *Britannia*,
but the same illustration first appeared in the 1607 edition.

of plain mouldings at the top. The sides have simplified versions of these mouldings
above and below enclosing a field which is decorated in relief. On the left side is a
representation of a bull walking towards the right (i.e. towards the front of the altar): he
is represented with his body in profile but his head in frontal view, and he is decorated
for sacrifice. The relief is low with some, but not much, surface detail. On the right side
is a simple garland looped up at the upper corners of the monument: it hangs in an arc
across the top of the field and down the sides, and there is a raised semi-circle above it.
The garland is rope-like without any particular details of its constituent fruits, etc., but
it does show some signs of a binding holding it together. Both the bull and the garland
presumably allude to the sacrificial offerings made to the god and the function of the
altar. The back was left roughly worked: this has clearly not been as exposed to the
elements as the rest of the surface of the altar and still shows clear tool marks.

Camden's publication of the altar ignored the decoration, representing the inscription
only without any interest shown in the monument itself (fig. 8). This is rectified by
Horsley, who presents not only a schematic drawing of the front but also drawings of the
decoration on both sides (fig. 9). These are not very accurate, as the top of the altar with
its bolsters and pediment is not properly shown, the bull is facing the wrong way, and

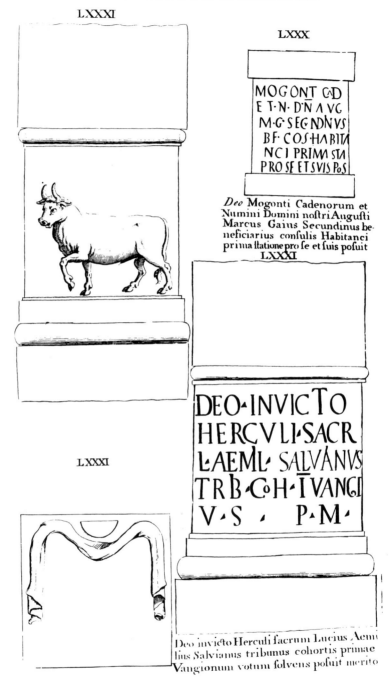

Fig. 9. Illustrations of altars (nos. 4 and 5). Horsley, *Britannia Romana*, p. 192 N.27

Horsley fails to recognize the garland as such. His interpretation of the last motif is however ingenious: 'an ornament not unlike a curtain, for I could not say it was a *feston*, and it is rather too large for a priest's veil. I imagined it to represent the *aulaeum* that separated the *adytum*, or some such thing; but of this I cannot be positive.'[11]

The inscription is quite well spaced and is fairly legible:

DEO INVICTO	Deo Invicto
HERCVLI SACR	Herculi sacr(um)
L AEMIL SALVIANVS	L(ucius) Aemil(ius) Salvianus
TR[I]B COH Ī VANGI	tr[i]b(unus) coh(ortis) I Vang(ionum)
V S L M	v(otum) s(olvit) l(ibens) m(erito)

Sacred to the invincible god Hercules. Lucius Aemilius Salvianus, tribune of the first cohort of Vangiones, willingly and deservedly fulfilled his vow.

In line 1 the final *O* is smaller than the other letters to fit it into the line; in line 2 *SACR* is very faint and difficult to read; in line 3 the *I* and *A* of *Salvianus* are ligatured; in line 4 the *I* of *Trib.* is missing, and the *C* of *COH* curls round the *O*. Both *I*s are elongated in this line.

L. Aemilius Salvianus also appears on the inscription recording the restoration of the South Gate of the fort (*RIB* 1234 – see under no. 2 above), which can be dated to A.D. 205–7, while another inscription (*CIL* VIII 2758) reveals he was buried at Lambaesis in Africa. He was not the only officer stationed at Risingham to dedicate an altar to Hercules (see *RIB* 1213 and 1214), and this may betray a particular reverence held by the first cohort of Vangiones for Hercules.[12] The formula in the last line of the inscription is conventional: it records the fulfilment of a vow, an agreement made between the dedicator and the god.

An intriguing footnote to this altar concerns the text found inscribed on a number of roofing tiles from a house at Bubbenhall in Warwickshire, one of which is preserved in the Cambridge Archaeological Museum (D 1978.1). These came to light when the roof of an old house was being repaired in 1877: a correspondent who merely calls himself 'Vicar' wrote in to *Notes and Queries* to say that seven tiles were found to have inscriptions on them, and he cites a text identical to that on the Risingham altar except that the last line reads 'VSPM' instead of 'VSLM': this in fact perpetuates the misreading of the last line of the altar's inscription as given by Camden and Horsley. The 'Vicar' estimated the house to be about two hundred years old at the time he was writing, which would suggest the tiles were made in the later part of the seventeenth century. Whatever the intention of the manufacturers, it seems they took their text from the published version of the inscription.[13]

Bibliography: *RIB* 1215; *CIL* VII 986; Camden, *Britannia* (1607), p. 663; Horsley, p. 235, Northumberland no. LXXXI, ill'd on p. 192 N. 27; Richmond, *HN* XV, p. 133, no. 11; Phillips, *CSIR*, p. 63, no. 190, pl. 41.

Fig. 10. Altar to Mogons (no. 5)

Fig. 11. Tombstone of the daughter of Blescius Diovicus (no. 6)

5. *Altar to the god Mogons* (figs. 9 and 10)

Found just before 1599 in the River Rede to the North of Risingham.[14] Now in the store of the Cambridge University Museum of Archaeology and Anthropology, inv. D 1970.6. Ht. 51 cm.; w. 34 cm.; d. 20 cm.

A plain altar with a simple broad fascia moulding at the top and bottom and between them a plain field containing the inscription on the front and left undecorated on the sides. The back is worked smooth and the top surface is flat. The surface of the stone is worn in places, especially down the left hand corner and there are also some chips missing down the right corner: in addition there is a large piece of stone missing at the front top left corner and a small piece at the top right edge.

The inscription is not very deeply cut and the strokes of the letters are fine: this, the weathering at the edges, and the fact that the stonecutter has tried to cram a lot of text into the space make the inscription difficult to read. I was not able to read the *DEO* that others have seen at the beginning of the inscription, placed on the upper moulding,

144

though the *O* is just about recognizable. (Horsley could not read it either, but Richmond claims it can be seen faintly on the stone and in his photograph.)

The text given follows that of *RIB*.

[D] E O	Deo
MOGONTI CAD	Mogonti Cad(… …)
ET. N. D. N̄.AVG	et N(umini) d(omini) n(ostri) Aug(usti)
M. G.SECVNDINVS	M(arcus) G(avius?) Secundinus
[B]F.COS.HABITA	[b(ene)]f(iciarius) co(n)s(ularis) Habita-
NCI PRIMA STAT	nci prima stat(ione)
PRO SE ET SVIS POSV[IT]	pro se et suis posu[it].

To the god Mogons Cad … … and to the Numen of our lord the emperor, Marcus Gavius Secundinus, consular beneficiarius on his first tour of duty at Habitancum, set this up for himself and his own.

In the second line the *C* curves round the small *A* in *Cad*; and in the fourth line in *Secundinus* the small *V* is contained by the *C*, and a small *I* is placed above and between the *D* and the second *N*.

This inscription was the subject of a lengthy commentary by Camden (1695 English ed., cols. 849–50):

From the former of these [i.e. the present inscription] some guess may be made that the place was called *Habitancum*; and that he who erected it was a Pensioner to a Consul, and Mayor of the Town. (For that the chief Magistrates of Cities, Towns and Forts were call'd *Primates*, the *Codex Theodosii* will abundantly teach us). Whether this god were the tutelar Deity of the *Gadeni*, whom *Ptolemy* makes next neighbours to the *Ottadini*, I am not yet able to determine; let others enquire.

Camden is right in some of his deductions: Habitancum is now generally agreed to be the Roman name of the fort at Risingham, and this inscription is still the only one known to mention Habitancum. But his interpretation of the post held by the dedicator is implausible, and the nature of the god Mogons is still not clear. In fact a beneficiarius consularis was a legionary soldier serving away from his legion, perhaps in this case serving as a district officer watching official movements and possibly collecting taxes: indeed it would not be surprising if he were acting as an intelligence officer in the strategic position of the outpost of Risingham.[15] The phrase 'prima stat.', misread and misinterpreted by Camden to mean 'primate', was taken by Horsley and others to apply to the fort itself, and to imply that this was the most northerly of the Roman stations at the time:[16] but is now generally agreed to refer to the fact that this was Secundinus's first posting as a beneficiarius, following the suggestion made by Birley. The formula used in the third line of the inscription suggests the altar was erected at some point in the third century when there was only one emperor:[17] given the rapid turnover at the time it is perhaps not surprising Secundinus chose not to name him.

The god Mogons has caused problems of identification: two rival views have emerged, one that he is a Germanic god, the other that he is local to this part of Britain. Collingwood and Wright in *RIB* suggest that 'Cad.' is a territorial epithet, possibly a

German pagus name,[18] but Birley states that the cult appears to have been confined to northern England, and agrees with Camden's identification of the 'Cad...' of the inscription as Gadenorum, of the Gadeni, a northern British tribe neighbouring the Ottadini (= the Votadini) according to Ptolemy. Various other inscriptions refer to what may be the same god: the nearest are from Old Penrith (*RIB* 921 – now lost) which reads 'Deo Mog(on)ti', and from Netherby (*RIB* 971) to 'deo Mogont(i) Vitire', while another from Risingham (*RIB* 1226 – now lost) is dedicated to 'deo Mouno Cad.'. An inscription from High Rochester (*RIB* 1269) is dedicated 'Dis Mountibus'. In no case is it clear that the god is either local or Germanic in origin. Mogons is accepted as a local god by Breeze and Dobson, who provide a small map showing where dedications to him have been found:[19] on balance there would be more evidence in favour of this view than the Germanic interpretation. Camden certainly attests to the folk memory of such a deity in this area (1695 English ed., col. 850):

The Inhabitants report, that the place was long defended by the god *Magon*, against a certain *Soldane* or Pagan Prince. Nor is the story wholly groundless; for that such a god was here worship'd, appears from these two Altars lately taken out of the River, and thus inscrib'd. (The text of this inscription and *RIB* 1226, now lost, follow.)[20]

Bibliography: *RIB* 1225; *CIL* VII 996, and p. 311; Camden, *Britannia* (1607), p. 662; Horsley, pp. xv and 234, Northumberland no. LXXX, ill'd on p. 192 N. 27; Birley, *Archaeologia Aeliana*, 4th ser., xii (1935), pp. 222–3; Richmond, *HN* XV, p. 137, no. 24, pl. facing p. 64.

6. *Tombstone of the daughter of Blescius Diovicus* (fig. 11)

Small tombstone seen at Risingham by Bainbrigg in 1601 (and by Camden and Cotton in 1599?).[21] Now on display in the Cambridge University Museum of Archaeology and Anthropology, inv. D 1970.11. Local buff sandstone.
Ht. (to apex of pediment) 71 cm.; w. 38 cm.; d. 9 cm.

The lower part of the tombstone consists of the inscription in a recessed panel with a plain frame. Above is a tall triangular pediment outlined by a groove. Inside is the crude portrait of a child, represented from the mid-chest up. The head is ill-defined and flat; the ears protrude upon either side of the face, the eyes are placed too near the top of the head, the nose is very linear, and the mouth is a mere slit. Her hair is represented by incised lines running back from her forehead. The figure is oddly placed in the space, as the head does not reach far up into the apex, while the lower part of the body overlaps the lower edge. The arms are held out to the sides, and it is possible the figure is meant to be holding the ends of a garland in her hands, with the garland hanging across the top edge of the inscription panel (Phillips however does not see this, but suggests she is holding a ball in her right hand). She is wearing a sleeveless tunic, the folds being indicated by a series of grooves. Horsley illustrates the tombstone with a line drawing, but this is not very accurate – he mistakes the ears for hair, for example – and does not add anything to our understanding of the motif. The deficiencies in the carving are not helped by later weathering, making the original rather amorphous forms more so. Phillips comments that 'The style of the carving is totally alien to the Graeco-Roman tradition of sculpture'. The sides and back are not worked smooth, but have been quite well finished.

Despite the weathering, the inscription remains fairly easy to read, although the spacing of the letters is a little eccentric.

D M	D(is) M(anibus)
BLESCIVS	Blescius
DIOVICVS	Diovicus
FILIAE	filiae
SVAE P	suae p(osuit).
VIXSIT	vixsit
ANVM	an(n)um
I ET DIE	I et die(s)
XXI	XXI.

To the spirits of the dead. Blescius Diovicus set this up to his daughter. She lived one year and twenty-one days.

The inscription is one of a number of funerary inscriptions found at Risingham: together these provide evidence that there was a *vicus* (civilian settlement) near the fort, although this has not been excavated. Salway follows Richmond in suggesting that the name is of Celtic origin, and that the family were native inhabitants of the settlement. Phillips indicates that the date is probably third century.

Bibliography: *RIB* 1254; *CIL* VII 1017; Camden, *Britannia* (1607), p. 662; Horsley, p. 238, Northumberland no. XC, ill'd on p. 192 N. 29; Richmond, *HN* XV, p. 140, no. 35; P. Salway, *The Frontier People of Roman Britain* (Cambridge, 1965), pp. 110–11 and 253, no. 99; Phillips, *CSIR*, pp. 97–8, no. 267, pl. 72.

High Rochester

The fort of High Rochester is some twenty miles further up Dere Street from Risingham, in an area north of Hadrian's Wall dominating the valley of the River Rede: after the withdrawal from Scotland it was the most northerly occupied fort known in Britain. It was founded in the first century by Agricola but replaced in stone in the second century under Lollius Urbicus, with further periods of rebuilding in the third and early fourth centuries. The inscription from High Rochester collected by Cotton belongs to the third century A.D., when the fort's main purpose was to police and control the area north of Hadrian's Wall: at this time one of the units stationed there was a unit of scouts or *exploratores*. The name of the unit (numerus exploratorum Bremeniensium) given in the inscription gives us the Roman name of the fort – Bremenium – as it was the unit of scouts then stationed at Bremenium.

Fig. 12. Altar or base dedicated to the goddess Roma (no. 7)

7. *Flat-topped altar or base with a dedication to the goddess Roma* (fig. 12)

Found at High Rochester, Northumberland, in or before 1601,[22] according to Camden in the ruins of a fort.[23] Now in the store of the Cambridge University Museum of Archaeology and Anthropology, inv. D 1970.1.

Ht. 95 cm.; w. 49.5 cm.; max. d. 25.5 cm.

The rectangular altar or base is fairly large, but shallow: it is described as an altar in the inscription, but has rather a narrow top surface for such a function, and Richmond describes it as a 'base'.

The decoration consists of a prominent inscription on the front with undecorated mouldings above and below: the first line of the inscription (D.R.S. – Deae Romae Sacrum) appears in larger letters in a plain rectangular field above the top moulding. The rest of the inscription is sandwiched between the upper and lower mouldings, but there is no frame enclosing the inscription down the vertical edges at the front corners. Instead the mouldings continue onto the sides of the monument, where the fields in between and

148

above and below are worked smooth but left plain and undecorated. The back was left roughly worked, and the top has been worked flat.

There is a little damage to the back edge of the top of the monument, and also down the top section of the front right hand corner. A hole has been drilled (presumably in modern times) into the top centre of the front face, cutting into the top of the *R* of *D.R.S.* Otherwise the condition remains good, with little weathering or chipping. The inscription is easy to read, with deeply cut, clear and well-spaced letters of even height.

D R S	D(eae) R(omae) S(acrum)
DVPL.N.EXPLOR	dupl(icarii) n(umeri) Explor(atorum)
BREMEN . ARAM	Bremen(iensium) aram
INSTITVERVNT	instituerunt
N̄.EIVS C ⊘ CAEP	n(atali) eius c(urante) Caep(ione)
CHARITINO TRIB	Charitino trib(uno)
V . S . L . M.	v(otum) s(olventes) l(ibentes) m(erito)

Sacred to the Goddess Roma. The duplicarii of the unit of Scouts of Bremenium set up this altar on Rome's birthday under the charge of Caepio Charitinus, tribune, willingly and deservedly fulfilling their vow.

The *I* and *B* in line six are ligatured, and various other letters are placed so close together as to be virtually ligatured.

This inscription, as Camden points out, gives us the Roman name for the fort at High Rochester (Bremenium). It was erected by duplicarii – soldiers on double pay as a reward for valour or for taking on extra responsibilities – and their commander who is named in the inscription as Caep(io?) Charitinus. The altar also attests to the presence of a unit of scouts in the fort. Horsley comments that:

The *exploratores* were, like our scouts, sent out to discover the enemy, or their country. When they were in garrison, it is probable they were generally placed in the more advanced stations, or such as were most conveniently situated for prospect, and discovering the first approach of the enemy; as also for guarding the passes against their inroads.

The altar dates to the third century A.D., when the fort was an outpost for the Northern frontier of Britain. (Camden also at this point in the *Britannia* comments on the frontiers of the empire and alludes to the fact High Rochester was a fort in advance of the Wall 'in the Enemy's territory'.) That this dedication was made here asserts the presence and importance of the goddess of Rome even in such a remote spot: the meaning of D.R.S. was not realized by Camden, but was by Horsley.

The meaning of the abbreviation *N. EIUS* has also caused some discussion. Hübner and Richmond expand the phrase as 'n(umini) eius' – to her divinity, but most more recent commentators have favoured 'n(atali) eius', suggesting the altar was set up on Rome's birthday, 21 April, a festival instituted by the Emperor Hadrian.[24] This festival, held on the traditional date of Rome's foundation, is also recorded among the anniversaries to be celebrated throughout the year by the 20th Cohort of Palmyrenes in the Calendar found at Dura Europos.[25]

Bibliography: *RIB* 1270; *CIL* VII 1037 and p. 312; Camden, *Britannia* (1607), p. 661; Horsley, p. 243, Northumberland no. XCV, ill'd on. p. 192 N. 32; *Journal of Roman Studies*, xxxiv (1944), p. 85; Richmond, *HN* XV, p. 149, no. 19, pl. opp. p. 64.

Halton Chesters

The site at Halton Chesters is a fort on Hadrian's Wall, $5\frac{1}{2}$ miles from Chesters and $7\frac{1}{2}$ miles from Rudchester. It was garrisoned by cavalry: in the third and fourth centuries the unit stationed there was the 500-strong ala I Pannoniorum Sabiniana, a cavalry unit originally raised in Pannonia (W. Hungary) named after someone called Sabinus, who raised the unit or was an early commander of it.[26] The dedicator of inscription no. 8, Messorius Magnus, belonged to this unit: the person commemorated was his brother (the name is now missing), who may also have been a cavalryman in the unit. He was from Noricum rather than Pannonia: Holder speculates that he may have been transferred to the unit on promotion, possibly in the aftermath of the Battle of Lugdunum in A.D. 197.[27]

8. *Fragmentary Tombstone of a Norican Tribesman* (fig. 13)

Seen by Bainbrigg at Halton in about 1600. Now in the store of the Cambridge University Museum of Archaeology and Anthropology, inv. D 1970.15.
Ht. 39.5 cm.; w. 53 cm.; d. 16 cm.

Only the lower part of the tombstone survives, and that is broken and chipped on all sides. The letters of the inscription are not very deeply cut, and are of uneven height. The inscription is now difficult to read, and the version below is taken from *RIB*.

///RMAT///	...]rmat[....]
[CIV]IS NORICI AN XXX	[civ]is Norici an(norum) XXX
[M]ESSORIVS MAGNVS	[M]essorius Magnus
[F]RATER EIVS DVPL ALIAE	[f]rater eius dupl(icarius) al⟨i⟩ae
SABINIANAE	Sabinianae
[F] C	[f(aciendum)] c(uravit).

... a Norican tribesman aged 30. Messorius Magnus, his brother, a duplicarius in the Sabinian cavalry unit, had this set up.

Several letters are ligatured: *A* and *N* in line 2, *R* and *I* in line 3, *V* and *P* in *DVPL*, and *AE* at the end of line 4; *FRATER* is very compressed, and in line 5 both the *I*s of *SABINIANAE* are ligatured with the first *N*. For the meaning of duplicarius see under no. 7 above.

The inscription is cited by Bainbrigg[28] and it seems that it was already damaged at the time he saw it (he describes it as 'haec mutilata inscriptio'). Bainbrigg and Camden also link this inscription with a relief of a man reclining on a bed. Camden's description is as follows (1695 ed., col. 855):

Near this place was digg'd up a piece of an old stone, wherein was drawn the pourtraiture of a

Fig. 13. Fragmentary tombstone of a Norican tribesman (no. 8)

Man lying on his bed, leaning upon his left hand, and touching his right knee with his right; together with the following Inscriptions...

Phillips has located what must be this relief built into a garden wall at Halton Castle: it is very weathered, but tallies with the description.[29] It is not certain whether the relief was part of the same tombstone as the inscription: the phrase used by Bainbrigg is 'cui adiungitur', but Camden (see above) merely suggests that the relief was found together with two inscriptions, without implying that it belonged to either of them. This type of image would not be unexpected on such a monument. It seems strange that Cotton would take the trouble to transport the inscription to Conington but not the relief if both were available to him – this may be an instance of greater interest being shown in inscriptions than in figured reliefs.

Bibliography: *RIB* 1433; *CIL* VII 571; Camden, *Britannia* (1607), p. 666; Horsley, pp. 214–15, Northumberland no. XVIII, ill'd on p. 192 N. 11.

Fig. 14. Altar to Jupiter and the welfare of Desidienus Aemilianus (no. 9)

Fig. 15. Altar to the Syrian goddess (no. 10), photographed lying on its side but shown here as if upright.

Housesteads

One altar in the Cotton collection was ascribed by Bainbrigg to a site he calls 'Chester in the Wall', called by the common people 'Busiegapp': this designation is followed by Camden.[30] In Cotton and Camden's day it was a no-go area: both Bainbrigg and Camden comment on the danger from robbers. According to Bainbrigg, 'Est is locus infestus excursionibus, et frequentionibus latrociniis expositus ad praedandum', while this is Camden's passage as it appears in the 1695 English translation (p. 848):

From hence the Wall bends about by *Iverton, Forsten* and *Chester in the Wall*, near *Busy-gapp*, noted for Robberies; where we heard there were forts, but durst not go and view them for fear of the *Moss-Troopers*.

LIII

LIV

DEAE SVRI +
AE SVB CALP
VRNIO AGE
ICOLA LEG·AVG
PR·PR·ALICINIVS
CLEMENS PRAEF
III·A·IOR

PRO SALVTE
DESIDIENIAE
LIANI·PRAE
ET SVAS·
POSVIT·V°T
O·SOLVIT·LIBE

NS TVSC°·ET BAS
SO COSS

Deae Suriae sub Calpur-
nio Agricola legatoAugu-
ftali propraetore Aulus Licinius Clemens praefectus
cohortis primae Hamiorum
[*vel cohortis* quartae Gallorum]

Pro salute Defidieni Ae-
liani praefecti et sua sacrum pofuit voto folvit
libens Tufco et Baffo con-
fulibus

Fig. 16. Horsley's illustration of altars no. 9 (on the right) and no. 10 (left) from *Britannia Romana*, p. 192 N.22

Horsley provides a further explanation:

The wild and western parts of the country were formerly, also, much harrassed by Moss-Troopers, who took that name from the mosses, where they usually had their fastnesses and places of retreat.[31]

It seems that Camden and Cotton avoided the area on their tour of Hadrian's Wall in 1599, but presumably Bainbrigg did visit the site as he records the inscription (albeit not very accurately), and his version of the text appears in Gruter's 1603 collection of inscriptions. Despite the difficulties of the area, Cotton clearly acquired the altar, probably by 1607, as the 1607 edition of Camden has a fuller and more accurate reading.

There has been considerable discussion of where exactly this site is. Horsley thought it was Chesterholm, Hodgson Carvoran, but Haverfield argued cogently for its identification as the site we now call Housesteads, and this has been generally accepted.[32]

153

Today Housesteads is 'the most famous and popular of all the wall-forts',[33] impressing visitors with its dramatic site and lonely situation. However, Camden himself continues the passage quoted above:

This *Chester*, we were told, was very large, insomuch as I guess it to be that station of the second [Cohort] of the *Dalmatians* which the Book of *Notices* calls *Magna*.

The cohors II Delmatarum is now thought to have been stationed at Carvoran: the units at Housesteads in the third century A.D. were the cohors I Tungrorum, a numerus Hnaudifridi, and a cuneus of Frisii, as several other inscriptions recovered from the site show.[34] None of these inscriptions is closely dated: that in Cotton's collection, by contrast, is (by a consular reference to A.D. 258), but does not mention which unit the dedicator was prefect of.

9. *Altar to Jupiter and the welfare of Desidienus Aemilianus* (figs. 14 and 16)

A large altar: for the find-spot see above. Now in the store of the Cambridge University Museum of Archaeology and Anthropology, inv. D 1970.9.

Ht. 103 cm.; w. 43 cm.; d. 34 cm.

The altar has suffered quite badly from weathering, which has blurred the decoration and makes the inscription difficult to read: the left-hand corner of the front in particular is damaged, and the first couple of letters in several lines cannot be read. The top surface of the altar has a depression for making offerings (the *focus*) flanked by bolsters at the sides and an undecorated triangular pediment at the front. There are deep mouldings at the top and bottom of the altar, enclosing the bulk of the inscription on the front (the last two lines spill over onto the base). The sides have the same mouldings above and below a field which is worked smooth but left plain. The back is roughly worked.

I O M	I(ovi) O(ptimo) M(aximo)
PRO SALVTE	pro salute
DESIDIENI AE	Desidieni Ae-
[MI]LIANI PRAEF	[mi]liani praef-
[ECTI] ET SVA SV[OR]	[ecti] et sua su[or]-
[VM] POSVIT VOT	[um] posuit vot-
[VM]Q SOLVIT LIBE	[um]q(ue) solvit libe-
[*on base*]	
NS TVSCO ET BAS	ns Tusco et Bas-
SO CO[SS]	so co[(n)s(ulibus)]

To Jupiter Best and Greatest, for the health of the Prefect Desidienus Aemilianus, both his own and his family's. He set this up and willingly fulfilled his vow in the consulship of Tuscus and Bassus. (N. Nummius Tuscus and Mummius Bassus were consuls in A.D. 258.)

Collingwood and Wright comment that the grammar of the text is muddled: presumably the prefect Desidienus Aemilianus was the dedicator of the altar, although the text does not explicitly say so. Several altars have been found at Housesteads dedicated to Jupiter

Optimus Maximus, but the most common formula links this with a dedication to the Numina of the emperors, and the dedication is by the unit under the command of a named prefect (see *RIB* 1584–8). Here the dedication is more personal: the prefect's vow and dedication are in his own interests, not those of his unit, and the unit he commanded is not named. The shape of the altar is also very like others found at Housesteads.

Bibliography: *RIB* 1589; *CIL* VII 769 and p. 310; Camden, *Britannia* (1607), p. 659; Horsley, p. 226, Northumberland no. LIV, ill'd p. 192 N. 22.

Melkridge/Carvoran

The fort at Carvoran may have existed before Hadrian's Wall, but it certainly seems to have been built or rebuilt in stone towards the end of Hadrian's reign. It lies not on the Wall itself but on the Stanegate behind it, and it defended the junction of the Stanegate and the Maiden Way from the South. In Hadrian's time the garrison was the first cohort of Hamians, a unit of Syrian archers, apparently the only unit of archers known for certain in Roman Britain. The unit was located at Bar Hill on the Antonine Wall during the occupation of Scotland, but it seems it returned to Carvoran after the retreat from Scotland, and was there at the time the inscription below was dedicated, in the period that Calpurnius Agricola was Governor of Britain (early in the reign of Marcus Aurelius). In the third century the garrison at Carvoran was different – the second cohort of Dalmatians.

10. *Altar to the Syrian Goddess* (figs. 15 and 16)

Bainbrigg and Camden say this altar was in Melkridge,[35] which is two miles from Haltwhistle and five miles from Carvoran: however, it appears to be associated with the fort of Carvoran, as the commander and unit mentioned in the inscription were stationed there. Either they set the altar up some distance from the fort, or it has been moved subsequently. It is now in the store of the Cambridge University Museum of Archaeology and Anthropology, inv. D 1970.4.
Ht. of main part *c.* 56 cm.; w. at the top 44.5 cm.; d. 32 cm.

The altar is roughly broken across, and in fact there appears to have been considerable weathering and flaking away of the lower part since Cotton and Camden's day, as less of the inscription can be read now (indeed Horsley comments on this: clearly much had flaked away even by the time he saw it).[36] All the edges and corners have also been chipped and worn.

The top surface of the altar appears to have been flat (though it is difficult to be certain of this as the altar is now stored upside down, and this surface too appears to have been weathered). The upper part of the front and sides was decorated with a series of elaborate mouldings: from the top down these consist of a row of half circles and a row of full circles containing daisy-like rosettes, a band of triangles, and a plain flat moulding; the moulding at the bottom is simpler. The inscription appears without a frame on the front, and the field on the sides is left plain and worked smooth. The back is also highly finished, with the profile of the upper mouldings worked, but no decorations on them.

The inscription is recorded as follows in *RIB*, which follows closely the reading in Camden: however, it is now very difficult to read anything below the third line:

+DEAE SVRI+	Deae Suri-
AE SVB CALP	ae sub Calp-
VRNIO AG[R]	urnio Ag[r]-
ICO[LA] LEG AV[G]	ico[la] leg(ato) Au[g](usti)
PR PR LIC[IN]IVS	pr(o) pr(aetore) Lic[in]ius
[C]LEM[ENS PRAEF]	[C]lem[ens praef(ectus)]
[CO]H I HA[MIORVM]	[co]h(ortis) I Ha[miorum]

To the Syrian Goddess, under Calpurnius Agricola, the emperor's propraetorian legate, Licinius Clemens, prefect of the first cohort of Hamians (set this up).

The crosses at either end of the first line are modern.

The first cohort of Hamian archers was a specialist unit that continued to recruit from the original area, in this case Syria.[37] A dedication to 'the Syrian goddess', therefore, was highly appropriate for the unit, and it seems that this was the only military unit stationed in Britain that is known to have worshipped this deity.[38] She is otherwise known as Cybele or the Great Mother, a goddess accepted into Rome as early as the late third century B.C.: despite attempts to Romanize and tame her she retained a rather exotic image. The inscription names both the unit's commander, Licinius Clemens, and the provincial governor, Calpurnius Agricola, both of whom appear again on another fragmentary inscription from Carvoran, also on part of an altar (*RIB* 1809). Licinius Clemens is otherwise unknown, but Sex. Calpurnius Agricola was in office A.D. *c.* 163-*c.* 166. He was probably sent to Britain to deal with unrest there, and clearly spent some time in the area of Hadrian's Wall, as he is mentioned in two dedicatory inscriptions from Corbridge (*RIB* 1137 and 1149).

Camden was quite taken with this altar, and provides the following commentary (1695 English ed., p. 848):

Now *Calphurnius Agricola* was sent against the *Britains* by [the Emperour] *M. Antoninus Philosophus*, upon the breaking out of the *British* wars, about the year of our Lord 170. at which time some Cohort, under his command, erected this altar to the Goddess *Suria*, who was drawn by Lions, with a Turret on her head and a Taber in her hand, (as is shewn at large by *Lucian*, in his Treatise *de Dea Syria*) and whom *Nero*, as sorrily as he treated all Religion, very zealously worship'd for some time, and afterwards slighted her to that degree, as to piss upon her.

The combination of triangles and discs as decorative mouldings has also been noted on altars from Bar Hill set up by the first cohort of Hamians while it was stationed on the Antonine Wall, probably in the period A.D. 142-*c.* 157, immediately before its arrival at Carvoran.[39]

Bibliography: *RIB* 1792; *CIL* VII 758; Camden, *Britannia* (1600), p. 719 bis; Horsley, pp. 225-6, Northumberland no. LIII, ill'd on p. 192 N. 22; Birley, *ANRW* xvi:2, 1978, p. 1516.

Fig. 17. Altar to Jupiter and Gordian III (no. 11)   *Fig. 18.* Altar to Fortune (no. 12)

Old Carlisle

The fort and *vicus* at Old Carlisle (some 10 miles from the modern town of Carlisle, near Wigton) have not been excavated, though remains are visible at the site and a number of inscriptions have been found there.[40] Camden mistakenly suggested the site was known as 'Castra Exploratorum': he appears to have visited the site on his tour of the north, and comments 'For spying of an Enemy you could not have a more convenient place; for 'tis seated upon a high hill which commands a free prospect all around the country'.[41]

11. *Altar to Jupiter and Gordian III* (fig. 17)

The altar seems to have been known since 1550, and appears in the first edition of Camden's *Britannia*.[42] It was found at Old Carlisle, and is now in the store of the Cambridge University Museum of Archaeology and Anthropology, inv. D 1970.12.
Ht. 74 cm.; w. 52 cm.; d. 21.5 cm.

The altar has a wide top and base with the inscription in a narrower field in between. There is a heavy plain moulding above the inscription, but the inscription is not enclosed

157

in a frame. Above again on the front is a design in shallow relief designed to suggest the ends of bolsters flanking a pediment, but the top surface of the altar is flat, and the bolsters have little shape to them. The sides have similar mouldings above and below a plain field. The stone is quite badly damaged and the surface of the inscription is pitted. This and the very small squashed letters make the inscription difficult to read: this was commented on by Horsley. The reading below is based on *RIB* 897:

I O M	I(ovi) O(ptimo) M(aximo)
PRO SALV[TE] IMPERATORIS	pro salu[te] imperatoris
M ANTONI GORDIANI P [F]	M(arci) Antoni Gordiani P(ii) [F(elicis)]
INVICTI AVG ET SAB[IN]IAE FVR	Invicti Aug(usti) et Sab[in]iae Fur-
IAE TRANQUILAE CONIVGI EIVS TO	iae Tranquil(lin)ae coniugi eius to-
TAQVE DOMV DIVIN EORVM A	taque domu divin(a) eorum a-
LA AVG GORDIA OB VIRTVTEM	la Aug(usta) Gordia(na) ob virtutem
APPELLATA POSVIT CVI PRAEST	appellata posuit cui praest
AEMILIVS CRISPINVS PREF	Aemilius Crispinus pref(ectus)
EQ NATVS IN PRO AFRICA DE	eq(uitum) natus in pro(vincia) Africa de
TVSDRO SVB CVR NONII PH	Tusdro sub cur(a) Nonii Ph-
ILIPPI LEG AVG PRO PRE[TO]	ilippi leg(ati) Aug(usti) pro pre[to(re)]
[AT]TICO ET PRAETEXTATO	[At]tico et Praetextato
COS	co(n)s(ulibus).

To Jupiter Best and Greatest, for the welfare of the Emperor Marcus Antonius Gordianus Pius (pious) Felix (fortunate) Invictus (invincible) Augustus and for his wife Sabinia Furia Tranquillina and the whole divine (i.e. imperial) house. The cavalry unit given the title 'Augusta Gordiana' on account of its valour set this up, its commander being the prefect Aemilius Crispinus who was born in the province of Africa and (comes) from Thysdrus. (They did this) under the charge of Nonius Philippus, the emperor's propraetorian legate, in the consulship of Atticus and Praetextus (i.e. A.D. 242).

The emperor in question is Gordian III (238–44), who as usual for this period is given an impressive array of titles in the inscription. Aemilius Crispinus was presumably so keen to point out that he was born in Thysdrus because this was where Gordian I (Gordian III's grandfather) was proclaimed emperor. Nonius Philippus was the provincial Governor of Britain at the time. Such dedications to Jupiter but also for the health and welfare of the reigning emperor are among the commonest Roman army dedications.

Bibliography: *RIB* 897; *CIL* VII 344; Camden, *Britannia* (1586), p. 454; Horsley, p. 276, Cumbria no. LV, ill'd on p. 192 N. 47; Collingwood, *CW* XXXVIII (1928), p. 115, no. 11; Birley, *CW* LI (1951), pp. 17–18.

Bowes

The fort at Bowes had the Roman name Lavatrae or Lavatris, and it guarded the eastern end of the Stainmore pass. The original Agricolan fort was replaced in the second century, and was repaired in the fourth century. The inscription in the Cotton collection, however, refers to the bath-house, which stood outside the fort walls: its site is still visible as a hollow, as building stone was plundered from here in the nineteenth century. The inscription records the rebuilding of the baths in A.D. 197–202, after they had been destroyed by fire. The inscription mentions two units: the first cohort of Thracians and the ala of the Spanish Vettones (see below).

12. *Altar to Fortune* (fig. 18)

Found before 1600 at Bowes;[43] now on display in the Cambridge University Museum of Archaeology and Anthropology, inv. D 1970.3.
Ht. 74 cm.; w. 42 cm.; d. 11.5 cm.

The altar is very plain, with little decoration apart from the inscription. There is a simple wide cyma/cyma reversa moulding above and below the inscription, which is not otherwise framed. These mouldings also appear on the sides of the altar. The top surface is flat, but only roughly worked: the extreme shallowness of the 'altar' means that it could scarcely have functioned as such. The condition of the stone is good, with little chipping or weathering, and the inscription, with its clear lettering and reasonably good spacing, is easily read. The first line is carved on the upper cornice, the rest on the main surface of the front.

DAE ♀ FORTVNAE	D(e)ae Fortunae
VIRIVS.LVPVS	Virius Lupus
LEG.AVG.PR.PR	Leg(atus) Aug(usti) pr(o) pr(aetore)
BALINEVM.VI	balineum vi
IGNIS.EXVST	ignis exust-
VM.COH.I.THR	um coh(orti) I Thr-
ACVM.REST[I]	acum rest[i]-
TVIT.CVRAN	tuit curan-
TE.VAL.FRON	te Val(erio) Fron-
TONE.PRAEF	tone praef(ecto)
EQ.ALAE.VETTO	eq(uitum) alae Vetto(num)

To the goddess Fortune. Virius Lupus, imperial propraetorian legate, restored the bath-house, burnt by the violence of fire, for the first cohort of Thracians. Valerius Fronto, prefect of the cavalry unit of Vettones, was in charge of the work.

Virius Lupus was governor of the province of Britain, A.D. 197–202, but as line 3 describes him as 'Leg. Aug.' and not 'Augg.' this must date to the period when Septimius Severus was sole Augustus, i.e. before Caracalla was elevated to this position in A.D. 198.

As indicated above, the mention of the two units has led to some confusion. According to other inscriptions (*RIB* 1028/9) the ala of Vettones was stationed at the fort of Binchester at this time.[44] The dating of these inscriptions, however, is not at all precise, and Collingwood and Wright in *RIB* supposed that the Vettones, stationed at Binchester, 'helped' the Thracians to rebuild their bath-house: according to them, the prefect of the cavalry unit of Vettones, being senior to the infantry commander at Bowes, is mentioned, whereas the latter is not. This view is also taken by Holder, but Wilson suggests a different scenario, with the Thracians arriving to replace the garrison of Vettones at Bowes shortly after the Vettones had finished the rebuilding of the baths – thus the Vettones did the donkey-work and the Thracians reaped the benefit.[45]

Camden in his commentary on this altar (1695 ed., col. 763) takes the opportunity both to castigate those who misread *balineum* as *Balingium* (and so tried to make it the name of the place) and to expand on the nature of Roman baths:

Baths were as much us'd by the Souldiers as any others, both for the sake of health and cleanliness (for daily, in that age, they were wont to wash before they eat;) and also that Baths, both publick and private, were built at such a lavish rate everywhere, that *any one thought himself poor and mean, that had not the walls of his Bath adorn'd with great and costly Bosses* [Seneca]. In these, men and women washed promiscuously together; tho' that was often prohibited both by the Laws of the Emperours and Synodical Decrees.

Bibliography: *RIB* 730; *CIL* VII 273; Camden, *Britannia* (1607), p. 658; Horsley, pp. 304, 352, Yorkshire no. I, ill'd on p. 192 N. 62; Wilson, p. 246.

Greetland near Halifax

The exact find-spot of the following altar has been the subject of some debate. A local antiquary, John Hanson, reported that it had been dug up in 1597 at a place called 'Thick Hollins': soon afterwards Camden saw it and described its location as 'Greetland'. A detailed analysis of the topography of the area appeared in the *Yorkshire Archaeological Journal* (1916–17), which to some extent elucidates the find-spot.[46]

13. *Altar to Victoria Brigantia* (figs. 19 and 20)

The altar was found in 1597 at Thick Hollins, now Bank Top, Greetland, two miles south of Halifax: according to Camden it was in the house of Sir John Savil at Bradley before it entered Cotton's collection. It is now on display in the Cambridge University Museum of Archaeology and Anthropology, inv. D 1970.2.
Ht. 53 cm.; w. 35.5 cm.; d. 25.5 cm.

The altar is quite small, but decorative and well finished. Although the top surface is basically flat it is provided with a series of raised and sunk features. In the centre is a circular indentation with a raised edge for offerings (the *focus*): this is flanked by two raised ridges. There are also four holes bored into the surface, and a raised edge round the outside. The top section of the front and sides of the altar is decorated with patterns in relief: on the front a rectangle above a series of arches, and on the sides similar arches below and crenellations above. The bottom section of the altar has a plain moulding with incised diagonal lines on the base of the front only. The profiles of the mouldings are

160

Fig. 19. Altar to Victoria Brigantia (no. 13), front

Fig. 20. Altar to Victoria Brigantia
(no. 13), right side

present on the back of the monument, but here they are undecorated. The main field on the front and right side has the inscriptions; on the left side and back it is worked smooth and left plain. The inscriptions are not contained in a frame.

The altar is quite chipped and worn at the edges, and the surface is weathered. The inscription is not easy to read, and the letters at the ends of the lines on the right side in particular are damaged.

[On the front]	
D VICT BRIG	D(eae) Vict(oriae) Brig(antiae)
ET NVM AVGG	et Num(inibus) Aug(ustorum)
T AVR AVRELIAN	T(itus) Aur(elius) Aurelian-
VS D D PRO SE	us d(edit) d(edicavit) pro se
E[T] SVIS S MAG S	e[t] suis s(e) mag(istro) s(acrorum)
[On the right side]	
ANTONIN[O]	Antonin[o]
III ET GETA [II]	III et Geta [II]
CO[S]S	co(n)s(ulibus)

161

To the goddess Victoria Brigantia and to the Deities of the emperors, Titus Aurelius Aurelianus gave and dedicated this for himself and his family while he was master of the sacred rites. In the third consulship of Antoninus and the second of Geta (A.D. 208).

The meaning of the last line on the front is not certain, and various possibilities have been suggested.[47]

The identification of the deity to whom the altar was dedicated was for some time hampered by a misreading of the first line by Camden and others as 'DVI CI BRIG': this Camden expanded as 'Dui civitatis Brigantium', that is, 'Dui' is a native British god, the tutelar deity of the Brigantes. Horsley also speculates on the nature of this Dui, citing Ward's theory that he was a British deity whose name was a corruption of Zeus, and presenting his own, that it is related to the deity from whom we derive the name for Tuesday.[48] In fact, the small letter inside the *C* of the first line is a *T* not an *I*, as Hübner realized, and the altar honours Victoria Brigantia along with the Numina of the emperors.[49]

This goddess of the Brigantes was the subject of a study by Joliffe, who suggests that Brigantia was created as a result of Severan reorganization of the Brigantes after a revolt in the area, and that the form 'Victoria Brigantia' belongs to an early phase in this development.[50] She points to the fact that, as with this altar, several of the dedicants to Brigantia have the family name Aurelius, suggesting recent enfranchisement, either of natives or of auxiliary soldiers, and that they show a desire to express loyalty to the ruling regime. She also suggests, however, that the identification of Brigantia with Victory, a goddess of the Roman armies, would not be 'entirely to the taste of the Roman government', and that this form of the goddess is only attested for a short period before A.D. 209, when the imperial family arrived in Britain and other aspects of the deity were stressed: thus she sees the establishment of the official Romanized cult of the goddess as an important part of the Severan pacification and reorganization of the area, but the Greetland altar belongs to the earlier phase of the development. Brigantia in her more developed form is typified by a relief found at Birrens, showing a more complex and syncretistic interpretation.[51]

Bibliography: *RIB* 627; *CIL* VII 200; Camden, *Britannia* (1600), p. 613; Horsley, pp. xxiii and 312–3, ill'd on p. 192 N. 65; F. Haverfield, *Yorkshire Archaeological Journal*, xxiii (1914–15), pp. 396–7; E. W. Crossley, *Yorkshire Archaeological Journal*, xxiv (1916–17), pp. 102–4; N. Joliffe, *Archaeological Journal*, vol. xcviii (1941), pp. 36–61, esp. p. 38.

Silchester

Silchester in Hampshire is the site of the Roman town Calleva Atrebatum, the civitas capital of the Atrebates. Excavations have taken place in the town on many occasions from 1864 onwards, but the remains of the massive walls must have been visible in the sixteenth century, when the tombstone now in Robert Cotton's collection was found in the area.

Fig. 21. Tombstone of Flavia Victorina (no. 14)   *Fig. 22.* Milestone (no. 15)

14. *Tombstone of Flavia Victorina* (fig. 21)

The tombstone is said to have been found in or before 1577 at Silchester, and already appears in the first edition of Camden's *Britannia* (1586). It was removed to Lord Burghley's house in London, and presumably was acquired by Cotton from there. Now in the store of the Cambridge University Museum of Archaeology and Anthropology, inv. D 1970.10.

Ht. 95 cm.; w. 60 cm.; d. 9.5 cm.

The tombstone is simple in form, but elegant, with the inscription contained in an undecorated moulded frame. The condition is generally good, with only a piece missing at the bottom left corner, but otherwise little damage or weathering. The inscription remains easily read, as the letters are of reasonably even height (except those deliberately elongated) and are well spaced.

MEMORIAE	Memoriae
FL.VICTORI	Fl(aviae) Victori-
NAE. T.TAM	nae T(itus) Tam(monius)
VICTOR	Victor
CONIUNX	coniunx
POSVIT	posuit

To the memory of Flavia Victorina. Titus Tammonius Victor, her husband, set this up.

163

In the first line the *A* and *E* of *Memoriae* are ligatured; in line two the *F* and *T* are elongated, and the final *I* is smaller and squashed; in both lines three and four the central *T* is elongated; in line five the central *I* is elongated; and in line six the *I* is smaller.

The message is simple and to the point: neither of the people named in the inscription is known from other sources, although a T. Tammonius Vitalis, son of Saenius Tammonius, is mentioned in another inscription from Silchester (*RIB* 67), a dedication to Hercules found in the forum: Wacher suggests the family was prominent in local civic life and that Roman citizenship had been granted for service as a local magistrate. Boon suggests a date in the third, or even the early fourth, century, as the 'Memoriae' formula is not an early one. This is the only tombstone found at Silchester.

Bibliography: *RIB* 87; *CIL* VII 8; Camden, *Britannia* (1586), p. 135; Horsley, p. 332, Hampshire no. I, ill'd p. 192 N. 75; G. C. Boon, *Silchester, The Roman Town of Calleva* (Newton Abbot, 1974), p. 186; J. Wacher, *The Towns of Roman Britain* (London, 1974), pp. 274–5.

Peterborough?

The final item in Cotton's collection is a milestone of unknown provenance: alone of all his collection it is not mentioned in any edition of Camden, and first appears in Horsley (1732, p. 278), who says he saw it at Conington. Horsley tentatively placed it in his section on Cumberland, in the Old Carlisle area, but he cheerfully admits that he does not know whether it should be put there:

I wonder much that this inscription, being amongst Sir *Robert Cotton's* collection and yet remaining at *Conington*, should not have been published before, and particularly that *Cambden* should have taken no notice of it. Where this inscription was first found, is not known; but I leave it in this place, because I know not where to dispose of it better.

However, it was noted in the *Journal of Roman Studies* for 1922, and subsequently by Collingwood in 1928, that the stone (Jurassic or oolitic limestone) does not belong to the Old Carlisle region, and in *RIB* it is suggested that the milestone may have been found locally, somewhere near Conington, which is some eight miles from Peterborough. This analysis has since been confirmed by the research of Jeffrey Sedgley, who points to the geological similarities between this and other milestones from Durobrivae (Water Newton, also near Peterborough) and Girton, Cambridge. He suggests the stones all came from nearby Barnack (Barnack Freestone or Rag). In this case the milestone may well have stood on Ermine Street.

15. *Milestone* (fig. 22)

For the provenance, see above. Now in the store of the Cambridge University Museum of Archaeology and Anthropology, inv. D 1970.14.
Ht. 115 cm.; w. (at top) *c*. 25 cm.; d. c. 19 cm.

This is a tall, rather irregularly shaped stone, basically rectangular with rounded corners at the front and also rounded off at the back. It is wider at the top and tapers a little towards the foot. A crack runs down the centre of the stone with partial filling (in mastic?) at the top where a V-shaped sliver is missing. The back of the stone was only roughly worked, and some of the tool marks are still visible here. The inscription is placed on the front face, but the ends of some lines run onto the curved surface at the right side. The letters are deeply cut but rather roughly formed, and the inscription is not very easy to read: I rely here on the reading in *RIB*. Several letters are ligatured.

D N FL IVL	D(omino) N(ostro) Fl(avio) Iul(io)
CRISPO	Crispo
NOB CAES	nob(ilissimo) Caes(ari)
FL CONS	Fl(avi) Cons-
TANTINI	tantini
MAXIMI	Maximi
PII FILIO	Pii filio
DIVI	divi
CONST	Const-
ANTI PI	anti Pi(i)
NEPOTI	nepoti

To our Lord Flavius Julius Crispus, most noble Caesar, son of Flavius Constantinus Maximus Pius, grandson of the deified Constantius Pius.

Crispus was the son of Constantine the Great and grandson of Constantius Chlorus; he himself was Caesar A.D. 317–26, so the milestone must date from these years. Unfortunately, although the inscription provides us at length with the titles and ancestry of the noble Crispus, it gives no clues about where it stood or the distance to the next town: such milestones were often designed to glorify the reigning emperor rather than to give meaningful and helpful directions to the traveller.

Bibliography: *RIB* 2239; *CIL* VII 1153, and p. 313; Horsley, p. 278, Cumbria no. LIX, ill'd on p. 192 N. 48; *Journal of Roman Studies* (1922), p. 281; Collingwood, *CW* XXVIII (1928), p. 119, no. 28; Jeffrey P. Sedgley, *The Roman Milestones of Britain: their Petrology and probable Origin*, British Archaeological Reports no. 18 (Oxford, 1975), p. 25, no. 26, and p. 7.

TABLE OF ABBREVIATIONS

ANRW	*Aufstieg und Niedergang der römischen Welt*
Breeze and Dobson	David J. Breeze and Brian Dobson, *Hadrian's Wall* (Harmondsworth, 1978)
Camden, *Britannia*	William Camden, *Britannia* – various editions are cited, including the first of 1586 and the 6th of 1600. Quotations are from the 1695 edition edited and translated by E. Gibson.
CIL	*Corpus Inscriptionum Latinarum*
CW	*Transactions of the Cumberland and Westmorland Antiquarian and Archæological Society*

Haverfield, *CW*   F. Haverfield, 'Cotton Iulius F.VI. Notes on Reginald Bainbrigg of Appleby, on William Camden and some Roman Inscriptions', *CW*, xi (1911), pp. 343–78

Holder   P. A. Holder, *The Roman Army in Britain* (London, 1982)

Horsley   J. Horsley, *Britannia Romana* (London, 1732)

Phillips, *CSIR*   E. J. Phillips, *Corpus Signorum Imperii Romani G. B. I*, 1. *Corbridge. Hadrian's Wall East of the North Tyne* (Oxford, 1977)

RIB   R. G. Collingwood and R. P. Wright, *The Roman Inscriptions of Britain I: Inscriptions on Stone* (Oxford, 1965)

Richmond, *HN*   I. A. Richmond, 'The Romans in Redesdale', *A History of Northumberland*, vol. xv, ed. M. H. Dodds (Newcastle, 1940), pp. 63–154

I would like to thank Dr Lawrence Keppie of the Hunterian Museum, Glasgow, for looking over an early draft of this paper and for making many useful suggestions, and Dr Robin Boast of the Cambridge University Museum of Archaeology and Anthropology for giving me access to the material in store. The photographs of the stones are reproduced with the kind permission of the Museum of Archaeology and Anthropology.

1 Two appeared in the first (1586) edition (nos. 10 and 12 here), three in the 1600 edition (nos. 2, 3, 4), and one (no. 15) never appeared in Camden.

2 BL, Cotton MS. Julius F. VI, f. 326 [309]; Haverfield, *CW*, p. 356. It appears for the first time in the 1607 edition of Camden's *Britannia*, on p. 664, and was probably recorded on Cotton and Camden's visit to the North in 1599.

3 Breeze and Dobson, p. 254; Holder, p. 117.

4 For the complexities of references to the numen/numina of the emperor(s) in Roman-British inscriptions, see D. Fishwick, 'The Imperial *Numen* in Roman Britain', *Journal of Roman Studies*, lix (1969), pp. 76–91.

5 BL, Cotton MS. Julius F. VI, f. 326 [309]; Haverfield, *CW*, p. 356.

6 Horsley, p. xv.

7 Phillips, *CSIR*, p. 73. Dr Keppie points out that by this date most of the cohort would be recruited from Southern England, and suggests that the use of Gallic motifs was therefore a deliberate retention of old regimental traditions.

8 BL, Cotton MS. Julius F. VI, f. 327 [310]; Haverfield, *CW*, p. 357; Camden, *Britannia* (1607), p. 662.

9 Holder, p. 123.

10 This is stated by *RIB*, but is presumably based on the fact that it appears in Camden's 1607 ed. and was collected by Cotton.

11 The copy of Horsley I consulted in the British Library (pressmark 806.i.1) has at this point (p. 235) a handwritten comment in the text 'I always thought it might be a priest's veil and a patera', and refers to Tacitus's *Annals*. This volume appears to have been owned by Dr J. Ward, presumably the authority whose opinion Horsley quotes in several places in his work, as the date of the bequest is 1761.

12 See D. Harrison, *Along Hadrian's Wall* (London, 1956), p. 261.

13 The exchange can be followed in *Notes & Queries* (1877), pt. 2 (July), pp. 28, 74, 133.

14 Camden, *Britannia* (1607), p. 662, and in BL, Cotton MS. Julius F. VI, f. 326 [309], quoted in Haverfield, *CW*, p. 357.

15 Richmond, p. 137; E. B. Birley and G. S. Keeney, 'Fourth Report on excavations at Housesteads', *Archaeologia Aeliana*, 4th ser., xii (1935), pp. 222–3.

16 Horsley, pp. xv and 234 ascribes the reading 'prima stat.' to Ward (see n. 11), and says the phrase 'shews that this station was then the most advanced to the north, unless we suppose (as an ingenious gentleman conjectures) that this expression only means, it being the first station beyond the wall.'

17 Fishwick, 'The Imperial *Numen* in Roman Britain', pp. 76–91.

18 This has been further elaborated by R. Embleton and F. Graham, *Hadrian's Wall in the Days of the Romans* (Newcastle upon Tyne, 1984), p.

281: 'Mogons was a Germanic God associated with the Rhineland from which the Vangiones came' – this assumes that Secundinus was in some way connected with the cohors I Vangionum which formed the garrison of Risingham in the third century, but there is no reason to suppose that he had any connection with this unit, and it is not mentioned in the inscription.

19 Breeze and Dobson, p. 263 and fig. 43c.

20 A similar comment appears, in Camden's handwriting, in BL, Cotton MS. Julius F. VI, f. 326 [309], quoted in Haverfield, *CW*, p. 357.

21 BL, Cotton MS. Julius F. VI, f. 326 [309]; Camden, *Britannia* (1607), p. 662.

22 Mentioned by Bainbrigg, BL, Cotton MS. Julius F. VI, f. 325 [308].

23 'Inter rudera vetusti castri reperta': Camden, *Britannia* (1607), p. 660.

24 For 'numini eius' see Hübner in *CIL* VII 1037; Richmond, *HN* XV, p. 149; for 'natali eius', *Journal of Roman Studies*, xxxiv (1944), p. 85; *RIB* 1270; Hassall in W. Rodwell (ed.), *Temples, Churches and Religion. Recent Research in Roman Britain*, B. A. R. British series, lxxvii (Oxford, 1980), p. 82.

25 J. Helgeland, 'Roman Army Religion', *ANRW*, xvi:2 (1978), pp. 1481–8.

26 Holder, p. 110.

27 Ibid., p. 73.

28 BL, Cotton MS. Julius F. VI, f. 353 [334]; Haverfield, *CW*, p. 374.

29 Phillips, *CSIR*, p. 96, no. 260, pl. 70.

30 BL, Cotton MS. Julius F. VI, f. 330 [312]; Camden, *Britannia* (1695), p. 848.

31 J. Horsley, *Materials for the History of Northumberland* in *Inedited Contributions to the History of Northumberland*, pt. i, (Newcastle upon Tyne, 1869), p. 5.

32 See Haverfield, *CW*, p. 357, for the arguments.

33 R. J. A. Wilson, *A Guide to the Roman Remains in Britain*, 3rd ed. (London, 1988), p. 291.

34 Breeze and Dobson, p. 244.

35 BL, Cotton MS. Julius F. VI, f. 345 [326]; Camden, *Britannia* (1600), p. 719 bis; (1607), p. 660.

36 Horsley, p. 226: 'the rest of it since Cambden's time is entirely gone, together with the outer or upper stratum of this part of the stone, deeper than the cut of the letters.'

37 Holder, p. 117.

38 Eric Birley, 'The Religion of the Roman Army: 1895–1977', *ANRW*, xvi:2 (1978), p. 1516.

39 L. J. F. Keppie, 'The Garrison of the Antonine Wall: Some New Evidence from Bar Hill', *Studien zu den Militärgrenzen Roms*, III: 13, Internationaler Limeskongress, Aalen 1983 (Stuttgart, 1986), pp. 53–7.

40 Wilson, op. cit., p. 253.

41 Camden, *Britannia* (1695), p. 829; Birley, 'The Roman fort and settlement at Old Carlisle', *CW*, li (1951), pp. 17–18.

42 Anon., BL, Harl. MS. 473, f. 15; Camden, *Britannia* (1586), p. 454.

43 As it appears in the 1600 edition of Camden's *Britannia*.

44 Holder, p. 110.

45 Wilson, op. cit., p. 246, suggests that the ala Hispanorum Vettonum was the garrison at Bowes until some time shortly before 208, when it was replaced by the cohors I Thracum.

46 Hanson: Bodl. MS. Dodsworth 58, f. 31v; for discussion, see *Yorkshire Archaeological Journal* (1914–15), pp. 396–7, where Haverfield introduces the discussion, and (1916–17), pp. 102–4, where E. W. Crossley presents a fascinating account of the detective work involved in leading to the conclusion that the 'Thick Hollins' of Hanson's account is now known as 'Bank Top': however, he failed to identify positively any remains of a Roman site the altar could have come from.

47 See *RIB* 627, notes to line 5, and Norah Joliffe, 'Dea Brigantia', *Archaeological Journal*, xcviii (1941), p. 38.

48 Camden, *Britannia* (1607), p. 563; Horsley, pp. xxiii and 313.

49 For this concept see under no. 1.

50 Joliffe, 'Dea Brigantia', pp. 36–61.

51 Joliffe, pl. 1; G. de la Bédoyère, *The Finds of Roman Britain* (London, 1989), pp. 144–5, fig. 87a; M. Henig, *Religion in Roman Britain* (London, 1984), p. 212, fig. 103.

AN EARLY SEVENTEENTH-CENTURY INVENTORY OF COTTON'S ANGLO-SAXON COINS

GAY VAN DER MEER

SIR Robert Cotton's cabinet of antiquities contained a large number of coins. He collected Greek and Roman, Ancient British, Anglo-Saxon, Norman and later English coins,[1] all very important relics of the ancient world and the English past. Like his manuscripts, they became the property of the nation after the death of his grandson in 1702, and, after several moves, were finally incorporated in the new British Museum in 1753.[2] The fire of 1731 in Ashburnham House does not seem to have damaged them. As no provenances of coins acquired by the Museum were recorded before 1837, it is no longer known in the majority of cases which specimens originated from the Cotton collection. In 1954 Michael Dolley, of the Department of Coins and Medals, together with his colleague Mrs Strudwick,[3] published an article in which they reconstructed the Anglo-Saxon portion of Cotton's cabinet on the basis of an eighteenth-century manuscript catalogue and the illustrations of Anglo-Saxon coins in John Speed's *History of Great Britaine* (1611). They came to the conclusion that the original Cotton collection had comprised at least 160 Anglo-Saxon coins, 125 of which could still be identified in the trays of the British Museum. Since then, an early seventeenth-century manuscript inventory of Cotton's Anglo-Saxon coins has come to light in the Netherlands which antedates the other catalogue by nearly a century and a half. It enlarges the number of 160 coins identified so far with fifty more specimens, twenty-five of which can be added with some certainty to the 125 already located in the British Museum. These 210 coins 'can claim to be regarded as the first scholarly collection of Anglo-Saxon coins ever to be put together'.[4] Its reconstruction is important, not only for its intrinsic historical interest, but also because it reveals traces of unrecorded finds and provides evidence of authenticity for coins under suspicion of being forgeries.

In 1954 Dolley and Strudwick had at their disposal a catalogue, compiled in 1748 by the antiquary Samuel Pegge (1704–96), and preserved in the Department of Coins and Medals. This manuscript lists the 128 Anglo-Saxon Cotton coins that were still together at that time (126 pennies and two unidentifiable sceattas). Pegge's motive for cataloguing them was probably that he knew the collection had been pilfered since Cotton's death, more than a century before. Some ten years later, the Rev. Andrew Gifford (1700–84), the first numismatist to be officially in charge of the collection, found that nine more coins had disappeared, but, on the other hand, he could round up thirteen strays, which had been found or had been returned to the Museum in the meantime. Afterwards five more coins must have been abstracted.

There was, then, a record of 141 coins which had certainly belonged to Cotton. Pegge remarked that of the thirty-four coins illustrated by Speed only fifteen were left. Though Speed had not claimed explicitly that he had drawn on the Cotton collection alone for his Anglo-Saxon coins, there was a tradition in 1748 that this was, in fact, the case. Dolley and Strudwick, therefore, added the nineteen missing Speed coins to the 141 registered specimens. Of the total tally of 160 coins thirty-five had gone astray.[5] Part of these missing coins could be identified as later acquisitions of the Museum, though one can never be absolutely sure that they are the original Cotton specimens. They may be die-duplicates.

The Museum Meermanno-Westreenianum at The Hague possesses two early seventeenth-century manuscript volumes with notes on numismatic subjects.[6] One of them contains notes on Greek, Roman, Byzantine and Jewish coins, and on engraved gemstones, while the second comprises lists of and notes on Merovingian, Carolingian and Arabic coins in various contemporary European collections. Among them, there is an inventory of Sir Robert Cotton's Anglo-Saxon coins, many of them quite unknown to either Speed, Pegge or Gifford. Also of interest are lists of twenty of Cotton's Ancient British coins, later illustrated by Speed, of seven of his Roman coins, and of five coins of William the Conqueror. In the first volume Cotton is mentioned only once, in connexion with some Roman coins which were sent to him in 1618.

These notebooks once belonged to the great French scholar Nicolas Claude Fabri de Peiresc (1580–1637) (fig. 1), and most of the notes are in his own hand.[7] He was the eldest son of a country nobleman with large estates in Provence. Like Cotton, at an early age he became interested in old books, manuscripts and antiquities, especially in coins, both ancient and medieval. Like Cotton, he had a share in the political life of his country as a councillor in the Parlement of Aix-en-Provence. He lived in that town for most of his life, though he had travelled extensively in his youth and lived in Paris from 1616 to 1623. Apart from his political work and the management of his estates, he filled his life with study, collecting, and, above all, with writing letters to a large circle of friends in France, England, the Low Countries, Germany and Italy. It is estimated that he wrote in all around 10,000 letters. Fortunately he kept copies of the letters he wrote himself. Many of them have been preserved, but of the letters he received in reply, most were probably destroyed, among them the letters Cotton must have written to him. It seems that after Peiresc's death, when his collections, papers and eighty-one volumes of notebooks were in his brother's house, his nieces used letters and pages of notebooks as wrappers around the cocoons of their silkworms and as hair curlers.[8]

Peiresc was a truly universal scholar. Among the many disciplines in which he was interested were archaeology, philology, natural history, horticulture, astronomy, mathematics, and oriental cultures. Between 1888 and 1898 Tamizey de Larroque edited

Fig. 1. Portrait of Nicolas Claude Fabri de Peiresc. Pierre Gassendi, *Viri illustris Nicolai Claudij Fabricij de Peiresc...Vita*, 3rd ed. (Hagæ-Comitum, 1655), frontispiece

part of his letters,[9] but he died before he could finish his project, which would have comprised eleven volumes at least. Many of Peiresc's letters and most of his notebooks are now in the Bibliothèque d'Inguimbert at Carpentras, not far from Aix. The British Library possesses a number of letters written by Peiresc to Cotton, Camden, Selden and Spelman, some in Latin, but most of them in French.[10] Peiresc's best friend and biographer, Pierre Gassendi, relates how Peiresc met these scholars, when he visited London for a month in 1606.[11] He was received several times by King James I, and was made very welcome by learned men and collectors, who showed him their manuscripts and antiquities. That must have given Peiresc his opportunity to study and catalogue Cotton's Anglo-Saxon coins. Everyone admired Peiresc's learning and acumen. After his departure he and Cotton exchanged letters until 1622. It has often been assumed that their correspondence came to an end then, because Cotton blamed Peiresc for taking four years to return one of his most precious manuscripts, the Cotton Genesis, after he had lent it to him. However, it was Camden who urged Peiresc repeatedly to send it back, not Cotton himself. The war between France and England, and Camden's death in 1623, were probably the main reasons why they stopped writing to each other.[12] Peiresc himself also generously gave or lent books and manuscripts to anyone who needed them for his studies. Like Cotton, he was always ready to help other scholars.

There are some intriguing passages in letters from Peiresc to Camden between 1617 and 1620.[13] On 11 December 1617 he writes that he would like to see a sample of what Cotton has started to have printed of his Anglo-Saxon coins.[14] In a letter of 25 August 1618 to a friend, one of the Dupuy brothers, he informs him that he has received from Camden a beautiful book about the seals and coins of the kings of England, but that it is too voluminous to send it to him. In his edition of the letters, Tamizey de Larroque noted that, after a long search, in which he was helped by several scholars in London and Paris, he had not succeeded in finding this book.[15] In 1619 Peiresc writes to Camden that one of his friends would very much like to have a copy of the book on Anglo-Saxon coins which Camden sent him the year before, but that he had told him that it would be difficult to find another copy, as they had only been issued for Cotton's private use. In 1620 he asks Camden to send another two copies. He clearly refers to a recently printed work, not to a written list. So far, no one has been able to identify this book.[16]

Peiresc possessed about 18,000 coins, 5,000 books, beautifully bound, and 200 manuscripts, apart from his eighty-one notebooks.[17] His younger brother, Palamède Fabri de Vallavez, who was devoted to him, inherited them after his death in 1637. When Vallavez died in 1647, his son, Claude de Rians, sold Peiresc's collections as soon as he could to various buyers. After some detours, a substantial part of the coins found their way into the Cabinet des Médailles of the Bibliothèque Nationale, and many of his books and manuscripts were acquired by the same institution. The majority of his notebooks, and other papers that had been preserved, were later brought together in Carpentras. Two notebooks that should have been there are the volumes with numismatic notes which are now at The Hague. Their pedigree can be traced back to the time just after Vallavez's death. Peiresc's nephew sold part of the coins to Achille d'Harlay, Count of Beaumont. Pierre Gassendi complains in the third edition of his biography (1655) that the two notebooks are in the possession of the buyer of the coins, who had got hold of the volumes by a trick, and that they have lain hidden in the buyer's house for seven years, of service to no one, being consumed by bookworms in the dark.[18] This is an exaggeration, for the owner looked after them very well, and had them bound and decorated with his coat of arms and his monogram (fig. 2). Afterwards, two other French collectors in succession owned them (Claude Gabriel de Boze and the Président de Cotte), until they were sold by auction in 1804 to the Dutch collector Pieter van Damme for 410 francs. When van Damme's books were sold in their turn in 1808, the Baron van Westreenen bought the two notebooks for two guilders and two stuivers. After his death the Dutch state acquired his collections, which are now housed in the Museum Meermanno-Westreenianum. There they were rediscovered at the end of the nineteenth century by French scholars like Delisle and Prou (see n. 7 below). However, at the time no one recognized the importance of the inventory of Cotton's Anglo-Saxon coins in the second volume. When I found it in 1961, I had photographs made of the relevant pages, which I showed to Christopher Blunt and Michael Dolley. They set to work at once to

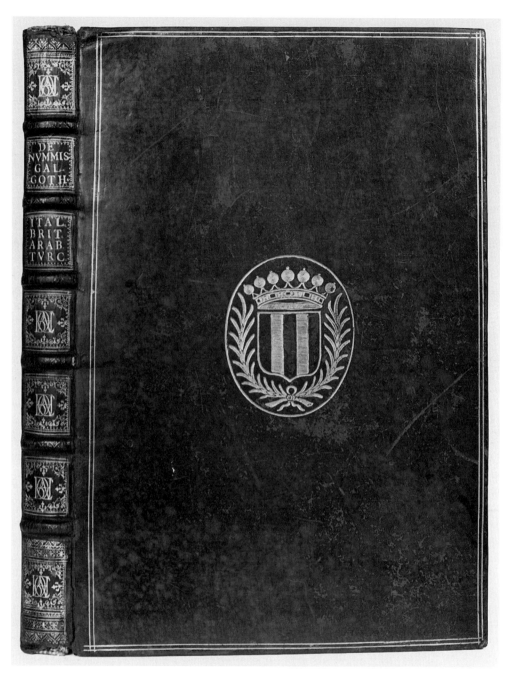

Fig. 2. Binding on Peiresc's second notebook, stamped with Achille d'Harlay's coat of arms. On the spine are his monogram and the title: *De Nummis Gal. Goth. Ital. Brit. Arab. Turc.* The Hague, Rijksmuseum Meermanno Westeenianum, MS 10 C 31

172

study Peiresc's Latin coin descriptions and remarks, and to arrange the coins in the right order. Peiresc lists 175 coins in all. Blunt and Dolley drew up a table in which the page numbers for each coin in Peiresc's notebook were plotted against the numbers in Pegge's catalogue and Speed's *History* respectively. It turned out that thirty-three of the coins in Pegge's catalogue of 1748 (with Gifford's additions) do not figure in Peiresc's lists. Cotton must have acquired them after Peiresc's visit in 1606. One wonders how many such additions went missing without a trace in the period between Cotton's death in 1631 and Pegge's catalogue. Also conspicuously absent from Peiresc's list, and, for that matter, from Pegge's catalogue as well, are two coins in Speed's book, namely the famous gold coin of the moneyer Pendraed from the time of Offa,[19] and a rare St Edmund memorial penny. Both are now back in the British Museum as later acquisitions. Cotton probably added them to his collection between 1606 and 1611, and they must have been lost before Pegge's check in 1748. Incidentally, the fact that thirty-three of the thirty-four coins illustrated by Speed (the Pendraed coin included) have now turned out to have actually belonged to Cotton vindicates the old tradition that Speed drew on his collection alone. Of the 175 coins in Peiresc's notebook fifty could now for the first time be given a Cotton provenance. Blunt and Dolley were able to trace the probable whereabouts of a number of these new specimens. 125 Cotton coins had already been located in the British Museum, and now twenty-five more pieces could be added to that tally with more or less certainty. Other rarities could be traced to the Hunterian collection in Glasgow, a few to the Ashmolean Museum, one to the Fitzwilliam Museum, and one to the Leeds University collection.[20] Of the rest, no present location could be established with any certainty, because they are common specimens. A few coins seem to be unrecorded, such as a penny of Edward the Elder's Hand type of the moneyer Fugel, which was also seen by Pegge in 1748, but cannot now be traced.

In 1961 Blunt, Dolley and I intended to write a paper on the new Cotton material, but for a variety of reasons nothing came of it then. Sadly, Christopher Blunt, Michael Dolley and Mrs Strudwick are no longer alive. However, the material is too interesting to be left unpublished. I shall restrict myself here to general observations about Peiresc's inventory. With the help of the table drawn up by Blunt and Dolley, I hope later to publish an annotated list of the fifty new coins in one of the English numismatic periodicals.

Some interesting conclusions can be drawn from the contents of the inventory. If we assume that Peiresc himself, actually at the time of his visit, noted down the coins which are not in Speed's book, then that means that Speed illustrated only a selection of Cotton's Anglo-Saxon coins, and that his collection was already very substantial in 1606. Dolley remarked in 1954 that, unfortunately, we know of no reference that would warrant our describing it as a sixteenth-century collection.[21] The fact that Cotton owned around 175 Anglo-Saxon coins as early as 1606 adds weight to the supposition that he had begun to collect them in the sixteenth century.

Dolley and Strudwick pointed out that a high proportion of Cotton's coins show a specific geographical pattern.[22] More than 80% of the 160 Cotton coins they knew then were struck north of the Thames. This led them to the conclusion that, as the Cotton estates were primarily in the Midlands, the cabinet had been built up in the main from local finds. The fifty new coins in Peiresc's notebook seem to confirm this pattern. Dolley's supposition that the Cotton cabinet drew heavily upon three unpublished finds, most notably a large hoard of pence of Edward the Elder, is also interesting.[23] Cotton possessed forty-four pennies of this king, more than a fifth of his whole collection. Thirty-eight of them were still together in 1748, two of which went missing afterwards. Three Edward the Elder coins in Peiresc's list, but not in Pegge's, have since then probably found their way back into the British Museum.

Of the sixty-nine coins that were lost in 1748 (the fifty new ones and the nineteen in Speed) a high percentage are early. The Mercian component had suffered most. For instance, no less than twenty-four coins of Offa, Coenwulf and Burgred, described by Peiresc, were no longer there in 1748. All in all, fifty-seven of the coins struck before Edgar's reform of the coinage of 973 must by that time have been stolen, as opposed to only twelve of the post-reform ones, i.e. nearly five times as many, whereas the ratio of pre-reform to post-reform coins in Cotton's collection was approximately three to one. Attempts to find out if any conclusions can be drawn from the provenance of coins probably recovered by the British Museum later on were unsuccessful. They are so diverse that it would be impossible to point a finger at any individual culprits. Dolley was surprised that a now common specimen like Cnut's Quatrefoil type was not represented in the Cotton collection.[24] Peiresc's list proves that there was at least one, now apparently lost.

Many of the 175 Anglo-Saxon coins in Peiresc's notebook, in fact 140, occur twice in two different sections. One section consists of a numbered list of four pages, in which the coins are arranged alphabetically under kings' names. This list stops after three coins of Harold I, but the numbers continue for a while, as if the writer intended to go on with his catalogue, but was prevented from finishing it. The king's name which follows in the alphabet after Harold (apart from Harthacnut, whose coins were listed under Cnut) is Offa. His coins are therefore absent from this numbered list. The letter forms of the Latin type descriptions are gothic, but the legends are in roman capitals. There are a few remarks in English in the margin. Exactly the same list, though much less neatly written, is to be found in Cotton MS. Titus B. VI, ff. 245r–246v. There it is headed by the caption *De Moneta*, but no mention is made of Cotton.[25] On the first page (fig. 3) of the neat copy of this same list in the notebook, however, Peiresc wrote the following text in his own handwriting:

Inscriptiones ord. alphabet. a D. Tato collectae ex Anglosaxonis antiquis nummis qui sunt penes virum Nobil. D. Robertus Cottonus Londini (Inscriptions in alphabetical order collected by Mr Tate, from the ancient Anglo-Saxon coins, which are at the London house of that noble man Sir Robert Cotton).

We may assume, therefore, that it was Cotton's friend Francis Tate who composed this list. Peiresc knew him, for in his biography Pierre Gassendi mentions Tate as being

174

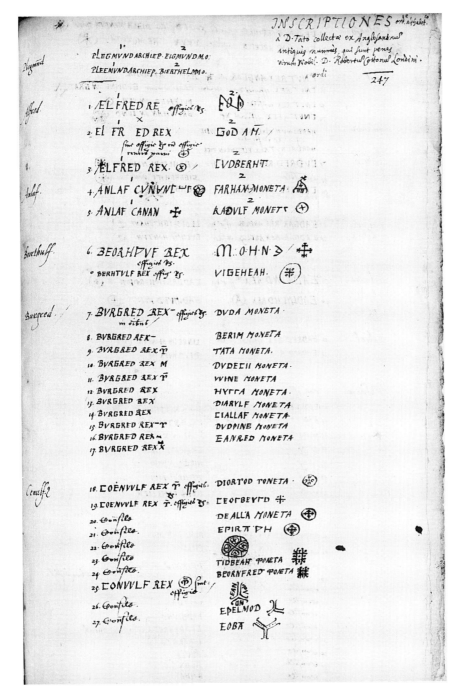

Fig. 3. First page of Francis Tate's list of Cotton's Anglo–Saxon coins, with Peiresc's note in the top right-hand corner. The Hague, Rijksmuseum Meermanno Westreenianum, MS 10 C 31, p. 247

175

present when Peiresc discussed some etymological questions with Camden.[26] Both the rough draft and the neat copy are written in the same hand. It seems plausible that the rough draft was made first, as several words were crossed out and corrected. The neat version was copied from it, but some new mistakes must have been made in the copying, for instance in the name of King Beorhtwulf, where the '1' was left out.

The second section, comprising seventeen pages, contains more elaborate descriptions of the same coins (but clearly not copied from Tate's list), and of thirty-one additional coins, ranging from Offa to William the Conqueror, in Peiresc's own handwriting. On several pages there are references to Cotton. It is difficult to decide which inventory was composed first. Probably Tate listed Cotton's coins some time before Peiresc's visit, while Peiresc made his own catalogue, and also received a copy of Tate's earlier list. Four of the coins Tate described apparently were not seen by Peiresc. However, if Tate's list were made after 1606 and sent over to Peiresc, it is difficult to explain how Peiresc could have noted down thirty-one more coins than Tate.

As for the correctness of the attributions to kings, Tate did not assign the kings to any kingdoms. With the exception of Archbishop Plegmund, who heads the list with two coins, they are arranged in strictly alphabetical order. Peiresc probably would not have been able to identify Cotton's Anglo-Saxon coins better than Cotton himself. He must have derived his identifications from Cotton's own notes, as Tate and Speed must also have done.[27] On the other hand, Camden, in the revised edition of *Britannia* of 1607, referred to Peiresc as the most noble, and as far as the antiquity of coins is concerned, by far the most learned and shrewd young man.[28] Of course, numismatic knowledge in the field of Anglo-Saxon coins was still in its infancy in the early seventeenth century. Dolley has pointed out that Pegge, in 1748, was still unable to distinguish the coins of Æthelstan of East Anglia from those of Æthelstan of All England.[29] Tate also mixed them up in his list. Peiresc recorded eight coins of Æthelstan and one of Eadmund, both kings of East Anglia, on a separate page under the heading *Nummi Saxonici*, with the remark that it had been difficult to put them in the right order, because the letter forms were much older than one would expect for the century in which the English kings Æthelstan and Eadmund ruled. But the coins which were really struck for Æthelstan and Eadmund of All England, he listed in the right place, after those of Edward the Elder (fig. 4). Peiresc assigned King Æthelweard of East Anglia to Mercia as a predecessor of Offa, with 714 as the alleged initial year of his reign, with the comment that it was not quite certain that these coins could be attributed to this king. One coin, however, of the same Æthelweard, of the same type, was entered under the heading *Ex Regno Nordanhimbrorum*, though with some doubt. It is true that he gave four coins of Edward the Confessor to Edward the Martyr, who is not otherwise represented in the collection, but Peiresc did see the difference between those and the coins of Edward the Elder. Of course, moneyers' names were often misread, both by Tate and Peiresc, though not always the same ones. It is clear, in any case, that a lot of thought was given to the identification of the kings who had struck the coins. No effort was made yet to identify the mints.

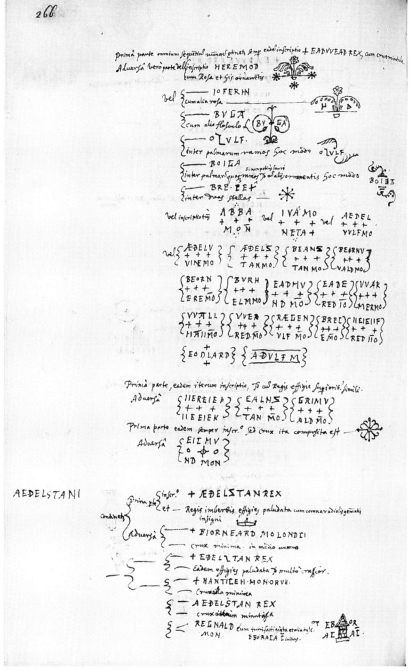

Fig. 4. Page from Peiresc's inventory of Cotton's Anglo-Saxon coins, showing coins of Edward the Elder (Wessex) and Æthelstan (All England). The Hague, Rijksmuseum Meermanno Westreenianum, MS 10 C 31, p. 266

177

In 1983 David Sturdy published drawings of five Anglo-Saxon coins which he had found in another manuscript that had once belonged to Peiresc, namely a volume containing notes on England, now at Carpentras.[30] These drawings were made by Peiresc's brother, Palamède Fabri de Vallavez, who visited England and the Low Countries in 1608. Before he left Paris, Peiresc sent him from Aix a long list of instructions, telling him whom he should visit and what he should do when he got there. One of these persons was of course Sir Robert Cotton.[31] Peiresc asked his brother to hand him a letter from himself, together with some *médailles* (i.e. Roman coins). He should ask Cotton to write to him, and should try to obtain, with Cotton's help, a coin of Carausius, one of Allectus and one of Laelianus, either in silver or in copper, for some of his friends, and he should try to get impresses of some English seals. Among the notes Vallavez made in England, Sturdy found the drawings of the five Anglo-Saxon coins, one of Cuthred of Kent, three of Offa, and one of Beornwulf of Mercia. He suggested that Cotton might have drawn Vallavez's attention to these, as recent finds, which Peiresc had not seen two years before. However, four of them are in Peiresc's own inventory of the coins he saw in Cotton's collection. The fifth is a coin of Beornwulf of Mercia, struck in East Anglia by the moneyer Eadgar.[32] It must have been added to Cotton's collection between 1606 and 1608, and it was still there when Pegge wrote his catalogue in 1748.

The other notebook in the Museum Meermanno-Westreenianum (MS. 10 C 30), with notes mainly on coins from the ancient world, contains only one reference to Cotton. At the top of p. 243, which shows a list of twenty-one Roman coins, Peiresc wrote that he had sent these coins to Cotton as a present in July 1618. There is a letter dated 4 July 1618 in the British Library,[33] in which Peiresc tells Cotton that he is sending him twenty-five or thirty coins of Antoninus Pius, Commodus, Severus and Caracalla, which will further Cotton's plans to assemble everything which the Romans made after their British conquests. Some of them are only casts, because he has not been able to find any originals, which he would much rather have sent him than these impressions. If he finds that they do not displease Cotton too much, he will take courage and get some more together.

Only one Anglo-Saxon coin features in this notebook (on p. 352), but without any mention of Cotton, in a list of Roman and Byzantine coins. It is a penny of Offa, struck by the moneyer Alred, not recorded by Speed or Pegge. The British Museum acquired a similar specimen in 1896,[34] but whether it is the very coin Peiresc described is not certain. It is possible that he saw it in a French collection, and the same is true for three other pennies listed in the other volume, with the medieval coins (10 C 31), on a separate page (p. 69; see fig. 5), inserted behind some pages describing Celtic coins in a French collection. One of them is a very rare coin of King Beorhtric of Wessex, of the moneyer Ecghard. Speed illustrated a similar coin of this king, therefore from Cotton's collection, now apparently lost. However, the specimen in Peiresc's notebook is a little different, and it also differs from the three other specimens known so far, all from attested finds.[35] This must be a fifth example, probably found in France, and now lost.

The two other coins on this same page are pennies of Offa, of the moneyers Eoba and

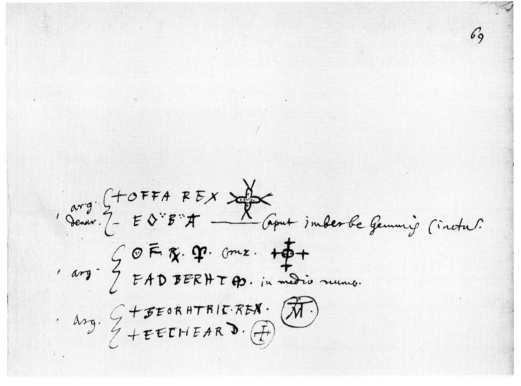

Fig. 5. Page from Peiresc's notebook, with three coins probably seen by him in (a) French collection(s). The Hague, Rijksmuseum Meermanno Westreenianum, MS 10 C 31, p. 69

Eadberht respectively, not known to Speed or Pegge. The Eoba coin is registered on two other pages as well, once on p. 101, with Merovingian and Carolingian coins in a French collection, and once on p. 271, with a description of impresses of seals of King Edgar and King Offa. Peiresc had seen these in the Abbey of St-Denis at Paris, attached to official Anglo-Saxon documents.[36] In the margin of that page, Peiresc remarks that the Eoba coin was found in Gallia Narbonensis, i.e. in the region of Narbonne in the South of France. Metcalf has pointed out[37] that an exceptionally large proportion of the coins of this moneyer have been found on the routeways leading through the Alpine passes towards Italy. He did not mention France, but travellers may have sailed to Bordeaux, made their way to Narbonne, and taken a ship to Italy from there.

The three Offa pennies of the moneyers Alred, Eoba and Eadberht must therefore probably be subtracted from the total of 210 registered Cotton coins.[38] It is possible, however, that Peiresc was able to get hold of them and send them to Cotton. In his letter to Cotton of 4 July 1618[39] the last line on the first page is intriguing. He writes:

Les monoyes d'Offa et de Beorhtricus, je les ay tant demandées qu'enfin ....

179

However, we shall never know what the next line was, unless Peiresc's own copy of this letter turns up, for the page is damaged, and the rest of the sentence has disappeared. Similar coins are in the British Museum now as later acquisitions, but they may not be the ones described by Peiresc.

A version of this paper appears in *Jaarboek voor Munt- en Penningkunde*, lxxxi (1994), pp. 215–33.

1 Kevin Sharpe, *Sir Robert Cotton 1586–1631* (Oxford, 1979), pp. 66–7.

2 John Walker, 'The Early History of the Department of Coins and Medals', *British Museum Quarterly*, xviii (1953), pp. 76–80.

3 R. H. M. Dolley and J. S. Strudwick, 'An Early Seventeenth-Century Collection of Anglo-Saxon Coins', *British Numismatic Journal*, xxvii (1954), pp. 302–12; R. H. M. Dolley, 'The Cotton Collection of Anglo-Saxon Coins', *British Museum Quarterly*, xix (1954), pp. 75–81.

4 Dolley and Strudwick, op. cit., p. 302.

5 If one subtracts the nine + five coins stolen after 1748 from the 141 recorded ones, 127 coins are left. Dolley and Strudwick identified 125 of them in the British Museum collection. The remaining two coins were probably sceattas, which were described so ambiguously by Pegge that they cannot now be identified. See Dolley, 'The Cotton Collection of Anglo-Saxon Coins', p. 76.

6 P. C. Boeren, *Catalogus van de handschriften van het Rijksmuseum Meermanno-Westreenianum* ('s-Gravenhage, 1979), pp. 90–1, MSS. 10 C 30–31. Nicolas Claude de Fabri de Peiresc (1580–1637), Tomus I: De Nummis Graecorum, Romanorum et Judaeorum. Tractatus de Monetis. Catalogi Rerum Antiquarum (paginae 1–716). Tomus II: Nummi Gallici, Gothici, Italici, Britannici, Arabici et Turcici (paginae 1–391).

7 For Peiresc's life and the history and contents of his two numismatic notebooks, see Pierre Gassendi, *Viri illustris Nicolai Claudii Fabricii de Peiresc Senatoris Aquisextiensis Vita* (Paris, 1641; 2nd ed., The Hague, 1651; 3rd ed., The Hague, 1655). My quotations are from the third edition. There is an English translation by W. Rand, *The Mirrour of True Nobility & Gentility. Being the Life of the Renowned Nicolaus Claudius Fabricius Lord of Peiresk* (London, 1657); Léopold Delisle, 'Un grand amateur français du dix-septième siècle Fabri de Peiresc', *Annales du Midi*, i (1889), pp. 16–34; M. Prou, 'Fabri de Peiresc et la numismatique mérovingienne', *Annales du Midi*, ii (1890), pp. 137–69; H. J. de Dompierre de Chaufepié, 'Un Manuscrit de Peiresc du Museum Meermanno-Westreenianum à La Haye', *Revue Belge de Numismatique*, lii (1896), pp. 107–20; idem, 'Een groot verzamelaar', *Tijdschrift voor Munt- en Penningkunde*, xvi (1908), pp. 37–69; P. Humbert, *Un amateur: Peiresc (1680–1637)* (Paris, 1933); Linda van Norden, 'Peiresc and the English Scholars', *Huntington Library Quarterly*, xii (1948–9), pp. 369–89.

8 L. Delisle, op. cit., p. 33; H. J. de Dompierre de Chaufepié, op. cit. 1908, p. 57; P. Humbert, op. cit., pp. 58 and 142.

9 Philippe Tamizey de Larroque (ed.), *Lettres de Peiresc*, 7 vols. (Paris, 1888–98).

10 Tamizey de Larroque states, *Lettres de Peiresc*, vol. i, p. 454, n. 4, that there are no copies of letters from Peiresc to Cotton at Carpentras, and that he has not found any letters from Cotton to Peiresc anywhere.

11 Gassendi, op. cit. (3rd ed., 1655), pp. 51–3. In the translation by W. Rand, pp. 99–100.

12 Peiresc had asked for the loan on behalf of a friend, the Jesuit priest Fronton du Duc, who wanted to collate the text with that of other Greek Bible codices. Also, Peiresc had commissioned the painter Daniel Rabel to copy the illustrations. Only two copies were made, now in the Bibliothèque Nationale, Fonds français 9530, ff. 31, 32. It is a pity they were not all copied, as most of the illustrations were lost or damaged in the fire of 1731. Peiresc warned Cotton that such a disaster might happen. See *Lettres de Peiresc*, vol. vii, pp. 766–9, 792, 796, 804, 807, 810–13, 821–3; Sharpe, op. cit., p. 97.

13 *Lettres de Peiresc*, vols. vii, p. 766; i, p. 7; vii, pp. 804–5 and 809.

14 'Je voudrois bien voir quelque eschantillon de ce qu'il a commencé de faire imprimer de ses monnoyes anglo-saxonnes'. *Lettres de Peiresc*, vol. vii, p. 766.

15 Ibid., vol. i, p. 7, n. 2.

16 In June 1618 Peiresc writes to Camden that he has heard that there will be a new edition of his *Britannia*. He will be glad to know whether this is true, how much progress Camden is making, whether Cotton's Anglo-Saxon coins will be inserted in it, and when one can expect to see them. However, Camden had to disillusion him. See *Lettres de Peiresc*, vol. vii, p. 783. Kevin Sharpe, op. cit., pp. 42 and 96, gives as his interpretation of the passage in Peiresc's letter of 11 Dec. 1617 to Camden that Cotton 'drew up a table of Saxon monies which was to be included in a revised edition of *Britannia*', but the voluminous book must have been of a different nature. Cf. also Van Norden, op. cit., p. 379, who seems to think that this book actually was a new edition of the *Britannia*.

17 M. Prou, op. cit., p. 143; H. Omont, 'Les manuscrits et les livres annotés de Fabri de Peiresc', *Annales du Midi*, i (1889), p. 317.

18 Gassendi, op. cit. (3rd ed., 1655), p. 296.

19 Colin Tite, 'Sir Robert Cotton and the gold Mancus of Pendraed', *Numismatic Chronicle*, clii (1992), pp. 177–81. Dr Tite established that this coin was, in fact, owned by Cotton.

20 This is probably the very coin Leeds University acquired in 1954 from Winchester Cathedral Library, to which it had been bequeathed by William Eyre in 1764. In the *Sylloge of Coins of the British Isles*, vol. xxi, *Coins in Yorkshire collections* (London, 1975), p. xxvii, Elizabeth J. E. Pirie convincingly argues that this coin (pl. XXXIV, no. 954) must be genuine, though its authenticity had been questioned. Peiresc's inventory proves that the coin existed in 1606, before the time when forgeries of Anglo-Saxon coins were produced.

21 Dolley and Strudwick, op. cit., p. 302.

22 Ibid., p. 306; Dolley, 'The Cotton Collection of Anglo-Saxon Coins', p. 78.

23 R. H. M. Dolley, 'Some Late Anglo-Saxon Pence', *British Museum Quarterly*, xix (1954), p. 60. See also 'The Cotton Collection of Anglo-Saxon Coins', ibid., pp. 77–8. Dolley announced a forthcoming paper with a reconstruction of this hoard, but such a paper does not figure in R. H. Thompson, 'The Published Writings of Michael Dolley, 1944–1983', in M. A. S. Blackburn (ed.), *Anglo-Saxon Monetary History: Essays in Memory of Michael Dolley* (Leicester, 1986), pp. 315–60.

24 Dolley and Strudwick, op. cit., p. 306. In 1777 coins of this type were still rare in English collections. One or more major hoards of Quatrefoil coins must have come to light in the last decades of the 18th century. See R. H. M. Dolley and D. M. Metcalf, 'Cnut's Quatrefoil type in English Cabinets of the Eighteenth Century', *British Numismatic Journal*, xxix (1958–9), pp. 69–81.

25 Mr Hugh Pagan kindly drew my attention to this list. I am grateful to the British Library for sending me reproductions of these pages, and of some letters written by Peiresc, referred to below.

26 Gassendi, op. cit. (3rd ed., 1655), p. 52.

27 It is now accepted that Cotton was in fact the editor of Speed's *History*: see David Howarth, 'Sir Robert Cotton and the Commemoration of Famous Men', *The British Library Journal*, xviii (1992), p. 26, n. 38, and reprinted above, p. 65, n. 38.

28 W. Camden, *Britannia* (London, 1607), p. 70. See also Gassendi, op. cit., (3rd ed., 1655), p. 53.

29 Dolley and Strudwick, op. cit., p. 304.

30 David Sturdy, 'N. C. Fabri de Peiresc and Five Early Anglo-Saxon Pennies in the Cotton Collection, Drawn c. 1608', *Numismatic Chronicle*, cxliii (1983), pp. 224–7.

31 *Lettres de Peiresc*, vol. vi, Appendice, p. 674.

32 Formerly attributed to Ceolwulf I: H. A. Grueber and C. F. Keary, *A Catalogue of English Coins in the British Museum, Anglo-Saxon Series*, vol. ii (London, 1887), no. 104.

33 Cotton MS. Julius C. III, f. 211.

34 B. M. Acq. 16, ex Montagu sale 1896. See also C. E. Blunt, 'The Coinage of Offa', in R. H. M. Dolley (ed.), *Anglo-Saxon Coins* (London, 1961), p. 57, no. 48. It is still the only specimen known with this spelling of the moneyer's name.

35 C. E. Blunt, 'XVII–XIX Century Manuscript Material on Anglo-Saxon Coins', in Harald Ingholt (ed.), *Centennial Publication of The American Numismatic Society* (New York, 1958), pp. 129–31.

36 Sulphur casts of these seals are in the British Library. See W. de G. Birch, *Catalogue of Seals in the Department of Manuscripts in the British Museum*, vol. i (London, 1887), p. 1, nos. 1 and 3. Miss Marion Archibald kindly gave me this reference.

37 D. M. Metcalf, 'Offa's Pence Reconsidered',

Cunobelin, The Yearbook of the British Association of Numismatic Societies, ix (1963), pp. 37–52 (at p. 38).

38 The Beorhtric coin remains included in the total of 210, because, when Blunt and Dolley drew up their table, they supposed it to be the coin illustrated by Speed, which has now turned out to be a different specimen.

39 Cotton MS. Julius C. III, f. 211.

A CATALOGUE OF SIR ROBERT COTTON'S PRINTED BOOKS?

COLIN G. C. TITE

THE inventory of the goods and chattels of Sir Robert Cotton taken on 20 May 1631, two weeks after his death, records that the upper study at Cotton House, Westminster, was furnished, *inter alia*, with 'i iron prese & ix presses wth printed bookes'.[1] This brief reference draws attention to a subject which has so far received very little consideration – the question of the history, character and present whereabouts of Sir Robert Cotton's library of printed books. In his monograph on the antiquary, Kevin Sharpe observes that

the fate of Cotton's printed books remains a mystery. We know that he owned many from the records of gifts sent by the French scholars and the dedications and expressions of thanks to Cotton by grateful English antiquaries. If he built up a considerable library of printed books, there is no evidence that he took the trouble to catalogue them separately – an omission which suggests a concentration on original material and collections of transcripts.[2]

It is, of course, for his superb collection of manuscripts, charters, rolls and coins that Cotton is primarily known. Much of this was catalogued either during his lifetime or that of his immediate successors and, in the case of the manuscripts, the system of Emperor pressmarks that he devised is still in use. If the printed books were ever organized systematically, the arrangement probably did not long outlive the termination of the family's direct interest in the library on the death of Sir John Cotton, grandson of Sir Robert, in 1702.[3] Certainly there no longer exists a block of Cottonian printed books in the British Library's holdings to parallel its collection of the family's manuscripts. Any printed books that arrived with the manuscripts at Montagu House after the creation of the British Museum in 1753 were destined to be absorbed into the Museum's general collections of printed books and, like other similar accessions, to lose whatever separate identity they may once have possessed.[4] Locating them today is therefore largely a matter of chance unless some piece of evidence exists to direct the searcher to a specific title. Furthermore, the hunt is complicated by the fact that, as with a number of manuscripts, some Cottonian printed books undoubtedly strayed from the library during the seventeenth century, well before its transfer to public ownership. Any search for the family's printed books must therefore take in other collections in addition to those of the British Library.[5] Clearly, work on tracing items in the printed book collection of the Cotton family would be substantially advanced by the identification of a catalogue of the volumes. There are three reasons for thinking that such a listing may have been undertaken. Firstly, Sir Robert Cotton supervised in detail the arrangement and listing of his manuscripts and it might therefore seem surprising if the printed books did not receive some degree of care. Secondly, the survival of catalogues of the printed books (as well as of manuscripts) belonging to other collectors of the period suggests that owners felt that organization and listing were desirable.[6] Thirdly, and most importantly, a list of printed books bearing on a preliminary folio the title 'Catalogus librorum Robert Cotton' is to be found in BL, Add. MS. 35213.

Is this list what it claims to be? A generation ago, Sears Jayne in his *Library catalogues of the English Renaissance* described it without hesitation as a catalogue of Cotton's printed books.[7] However, while this is possible, the manuscript as a whole and this list in particular present a number of problems which must be confronted before the authenticity of the catalogue can be accepted.

Add. MS. 35213 is a composite manuscript in four broad sections. Briefly, its first four folios are a catalogue of printed books and manuscripts belonging to John Dee (who died in 1608).[8] Folios 5r–32r contain a catalogue of manuscripts owned by Henry Savile of Banke (d. 1617),[9] while ff. 33r–44r consist of a number of separate memoranda. The remainder of the volume is almost wholly taken up by the so-called list of Cottonian printed books on ff. 46r–83v.[10] Of these sections, Sir Robert Cotton's connection with the second and third can be clearly established. In the margins of the second section, the Savile catalogue, marking a number of manuscripts – some of which later became Cottonian – are to be found the clover leaf sign and the astronomical sign of Venus which appear not only in another Savile catalogue, BL, Harl. MS. 1879, ff. 1r–10r, which undoubtedly went to Cotton,[11] but also in Cotton's own catalogue of his manuscripts in Harl. MS. 6018. In itself, the evidence from these signs is obviously not conclusive – Cotton was not alone in using such marks in the early seventeenth century – but annotations in his hand are also to be found in the Savile catalogue in Add. MS. 35213. Of these, the most telling appears against an entry of a manuscript which is now BL, Cotton MS. Claudius D. VII: this has been noted in Cotton's hand as lent to Lord William Howard of Naworth and this same annotation is repeated, again by Cotton, against the entry for the same manuscript in his catalogue in Harl. MS. 6018 which he began in 1621. As this borrowing is also noted in a separate list of loans compiled by Cotton and outstanding in April 1621, the Savile catalogue must have been in use as one of his working records shortly after Savile's death in 1617, while the loan to Lord William noted in all three places must surely refer to one and the same borrowing.[12]

Several of the memoranda which occupy ff. 33r–44r, the third section of Add. MS. 35213, are also clearly associated with Cotton. Folio 33r, a list of books that Sir Robert had from the arms painter and genealogist, Jacob Chaloner, and f. 34rv, noting exchanges of manuscripts with Patrick Young, Royal Librarian, are in Cotton's hand. Folios 35r–36v are not, but they are a version of similar entries in the catalogue of Cotton's manuscripts in Harl. MS. 6018. Folios 37r–43v are further lists by Cotton, mainly of manuscripts, most of which can be identified. Folio 44r is a record of four

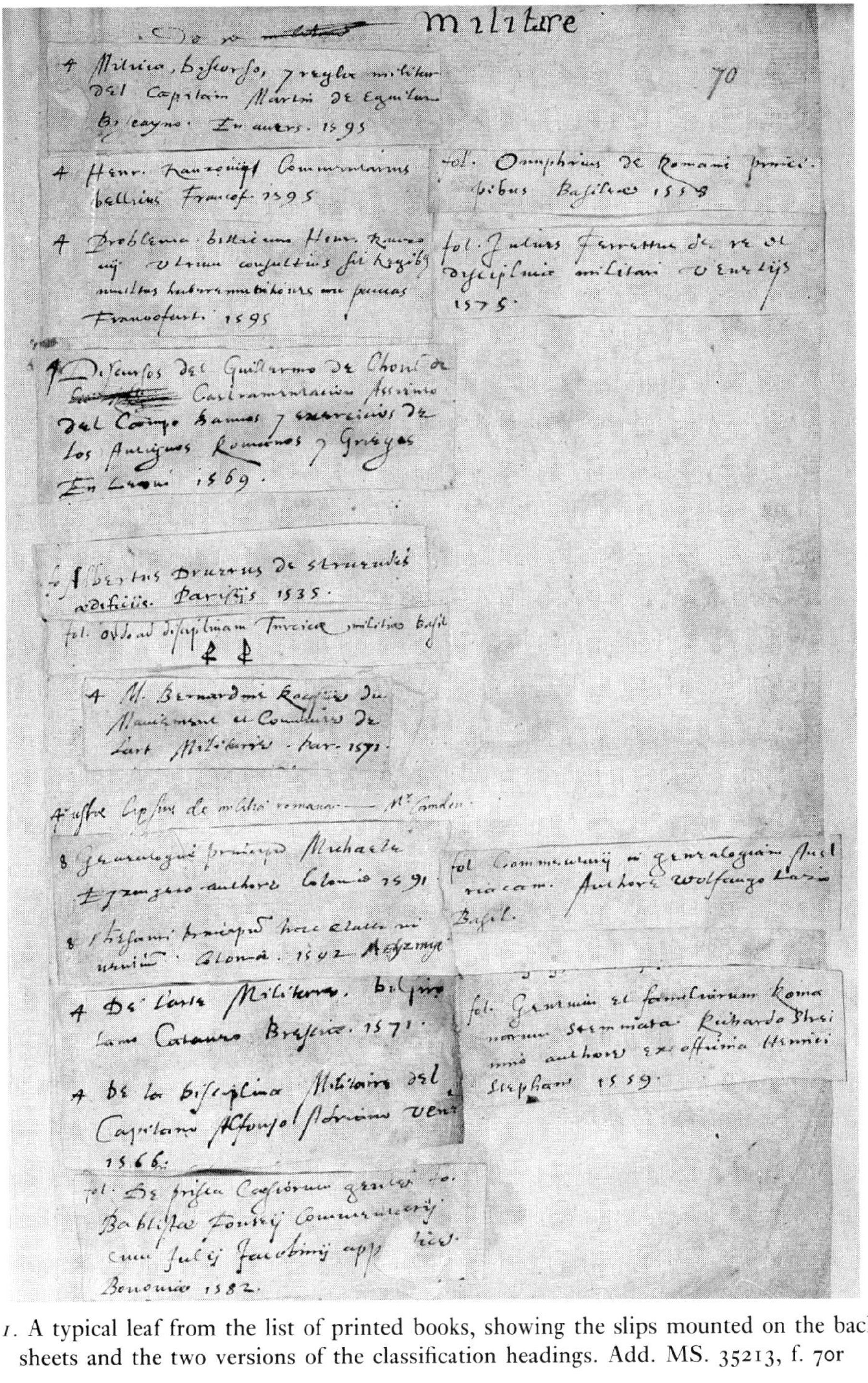

Fig. 1. A typical leaf from the list of printed books, showing the slips mounted on the backing sheets and the two versions of the classification headings. Add. MS. 35213, f. 70r

185

borrowings of manuscripts, at least one of which appears to come from the Cotton library. However, this folio must be a later insertion as it cannot date from before 1634, three years after Cotton's death.[13]

Enough has perhaps been said to establish that the context of the list of printed books on ff. 46r–83v of Add. MS. 35213 is Cottonian. Moreover, the fact that the manuscript is no longer a part of the familiar Cotton series need not cause concern: the same is true not only of Harl. MS. 6018 but of two others of the early Cotton catalogues of manuscripts, Add. MSS. 36789 and 36682.[14] Nevertheless, the list itself requires close scrutiny. It is composed almost entirely of titles written originally on larger sheets which were subsequently cut up. The resulting slips, with one or more titles on each, were then rearranged and mounted on the backing sheets which now form the folios of Add. MS. 35213.[15] The rearrangement was in accordance with a subject classification whose categories have been written, often in duplicate (one version scribbled, the other more carefully inscribed), at the tops of the pages (fig. 1). There is a very large number of these headings – 'Religio', 'Historia Ecclesiastica', 'Politicae', 'Ethicae', 'Astronomia', 'Cronologiae', 'Italia', 'Germanie scriptores', 'Turcay scriptores', 'Hungaria', 'Tartaria', 'Militare', 'Antiquitates', 'Epistolae', 'De Artitectura' [sic] – to mention fewer than half of them. Within these classifications it appears that an attempt has been made to group volumes of a similar size together but this system frequently breaks down, suggesting that not all the slips were available for mounting at the outset. The hand predominantly responsible for the titles on the slips has yet to be firmly identified:[16] it is possible that the writer was a friend or servant of Cotton, engaged on listing his printed books. However, for two reasons it seems unlikely that this is what he was doing when he produced all, or at least the bulk, of this list. He has recorded, in some detail, the titles of approximately 575 books, often giving their size and normally the place and date of publication as well. None of the dates of publication he records is later than 1595. In that year Cotton had most of his career as a collector ahead of him: if this is a list of his books it is perhaps surprising that it was not kept up-to-date.[17] Another objection to accepting the list as Cottonian stems from the identity of the person responsible for establishing the classification system within which the pasted slips were arranged. As has already been mentioned, there are two types of heading to the backing pages: one is in a scribbled hand, the other in a more careful display script. There can be no doubt that the scribbled hand wrote first, to have its work duplicated by the second script.[18] The scribbled hand is obviously not that of a professional scribe nor of Sir Robert Cotton, nor at present is its identity known. But it is almost certainly the same hand as that which records a loan of books on f. 84v (fig. 2).[19] This loan appears to be dated 1579 and part of its wording makes it clear that the writer is also the owner of the books lent.[20] In 1579 Cotton was eight years old and could not have had any connection with this loan. The likelihood is that whoever made the loan also established the classification system laid down by the scribbled headings and, indeed, owned the books listed on the pasted slips, employing an assistant to do this work. If this is correct it fits in with the terminal publication date of 1595 for items recorded on the slips. The owner must belong to the generation

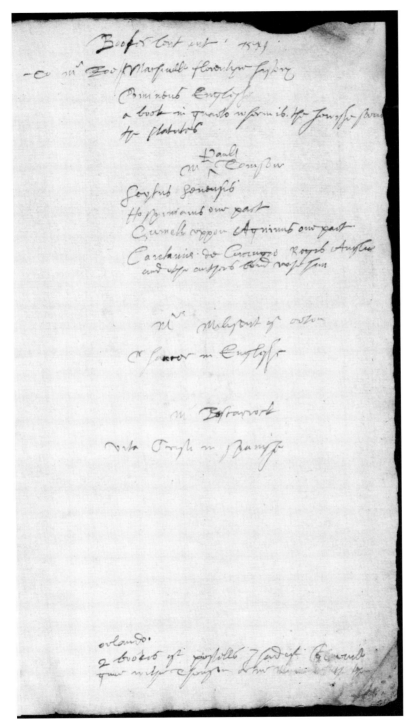

Fig. 2. A loan of books, apparently dated 1579, and almost certainly in the same scribbled hand as writes classification headings to the list of printed books. Add. MS. 35213, f. 84v

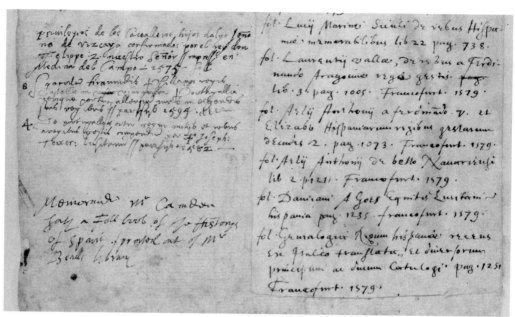

Fig. 3. A memorandum in Cotton's hand recording that Camden 'hath a Foll book of the Historye of Spain ...'. Above this is an entry by another hand which annotates the printed books list. Add. MS. 35213, f. 60v (lower part)

immediately senior to Cotton's and would therefore be reaching old age by around 1600.

However, if Sir Robert Cotton did not commission the list it does not follow that it has no connection with him or that he did not own, or fall heir to, some or all of the books in it. In the same way as he must have taken over the Savile catalogue, as well as some of the manuscripts described in it, he may equally have adopted both the catalogue and some of the volumes of printed books. Part of the evidence which points to this possibility is of a similar nature to that which has been discussed in relation to the Savile catalogue: the list of printed books has been annotated in at least two hands, one of which is undoubtedly that of Sir Robert Cotton (fig. 3). Moreover, as I shall suggest shortly, the context of several of these annotations is Cottonian; but first it may be useful to consider their general purpose and character. Annotations are to be found both on the mounted slips and on the backing pages on which the slips are mounted. Occasionally, they have been partly obscured by a slip or cropped when the slip was cut up, indicating that some slips at least were added or moved after the annotations were made.[21] Sometimes the annotations record an additional title or note a further piece of information[22] but the most interesting are notes of loans, either of new titles which are written, with the name of the borrower, on the backing sheets, or of existing titles, where the slip is annotated (fig. 4). Seven borrowers are recorded: 'Mr Tomson my lord

188

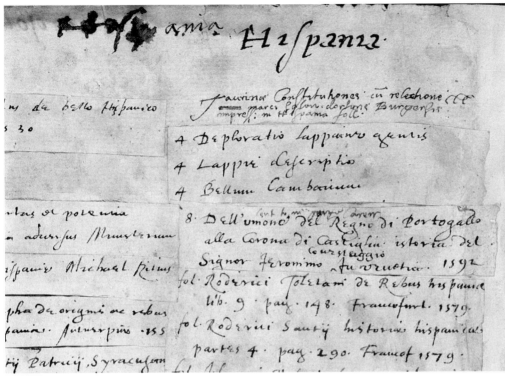

Fig. 4. A loan to George Carew is recorded in the right-hand column. Add. MS 35213, f. 60v
(detail of upper part)

tresorers chaplein', 'Mr Camden', 'Mr Cope', 'Mr George Carew', 'Mr Tat', 'John Neell' and 'Mr Beston'.[23] Of these, the last two are at present unidentified but the remaining five were all members of Sir Robert Cotton's circle and borrowers or donors of manuscripts. 'Mr Tomson' is Paul Thomson of Trinity College, Cambridge; he lived until 1617 and was successively chaplain to Lord Burghley and to James I.[24] William Camden (d. 1623) needs no introduction. 'Mr Cope' is Sir Walter Cope who combined a career in government and politics with antiquarian interests, was knighted in 1603 and died in 1614.[25] George Carew is the future earl of Totnes, diplomat, administrator in Ireland and collector of Irish papers and manuscripts, who was raised to the peerage as Baron Carew in 1605.[26] 'Mr Tat' is Francis Tate, secretary of the Elizabethan Society of Antiquaries, who died in 1616.[27] The styles by which Cope and Carew are recorded indicate a terminal date by which, presumably, the records of their borrowings must have been made, and such a chronology agrees with what was said earlier about the date of compilation of the original catalogue of printed books and the possibility that Cotton inherited it around 1600 to use it, at least for the time being, as a working record in much the same way as he used the Savile catalogue.

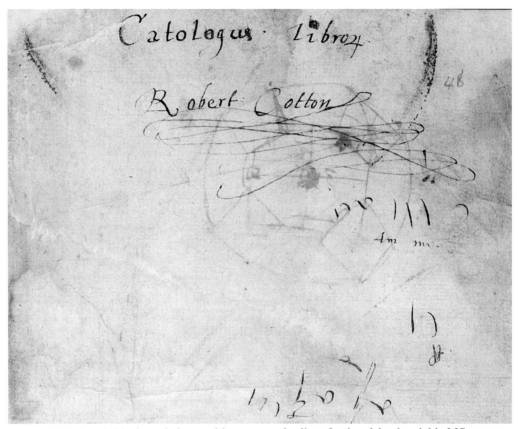

Fig. 5. A leaf probably intended as a title page to the list of printed books. Add. MS. 35213, f. 46r (upper part)

In addition, three other detailed pieces of evidence may be advanced for Cotton's ownership of the catalogue of printed books. Firstly, it will be recalled that the backing sheets are headed with broad subject classifications and that these often appear twice, once in a scribbled hand which is then duplicated by a more careful display script (figs. 1, 4). For what it is worth, this habit of duplicating a rough heading by presenting it in a more formal way is to be found in many of the volumes of letters and papers among the Cotton manuscripts where it is undoubtedly a consequence of Cottonian ownership. Secondly, although the two hands of these headings have not been identified, a third hand which occasionally provides a heading is almost certainly Cotton's.[28] Finally, weight must be given to the title of f. 46r, 'Catalogus libror*um* Robert Cotton', which precedes the list of printed books and which is in an early seventeenth-century hand (fig. 5). This title, rough though it is, is probably intended to relate to the contents of the leaves which follow it.

My suggestion is, then, that Sir Robert Cotton took over a previous owner's catalogue of printed books in Add. MS. 35213 and that there is a good chance that, as in the case of the Savile catalogue, at least some of the volumes listed in it entered his possession at much the same time. Whether, or to what extent, this catalogue does reflect the contents of his 'presses wth printed bookes' and whether it may be possible to establish the identity of its and their original owner is likely only to be determined when the catalogue is edited, a task that would seem well worth undertaking. In conclusion, however, a final point, both negative and positive, should be made. It remains a matter of concern that the catalogue, if it is Cottonian, was not kept up-to-date. We can only guess at the reason but perhaps the task of arranging the manuscripts, especially the volumes of letters and papers, was such a monumental one that little opportunity remained for listing printed books. Nevertheless, although Cotton may not have persisted with the catalogue or continued to use it to note loans, he and later his son did not entirely neglect to keep records of their printed books. Scattered notes and occasionally rather fuller lists of loans of these are to be found interspersed among the records of manuscripts borrowed which are now on ff. 147r–190r of Harl. MS. 6018.[29] As with other contemporary lists of this type, problems arise both of identification and of distinguishing manuscripts from printed books, but a rough count of titles, where these are identifiable, indicates that approximately half of those which might reasonably be expected to feature in the Additional MS. list do so. One block of loans shows a particularly striking coincidence with the printed book catalogue. In 1635 Sir William Howard, probably the brother-in-law of Sir Thomas Cotton, Sir Robert's son, borrowed thirteen titles. Of these eight or nine are listed in the catalogue of printed books.[30] While the existence of multiple copies of printed books naturally renders such evidence less compelling than in the case of manuscripts, it is a further indication that the catalogue in Add. MS. 35213 may well be a valuable key to Sir Robert Cotton's library of printed books.

Professor Robin Alston, Arthur Searle and Professor Andrew Watson kindly read this article in draft. I am grateful for their valuable comments.

1 BL, Cotton ch. i. 16. The inventory makes no mention of manuscripts.

2 Kevin Sharpe, *Sir Robert Cotton 1586–1631. History and politics in early modern England* (Oxford, 1979), p. 57.

3 For a brief account of the early history of the library see the introduction to my edition of Thomas Smith's *Catalogue of the manuscripts in the Cottonian library 1696* (Woodbridge, 1984).

4 It is possible that Cotton's printed books, as a group, never reached the British Museum. It has not, I think, been previously noticed that the act of Parliament (12 & 13 William III, c. 7) which

legislated for Sir John Cotton's gift of the library to the nation makes no mention of printed books, although it defines the scope of the donation fairly precisely: '… Manuscripts, Written Books, Papers, Parchments, Records, and other Memorials … together with all Coins, Medals, and other Rarities and Curiosities …'.

5 John Sparrow found 41 printed books in Selden's library (and now in the Bodleian Library) bearing Cotton's signature: 'The earlier owners of books in John Selden's library', *Bodleian Quarterly Record*, vi (1931), pp. 165–6. Richard L. DeMolen recorded Cottonian printed books now in the Folger Shakespeare Library, Washington D.C., and in the National Library of Wales, Aberystwyth: 'The library of

William Camden', *Proceedings of the American Philosophical Society*, cxxviii (1984), pp. 342, 382.

6 See Sears Jayne, *Library catalogues of the English Renaissance* (Berkeley and Los Angeles, 1956; reissued Godalming, 1983) and Professor R. C. Alston's handlist, 'Library Catalogues, Lists of Manuscripts and Printed Books in The British Library Department of Manuscripts', which is available in the British Library. I am engaged on a history of Sir Robert Cotton's manuscript collection.

7 Sears Jayne, *Library catalogues*, p. 157.

8 List B in R. J. Roberts and Andrew G. Watson (eds.), *John Dee's Library Catalogue* (Bibliographical Society, London, 1990).

9 Edited by Andrew G. Watson, *The manuscripts of Henry Savile of Banke* (London, 1969).

10 The final folio, 84, is written only on the verso. Its significance will be discussed later.

11 Watson, p. 14. Of the sixteen manuscripts marked by the clover leaf sign, ten (Watson, nos. 10, 12, 70, 102, 176, 183, 211, 218, 226, 233) either certainly or possibly entered the Cotton collection.

12 Add. MS. 35213, f. 10rv; Harl. MS. 6018, ff. 120r, 149r; Watson, pp. 14–15, 21 (no. 20). Cotton was also responsible for the addition 'a monacho Lanercostensis monasterii in Com*itatu* Cumberlandiae' to the same Savile catalogue entry (an authorship which he also records in the April 1621 loans record) and for noting the loan of another manuscript (Watson, p. 22, no. 23) to 'my lord Carew'. The return of Claudius D. VII from Lord William Howard must be reflected by the duplicate entry for it on f. 135r of Harl. MS. 6018.

13 Sir William Le Neve, knighted in 1634, is mentioned in one of the items. The volume which is likely to be Cottonian (probably Tiberius E. I) is noted 'titled by Mr James'. Richard James became Cotton's librarian around 1625 and was responsible for writing many contents tables into manuscripts.

14 See my article, 'The early catalogues of the Cottonian library', *British Library Journal*, vi (1980), pp. 144–57. Add. MS. 35213 was previously owned by the Fairfax family and then by Sir Thomas Phillipps whose number 10701 appears on f. 46r, the title page to the list of printed books, and elsewhere in the volume. The repetition of this numbering, together with the presence of a variety of post-seventeenth-century foliations, may indicate that the manuscript has been reordered in the last two centuries, but the fact that so much of it is Cottonian makes it likely that Sir Robert was originally responsible for bringing it together in something like its present form.

15 Evidence of rearrangement is provided by a slip at the foot of f. 75r. This has the catchwords 'Annales pipini' and must have led on to the entry, now on f. 58v, which begins 'fol. Annales Pipini...'.

16 It is possible that the entries are by Nicholas Charles, Lancaster Herald, who died in 1613. I am grateful to Ann Payne for advice on Charles's hand. Occasional slips are in another hand: examples are on ff. 51r, 63r. Equally occasionally, slips record manuscripts rather than printed books (ff. 51v, 57r).

17 Unless, of course, as Kevin Sharpe suggests, Cotton's interests had turned to original material.

18 See, for example, the headings on f. 70r (fig. 1).

19 F. 84v is bound into the manuscript upside down. However, it is of the same paper type as the backing sheets of the booklist proper and shares their watermark. The loan it records is of a dozen items. Several descriptions are inexact but six or seven appear to refer to printed books. For only one of these ('the statutes') is there a parallel entry in the main booklist (on f. 71v). This is disappointing but some years may separate the list on f. 84v from the main list. The scribbled hand is also responsible for some rough notes on ff. 80r and 81r. These two folios carry no mounted slips and may have been displaced from the end of the main list, but they share its paper type and watermark.

20 The entry runs: '2 bookes of postells I had of Glenvill'. (The reading of Glenvill is uncertain.) The figure '7' in the date is curiously formed but no other reading seems plausible (fig. 2).

21 For example, notes of loans to Camden on ff. 52r and 70r (see fig. 1, left-hand column) are partly obscured by mounted slips and f. 49r carries a slip whose annotation (also recording a loan) has been cropped.

22 For example, on f. 60v (where three titles have been written on the backing page: see fig. 3), on f. 59v (an addition to a title on a slip), and on f. 70v (a title added to a slip).

23 Tomson: ff. 47v, 49r, 51v; Camden: ff. 50v, 52r,

58v, 70r (fig. 1, left-hand column); Cope: f. 51v; Carew: ff. 52v, 60v; Tat: f. 71v; Neell: f. 73r; Beston: f. 77v.

24 John Venn and J. A. Venn, *Alumni Cantabrigienses. Part I: From the earliest times to 1751*, 4 vols. (Cambridge 1922–7); BL, Lansd. MS. 83, ff. 126r–127v; BL, Eg. MS. 2877, f. 161r. He features, as do the other four, in the memoranda and loans lists at the end of the Cotton catalogue, Harl. MS. 6018. He is also one of the borrowers noted on f. 84v of Add. MS. 35213 (where he is recorded as being lent a copy of the *Bibliotheca Sancta* of Sisto da Siena, a work which is also listed as on loan to him in Harl. MS. 6018, f. 156r). I am grateful to Pamela Selwyn for identifying Thomson and to Pauline Croft for advice about him.

25 *D.N.B.*; Andrew G. Watson, 'The manuscript collection of Sir Walter Cope (d. 1614)', *Bodleian Library Record*, xii (1987), pp. 262–97.

26 *D.N.B.*; R. A. Skelton and John Summerson, *A description of maps and architectural drawings in the collection made by William Cecil, first Baron Burghley now at Hatfield House* (Oxford, 1971), p. 17.

27 *D.N.B.*

28 For example, it writes 'Dania' on f. 56r and 'Rodium' on f. 64r.

29 I hope shortly to publish a paper on a loan of printed books made by Cotton to John Selden in 1622.

30 The Howard loan is on f. 181r of Harl. MS. 6018. The entries which can also be found in Add. MS. 35213 are: 1. 'Descriptio Britanie' (on f. 57r of the Add. MS., if this loan is of Camden's *Britannia*); 4. 'Gregorii Fabritii Chemnisensis' (f. 75r); 6. 'Nove Saxonum Historie' (f. 55r); 7. 'Mathei Castritii Dar[m]statini' (f. 50r); 8. 'Pantheon. folio' (f. 51v); 9. 'Danica Historia. folio' (f. 56r); 10. 'James [= Johannes] Turpinus. folio' (ff. 59r, 75r); 11. 'Davidis Chitrei [= Chytraeus]. folio' (f. 65r where, however, the volume listed is octavo); 12. 'Wolphangus Latius. folio' (ff. 50v, 61r, 70r).

SOME CLASSIFIED CATALOGUES OF THE COTTONIAN LIBRARY

E. C. TEVIOTDALE

COLIN TITE has recently drawn our attention to the many manuscript catalogues of the Cotton collection copied in the seventeenth century and has initiated a reconsideration of their role in our understanding of the formation and early history of the Cottonian Library.[1] It is my intention here to consider a group of catalogues copied when the library was in the hands of Sir John Cotton (1621–1702), the eldest grandson of the library's founder.[2] This group consists of eight classified lists of the collection, one of which survives only as a fragment. There is a complicated network of similarities among them, which could only be analysed in full if a complete comparative edition were made. This would be an enormous task, and I do not claim to have undertaken it. In the absence of an exhaustive study, however, some observations on the origin, the contents, and the owners of these manuscripts might be of interest.

Before turning to the manuscripts that will principally occupy us here, a few remarks about the Cottonian manuscripts themselves are in order. The majority of codices in the Cotton collection are volumes comprised of several discrete items (sometimes hundreds of discrete items) bound together only after they came into the Cottonian Library. In compiling a classified catalogue of the collection, each item in a given manuscript would have to be considered and listed separately, particularly as its character might be quite different from that of surrounding items. It should also be remembered that the chief collecting interest of the library's founder, Sir Robert Cotton (1571–1631), was English history, and any classification scheme for the library would be rather more detailed for English history than for other subjects.

The surviving classified lists of the collection include six paper codices whose seventeenth-century owners can be traced, a fragment of a similar paper codex, and a large parchment document. The latter two present rather different problems from the first group, so I shall proceed to them from a discussion of the six paper codices, which are:

Cambridge, Magdalene College, Pepys MS. 2427, ff. 33–186[3]
Cambridge, Trinity College, MS. O.4.12 (James 1243)[4]
London, British Library, Harl. MS. 694, ff. 214–288[5]
London, Inner Temple Library, Petyt MS. 538/40, ff. 1–172, 181–189[6]

Maidstone, Kent County Archives, Doc. U1121 Z19[7]
Oxford, Bodleian Library, MS. Tanner 273 (SC 10099)[8]

These catalogues are arranged according to subject. Each entry includes a description of an individual item (occasionally a group of items within a single codex) followed by the pressmark of the manuscript (occasionally the pressmarks of more than one manuscript). Only very rarely is any indication given of that item's position within the manuscript. It is not uncommon for a series of entries from one manuscript to appear together, in which case the pressmark generally will not be repeated but the word 'ibidem' will take the place of the pressmark in the later entries. There tend to be patches of entries from a single shelf together, but there is no systematic progression through the presses within each category. These catalogues would serve a user of the library well. Having perused the entries under the subject that interested him in the catalogue, he would be directed to a particular volume. Once he had the manuscript in hand, he could consult a table of contents at the front of the volume, if one was present, in order more precisely to locate the item that he sought.

Tite has already intimated that the six classified lists in codex format rely on the same or closely related exemplars, and this is indeed the case.[9] All six are prefaced by an identical table of contents. In four of the manuscripts, this table is supplied with page references, identical in all four, not to the attached catalogue but to another earlier version of the catalogue.[10] In the remaining two codices, the table was copied without page references, and then page references to the catalogue at hand were added later.[11] Here follows a transcription of the table of contents as it appears in Petyt 538/40, one of the four manuscripts in which the page references to an earlier version of the catalogue have been faithfully copied and one of the most carefully copied and corrected manuscripts of the group:

History of England and other Countries p. 1
Theologicall bookes and Ecclesiasticall history p. 37
Lives of Saints p. 91
Revennues, Priviledges, Foundations, Charters of Monasteries Churches and hospitalls p. 105
Prophecyes pa: 117
Lawe
    Civill and Canon p: 126
    Co[m]mon p. 123
Affaires of State between England &
    Italy p. 133
    Spaine p. 134
    France p. 139
    Low Countryes p: 145
    Scotland p. 151
    Ireland p: 152
    Denmarke p: 157

196

It will be apparent at a glance that the vast majority of the classifications relate to the history of England. It should also be remarked that the page references are not always consecutive and that one subject, 'Of Particular Persons of England', bears no page reference.[12] This suggests that there was another version of the catalogue that presented the subjects in the order of their appearance in the table. Support for this hypothesis is to be found in the title of three of the surviving manuscripts: 'Catalogus Bibliothecae Cottonianae Anno 1674 continet folia 86'.[13] None of the six surviving manuscripts contains eighty-six folios, and the manuscript implied by the page references in the table of contents would be about 270 pages long (135 folios if both sides were used and 270 folios if only the rectos were written on). We have evidence, therefore, for two lost versions of the classified list, a 'paginated catalogue' and an '86 folio catalogue'. The former would have been copied from the latter, taking over the title (with its reference to the size of the earlier catalogue) and the table of contents, but differing from its model in the arrangement of the body of the catalogue (hence non-consecutive page references in the table). The four surviving manuscripts with the faithfully copied irrelevant page references must, of course, rely on the paginated catalogue rather than the '86 folio catalogue', and it can be shown by the arrangement of the subjects within the body of the surviving codices that they all rely on the paginated catalogue.

An assessment of the arrangement of the surviving catalogues is complicated by three factors: (1) the classifications are not always explicitly labelled;[14] (2) the heading in the body of the catalogue does not always agree with the wording in the table of contents;[15] and (3) one section has been mislabelled.[16] Nevertheless, an analysis of the entries themselves reveals that most of the subject divisions given in the table of contents are reflected in the six extant catalogues, but they appear neither in the order in which they are presented in the table nor in the order implied by the page references. Indeed, no two surviving versions of the catalogue present the classifications in exactly the same order. They share, however, certain patterns in their arrangement, and these all derive from the order of the paginated catalogue. Also, two of the copies include numbers in the left margin of the body of the catalogue that accord with pages of the paginated catalogue.[17] Furthermore, none of the extant catalogues includes a section on particular persons of England, the very section that we surmised was missing from the paginated catalogue.

All of the surviving lists, as originally copied, are also missing the following categories: 'Of Princes', 'The King's House', 'Of Queens', 'Great Officers of State', 'Rights of Kings to several Crowns', 'Of Heraldry', 'Of Knights', and 'Of War' (that is pp. 181–206 of the paginated catalogue). These subjects were ultimately transcribed into

Petyt 538/40 but are clearly a later addition.[18] This provides an important clue for understanding the transmission of the text of the paginated catalogue to the manuscripts we have today. The exemplar for these six codices, most probably the paginated catalogue itself, was not a bound codex but was either a series of unbound gatherings or loose sheets bundled into sections. The portion that comprised pp. 181–206, it would seem, was not routinely available. This explains both the variety of arrangements and the haphazard labelling among the six copies, for a copyist could well be confused or misled by an exemplar in pieces, particularly in transcribing a text as monotonous as a catalogue and in the absence of a running head or careful labelling in the exemplar.

The problem of organizing a copy of the catalogue would have been exacerbated if the portions of the exemplar were not all available at once to a copyist, and this situation may well have obtained. The six catalogues we know today show no sign of having been produced centrally. Some were copied by a single hand, others by more than one. They are on a variety of papers, and no single paper is present in more than one copy.[19] It is entirely possible, therefore, that someone who wanted a copy of the catalogue would receive portions of the exemplar as they were needed. Indeed, the exemplar may have been divided into portions in order to facilitate its speedy reproduction. Four of the surviving copies of the classified list bear the date 1674, and it is reasonable to assume that they would not have been copied much after that date. This assumption is confirmed for Petyt 538/40, into which another brief catalogue dated 30 March 1675 has been entered after the bulk of the Cotton catalogue was copied.[20] The others probably date from around the same time, but we cannot be absolutely certain.[21]

The six copies of the catalogue were owned by scholars and clergymen, most of whom were of Sir John Cotton's generation, and there is no compelling reason to doubt that they were made for those men. The manuscript in Magdalene College, Cambridge, was owned by Samuel Pepys (1633–1703), the famous diarist. Sir John and he were certainly acquaintances by 1675, when they together advocated a large allocation for the building of new ships for the Royal Navy in a House of Commons debate.[22] In later years, Pepys would borrow many manuscripts from the collection,[23] and he was quoted as saying he considered the Cottonian Library one of the jewels of the crown of England.[24]

Trinity College O.4.12 belonged to Thomas Gale (1635/6–1702), who was High Master of St Paul's School at the time this manuscript would have been copied. He was the greatest scholar among those who possessed copies of this catalogue, and he used the library extensively.[25] In the preface to the third volume of his *Historiae Anglicanae Scriptores* (1691), Gale praised the quality of the Cotton collection and the generosity of its owners in allowing access.[26] Thomas Smith (1638–1710), who prepared the first printed catalogue of the Cotton collection (1696), mentioned therein Gale's having used the library.[27]

The copy of the classified list included in Harley 694 was owned by Edward Stillingfleet (1635–99), who was appointed Bishop of Worcester in 1689.[28] His study of English church history, *Origines Britannicae*, was published in 1685.[29] Of his acquaintance with Cotton, we know only that Sir John was selected by the House of Commons to invite Stillingfleet to preach to the House in 1666.[30]

William Petyt (*c.* 1641–1707), most of whose writings dealt with the history of Parliament, owned the copy in the Inner Temple Library. Although little of his correspondence survives, we have a copy of a letter he wrote to Sir John Cotton in 1676 concerning the origins of Parliament.[31] Petyt used many Cotton manuscripts,[32] and he, like Gale, was mentioned by Smith in his history of the collection.[33] Petyt had an emperor order catalogue of the Cottonian Library in addition to the classified list, and this emperor order catalogue was most probably one of the authorities consulted in the emendation of his classified list.[34] Petyt's classified list was originally of the same extent as the others but was subsequently expanded by the addition of the subjects on pp. 181–206 of the paginated catalogue.[35]

A list of 'Books given to Sir John Cottons Library by John Marsham, Esq.' has been written at the end of Kent County Archives Doc. U1121 Z19.[36] This John Marsham would almost certainly have been the younger Sir John Marsham, who was particularly interested in English history. The elder Sir John (1602–85), the Egyptologist, was knighted in 1660 and created baronet in 1663, and it is unlikely he would have been referred to as 'John Marsham, Esq.' in the 1670s.[37] Sir John Marsham the younger, on the other hand, would not have taken the title 'Sir' until he inherited the baronetcy on the death of his father in 1685. Many entries in this catalogue have been marked in the margin, including some for items that Sir John Marsham the younger had transcribed.[38] One is tempted to hypothesize that the gift of manuscripts to the Cotton collection was in exchange for the classified list itself, which would indicate that the list was made for the son, but we cannot be certain for which Marsham the catalogue was copied.

William Sancroft (1617–93) owned Tanner 273. His name is inscribed at the head of the manuscript: 'W: Cant.' Sancroft did not become Archbishop of Canterbury until 1678, but he may have owned the manuscript earlier.[39] He marked several entries on church history in the margin of his copy. If we are to believe Thomas Smith, Sancroft did not think very highly of his catalogue:

To help me to realise the purpose to which I clung [i.e., the preparation of a new catalogue of the Cotton collection] I consulted the most reverend father and lord in Christ, William Sancroft, the late archbishop of Canterbury, while he was still living at Lambeth, and he approved of the idea and poured charming encouragement into my ready ears to revise or rather reconstruct the old catalogues which were mutilated and imperfect, teeming, as he said, with a thousand errors.[40]

A fragment of a manuscript like the six discussed thus far forms a part of MS. Rawlinson D.901 in the Bodleian Library.[41] It bears no marks of previous ownership, not even an earlier pagination or foliation, and its provenance cannot be traced further back than 1893, when it was bound into Rawlinson D.901 from Rawlinson fragments.[42] It is a genuine fragment, and not a selective listing.[43] There are far too few entries to a page for it to be a fragment of the '86 folio catalogue', and the absence of any pagination makes it unlikely that it is a fragment of the paginated catalogue. It is most probably,

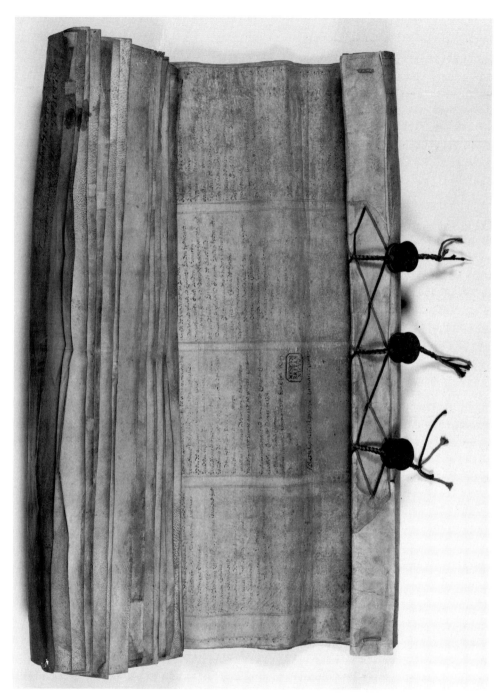

Fig. 1. Add. MS. 8926

therefore, all that remains of another copy of the classified list that circulated in the 1670s.

It is likely that Henry Powle (1630–92) owned, or at least used, a copy of the classified list. 'A Catalogue of the Manuscripts in Sir Robert Cottons Library reduced under severall heads' occupies a page of MS. Additional C.40 in the Bodleian Library, which once belonged to him.[44] It consists of a version of the table of contents familiar from the six paper codices. It is, however, different in intriguing respects. The page references are mostly those of the faithful copies of the table of the paginated catalogue, but the order of presentation of classifications is not quite the same, the wording is not quite the same, and three categories are missing.[45] The changes seem to reflect an attempt to make better order of the more familiar table. This table certainly does not, however, present the categories in the order implied by the page references, so it does not directly reflect the shape of the paginated catalogue. On the verso of the page on which the table is written is 'A note of some choyse MS. remaining in the sayd Library'.[46] This gives brief descriptions and emperor pressmarks of about thirty items, with page references to the classified list. The entries are not identified according to classification, however, and they appear neither in the order of their appearance in any surviving copy of the classified list nor in emperor order. These entries in Additional C.40 provide, therefore, somewhat puzzling evidence for the further dissemination of the classified list.

The last manuscript of our group, Additional MS. 8926 in the British Library (fig. 1), is a large parchment document of twenty folios stabbed at the bottom edge and tied with string and coloured silks, to which are attached three seals, all melted.[47] It is written in a single elegant formal hand. This manuscript attracted the attention of Joseph Planta when he was preparing the now standard catalogue of the Cotton collection.[48] It was not incorporated as an Additional Manuscript by the British Museum until c. 1832, and it seems to have been among the Cotton Manuscripts when Planta knew it.[49] It differs from the paper codices in the complete absence of the table of contents and of pressmarks. The subjects are familiar from the paper manuscripts, and they are presented in the order of the paginated catalogue. The subject 'Of Particular Persons of England', apparently missing from the paginated catalogue and certainly missing from the paper codices, is missing here as well.[50] The parchment manuscript would have been copied, therefore, from the same exemplar as the others. It was copied later than the others, however, for it includes an extra section, headed 'Roberti Grosthed Episcopi Lincoln opera', which contains entries for dozens of items in manuscripts returned to the Cottonian Library from Westminster Abbey.[51] These manuscripts left the library in Sir Robert's time and were definitely at Westminster at the time the classified list was originally drawn up.[52] Thomas Smith alluded to their return in his catalogue of 1696, claiming that they had been estranged from the library for sixty years, but we do not know precisely when these manuscripts came back to the Cotton collection.[53]

The parchment document could be the schedule mentioned in an act of Parliament of 1701 concerning the transfer of the collection into public hands.[54] Its pretentious format suggests that it may have been made in connection with the gift of the collection to the nation. Whereas the paper codices constituted a sort of publication of the library's contents to scholars, the parchment copy would have been made for another purpose. It would prove impractical for locating material in the library because of the absence of pressmarks, and it must have been copied more for ostentation than for utility, most likely, I think, when the Cottonian Library was bequeathed to the nation at the turn of the century.

It remains to consider when, how, and by whom the classified list was originally drawn up. Although the exemplar for the manuscripts we have today was undoubtedly dated 1674, it need not have been made in that year. There is some evidence that the list was compiled over several years. As already mentioned, there is no systematic progression through the presses within each category. One has the impression that parts of the list were begun in a fairly systematic fashion (the large classifications start with a series of entries from Julius) but that this was abandoned and the work then proceeded more casually. The section of documents relating to monasteries, churches, and hospitals must already have been partially compiled when the entries were made for three manuscripts (Claudius A. XIII, Nero E. VII, and Otho B. XIV) given to the Cottonian Library in 1670 by Samuel Roper (1633–78).[55] The entries for these manuscripts appear together in a sequence near the end of the section and would have been added when the manuscripts were assigned pressmarks shortly after their arrival.[56] Titus C. XVI and Titus C. XVII, given by Sir Edward Walker (1612–77), were clearly also a late addition to the list.[57] These factors point to work on the classified list having spanned some years beginning in the 1660s.

The classified list was partially, and probably mostly, prepared from an emperor order catalogue of the collection. Items from manuscripts that had been out on loan for decades or had been missing since the mid 1650s are to be found among the entries in the classified list.[58] The list was not, however, exclusively compiled from an old catalogue, as attested by the inclusion of acquisitions as recent as the Roper gifts. The classified list, therefore, reflects the state of the collection as it would have been in the 1670s, had manuscripts not become estranged from the collection.[59] The list would seem to have been updated even after the paper codices were copied. The parchment copy includes an entry for Vespasian E. XXVI, absent from the paper copies, as the last item in the section of documents relating to monasteries, churches, and hospitals.[60] This manuscript, a gift from Anchitell Grey (d. 1702), was a late addition to the collection.[61]

Finally we come to the question of the authorship of the classified list. Sir John Cotton did not attend to the maintenance of the collection himself. He spent most of his maturity at his villa at Stratton, Bedfordshire.[62] He would have had neither the inclination nor the opportunity to prepare the classified list, although he probably would have authorized its reproduction in 1674. If one person was largely responsible for the compilation of the classified list, that person most probably would have been Sir William Dugdale (1605–86). It was he who claimed in his autobiography to have been given free access to the library by Sir Thomas Cotton (1594–1662) in the early 1650s, to have sorted much material, and to have arranged for the binding of some eighty volumes around that time.[63] It was also Dugdale who wrote the *ex dono* inscriptions in the codices whose entries appear to represent late additions to the classified list, both before and after the publication in 1674.[64] Between the death of John Selden (1584–1654) and the advent of Thomas Smith,[65] no scholar was more closely associated with the Cottonian Library than Dugdale.[66] He might have made some partial lists in connection with the sorting and binding of state papers in the early 1650s, or he might have begun by drawing up lists in connection with his work for the *Monasticon Anglicanum* (1655–73) or his *Antiquities of Warwickshire* (1656), and only later conceived of a classified list of the whole of the collection. We have no compelling evidence that Dugdale compiled the classified list, but he certainly had the opportunity to do so.

I would like to offer the following provisional conclusions, which await refinement, refutation, or confirmation once a comparative edition of the manuscripts has been made. The classified list was compiled, perhaps by Dugdale, during the 1660s and 1670s from an emperor order catalogue and also from the manuscripts themselves. A version of that list, the 'paginated catalogue', served as the exemplar for the eight surviving manuscripts. The paper codices, copied in the 1670s for scholars and clergymen, constituted a limited publication of the contents of the library. The parchment document was copied later, perhaps in connection with the donation of the collection to the nation around the turn of the century.

1 Colin G. C. Tite, 'The Early Catalogues of the Cottonian Library', *British Library Journal*, vi (1980), pp. 144–57.

2 This group was defined by Tite, *Catalogue of the Manuscripts in the Cottonian Library (1696)... reprinted from Sir Robert Harley's Copy, annotated by Humfrey Wanley, together with documents relating to the fire of 1731* (Cambridge, 1984), p. 14.

3 C. S. Knighton, *Catalogue of the Pepys Library at Magdalene College Cambridge*, V, ii: *Modern Manuscripts* (Woodbridge, 1981), pp. 63–4; M. R. James, *Bibliotheca Pepysiana: A Descriptive Catalogue of the Library of Samuel Pepys*, III: *Mediaeval Manuscripts* (London, 1923), pp. 103–5; *Catalogi librorum manuscriptorum angliae et hiberniae* (Oxford, 1697), vol. ii, pt. i, p. 209 (no. 6793). I am grateful to Richard Luckett, Pepys Librarian, for permission to examine this manuscript.

4 Montague Rhodes James, *The Western Manuscripts in the Library of Trinity College, Cambridge, Volume III containing an account of the manuscripts standing in class O* (Cambridge, 1902), p. 262; *Catalogi librorum manuscriptorum*, vol. ii, pt. i, p. 190 (no. 6051). I am grateful to

D. J. McKitterick, Librarian at Trinity College, for permission to examine this manuscript.

5 *A Catalogue of the Harleian Manuscripts, in the British Museum* (London, 1808), vol. i, pp. 407–8.

6 J. Conway Davies, *Catalogue of Manuscripts in the Library of the Honourable Society of the Inner Temple* (Oxford, 1972), pp. 835–6. I am grateful to W. W. S. Breem, Librarian and Keeper of Manuscripts of the Honourable Society of the Inner Temple, for permission to examine this manuscript and other materials in the Petyt collection.

7 There is no published catalogue of the collection of the Kent County Archives. The 'unofficial catalogues' can be consulted at the archives. The Marsham material was catalogued by F. Hull, Mar.–Apr. 1966.

8 Alfred Hackman, *Catalogi codicum manuscriptorum bibliothecae bodleianae*, IV: *Codices viri admodum reverendi Thomae Tanneri, S.T.P.* (Oxford, 1860; reprint, 1966), col. 658.

9 Tite, *Catalogue of the Manuscripts*, p. 14.

10 Pepys 2427, Trinity College O.4.12, Petyt 538/40, and Kent County Archives Doc. U1121 Z19. Some of the page references have been

effaced in Kent County Archives Doc. U1121 Z19, and page references for the volume at hand have been entered in their place.

11 Harley 694 and Tanner 273.

12 It probably once occupied pp. 207–10 of that catalogue, but was removed before the page references were entered into the table. 'Of War' only contains a handful of entries and could not have occupied all of the space between pp. 206 and 211 (see Petyt 538/40, f. 189r).

13 Pepys 2427, Harley 694, Petyt 538/40. In Kent County Archives Doc. U1121 Z19, the title has been written as in the other three, but without the number of folios; then the number of folios of the volume at hand (129) has been added.

14 For example, 'Acta Concilii' and 'Of Merchandise and Moneys' are present in all six codices, but are not labelled as such.

15 For example, the section 'Abstracts out of ancient records' is headed 'Rotula Recorda Registra Chartuaria &c' in Harley 694 (f. 261r).

16 The section labelled 'Miscellanea' beginning on f. 270r of Harley 694 is actually a part of the section 'Theological Books and Ecclesiastical History'.

17 Trinity College O.4.12, ff. 23r–31r, 45r–50r, 78r–90v; Harley 694, ff. 270r–273v. Some of these numbers do not appear in consecutive order, and it is apparent that the pages within the section 'Theological Books and Ecclesiastical History' were scrambled in the exemplar. This has led to inaccurate implications of pressmarks in the catalogues we have today. If the first entry at the top of a page in the exemplar had 'ibidem' rather than a pressmark and that page was copied out of order, the wrong pressmark would then be implied, because the nearest preceding pressmark would not be the correct one. The numbers do not occur in consecutive pairs, which suggests that only one side of each leaf was written on in the paginated catalogue.

18 The bulk of the Cottonian catalogue in Petyt 538/40 (ff. 1–172) was copied by a single scribe. Another hand has carefully corrected and emended the work of the first and has written the portion containing the missing categories (ff. 181–189).

19 I have not made a comparative palaeographic study of these manuscripts.

20 F. 179.

21 They surely would have been copied before 1687, when Sir John Cotton wrote to Thomas Smith (30 June): 'Truly (Sir) we are fallen into so dangerous times, that it may be more for the advantage of my private concerns, & the publick too, that the library should not be too much known. There are many things in it, which are very crosse to the Romish interest, & you know what kind of persons the Jesuits are'. (Oxford, Bodleian Library, MS. Smith 48 [SC 15655], p. 253).

22 Cotton made his most important speech in Parliament as he moved for this allocation (Anchitell Grey, *Debates of the House of Commons from the year 1667 to the year 1694* [London, 1763], vol. iii, pp. 323–33; Basil Duke Henning, *The House of Commons 1660–1690*, The History of Parliament (London, 1983), vol. ii, pp. 139–40).

23 For the loans, see the correspondence between Pepys and Thomas Smith contained in Oxford, Bodleian Library, MS. Smith 53 (SC 15660) and MS. Smith 65 (SC 15671).

24 A letter from Humfrey Wanley to Arthur Charlett, 13 May 1698 (Henry Ellis, *Original Letters of Eminent Literary Men of the Sixteenth, Seventeenth, and Eighteenth Centuries* [London, 1843], pp. 259–61).

25 On Gale's scholarship, see David C. Douglas, *English Scholars 1660–1730*, 2nd ed. (London, 1951), pp. 59–61, 170–74, and *passim*.

26 Thomas Smith quoted this passage in his catalogue of the Cottonian manuscripts (*Catalogus librorum manuscriptorum bibliothecae Cottonianae* [Oxford, 1696], p. L).

27 Smith, *Catalogus*, p. XLII.

28 The entry for Stillingfleet in *Fontes Harleiani* is somewhat misleading. The table of contents at the beginning of this volume originally listed only the first nineteen items in the manuscript (a series of catalogues of libraries in a single hand and on the same paper). The Cottonian catalogue is in several hands and on different papers and is a later addition to the table of contents. Nevertheless, it is almost certain that this Cottonian catalogue belonged to Stillingfleet and came into the Harleian collection together with the other Stillingfleet manuscripts, not only because it is now bound into a volume with other Stillingfleet material, but because two catalogues of Stillingfleet's manuscripts include entries for a catalogue of the Cotton collection (London, BL, Harl. MS. 7644, f. [1]v and Oxford, Bodleian Library, MS. Rawlinson D.878, f. 78r). Cf. Cyril

Ernest Wright, *Fontes Harleiani: A Study of the Sources of the Harleian Collection of Manuscripts preserved in the Department of Manuscripts in the British Museum* (London, 1972), p. 316, and C. E. Wright and Ruth C. Wright (eds.), *The Diary of Humfrey Wanley, 1715–1726* (London, 1966), p. xix.

29 See Douglas, *English Scholars*, pp. 198–200.

30 Henning, *The House of Commons*, vol. ii, p. 139.

31 London, Inner Temple Library, Petyt MS. 538/17, f. 482.

32 A list of Cottonian manuscripts consulted by Petyt is included as an appendix to Conway Davies's catalogue of the manuscripts in the library of the Inner Temple (*Catalogue*, pp. 1347–8).

33 Smith, *Catalogus*, p. XLII.

34 London, Inner Temple Library, Petyt MS. 538/41. Some of the corrections reflect archaisms in his emperor order catalogue and thus would have been made from it rather than from the manuscripts themselves.

35 Ff. 181–189.

36 F. 129r.

37 *D.N.B.* under Marsham.

38 Transcripts from Cottonian manuscripts made for Marsham are preserved in the Kent County Archives Office (Docs. U1121 Z53/3 & 6 and U1121 Z54/2–6).

39 There is an entry for this catalogue in a manuscript catalogue of Sancroft's manuscripts, dated 1721 (Oxford, Bodleian Library, MS. Carte 263, f. 110r).

40 Smith, *Catalogus*, 'lectori' (not paginated), transl. Godfrey E. Turton (Tite (ed.), *Catalogue of the Manuscripts*, p. 23).

41 Oxford, Bodleian Library, MS. Rawlinson D.901 (SC 13667), ff. 148–181. William Macray, *Catalogi codicum manuscriptorum bibliothecae bodleianae: Partis quintae, fasciculus quartus: Viri munificentissimi Ricardi Rawlinson, I.C.D.* (Oxford, 1898), cols. 100–1.

42 Macray, *Catalogi*, col. 101. The hand responsible for this fragment is quite like that of Pepys's copy of the classified list. Their resemblance ought to be more closely examined, especially as some Pepys material found its way into the Rawlinson collection (Falconer Madan, *A Summary Catalogue of Western Manuscripts in the Bodleian Library at Oxford*, vol. iii (Oxford, 1895), p. 178).

43 Its arrangement is particularly chaotic, with fragments of the alphabetical section interspersed among the subject divisions.

44 Oxford, Bodleian Library, MS. Additional C.40 (SC 27837), p. vii. Madan, *A Summary Catalogue*, vol. v, pp. 368–9. Colin Tite brought this manuscript to my attention. Powle owned an emperor order catalogue of the Cotton collection that was substantially expanded and revised on the authority of the published catalogue of 1696: Rawlinson D.901, ff. 1–147 (Macray, *Catalogi*, cols. 100–1).

45 The numbers of the references generally agree with those in the four faithful copies, but in the few instances in which they are qualified, they are said to be folio rather than page numbers. This contributes to the suspicion that only the rectos of leaves were written on in the paginated catalogue (see n. 17). The categories that are entirely missing are: 'Of Particular Persons of England', 'Of Particular Cities and Towns in England', and 'Of Universities and Colleges'. These would not have been strictly contiguous in the paginated catalogue.

46 P. viii.

47 'Catalogue of Additional Manuscripts Nos. 6666–10018', p. 56 (an unpublished catalogue available in the Students' Room of the Department of Manuscripts).

48 Joseph Planta, *A Catalogue of the Manuscripts in the Cottonian Library deposited in the British Museum* (London, 1802), p. xi. Planta thought that the parchment list was much older than it possibly can be (see Tite, 'The Early Catalogues', p. 147).

49 Planta, *Catalogue*, p. xi. The date of its incorporation as an Additional Manuscript is suggested by its number. Additional MSS. 8928–8976 were received into the Department of Manuscripts in 1832 ('Catalogue of Additional Manuscripts Nos. 6666–10018', p. 56).

50 It does, however, include the categories on pp. 181–206 of the paginated catalogue.

51 Otho C. XII–XVI and Otho D. X–XI. J. Armitage Robinson and Montague Rhodes James, *The Manuscripts of Westminster Abbey*, Notes and Documents concerning Westminster Abbey, 1 (Cambridge, 1909), pp. 27, 34–9, 50–2 (beware the misidentification of some of the Cotton manuscripts in this publication).

52 The copies of the classified list owned by Gale and Sancroft include the following entry at the appropriate place in the alphabetical portion:

'Roberti Grostest opera fuere in hac bibliotheca nunc translata sunt in Westmonasteriensem' (Trinity College O.4.12, f. 105v and Tanner 273, f. 134r).

53 Smith, *Catalogus*, 'lectori' (not paginated).

54 The statute states that all the manuscripts 'are particularly mentioned and named in a Schedule now remaining in the said Library' (*The Statutes of the Realm*, vol. vii, p. 642). It goes on to specify one of the duties of the keeper once he is appointed: '... he shall cause another Schedule to be made in Parchment which shall contain not only the Names and Titles of all the said Manuscripts Parchments Written Papers Records and other Memorialls but also the Number of the Pages and Folio's thereunto belonging...' (Ibid., vol. vii, p. 643). The schedule 'now remaining in the said Library' was clearly considered inadequate, as well Add. MS. 8926 might be.

55 Two different cartularies were given the pressmark Otho B. XIV during the course of the seventeenth century. I refer here to the second manuscript to be given that pressmark, a Lenton cartulary. Although Otho B. XIV was destroyed in the fire of 1731, we know that it was once owned by Samuel Roper (G. R. C. Davis, *Medieval Cartularies of Great Britain: A Short Catalogue* (London, 1958),p. 62). Claudius A. XIII and Nero E. VII have dated *ex dono* inscriptions, and it seems reasonable to assume that all three manuscripts were given in 1670.

56 Kent County Archives Doc. U1121 Z19 is missing the entry for Nero E. VII, presumably due to a scribal error.

57 These manuscripts were numbered Titus C. XVII and Titus C. XVIII when they first entered the collection (and carry those pressmarks in the classified list). These both have *ex dono* inscriptions. The classification 'History of England and other Countries' is arranged as follows: anonymous chronicles and histories, attributed chronicles and histories (in alphabetical order), histories arranged chronologically by reigning English monarch. The entries for Titus C. XVI (Mandeville, *Travels*) and Titus C. XVII (Geoffrey of Monmouth, *Historia britonum*) appear together at the end of the alphabetical sequence.

58 For example, the Cotton Genesis (Otho B. VI) was lent to the Earl of Arundel in 1630 (BL, Harl. MS. 6018, f. 178v) and was bought back

for the library not long before 1696 (Smith, *Catalogus*, 'lectori' (not paginated)), but it is listed in the classified catalogue. Similarly, Tiberius B. VII (William Thorne, *Chronicle*), missing according to a checklist made in 1656 (BL, Add. MS. 36682, f. 1r, where it is mistakenly listed as an Augustus manuscript) and never recovered, is recorded in the classified catalogue.

59 Here follows an outline of changes in the shape of the collection as reflected in the first emperor catalogue (Add. MS. 36682) and as reflected in the classified list: when the classified list was made, Caligula B had 10 volumes, Caligula C had 9, Caligula D and E each had 12, Nero C had been extended to 12 volumes, Nero E had been extended to 7, Galba E had been extended to 12, Otho D had been extended to 11, Vespasian E had 25 volumes, Vespasian F had 11, Titus C had been extended to 18 volumes, Titus D had been extended to 27, Faustina C had 11 volumes, Faustina D had 4, Faustina E had 15 (?), Faustina F had 1 volume. No manuscripts are classed in the Augustus press in the classified list. It should be remembered that the first emperor catalogue, no less than the classified list itself, seems to have been compiled over a period of some years, and we do not know to what extent it is complete or accurately reflects the actual holdings at the time it was drawn up. On the dating of the first emperor catalogue, see Tite, 'The Early Catalogues', pp. 148–50.

60 It is included as a marginal addition in Petyt 538/40 (f. 127v).

61 The gift is recorded in an *ex dono* inscription in the manuscript (f. 2r). We do not know when the manuscript came into the Cotton collection.

62 *D.N.B.* under Cotton.

63 William Dugdale, *Life, Diary, and Correspondence*, ed. William Hamper (London, 1827), p. 24.

64 That is: Claudius A. XIII, Nero E. VII, Vespasian E. XXVI, Titus C. XVI, and Titus C. XVII. Colin Tite has kindly confirmed the identification of Dugdale's hand. I am most grateful to him for his counsel and encouragement in the preparation of this article.

65 Smith first proposed preparing a new catalogue in a letter to Sir John Cotton dated 23 June 1687 (Oxford, Bodleian Library, MS. Smith 59 [SC 15666], p. 181), but he did not begin work on the new catalogue until 13 Apr. 1694 (see Smith 59,

p. 232). Smith and Cotton were on friendly terms, Smith having already visited Sir John's country home, by 1686 (see Smith 48, pp. 247–248). I am grateful to Martin Kauffmann for assistance on this point and on other matters pertaining to Bodleian manuscripts. The correspondence between Smith and both Sir John and his half brother Sir Robert deserves closer scrutiny.

66 *D.N.B.* under Cotton. He has written pressmarks and tables of contents in a number of Cotton manuscripts (I owe this point to Colin Tite).

Thomas Smith mentioned Dugdale several times in his history of the library (*Catalogus*, pp. XXXI–XLVI), and he acknowledged Dugdale as a predecessor in his address to the reader (Smith, *Catalogus*, 'lectori' [not paginated]). If Dugdale supervised the copying of the classified list, he might have withheld the portion of the exemplar that was not routinely available (pp. 181–206 of the paginated catalogue) because it included the section of genealogies, which he needed as he prepared his *Baronage of England* (1675–6) for the press.

THE ROYAL LIBRARY AS A SOURCE FOR SIR ROBERT COTTON'S COLLECTION: A PRELIMINARY LIST OF ACQUISITIONS

JAMES P. CARLEY

PUBLIC Record Office, Augmentation Office, Misc. Books 160 (E. 315/160), ff. 107v–120r, contains an alphabetical list of 910 books, printed and manuscript, found in the Upper Library at Westminster Palace in 1542.[1] At approximately the same time the inventory was compiled, so it would appear, a number was entered into each book: this number corresponded to the place where the book occurred in the alphabetical sequences established by the list. Slightly afterwards, probably around 1550, more books came to Whitehall – presumably from Hampton Court and Greenwich – and these too were put into alphabetical order and an inventory number inserted.[2] Somewhat later the printed and manuscript books were separated.[3]

The form of the inventory number inserted in each book is characteristic: it is always found on an upper recto corner of an early folio, and always takes the form 'No — —'. Most of the manuscripts found in the Upper Library at Westminster Palace, and it is manuscripts alone that I shall be discussing in this paper, were rescued from monastic houses at the time of the Dissolution[4] and many have remained in the royal collection ever since. Not every title in the inventory, however, can be matched with a surviving royal book: indeed, approximately half disappeared at some point after 1542. The first major disruption, it would seem, must have occurred shortly after Henry VIII's death in 1547, in the period when Traheron, a radical evangelist, was librarian and when Edward VI's injunctions concerning the destruction of popish books were promulgated.[5] Throughout Elizabeth's reign, too, books trickled out. Unwanted items, duplicates and such, went to interested individuals: Sir Thomas Pope (1507?–59), William, Lord Howard of Effingham (d. 1573), Sir John Fortescue (d. 1607), and others.

During the librarianships of Sir Peter Young (d. 1628) and his son Patrick Young (d. 1652), the situation improved and Sir Thomas Bodley, for example, was blocked in his scheme to remove books *en masse* to his own collection in Oxford. Nevertheless, individual items did continue to migrate. James Ussher (1581–1656) took possession of several manuscripts, including the beautiful illuminated psalter which survives as Trinity College, Dublin, MS. 53. Sir James Balfour of Denmilne (1600–57) acquired at least three manuscripts which are now in the Advocates Library in Edinburgh. Thomas Reid (d. 1624), Latin Secretary to James I and associated with Young in the translation into Latin of James's English writings, was given a luxurious bestiary, now Aberdeen,

U.L., MS. 24. Young, moreover, kept a certain number of books for himself, two of which can now be found in Oxford as Bodleian, Cherry MSS. 3 and 4.[6] Young's principal dealings, however, seem to have been with Sir Robert Cotton (1571–1631), with whom he made a variety of exchanges.[7] The following is a list of manuscripts, or parts of manuscripts, known to have been at Westminster in 1542, which migrated to Cotton's collection in the early seventeenth century.

1. *Cotton Vespasian B. XII* (s. xv^2).

Among the post-1542 losses from the royal library, i.e. books no longer in the royal collection as such, is a text entitled 'Hunting and Hauking', whose inventory number should be 'No. 373'. At first glance this title would seem to pertain to a printed book, the well known *Book of Hawking, Hunting and Blasing of Arms* (*The Book of St Albans*),[8] but, in fact, this is not the case. Rather, it describes a manuscript, Cotton Vespasian B. XII, which has the characteristic identifying number on f. 3r (fig. 1).[9] Vespasian B. XII is a relatively elegant illuminated book which is made up of two texts:[10] [a] William Twiti (d. 1328). *Art of Hunting* (ff. 3r–9r). This is the Middle English version of Twiti's *L'Art de Vénerie* with a metrical introduction and three illustrations of the hunt and chase.[11] [b] Edward of Norwich, second Duke of York (d. 1415). *The Master of Game* (ff. 10r–106r). His partial translation, with additions (written between 1406–13), of the *Livre de la Chasse* (1378) of Gaston III, Comte de Foix, undertaken for Henry V while he was still Prince of Wales.[12] Although the text survives in a number of copies, the presentation copy appears to be lost.[13]

Kathleen L. Scott has noted that decorations in Vespasian B. XII closely resemble work in a group of texts whose production may well be associated with Bury St Edmunds or Clare in the 1460s.[14] From her analysis of these manuscripts, Scott postulates that there must have been a group of wealthy provincial patrons acquiring books at this period and possibly having them illuminated in a single shop: 'The district may in fact have had only one illuminator's shop where a local, well-to-do buyer or his scribe/agent could have his books done (unless the buyer wished to go to the extra expense of sending a book to London).'[15]

Most of the manuscripts examined by Scott are copies of works by John Lydgate, several of which descend from BL, Harl. MS. 2278, the text of Lydgate's Lives of Saints Edmund and Fremund prepared for presentation to Henry VI after his prolonged visit to Bury St Edmunds in the Winter and Spring of 1433–4.[16] Vespasian B. XII would, of course, also appeal to an aristocratic book purchaser and the possibly incomplete and partially erased arms which occur on ff. 10, 12 and 47v support the hypothesis of production for such an owner.[17] On ff. 1v, 106v, 107v, 108r, moreover, there are various annotations and scribblings which name specific individuals. On f. 1v the following notes appear in a very late fifteenth-century hand: 'Johannes Herberts/Johannes of the pantry/Item payyde vnto gorge strokybe[?] xx l'. Herbert's name turns up elsewhere; particularly interesting is the reference on f. 108r: 'Iste lyber constat Johannes Harbytt'.

Alle suche dysport as woydyth ydilnesse
It syttyth every gentilman to knowe
ffor myrthe anneyed is to gentilnesse
Qwerfore among alle op as y trowe
To knowe the craft of houtyng and to blowe
As thys book shall witnesse is one the beste
ffor it is holsum plesaunt and honest
And for to sette yonge hunterys in the way
To venery y caste me fyrst to go
Of wheche. iij bestis be that is to say
The hare the herte y wulfhe the wylde boor also
Of venery for sothe y be no moe
And so it shelwith here in portetelure
Wher euy best is set in hys figure

Fig. 1. Cotton MS. Vespasian B. XII, f. 3r

210

What these notes suggest, then, is that the book came to the Royal Household with a John Herbert who was an Officer of the Pantry.[18] On f. 108r there is an erased inscription of ownership, and just below this the name 'Master Sapcot' appears. It seems likely that the reference here is to Sir John Sapcote (1448–1501), who was Squire of the Body 1472–85, and Knight of the Body 1485–1501.[19] Another individual is named on f. 108r, i.e. 'Henr. Branford' (possibly 'Bramford'): his name seems to be in a slightly later script.[20]

From all this one can conclude that Vespasian B. XII was produced in East Anglia for the individual whose erased arms appear in it. It may be he was a member of the Waldegrave family, although this is not certain. At some point the book came into the possession of John Herbert and was brought by him into the Royal Household, presumably shortly before 1500. Whether or not it passed from him to Master Sapcot or Walter Herbert is not clear; they may simply have been interested readers. (Whatever else, it is precisely the sort of book which would have appealed to courtiers.) Nor is there any indication of how it moved from private ownership into royal hands. The various jottings on the flyleaves make it seem improbable that it was a gift and unreturned borrowing would seem the most likely channel. To date, however, no independent documentary evidence has turned up to confirm this hypothesis and so the matter must remain within the realms of speculation.

2. *Cotton Tiberius E. I* (*Redbourn, s. xiv*).

In the 1542 list No. 845 is described as 'Sanctilogium Io. de Anglia'. According to his *Index Britanniae Scriptorum*, moreover, John Bale saw a copy of 'Sanctilogium Ioannis de Anglia' among the books in the king's library.[21] The reference quite clearly must be to John of Tynemouth's *Sanctilogium Angliae*, which survives, unedited, as the badly scorched Cotton Tiberius E. I, from Redbourn Priory.[22] Unfortunately, no inventory number can be detected in Tiberius E. I because of severe damage from the fire at Ashburnham House in 1731, but there is strong corroborating evidence to support the hypothesis that this manuscript came to Cotton from the royal collection. Cotton Tiberius E. I is a unique copy of the *Sanctilogium Angliae*. The next title in the 1542 inventory is 'Sanctilogium Guidonis': the only known copy of Guido de Castris's *Sanctilogium* survives as Royal 13 D. IX; it comes from Redbourn Priory and has the inventory number 846. These two manuscripts are the only identified survivors from Redbourn and they are very similar in their contents, which suggests that they would have both caught the eye of the individual collecting for the King at the time of the Dissolution. If Cotton Tiberius E. I is not identified as No. 845, moreover, then there must have been another copy of the same text which escaped the Dissolution and which Cotton acquired in some unknown manner from an equally unknown collector. At the same time, too, the Westminster copy would have had to have disappeared from the royal library, leaving no trace. The likelihood of this concatenation of events must certainly be almost nil.[23]

3. *Cotton Vitellius E. VII, ff. 13–70 (Bardney, s. xiii–xiv)*.

Around 1530 Henry VIII himself or one of his agents placed a cross beside the titles of five books from a list compiled at the Benedictine abbey of St Peter, St Paul and St Oswald at Bardney, Lincolnshire, and these volumes were subsequently removed to the royal collection.[24] Four can be identified, as would be anticipated, as surviving manuscripts from the Old Royal Library and all four carry Westminster inventory numbers. The fifth, the Latin version of the *Ancrene Riwle*, described in the Lincolnshire list as 'Vita anachoritarum utriusque sexus', is no longer in the royal collection, but survives in Cotton Vitellius E. VII.[25] Vitellius E. VII, which was badly damaged in the 1731 fire, is a made-up volume and was undoubtedly put together by Cotton himself. In the catalogue of 1621 + found in Harley 6018 it appears as number 181 (f. 85r): '1. Vita regis et martiris Aedelberti, Davidis archiepiscopi Meneuensis, sancti Patricii per Giraldum Cambrensem. 2. Regula domini Aelredi abbatis de institucione inclusarum et ordo includendi famulam Dei./De vita Anachoretarum utriusque sexus auctor Robertus Lincolnensis.'[26] Given the division into three sections, and the slash is equivalent to an actual number in this respect, it is tempting to speculate that Aelred of Rievaulx's *De Institutione Inclusarum* was not part of the manuscript as it came from Bardney (and this is certainly the case for the earlier saints' lives) but was rather a Cotton insertion.[27]

Although the manuscript is too badly burned for any inventory number to show, it can be established that it did go from Bardney to Westminster: the title for entry 902 in the inventory is identical to that in the Lincolnshire list, i.e. 'Vita anachoritarum utriusque sexus'. According to the description in Thomas Smith's 1696 catalogue 'Hunc librum Frater Robertus de Thorneton, quondam Prior, dedit Claustralibus de Bardenay.'[28]

4. *Cotton Otho A. XV, ff. 1–80 (Rochester)*.

Number 42 in the Westminster inventory is described as 'Acta gestorum pontificum', but there is no matching book in the modern royal collection. In his list 'ex bibliotheca anglorum regis' Bale noted a work with the title 'Acta pontificum', presumably the same volume.[29] Given this title, moreover, one can postulate that it might have been a copy of Pseudo-Anastasius Bibliothecarius's *Liber pontificalis*[30] which went missing. Although there are no longer any copies of this work in the old royal collection, one was found in Cotton's library as Otho A. XV, ff. 1–80. Unfortunately, this manuscript was destroyed in the fire of 1731 – as Madden notes, 'No portion of this MS. has been recovered'[31] – and so it is not possible to see if there was a royal inventory number in it.

The medieval provenance can, however, be determined through the evidence of two individuals and this in turn increases strongly the likelihood that Otho A. XV is the missing No. 42. In his Catalogue Thomas Smith asserted a Rochester provenance for Otho A. XV: 'Liber olim erat S. Andreae Roffensis: continuatur ad Stephanum inclusiue.'[32] Earlier in the century Richard James had compared a manuscript of the *Liber pontificalis* with a printed copy of the *editio princeps* (Mainz, 1602), now in Corpus

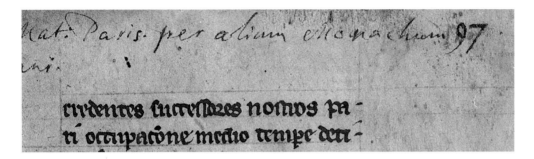

Fig. 2. Cotton MS. Claudius D. VI, f. 101r (top right-hand corner), showing where the
Westminster inventory number '1056' has been erased

Christi College, Oxford, and made various observations on a front flyleaf of the printed
version.[33] That he was dealing with Otho A. XV, which must therefore have had a
Rochester ex libris, is certain since he stated that his notes came 'Ex cod. Cottoniano qui
olim erat claustri Roffensis per petrum praecentorem, cum quo simul habere petri
alfonsis Iudaismus.' In Otho A. XV, as it was put together by Cotton, the *Liber
pontificalis* is followed by Petrus Alfonsi's *Dialogus aduersus Iudaeos.* Neither Smith nor
James includes the *Dialogus aduersus Iudaeos* as part of the Rochester book: in both cases
the citation of the Rochester ex libris comes before the reference to Petrus's text. This,
too, ties in with the evidence found in an entry in a twelfth-century catalogue inserted
into the *Textus Roffensis*: 'Acta beatorum pontificum i vol'.[34]

Granted, the case for a royal link as outlined above is based on circumstantial
evidence. What is important to remember, however, is that well over half of the surviving
Rochester books were gathered into the library at Westminster at the time of the
Dissolution.[35] There is, therefore, statistically a strong chance that any surviving book
with a known Rochester provenance was moved from Rochester to Westminster by 1542.
The probability increases greatly if the book can be matched with a title in the
Westminster inventory. It is made almost certain when its subsequent history follows a
well-known, in this case the single most common, pattern through which royal books
were 'de-accessioned' in the period after Henry's death.

5. *Cotton Claudius D. VI, ff. 101–220 (C) + Royal 14 C. I, ff. 1–22 (R) (St Albans, s. xiv
in.).*[36]

No title in the Westminster inventory as such describes the writings of William
Rishanger. Yet, in his entry on William Rishanger, where he gave six titles with incipits,
John Bale named the royal library as his source of information.[37] Since Bale examined
the royal library after the second group of books (nos. 911–1450) was brought to
Whitehall and since Rishanger's name does not appear in the Westminster inventory per
se, one can assume that Rishanger must have figured among the higher numbers. As it

happens, all of Rishanger's works (or at least works subsequently associated with his name) survive in unique copies and all, with one possible exception, are found either in Claudius D. VI or Royal 14 C. I (hereafter C and R).[38] The first item listed by Bale, *The Account of the Barons' War*, is found on ff. 101r–118v of Claudius D. VI. Under ultra-violet light, moreover, a Westminster inventory number (No. 1056) can be found on f. 101 (fig. 2). In the late-medieval manuscript, then, *The Account of the Barons' War* must have come first, just as Bale's entry suggests. (The location of the inventory number also shows that the copy of Matthew Paris's *Abbreviatio Chronicorum* and related materials in Claudius D. VI, ff. 2–100, cannot have been part of the original manuscript, or at least of the manuscript which travelled from St Albans to Westminster Palace.)[39] Partially erased foliation establishes that the *Opus Chronicorum*, covering the years 1259–97 (C, ff. 119r–137v), followed. Before Bale's third title, 'De controuersia habita super electione regni Scotie' (C, f. 138r + v), there were two other items which Bale did not list: a Life and Miracles of St Louis (now R, ff. 7r–10r), and a chronicle fragment covering the years 1285–1307, beginning *De obitu Alfundi filii regis* (R, ff. 11v–19v + 3 blanks). Next came a narrative of the Great Cause (1291–2), called by modern historians the *Annales Regni Scotiae* and known to Bale as 'Super constituto rege Ioanne Balliolo' (now C, ff. 139r–164v). This was followed, as is still the case, by sections of chronicle (not recorded by Bale): *Mox idem Iohannes* (1292–1300) (C, ff. 165r–176v), *De tempore regis Edwardi* (1299–1300) (C, ff. 177r–184v), a poem *De bello Scotico* (C, ff. 184v–186r + 1 blank), and another chronicle section (1295–1300), beginning *Eodem anno peciit et obtinuit rex Edwardus* (C, ff. 188r–190r). The next item in the late medieval manuscript, a copy of Edward I's letter to Pope Boniface VIII asserting England's historical right to Scotland (Bale's 'De iure quod habet rex ad Scotiam'), is now found as R, ff. 1r–4r; afterwards there are twelve lines of verse (f. 4r + v) with the heading: 'De ista materia cronigraphus metrice scribens breuiter sic ait'. This section was succeeded by Rishanger's *Quedam recapitulatio breuis de gestis domini Edwardi*, covering 1297–1307 (now R, ff. 4v–6v; +C, ff. 191r–192v) (figs. 3, 4).[40] This was followed in turn by a brief rhymed chronicle of the kings of England (C, f. 193r). After a blank verso we then find the *Annales* (1307–22) normally associated with John de Trokelowe but ascribed to Rishanger by Bale (C, ff. 194r–212r). The text headed 'Incipiunt Cronica Fratris Henrici de Blaneforde' begins on f. 212r (1323) and breaks off incomplete in the year 1324 on f. 217v: clearly leaves have been lost at the end of the manuscript.

The form the manuscript took in the later Middle Ages and throughout its 'royal incarnation', the arrangement I have just outlined, represents an elaboration and 're-shuffling' of a somewhat different manuscript (as earlier quire signatures indicate), itself made up of previously independent booklets.[41] This is not, however, the final metamorphosis. Among the exchanges between Cotton and Patrick Young recorded in Add. MS. 35213, the fourth entry reads: 'Marianus Scotus et Bartholomew de Cotton. Foll new bound.' In the Harley 6018 exchange list the twenty-second entry states: 'Lent him [presumably Young] my Marianus Scotus and Bartholl de Cotton in Foll.' Cotton's reference is to the present Cotton Nero C. V which begins with a description of Britain

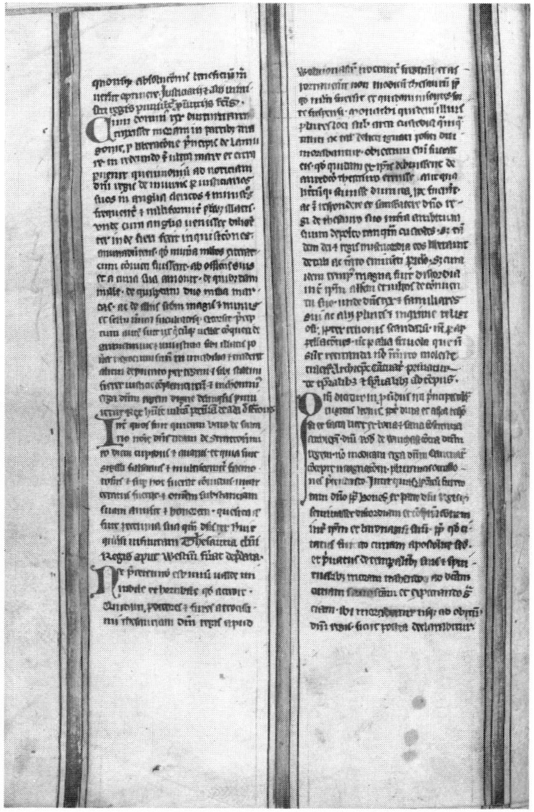

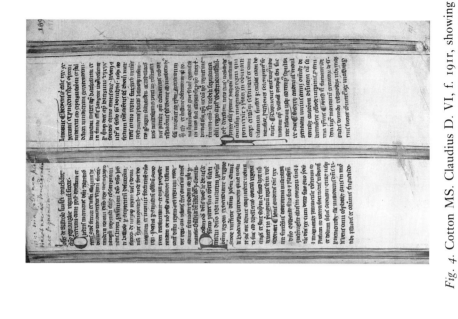

Fig. 3. Royal MS. 14 C. I, f. 6v, showing the continuity of layout with Cotton MS. Claudius D. VI, f. 191r

Fig. 4. Cotton MS. Claudius D. VI, f. 191r, showing the continuity of layout with Royal MS. 14 C. I, f. 6v

taken from Henry of Huntingdon's *Historia Anglorum* and attributed here (as elsewhere) to Marianus Scotus (from Worcester), followed by Bartholomew Cotton's *Historia Anglicana* (from Norwich).[42] This copy of Bartholomew's history (ff. 162–254) was formerly part of Royal 14 C. I, that is when the manuscript began with the present ff. 20–137 and was made up of Martinus Polonus's *Cronica* (ff. 20–79) followed by Geoffrey of Monmouth's *Historia Regum Britanniae* (ff. 80–137).[43] Originally, then, Bartholomew came after the latter text, which in fact constitutes its first book.[44] Sir Robert Cotton's division of Bartholomew's chronicle into component parts and his incorporation of the second and third books (i.e. Bartholomew's own chronicle) into a new manuscript (Nero C. V) for his own collection makes good sense: presumably the *Historia Regum Britanniae* itself would represent a duplicate and would be of no interest. After the detachment of books two and three, that is Bartholomew proper, what would remain would be a manuscript containing Martinus Polonus and Geoffrey, i.e. the skeleton of the present 14 C. I.

At approximately the same time as he put together Nero C. V, Cotton must have obtained Claudius D. VI in its late-medieval form from Young. He had also acquired the autograph copy of Matthew Paris's *Abbreviatio Chronicorum*[45] with which Claudius D. VI would have matched textually (i.e. the *Opus Chronicorum* begins chronologically more or less where the *Abbreviatio Chronicorum* ends) and in terms of layout (i.e. the characteristic Matthew Paris/St Albans banded margins). The *Abbreviatio Chronicorum* was therefore inserted at the beginning of Claudius D. VI, that is immediately before *The Account of the Barons' War*. Concurrently, quite distinct sections of Claudius D. VI – (i) ff. 108–113 (by medieval foliation) containing Edward I's Letter and the beginning of Rishanger's *Quedam recapitulatio*; and (ii) ff. 38–52 (by medieval foliation) containing the Life and Miracles of St Louis and the chronicle fragment *De obitu Alfundi* – were removed and placed at the beginning of 14 C. I.[46] Even more extraordinary is the fact that a memorandum which had been written in the bottom margin of the opening leaf of *The Account of the Barons' War*, 'Memorandum quod ego frater Willelmus de Rishanger cronigraphus, die inuentionis sancte crucis, anno gratie m°.ccc^{mo}.xii°, qui est annus regis Edwardi filii regis Edwardi quintus, habui in ordine xli annos et in etate lxii annos. Hic est liber Sancti Albani', was cut out and glued onto the bottom of f. 1 of Edward's Letter, that is at the beginning of the newly formed 14 C. I.[47]

The reason for the creation of the new Cotton manuscript, 'Matthew Paris Historia minor in parchment bound up with my armes and Rishanger with it',[48] seems obvious: Claudius D. VI in its present form gives a chronologically complete account of English history from 1000 to 1324+. On the other hand, Royal 14 C. I does not present a coherent whole and there is no relationship between the opening St Albans part of the manuscript and its Norwich sequel. More importantly, there does not seem to be any logical reason either for the excision of the St Albans fragments from Claudius D. VI or for their relocation in this entirely alien context.

216

Fig. 5. Royal MS. 13 A. XXI, f. 14r (top right-hand corner)

6. *Cotton Vespasian B. XI, ff. 2–61 + Royal 13 A. XXI, ff. 12–150 (Hagnaby, s. xiv in.).*[49]

Unlike most of the Westminster books which managed to remain in the Old Royal Library, Royal 13 A. XXI has undergone changes: both additions and deletions. What can be seen as the core unit consists of ff. 12–150, made up of Honorius of Autun's *Imago Mundi*, followed by Wace's *Roman de Brut* and Geoffrey Gaimar's *Estoire des Engles*.[50] On f. 14r, that is on the third folio of what would have been the medieval manuscript, the characteristic Westminster inventory number has been entered: No. 1146 (fig. 5). The copy of a section of the Biblical paraphrase in Old French verse by Herman de Valenciennes which makes up ff. 2–11 of the present manuscript, therefore, must be a later addition, presumably inserted at the time other materials were removed.

In the Lincolnshire list of books marked for removal to the royal collection there are two entries for Hagnaby.[51] The first refers to a 'Cronica regum Anglie ab anno domini millesimo usque ad annum eiusdem millesimum cccuiimum'. This title is very specific in its chronological boundaries and must refer to Cotton Vespasian B. XI, ff. 2–61, one of the three known Hagnaby survivors.[52] It is clear, then, that this text must have gone directly from Hagnaby to the royal library, and that Cotton must have acquired it from Young, at the time of their various exchanges. However, there are no signs of an inventory number at the beginning of Vespasian B. XI, as there would have been if it had been the opening text in one of the royal manuscripts: one must assume therefore that it was not the first item in the manuscript which came to the royal collection in the 1530s.[53] A comparison of Royal 13 A. XXI, ff. 12–150 and Vespasian B. XI, ff. 2–61 shows that they are extremely similar, both in terms of layout and script,[54] and it would seem obvious that the chronicle section of Vespasian B. XI was attached to the end of Royal 13 A. XXI at the time the manuscript was brought to the royal library.[55] This hypothesis seems confirmed by Bale's reference to a copy of 'Imago mundi, cum chronica anglorum' which he saw in the royal library.[56]

In the exchange list found in Add. MS. 35213, the twelfth item, which appears as 'Book that I had of Mr Young', is 'A Cronicle part of Imago Mundi 4o.' One can only presume that the term 'part' relates to Cotton's removal of what is now the opening text of Vespasian B. XI from its larger framework. A second entry (item 38) refers to the manuscript after the chronicle section had been excised: among books 'To be given back', is the 'Imago Mundi in Black Valur and Bossed'. When he removed the chronicle, moreover, and before he returned the manuscript to Young, Cotton must also have inserted the (useless from his point of view) ten folios at the beginning of Royal 13 A. XXI.

Folios 151–192 of Royal 13 A. XXI once formed part of a single manuscript at Kirkham Abbey, of which another text in Vespasian B. XI was also a portion.[57] The opening section of the Kirkham manuscript consisted of what is now Arundel 36. This was followed by a copy of Aelred of Rievaulx's *Vita S. Edwardi*, which is found as ff. 84–125, 125* of the modern Vespasian B. XI. Late sixteenth-century foliation indicates that ff. 151–192 of Royal 13 A. XXI (beginning with Jerome's *De uiris illustribus*) came next. As the description in Bernard's *Catalogi Librorum Manuscriptorum Angliae et Hiberniae* establishes, there was also a now lost copy of Isidore of Seville's *De patribus ueteris et noui Testamenti*, which would have come after Gennadius's *De uiris illustribus* and before Isidore's *De uiris illustribus*, that is between the present ff. 170 and 171.[58] Presumably, an unknown owner, the individual who must have acquired the manuscript at the time of the Dissolution, removed Isidore's *De patribus ueteris et noui Testamenti* for his own purposes. Later, Henry Savile of Banke acquired the first fifty-six folios (now BL, Arundel MS. 36) in fragmentary form and he retained these (with other unrelated materials) in a loose cover. Cotton must have obtained other parts of the manuscript, keeping Aelred of Rievaulx's *Vita S. Edwardi* for his own collection and inserting the other extraneous matter at the end of Royal 13 A. XXI to fill up the gap left by the removal of the Hagnaby chronicle.

7. *Cotton Otho D. VIII, ff. 174–233v + Royal 13 D. I (St Peter-upon-Cornhill, London, s. xiv ex.).*[59]

A manuscript which has been analysed by historians and art historians alike is Royal 13 D. I, a late-fourteenth-century collection of historical texts from the church of St Peter-upon-Cornhill, London.[60] It was one of the books gathered up for the royal collection in the sixteenth century and was numbered 708 (fig. 6) in the Westminster sequence. The second booklet (now removed to form a separate codex, Royal 13 D. I*) stands apart from the rest of the manuscript in terms of layout and contents: it is a portion of an illuminated mid-fourteenth century psalter, other stray leaves of which have survived as binding fragments in a variety of manuscripts throughout the Cotton collection.[61] Although the psalter has internal characteristics which would hint at a northern Pentatiuk and sainctes Lyves, thother of medicine.' The second manuscript, from medieval times and must therefore have come to London in an early period. What is difficult to explain, nevertheless, is why Cotton would have borrowed the manuscript and removed some, but not all, of the leaves from the psalter booklet to use as flyleaves in his own books.

The title in the Westminster inventory which matches the entry for 708 clearly

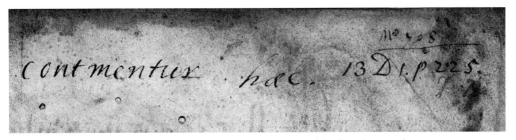

Fig. 6. Royal MS. 13 D. I, f. 2r (top right-hand corner)

describes 13 D. I but, in fact, is not a perfect fit: it gives as the second and third items not the psalter but rather (i) 'Cronica Nich. Triuet', and (ii) 'parua prophecia de regibus Anglis'. There are about fifteen known surviving copies of Nicholas Trevet's *Annales* and one of these is found as ff. 174–231r of Otho D. VIII. Otho D. VIII is a composite manuscript, badly damaged in the fire of 1731, in which ff. 174r–233v constitute a separate booklet. The *Annales* are, moreover, followed by materials which can quite comfortably be described as 'parua prophecia de regibus Anglis'.[62] Even though the booklet is badly damaged, it is clear that the hand is identical to that of Royal 13 D. I; the layout also matches, and both manuscripts have later annotations by the same individual. There can be no doubt, then, that Otho D. VIII, ff. 174–233v, represents the missing section of 13 D. I, as described in the Westminster inventory.

At the time when Cotton borrowed Royal 13 D. I from Patrick Young he must already have owned the psalter, which he presumably considered to be of no particular historical significance. When the *Annales* booklet was removed the manuscript may have lacked bulk, therefore requiring stuffing with waste materials which were already to hand, i.e. a section of the psalter, or it may be that these waste materials were incorporated into the altered manuscript by mistake, perhaps during rebinding. Either alternative, of course, explains why some leaves of the psalter turned up in a block in Royal 13 D. I, whereas others occurred as binding fragments in other Cotton manuscripts.

8. *Cotton Vespasian D. XXI, ff. 18–40 + Bodleian Library, Laud Miscellaneous 509 (s. xi²).*[63]

In the Westminster inventory the title for item no. 129 is unusual in that it describes two manuscripts rather than one: 'Bookes written in tholde Saxon tonge two. thone of the Pentatiuk and sainctes Lyves, thother of medicine.' The second manuscript, from Winchester, still remains intact in the Royal Library: it is known to modern scholars as Bald's Leechbook (Royal 12 D. XVII) and it carries the number 129 on f. 1r.[64]

The first manuscript, however, has had a more complex history. At some point after it came to Westminster it was divided into two parts which survive as Oxford, Bodleian Library, MS. Laud Miscellaneous 509, and Cotton Vespasian D. XXI, ff. 18–40. As the modern shelfmark makes clear, the second of these component parts, the Old English

219

Fig. 7. Royal MS. 15 A. XXII, f. 2r (top right-hand corner), showing where the Westminster inventory number '823' has been erased

prose translation of Felix's *Vita sancti Guthlaci* and the related homily,[65] must represent a Cotton acquisition. Cotton, moreover, combined this text with a copy of pseudo-Nennius's *Historia Brittonum* to form Vespasian D. XXI.[66] In Harley 6018, f. 154r, among a list of books outstanding at 20 December 1606, there is a reference to William Camden's having borrowed 'Nennius and vita Sancti Guthlaci *8vo*', which establishes that the dismemberment and recombination must have taken place before this date.[67]

Laud Misc. 509 contains the text which originally came before the *Vita S. Guthlaci*, that is, a copy of the Old English Hexateuch, preceded by Ælfric's preface and followed by his summary of the Book of Judges and some other pieces.[68] The inventory number, i.e. No. 129, is found on f. 2r.[69] As it happens, Cotton lent what is now Laud Misc. 509 to William Lisle (1569?–1637), and this loan was still outstanding on 23 April 1621. Ker assumed that it went from Lisle to William Laud, Archbishop of Canterbury (d. 1645), whose inscription: 'Liber Guil: Laud Archiepi: Cant: & Cancellar: Universitatis Oxon 1638' appears on f. 1r, and passed from Laud to Bodley in 1639. There is, as Tite has observed, one problem with this scenario, since Richard James transcribed material from the first folio into one of his notebooks in a context which it makes it seem certain that the manuscript must have been in the Cotton library when he made the transcription. Since James did not work for Cotton before *circa* 1625, this suggests that the manuscript must have come back to Cotton from Lisle before going to Laud.

9. *Cotton Vespasian D. XXI, ff. 1–17 + Royal 15 A. XXII (Rochester, s. xii¹).*

Cotton was keenly interested in pseudo-Nennius's *Historia Brittonum* and owned three copies of the Harleian recension of this text. These are closely related: one (Vespasian B. XXV [s. xii¹], from Christ Church, Canterbury) forms part of a manuscript which has remained intact from medieval times; the other two, both from Rochester, have been excised from manuscripts still in the royal library.[70] Royal 15 A. XXII carries a now erased Westminster inventory number 823 (fig. 7) and the corresponding entry roughly describes the contents: 'Solinus de mirabilibus mundi. historia Troianorum. Pergesis de situ terrae. Prophecia Sybillae. Segardus de miseria hominis et historia Britonum'. An earlier description of the manuscript is found in the *Textus Roffensis* catalogue: 'Solinus et dares, et liber pergesis i. de situ terrae prisciani grammatici urbis romae, et vaticinium sybillae, et historiam britannorum in i vol.'[71] On f. 1v, moreover, there is a medieval list

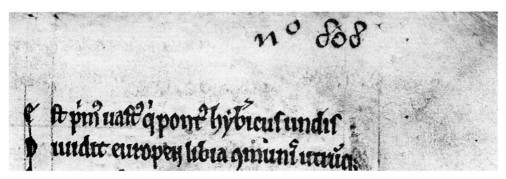

Fig. 8. Royal MS. 15 B. XI, f. 3r (top right-hand corner)

of contents which matches the first five items in the Westminster inventory: '⟨D⟩e mirabilibus tocius mundi; ⟨H⟩istoria troianorum; ⟨L⟩iber pergesis de situ terre; ⟨P⟩rophetia sybille; ⟨V⟩ersus Segardi de miseria hominis et penis inferni'. After these entries, however, two further titles, which can just be made out with the aid of ultra-violet light, have been erased: '⟨H⟩istoria Britonum' and '⟨D⟩e miraculis Britannie'.[72]

As there are only two 'dismembered' copies of the combined *Historia Brittonum* and *De miraculis Britanniae* in the Cotton library (Vitellius A. XIII, ff. 91–100, and Vespasian D. XXI, ff. 1–17), the first of which indisputably forms part of 15 B. XI, it would seem logical to assume that Vespasian D. XXI, ff. 1–17, represents the missing section of 15 A. XXII to which the erased entries pertain.[73] It is this copy of the *Historia Brittonum*, too, which Richard James described in his contents list in Vespasian D. XXI as 'Antiquissimum exemplar Nennii in quo plura continentur quam in aliis'[74] and which Cotton lent to Camden before December 1606.[75] There are several other references to Vespasian D. XXI in the loans lists in Harley 6018: on f. 162v Cotton recorded a loan to Francis Tate (d. 1616) of 'Nennii Historia my Best Coppy et vita Gutlaci in Saxon 8° bound with my armes'; and on f. 176r he noted that he had lent to 'Mr Francis Tate late of the Midle Temple', 'Nennii Historia et vita Guthlaci. bound with my armes 8° clasp'. On 7 July 1640 Sir Thomas Cotton lent 'Antiquissimus Exemplar Nennii', presumably Vespasian D. XXI, to William Watts.[76]

10. *Cotton Vitellius A. XIII, ff. 91–100 + Royal 15 B. XI (Rochester, s. xiii¹).*

Royal 15 B. XI, as it came into the royal library from Rochester as No. 808 (fig. 8), was a closely related, slightly later version of Royal 15 A. XXII + Cotton Vespasian D. XXI, ff. 1–17. In this case, Cotton's removal of the *Historia Brittonum* and the *De miraculis Britanniae* after f. 66v, necessitated the severing of the last leaf of the *De excidio Troiae* of 'Dares Phrygius'.[77] The *Prophetia Sybillae* (now ff. 67r–69v) originally followed the *De miraculis* and began a new quire. After the *Prophetia Sybillae* there is evidence of further tampering: somebody, presumably Cotton, has inserted a copy of Gilbertus Universalis's *Glossa in Jeremiah* (ff. 70–101v), a text completely unrelated in terms of

221

layout and script. Based on the parallels with Vespasian B. XXV and Royal 15 A. XXII one can assume, moreover, that a (now lost) copy of Segardus Iunior of St Amar's *De miseria hominis* was removed from this spot before the *Glossa* was inserted.

The entry for Vitellius A. XIII in the 1621 'Catalogus Librorum Manuscriptorum in Bibliotheca Roberti Cottoni' (Harley 6018, ff. 25–26) includes only the 'Liber chartarum domus Certeseye', (given to Cotton by Arthur Agarde): the *Historia Brittonum* and other materials must have been added later. By the time of the compilation of the catalogue of *circa* 1638 (Add. MS. 36682) the manuscript had taken its modern form.

CONCLUSIONS

In the essay on the history and contents of the library which accompanied his catalogue, Smith provided the following headings to categorize the collection: (i) manuscripts written in the Anglo-Saxon tongue; (ii) cartularies of monasteries; (iii) lives and passions of the saints and martyrs; (iv) genealogical tables; (v) histories, annals and chronicles; (vi) original records of the kingdom.[78] Kevin Sharpe, moreover, has perceived a process of evolution within these categories: 'Cotton's initial interest in Saxon and early ecclesiastical material widened to embrace medieval chronicles, foreign works, and documents illustrating recent and contemporary affairs, whilst he continued to search for Saxon manuscripts. Cotton's developing interests created a library which contained a wealth of material for ecclesiastical history; the history of families, offices, and institutions; and the story of the kings of England from Saxon times.'[79] The royal acquisitions fall very neatly into this pattern.[80] The earliest item to have come from Young may well have been the Anglo-Saxon copy of the Hexateuch and the *Vita Sancti Guthlaci* (Laud Misc. 509 + Vespasian D. XXII, ff. 18–40). Cotton also acquired at least one of his copies of the *Historia Brittonum* (Vespasian D. XXII, ff. 1–17) before 1606. Later came histories of the church (Otho A. XV) and the works by medieval chroniclers (Claudius D. VI; Vespasian B. XI, ff. 1–61; Otho D. VIII, ff. 174–233). There is a volume of saints' lives (Tiberius E. I) and a Latin translation of the *Ancrene Riwle* with related texts (Vitellius E. VII).[81] At first glance Vespasian B. XII might appear to stand apart from Smith's categories, a book chosen simply as an object of beauty, one of the 'jewels woven in a purple cloak [to] add a new and powerful brilliance'.[82] In fact, it probably relates to Cotton's interest in 'genealogical tables' and is one of the texts which 'throws light on everything pertaining to nobility', 'reports of acts of defiance, challenges, duels, plays, pageants and equestrian manoeuvres which we call tournaments…'.[83]

On a more general level, what a number of these examples illustrate dramatically is the fact that seventeenth-century collectors (in the manner of their sixteenth-century predecessors such as Matthew Parker)[84] did not share our respect for the integrity of the manuscript as a historical artefact.[85] Their concern was for individual items, which of course was perfectly reasonable in a period when so much material was still unprinted and more or less inaccessible.[86] It is only in modern times, really very modern times,

222

that scholars have begun studying carefully the context in which individual works appear.

Pamela R. Robinson has written perceptively about the role of the booklet in composite manuscripts and has shown how in earliest form a single quire or group of gatherings could circulate independently before being brought together as part of a single manuscript.[87] In her definition Robinson focuses on the self-contained aspect of the booklet, reminding us that 'The beginning and end of a "booklet" always coincides with the beginning and end of a text or a group of texts'.[88] What she emphasizes, then, is the possible independent origin and circulation of the component parts of a medieval manuscript. The examples above remind us that we must also remember the opposite end of the process: the putting asunder, which is always a much more violent enterprise, of what seemed to have been permanently joined together. When dealing with manuscripts made up of multiple units scholars should, therefore, be suspicious of odd juxtapositions, as in the case of the Matthew Paris/William Rishanger texts, or 'sore thumbs' such as in the case of the psalter inserted into Royal 13 D. I. Our reverence for the manuscript as such may well make us overlook what was going on in early modern times or even before.[89]

Michelle Brown has provided helpful palaeographical information and Nigel Ramsay has made various suggestions. My greatest debt, however, is to Colin Tite, who has read the whole article carefully several times and has enlightened me on general as well as specific points.

1 The list forms a section in a complete inventory of 'all suche our Money, Iuells, Plate, Vtensiles, Apparell, Guarderobe stuff and other our Goods, Catalls, and things as Anthony Denny keper of our Palloice at Westminster shall stande chargid with' (f. 1r). Denny was first styled Keeper of Westminster Palace on 31 Jan. 1537. On the Westminster inventory, see James P. Carley, 'John Leland and the Foundations of the Royal Library: the Westminster Inventory of 1542', *Bulletin of the Society for Renaissance Studies*, vii (1989), pp. 13–22.

2 On the three libraries established, primarily as repositories for monastic books, during Henry's reign, see Carley, 'Leland and...the Royal Library', p. 14; also Carley, 'Greenwich and Henry VIII's Royal Library', in David Starkey (ed.), *Henry VIII: A European Court in England* (London, 1991), pp. 155–9. When Bartholomew Traheron became King's Librarian in 1549 he was specifically empowered by his letters patent to bring books from the other libraries to Whitehall (as Westminster Palace was generally

termed by the early 1540s). The second, later, alphabetical sequence carries the numbers 911–1450.

3 See James P. Carley, 'Books Seen by Samuel Ward "In Bibliotheca Regia", *circa* 1614', *British Library Journal*, xvi (1990), pp. 89–98, at 97, n. 16.

4 On John Leland as a collector of monastic manuscripts in the 1530s, see 'John Leland and the Foundations of the Royal Library', pp. 13–14.

5 On this topic, see Owain Tudor Edwards, 'How Many Sarum Antiphonals Were There in England and Wales in the Middle of the Sixteenth Century?', *Revue Bénédictine*, xcix (1989), pp. 155–80, at 155–6, 169–72.

6 Francis Cherry (d. 1713) got the manuscripts from Leigh Atwood, whose ultimate source was his maternal ancestor Patrick Young. (Young's daughter Elisabeth married John Atwood, of Broomfield.) On Young as a collector, see also Teresa Webber, 'Patrick Young, Salisbury Cathedral Manuscripts and the Royal Collection', *English Manuscript Studies 1100–1700*, ii (1990), pp. 283–90.

7 References to Cotton's exchanges with Young are found in two manuscripts: BL, Harl. MS. 6018, f. 159v, and BL, Add. MS. 35213, ff. 34v + r (leaf reversed in binding). Colin Tite,

who is producing a complete edition of all Cotton's exchange lists and who has kindly permitted me to see his typescripts, dates these exchanges to *c*. 1616. See his '"Lost or Stolen or Strayed": a Survey of Manuscripts Formerly in the Cotton Library', *British Library Journal*, xviii (1992), pp. 111–13, and reprinted below, pp. 266–8.

8 See A. W. Pollard and G. R. Redgrave, *A Short-Title Catalogue of Books Printed in England, Scotland and Ireland ... 1475–1640*, 2nd ed., rev. W. A. Jackson, F. S. Ferguson and Katharine F. Pantzer (Oxford, 1976, 1986), no. 3308.

9 Dr Tite first pointed out to me that Vespasian B. XII carries a Westminster inventory number. I also thank Kathleen Scott for providing me with information about this manuscript from her unpublished notes. Cotton's librarian, Richard James (1592–1638), appears to have taken extracts: see Oxford, Bodleian Library, MS. James 11 (*SC* 3848), pp. 57–60.

10 There is some disagreement among art historians about just how de luxe the manuscript really is. What is generally accepted, however, is that it is not grand enough to have been a royal presentation copy.

11 The *Art of Hunting* survives in five manuscripts, two in Anglo-Norman and three in Middle English: see William Twiti, *Art of Hunting. 1327*, ed. Bror Danielsson (Stockholm, 1977); also Gunnar Tilander, *La Vénerie de Twiti* (Uppsala, 1956). On John Gifford, who is given as joint author in Vespasian B. XII, f. 9r, see Danielsson, pp. 34–5. Plate II in *Art of Hunting*, ed. Danielsson, shows the Westminster number. Danielsson, who would date the script to *c*. 1430 (p. 40, n. 2), describes this text as 'inferior' (p. 37).

12 See W. A. and F. Baillie-Grohman (eds.), *The Master of Game by Edward, second duke of York* (London, 1904); they edit, or at least give 'a modern rendering', from this manuscript, which is described as the best of the existing nineteen MSS. of the 'Master of Game' (p. xxvi).

13 See J. J. G. Alexander, 'Painting and Manuscript Illumination for Royal Patrons in the Later Middle Ages', in V. J. Scattergood and J. W. Sherborne (eds.), *English Court Culture in the Later Middle Ages* (London, 1983), pp. 141–62, at 158; also Jeanne E. Krochalis, 'The Books and Reading of Henry V and His Circle', *The Chaucer*

Review, xxiii (1988), pp. 50–77, at 65, who mistakenly cites it as Cotton Vespasian B. XI.

14 Kathleen L. Scott, 'Lydgate's Lives of Saints Edmund and Fremund: A Newly-Located Manuscript in Arundel Castle', *Viator*, xiii (1982), pp. 335–66, at 345, 346, 365–6.

15 Scott, 'Lydgate's Lives', p. 365.

16 This manuscript has a Westminster inventory number (No. 467) and is listed as 'Lyf of St Edmonde' in the inventory. Presumably it went to a royal collection soon after its production.

17 Both Ann Payne and Nigel Ramsay have kindly tried to decipher the arms for me. As Mrs Payne has suggested, it would seem possible to make a tentative reconstruction: Quarterly, I., Party per pale argent & gules (Waldegrave): II. & III., Barry of 10, argent & azure (Montchesny); IV., ? a maunch gules. Sir Richard Waldegrave (d. 1434) of Bures St Mary, Suffolk, did indeed marry Jane, daughter and heir to Sir Thomas Montchesny (d. 1450), and they had a son Sir William Waldegrave, who in turn had two sons of his own.

18 I have not been able to find any other references to John Herbert in the Royal Household and his name does not appear among the Officers of the Pantry in 1509. Nor does he appear in other published documents for the period. The manuscript was owned by more than one member of the Herbert family since Walter Herbert is given as owner on f. 107v and the name G[ualterus?] Herbert is found on f. 108r. It is possible that the reference here is to Sir Walter Herbert, who married Anne Stafford (cousin of Henry VII's Queen Elizabeth) in 1499. I thank Dr David Starkey for this reference and for many helpful suggestions concerning the owners of Vespasian B. XII and possible means by which it may have found its way into the royal library.

19 See J. C. Wedgwood & A. D. Holt, *History of Parliament. Biographies of the Members of the Commons House 1439–1509* (London, 1936), pp. 740–1. I owe this reference to Dr Ramsay.

20 There may well be a link with Bramford in Suffolk.

21 See *Index Britanniae Scriptorum. John Bale's Index of British and Other Writers*, ed. R. L. Poole and Mary Bateson, with an Introduction by Caroline Brett and James P. Carley (Cambridge, 1990), pp. 177, 516.

22 For a description see Carl Horstman (ed.), *Nova Legenda Anglie*, 2 vols. (Oxford, 1901), vol. i, pp.

xi–xvi. Horstman edited from a printed version – Wynkyn de Worde's *Nova Legenda Angliae* (1516) – which was taken from John Capgrave's fifteenth-century re-arrangement of the *Sanctilogium Angliae* itself.

23 Interestingly, the Benedictine Augustine Baker (1575–1641) compiled information, dated 29 Mar. 1637, concerning Tiberius E. I, which is found in Jesus College, Oxford, MS. 77, ff. 63r–64v. He wrote (f. 63v): 'In praedicto autem manuscripto (sed recentiori manu) refertur quendam Iohannem Anglicum monachum sancti Albani (de quo est legere in Pitsaeo) fuisse Authorem primitivum istius operis scilicet legendae sanctorum maioris Britanniae et Hiberniae.' It is possible that the note seen by Baker was what provided the information for the entry in the 1542 inventory; alternatively, he could be quoting from a note made by the 1542 cataloguer himself.

24 See James P. Carley, 'John Leland and the Contents of the English Pre-Dissolution Libraries: Lincolnshire', *Transactions of the Cambridge Bibliographical Society*, ix, pt. 4 (1989), pp. 330–57, at 355.

25 See Charlotte D'Evelyn (ed.), *The Latin Text of the Ancrene Riwle*, E.E.T.S., o.s., no. 216 (London, 1944). D'Evelyn gives a description of this manuscript, the earliest and most complete of the four surviving copies of the Latin text of the *Ancrene Riwle*, on pp. xiii–xiv. Cotton also owned three copies of the English version of the *Ancrene Riwle* and one of the French.

26 The last text in the manuscript was (and is) a copy of the pseudo-Robert Grosseteste, *De Oculo Morali*, and this would presumably account for the attribution of the *Ancrene Riwle* to Grosseteste. The *De Oculo Morali* begins on f. 53v of the surviving manuscript: it is not listed by Thomas Smith in his catalogue of 1696, but it does appear in the report drawn up after the fire; see Thomas Smith, *Catalogue of the Manuscripts in the Cottonian Library 1696*, intro. C. G. C. Tite (Cambridge, 1984), p. 97 and Appendix B.

27 The section containing the *De Institutione Inclusarum*, it seems, has disappeared completely. The *Ancrene Riwle* is found on ff. 14–48, although the order is somewhat jumbled: 41, 14, 25, 32, 33 + 34, 31, 38, 39, 40, 27, 28, 29, 30, 24, 35, 36, 37, 17, 18, 19, 20, 21, 22, 15, 16, 23, 42, 43, 44, 45, 46, 47, 48. Bruce Burnam, Centre for

Medieval Studies, University of Toronto, has kindly informed me that the *Ancrene Riwle* is succeeded by the Dublin Rule, edited without reference to this manuscript by P. L. Oliger, 'Regulae tres reclusorum et eremitarum Angliae sac. XIII–XIV', *Antonianum*, iii (1928), pp. 151–90, 299–320, at 170–90: see also Hope Emily Allen, 'Further Borrowings from "Ancren Riwle"', *Modern Language Review*, xxiv (1929), pp. 1–15, at 1–2. I have not been able to locate the source for the fragments which survive as ff. 13, 26. These appear to be in the same hand as the text of the *Ancrene Riwle* and if it happens that they formed part of the *Ordo Includendi famulam Dei* following Aelred's *De Institutione Inclusarum* then my hypothesis concerning Cotton's role in the formation of this portion of the manuscript must be abandoned.

28 See Smith, *Catalogue of the Manuscripts in the Cottonian Library*, p. 97. Smith gives Simon of Ghent as author and D'Evelyn (*The Latin Text*, p. xiv) assumes that the manuscript originally contained an ascription to him. As Dr Tite has observed (private communication), Smith's description is based on the entry in an unpublished catalogue compiled in the 1630s (BL, Add. MS. 36682, f. 72r): 'Liber Simonis de Gandauo Episcopi Sarum De uita solitaria sororibus suis anachoritis apud Tarente talis n. inscriptio eius habetur in exemplari bibliothecae Magdal. Oxon.'

29 *Index Britanniae Scriptorum*, p. 516.

30 Printed PL 127.

31 Smith, *Catalogue of the Manuscripts in the Cottonian Library*, Appendix B.

32 Ibid., p. 68; see also Ker, *Medieval Libraries*, p. 161.

33 Corpus Christi College, Oxford, LD. 7 c. 13. I thank David Cooper, the librarian at Corpus Christi College, for providing generous access to the book at short notice and for allowing me to xerox pertinent materials.

34 See Mary P. Richards, *Texts and Their Traditions in the Medieval Library of Rochester Cathedral Priory* (Philadelphia, 1988), p. 36. Richard James, presumably quoting from the manuscript itself, gave a title which matches precisely the *Textus Roffensis* entry: 'Acta Beatorum pontificum vrbis Romae'. Bale's version is slightly abbreviated.

35 On possible reasons for this, see Carley, 'John

Leland and the Foundations of the Royal Library', p. 19.

36 For a more detailed discussion, see James P. Carley, 'William Rishanger's Chronicles and History Writing at St. Albans', in Jacqueline Brown and William P. Stoneman (eds.), '*A Distinct Voice*'. *Medieval Studies in Honor of Leonard E. Boyle, O.P.* (Notre Dame, Indiana, 1997), pp. 71–102.

37 See *Index Britanniae Scriptorum*, pp. 145–6; also p. 515: (1) 'Chronicon seu narrationem de bellis apud Lewes et Euesham'; (2) 'Opus chronicorum ad Ioannem abbatem, ab A.D. 1259 ad suam etatem'; (3) 'De controuersia habita super electione regni Scotie'; (4) 'Super constituto rege Ioanne Balliolo'; (5) 'De iure quod habet rex ad Scotiam'; (6) 'Annales regis Edwardi primi'.

38 See Antonia Gransden, *Historical Writing in England ii: c. 1307 to the Early Sixteenth Century* (London, 1982), pp. 4–5.

39 Madden seemed to have been aware of this fact and observed: 'It [the *Abbreviatio Chronicorum*] is preserved in the Cottonian collection, under the press-mark Claudius D. VI., and has been bound up with other historical works, composed by monks of the abbey of St. Alban in the 14th century.' See F. Madden (ed.), *Matthaei Parisiensis...Historia Anglorum...*, 3 vols., RS. xliv (London, 1866–9), vol. iii, p. 155. Generally speaking, however, scholars treat Claudius D. VI as a single integrated St Albans manuscript, beguiled perhaps by the congruity of layout between the component parts. See, for example, the comments of E. L. G. Stones and G. G. Simpson (*Edward I and the Throne of Scotland, 1290–1296: an Edition of the Record Sources for the Great Cause*, 2 vols. (Glasgow, 1978), vol. i, p. 63): 'Item 3 [the *Abbreviatio Chronicorum*], however, (which is written in the autograph of Matthew Paris), is arranged in two columns on each page, with margins in bands of different colours. This same arrangement persists as far as the end of item 12 [a chronicle fragment preceding the *Annales* attributed to John de Trokelowe], which suggests that the compilers, after the death of Matthew Paris, were filling up a manuscript which had been prepared in blank, with coloured margins, for his use. If so the original unity of the manuscript is not in doubt, at any rate as far as item 12.' For a salutary discussion of the dangers of mis-attribution on the basis of Cotton's made-up volumes, see C. E. Wright, 'The Elizabethan Society of Antiquaries and the Formation of the Cottonian Library', in Francis Wormald and C. E. Wright (eds.), *The English Library Before 1700* (London, 1958), pp. 176–212, at 204–5.

40 This is the only 'Rishanger' text in which he actually named himself as author: 'Frater Willelmus de Rissanger, cronicator, de multis pauca tangendo, ad dei honorem et anime regie recommendacionem redigit in scripturam' (f. 4v).

41 See n. 36, above.

42 In one of his letters, dated by its modern editor to early in 1613, Young also refers to this manuscript: 'John, deliver unto your master Sr. Robert, with my humble duties and hartiest commendations, two Bookes which I borrowed of him: Elmerus his Epistles, and Fulcherus Carnotensis his Historie, which is printed in Bongarsius booke, otherwise then Sr Robert did thinke. Desire his Worship to leane me Marianus his Chronicon, and his other Worke, for the tyme he is in the countrie, and deliver them unto this bearer I praye yow. Pa Young.' See J. Kemke, *Patricius Junius (Patrick Young) Bibliothekar der Könige Jacob I und Carl I von England* (Leipzig, 1898), p. 19.

43 The text ends on f. 137r, which is followed by a blank verso.

44 Although they have strong physical similarities which indicate the same scriptorium, Martinus's chronicle and Geoffrey's history were not necessarily joined together originally; the *Historia Regum Britanniae* begins a medieval foliation (ff. 1–58) completed by Bartholomew's chronicle (ff. 59–152), in which Martinus is not included. Nor does the subsequent portion (ff. 255–85) of Nero C. V, which is also very similar in hand and layout, have this foliation.

45 The *Abbreviatio Chronicorum* has the signature of Richard Hutton (which Madden misread as Hatton) on f. 9v.

46 That these did not simply fall out when the *Abbreviatio Chronicorum* was inserted is apparent, since the process involved the splitting of quires.

47 In 1860 Madden reinserted it in its rightful place on f. 101r of Claudius D. VI.

48 Harley 6018, f. 160v, where Cotton also noted that 'Mr Young or Mr Allington of the pip office had it.'

49 For a further discussion of these manuscripts, see Tite, '"Lost or Stolen or Strayed"', p. 112, and reprinted below, p. 267.

50 For a description, see Warner and Gilson, *Royal Manuscripts*, vol. ii, pp. 86–7.

51 See Carley, 'Lincolnshire', pp. 355–6.

52 For a description, see J. Planta, *Catalogue of the Manuscripts in the Cottonian Library Deposited in the British Museum* (London, 1802), p. 440; also A. Gransden, *Historical Writing in England [i:] c. 550 to c. 1307* (London, 1974), p. 406, n. 20. For another survivor see Ker, *Medieval Libraries of Great Britain*, p. 94.

53 With one exception, which presumably went to Greenwich or Hampton Court, all the starred items from Lincolnshire libraries travelled to Westminster: see Carley, 'Lincolnshire', pp. 354–7. That the Hagnaby list begins with a reference to the chronicle, rather than anything that came previously in the manuscript, does not pose a problem: the list mentions materials of possible interest to Henry and does not necessarily begin with the first text in a given manuscript.

54 See also the form of the pointing finger found in the margin of both manuscripts.

55 Andrew G. Watson makes the same point in his *Supplement to the Second Edition* of N. R. Ker, *Medieval Libraries of Great Britain* (London, 1987), p. 38.

56 *Index Britanniae Scriptorum*, p. 515. There is also a sixteenth-century label of the type found in the Westminster books, now pasted in at the beginning of Royal 13 A. XXI, which reads 'Imago mundi et cronica regum anglie. Galice.' This second reference here would pertain to Wace or Gaimar.

57 Using catalogue entries and medieval foliation Andrew G. Watson, *The Manuscripts of Henry Savile of Banke* (London, 1969), Appendix I, pp. 74–7, has provided a detailed analysis of the various texts, as well as their modern provenance, which made up the original Kirkham manuscript.

58 In order to extract the *De patribus* it was also necessary to remove a section at the end of the Gennadius text and one at the beginning of Isidore's *De uiris illustribus*; see Warner and Gilson, *Royal Manuscripts*, vol. ii, p. 87.

59 For a more complete discussion, see James P. Carley and Colin G. C. Tite, 'Sir Robert Cotton as Collector of Manuscripts and the Question of Dismemberment: British Library MSS. Royal 13 D. I and Cotton Otho D. VIII, ff. 174r–233v', *The Library*, 6th Series, xiv (1992), pp. 94–9.

60 For a full description see Julia C. Crick, *The Historia Regum Britannie of Geoffrey of Monmouth. III. A Summary Catalogue of the Manuscripts* (Cambridge, 1989), no. 111.

61 On the psalter see L. F. Sandler, *Gothic Manuscripts, 1285–1385*, 2 vols., A Survey of Manuscripts Illuminated in the British Isles 5 (Oxford, 1986), vol. ii, no. 131. On the various fragments see Carley and Tite, 'Sir Robert Cotton as Collector of Manuscripts', p. 96, no. 10. For a sample leaf, see below, Tite, '"Lost or Stolen or Strayed"', p. 291, fig. 6.

62 These include lists of Anglo-Saxon kings, the *Revelationes* attributed to St Methodius of Olympus, a *Narracio de Visione S. Thome Cantuariensis*, and the *Prophetia Hermerici*.

63 See also Tite, '"Lost or Stolen or Strayed"', pp. 110–11, and reprinted below, pp. 265–6.

64 See T. O. Cockayne (ed.), *Leechdoms, Wortcunning, and Starcraft of Early England*, 3 vols., RS. xxxv (London, 1864–6), vol. ii; also C. E. Wright (ed.), *Bald's Leechbook. British Museum Royal 12 D. xvii*, E.E.M.F. 5 (Copenhagen, 1955); Roland Torkar, 'Zu den ae. Medizinaltexten in Otho B. XI und Royal 12 D. XVII. Mit einer Edition der Unica (Ker, No. 180, art. 11a–d)', *Anglia*, xciv (1976), pp. 319–38; Audrey L. Meaney, 'Variant versions of Old English medical remedies and the compilation of Bald's *Leechbook*', *Anglo-Saxon England*, xiii (1984), pp. 235–68. Ker, *A Catalogue of Manuscripts Containing Anglo-Saxon* (Oxford, 1957), no. 264, misreads the inventory number as 139.

65 For full bibliographical references, see Jane Roberts, 'An Inventory of Early Guthlac Materials', *Mediaeval Studies*, xxxii (1970), pp. 193–233, at 202–3.

66 Presumably at this same time the third section (ff. 41–71) containing Sedulius's *Carmen Paschale* was added after the *Vita S. Guthlaci*. For the first seventeen folios see below, no. 9.

67 As Tite observes, it is possible to be even more specific. The form of Cotton's signature on both f. 1 (*Historia Brittonum*) and f. 18 (*Vita S. Guthlaci*) – in a version he used almost invariably after he was knighted in 1603, i.e. Robert Cotton Bruceus (or variants thereof) – combined with the fact that both sections have the signature and

must therefore earlier have been discrete booklets suggest that they were brought together between 1603–6. (For reservations concerning dating firmly on the basis of Cotton's signature alone, see Wright, 'The Elizabethan Society of Antiquaries', p. 200; Tite, 'Introduction' to Smith, *Catalogue of the Manuscripts in the Cottonian Library*, p. 2; also Tite, '"Lost or Stolen or Strayed"', p. 110, reprinted below as p. 265, and n. 18.)

68 See S. J. Crawford (ed.), *The Old English Version of the Heptateuch, Ælfric's Treatise on the Old and New Testament and his Preface to Genesis*, E.E.T.S., O.S. 160 (1922), reprinted with the text of two additional manuscripts transcribed by N. R. Ker (London, 1969). See also C. R. Dodwell and Peter Clemoes (eds.), *The Old English Illustrated Hexateuch* (Copenhagen, 1974), pp. 13, 42; also Andrea B. Smith, *The Anonymous Parts of the Old English Hexateuch: A Latin-Old English/Old English-Latin Glossary* (Cambridge, 1985). At least one leaf has been lost.

69 See Ker, *A Catalogue*, no. 344, who misreads it as 159. It should be pointed out, however, that cropping makes the '2' almost totally illegible.

70 On the close links between Christ Church, Canterbury and Rochester, and the frequent copying of Canterbury texts by Rochester scribes, see Richards, *Texts and Their Traditions*, pp. 3–8, 10, 77–8, 84, 121–3. In this case, however, the Christ Church Canterbury text (Vespasian B. XXV) descends from a Rochester exemplar, i.e. Vespasian D. XXI, and indeed may well have been written at Rochester.

71 See Richards, *Texts and Their Traditions*, p. 32. As she notes, however, the description could possibly pertain, although this is less likely, to Royal 15 B. XI + Cotton Vitellius A. XIII, on which see below.

72 Cotton seems to have erased entries from contents' lists after he removed texts; see Carley and Tite, 'Sir Robert Cotton as Collector of Manuscripts'.

73 Vespasian D. XXI has been heavily cropped but the written space and number of lines per page match roughly, as do some of the rubricated capitals (see, for example, Royal 15 A. XIII, f. 90v and Vespasian D. XXI, f. 1r). See also David N. Dumville, 'The *Liber Floridus* of Lambert of Saint-Omer and the *Historia Brittonum*', *Bulletin of the Board of Celtic Studies*, xxvi (1974–6), pp. 103–22, at p. 103 (reprinted in *Histories and Pseudo-histories of the Insular Middle Ages* [Aldershot, 1990]), who appears to take the original unity of these two manuscripts as certain.

74 In the *Catalogue of the Manuscripts in the Cottonian Library*, p. 115, Smith called it 'Exemplar uetustum & emendatum'.

75 See above, p. 220.

76 Cotton Appendix XLV, art. 13, f. 8. I thank Dr Tite for this and the above references.

77 Smith, *Catalogue of the Manuscripts in the Cottonian Library*, p. 83, listed the 'Fragmentum historiae Trojanae ex Darete Phrygio, aliisque'. He also referred to the *Historia Brittonum* as 'Nennius. Exemplar antiquum & nitidum'. Richard James's list of contents in the manuscript itself describes the *Historia Brittonum* as 'Nennii antiquum exemplar'. Interestingly, Cotton has entered directions to the binder on a flyleaf of Vitellius A. XIII: 'Bind this very fair and strong / cut it smoth on all sides…and Fillett it Fair with Flowers / and press it well and smoth.' (See Wright, 'The Elizabethan Society of Antiquaries', p. 206.)

78 Smith, *Catalogue of the Manuscripts in the Cottonian Library*, 'A History and Synopsis of the Cotton Library', pp. 47–57.

79 *Sir Robert Cotton 1586–1631: History and Politics in Early Modern England* (Oxford, 1979), p. 54.

80 This group constitutes an important indicator, it seems to me, because it represents texts which Cotton made a determined effort to acquire, not just items which fell his way. According to Sharpe it seems unlikely that Cotton ever actually purchased books; see *Sir Robert Cotton*, pp. 61–2. For a slight qualification, however, see Tite, 'Introduction', p. 4.

81 Smith refers specifically, and somewhat apologetically, to Tiberius E. I: 'It is a work of no small value because of the relics of genuine antiquity found among a mass of rubbishy fables.' In general, Smith – profoundly anti-Catholic – appears to have been rather uncomfortable with Cotton's interest in the 'lives and passions of saints and martyrs': '…these monks corrupted the truth with a mixture of stories of a different sort, feeding the credulity of the superstitious in a vicious and ignorant age with inventions tacked on by dull minds and designed less to teach than to mislead.' *Catalogue of the*

Manuscripts in the Cottonian Library, 'A History and Synopsis', p. 54.

82 Ibid., 'A History and Synopsis', p. 46.

83 Ibid., 'A History and Synopsis', p. 55.

84 See R. I. Page, *Matthew Parker, Archbishop of Canterbury and his Books* (Kalamazoo, 1993).

85 Even among modern scholars there has been a tendency to apply modern standards and to blame Cotton and his contemporaries for their dismemberment of composite manuscripts. In his hostile review (*Medium Aevum*, xxix (1960), pp. 144–7, at 146) of C. E. Wright's commendation of Cotton as a preserver of manuscripts (in *The English Library Before 1700*), N. R. Ker quoted with approbation Gilson's comments from his introduction to the catalogue of Savile of Banke: 'Sir Robert had absolutely no conscience in the matter of destroying a book's identity, cutting MSS. in pieces and rebinding them with others...'

86 See Sharpe's comments (*Sir Robert Cotton*, pp. 68–9) on this topic: 'It was not at all unusual to divide manuscripts... Cotton viewed his library as a working collection and adopted an arrangement that was utilitarian rather than bibliographically correct by modern standards. He headed manuscripts with new titles, marked them with marginal notes, and bound them with other papers on the same subject. He evidently rebound the bulk of them... Things were bound together that were consulted together. Often it is hard to see any logic in the compilations.'

87 'The "Booklet": A Self-Contained Unit in Composite Manuscripts', *Codicologica*, iii (1980), pp. 46–69. See also Julia Boffey and John J. Thompson, 'Anthologies and Miscellanies: Production and Choice of Texts', in Jeremy Griffiths and Derek Pearsall (eds.), *Book Production and Publishing in Britain 1375–1475* (Cambridge, 1989), pp. 279–315.

88 'The "Booklet"', p. 47.

89 This is a point which Robinson ('The "Booklet"', p. 56) also makes: 'when studying a composite manuscript it is necessary to establish that it represents a medieval collection and not the whim of a post-medieval collector.'

SIR ROBERT COTTON'S RECORD OF A ROYAL
BOOKSHELF

JANET BACKHOUSE

OUR knowledge of the early history of the English royal library, conveniently sketched out by Warner and Gilson in 1921,[1] has been considerably amplified in recent years.[2] An edition of the vital Westminster library catalogue of 1542 is now in preparation and will be of major advantage to future students.[3] However, the Tudor rulers of England, like other noble owners of large quantities of books, did not confine the storage of reading matter to a single one of their many residences, nor to one specially designated apartment in any house. It is increasingly clear that the Westminster list by no means reflects even the entire royal collection of books in the one major palace at the time it was drawn up. The existence of substantial libraries in other royal residences is recorded in the inventories of Henry VIII's possessions taken soon after the accession of Edward VI and individual volumes appear variously among the diverse contents of private apartments, alongside hawks' hoods, dog collars, spectacles, scissors, knitting needles and other minor paraphernalia of everyday life.[4] References to the contents of the royal library during the latter part of the sixteenth century are scanty, though all three of Henry VIII's children are known to have been interested in books and each quite frequently received them as gifts on appropriate occasions. Such books seem often to have been set aside for personal use. The New Year gift rolls of Elizabeth's reign show that, although some volumes were at once assigned to Thomas Knyvett, who apparently had charge of the library, the Queen herself not infrequently took possession of books that caught her personal fancy.[5] Others were placed in the hands of her principal gentlewoman of the Privy Chamber, Blanche Parry,[6] or her successor Mary Radcliffe, who also took charge of gifts of clothing and personal jewellery.

A brief and hitherto unnoticed list of manuscripts in one of the private apartments at Whitehall, probably written during the early years of the reign of James I, seems to record a small cache of volumes placed there in the time of Elizabeth and is of particular interest because it mentions identifiable items not previously associated with royal ownership. This list appears on the recto of a vellum flyleaf at the end of Cotton MS. Vespasian B. IV and is clearly in the hand of Sir Robert Cotton himself (fig. 1). The leaf, now numbered f. 25, was originally a pastedown. Traces of the fabric covering of the boards appear round three sides, matching similar traces on the corresponding leaf at the

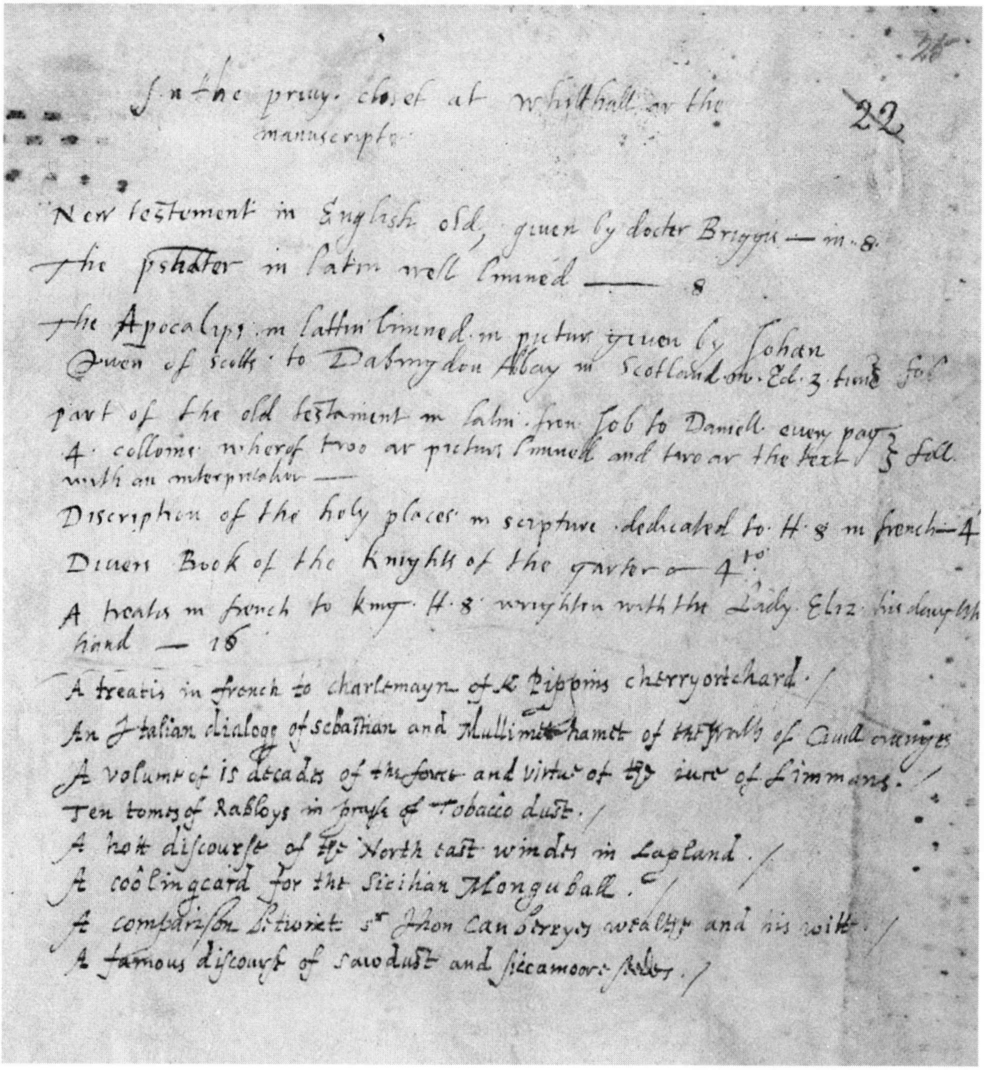

Fig. 1. The two book lists. Cotton MS. Vespasian B. IV, f. 25

front of the volume. The manuscript itself was once a royal book, containing two Latin poems addressed to Henry VII in 1497.[7] The list reads as follows:

In the priuy closet at Whitthall ar the manuscripts
New testement in English old, giuen by docter Briggis — in 8
The psalter in latin well limned — 8
The Apocalips in lattin limned in picturs giuen by Johan Quen of Scotts to Dabingdon Abbay
  in Scotland on Ed. 3 time — fol

231

Part of the old testament in latin from Job to Daniell euery pag 4 colloms wherof two ar picturs limned and two ar the text — foll

Discription of the holy places in scipture dedicated to H. 8 in french — 4^t

Divers Book of the knights of the garter — 4to

A treatis in french to king H. 8 wrighten with the Lady Eliz. his daughter hand — 16

This is immediately followed by a second list, in a different and more florid hand but apparently in the same ink, parodying a library list thus:

A treatis in french to Charlemayn of K Pippins cherry orchard

An Italian dialogg of Sebastian and Mullimethamet [sic] of the Worth of Civill oranges

A volume of 15 decades of the force and virtue of the iuce of Limmans

Ten tomes of Rabloys in prayse of Tobacco dust

A hott discourse of the North east windes in Lapland

A coolingcard for the Sicilian Monguball

A comparison betwixt Sr Jhon Canberryes wealthe and his witt

A famous discourse of sawdust and siccamoore seedes

The hand of this second list has so far resisted identification.

One of the descriptions on Cotton's list, that of the illuminated psalter, is too vague to allow of reasonable identification.[8] Two of the other items can, however, be equated immediately with manuscripts in the Royal collection in the British Library. The English New Testament given by 'docter Briggis' is Royal MS. 1 A. XII, an early fifteenth century copy of the revised Wycliffite text presented to Elizabeth by her chaplain John Bridges, Dean of Salisbury, as a New Year offering in an unspecified year. The volume retains its presentation binding of faded blue velvet, with impressions of the original bosses and clasps in the form of roses and fleurs de lys. The fifth item, the 'discription of the holy places in scripture', is almost certainly Royal MS. 20 A. IV, Marcel Brion's 'Tresample description de toute la Terre Saincte', a French treatise offered to Henry VIII about 1540. In 1547 this book, described as 'the description of the holy lande and [sic] a boke couered w^t vellat enbrawdred with the kings armes declaring the same, in a case of blacke leather with his graces Armes', was in 'the litle Study called the newe Librarye' in the Palace of Westminster.[9] The lavish and distinctive embroidered binding survives to this day[10] but the wording of the 1547 inventory entry perhaps suggests that the manuscript was originally supplemented by a map.

Books of the knights of the Garter (item 6) and similar heraldic records were standard New Year gifts to the monarch from Garter King of Arms. A series of nine such manuscripts, all still bound in crimson velvet and trimmed with gold, appeared on the London market in 1986.[11] They had been prepared for Elizabeth by Sir Gilbert Dethick between 1569 and 1580. In 1577 and 1597 annotations on surviving gift rolls record that Garter's offerings were handed into the care of Blanche Parry and Mary Radcliffe respectively.[12]

The Lady Elizabeth's treatise in French, addressed to her father, King Henry VIII (item 7), may have been the little manuscript shown to Paul Hentzner in 1598 as one of

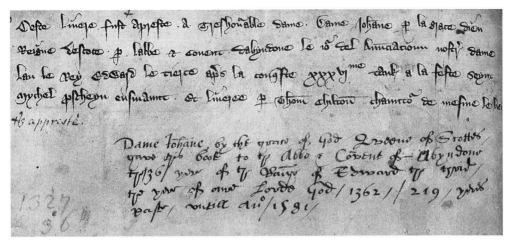

Fig. 2. Fourteenth-century inscription in the Abingdon Apocalypse, recording the loan of the book to Queen Joan of Scotland. Below is the mistranslation added by Stephen Batman. Add. MS. 42555, f. 4v (detail)

the special treasures of the palace.[13] Elizabeth's youthful translations are well documented and two have survived. The earlier, her English version of Marguerite of Angoulême's 'Mirror of the Sinful Soul', addressed to Queen Catherine Parr as a New Year gift in 1545, is now Cherry MS. 36 in the Bodleian Library.[14] The second, and more ambitious, Queen Catherine Parr's own 'Prayers and Meditations', translated by the Princess into Latin, French and Italian and offered to her father at New Year 1546, remains among the Royal Manuscripts as MS. 7 D. X. It is, however, unlikely to be the book mentioned by Cotton, as its dedication is in Latin and the dedication quoted by Hentzner is actually in French.[15]

The two remaining items, both described in some detail by Cotton, seem to be identifiable with two major thirteenth century illuminated manuscripts, neither of which has ever before been associated with the English royal library. The first (item 3) is, beyond all doubt, the Abingdon Apocalypse, now Additional MS. 42555 in the British Library. The second (item 4) seems to be a volume of the *Bible moralisée*.

As recorded by Cotton, the Abingdon Apocalypse does contain, at f. 4v, an English inscription describing the gift of the manuscript *to* Abingdon *from* Queen Joan of Scotland. This is, in fact, a mistranslation of the original Latin which precedes it, which records the loan of the manuscript *to* Joan *by* the abbot and community (fig. 2). The loan was to run from Lady Day (25 March) to Michaelmas (29 September) 1362 and the interests of the abbey were safeguarded not only by this formal entry but also by a further note, on f. 83, recording the number of folios 'escriptes & enlumines' contained in the volume. The implied misgivings of the lenders may have been justified. Queen Joan, younger sister of Edward III, died in the late summer of 1362 and there is no way of

233

telling whether the monks of Abingdon ever retrieved their property. A fifteenth-century inscription of f. 1v, reading 'precii xiijs', may indicate that they did not.

The mistranslation noticed by Cotton is in the hand of Stephen Batman (d. 1584) and is dated 1581. Batman had been domestic chaplain to Archbishop Parker (d. 1575), who employed him to collect manuscripts for the library which subsequently passed to Corpus Christi College, Cambridge. Batman was, however, a bibliophile and antiquarian in his own right and a number of manuscripts contain inscriptions in his hand.[16] Alongside the note on f. 83 of the Abingdon Apocalypse he has written 'a me batman', but whether this implies that he owned the manuscript or merely that he had checked the accuracy of the fourteenth-century librarian's collation is unclear. For the last two years of his life Batman was domestic chaplain to Henry Carey, Lord Hunsdon, Elizabeth's first cousin on her mother's side and even possibly her half-brother. He was Lord Chamberlain of her household in 1583. It is possible therefore that it was through Hunsdon that the Apocalypse passed into royal hands, a very suitable gift in view of its fourteenth-century associations. How it passed out again, after Cotton had seen it, we do not know, as there is no further evidence of ownership before the late eighteenth century. In view of its newly-recognized royal connections, it is, however, interesting to remark the remaining traces of a crimson velvet binding.

The last of the seven items seems to be a single Old Testament volume of the *Bible moralisée*, which is typically laid out with two columns of miniatures and two of accompanying text on every page. No extant manuscript corresponds exactly with what Cotton has written, but the volume now in the Bibliothèque Nationale in Paris is close enough to be a possible candidate.[17] The Paris manuscript, MS. lat. 11560, is the second portion of a complete four-volume Bible. It begins, as described by Cotton, with the final passages of the Book of Job but it ends with Zacharias and the last portion of Daniel occurs on f. 213b of the 222 folio volume. However, the other three volumes of the set are all in England and there is every reason to suppose that they were here at the end of the sixteenth century. The first, containing the initial books of the Old Testament, is now MS. Bodley 270b in Oxford. It was given to Bodley in 1604 by Sir Christopher Heydon, writer on astrology, having already been in England for more than a century, for a fifteenth-century note recording the collation (f. 224v) is written in English.[18] The two remaining volumes, containing Maccabees and the New Testament, are Harley MSS. 1526 and 1527 in the British Library. They were acquired for Lord Oxford from the library of the antiquary John Kemp (d. 1717), which was sold up in 1721. Kemp had purchased them in 1711 from the bookseller William Innys at a cost of £40.[19] The signature of an unidentified fifteenth-century Englishman named John Thwayte occurs on the flyleaf of Harley MS. 1527, indicating that it too had spent a long period in England. The Paris manuscript has no recorded history before its appearance in the collection of Pierre Séguier (d. 1672), who was Chancellor of France from 1653. It is quite possible that the entire *Bible moralisée* was in England during the sixteenth century and that the one volume left the country during the troubles of the seventeenth century. It is worth recalling that a Psalter of St Louis, identifiable as the Ingeborg Psalter now in the Musée Condé at Chantilly, is said to have been in the English royal collection, having been presented to Mary I by Philip of Spain at the time of their marriage, and to have made its way out of the country in or about 1649 through Pierre de Bellièvre, French ambassador to London in that year.[20] It is of course very tempting to equate the Ingeborg Psalter with the 'psalter in latin well limned' of Cotton's list, but unfortunately its size does not support the identification.[21]

Cotton described the books on his list as being 'in the priuy closet at Whithall', but it is not clear from existing descriptions of the royal apartments exactly which room he had in mind. The royal apartments were on the first floor and included a number of small rooms as well as the larger and more formal ones. The most detailed source of information is the inventory of King Henry VIII's goods and chattels, taken in 1547 and now Harley MS. 1419 A in the British Library. It enumerates small, often personal and everyday items in 'the Study at the hether ende of the Longe Gallerie' (ff. 113–114), 'the kynges secrete studie called the Chaier house for the furnyture of the same' (ff. 115–118v), 'the study nexte the kyngs olde Bedde chambre' (ff. 151–158v) and 'the litel Study called the newe Librarye' (ff. 186–188v).[22] The third of these apartments housed (f. 157) 'A booke of paternes for phiosionamyes', against which is recorded 'taken by the kings maiestie hymselfe 12° Novembre 1549'. This has been reasonably identified with the Holbein drawings of personalities at the court of Henry VIII, now at Windsor.[23] In the 'newe Librarye' were cupboards and drawers containing a variety of documents including (f. 187) 'upon two Shelues paternes for Castles and engynnes of warre'[24] and the description of the Holy Land mentioned above. A small room described as 'the kinges rich cabonett' was fitted out with new cupboards, shelves and drawing tables for Charles I in 1630–1.[25] This has been tentatively equated with 'her ma[tes] Cabanett' redecorated for Elizabeth by George Gower in 1588–9[26] and it is at least possible that one particular small room in the palace was the customary repository for books and documents used privately by the sovereign. Four of the seven manuscripts on Cotton's list were certainly gifts to Elizabeth or her father, Henry VIII. It seems extremely likely that all seven fall into the category of individual offerings taken in charge either personally by the sovereign or by someone in close attendance, rather than being assigned to the keeper of the royal library proper. Certainly, neither of the two items still among the Royal Manuscripts in the British Library can be recognized in any of the early royal library catalogues.

During the early years of James I's reign Cotton enjoyed the royal favour and was a frequent visitor in the palace of Whitehall. It was probably at this time that he saw and listed the cache of manuscripts in the privy closet.[27] His interest was doubtless not untinged with covetousness. The Cotton collection boasts a significant number of manuscripts originally owned by members of the royal family and this varied little group would have been very much to his taste.

1 G. F. Warner and J. P. Gilson, *Catalogue of Western Manuscripts in the Old Royal and King's Collections* (1921), introduction.

2 See T. A. Birrell, *English Monarchs and their Books: from Henry VII to Charles II*, The Panizzi Lectures, 1986 (London, 1987); J. Backhouse 'Founders of the Royal Library: Edward IV and Henry VII as Collectors of Illuminated Manuscripts', *England in the Fifteenth Century*, Proceedings of the 1986 Harlaxton Symposium (1987), pp. 23–41.

3 In the present context Westminster and Whitehall are synonymous. The relationship of the two adjoining palaces is studied in H. M. Colvin (ed.), *The History of the King's Works*, iv, pt. ii (1982), pp. 286–343. The 1542 catalogue is currently being edited by James P. Carley.

4 The relevant inventories occur in Harley MSS. 1419 A and B.

5 For a list of surviving New Year Gift Rolls, see A. J. Collins, *Jewels and Plate of Queen Elizabeth I: the Inventory of 1574* (1955), pp. 247–53.

6 See C. A. Bradford, *Blanche Parry, Queen Elizabeth's Gentlewoman* (1935).

7 How Cotton himself came by this manuscript is unclear. It is tempting to suppose that it was originally one of the books which he found in the 'priuy closet' and that he abstracted it as a suitable place in which to note down his list. However, the opening page of the text, now f. 3, is inscribed 'phillips . 1600 . sept' in a contemporary hand. Some further writing at the head of this leaf has been obliterated. I am very grateful to Colin Tite for his notes on the manuscript. It is apparently not actually recorded among Cotton's books until about 1631, though this is not a clear indication that he did not own it earlier. However, 'phillips' has not yet been identified.

8 Cotton describes the psalter as octavo, the same size as Dr Bridges's Bible. The latter measures approximately 210 × 145 mm. Of the obvious candidates still in the Royal collection, the nearest in size is Henry VIII's personal psalter (MS. 2 A. XVI), which measures 205 × 140 mm. Queen Mary's Psalter (MS. 2 B. VII), certainly 'well limned', is 275 × 175 mm. The lavish 13th cent. psalter (MS. 1 D. X) is a substantial 350 × 240 mm., larger than the Apocalypse, 330 × 205 mm., which Cotton classes as folio.

9 Harley MS. 1419 A, f. 187.

10 Reproduced in A. Payne and R. Marks, *British Heraldry from its Origins to c. 1800* (1978), p. 113.

11 Sotheby's sale catalogue, 18 Dec. 1986, lot 203.

12 The 1577 roll is in the Public Record Office, Chanc. Misc. 3/39. The 1596/7 roll, untraced by Collins, op. cit., was sold at Sotheby's, 14 Mar. 1967, lot 201. Photographs are available in the British Library as MS. Facs. 672.

13 P. Hentzner, *Itinerarium Germaniae, Galliae, Angliae, Italiae* (Nuremberg, 1612), p. 127. He describes the 'Bibliotheca Reginae' as being well supplied with books in Greek, Latin, Italian and French, all bound in velvet, chiefly red, with clasps of gold and silver and sometimes with pearls and precious stones set in the bindings.

14 Fully reproduced in P. W. Ames (ed.), *The Mirror of the Sinful Soul* (1897).

15 Loc. cit. Although Hentzner's original text is in Latin, he gives Elizabeth's dedication in French.

16 The Bodleian Library furnishes a number of examples, viz.: MS. Bodley 155, 'Stephan Batman the true onor of thys booke, which coste xx'; MS. Bodley 480, 'S. and B. belonges to me; ijs'; MS. Bodley 801, 'Stephanus Battemanus huius librj possesor'; MS. Auct. F. 5. 29, 'Stephanus Batman to his phrend Camden (?)'. Batman was in addition responsible for MS. Douce 363, an illustrated copy of Cavendish's Life of Wolsey, in a volume that also contains material by Dr John Dee. His career and writings are outlined in the *D. N. B.* and references are given by M. B. Parkes in G. Chaucer, *Troilus and Criseyde, a Facsimile of Corpus Christi College MS. 61*, ed. M. B. Parkes and E. Salter (1978), p. 12.

17 I am very grateful to my colleague François Avril, who kindly answered my questions about the Paris volume. All four volumes of this famous manuscript were reproduced between 1911 and 1927 by the Société française de reproductions des manuscrits à peintures, with an introduction by A. de Laborde. However, each page of the *Bible moralisée* is painted on one side only and the intervening blank openings were not (understandably) included in the facsimile. The pages were, in addition, much cut down. Much of the bibliographical evidence, in the form of quire marks and inscriptions, is therefore omitted from the edition.

18 The collation note is dated to the 15th cent. in the Bodleian catalogues. It is actually very

crudely written and hard to date, but must be much earlier than Heydon's donation in 1604.

19 C. E. Wright, *Fontes Harleiani* (1972), pp. 203, 209, 329 and 398. Wright suggests that the two Harley volumes were also owned by Heydon, but this appears to be based merely on the known history of the volume in Oxford.

20 Warner and Gilson, op. cit., vol. i, pp. xxii–iii.

21 The Ingeborg Psalter, MS. 1695 at Chantilly, measures 304 × 204 mm.

22 The personal use of favourite books by the monarch is perhaps accurately reflected in the miniature of Henry VIII seated reading in his bedchamber, Royal MS. 2 A. XVI, f. 3.

23 See the exhibition catalogue *Holbein and the Court of Henry VIII*, Queen's Gallery 1978–9, pp. 11–13.

24 Drawings and designs of this type are among the items grouped in MSS. Augustus in the Cotton collection.

25 *The King's Works*, iv, pt. ii, pp. 341–2.

26 Ibid., p. 318.

27 It is perhaps worth noting the botanical emphasis of the titles in the facetious list that follows Cotton's notes. Birrell, op. cit., p. 26 has drawn attention to James I's personal interest in books on fruit and, indeed, on tobacco, and it is just possible that this offers a supplementary indication of the date at which the two book lists were written into Cotton MS. Vespasian B. IV.

CAMDEN, COTTON AND THE CHRONICLES OF THE NORMAN CONQUEST OF ENGLAND

ELISABETH M. C. van HOUTS

The collaboration between William Camden (1551–1623), the Clarenceux King of Arms, and his pupil Sir Robert Cotton (1571–1631) in antiquarian studies is well known.[1] Whereas Camden developed the principles on which the study of history should be based, Cotton provided the raw material by gathering together what, judged by quality rather than quantity, was the most important collection of medieval manuscripts owned by a single person. The range of his collection of medieval chronicles was unrivalled in Western Europe and his generosity towards scholars enabled them to borrow his manuscripts in order to print their texts and make them available to a larger public. In some cases these early editions are now our only witnesses for texts of which no manuscripts any longer survive.[2] In this article I shall discuss the contributions made by Camden and Cotton to the process of editing and publishing the chronicles of the Norman Conquest of England in 1066.

By 1586, when William Camden, Robert Cotton and others founded the Elizabethan Society of Antiquaries, only medieval chronicles relating to the Anglo-Saxon past of England had been published, such as Gildas's *De Excidio* (1525), Bede's *Historia Ecclesiastica* (1565), Asser's *Life of Alfred* (1574) and Geoffrey of Monmouth's *Historia Regum Britanniae* (1508, 1517), or general works on English history, like the *Brut* and *Polychronicon* (1480), John Hardyng's *Chronicle* (1543), and the collection published by Matthew Parker in the years 1567 to 1574 comprising Matthew Paris's *Chronica Majora*, Thomas Walsingham's *Historia Anglorum* and *Ypodigma Neustriae* as well as Asser's biography of Alfred.[3] None of the works describing Anglo-Norman relations in the eleventh century, like Dudo of Saint-Quentin's *De moribus et actis primorum Normanniae Ducum* and the *Encomium Emmae Reginae*, or, indeed, the contemporary sources for '1066', William of Jumièges's *Gesta Normannorum Ducum* and the *Gesta Guillelmi ducis Normannorum et regis Anglorum* by William of Poitiers had been edited, nor the chronicles written at the beginning of the twelfth century by Henry of Huntingdon, William of Malmesbury, 'Florence' and John of Worcester and Orderic Vitalis. Yet, by the time Sir Robert Cotton died in 1631 all these histories had been published once, some even twice, in England and in France and the majority of them were edited on the basis of Cotton manuscripts.[4] However, important texts like the *Anglo-Saxon Chronicle*, or the history of the kings of the English by Simeon of Durham, also represented by

238

manuscripts in the Cotton collection, were not printed until several decades after Sir Robert's death. Consequently, study of these chronicles, until respectively 1643 and 1652, was only possible if one had access to the manuscripts themselves or to copies made of them.[5] But, before we assess the contributions made by William Camden and Robert Cotton, it is necessary to find out more about their interest in the history of the Norman Conquest of England.

That scholars were interested in the impact of the Norman Conquest of England on the English people is clear from the works of, for example, John Steed and Samuel Daniel.[6] Both historians took great care in their reconstruction of the past using a mixture of original sources and later narratives. They carefully distinguished between the comments of the medieval historians and their own. They were also aware of the problems of vocabulary, especially with regard to early offices and titles. Their analysis is nowhere more impressive than in their attempts, and indeed in those of others like John Seldon or Sir Henry Savile, to solve such eternal questions as to the origins of institutions or laws; were they Anglo-Saxon or Norman? Historical research, certainly in the days of the Society of Antiquaries, arose from a combination of factors: some utilitarian and some purely intellectual.[7] Justification of the independence of the English Church after King Henry VIII's divorce from Catherine of Aragon and its religious and political consequences for England's relations with Rome and the rest of Europe played as large a role as a purely 'scientific' approach to the medieval past. Apart from these problems of state there were many other reasons why inspection of original source material could help. Matters of right of title to property, or exercise of rights of local taxation, resulted in the study of manuscripts and documents in order to find precedents. Kevin Sharpe in his study of Sir Robert Cotton gives several examples of the utilitarian nature of historical research in Sir Robert Cotton's time.[8] Most recently, Roger Manning has shown that Cotton himself delved into the medieval documents of his own estates at Conington in order to support his case in law suits with his tenants.[9] Research into the Anglo-Norman period, therefore, had as much to do with contemporary society and politics as with a wish to reconstruct the events of '1066'. However, in his writings Sir Robert proved to be capable of sound and original historical argument with regard to some of the effects of the Norman Conquest of England. Three centuries before J. H. Round published his analysis of the introduction of knight-service into England, Cotton had set out the same conclusions in a paper published posthumously, using most of the arguments put forward by Round.[10] It is here unimportant whether or not we now agree with Cotton and Round. The important point is that Cotton, and indeed his mentor Camden, used medieval manuscripts and documents for original historical research. Both, however, realized that the only way forward in the study of history was to provide scholars with the original texts. Their greatest contribution to the field of Anglo-Norman studies was their involvement in the production of editions.

We cannot claim that any action on the part of the young Cotton influenced the appearance in print of the chronicles of 'Florence' of Worcester, edited by Lord William Howard in 1592, or of Henry of Huntingdon and William of Malmesbury, edited by Sir

Henry Savile in 1596.[11] It is, however, interesting that relatively few manuscripts of these three authors, as far as we know, were ever in the possession of Sir Robert Cotton. I have found no Cotton manuscript of either 'Florence' or his continuator John of Worcester, and only one manuscript of Henry of Huntingdon's *Historia Anglorum* (London, BL, Cotton Vespasian A. XVIII) and one of each of William of Malmesbury's *Gesta Regum* (Cotton Claudius C. IX) and *Gesta Pontificum* (Claudius A. V; fig. 1).[12] This is a surprisingly small number considering the fact that all three texts were written in England and that they have survived in many copies. Moreover, none of these Cotton manuscripts was, as far as we know, used for the Savile edition of 1596.[13] It is not until after the turn of the century that we can establish links between Cotton manuscripts and printed editions directly concerned with Conquest chronicles.

The first is William Camden's collection of texts published under the title *Anglica, Normannica, Hibernica, Cambrica, a veteribus scripta. Ex quibus … plerique nunc primum in lucem editi ex bibliotheca Guilielmi Camdeni …* at Frankfurt in 1602.[14] In his preface to Fulke Greville, Camden states that he included some of the works which had already been edited, like those of Asser and of Thomas of Walsingham, because the editions were rare in England.[15] From our point of view the most important text edited here is William of Jumièges's *Gesta Normannorum Ducum*, the first prose account of the Norman Conquest, written within four years of the event. This chronicle was revised and interpolated several times and the early printed editions all contain the text as revised by Robert of Torigni, monk of Bec, *circa* 1139.[16] Collation of the text of Camden's edition with the surviving manuscripts shows that Camden conflated two manuscripts, now Cotton Nero D. VIII and Cotton Vitellius A. VIII, ff. 5–100, of which the latter was the more important.[17] According to the subtitle of his edition, Camden used manuscripts from his own library. This statement would suggest, therefore, that in 1602 the two manuscripts belonged to Camden, and that they passed to Cotton in 1623 as part of Camden's bequest to him.[18] This conclusion is not so straightforward as it seems, for Cotton's catalogue of 1621, two years before Camden died, already lists Nero D. VIII (fig. 2), as well as other manuscripts used by Camden for his 1602 edition, which as I suggested above would have been his own.[19] Either Camden had already given manuscripts to Cotton before he died, or Cotton listed books borrowed from Camden as his own. Alternatively, the book collections of both men were so intermingled – and this is suggested by a specification in Camden's will according to which Cotton was advised to search for his own books lent to Camden in Camden's house first – that neither of them knew precisely which book belonged to whom. How Camden acquired his manuscripts in the first place is unknown.

Vitellius A. VIII, together with Cambridge, Gonville and Caius College 177/210, forms a manuscript from Reading Abbey written in the second half of the twelfth century.[20] It is closely related to Robert of Torigni's autograph manuscript of the *Gesta* from Bec (Leiden, UB BPL 20), because it is the only medieval copy which contains some of Robert's later alterations. The other contents of the Reading codex is also a copy

240

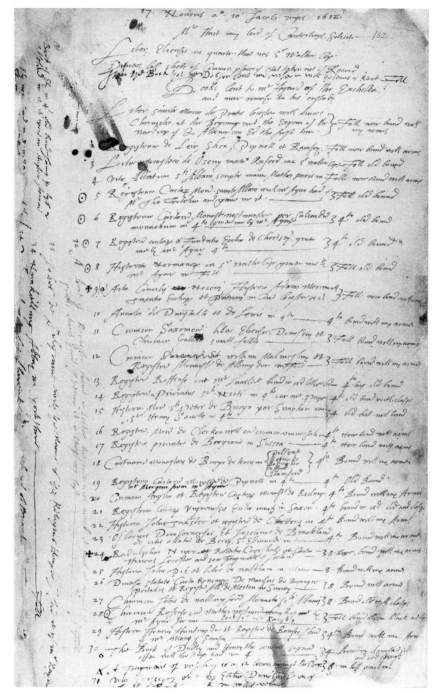

Fig. 1. A list of books lent by Cotton to Agarde, including (12) William of Malmesbury's *Gesta Regum* and (29) Henry of Huntingdon's *Historia*. Harl. MS. 6018, f. 162

241

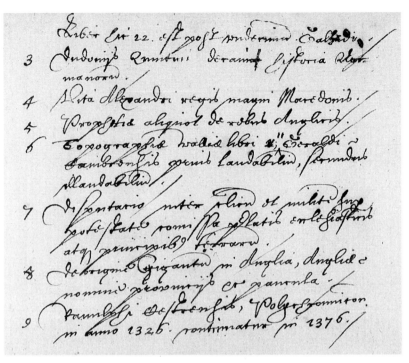

Fig. 2. Part of the entry in Cotton's 1621 catalogue for the MS. now known as Nero D. VIII. Harl. MS. 6018, f. 91 (detail)

of Robert's manuscript. The Reading manuscript was probably split up before 1600. In 1560 the Cambridge part was given by Ethelbert Burdet, who owned more Reading books, to William Harrison and as part of the library of one William Moore (1590–1659) it was bequeathed to Gonville and Caius College. The London part was used, as we have seen, by Camden in 1602 and a third part, Nennius's *Historia Brittonum* which once followed the *Gesta*, is still lost.

The manuscript of Nero D. VIII has a more obscure history.[21] The part which interests us here, ff. 3r–175v, is written in a single hand from the end of the twelfth or the beginning of the thirteenth century. It is the only surviving manuscript of the *Gesta Normannorum Ducum* where a full text of Dudo of Saint-Quentin's history of the dukes of Normandy is followed by a conflation of two different *Gesta* versions woven together by several short passages which do not occur anywhere else. The significance of the unique combination lies in the fact that around 1200 someone in England intelligently collated several different *Gesta* manuscripts. He, or she, displays a philological and critical interest in the text which is rare for its time as far as chronicles are concerned. This reason alone makes it frustrating that we do not know where the manuscript was written. William Camden's use of it in 1602 is the first glimpse we have of it.

William Camden also included in his 1602 edition a short text which he thought might have been the work of William of Poitiers, a contemporary of William of Jumièges and biographer of William the Conqueror: a *fragmentum ... de vita Gulielmi Conquestoris*. In fact, the text is not William of Poitiers's but a combination of two excerpts from the *Historia Ecclesiastica* of Orderic Vitalis, concerning the trial of Bishop Odo of Bayeux and the final bequests and death of William the Conqueror.[22] The manuscript is Cotton Vespasian A. XIX, ff. 104–121, which, like the two *Gesta Normannorum Ducum* manuscripts, first belonged to Camden and then to Cotton.[23] It is written in an early fifteenth-century hand and decorated with gold. The name of William the Conqueror is consistently written in gold. The rubric on f. 104r (fig. 3) states that it is a direct copy of a manuscript of Saint-Etienne at Caen, which Orderic's modern editor, Marjorie Chibnall, identified as being Vatican, Reg. Lat. 703 B.[24] At present the fragment is bound with material from Ely, but the connection is no doubt accidental for Camden says in his edition that the fragment had come from France as war booty at the time of King Henry V (1413–22). In fact the manuscript was not looted in France by the English, but presented by the monks of Caen to King Henry V, when after the Treaty of Troyes in 1420 Normandy once again came under English rule. The excerpts from Orderic together with other documents transcribed at the same time formed part of an appeal by the monks for the restitution of their English possessions. All the texts illustrate William the Conqueror's legacy to Saint-Etienne of Caen of his regalia which in the time of his son William Rufus were exchanged for several English manors. It was these manors which the monks claimed back in the early 1420s.[25] How the manuscript came to be bound up with Ely material is unclear, but the Caen provenance of the fragment is beyond any doubt. Camden's assumption that he had found part of William of Poitiers's biography of William the Conqueror is, however, an important indication of the state of knowledge about this author in 1602. The misidentification proves that though he knew of William of Poitiers, he had not seen the text itself. It also strongly suggests that Sir Robert Cotton had not yet acquired his own copy.

By the beginning of 1618 a copy, probably an eleventh or early twelfth-century manuscript (see below), was in the possession of Cotton.[26] We know this because the manuscript is mentioned in a series of letters exchanged between William Camden, on behalf of Sir Robert Cotton, and their colleague Nicholas de Peiresc (1580–1637), the French antiquary, who with André Duchesne (1584–1640) was preparing a new collection of texts by Anglo-Norman writers. This edition was published in the summer of 1619 under the title *Historiae Normannorum Scriptores antiqui ... ex mss codd. omnia fere nunc primum edidit*. In February 1618 De Peiresc wrote to Camden saying that the edition had gone to press and, in a now lost letter, he must have asked for a copy of William of Poitiers for in March he wrote again to acknowledge its arrival.[27] Unfortunately the copy contained many mistakes and he asked Camden to mediate between him and Sir Robert Cotton to let him have the original. This was duly sent to him on 2 April and described by De Peiresc a few weeks later as follows:

l'autographe du fragment de Guillelmus Pictavinus bien conditionné ... J'ay pris fort grand plaisir

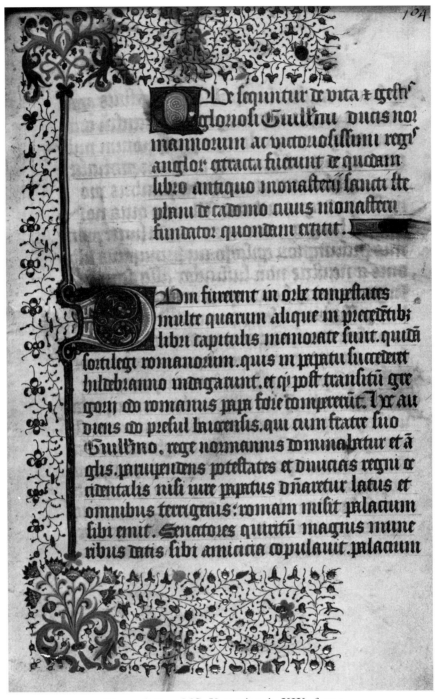

Fig. 3. Cotton MS. Vespasian A. XIX, f. 104

de le voir et crois veritablement qu'il soit escrit du tems meme de l'autheur; car le caractere n'est point plus moderne que cela. Esperant qu'il s'en tirera encore quelque correction á mesure qu'il s'imprimera.[28]

He also explained that he was still unable to find the complete copy of William of Poitiers which he knew was in the possession of Pierre Pithou (d. 1596) and he added that he would send the first quire of the edition to give Camden and Cotton an idea of the contents.[29] In his letter of 17 June he confirmed that William's text was in the press.[30] Then in August he wrote apologetically, presumably in response to a reproachful letter from Camden, that he would rewrite the first page of the preface which contained the acknowledgements. Apparently Camden, and possibly Cotton as well, had complained that the acknowledgement to Cotton was inadequate, for De Peiresc wrote:

Nous tascherons de faire refaire la feuille ou est mentionné Monsieur Cotton, pour y ajouter le mot Anglus, qui s'est oublié par inadvertance.... Et memes desireroit on d'y ajouter un eloge en sa recommandation, pour lequel je vous avois prié de nous envoyer un peu d'instruction tant de ses qualitez que des affaires, ou il peut avoir esté employé pour le public, affin d'en faire la plus honnorable mention que nous pourrons.[31]

Camden surely did his best in providing De Peiresc and Duchesne with a brief which resulted in the following eulogy:

Huius [the *Encomium*] ut et sequentis authoris Guillelmi Pictavini scripta debentur viro perillustri D. Roberto Cottono Anglo, non solum familiae vetustate ac splendore, quae honoratissimas cognatione complexa est, atque equestris ordinis dignitate Baronetta: sed etiam eruditione multifaria, nec non felicissima industria in congerenda antiqua rarissimorum librorum numerorum supellectile, quam pro candore omnibus studiosis libentissime aperit, commendatissimo.[32]

The reference to William of Poitiers's manuscript in this preface is the last proof of its existence we have. What happened to this manuscript and its copy sent earlier by Camden remains a mystery. Either it was never returned and remained in France, where for all we know it may still lie undiscovered in some library. If, however, this were the case it is strange that the manuscript was never mentioned again in the correspondence of De Peiresc and Camden. Or, it was returned to Camden and Cotton, but not used any more because of the existence of the text in print, and presumably perished in the fire of 1731. But this explanation does not answer the question why, if the manuscript had come back to England, it was not listed in Thomas Smith's Cotton catalogue of 1696.[33]

None of the other manuscripts of William of Poitiers which existed in the Middle Ages, nor the complete copy mentioned by De Peiresc as being in the possession of Pierre Pithou, has ever been found.[34] The Norman copies available to Orderic Vitalis *circa* 1109–41 at Saint-Evroult, and to Milo Crispin and Robert of Torigni in the mid-twelfth century at Bec have left no trace in the library records of these monasteries.[35] In England at least two copies circulated in the second half of the twelfth century: one at St Paul's in London where it was excerpted by Ralph of Diceto and the other at Ely where the monk Richard used it for his *Liber Eliensis*.[36] The Cotton fragment was probably one of the two English manuscripts, or a copy of one of them, rather than one of the Norman manuscripts. But despite the fact that the loss of William the Conqueror's biography is irretrievable we should be grateful to Cotton that he preserved it just long enough for it to have been printed by De Peiresc and Duchesne in 1619. Their edition provided more links with William Camden and Sir Robert Cotton than through William of Poitiers alone.

The *Encomium Emmae Reginae*, a biography of Queen Emma, widow of King Ethelred and King Cnut of England, written *circa* 1040 by a Flemish monk at the request of Emma herself was also included in the Anglo-Norman collection.[37] As in the case of William of Poitiers, the French editors only had access to Sir Robert Cotton's copy. There are no details of this manuscript in the correspondence of De Peiresc and Camden, but the few references we have suggest that what was sent to France was a late copy rather than an early medieval manuscript. The most important reference occurs in the letter of 5 March 1618, where De Peiresc explained that the marriage of Emma, who was Norman, to King Ethelred ultimately led to her nephew's conquest of England in 1066 and that this was sufficient reason to include the *Encomium*:

J'ay receu L'Encomium de votre Reyne Emme, que nous ferons imprimer en son rang et ordre dans le recueil des Historiens de Normandie. C'est bien la verité, qu'il appartient plus à l'Angleterre qu'à la Normandie; mais il ne sera pas tant mal seant entre ceux de Normandie, puis qu'elle [Emma] estoit Normande; et que son alliance fust la premiere planche aux conquete de Guillaume son neveu. Il se trouve si peu d'Ecrivains de ce siecle la, que je n'en scauroit point negliger.[38]

This passage also confirms that the text was printed from a Cotton manuscript, a statement which we again find in the preface of the 1619 edition.[39] Several manuscripts of the *Encomium* have survived of which BL, Add. MS. 33241 from the mid-eleventh century is the most important.[40] Although of continental origin, at the end of the Middle Ages it belonged to St Augustine's in Canterbury and in the early nineteenth century it was owned by the tenth Duke of Hamilton after which it was finally acquired by the British Museum in 1887. The other copies are a manuscript written *circa* 1624 by the Welsh antiquary Robert Vaughan (1592–1667), now Aberystwyth, NLW, MS. Hengwrth 158; a manuscript written in the late eighteenth century, now BL, Add. MS. 6920; and a lengthy sixteenth-century excerpt, now Paris, BN Lat. 6235. Of these, the Vaughan manuscript is the most important for it indirectly provides the clue for solving the problem of which manuscript was owned by Cotton and sent to De Peiresc.

Robert Vaughan wrote that he copied the *Encomium* from a manuscript which in turn had been copied by Thomas Talbot in 1566 from a medieval manuscript.[41] Alistair Campbell, the most recent editor of the *Encomium*, established beyond doubt that this must have been the mid-eleventh-century London manuscript. Talbot's copy of 1566 is lost, but a comparison of Vaughan's text with the Duchesne edition strongly suggests that what was sent to France in 1618 was a careless copy of Talbot's text.[42] What

Campbell did not know, but what is a well-established fact now, is that Sir Robert Cotton acquired manuscripts and notebooks of his older colleague and co-founder of the Society of Antiquaries, Thomas Talbot, one-time Clerk of the Records.[43] Therefore we may conclude that in 1617 or 1618 Camden or Cotton had a copy made of Talbot's *Encomium* which was sent to France. Talbot's own manuscript presumably remained in England where within six years it was copied by Robert Vaughan. This reconstruction supports my earlier suggestion that De Peiresc received the text of the *Encomium* written in an early seventeenth-century hand. The whereabouts of the early medieval *Encomium* copy from St Augustine's at Canterbury were unknown, it seems, to either Camden or Cotton.

Duchesne also printed William of Jumièges's *Gesta* in 1619. In his preface he explained that he used Camden's edition, which of course was based on two Cotton manuscripts, and that he had made several emendations with the help of some French manuscripts from the collection of De Thou.[44] His text, however, is substantially that of Camden. This raises the interesting point that the English and French antiquaries co-operated to an extraordinary degree with each other, and that, as far as we know, matters of copyright were not raised. Camden, even if he had wished to object, was not really in a position to do so because he had done exactly the same in 1602 when he reprinted some of Matthew Parker's editions from the 1570s. As far as Dudo of Saint-Quentin's history of the dukes of Normandy is concerned, there is no evidence that Duchesne used, or had asked for, any of the manuscripts which we know were owned by either Camden or Cotton.[45] According to his preface, he printed Dudo's text from two manuscripts in French ownership: one of François d'Amboise and the other of Jacques Sirmond.[46]

On 15 July 1619 De Peiresc sent two copies of Duchesne's edition to Camden. One was for himself and the other for Sir Robert Cotton.[47] Unfortunately, due to the loss or dispersion of Cotton's printed book collection his personal copy of this edition is lost.[48] We cannot therefore be sure if he ever collated any of its texts with his own manuscripts. The Duchesne edition also contains a mass of material relating to the genealogies of French and English families. Although no documents or texts from this section are specifically mentioned in the preface as having come from the Cotton collection, the De Peiresc and Camden correspondence of the years 1618 and 1619 is devoted primarily to these genealogies. The letters contain many requests for manuscripts either from Sir Robert Cotton or from other manuscript collections in England, notably the Cambridge and Oxford colleges, to verify the details from French sources. It is a pity that we do not have Camden's answers to these queries, for in his position as King of Arms and herald his knowledge must have been particularly valuable.

The editions of Anglo-Norman chronicles by Camden and Duchesne based on Cotton manuscripts are amongst the most important evidence illustrating the value of Sir Robert's collection for texts from the period of the Norman Conquest of England. Apart from these two editions there was one more for which Cotton provided a key witness. This was John Selden's edition of Eadmer of Canterbury's *Historia Novorum* written in the first two decades of the twelfth century.[49] Only two manuscripts of this text are known. One, possibly Eadmer's autograph, is now Cambridge, Corpus Christi College MS. 452, and the other Cotton Titus A. IX. The latter is a thirteenth-century manuscript from Haughmond Abbey in Shropshire, which John Selden borrowed from Sir Robert Cotton for his edition of 1623. In his preface he referred to the Duchesne edition for the texts of William of Poitiers and Orderic Vitalis, which although not written by English authors, were, he said, important for the history of England. He added that one should not avoid studying these Norman texts:

Normannorum enim rebus vetustis adeo nostrae plerunque intermistae sunt ut non sine ignavia aut inscitia praeteriri illae possint, si quis de nostris diligentius consulat.[50]

In the same preface he also thanks Sir Robert Cotton for the use of his manuscripts. His effusiveness was no doubt inspired by the praises of Duchesne and De Peiresc which he may well have tried to surpass:

Codices autem Mss quos testes sine loco et nomine laudamus, omnes (uti etiam ipsum unde haec editio) suppeditabat instructissima illa, et quantivis precij, bibliotheca Nobilissimi eruditissimi, mihique amicissimi viri ROBERTI COTTONI Equestri dignitate, et ea, quam Baronetti, dicimus, clari, qui non modo comparandis ingenti sumptu libris Mss. ijsque selectissimis, sed etiam humanissime ijs atque propensissimo in bonarum literarum et rerum civilium studiosos animo communicandos, immortalem tam apud exteros quam populares meritissimo nactus est famam.[51]

Besides the narrative sources for the history of the Norman Conquest of England preserved amongst the Cotton Manuscripts, Sir Robert collected cartularies and several so-called cartulary-chronicles. They were drawn up in England within three generations after 1066 as a record of land transactions both before and after the Conquest.[52] They are of extraordinary value because in many cases they contain the texts, in the vernacular or translated into Latin, of Anglo-Saxon documents, which themselves have disappeared. The most spectacular examples concern those of Ramsey Abbey, Ely Cathedral, Abingdon and Worcester.[53] None of these was published during Cotton's lifetime, but they were used by scholars like John Selden and Sir Henry Savile amongst others for their historical studies. As early as the 1590s the antiquarian Arthur Agarde (1540–1615), for example, referred to the loan of a book entitled *Restauratio ecclesiae de Ely*, which is almost certainly to be identified as Cotton Titus A. I, ff. 3–56, containing Book II of the *Liber Eliensis*.[54]

There is another reason why this group deserves attention here. The Ramsey cartulary and the Winchester cartulary, which dates from the fourteenth century, were each bound together by Sir Robert Cotton with short Anglo-Norman histories.[55] The Ramsey collection contains an unrelated quire with a text entitled *Quedam exceptiones de historia Normannorum et Anglorum*,[56] whereas the Hyde Abbey manuscript has an equally separate chronicle written probably at St Pancras at Lewes, known under the misleading title of the 'Hyde Chronicle'.[57] Both are unique copies of short chronicles written early in the twelfth century in the Anglo-Norman realm which contain information not to be found elsewhere. For example, the *Quedam exceptiones* affords independent evidence about the FitzOsbern family, in particular Bishop Osmund of Exeter, and provides us with the only reference to William de Vauville as the first castellan of Exeter. The 'Hyde' Chronicle is an important source not only for pre-Conquest England and in particular for Earl Harold's family, but also for the history of England and Normandy in the 1110s and 1120s. Thus, it gives an independent account of the Battle of Brémule in 1119. Both chronicles are written in a Latin which is sometimes clumsy and not very refined. They are not products of the great historiographical schools of Saint-Evroult, Bec, Worcester, Malmesbury or Canterbury, but in their own modest way they represent traditions, some of which are undoubtedly oral, which, if they had not been written down, would have been lost. The fact that these chronicles, too, were saved for posterity by Sir Robert Cotton is as remarkable as his rescue of the more famous and well-known chronicles relating the history of the Norman Conquest.

1 C. E. Wright, 'The Elizabethan Society of Antiquaries and the formation of the Cottonian library', in F. Wormald and C. E. Wright (eds.), *The English Library before 1700* (London, 1958), pp. 176–212; M. McKisack, *Medieval History in the Tudor Age* (Oxford, 1971), pp. 155–69; H. Trevor-Roper, *Queen Elizabeth's First Historian: William Camden and the Beginnings of English 'Civil History'*, 1971 Neale Lecture in English History (London, 1971); K. Sharpe, *Sir Robert Cotton 1586–1631. History and Politics in Early Modern England* (Oxford, 1979).

2 For the example of William of Poitiers's biography of William the Conqueror, see pp. 243–5.

3 The works are listed in E. P. Goldschmidt, *Medieval Texts and their First Appearance in Print*, Transactions of the Bibliographical Society, Supplement, xvi (1943).

4 For Henry of Huntingdon and William of Malmesbury, as well as for 'Florence' and John of Worcester, see below n. 11. The *Historia Ecclesiastica* of Orderic Vitalis was published by André Duchesne in 1619, see p. 158.

5 The *editio princeps* of the Anglo-Saxon Chronicle was edited by Abraham Wheloc (1593–1653) and published as an appendix to his edition of Bede's *Ecclesiastical History* (Cambridge, 1643) on pp. 503–70. Wheloc called it the *Chronologia Saxonica* and based his edition on the Parker manuscript (Cambridge, Corpus Christi College 173) and Cotton Otho B. XI. Modern editions of respectively the A and G versions of the Anglo-

Saxon Chronicle are *The Anglo-Saxon Chronicle. A Collaborative Edition, Vol. 3: MS A*, ed. J. M. Bately (Cambridge, 1986), and *Die Version G der Angelsächsischen Chronik. Rekonstruktion und Edition*, ed. A. Lutz (Munich, 1981). Simeon of Durham's Chronicle was published by Roger Twysden (*Historiae Anglicanae Scriptores X ex vetustis manuscriptis nunc primum in lucem editi* (London, 1652)).

6 John Steed, *The History of Great Britaine* (London, 1611) and Samuel Daniel, *The First Part of the Historie of England* (London, 1612). The latter text has been published in a modern edition: *The Complete Works in Verse and Prose of Samuel Daniel*, ed. A. R. Grosart, 5 vols. (New York, 1896), vol. iv, pp. 69–299. I am very grateful to John Gillingham and Colin Tite for their comments on the earlier version of this paragraph. For the problem of '1066' as a subject, see D. C. Douglas, 'The Norman Conquest and British historians', in *Time and the Hour. Some Collected Papers of D. C. Douglas* (London, 1977), pp. 57–76, and C. Brett, 'John Leland and the Anglo-Norman historian', in R. Allen Brown (ed.), *Anglo-Norman Studies XI. Proceedings of the Battle Conference 1988* (Woodbridge, 1989), pp. 59–76.

7 The development of antiquarian studies is discussed, amongst others, by McKisack, *Medieval History*, and R. Southern, 'Aspects of the European tradition of historical writing. 4. The sense of the past', *Transactions of the Royal Historical Society*, 5th ser., xxiii (1973), pp.

243–63 and especially 256–63. For criticism of both authors' underestimation of the value of antiquarian studies in the fifteenth century, see A. Gransden, 'Antiquarian studies in fifteenth-century England', *Antiquaries Journal*, lx (1980), pp. 75–97, and A. Gransden, *Historical Writing in England, ii: c. 1307 to the Early Sixteenth Century* (London, 1982), pp. 454–79.

8 Sharpe, *Sir Robert Cotton*, pp. 19–25.

9 R. Manning, 'Antiquarianism and the seigneurial reaction: Sir Robert and Sir Thomas Cotton and their tenants', *Historical Research*, lxiii (1990), pp. 277–88.

10 Douglas, 'The Norman Conquest', p. 67; Sharpe, *Sir Robert Cotton*, p. 24. In general, see C. Brooks and K. Sharpe, 'History, English law and the Renaissance', *Past and Present*, lxxii (1976), pp. 133–42.

11 *Chronicon ex Chronicis...accessit etiam continuatio usque ad annum Christi 1141* (London, 1592); for this edition, see McKisack, *Medieval History*, pp. 61–2. *Rerum Anglicarum Scriptores post Bedam ex vetustissimis codicibus manuscriptis nunc primum in lucem editi* (London, 1596; repr. Frankfurt, 1601).

12 For Henry of Huntingdon's manuscripts, see D. E. Greenway, 'Henry of Huntingdon and the manuscripts of his Historia Anglorum', R. Allen Brown (ed.), *Anglo-Norman Studies IX. Proceedings of the Battle Conference 1986* (Woodbridge, 1987), pp. 103–26. Dr Greenway, however, does not include manuscripts containing excerpts or fragments of Henry's Historia. Sir Robert Cotton certainly possessed one Henry of Huntingdon manuscript, though this is not necessarily Cotton Vespasian A. XVIII, by 1612 for it is listed as one of the books he lent in that year to Arthur Agarde (Harl. MS. 6018, f. 162r). The Cotton copies of the chronicles of William of Malmesbury are discussed in *Willelmi Malmesbiriensis monachi de gestis regum Anglorum*, ed. W. Stubbs (London, 1889), vol. ii, pp. lxxiii–iv (Cotton Claudius C. IX), and *Willelmi Malmesbiriensis monachi de gestis pontificum Anglorum libri quinque*, ed. N. Hamilton (London, 1870), p. xx (Cotton Claudius A. V). Other works of William of Malmesbury have survived in Cotton manuscripts: the Miracles of St Andrew (Nero E. I, Tiberius A. XII and Tiberius B. III), the Commentary on the Lamentations of Jeremiah (Cotton Tiberius A. XII), the Miracles of the Blessed Virgin (Cotton Cleopatra C. X), see *Willelmi...de gestis regum Anglorum*, ed. Stubbs, vol. ii, pp. cxx–cxxxvii. The *Gesta Regum* manuscript, Cotton Claudius C. IX, was in Cotton's possession by 1612; see Harl. MS. 6018, f. 162r (list of books lent to Arthur Agarde).

13 Savile does not give details of the manuscripts he used. For suggestions as to the Henry of Huntingdon manuscripts used, see Greenway, 'Henry of Huntingdon', p. 103, n. 2.

14 Another edition was published one year later, also at Frankfurt. For the discrepancies between the two, see *British Museum. General Catalogue of Printed Books*, vol. xxxii (1965), col. 609.

15 *Anglica, Normannica...scripta*, ed. Camden, sig. *** 2v.

16 E. M. C. van Houts, *Gesta Normannorum Ducum. Een studie over de handschriften, de tekst, het geschiedwerk en het genre* (Groningen, 1982), and *The Gesta Normannorum Ducum of William of Jumièges, Orderic Vitalis and Robert of Torigni, i: Introduction and Books I–IV* (Oxford, 1992).

17 Van Houts, *Gesta*, p. 10, and *The Gesta Normannorum Ducum*, ed. van Houts, vol. i, p. cxxviii.

18 For the bequest, see *G. Camdeni et illustrium virorum ad G. Camdenum epistolæ...præmittitur G. Camdeni vita*, ed. T. Smith (London, 1691), pp. lxv–lxvi, and Sharpe, *Sir Robert Cotton*, p. 58.

19 Harl. MS. 6018, ff. 90r–91r, no. 194 (Cotton Nero D. VIII) and f. 66r, no. 132 (Cotton Vespasian A. XIX), see below.

20 Van Houts, *Gesta*, pp. 239–41, and *The Gesta Normannorum Ducum*, ed. van Houts, vol. i, pp. cxii–cxiii.

21 Van Houts, *Gesta*, pp. 196–8, 244–6; *The Gesta Normannorum Ducum*, ed. van Houts, vol. i, pp. xcvi–xcvii, cxiv–cxv, and *The Historia Regum Britannie of Geoffrey of Monmouth, iii: A Summary Catalogue of the Manuscripts*, ed. J. C. Crick (Cambridge, 1989), pp. 149–52.

22 *The Ecclesiastical History of Orderic Vitalis*, ed. M. Chibnall, 6 vols. (Oxford, 1969–80), vol. iv, pp. 38–42 and 80–108.

23 *The Ecclesiastical History*, ed. Chibnall, vol. i, p. 121, where a fourteenth-century date is suggested. It is listed as no. 132 in Cotton's 1621 catalogue (Harl. MS. 6018, f. 66r).

24 *The Ecclesiastical History*, ed. Chibnall, vol. i, p. 121.

25 D. Matthew, *The Norman Monasteries and their English Possessions* (Oxford, 1962), pp. 132–3, 172–3, and B. English, 'William the Conqueror and the Anglo-Norman succession', *Historical Research*, lxiv (1991), p. 232 nn. 44, 45.

26 For the history of the Cotton manuscript of William of Poitiers's biography of the Conqueror, see *Guillaume de Poitiers, Histoire de Guillaume le Conquérant* (Paris, 1952), pp. l–lv, and R. H. C. Davis, 'William of Poitiers and his History of William the Conqueror', in R. H. C. Davis and J. Wallace-Hadrill (eds.), *The Writing of History in the Middle Ages. Essays presented to Richard William Southern* (Oxford, 1981), pp. 71–101 at 91–101. Neither John Steed nor Samuel Daniel used William of Poitiers's history in their works published in 1611 and 1612 respectively. Colin Tite kindly pointed out to me that probably in *c.* 1612 John Speed borrowed from Robert Cotton a text which might have been William's, for an entry in the Cotton catalogue (BL, Harl. MS. 6018, f. 160) reads: 'Vita Willimi Conquestoris in 8 old but new bound it is the best'.

27 *G. Camdeni…epistolae*, ed. Smith, no. clxxii, pp. 216–17 (10 Feb. 1618), no. clxxvi, pp. 222–3 (5 Mar. 1618).

28 Ibid., no. clxxxv, pp. 231–4 at 231 (29 Apr. 1618).

29 Ibid., no. clxxxv, pp. 231–4 at 232.

30 Ibid., no. cxci, pp. 241–3 at 242.

31 Ibid., no. cxcviii, pp. 252–5 at 254.

32 *Historiae Normannorum…Scriptores*, ed. Duchesne, p. a iij verso.

33 *Catalogus librorum manuscriptorum bibliothecae Cottonianae*, ed. T. Smith (Oxford, 1696). The catalogue of Cotton manuscripts of 1621, Harl. MS. 6018, contains as item 102 (f. 58r) an unidentified text, 'Fragmentum vitae Will[elm]i .i.', which according to Dr Colin Tite is now lost.

34 R. H. C. Davis pointed out that some of Pithou's manuscripts came into the possession of the Marquis de Rosanbo, see 'William of Poitiers', pp. 95–6. However, the Rosanbo collection was split up and sold; there is no trace of William of Poitiers (P. O. Kristeller (ed.), *Iter italicum…*, (London–Leiden, 1983), vol. iii, p. 344).

35 *The Ecclesiastical History*, ed. Chibnall, vol. ii, pp. xviii–xxi; P. Bouet, 'Orderic Vital, lecteur critique de Guillaume de Poitiers', in C. Viola (ed.), *Mediaevalia Christiana xie–xiie siècles. Hommage à Raymonde Foreville de ses amis, ses collègues et ses anciens élèves* (Paris, 1989); *The Gesta Normannorum Ducum*, ed. van Houts, vol. i, pp. lxxxviii–lxxxix.

36 Davis, 'William of Poitiers', p. 100; *Liber Eliensis*, ed. E. O. Blake (London, 1962), pp. xxvii–xxix.

37 *Encomium Emmae Reginae*, ed. A. Campbell (London, 1949).

38 *G. Camdeni…epistolae*, ed. Smith, no. clxxvi, pp. 222–3, at 222.

39 *Historiae Normannorum…Scriptores*, ed. Duchesne, p. a iij verso, and *Encomium*, ed. Campbell, pp. xiii–xiv.

40 For the manuscripts, see *Encomium*, ed. Campbell, pp. xi–xvii. A photograph of BL, Add. MS. 33241, ff. 1v–2r, showing Queen Emma with her sons Edward and Harthacnut and the beginning of the dedicatory letter, can be found in J. Backhouse and L. Webster (eds.), *The Golden Age of Anglo-Saxon Art* (London, 1984), pp. 144–5, no. 148.

41 *Encomium*, ed. Campbell, p. xiii: 'transcriptū et excerptū a vetustissi [*sic*] exemplari manuscripto per Thom. Talbot, anᵒ Dni 1566'.

42 Ibid., pp. xiii–xiv.

43 Wright, 'The Elizabethan Society', pp. 197–8, 199; Sharpe, *Sir Robert Cotton*, p. 17; excerpts from Thomas Talbot's notebook, Cotton Vespasian D. XVII, are printed in A. G. Watson, *The Manuscripts of Henry Savile of Banke* (London, 1969), pp. 78–82.

44 *Historiae Normannorum…Scriptores*, ed. Duchesne, p. a iiij recto; van Houts, *Gesta Normannorum Ducum*, pp. 11–12, and *The Gesta Normannorum Ducum*, ed. van Houts, vol. i, p. cxxviii.

45 Cotton Nero D. VIII and Cotton Claudius A. XII. The latter was listed in Cotton's catalogue of 1621; see Harl. MS. 6018, f. 115v (no. 313). See also G. Huisman, 'The manuscript tradition of Dudo of Saint-Quentin's *Gesta Normannorum*', in R. Allen Brown (ed.), *Anglo-Norman Studies VI. Proceedings of the Battle Conference 1983* (Woodbridge, 1984), pp. 122–35, at 125, 126–7.

46 *Historiae Normannorum…Scriptores*, ed. Duchesne, p. a iij recto + verso.

47 *G. Camdeni…epistolae*, ed. Smith, no. ccxxi, pp. 281–3 at 282; Sharpe, *Sir Robert Cotton*, p. 58 n. 68.

48 Sharpe, *Sir Robert Cotton*, p. 57.

49 *Eadmeri monachi Cantuariensis Historiae*

Novorum sive sui saeculi libri vi…in lucem ex bibliotheca Cottoniana emisit Ioannes Seldenus et notas porro adjecit et spicilegium (London, 1623).

50 Ibid., p. vii.

51 Ibid., p. vi.

52 J.-Ph. Genet, 'Cartulaires, registres et histoires: l'exemple anglais', in B. Guenée (ed.), *Le métier d'historien au Moyen Age. Etudes sur l'historiographie médiévale* (Paris, 1977), pp. 95–138; Gransden, *Historical Writing*, vol. i, pp. 269–79.

53 *Chronicon Abbatiae Rameseiensis*, ed. W. D. Macray (London, 1886); *Liber Eliensis*, ed. Blake; *Chronicon Monasterii de Abingdon*, ed. J. Stevenson (London, 1858); *Hemingi chartularium ecclesiae Wigorniensis*, ed. T. Hearne (Oxford, 1723), and N. R. Ker, 'Hemming's Cartulary' in *Studies in Medieval History presented to F. M. Powicke* (Oxford, 1948), pp. 49–75.

54 Sharpe, *Sir Robert Cotton*, p. 19 n. 14; *Liber Eliensis*, ed. Blake, pp. xxv, 65, 72. For A. Agarde, see McKisack, *Medieval History*, pp. 85–93.

55 *Liber de monasterii de Hyda*, ed. E. Edwards (London, 1866).

56 Cotton Vespasian A. XVIII, ff. 157r–162v: E. M. C. van Houts (ed.), *The Gesta Normannorum Ducum of William of Jumièges, Orderic Vitalis and Robert of Torigni. ii: Books V–VIII* (Oxford, 1995), Appendix.

57 Cotton Domitian XIV, ff. 4r–21v, edited in *Liber de Hyda*, ed. Edwards, pp. 283–321.

ARTHUR AGARDE AND DOMESDAY BOOK

ELIZABETH M. HALLAM

ARTHUR AGARDE, Deputy Chamberlain of the Exchequer from 1570 to 1615 and an associate of Sir Robert Cotton, was the founder of scholarly work on Domesday Book.[1] He brought to his office a new academic and archival dimension, by sorting, calendaring and listing the records in his care, and by compiling a searcher's guide to the Exchequer records, so that subsequent generations were to remember him as, to quote his epitaph in the cloisters at Westminster Abbey, a '*diligens scrutator*' of the royal records. Also a scholar and antiquarian, he had interests which ranged far beyond the Treasury of Receipt; and, having gained a profound knowledge of Domesday Book in the course of his official duties, he was the first to assess its historical significance and interpret its contents.

This short article briefly examines Agarde's career and achievements and sets him in the context of contemporary developments in the practices of record keeping. His role as an antiquary and his links with Cotton and his circle are also explored. Recently discovered manuscript material is then discussed which emphasizes the extent of Agarde's interest in and understanding of the Conqueror's survey and highlights his key position in early Domesday studies.

Agarde was born in Derbyshire in about 1540. He studied at Cambridge, trained as a lawyer, and was admitted into the Exchequer as a clerk.[2] In 1570 he was granted one of the two offices of Deputy Chamberlain at the Treasury of Receipt by Sir Nicholas Throckmorton and this he was to fill with distinction for the next forty-five years.[3] The traditional tasks of these functionaries, which had evolved with their office in the thirteenth century, were threefold: care and custody of the records, making searches and copies for administrative and legal purposes, and striking tallies.[4] Much of the day-to-day work was performed by the anonymous clerks working for them.

Agarde's tenure of one of the twin offices saw an enhancement in the status and responsibilites of both, in part due to the high quality of his work and in part to reforms in Exchequer practices. A reorganization in the 1570s severed earlier ties of the Pells officials with the Treasury of Receipt and left the Deputy Chamberlains in sole control of the records. Moreover, in 1574 Thomas Burrow, Agarde's colleague, retired, leaving Agarde at an early stage in his career as the more senior of the two officers.[5] A reconstruction of the Exchequer buildings provided a new repository for the records and more spacious accommodation for their custodians,[6] and this doubtless helped Agarde in his sorting and digesting of the documents in his care – for which his normal fees were augmented by an extra £40 *per annum* in 1609.[7]

The industry and accuracy which Agarde brought to bear in his work are shown in the abstracts and indexes to plea rolls, assize rolls and other records which he and his subordinates made, a number of which still remain the principal means of reference to the records they describe.[8] Some he bequeathed to the Treasury of Receipt. Others he left to his friend Sir Robert Cotton, thereby arousing a considerable degree of official indignation: the bequest was unsuccessfully contested in 1615 by Sir Thomas Wilson, Keeper of the State Papers.[9] So valued were these manuscripts by subsequent generations that later in the seventeenth century an anonymous antiquarian collected or commissioned transcripts of many, in memory of Agarde.[10]

Agarde took his duties as a custodian of the records seriously, and wrote a treatise, completed in 1610 with the help of Cotton and Sir Walter Cope, to guide his fellow record keepers and other searchers. Known as the *Compendium Recordorum*, the treatise – which was widely copied – catalogues the contents of the four treasuries of the Exchequer.[11] The text also benefitted Agarde's fellow antiquaries; for example, one copy was made by him and bound specially for Sir Julius Caesar in 1610 and a second was produced for William Cecil, Earl of Salisbury, in the same year. In his introductory note to the Salisbury volume, Agarde describes his labours in sorting the records and expresses his indebtedness to the Earl and to Cotton.[12]

The problems confronting Agarde and his peers are brought vividly to life in the preface to this treatise. The documents are, Agarde says, constantly under threat from fire, water, rats and mice and from being misplaced; and worst of all, from being taken away altogether. The value of this work was stressed by Thomas Powell, who printed parts of it in 1631 as his *Repertorie of Records*. In the same work, he drew also on Agarde's legacy in his many interesting comments about the care and custody of Domesday Book and other documents. 'In searching the Booke of Domesday', he observes, 'is to bee avoyded, laying bare hands or moysture, upon the writing thereof, and blotting'.[13]

As a Deputy Chamberlain, Agarde was one of the leaders of a generation of record keepers who emerged from the bureaucratic obscurity surrounding their predecessors to become recognized as scholars and archivists as well as custodians and copyists. During Elizabeth I's reign it was belatedly realized in government circles that the archives of state had fallen into confusion so great that official business was impeded. The records were divided between numerous different jurisdictions and repositories and were, in many cases, neglected and unsorted.[14]

Attempts were subsequently made to remedy matters. In the first decade of the seventeenth century, the sovereign's personal library of State Papers was gradually sorted and methodized by Thomas Wilson, who became joint Keeper of the State Paper Office, a new post, in 1610.[15] Vigorous efforts were made in the 1580s by the Keeper of the Tower archives, William Bowyer, to end the long-standing and problematical division of the Chancery records between the Tower and the Rolls Chapel. His initiatives met with no success, although Bowyer at least began to reorganize and catalogue the documents in his charge.[16] In 1601 one of his successors, the celebrated antiquarian William Lambarde, presented the elderly Queen Elizabeth with a 'pandect' which described the contents of his archive in detail. He expounded his work to Her Majesty in person, and she is said to have showed considerable interest in what he had to say.[17] Bowyer, Lambarde, and other custodians of the Tower records, such as Sir Thomas Heneage and Thomas Talbot, were a new kind of record keepers, men who combined the skills of scholars, organizers and archivists.[18]

Nor was this new approach confined to the archives of state. At Exeter, John Hooker rearranged and catalogued the city muniments for the Mayor and Corporation,[19] and similar work was undertaken in the City of London by Robert Smith, a protégé of William Fleetwood, the City Recorder. As holder of the Comptrollership of the Chamber and other offices, Smith had responsibility for the City's estates, and he compiled a series of transcripts, calendars and indexes of the corporation archives, with official backing.[20] His efforts were primarily a response to the needs of London's dignitaries to use these records for their burgeoning legal and administrative activities, and similar practical considerations seem to have underlain much of the archival work undertaken at this time.

There was, however, also a scholarly dimension to all this activity, and it is significant that Smith's patron, Fleetwood, was, like Heneage, Talbot, Lambarde and Agarde, a lawyer by training and a fellow of the Elizabethan Society of Antiquaries. Constituted in about 1586, its members were 'gentlemen of great abilities..., [who] applied themselves to the study of the antiquities and history of this kingdom, a taste at that time very prevalent, wisely forseeing that without a perfect knowledge of those requisites, a thorough understanding of the laws of their native land could not be attained'.[21] Politicians, lawyers, scholars and record keepers all had their place in this select and influential fraternity.[22]

Agarde was an early member of the society, to which he delivered papers on a wide range of topics, from the etymology of 'Duke' to the origins and privileges of heralds.[23] These show his acquaintance with a wide range of sources outside as well as inside the Treasury of Receipt. Sir Robert Cotton's library was at his disposal, and many of the cartularies and chronicles he cited had been borrowed from this important collection.[24] But Agarde was always at his most secure when quoting record sources, and was unabashed in his bias towards English rather than foreign topics of study.[25]

The Antiquaries seem to have found his knowledge of Domesday Book particularly impressive. In 1599 he lectured to them on measurements of land, citing much material from the survey.[26] Even more important was his treatise on the Book, a copy of which passed to Sir Robert Cotton with other memorabilia of the Elizabethan Society of Antiquaries (fig. 1). Its significance was to be recognized by future generations as the first systematic attempt to explain the origins of Domesday Book.[27] In it Agarde identified the questions put by the commissioners in the *Inquisitio Eliensis*, an ancient register he had presented to and later borrowed back from Cotton.[28] Cotton had also lent him a copy of

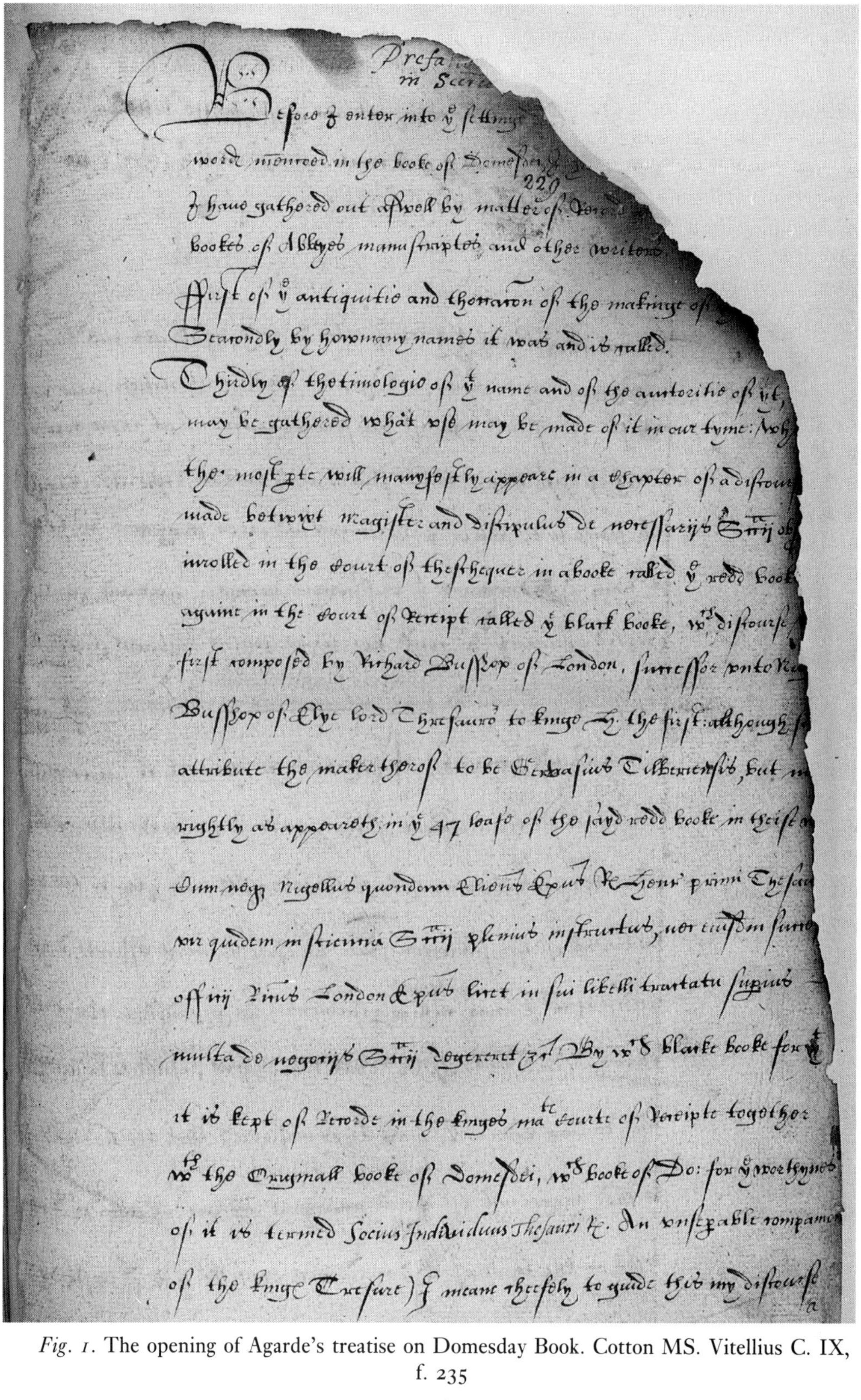

Prefa[...]
in Secre[...]

Before I enter into ye settinge [...]
word menconed in the booke of Domesda[y] [...]
229
I have gathered out aswell by matter of recor[d] [...]
bookes of Abbyes manuscriptes and other writers.
ffirst of ye antiquitie and thoccacion of the makinge of [...]
Secondly by howmany names it was and is called.
Thirdly of thetimologie of ye name and of the autoritie of yt,
may be gathered what use may be made of it in our tyme: wh[ich]
the most pte will manyfestly appeare in a chapter of a discou[rse]
made betwixt Magister and discipulus de necessariis Sccij ob[...]
inrolled in the Court of thexchequer in a booke called ye redd boo[k]
againe in the Court of Receipt called ye black booke, wch discourse
first composed by Richard Bisshop of London, successor unto Ric[hard]
Bisshop of Elye lord Thresaurer to kinge H. the first: although so[me]
attribute the maker thereof to be Gervasius Tilberiensis, but m[...]
rightly as appeareth in ye 47 leafe of the sayd redd booke in theise [...]
Cum neque Nigellus quondam Elien[sis] Epus R[egis] Henr[ici] primi Thesau[rarius]
vir quidem in Scientia Sccij plenius instructus, nec eiusdem succe[ssor]
officij Ricus London Epus licet in sui libelli tractatu suppius
multa de negotiis Sccij dixerint &c. By wch black booke for yt
it is kept of recorde in the kinges matie Courte of receipte togeather
wth the Originall booke of Domesdei, wch booke of Do: for ye worthynes
of it is termed Socius Individuus Thesauri &c. An unseparable companion
of the kinge Tresure) I meane therfore to guide this my discourse

Fig. 1. The opening of Agarde's treatise on Domesday Book. Cotton MS. Vitellius C. IX, f. 235

the *Dialogus de Scaccario*,[29] from which he quoted the now celebrated passage explaining why Domesday Book was so-called, and suggesting reasons for its compilation. Subsequent Domesday scholarship was to build on these discoveries by Agarde.[30]

Individuals, too, profited from Agarde's expertise on the survey. In the first part of his *Archæologus*, published in 1626, Sir Henry Spelman, fellow antiquary, praised Agarde for the excellence of the copies he had made him from Domesday.[31] Another searcher at the Treasury of Receipt, Sir George Buck, historian, poet and James I's Master of the Revels, acknowledged on the first page of his collection of Domesday memorabilia that he had benefited from Agarde's wise counsels about the Book's history.[32] And in writing his county histories Cotton always began his entries about manors with an appropriate Domesday extract.[33]

Agarde had gained his familiarity with the Domesday text from many years of making searches in and copies from its pages for official purposes. A number of Domesday exemplifications written and validated by him have survived, penned, in accordance with the practice established a century earlier, in an imitation Caroline minuscule hand.[34] As he scrutinized the survey, Agarde made annotations on its folios, ranging in content from a helpful hint on locating the entry for Derby to a signed and dated observation about the Kentish *sulung*.[35] He also gathered a miscellaneous collection of Domesday-related notes and jottings, including an extent and an inquisition both dating from the thirteenth century, which he seems to have kept with the Book. His successors continued the tradition, and in the nineteenth century the whole collection thus amassed was bound up with Great Domesday as its preliminary folios.[36]

Agarde's knowledge of Domesday's contents was founded on meticulous scholarship. He maintained an alphabetical glossary, acting as an expanded *index rerum* to the survey, which he augmented and updated, probably over the course of many years, as he came across additional material. Since 1892 this glossary has been in the Bodleian Library, Oxford, to which it was sold by a Mr Nicholson after its rejection by the British Museum.[37] The manuscript's authorship was unrecognized at that time and it remained unidentified until 1985. The present author then inspected it and discovered that although it is unsigned, its handwriting, layout and contents identify it as Agarde's work.

Most of the sixty-three folios in this manuscript contain a list of terms – such as 'Alnetum' and 'Alodium' – arranged letter by letter, with copious and detailed explanations and references to the Domesday text by landholder and manor. The headings, and the names of the counties, are rubricated in a style typical of their author.[38] At the end are extracts from works often quoted by Agarde in connection with the survey, the *Grand Coustoumier de Normandie* and the *Inquisitio Eliensis*.[39]

In the 1630s Thomas Powell praised a work by Agarde which was kept in the Treasury of Receipt and which was of great value to those who sought to read and interpret Domesday. His description fits the glossary better than any of Agarde's other Domesday works,[40] suggesting that this manuscript was used and appreciated for some years after its author's death. However, it was subsequently lost sight of until the late nineteenth

257

century, and only now is its identity as an example of Agarde's meticulous Domesday scholarship apparent once more.

A final example of Agarde's scholarly work on Domesday is a two-volume abstract of the Book, the original manuscripts of which have similarly come to light only recently. The Great Domesday section is in private hands, the Little Domesday section in the British Library.[41] Although again neither part bears his signature, the distinctive writing and the contents leave no doubt as to the authorship.[42] The Great Domesday volume has retained its original vellum binding. Its information appears in the same order as in its exemplar, but in an abbreviated form: for example, the first eight Surrey landholders, who in Great Domesday occupy four folios, here take up only one.[43] As Domesday Book had not yet been given folio numbers, let alone an index of places and names, this was a highly practical way of navigating its complexities.

The amount of detail given about each entry in the abstract varies, the Dover entry on f. 1 being far fuller than those which follow. The layout of the pages is reminiscent of the alphabetical glossary described above and of some of Agarde's abstracts of records.[44] Each page has a large heading giving the county, often written in Domesday script, and the names of the landholders prefixing the summaries of their holdings are rubricated. A number of jottings appear in the manuscript which are very much on a par with its author's annotations in Great Domesday,[45] as are the marginal signs depicting pointing hands and used to emphasize items of interest.[46]

The Little Domesday volume has the same layout, and although there are no jottings in its pages it is quite clearly a continuation of the Great Domesday abstract. Its original binding has been lost, and a later owner, who added to its first and last folios the Little Domesday colophon and other notes, stated that this ancient breviary was by an author unknown.[47]

These manuscripts apparently mark the first complete summary of Domesday Book to have been made since the thirteenth century, when a number of abstracts had been compiled for both private and public use.[48] In the intervening centuries résumés of Domesday information on particular manors or topics had been made by the Book's custodians for legal or administrative purposes. The codification of royal forest rights undertaken in 1316 to mollify baronial resentment against Edward II's oppressions is an example.[49] Agarde's abstract would have proved a useful repertory for anyone conducting similar searches in future.

The frequency with which Domesday was used for such purposes was, however, fast diminishing, and the jottings which Agarde made in the Great Domesday abstract suggest that he intended it primarily for antiquarian purposes. His scholarly friends must have greeted it with enthusiasm: there are three exact contemporary copies of both volumes in the British Library alone. One, made for the lawyer, scholar and collector Joseph Holand, is dated 5 March 1598, showing that Agarde had completed his own text by then.[50] The second, undated, is attributed to the leading antiquary and friend of Agarde, William Camden,[51] and the third, undated and anonymous, is of a similar period.[52] Two of them passed to the Cottonian Library, and that perhaps explains why

Agarde's original volumes, which he bequeathed to Cotton with his other manuscripts, were not retained in that collection.[53]

After Agarde's death knowledge of his abstracts and their value faded. Antiquarians such as Sir Simonds D'Ewes, who was working on the Book only a few decades later, knew nothing of their existence, and had to make their own summaries *ab initio*.[54] But while Agarde's abstracts fell into oblivion, the fruits of his historical work on Domesday Book remained well-known after his death and, built on by some of his successors and by later antiquarians, passed into the mainstream of Domesday studies.

John Bradshaw, Deputy Chamberlain from 1613 to 1633, assiduously compiled a short tract about Domesday in 1618, clearly based on Agarde's work.[55] On 10 October 1627 he copied out the passage from the *Dialogus de Scaccario* identified by Agarde and explaining why the Book was so-called, into the preliminary pages of Great Domesday. Incongruously, he used the mock-Domesday script which the Deputy Chamberlains employed for Domesday exemplifications – for a work which had been written almost a century later.[56] But this placing of the passage at the start of the text of Great Domesday ensured that future generations consulting the Book would not lose sight of its significance. Bradshaw was also the likely source of the comments in Thomas Powell's *Repertorie of Records* about the care and custody of Domesday,[57] practices still observed by its modern guardians.

This approach to safeguarding Domesday and advising on its contents was carried forward by several subsequent Deputy Chamberlains, who had no hesitation in inscribing further helpful hints and comments in Domesday Book and adding to the notes and jottings which were to be bound up with it, very much in the tradition of Agarde. One was Edward Fauconberg, who foliated Great Domesday and Little Domesday,[58] and another Peter Le Neve, who in 1708 became the first President of the refounded Society of Antiquaries. Well known by his scholarly contemporaries for his willingness to share his knowledge and understanding of the survey, he added comments and folio numbers to several of Agarde's annotations in the Book and its preliminary folios, while inserting yet further notes himself.[59]

The value of Agarde's treatises about – and drawing upon – Domesday were recognized when in the eighteenth century they found their way into print. In 1720 Thomas Hearne, assiduous scholar and editor of texts, published some in his *Collection of Curious Discourses Written by Eminent Antiquaries*, amongst a selection of the papers of the Elizabethan Antiquaries.[60] More were added when this work was expanded and reprinted in 1770. One, Agarde's important treatise on Domesday, had meanwhile been reprinted in the *Registrum Honoris de Richmond* by Roger Gale, who had also discovered, and who printed in the same volume, his discussion of measurements of land. In the preface Gale pays tribute to Agarde as a most eminent antiquarian, stating that although Hearne has already published one of the tracts, they are of great importance and deserve a wider audience.[61] From then on, their availability to Domesday scholars was ensured, and Agarde's treatise on Domesday is, in the Gale edition, the earliest work to appear in the definitive modern bibliography of Domesday Book.[62]

I would like to thank Miss M. M. Condon and Dr A. S. Bevan for their helpful comments on this paper, and Mr J. Hotson for drawing my attention to the Agarde manuscript in his possession and making it available for me to study.

1 E. M. Hallam, 'Nine Centuries of Keeping the Public Records', in P. Spufford (ed.), *Records of the Nation* (Woodbridge, 1990), pp. 23–42, esp. pp. 23, 36.

2 T. Hearne, *A Collection of Curious Discourses Written by Eminent Antiquaries*, 2nd edn., 2 vols. (London, 1771), vol. ii, pp. 421–2. This is an expanded version of Hearne's first edition, published in 1720.

3 J. C. Sainty, *Officers of the Exchequer*, List and Index Society, Special Series, vol. xviii (1983), p. 176.

4 E. M. Hallam, *Domesday Book through Nine Centuries* (London, 1986), pp. 56–8. For lists of the Deputy Chamberlains, see Sainty, pp. 168–77.

5 C. D. H. Coleman, 'Arthur Agarde and the [Deputy] Chamberlainship of the Exchequer', *Derbyshire Archæological Journal*, c (1980), pp. 64–6, esp. p. 68, n. 29.

6 H. M. Colvin *et al.* (eds.), *The History of the King's Works*, 1485–1660, vols. iii (London, 1975), pp. 77–8; iv (London, 1982), pp. 294–5.

7 P.R.O., E 403/1706: payment of 24 Feb. 1609, noted in Sainty, *Officers*, pp. 164–5.

8 Many of these are preserved among 'Agarde's Indexes' in P.R.O., IND 1/17083–17122; others (e.g. Add. MS. 25161) are in the BL. Not all of 'Agarde's Indexes' are in Agarde's own hand and some were probably compiled by clerks under his supervision.

9 P.R.O., PROB 10/323; SP 14/81, no. 69.

10 Stowe MSS. 527–531.

11 There are copies of all or part of this in P.R.O., IND 1/17126 and IND 1/17128, plus Lansdowne MS. 127, Harl. MS. 94 and Add. MS. 25256. Printed in part in F. Palgrave (ed.), *Kalendars and Inventories of the Exchequer*, vol. ii (London, 1836), pp. 311–35.

12 Harl. MS. 94; Salisbury MS. 252 noted in HMC *Salisbury*, xxi, p. 272.

13 T. Powell, *The Repertorie of Records* (London, 1631), p. 132; Hallam, *Domesday Book through Nine Centuries*, pp. 61, 116; E. M. Hallam, 'Annotations in Domesday Book since 1100', in A. Williams and R. W. H. Erskine (eds.), *Domesday Book Studies* (London, 1987), pp. 136–50, esp. p. 141.

14 R. B. Wernham, 'The Public Records in the Sixteenth and Seventeenth centuries', in L. Fox (ed.), *English Historical Scholarship in the Sixteenth and Seventeenth Centuries* (Oxford, 1956), pp. 11–30.

15 *Thirtieth Report of the Deputy Keeper of Public Records* (1869), app. vii, pp. 225–6.

16 Wernham, 'The Public Records', pp. 17–18.

17 Stowe MS. 543, ff. 55–58; M. McKisack, *Medieval History in the Tudor Age* (Oxford, 1971), pp. 75–82.

18 Ibid., pp. 77–8; E. M. Hallam, 'The Tower of London as a Record Office', *Archives*, xiv (1979), pp. 3–10, esp. pp. 5–6.

19 McKisack, *Medieval History*, p. 93.

20 P. Cain, 'Robert Smith and the Reform of the Archives of the City of London', *London Journal*, xiii (1987–8), pp. 3–16. My thanks to Mr Cain for discussions about Smith and his work.

21 Hearne, *Curious Discourses*, vol. i, introduction, p. iv.

22 K. Sharpe, *Sir Robert Cotton, 1586–1631: History and Politics in Early Modern England* (Oxford, 1979), p. 198; McKisack, *Medieval History*, pp. 155–69.

23 Examples of attendance lists of the Society, including Agarde's name, are in Harl. MS. 5177, f. 141; Cotton MSS. Cleopatra E. I, f. 11v; Faustina E. V, f. 108v. These manuscripts, plus Cotton Titus C. I and Stowe MS. 1045, all contain papers and notes by Agarde produced for the Society of Antiquaries, and are printed in Hearne, *Curious Discourses*.

24 Harl. MS. 6018 (catalogue of the Cottonian Library), ff. 155, 162, 165 and 176 lists some. On Agarde's loan of the Osney cartulary, see Colin G. C. Tite, '"Lost, stolen or strayed": a survey of manuscripts formerly in the Cotton library', *British Library Journal*, xviii (1992), p. 113, and reprinted below, p. 268.

25 Hearne, *Curious Discourses*, vol. ii, p. 160; McKisack, *Medieval History*, pp. 89–90; Sharpe, *Cotton*, pp. 22–3.

26 Cotton MS. Faustina E. V, ff. 15v–18, printed in T. Gale (ed.), *Registrum Honoris de Richmond* (London, 1722), app. ii.

27 Cotton MS. Vitellius C. IX, ff. 235–239v, printed in Hearne, *Curious Discourses*, vol. i, pp. 43–50, and in Gale, *Registrum*, app. i.

28 Cotton Tiberius A. VI (the *Inquisitio Eliensis*), f. 38, annotation and Bodleian MS. Top. gen. c. 22, f. 52, for Agarde's gift of the manuscript in 1609; Harl. MS. 6018, ff. 162, 165, for Agarde's later loan from Cotton.

29 Harl. MS. 6018, f. 176 (the manuscript of the *Dialogus*, known as 'Gervase of Tilbury', later passed from Agarde to Sir Fulke Greville). There are also copies of the *Dialogus* in both the Red Book and the Black Book of the Exchequer (P.R.O., E 164/2 and E 164/12). Agarde would have had ready access to both.

30 Below, nn. 60–1.

31 H. Spelman, *Archæologus. In Modum Glosarii*, vol. i (London, 1626), p. 220.

32 Lansdowne. MS. 310, f. 1.

33 Sharpe, *Cotton*, p. 24.

34 E.g. P.R.O., SP 14/71, no. 37; Hallam, *Domesday Book through Nine Centuries*, pp. 60–1, 212 and app. iv, nos. 5–10.

35 P.R.O., E 31/2 (Great Domesday), ff. 1v, 272r; Hallam, 'Annotations in Domesday Book', pp. 140–6, for a detailed discussion of these; C. Thorn, 'The Marginal Notes and Signs in Domesday Book', in Williams and Erskine, *Domesday Special Studies*, pp. 113–35, esp. pp. 133–4.

36 Hallam, *Domesday Book through Nine Centuries*, p. 117; below, nn. 58–9.

37 Bodleian MS. Top. gen. c. 22.

38 E.g. P.R.O., IND 1/17112.

39 Bodleian MS. Top. gen. c. 22, ff. 52, 53v.

40 Powell, *Repertorie*, p. 133.

41 The Great Domesday abstract is in the possession of Mr J. Hotson. The Little Domesday abstract is Harl. MS. 5167.

42 The watermark in both reinforces the late-16th

century date: cf. C. M. Briquet, *Les Filigranes, dictionnaire historique des marques du papier*, vol. ii (Geneva, 1977), p. 396, nos. 7210–11.

43 Hotson MS., f. 7; P.R.O., E 31/2, ff. 2v–5v.

44 Above, n. 38.

45 E.g. Hotson MS., f. 51v.

46 E.g. Ibid., f. 20v; Thorn, 'Marginal Notes', pp. 133–4.

47 Harl. MS. 5167, ff. 1, 18.

48 Hallam, *Domesday Book through Nine Centuries*, pp. 42–7.

49 Ibid., pp. 66–7.

50 Cotton MS. Faustina C. XI, ff. 61–160 (text), f. 160 (dating); R. A. Caldwell, 'Joseph Holand, Collector and Antiquary', *Modern Philology*, xl (1943), pp. 295–301, esp. p. 298.

51 Cotton MS. Julius C. I; *A Catalogue of the Manuscripts in the Cottonian Library Deposited in the British Museum*, vol. i (London, 1802), p. 8.

52 Lansdowne MS. 329.

53 P.R.O., PROB 10/323.

54 Harl. MS. 623; Hallam, *Domesday Book through Nine Centuries*, pp. 118–20.

55 P.R.O., SP 14/103, nos. 56–7.

56 P.R.O., E 31/2, f. o; Hallam, 'Annotations in Domesday Book', pp. 146–7.

57 Powell, *Repertorie*, p. 132.

58 Hallam, 'Annotations in Domesday Book', pp. 146–7.

59 Ibid., pp. 147–8, and eadem, *Domesday Book through Nine Centuries*, pp. 128–9.

60 Hearne, *Curious Discourses*; Hallam, *Domesday Book through Nine Centuries*, p. 130.

61 Gale, *Registrum Honoris de Richmond*, preface, p. xxxiii and apps. i–ii.

62 D. Bates, *A Bibliography of Domesday Book* (Woodbridge, 1985), p. 3, no. 103.

'LOST OR STOLEN OR STRAYED': A SURVEY OF MANUSCRIPTS FORMERLY IN THE COTTON LIBRARY

COLIN G. C. TITE

THE manuscript collection that was founded by Sir Robert Cotton in the 1580s passed by inheritance first to his son, Thomas, and then to his grandson, John. In 1702, on the death of John and in accordance with the intentions of Sir Robert, it became national property, and fifty years later it entered the British Museum as one of the foundation collections. This orderly succession, disturbed only by the damage wrought by fire in 1731, does not appear to provide occasion for the haemorrhaging that often occurs in a great collection on the death of its founder or the immediate heirs. In consequence, little attention has been given to the losses that the Cotton library suffered while in private ownership and, although a few instances are well known, the reputation of Sir Robert as a collector who was certainly acquisitive and perhaps greedy, and of his successors as men who regarded themselves as custodians of a holy relic, has conveyed the impression that the manuscript library remained substantially inviolate.

Yet volumes did leave the collection, and in significant numbers. The Cotton library was a working collection, certainly in Sir Robert's time although perhaps less so in that of his son and particularly his grandson. Moreover, the possession of books and papers which were not easily available, if at all, elsewhere gave the family importance and influence in the scholarship and politics of the time. Within those circles, manuscripts could be employed as the currency of influence and as a mark of favours done : Sir Robert Cotton certainly received books for these reasons and it would be surprising if he did not initiate such transactions himself. Considerations such as these point to a variety of reasons why his manuscripts might wander – through gift, exchange, loan leading to loss, to which might be added disposal of duplicates or of items of small interest, sometimes by sale.

It is by no means possible to explain the motivation for the alienation of every manuscript that the library lost. Neither the route nor the date is always clear, so that we often lack the types of information that might make it possible to estimate the importance of the manuscript to the library's owners. Moreover, we need to bear in mind that a volume that seems significant to us was not necessarily so to the Cottons, while a manuscript that they regarded as of primary importance may seem less so in the light of later scholarship. Nevertheless, a survey of manuscripts that strayed can tell us something about motivation and it can also give some insight into the habits of, particularly, Sir Robert Cotton himself as a collector.

Inevitably, in dealing, as we must, with a considerable number of manuscripts, there is a danger of missing the wood for the trees and I have therefore endeavoured to group together volumes that are linked in some way by common themes.[1] As significant numbers of manuscripts left the Cotton library for other early-seventeenth-century collectors or for collections that were formed or active at that time, we shall begin with these, dealing with them in broad chronological order.

I

A decade after Cotton began his collecting activities, Sir Thomas Bodley resolved to devote his retirement from affairs of state to re-creating the public library at Oxford. To this end, as is well known, he solicited donations and benefactions, and Cotton was one of the early contributors. As far as we can tell, the very first gift of books that Cotton made to anyone was his donation to the Bodleian Library in 1602–3. The gift consisted of about a dozen volumes which, with the exception of a commentary on the canticles (Harl. MS. 988) to which we shall return, are listed in the Library's Register of Benefactors[2] under the year 1603 and are still at Oxford. Of these eleven, five bear Cotton's *ex dono* inscription, usually in the form of a *votiva ara*, with the wording 'GENIO LOCI BODLEO RESTITV. BONO PUBLICO ROBERT: COTTON CONNINGTON: HAC LL.M.DD.' or minor variations of this, and the date 1602.[3]

The volumes carrying this inscription are MS. Bodl. 630 (*SC* 1953), a fifteenth-century volume of theological treatises originally from Syon Abbey; Bodl. 116 (*SC* 1978), an early-thirteenth-century manuscript of St Gregory's *Liber Pastoralis*[4] and the *De Institutione Novitiorum* of Hugh of St Victor (undated inscription); Auct.F.2.27 (*SC* 2310) an early-fifteenth-century Italian manuscript of Lactantius's *Divinae Institutiones*; Bodl. 422 (*SC* 2321), a late-twelfth-century volume of the 'Homilies' of Origen; and Bodl. 336 (*SC* 2336), an early-fourteenth-century *Legenda Sanctorum* (of Jacobus de Voragine) from Christ Church, Canterbury. Four further manuscripts do not bear the full *ex dono* inscription but have some version of 'Ro: Cotton Conningtonensis', with or without a date. They are Bodl. 56 (*SC* 1995) a late-fifteenth-century copy of Werner Rolewinck's *Paradisus Conscientiae*; Bodl. Or. 46 (*SC* 2606), a manuscript in Hebrew of a part of the Old Testament; Auct.D.2.14 (*SC* 2698), the so-called 'Gospels of "St Augustine"', a precious manuscript written in Italy in the seventh century; and Bodl. Or. 135 (*SC* 3086), a volume of miscellaneous writings, including grammars and fables, in Hebrew. The two remaining volumes listed in the Register of Benefactors – almost certainly correctly identified as Bodl. 343 (*SC* 2406), a twelfth-century manuscript of sermons in Old English and Latin, and Bodl. Or. 24 (*SC* 3002), prayers in Hebrew – have no inscriptions.[5]

The history as a Cotton stray of another manuscript, Harl. MS. 988, a commentary on the canticles, requires rather fuller consideration. Although it is not to be found in the Register of Benefactors, it possesses the *votiva ara* and full inscription dated 1602, as in the first five manuscripts already discussed. However, despite these indications that it was intended to form part of Cotton's gift, a different history has been constructed for it. In correspondence with Humfrey Wanley in 1714, Thomas Hearne claimed, although without citing any evidence, that it had originally been donated to Oxford by Duke Humfrey and that 'Sr Robert gave it to Sr Thomas Bodley, to be restored again to its place', adding however that he was 'apt to think that thro' multiplicity of other business it was neglected to be brought' to Oxford. In his reply Wanley disputed Hearne's claim that the manuscript had ever belonged to Duke Humfrey, but Macray in his *Annals of the Bodleian Library* lent further support to Hearne's contention, though on the distinctly slender ground that as two treatises on the canticles had been listed in Humfrey's gift this manuscript must have been one of them. Macray also maintained that the inscription in the manuscript was 'intended to commemorate his [i.e. Cotton's] returning it to the University Library in 1602', presumably (and, I suggest, erroneously) taking the verb *restituo* to refer to the restoration of the book rather than the restoration of the library.[6]

Given the close similarity between the inscription in Harl. 988 and that in the group of five manuscripts which undoubtedly formed part of Cotton's gift, the chance must surely be that Harl. 988 was intended as a part of that gift. Why, then, is it not to be found in the Register of Benefactors? Could it be that it arrived separately and therefore did not earn a listing?[7] We can at present do no more than speculate but if the manuscript did indeed reach Oxford it was not to remain there: it passed into the hands of Edward Stillingfleet (1635–99), bishop of Worcester, from whose collection it was bought by Robert Harley in 1707.[8]

Apart from pointing up the history of Harl. MS. 988, some emphasis has been given to the *ex dono* and other inscriptions in these manuscripts because they make it quite clear that at this period in his life Cotton wished to be known as 'of Conington', the location of his principal manor.[9] In the past, it has often been stated that, on the accession of James I in 1603, he added the name 'Bruceus' after his signature to indicate his kinship with the new Scottish Stuart king and the presence of this embellishment has sometimes been used as a guide to the date of his acquisition of a manuscript. The donation to the Bodleian, of course, antedated James's accession but as will be seen later Cotton's practice was not as consistent as has been suggested: in particular, 'Conningtonensis' was to have a half-life.[10]

Cotton's gift to the Bodleian Library was of no low quality and it is worth asking whether he is likely to have gathered these manuscripts specifically for the purpose of this donation or whether he already had them on his shelves. While there is no firm evidence either way, the chances probably favour the former, at least for those with the *votiva ara* or with no inscription at all. None of the volumes has a Cotton binding[11] and, with the exception of Bodl. Or. 46, the Hebrew manuscript of part of the Old Testament, which has a contents table in Cotton's hand, they exhibit virtually no annotations which might suggest ownership by him over any length of time.[12] On the other hand, Henry Savile, provost of Eton, in a letter to Cotton, probably dating from this time and arranging for Bodley to accompany Savile on a visit to Cotton, jestingly advised Cotton to put out of sight any books he would be loath to part with.[13]

Several more former Cotton volumes were accessions to the Bodleian collection in the early seventeenth century. MS. Bodl. 181 (*SC* 2081) must have been one of Cotton's first manuscripts: his signature, a plain unadorned 'Robertus Cotton', followed by '18/1588/19/1589', a record of his age in those years, is clearly visible on the first folio. The volume is a fifteenth-century copy in vellum, chiefly consisting of the *De Regimine Principum* of Egidius Romanus and the pseudo-Aristotelian *Secretum Secretorum* (of the second of which Cotton was later to own another copy, BL, Arundel MS. 59, discussed in section VI, below). It is not known when Cotton parted with it but the manuscript was given to the Bodleian, perhaps in 1612, not by Cotton but by the then Somerset Herald, Robert Treswell.[14]

The second is a particularly important manuscript. Auct.D.4.2. (*SC* 3055) is a copy of the psalter and canticles written in the mid-thirteenth century in The Netherlands. Its rare binding, with pictures of the Virgin and the Annunciation in silver covered in translucent enamel and surrounded by a border of silver-gilt foliage, is possibly contemporary and is the only example of its type in the Bodleian.[15] How Cotton acquired the manuscript we do not know but its subsequent history is better documented. Two inscriptions tell the story. On f. 4r Cotton has written 'Doctissimo Medico et amico Willi° Butler Cantab: Robertus Cotton Coningtonens. / LL. ·MM. D·D. / 1614', while the gift to the Bodleian on 15 July 1648 'ex dono nobilissimae D. Annae Sadler uxoris Radulphi Sadler de Stonden in Comitatu Harford Armigeri' is recorded on f. 3v. Butler was the famous Cambridge doctor, renowned for both his skill and his eccentricity, who was called in to treat Cotton when he was ill at Cambridge in 1614: no doubt the book was a token of gratitude.[16]

It has long been recognized that Bodl. MS. Laud Misc. 509, a translation into Anglo-Saxon of parts of the Hexateuch, together with Ælfric's homily on Judges, which was given by Archbishop Laud to the Bodleian in 1639, once belonged to Sir Robert Cotton.[17] What requires further investigation, however, is the route by which it strayed from his collection. The volume originally belonged to the Royal library, at which time it also incorporated a life of St Guthlac. Cotton separated out the Guthlac at some point between about 1603 and 1606 and used it to form one of the three parts of a new volume he was creating, now Vespasian D. XXI.[18] Much later, he lent what is now Laud Misc. 509 to William Lisle, the Cambridge scholar, and Neil Ker suggested that, as a number of other manuscripts went from Lisle to Laud, it was this loan which explained Cotton's loss of the manuscript.[19] However, other evidence (which Ker also noted) renders this unlikely. The loan to Lisle was outstanding at 23 April 1621 but there survives an extract, made by Richard James, Cotton's librarian, from the manuscript when it was clearly still in the Cotton library. As James was certainly not working for Cotton before April 1621 the manuscript must have returned from this loan to Lisle, to be lost at a later date. This might even have occurred through a second loan to Lisle: he died in 1637 and Laud's inscription of ownership in the manuscript is dated 1638.[20]

Three volumes now among the Digby manuscripts at the Bodleian also passed through the Cotton library. The greater part, and probably the whole, of MS. Digby 76 (*SC* 1677), a copy of the works of Roger Bacon and others, belonged from 1556 to John Dee, from whose library Cotton no doubt obtained it. It is entered towards the end of the Cotton library catalogue of the early 1620s, Harl. MS. 6018, and the inventory number there assigned to it (no. 405) is still to be seen on f. i[v]. The contents list on f. iii[r] is in the hand of Richard James. It was presented to the Bodleian Library by Sir Kenelm Digby in 1634, together with his other manuscripts, and may have been part of a transaction between Cotton and Digby, possibly involving Thomas Allen of Oxford, of which no record survives.[21]

Digby 96 (*SC* 1697), a twelfth-century manuscript from Abingdon Abbey of Godwin's *Meditationes*, was also owned by Cotton in the early 1620s. It, too, is entered in his catalogue in Harl. MS. 6018 and its inventory number there, '359', can still just be read at the top margin of its first folio. As with Digby 76, we do not know how it reached Digby from Cotton but it was included in the gift to the Bodleian in 1634.[22]

Finally, Digby 178 (*SC* 1721), a late-medieval collection of scientific treatises, was formed by Cotton, probably in the mid-1620s, from parts of two manuscripts that had belonged to John Dee.[23] Cotton had Richard James write the contents list which still remains on f. 1r and shortly afterwards gave the manuscript to Thomas Allen who bequeathed it to Digby in 1632 who, in turn, gave it to the Bodleian Library two years later.[24]

II

As part of a complicated exchange of manuscripts with Patrick Young, the Royal librarian, in about 1616, a number of Cottonian volumes entered the Royal library.[25] Cotton's 'Horrac very old with a gloss 8[o]' is now BL, Royal 15 B. VII, a twelfth-century manuscript,[26] while his 'Eutropius and paulus Diaconus. Foll.', another twelfth-century manuscript, is Royal 15 C. VI.[27] 'Philistratus grece fair wrighten. 4[o]' is now Royal 16 C. XXIII, a fifteenth-century manuscript in Greek which Cotton had acquired from 'Mr Tomson', recently identified as the Biblical scholar, Richard Thomson, who died in 1613.[28] The identity of 'Cesar Comentary Foll fair' is not completely certain but the entry very likely refers to Royal 15 C. XV.[29] 'Constantini Manassis historia Greca Carmine. 8[o]', also described as 'in paper',[30] is probably Royal 16 C. VII. Although without illumination or other decoration, this fifteenth-century manuscript, which is indeed on paper, is quite fairly written; it is also the sole copy of this work now in the Royal library. Finally in this group, 'A greek Manuscript in paper de Anima etc. Foll.' is probably Royal 16 C. XXV, a sixteenth-century copy of Aristotle's treatise, together with extracts from Plato, and the only volume to answer this description now to be found in the Royal library.[31]

266

It can also, I believe, be demonstrated that part of Royal 13 A. XXI once belonged to Cotton. For some time, scholars have known that the copy of the *Imago Mundi* and two chronicles in French which are now ff. 12r–150r of Royal 13 A. XXI and the English chronicle found in ff. 2r–61v of Cotton Vespasian B. XI were once united and that the original, combined volume came from Hagnaby Abbey, Lincolnshire.[32] What was not understood was how and when the division occurred. However, two entries in the transaction between Cotton and Young of *c.* 1616 appear to provide the explanation and to establish beyond doubt that Cotton was responsible. In one part of that list he records 'A Chronicle part of Imago Mundi 4[0]' as a 'Book that I had of Mr Young', while in another section, headed 'To be given back', he enters 'Imago Mundi in Black Valur and Bossed'.[33] The first entry must surely refer to the combined volume of which Cotton retained the chronicle now in Vespasian B. XI, the second entry to the part of it that he returned, now in Royal 13 A. XXI.[34] This transaction, of course, illustrates the lengths to which Cotton would go to secure manuscripts he wanted – in this case an item very much in line with his well-known wish to gather materials related to the history of England – but it also sheds light on another.

These two sections of Vespasian B. XI and Royal 13 A. XXI are not the only material to link the two manuscripts. The copies of, *inter alia*, the *Vita Edwardi Confessoris* in ff. 84r–125*v of B. XI and of Jerome in ff. 151r–192v of 13 A. XXI once formed part of a manuscript from Kirkham Priory.[35] As it is hardly possible that the Kirkham manuscript would have been divided between the same two volumes as the Hagnaby manuscript unless the same hand were responsible for both operations, it seems safe to conclude that it was Cotton who was making the division – and at much the same time as he was at work on the Hagnaby manuscript. Indeed, this seems the only possible conclusion, for if Cotton were not responsible it would be necessary to argue that the Hagnaby and Kirkham manuscripts were already bound together in the Royal library before he removed his sections, an altogether unlikely state of affairs.[36] If this argument carries conviction, it follows that ff. 151r–192v of Royal 13 A. XXI once belonged to Sir Robert Cotton or at least passed through his hands, while his reason for retaining the *Vita Edwardi* is similar to that underlying his acquisition of the chronicle from Hagnaby.[37]

Lastly, in this section, it will be convenient to deal here with another manuscript, 'Fortescue in paper de legibus Anglie', which was received by Cotton in this same transaction with Young, although, unlike those already discussed, it was not to return to the Royal library. There is no copy now in the Cottonian collection of this well-known treatise by Sir John Fortescue in praise of the English laws and Cotton's manuscript has not hitherto been identified, but there can be no doubt that it is now Cambridge University Library, MS. Ff.5.22, a fifteenth-century volume, written on paper, with the signature, 'Ro: Cotton', on its first folio.[38] It is not known how or when it left his library.

III

Another exchange, probably occurring at much the same date as the transaction with

Young and with equally obvious benefits to Cotton, explains the departure from his collection of the cartulary of Osney Abbey, which is now in the Chapter Library, Christ Church, Oxford. According to a note on f. i^r in Cotton's hand and signed 'Robert Cotton', he 'delivered [it] to Mr Phillip King Esquier Auditor of...Christchurch...' and 'had in a thankfull remembrance from them a Book called Annales Burtonensis'. Cotton's leather binding survives on the cartulary, although attempts have been made to deface the coat of arms, while the Burton annals are now the first article in Vespasian E. III. The transaction must have occurred between 1612 and 1621, probably towards the end of that period: although Cotton himself does not help us by adding only '31 May' to his record of the exchange, what is clearly the Christ Church manuscript was on loan from him to Arthur Agarde on 18 July 1612, while the Burton annals had reached him before 23 April 1621 when they were lent to Richard Montague, the future bishop of Norwich. By then, if not a good deal earlier, Cotton also owned another, older version of the Osney cartulary, now in Vitellius E. XV, which had the advantage, not shared by the Christ Church manuscript, of incorporating some English chronicle material in its first few folios.[39]

A few years previously, Cotton had given the cartulary of Luffield Priory, Northants, now Cambridge University Library, MS. Ee.1.1, to his friend and fellow collector, the antiquary Francis Tate who, as a native of the county, can be presumed to have had a particular interest in the house. The *ex dono* inscription, in Tate's hand, is on the first folio, together with the date, 28 November 1609.[40] Later, some of Tate's notebooks were to enter Cotton's library.

IV

James Ussher, later archbishop of Armagh, was a regular user of and frequent borrower from Cotton's library in the early years of the seventeenth century. While Cotton and Bodley were building up their libraries, Ussher was engaged on a similar task – soliciting donations for the newly established foundation at Trinity College, Dublin.[41] This and Ussher's own interests account for a number of manuscripts that left Cotton's hands, and it is striking how many of them relate to the teachings of the fourteenth-century theologian, John Wyclif. Of these manuscripts, TCD MS. 244 (C.3.12) has one of the better-documented histories. This volume of tracts by Wyclif was given by John Bale in 1552 to Francis Russell, afterwards second earl of Bedford.[42] In his will, Russell (d. 1585) left his Wycliffite books to William Cecil; thus the latter may well have owned this manuscript before it reached Cotton who wrote his name, with the addition of 'Bruceus', at the foot of the first folio.[43] We do not know when the manuscript was transferred to Ussher but it must be the first item mentioned in a letter that Ussher wrote to Camden on 30 October 1606:

Sir *Robert Cotton* made half a promise of some Manuscripts unto our Library: if he would be pleased to spare *Wickliffe's Homilies* and his *Lanthorn of Light*, with another volume, wherein the examination of *Thorpe* is, it should very gratefully be accepted...[44]

268

There is at present no evidence to show whether Cotton granted Ussher's second request, but there is no doubt that he owned at least one copy of the 'Lanterne', which he had obtained from Robert Beale, the Elizabethan diplomat and antiquary (d. 1601), and which he may have lost in consequence of a loan to Robert Bowyer.[45] Neither of the two surviving copies of the 'Lanterne' – Harl. MSS. 2324 and 6613 – bears evidence of either Cotton's or Beale's ownership but, of the two, perhaps Harl. 2324 is the more likely to have been Beale's copy.[46]

The third volume sought by Ussher must be Bodl. MS. Rawlinson C. 208 (*SC* 12070), the only surviving Middle English copy of the examination of the Oxford Wycliffite, William Thorpe, before Archbishop Arundel in 1407. This manuscript was certainly owned by Cotton – 'Rob. Cotton Bruceus 1599' is written at the foot of f. 1r – and given its rarity and the fact that a number of Ussher manuscripts are to be found among the Rawlinson collection it is very likely that Cotton did indeed grant Ussher's request and that this is the manuscript that he gave.[47]

Ussher also obtained from or through Cotton two or three manuscripts previously owned by Henry Savile of Banke. The first is now TCD 215 (B.5.4), a volume containing anti-Wycliffite tracts. Cotton entered this on ff. 133r + v (no. 374) of the catalogue of his manuscripts in Harl. MS. 6018, which he started to draw up in 1621[48] and he also wrote the list of contents on f. 1r. The second volume, TCD 189 (B.2.4), is an early-fifteenth-century manuscript of the *Summa in Questionibus Armenorum* of the eminent Oxford scholar and archbishop of Armagh, Richard FitzRalph, one of the influences on Wyclif, and of the *Summa Theologica* of Henry of Ghent. It has long been known that this manuscript passed from Savile to Ussher and thence to Trinity College, but that Cotton was the intermediary, and perhaps for a time the owner, is established by the summary of contents which he has written on both the flyleaf and the first folio.[49]

Another former Savile manuscript may well have been split up by Cotton. Cleopatra B. VI, one of his 'made-up' volumes, contains two articles which came to Cotton from Savile: ff. 206r–233v, a copy of the *Elucidarium* of Honorius Augustodunensis, had been a separate volume in Savile's library; ff. 190r–205v, which consists of Hugh of Fouilloy's *De Duodecim Abusionibus Seculi*, followed by a treatise on the Virgin and by prayers in verse, is a fragment of another Savile manuscript, of which the remainder is TCD 301 (C.3.19).[50] The juxtaposition of these two Savile manuscripts in Cleopatra B. VI must therefore make it likely that it was Cotton who was responsible for dismembering the second volume, then to pass on the balance, a manuscript which opens with a treatise on the Seven Deadly Sins, to Ussher. If this is correct, we are here dealing with another example of the activity described above (section II) in connection with Vespasian B. XI and Royal 13 A. XXI. Dismemberments such as these, when taken together, prompt a wider reflection. Even the most cursory examination of the manuscripts owned by late-sixteenth-century collectors shows (what is widely recognized) that quite frequently those volumes suffered the fate of being divided, one part going to Cotton and other sections arriving at a different destination. What has not so often been asked is how and when this happened. However, as groups of these manuscripts are studied together, it is becoming increasingly likely that Cotton will be seen to have played a key role, as agent in dividing and passing on material as well as in keeping it.[51]

A related theme may underlie the story of the next manuscript. It has been suggested that Cotton owned the fragment of the chronicle of Martinus Polonus and the so-called 'Annals of St Mary's, Dublin', now ff. 1r–2r and 2v–13v of TCD 175 (E.3.11).[52] Although there is no evidence in the manuscript itself to establish Cotton's ownership, James Ware, the Irish antiquary, says that extracts that he made in the 1620s, now in Add. MS. 4787, were taken from a copy of the 'Annals' in Cotton's library, recording it as having an *explicit* which agrees with that in TCD 175. However, in letters of 1627 and 1629 to Cotton, Ware adds a complicating twist, asking him to procure the use of some Irish annals then in the possession of George Carew, earl of Totnes. If this is – as seems likely – the same manuscript as that in TCD 175, it may be that Cotton was therefore merely the handling agent rather than the owner.[53] On the other hand, it is interesting to note that bound with the chronicle and annals in TCD 175 are two further booklets – a volume of saints' lives and a copy of Richard FitzRalph's *De Pauperie Salvatoris*. While the presence of an early pressmark of Trinity College at the beginning of the saints' lives suggests that the component parts were brought together only after they reached Dublin, the fact that Ussher had earlier been interested in Cotton's Wycliffite material may be suggestive.[54]

Two more manuscripts remain to be considered in this group. Cotton certainly passed on to Ussher a late-fourteenth-century manuscript of the *Eulogium Historiarum*, now TCD 497 (E.2.26), which he had been given by Camden in 1609 and of which, by the early 1620s, he had another copy (now Galba E. VII).[55] However, his ownership of another volume, TCD 176 (E.5.28), can almost certainly be ruled out. This manuscript of Goscelin's lives of saints has been tentatively assigned to him on the basis of an inscription in pencil, 'Sum Cottoni', on its second folio. While the hand is probably of the seventeenth century, the form of words is a wholly unusual indication of Cotton's ownership. Moreover, although the manuscript was given to Trinity College by Ussher, it had previously appeared in a list of books belonging to that library in February 1601. Firmer evidence of a connection with Cotton is therefore needed before we should take the inscription too seriously.[56]

V

Four manuscripts passed from Cotton to his friend and fellow antiquary, Sir Simonds D'Ewes, and thence to Robert Harley. The first, Harl. MS. 105, a twelfth-century life of St Augustine by Goscelin, had formed part of an exchange of manuscripts between the two men in March 1625: a record of this transaction is to be found on f. 1r of the Harleian volume and in a somewhat ambiguous note among the Cotton loans memoranda.[57] At much the same time, between Christmas 1624 and Lady Day 1625, D'Ewes bought for two shillings, presumably directly from Cotton, a late-thirteenth-century copy of the gospels and psalter, originally from Ely and now Harl. MS. 547.[58]

The other two manuscripts changed hands at unknown dates. They are Harl. MS. 513, a treatise on commodities and money written in 1610 by the merchant, Gerard Malynes, and Harl. MS. 525, a fifteenth-century volume of English poetry.[59] The last three of these manuscripts carry Cotton's signature, in various forms, on the first folio.[60]

None of the four volumes is listed in Harl. MS. 6018, the catalogue which Cotton began in 1621,[61] and, while that catalogue is not complete, it is unlikely that all four would have escaped listing if Cotton had owned them at the time. The probability is, therefore, that – at least in the case of the two volumes which passed to D'Ewes in 1624–5 – Cotton did not long retain them in his possession, perhaps an indication that neither was of any lasting interest to him.[62]

VI

At the end of the 1620s Cotton lent some of his choicest manuscripts to the Earl Marshal, Thomas Howard, earl of Arundel. Cotton had been associated with Arundel since 1614 and was firmly under his patronage from 1618, while in 1625 and again in 1628 he was returned to Parliament for Howard seats. The two men shared scholarly interests and Arundel had certainly been borrowing from Cotton's library since 1621: he was clearly in a position to gain access to its finest resources.[63]

During the library's closure in and after 1629, in a list probably prepared to take account of borrowings extant at that time, Arundel had in his possession seven manuscripts, at least two of which became certain strays. These were 'An Auncient Coppie of the Psalms. literis maiusculis, in latin, and pictures...', the famous Utrecht Psalter, a manuscript of outstanding importance, and 'A booke in a large fol thine, parte of a Massebooke lymmed faire, haveinge the Lord Lovells picture in the beginninge...', which is undoubtedly the Lovel Lectionary, now Harl. MS. 7026. A third borrowing, 'An Auncient Coppie of Genesis in Greeke in Capitall letters and pictures...', is the well-known Cotton Genesis, Otho B. VI, which was lost to the library at this time and repurchased by Sir John Cotton half a century later, only to be almost completely destroyed in the fire of 1731.[64]

The remaining items in the loan to Arundel will be dealt with shortly but at this point we should pause to consider a feature of the Utrecht Psalter which, it will now be argued, throws light on the state of development of the Cotton library at the time of this loan. The rearrangement of the collection under pressmarks named after early Roman emperors was probably begun in the late 1620s and, interrupted by the closure of the library, was to be completed in the 1630s. The change is reflected in the two contemporary catalogues, the dates of which have been established from other evidence in an attempt to pinpoint this evolution.[65]

The dating of these catalogues and of the rearrangement of the library can, however, now be confirmed from another direction: the psalter has inscribed on the front pastedown its Emperor pressmark, Claudius C. VII, in a hand which is certainly that of one of Sir Robert Cotton's scribes. The existence of this pressmark establishes that a part

271

at least of the Emperor system was in place before the psalter was lent to Arundel, always providing that he did not return it to the library for it to be lost in a subsequent loan. This last point is of some interest as the circumstances and timing of the loss of the manuscript to Cotton have been the subject of debate. A century ago Walter de Gray Birch suggested that Arundel might have returned the manuscript and this possibility has been examined in the recent facsimile edition of the psalter by Koert van der Horst and Jacobus Engelbregt.[66] However, their conclusion that the loan to Arundel was the occasion of the manuscript's alienation from the Cotton library carries even more conviction when set in the context of the remainder of the Arundel loan. As already stated, the Lovel Lectionary, Harl. 7026, was no doubt lost in consequence of this loan and the Genesis was long absent. We may now return to the remaining items in Arundel's borrowing: these will provide further supporting evidence for the contention that the Utrecht Psalter was lost at this time and, therefore, for the claim that the rearrangement of the library was then in progress.

Four more manuscripts were listed in the memorandum: 'A booke of the order of the Garter St Michaell the Golden Fleece Rolles of Precedency and other things…folio', 'Insulae Archipelagi descriptio and divers other tracts…8ᵛᵒ', 'The Coronation of K. Hen: 3. Mr Thinnes booke of the Earle Marshalls Office wᵗʰ theire Armes in Mettell dedicated to the Earle of Nottingham, with the Statuts of the knights of Jerusalem…8ᵛᵒ', and 'Discourses of State wherein there is in my Lord Treasorer Burleighes hand A meditation of the Raigne of Queene Eliz:…folio'. With the exception of the second item, Christoforo Buondelmonti's description of the Greek islands, now Vespasian A. XIII, none of these manuscripts is now in the Cotton library and they seem to have disappeared altogether.[67] It is almost inconceivable that Sir Robert Cotton would have been willing to part with such important manuscripts: whatever he may have felt about the theological volumes, he would certainly have been interested in the historical and heraldic manuscripts. The probability is that his death in 1631 while the library was still closed, followed by Arundel's own death abroad in 1646, must have a substantial bearing on the matter. We can therefore safely conclude, from an examination of these loans, that accident as well as intention played its part in the alienation of Cotton manuscripts.

Apart from manuscripts which strayed from the Cotton library as a consequence of this loan, a further three or four manuscripts in the collection formed by Thomas Howard, earl of Arundel, and now at the British Library, once belonged to Cotton. To the first of these, some uncertainty attaches. Arundel MS. 16, a twelfth-century manuscript of the life of St Dunstan by Osbern, has been annotated and supplemented by Archbishop Parker's secretary, John Joscelyn, a number of whose books Cotton received. This may well be one of them but unfortunately the erased signature on the first folio has been treated with a reagent; while the style could certainly be Cotton's, all that can now be read is 'R [   ]on'.[68]

However, both Arundel 20 and Arundel 59 undoubtedly belonged to Cotton. Arundel 20 is a fifteenth-century manuscript of the life of St Catherine by John Capgrave, together with treatises on the Ten Commandments and the Seven Deadly Sins. Once owned by Cotton's friend and fellow antiquary, George Carew, whose signature is found on the first folio, it was in Cotton's hands by the early 1620s: our knowledge of his ownership is derived from the detailed entry for this manuscript in Harl. MS. 6018 (f. 77r, no. 162) but it is not yet known when he lost it.[69]

Arundel 59 is a copy in paper of Thomas Hoccleve's poem, *De Regimine Principum*, followed by John Lydgate's *Secretum Secretorum* (of the second of which Cotton had previously owned another manuscript, MS. Bodl. 181, discussed in section I). The manuscript has Cotton's signature and the date, 1610, at the foot of the first folio, while the 'Jo: Starkey' who signs at the top of the same leaf probably provides the clue to Cotton's possession of the volume. Starkey was also a former owner of Cotton Julius E. VI, a manuscript which came to Cotton via Henry Savile of Banke; if this Starkey is the man who was father of Ralph Starkey, a close associate of Cotton, he died in about 1613.[70]

Although nothing is yet known about the route by which these three manuscripts strayed, the path followed by another Arundel manuscript can be plotted with greater certainty, to show rather appropriately an intimate personal possession of one of Cotton's patrons, the earl of Northampton, passing through his hands to another, the earl of Arundel, who was also Northampton's great-nephew. The clue is provided by a loan to Francis Fowler, secretary to the Spanish ambassador, Count Gondomar, of the 'Prayers of my lord of Northampton in velom and bound in whitt velom'. Apart from the binding, the description accords precisely with the book of prayers in Northampton's own hand which is now Arundel MS. 300. Cotton presumably received it on Northampton's death in 1614. Fowler himself died in Spain in 1619 and, while it is possible that the manuscript was never returned by him, it is interesting that it was at much this time that Cotton was working to secure Arundel's patronage.[71]

The final manuscript to be considered in this group is the Glastonbury cartulary, 'Secretum Abbatis', now Bodl. MS. Wood empt. I (*SC* 8589) and formerly in the Arundel collection. According to Sir Frederic Madden, it was once owned by Cotton and it is certainly true that his library possessed a 'booke of Glassenbury', while the term 'book', as used in this manner in his loans memoranda, normally indicates a monastic register. This Cotton volume was lent to William Seymour, earl of Hertford, in June 1638 and to John Selden, probably at much the same time, and although the record of the loan to Selden has been deleted, doubtless indicating the return of the manuscript, that to Hertford has not.[72] Moreover, Ussher tells us quite independently, in notes also made in 1638, that the 'Secretorum Domini Abbatis' was then in the library of the earl of Arundel,[73] so that, on grounds of dating, it is just possible that MS. Wood empt. I once belonged to the Cotton library. On the other hand, there is nothing in the manuscript itself to confirm this and, as the volume had been owned in the sixteenth century by a previous member of the Howard family, Madden's proposition should surely be treated with some scepticism.[74]

Another member of the Howard clan was also an intimate of the Cottons. Lord William Howard was Arundel's uncle and Northampton's nephew, and one of his daughters, Margaret, married Sir Robert Cotton's son, Thomas. Lord William shared scholarly interests with Sir Robert and books passed between the two men. It is very probable that he would have received some of Cotton's manuscripts but so far only one likely candidate has been identified. This is National Library of Australia, Canberra, MS. 1097/41, a late-sixteenth-century manuscript of Gregory Martin's *Roma Sancta*, an account of the churches and other holy places of Rome. Martin had been tutor to Lord William Howard but left for Douai in 1569 or 1570 when the boy was barely seven years old. Later, at Rheims, Martin worked on the English translation of the Bible and he also spent time in Rome. The manuscript of *Roma Sancta* was completed in 1581, shortly before his death in the following year.

G. B. Parks, printing the work for the first time twenty years ago, attempted to establish the wanderings of the only surviving manuscript, and notes that John Pits, in his *De Rebus Anglicis* published in 1619, records it as being at Dieulouard in Lorraine, a Benedictine house founded in 1608. After this it disappears from sight, to reappear in 1832 in the possession of the Catholic Lords Clifford of Chudleigh, Devon.[75] However, Parks was unaware of Cotton's likely role in the story. In a list of books 'formerly lent out…and…not receaved back this 20 May 1617' Cotton notes 'Gregory Marten his discription of Rom in paper new wrighten, and thick. a book of not. Foll'. The borrower was Lord William Howard and another of Cotton's several references to the book establishes that it was still out on loan to him four years later.[76] Given Martin's previous association with Lord William, the latter's interest in the book is obvious as also is the possibility that he would have wished to retain it. Moreover, the apparent conflict between the date of Cotton's loan of 1617 and Pits's reference to it in his work of 1619 is easily resolved: his book, published posthumously, was completed in 1613, three years before his death.[77] Unless, therefore, there once existed other copies of the manuscript, Cotton must have received the book from Dieulouard at some point between 1608 and 1617, possibly to satisfy a direct request from Lord William.[78] Further light may in due course be thrown on the history of this manuscript when the hand which annotates it, challenging certain of its statements, is firmly identified,[79] but for the present it seems probable that the volume now in Australia is that which once belonged to Sir Robert Cotton.

Lord William's son, Sir William Howard, inherited some of his father's scholarly interests and was also a borrower from the Cotton library when Sir Thomas owned it.[80] He must have been responsible for the removal of the manuscript which is now Add. MS. 15673, a volume of *c.* 1500 which opens with a sermon of St John Chrysostom and continues with the *Speculum Regis Edwardi tertii* of Simon Islip.[81] There are two main reasons for assigning this volume to the Cotton collection: firstly, it has a contents table in the hand of Richard James, who was the family's librarian from about 1625 and who wrote many such *elenchi* in its manuscripts;[82] and, secondly, among the Cottonian memoranda there is a record of a loan on 11 May 1640 to Sir William Howard of a book containing '6 tracts. whereof the second is Speculum Regis Edwardi 3[tii] per Simonem Islep...'.[83] As the Howard loan is not deleted, it is more than likely that it explains this loss from the Cotton collection (particularly as the entry for another volume borrowed by him at the same time has been scored through), but, much more significantly, Richard James's *elenchus* to Add. MS. 15673 enumerates six articles, of which the *Speculum* is the second.

A further point should be made now about Add. MS. 15673, although the matter will be considered again later. While there is no doubt that the manuscript was still in the library in 1640 it had not been allocated a pressmark in accordance with the Emperor system, despite the fact that this arrangement was apparently by then fully in place.[84]

VIII

We now need to turn our attention to manuscripts which did not go directly to the well-known early-seventeenth-century collectors or to the collections that were formed or in use at that time. Of the remaining stray manuscripts, some were at a later date to enter the great national collections; others were dispersed more widely.

First there is a group of seven manuscripts, largely products of the sixteenth or seventeenth centuries, which are either heraldic in content or connection, or which were designed for ceremonial or commemorative purposes.

Bodl. MS. Ashmole 765, a painted, neatly written manuscript composed in 1585 by William Smith, later Rouge Dragon, and entitled 'The Vale Royall of England, or, Countie Pallatine of Chester', once belonged to Sir Robert Cotton. As recorded on its title page, Cotton's son Thomas gave it to Roger Norton, probably for publication. The eventual edition, by Daniel King in 1656, was made from this manuscript and Elias Ashmole later bought the original from the arms painter, Sylvanus Morgan.[85]

Folger Shakespeare Library, Washington DC, MS. V.a.199, is another manuscript by the same William Smith. It is an account of abuses committed by arms painters to the prejudice of the Office of Arms, a matter of concern in the late sixteenth century, and one that would also have interested Cotton, whose signature is at the foot of f. 1r. The small volume is bound in contemporary cream vellum with gilt decorations. According to a note on the flyleaf, it was in the hands of Peter Le Neve, Norroy King of Arms, in 1704 but by what route it arrived there is unknown.[86]

A volume of historical miscellanea, now Add. MS. 4712, is, despite a few later additions, largely Cotton's creation: many of its articles are written by a scribe who undoubtedly worked for him.[87] His signature, 'Robertus Cottonus Conningtonensis', dated 1602, is on f. 3r preceded on f. 1r by that of Sir Richard St George as Clarenceux, a post to which he was appointed in 1623. It is likely that the manuscript changed hands at around that date for there is a loan to St George, outstanding in 1621, of 'A Book of the Orders in Court in velom bound and divers other things...in $4^{[o]}$', which matches very well ff. 3r–22r of the volume.[88]

A further volume, strongly heraldic in both content and provenance, is Add. MS. 6113, late-fifteenth- and sixteenth-century collections relating to royal and noble creations, christenings and coronations. In part the work of William Colbarne, York Herald from 1565, it was bought by Cotton from the arms painter, Jacob Chaloner, who had it to dispose of among the books of William Dethick, Garter, who died in 1612.[89] Cotton's signature, without 'Bruceus', is on the first folio and the volume is likely to have been one of a group of books lent to Camden in July 1617 which were apparently never returned.[90]

Camden is also very probably the borrower responsible for the loss of a handsome copy of the discourse on Knights of the Bath and Knights Bachelor by Francis Thynne, Lancaster Herald, which is now Add. MS. 12530. This manuscript must surely be the copy that Thynne prepared for presentation to James I: it has the king's arms opulently emblazoned on the reverse of the title page as well as a fine binding of brown leather where the royal arms are repeated together with the fleur-de-lys, both gilded as are the edges of the pages. All this accords well with Cotton's description of the volume lent to Camden: 'Mr Thine Book of knights of the bath bound up in red lether and gilt for the king. Foll.' and if this identification is correct it is a matter worthy of note that the manuscript was lost in turn by both the Royal and the Cottonian libraries.[91]

Harl. MS. 6257 may be another presentation volume to have belonged to both libraries. The manuscript is a copy of 'A Dutifull Defence of the Lawful Regiment of Women', written in the 1580s by Henry Howard, later earl of Northampton.[92] The volume contains the dedication to Queen Elizabeth and is one of a number of copies, some of which were prepared for presentation to Court officials. This one contains annotations in Northampton's hand and, if he parted with it, it must later have been returned to him as his *ex dono* inscription, almost certainly addressed to Cotton, is at the foot of the title page.[93] The date of Northampton's gift is 1613, the year before his death, and Cotton's loss of the manuscript is no doubt to be explained by its loan to Ralph Starkey, which was still outstanding in April 1621.[94]

The story of another recently written manuscript with royal connections is rather unusual. In about 1677 Sir William Dugdale asked Sir Thomas Herbert to write a memoir of Charles I during the period when Herbert attended the king, the last two years of Charles's life. The result was *Threnodia Carolina*, Herbert's autograph copy of which is now Harl. MS. 7396. After making a copy of Herbert's work, Dugdale records that he deposited the original 'for the better preservation of so excellent a memoriall...amongst those choyse Manuscripts at Westminster, belonging to Sr Iohn Cotton...Grandson and heire to Sr Robert Cotton...'.[95] There is no reason to doubt Dugdale's word, particularly as he was responsible for the accession of a number of manuscripts to the Cotton library in the middle years of the seventeenth century. However, Herbert's memoir did not receive an Emperor pressmark – a subject to which we shall later return – nor is its date of accession to the Harleian library known. In fact, it may be that its transfer from the one to the other collection was an accident of arrangement, either while both were together at Cotton House or after the two libraries arrived at the British Museum in the mid-eighteenth century: indeed, a tart note among the records of the British Library's Department of Manuscripts virtually blames the transfer on 'the same *blundering* of Nares, Planta, & others, which has mis-placed several other Cotton MSS among the *Additional* and *Harleian* Collections'.[96] If this is indeed the correct explanation it serves to remind us of another means by which manuscripts might stray.

IX

Two volumes of antiquarian collections by contemporaries of Cotton also passed through his hands. Harl. MS. 2223, a volume which contains papers in the autograph of the antiquary Thomas Talbot, was undoubtedly once owned by Sir Robert Cotton, although suggestions that he also compiled it appear to be without foundation.[97] When and how it was lost to the Cotton library is unknown, as also is the route by which it reached the Harleian library. The other volume, now section A of Bodl. MS. Dodsworth 20 (*SC* 4162), contains collections which are in part in the hand of William Camden and the probability is that these reached Cotton in Camden's bequest to his friend and former pupil on his death in 1623. They remained in the library for at least the next decade: the manuscript still bears the Cotton Julius B. X pressmark and it was entered in Add. MS. 36682, the first catalogue to be drawn up on the Emperor basis. But it was missing by early 1657 and a note by Thomas Smith in his own annotated copy of the catalogue he published in 1696 asks 'whether my Lord Hatton hath not this book...'.[98] However, in noting this possibility, Smith must have been relying on received information because the last of Dodsworth's manuscripts had reached the Bodleian in 1683–4, well before Smith became librarian to Sir John Cotton.

X

A number of volumes, primarily working records, of legal and parliamentary material also strayed from the Cotton library. We should first consider three volumes of English statutes and writs – one at the Bodleian, another at Cambridge and the third in private ownership. Bodl. MS. Douce 139 (*SC* 21713), a composite manuscript written in the thirteenth century, has Sir Robert Cotton's arms on both covers in the less common version of four quarterings. The name, 'Henry Ferrers', appears several times at the start of the second of the three sections of which the manuscript is composed. This may be the Warwickshire antiquary of that name who died in 1633 but the note is not in Ferrers's normal secretary script, nor is there any record in Cotton's memoranda that the volume was either received from or passed to Ferrers, or indeed anyone else.[99]

Cambridge University Library, MS. Ff.1.32, a fifteenth-century register of writs, displays Cotton's signature, 'Ro: Cotton', on its first folio and may well be the

277

manuscript entered at no. 324 of Harl. MS. 6018, his catalogue of the early 1620s: 'Registrum Brevium iuris Anglicani peramplum et accurate scriptum. tempore Hen. quarti'. It is not, however, readily identifiable in the next catalogue of 1631–2, Add. MS. 36789, and may therefore have left the collection before Cotton's death.[100]

The third volume of statutes and writs, Holkham Hall, Norfolk, MS. 752, a fourteenth-century manuscript, is less certainly connected with him. Although 'Robert Cotten me possidet' is written on the flyleaf, the inscription is not by Cotton who never spelled his name in this way. Nor, on balance, does it appear to be by Sir Edward Coke who would, of course, have been the most likely conduit by which a manuscript of Cotton's might have reached the Holkham collection. At present, therefore, the question of Cotton's ownership of the volume must remain open, although naturally the book is of the type that he would have collected.[101]

Another of Cotton's legal manuscripts to have come to rest in Cambridge is his fourteenth-century copy of the treatise known as 'Britton', a summary of Bracton, now in CUL, MS. Hh.4.6.[102] His signature appears on both the flyleaf and f. 3r, on the second occasion with the date, 1598. However, the manuscript is not mentioned in any of the Cottonian records and we do not know how or when it left the library.

Two volumes of transcripts of medieval parliamentary records also strayed from the collection. These were, no doubt, among the products of the campaign to edit the statutes which was under way during the second decade of James I's reign and in which Cotton appears to have participated.[103] Indeed, he may well have commissioned them, although neither is in his hand. They are Add. MS. 33216, an abridgement of the parliament rolls from the reigns of Edward II to Richard III, and National Library of Wales MS. 17048 D, a transcript of rolls, of writs of summons and of writs for the payment of members, 4-51 Edward III.[104] The Additional manuscript bears no signature or annotations by Cotton but his arms, taken from a previous binding, are mounted on the inside of both covers and the engraved title page is of a type provided by Cotton in a number of his manuscripts.[105]

The manuscript bought by the National Library of Wales in 1945 has Sir Robert Cotton's signature, with the addition of 'Bruceus', on the first leaf of the text, while the running titles in display script, designed as a guide to the appropriate parliament, are of a type often found in the Cottonian state paper volumes. We cannot be certain when these manuscripts left the Cotton library but a loan to Selden in 1640 of 'The abridgment of all yᵉ Records of Parliament in yᵉ Tower. from the 1. of Ed. 3. unto yᵉ end of Rich. 3.' could explain the departure of the first.[106]

The signature, 'Ro: Cotton Bruceus', at the beginning of Oxford, Queen's College, MS. 54, is the reason for assigning this late-fifteenth-century collection of ecclesiastical precedents to his library,[107] while a loan to 'Mʳ Lamb and Docter Hickman' of 'A large thike book in parchment of presidents in the Court Ecclesiasticall of good uss. Foll in lether and bord clasped' probably accounts for its departure.[108] This description fits MS. 54 well and, although the clasps no longer survive, the present binding is post-Cottonian. The loan presumably dates from between 1615, when John Lambe and Henry Hickman were jointly appointed to office in the diocese of Peterborough, and 1621, when Lambe was knighted.[109]

A volume undoubtedly created by Cotton is Add. MS. 46410, collections relating to the Court of Chancery. Some of the transcripts must have been done for him and his notes, designed to provide a scheme of arrangement for the volume, are still clearly visible.[110] The dating of a number of the articles suggests that the manuscript was assembled soon after 1618 and it is probably the volume which was out on loan to the Lord Keeper before 23 April 1621.[111] Later it was allocated the Cottonian pressmark, Claudius B. VIII, and the loan which may have occasioned its loss was that to the earl of Manchester on 13 July 1640.[112] At any rate, it must have gone before the death of Robert Cotton's son, Thomas, in 1662, because he was responsible for an interesting alteration in the catalogue of the manuscripts that was the first to be based on the Emperor arrangement, when he transferred to the vacant Claudius B. VIII position his father's copy of the Samaritan Pentateuch, previously listed as Tiberius A. I.[113]

Another volume of Chancery material, a precedent book for the years 1509–58 in the hand of more than one copyist, apparently also belonged to Cotton. His signature is on f. 1r but this is the only indication of his ownership and there is apparently no evidence to establish how or when he lost the book.[114]

Add. MS. 25248 is a volume of collections relating to the antiquity and authority of the Court of Requests, from the reign of Edward VI to that of James I, composed by Richard Oseley, clerk of the 'King and Queenes Counsell' at the instigation of the Lord Treasurer.[115] Although a copy, it is exactly the type of work that would have interested Cotton but there is no record of it in his ownership. It is certain, however, that it belonged to his son, Thomas, as he gave it away 'ex studio suo antiquitatum' in August 1638 to one Robert Bernard.[116]

Lastly, in this group, Cotton's signature with the addition 'Bruceus' establishes his ownership of Bodl. MS. Tanner 212 (*SC* 10038), an examination of the jurisdiction of the Lord Admiral of England, written in the later years of Elizabeth I's reign by William Fleetwood, Recorder of London from 1571 to 1591. The copy, largely in one scribal hand, presumably came to Cotton after Fleetwood's death in 1594 and a loan of 'My Book of the Admirall pattent and Jurisdiction. Foll. Whitt.' to Sir Daniel Dunn, the Admiralty judge who died in 1617, may explain its loss.[117]

XI

Manuscripts in another category of working records, volumes concerned with the family's estates, also left the ownership of the Cottons. One such is now Add. MS. 29611, a mid-sixteenth-century survey chiefly of lands in the manor of Falkworth, Huntingdonshire, then belonging to Sir Edward Montagu. In the early decades of the following century when both Robert and Thomas Cotton were engaged in lawsuits with their tenants, one of their principal antagonists and victims, Robert Castle, possessed messuages in Falkworth, the lordship of whose manor had by then passed to the Cottons.[118] The manuscript has Robert Cotton's signature on f. 2r while on the previous folio is written 'Sr John Cottons Book'. Although this inscription is not in the hand of Sir Robert's grandson, it must indicate that the volume remained in the family's ownership at least into the late seventeenth century, when it might still have possessed utilitarian value. By the middle of the following century, however, when the direct Cotton line died out and the estates were broken up, the manuscript would have been an obvious candidate for disposal, although it is not known when or how it was lost.[119]

It is probable that throughout its time in the possession of the Cottons this volume would have been regarded as an estate document rather than an item in the library, and there is certainly no indication that it ever received an Emperor pressmark or was entered in a library catalogue. The chances are, too, that it would normally have been kept at Conington, the principal manor, rather than in London, and therefore would have stood no chance of being incorporated into the collection. However, such reflections do suggest questions about the range and scope of the Emperor sequence which the next group of manuscripts to be considered will pose more insistently.

In private ownership at Elton Hall, Peterborough, are four manuscripts which belonged to the Cottons.[120] Chiefly concerned with the family's estates and divided broadly by manor, hundred or village, they must have been taken to Elton when Sir Robert's grand-daughter, Frances, married Thomas Proby in 1661. They are written in various hands, some of them those of professional copyists, but all except the Elton volume (Volume II) have annotations by Sir Robert and Sir Thomas Cotton.[121] They were obviously compiled for practical purposes and yet their presentation indicates that they were not merely regarded in this way. Each of the four small folio volumes has an original (and well-preserved) Cottonian binding in leather with the coat of arms on both covers; these bindings are of the same quality as the few of Cotton's own that survive elsewhere, including the handful among the Emperor sequence. The work must have been done in London where Cotton used the binders and clasp makers of Warwick Lane and Paternoster Row.[122] Volume III (surveys of Glatton and Holme in 22 Elizabeth I and of Glatton in 11 James I) still bears Sir Robert's instructions to his binder, evidence that he bestowed the same care upon it as upon any of his finest manuscripts: 'A leafe of parchment befor and behind and cute the Book small'. The flyleaves of vellum are still in place.[123] Volume IV (Glatton, Holme and Conington) has been provided with an engraved title page, a practice which, as already mentioned, was adopted in many volumes in the Emperor arrangement.[124]

All together, therefore, the impression that these Elton Hall volumes create is that they were designed for the shelves of a library rather than for the archives of a country estate. Nevertheless, they were not incorporated into the Emperor arrangement, unlike other volumes of working papers such as letters to Cotton and proceedings both official and unofficial in which he was engaged.[125] Perhaps this was an oversight, perhaps they were not kept in London, but it does raise the question of the extent and scope of the Emperor sequence and therefore the possibility, already hinted at in connection with Add. MS. 15673 and Harl. MS. 7396 (sections VII and VIII, above), that there were manuscripts in the library that were not incorporated into it.[126]

XII

The last group of manuscripts to be discussed, fifteen in number, is, inevitably, a miscellaneous one. It opens with three volumes of chronicles.

The work of Richard James, librarian from about 1625 to 1638, is the main reason for assigning BL, Lansdowne MS. 204 to Cotton's ownership. This large, early-fifteenth-century manuscript, a copy of John Hardyng's 'Chronicle of Britain', was owned by William Bowyer in 1566 and used by John Stow.[127] Cotton almost certainly wrote the title on f. 2r, 'A Chronicel of Britane gathered out of divers auters the auter unknown', and this must pre-date Richard James's contents list on the same page where Hardyng is named as author. Unfortunately, there is no record of the manuscript in any of the Cotton catalogues or loans lists to clinch the question of ownership or to indicate when it may have been lost, but it eventually came into the possession of the Gerard family, earls of Macclesfield in the late seventeenth century.[128]

There is good evidence that National Library of Wales, Llanstephan MS. 175, once belonged to Cotton. This manuscript contains a copy of the *Historia Brittonum* bound with a chronicle of England from Brutus to 1307, and is certainly of the type to interest Cotton. The case for his ownership, however, is based on the use that James Ussher made of a manuscript which, for textual reasons, fits Llanstephan 175 and which, according to his testimony, was in the Cottonian library.[129] Moreover, while no firm indication of Cotton's ownership survives in the volume itself, it is possible that the quire signatures are by him. As to the loss of the volume, the arms of Sir Edward Dering, found on both covers, may explain this: another of Cotton's missing manuscripts, to be discussed next, passed to Dering who provided Cotton, between 1623 and 1630, with a number of important charters, including a copy of Magna Carta. It may therefore be that the Llanstephan manuscript was part of some sort of exchange or thank offering.[130]

Against the entry for no. 396 in the catalogue, begun in 1621, in Harl. MS. 6018, Cotton has written 'Sr Edward Dering hath this book'. The entry undoubtedly relates to Cambridge University Library, Add. MS. 3578, a late-fourteenth-century volume of chronicle material which has not previously been identified as owned by Cotton.[131] It still has the Dering crest on both covers and it must clearly have changed hands at much the same time as Cotton was acquiring his Dering charters.[132]

Historical material of a rather different type, in Cambridge University Library, MS. Mm.5.14, also may have belonged to Cotton. Consisting largely of a copy of the *Historia Troiana* by the Sicilian judge, Guido della Columna, this fifteenth-century Latin manuscript has Robert Cotton's name on ff. 1r and 207v in Greek lettering. The appearance of the inscription is, naturally, quite unlike that of his customary signature and, in the absence of any similar examples or of other specimens of Cotton's Greek script, this evidence should perhaps be treated with some caution as an indication of his ownership. The manuscript bears no other marks to connect it with Cotton, nor is it listed in any of his records.[133]

However, the Wycliffite version of the New Testament, now Cambridge, Magdalene College, Pepys Library MS. 2073, certainly once belonged to Cotton. The handsome volume contains a prayer for the soul of William Weston 'lord of senct Johans Jerusalem' who had died on 6 May 1540, together with the names of Edmond Herenden and Thomas Bache in a sixteenth- or possibly early-seventeenth-century hand. The evidence that ties it to Cotton is an inscription by Edmund Randolph, the friend to whom Cotton gave it on 23 March 1607.[134]

Another volume of Wycliffite writings, Norwich Castle Museum MS. 158.926/4g3, is signed 'Ro: Cotton: Conningtonensis' at the foot of the first folio.[135] In view of the form of signature, it is likely that the volume was a fairly early accession to the library; moreover, as it is possibly the only Cotton manuscript to have retained its original binding (of wooden, leather-covered boards), it is unlikely to have remained there long. Its loss may be explained by one of two loans made in the few years before 1615[136] but after its spell in Cotton's ownership it disappears from view for two centuries, only to reappear in the early nineteenth century.[137] As with other such volumes, Cotton's records once again provide us with a glimpse of bright light in an often lengthy period of obscurity.

A manuscript which has so far defied efforts to discover anything about its immediate pre- or post-Cottonian provenance is Cardiff Public Libraries MS. 1–381. This opens (ff. 1r–8ov) with the *Vita S. Winwaloi*, a thirteenth-century manuscript from the Benedictine priory at Dover, followed (ff. 81r–146v) by a twelfth-century collection of saints' lives, originally at the Benedictine nunnery at Barking; the two parts were probably combined by Cotton. His signature could once be read at the top of the first folio but now only the date, 1601, survives.[138] Inscriptions and the name, 'John Greene', written in a hand of the eighteenth or nineteenth century on ff. 13r, 57v and 58r, may be those of a later owner.[139]

The only firm evidence to link Bodl. MS. Add. C. 181 (*SC* 29209) with the Cottonian library is the signature of Sir Robert's son, Sir Thomas (d. 1662), on the first folio. The manuscript is a twelfth-century copy of St Augustine's *Contra Julianum*, one of his writings against the Pelagians, and came from the abbey of Bury St Edmunds. It received no Emperor pressmark and may therefore have remained in the library for only a short time.[140]

Add. MS. 5475, a sixteenth-century record of ecclesiastical taxation, has a contents table by Richard James and still had the Cotton coat of arms on its binding in the eighteenth century. By then, however, it had passed into the hands of Peter Le Neve, Norroy King of Arms from 1704,[141] who also had the Folger Shakespeare Library manuscript discussed above (section VIII), although, as in the case of that volume, the route and date of departure of the Additional manuscript from the Cotton library are unknown.

We owe to Anthony Wood our knowledge of the later history of Bodl. MS. Barlow 49 (SC 6414), ff. 4r–56v, a manuscript once owned by John Dee. Wood tells us that this section, a fifteenth-century copy of the constitutions and letters of Bishop Grosseteste, was lent by Sir Thomas Cotton to Dr John Prideaux, bishop of Worcester from 1641, who never returned it.[142] Evidence of Robert Cotton's ownership is to be found in this part of the volume in the form of a plain 'Rob. Cotton' (possibly written by Richard James) on f. 4r and it is probable that Cotton acquired it direct from Dee. As to the remainder of MS. Barlow 49 – a register of documents relating to the manor of Faringdon, Berkshire (ff. 58r–114v), and a cartulary of the college of Holy Trinity, Pontefract (ff. 115r–165v) – these, too, must have been owned and then united in the one volume by Cotton: the seventeenth-century covers to the manuscript bear his arms, while the contents table on f. 1r, where all three parts are enumerated, is by Richard James.[143] Although it is difficult to see what theme unites the three parts, the manuscript is precisely of the type that Cotton was inclined to create. The whole was lost as a consequence of the loan to Prideaux.[144]

The fact that the Royal and the Cottonian libraries were housed together by about 1714, first in Cotton House and other private residences and then in the British Museum, may account for the wandering of the following three manuscripts. It has been suggested that article 8, ff. 31r–34r, of Royal Appendix 85 was once in the Cotton library. The volume is a collection of fragments, probably one of the volumes formed during attempts to repair the damage caused by the fire of 1731 which affected both libraries. As two other leaves (ff. 35 and 55) from the volume have been identified as belonging to Cotton manuscripts, to which they were restored early in this century, it is possible that article 8, a much damaged section of a register of Nostell Priory, was also once part of the Cotton collection, although there is no means of establishing this from the leaves themselves.[145]

However, two other Royal manuscripts certainly were. Royal 2 A. XXI, a fifteenth-century manual from South Charford Church, Hampshire, was, according to an inscription on f. 1r of the book, given to the library by Antony Warton, vicar of Godalming, on 13 May 1703, eight months after Sir John Cotton's death and the consequent gift of the library to the nation. It thus entered the library at the time when a survey of the bequest was being made but it was not given a place in the Emperor sequence. It has been suggested that its transfer to the Royal library may have been the work of Richard Bentley or of his deputy David Casley when they were responsible for both collections in the early eighteenth century, but there can be no certainty about this.[146] The second volume, Royal 15 A. XXI, a fifteenth-century manuscript of the *Thebais* of the Roman poet Statius, was once owned by Ben Jonson who, as a member of Cotton's circle, may have given it to him, but when it, too, left the Cotton library is unknown.[147]

BL, Sloane MS. 2423, a small fifteenth-century volume of the laws of Oleron and other similar material, was presented by Cotton to the French scholar, Nicolas Claude Fabri de Peiresc, in 1606, perhaps during the latter's visit to England in that year. The *ex dono* inscription is on the first folio and the gift must have been an appropriate start to a friendship that was long to endure.[148]

Finally, Sloane MS. 3189 is probably a former Cotton manuscript. This is a copy of John Dee's 'Book of Enoch', written in the hand of his coadjutor, Edward Kelly. It bears no physical marks to connect it with the Cotton library but when Elias Ashmole borrowed it to make his own copy he noted that 'the Booke of Enoch in Sr John Cottons Library, was written by E. K. hand'.[149] It is not known when or how it left the Cotton library but Ashmole's borrowing is a very possible occasion.

XIII

An examination of the Cotton memoranda and correspondence, and of the records of contemporaries, establishes the existence of a by no means insignificant number of manuscripts which, once owned by the Cottons, have since disappeared. What, for instance, happened to the 'Registru*m* S*a*nctae Mariae Ebor*acensis* I had of Mr Bradshawe. unbound' that was on loan to Roger Dodsworth in 1621–2, presumably the same manuscript recorded by Dugdale twenty or more years later as in the possession of Sir Thomas Cotton?[150] What, too, became of the Bermondsey cartulary which probably passed to Selden,[151] or of the composite volume which opened with a copy of the 'Dialogue of the Exchequer' and included another manuscript of the *Historia Brittonum*?[152] Sadly, the trail has gone dead on Sir Robert Cotton's manuscripts of the *Encomium Emmae Reginae* and William of Poitiers which he lent to the French scholar, André Duchesne.[153] Where, too, is the register of Winchcombe from which Augustine Vincent made extracts while it was in Cotton's possession in 1622 and which was later recorded by Dugdale as in Sir Thomas Cotton's ownership? Could it have been the cartulary that was destroyed in the Great Fire of London of 1666?[154] Dugdale also lists as in the Cottonian library registers of Chester, Croyland and, possibly, Belvoir, which have yet to be identified.[155]

As the Cottonian records are studied, it will become apparent that other manuscripts, once in the library, are missing. Some have probably disappeared for ever but others may yet be lurking, unrecognized, on the shelves of public and private collections. A survey, such as this, of stray manuscripts is, in consequence, never complete: there is always the possibility, fortified by optimism, that fresh discoveries will be made. Therefore, with this in prospect, I have appended to this paper photographs of the two versions of the Cotton coat of arms (fig. 1), of samples of Sir Robert and Sir Thomas Cotton's hands (figs. 2, 3) and of Cottonian manuscript contents tables drawn up by Richard James (fig. 4) and by another well-known, though unidentified, contemporary hand (fig. 5). One of the illustrations (fig. 4) shows an inventory number corresponding to the entry for the manuscript in the Cottonian catalogue in Harl. MS. 6018. Several of the entries in that catalogue have yet to be identified: the appropriate numbers, together with an indication of the nature of the entry, are therefore listed in the appendix, below.

Fig. 1. The two versions of Sir Robert Cotton's coat of arms. C. J. H. Davenport, *English Heraldic Book-stamps* (London, 1909), pp. 126, 127 (details)

This survey has considered more than eighty manuscripts that strayed from the Cottonian library in the century and a half before it entered the British Museum in the 1750s. Even this number, a bare minimum figure, is an indication of the extent to which the library was a fluid, changing collection throughout those years. In view of its nature and the use to which it was put by the intelligentsia of early Stuart England, this is hardly surprising[156] but that approximately one in ten of its manuscripts strayed is some indication of Sir Robert Cotton's attitude towards his collection. Eager harvester he may have been, miser he was not. Indeed, the extent of the losses suggests a certain casualness in safeguarding the integrity of the collection, a matter in which the evidence of the loans records indicates that Sir Robert was less meticulous than his son.[157] Clearly, some departures were more deliberate than others, a consideration which makes it difficult to establish the degree of selection that was applied to distinguishing the manuscripts that wandered from those that were kept, but there is little surprise in discovering that the earl of Arundel was the recipient of the most outstanding strays.

In 1612, a quarter of a century after the opening of his career as a collector, Cotton received letters from his friend, Edmund Bolton, the antiquary and historian, in praise of his library. In one passage, commenting on the rarity of some of the manuscripts, Bolton compared Cotton jokingly to '[t]hat ancient bane of commonweal Monopolie': the importance of the collection was, of course, by then firmly established.[158] Those of

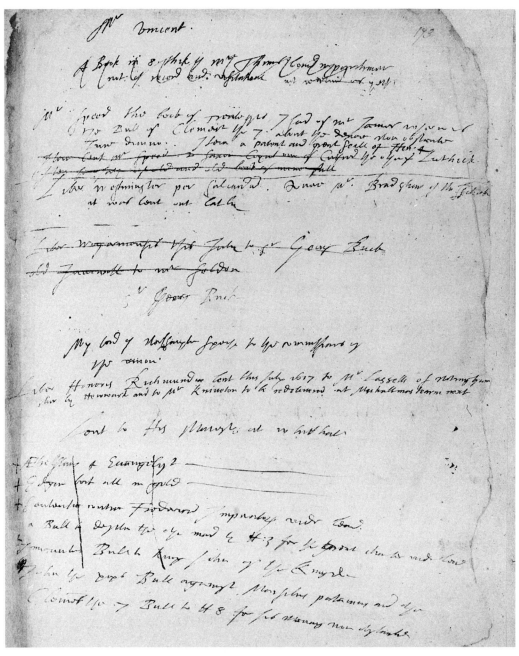

Fig. 2. Sir Robert Cotton's hand. His italic script is commonly more carefully written than his secretary script. Harl. MS. 6018, f. 173r

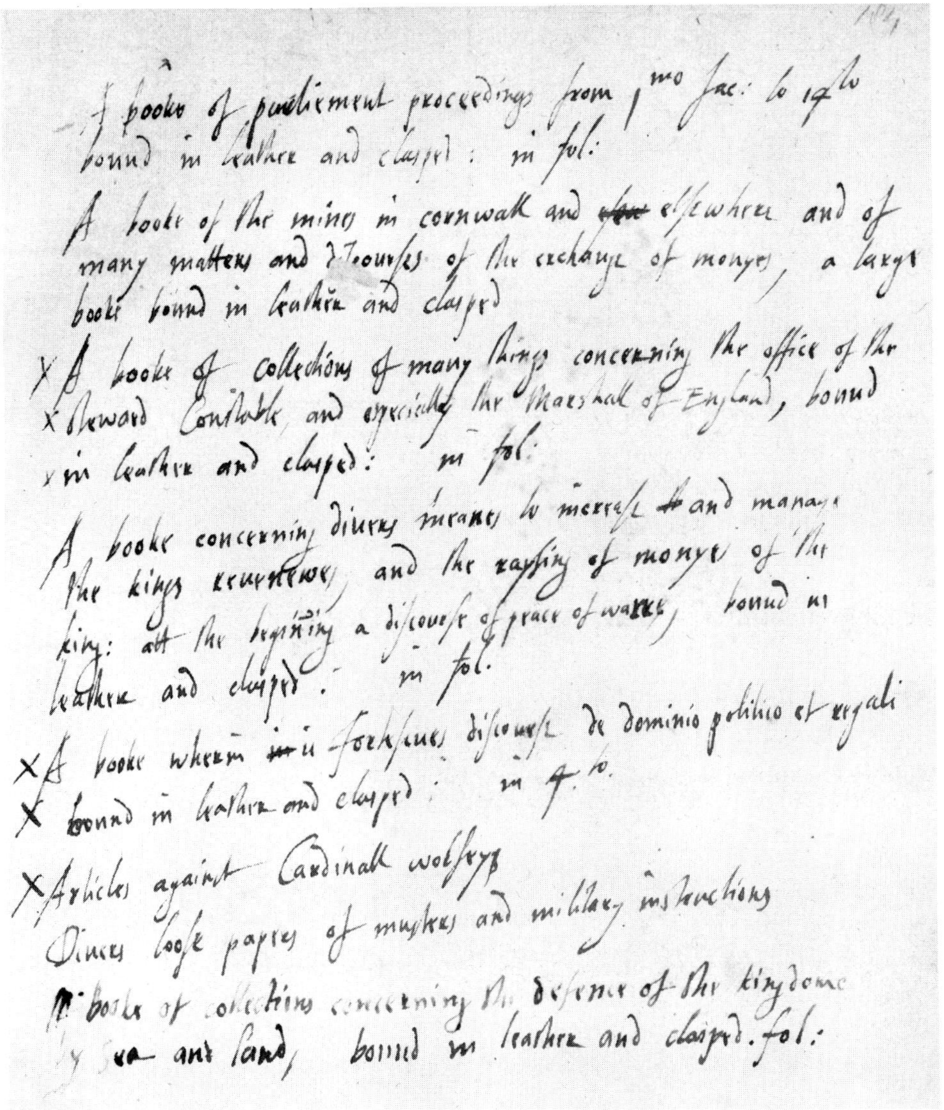
A booke of parliement proceedings from 1mo Jac: to 14to bound in leather and clasped: in fol:

A booke of the mines in cornwall and elsewhere and of many matters and discourses of the exchange of monyes, a large booke bound in leather and clasped

X A booke of collections of many things concerning the office of the Steward Constable and especially the Marshall of England, bound in leather and clasped: in fol:

A booke concerning divers meanes to increase and manage the kings revenewe, and the raysing of monye of the king: att the beginning a discourse of peace of warre, bound in leather and clasped: in fol.

X A booke wherein is fortescues discourse de dominio politico et regali bound in leather and clasped: in 4to.

X Articles against Cardinall wolseys

Divers loose papers of musters and military instructions

A booke of collections concerning the defence of the kingdome by sea and land, bound in leather and clasped. fol:

Fig. 3. Sir Thomas Cotton's hand. Harl. MS. 6018, f. 184r

Cotton's manuscripts that wandered, some of them unique copies, not only give an insight into its evolution but also offer us a representative sample of a remarkable library, from its work-a-day volumes to its choicest texts.

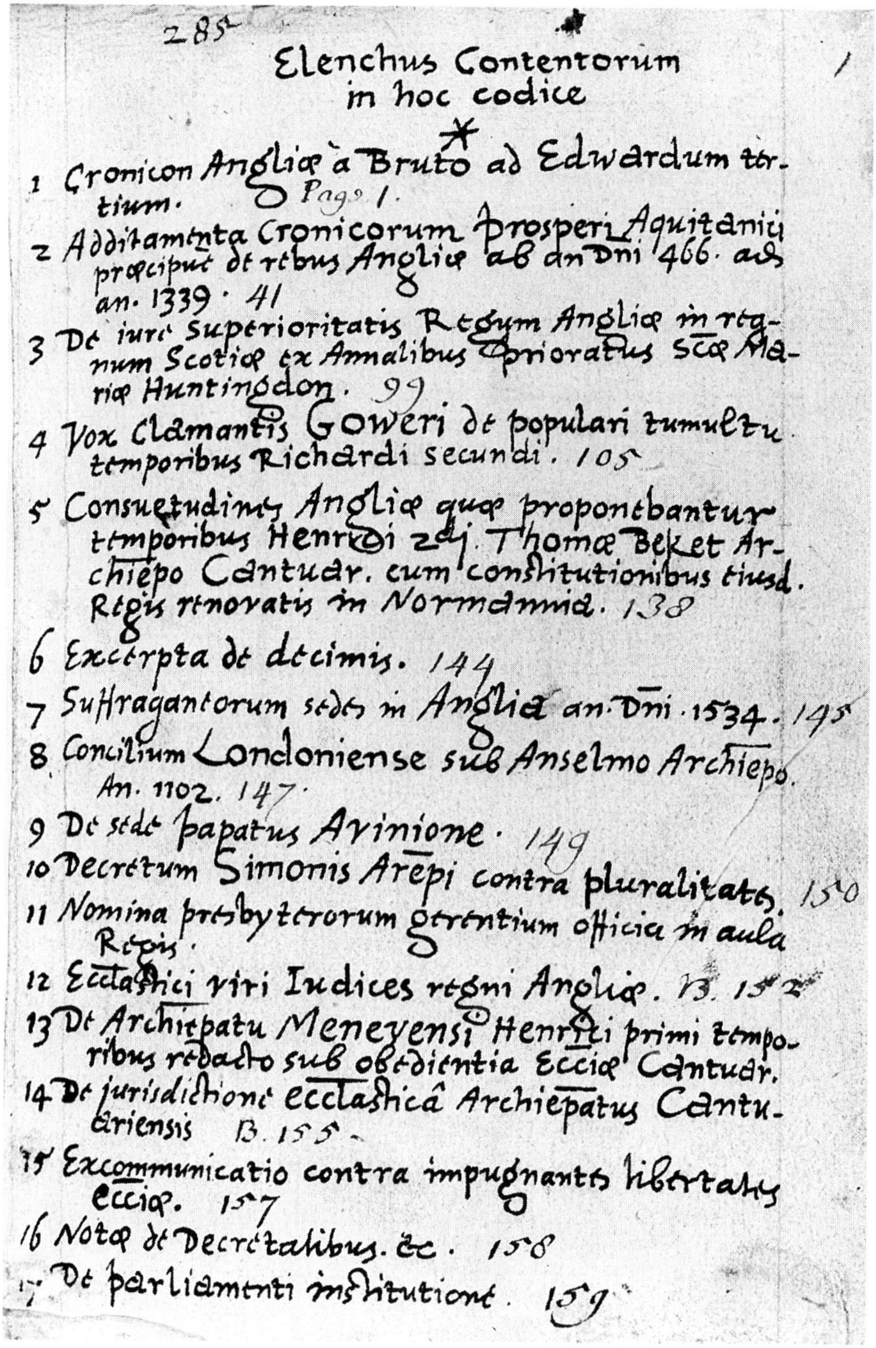

Elenchus Contentorum
in hoc codice

1 Cronicon Angliæ a Bruto ad Edwardum tertium. *Pag. 1.*

2 Additamenta Cronicorum Prosperi Aquitaniu præcipue de rebus Angliæ ab an Dni 466. ad an. 1339 . 41

3 De iure superioritatis Regum Angliæ in regnum Scotiæ ex Annalibus Prioratus stæ Mariæ Huntingdon . 99

4 Vox Clamantis Goweri de populari tumultu temporibus Richardi secundi. 105

5 Consuetudines Angliæ quæ proponebantur temporibus Henrici 2ij Thomæ Beket Archiepo Cantuar. cum constitutionibus eiusd. Regis renovatis in Normannia. 138

6 Excerpta de decimis. 144

7 Suffragantorum sedes in Anglia an. Dni. 1534. 145

8 Concilium Londoniense sub Anselmo Archiepo. An. 1102. 147.

9 De sede papatus Avinione . 149

10 Decretum Simonis Arepi contra pluralitates 150

11 Nomina presbyterorum gerentium officia in aula Regis.

12 Ecclashci viri Iudices regni Angliæ. B. 152

13 De Archiepatu Menevensi Henrici primi temporibus redacto sub obedientia Ecciæ Cantuar.

14 De iurisdictione ecclashca Archiepatus Cantuariensis B. 155

15 Excommunicatio contra impugnantes libertates Ecciæ. 157

16 Notæ de Decretalibus. &c. 158

17 De parliamenti institutione. 159

Fig. 4. Part of the contents list to a manuscript, in the hand of Richard James. The inventory number from Harl. MS. 6018 is at the top of the page. Cotton MS. Titus A. XIII, f. 1r

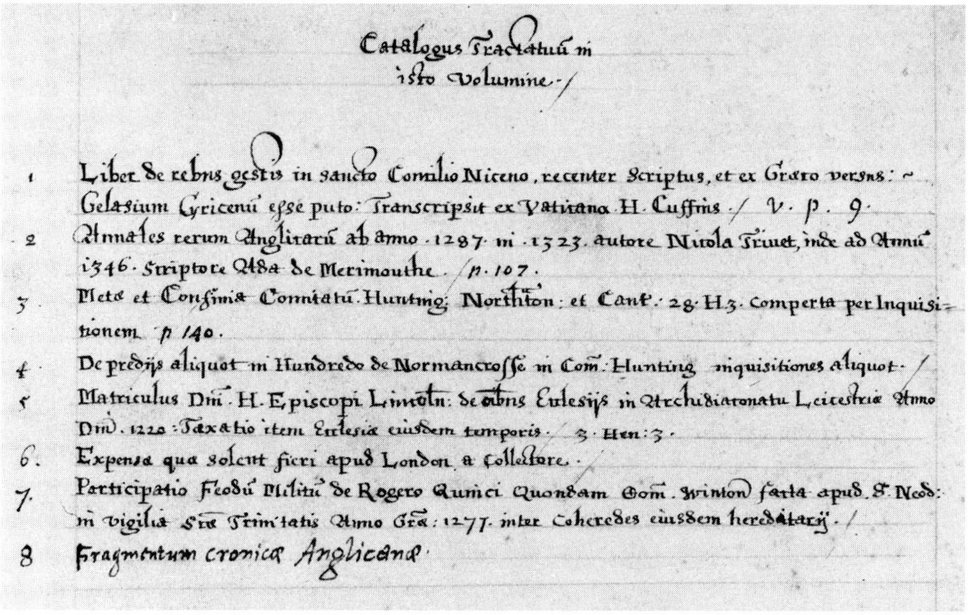
Catalogus Tractatuū in
isto Volumine./

1 Liber de rebus gestis in sancto Concilio Niceno, recenter Scriptus, et ex Græco versus: ~
Gelasium Cyricenū esse puto: Transcripsit ex Vaticana H. Cuffins ./ v. p. 9.
2 Annales rerum Anglicarū ab anno .1287. in .1323. autore Nicola Triuet, inde ad Annū
1346. Scriptore Ada de Merimouthe. /p. 107.
3 Meta et Confinia Comitatu. Hunting: Northton: et Cant.: 28. H3. comperta per Inquisi-
tionem p 140.
4 De predijs aliquot in Hundredo de Normancrosse in Com: Hunting inquisitiones aliquot. /
5 Matriculus Dni. H. Episcopi Lincoln: de oibus Ecclesijs in Archidiaconatu Leicestrie Anno
Dni. 1220: Taxatio item Ecclesie eiusdem temporis. 3. Hen: 3.
6. Expensa qua solent fieri apud London. a Collectore.
7. Participatio Feodū Militū de Rogero Quinci Quondam Com. Winton facta apud S. Neots:
in vigilia Ste Trinitatis Anno Gra: 1277. inter Coheredes eiusdem hereditarij. /
8 Fragmentum Cronice Anglicane

Fig. 5. Contents list to a manuscript, in the hand of an unidentified scribe employed by the Cottons. The addition at the foot is by Richard James. Cotton MS. Nero D. X, f. 2r

A SUPPLEMENTARY NOTE

Since this article was first published, another important Greek manuscript has come to light as once owned by Sir Robert Cotton. This is the *Lexikon* of Photius, now Cambridge, Trinity College MS. O.3.9, written probably in the early eleventh century and the only manuscript of the work known before the late nineteenth century. In a monograph published in Modern Greek in 1967, K. Tsantsanoglou pieced together much about the early modern ownership of the work but his conclusions seem not to have reached an English audience. According to his account, the manuscript had been discovered in Florence in 1598 and brought to England soon afterwards by Richard Thomson, the Biblical scholar who died in 1613.

Among its subsequent owners or users, Tsantsanoglou then pointed to Isaac Casaubon (who was consulting it in 1603), Robert Cotton and Patrick Young, but more detailed circumstances of this changing ownership were not known to him.[159] However, some of the uncertainties can now be removed because one of the entries in the series of loans to and exchanges with Patrick Young, the Royal librarian, that took place in about 1616 (for which see Section II above) fits the manuscript precisely. Cotton listed 'Photii lexicon Grece that I had of Duch Tompson Foll bound with my armes',[160] and although he does not state whether he is giving or lending it to Young the chances must favour the former: others of the manuscripts in the list are now in the Royal library. 'Dutch

Thomson' was the name by which Richard Thomson was known and Cotton's statement that he was the source eliminates the possibility (suggested by Tsantsanoglou) that Casaubon might have been the supplier.[161] Cotton's record also establishes that the manuscript was once embellished with his coat of arms, in accordance with his frequent practice. The volume at Cambridge was rebound, probably in the late seventeenth century, and no longer displays any arms, but an interesting repair to it must be Cotton's work. The binding has been strengthened with stubs taken from the same fourteenth-century psalter from which leaves were removed to provide similar material in twenty-six Cottonian manuscripts.[162] It is likely that this psalter, now in part reconstituted as Royal 13 D. I*, was being dismembered for these purposes in about 1612.[163] If so, Cotton must have owned the Photius for some years before parting with it to Young, *circa* 1616. (A leaf from the psalter is reproduced in fig. 6, as it may well be that further fragments from it are yet to be discovered in other manuscripts.)

Cotton's ownership of another important document is less securely established but as he undoubtedly handled a loan of it in 1611 and again in 1616 and may have had possession of it in the intervening period, it warrants a brief mention here. The Irish version of the *Modus Tenendi Parliamentum*, in the exemplification of 1419 issued under the Great Seal of Ireland, was known to English antiquaries in Cotton's time. The only surviving medieval copy of this, now MS. EL 1699 at the Huntington Library, California, once belonged to the Ellesmere library. As will be seen, this ownership alone makes it very likely that this was the manuscript that Cotton handled but added support comes from a seventeenth-century transcript, almost certainly made from the exemplification of 1419, which states that it is a true copy of a manuscript then 'remayning in ye hands of Sr Ro: Cotton. Knight'.[164] Further crucial evidence is provided by Cotton's loans records. The first of these, dated 4 May 1611, is a borrowing by 'Sir James Lee Attorney of the Court of Wards' of '... modus tenendi parlamentum sealed with the seal of Ireland about Hen. 5. time'. The entry has been crossed through, usually an indication of the return of a loan, but in the margin Cotton has added, and not deleted, 'This I had back and my Lord Chancelor hath it'.[165] If this addition was made before 1617 the Lord Chancellor would have been Lord Ellesmere and the borrowing would very probably explain his acquisition of the manuscript. Cotton's second loans record, part of a disorderly list, is less clear: the borrower and date are given as 'Mr Ro. Bowier the last Session. 1616' and the entry reads 'Item he had from the Clark of the Parlament Modus tenendi Parlamentum under the Seall of Ireland'.[166] But as Bowyer was himself clerk of the parliaments in 1616, the borrowing seems to make little sense unless the clerk of the *Irish* parliament is intended. Nor does it appear (to judge from the wording) that Cotton was himself initiating this loan. Nevertheless, a further note indicates that the manuscript was returned to him, although whether this was before or after the Lord Chancellor's borrowing there is at present no means of knowing. It must, therefore, remain an open question whether Cotton's control over the Irish *Modus* was sufficient to justify assigning it, for a time, to his ownership. While it was certainly the type of manuscript he would have wished to acquire, it was also a

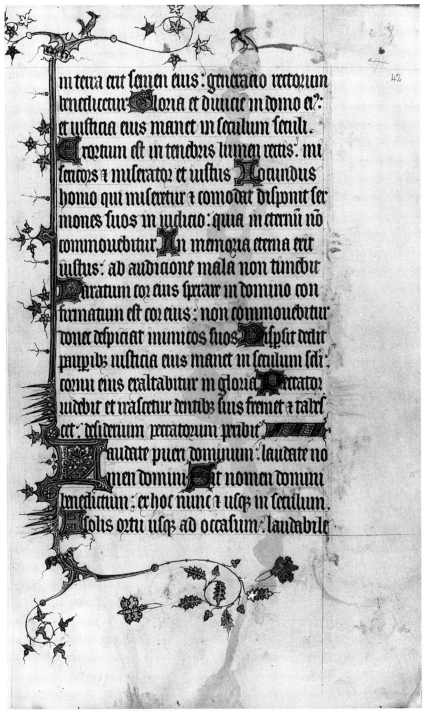

Fig. 6. Leaf from an illuminated mid-fourteenth century psalter, some of whose folios were cut up and used, in about 1612, as binding material in a number of Cottonian manuscripts (see p. 290, above). Royal MS. 13 D. I*, f. 42r

document of procedural significance to the Irish parliament, whose first meeting since 1586 took place in 1613: it can therefore hardly have been the type of record that could have passed easily and unchallenged into his ownership.[167]

Further information is now available about National Library of Wales MS. 17048D, the transcript of parliamentary records for 4-51 Edward III discussed in Section X. The fact that the manuscript is bound in white vellum and was once tied with green string enables it to be identified with two loans among Cotton's records and establishes its provenance. The first loan was made to 'Mr Attorney Generall Sir John Hubbard' and was of 'A volume of the parlament Rolls in Ed 3 time that was Mr Henages. Foll bound in velom past gren strings'.[168] 'Mr Henage' is Michael Heneage, who from about 1578 until his death in 1600 was one of the keepers of records in the Tower of London: in view of his ownership, my suggestion (above p. 278) that Cotton himself may have commissioned production of the manuscript obviously falls. The identity of the borrower, however, presents some difficulty. Sir John 'Hubbard', or Hobart, was never Attorney-General but his father, Sir Henry, held the office from 1606 to 1613 and John was knighted in 1611: the error, if that is what it was, is understandable. Despite the apparent confusion in the record, this borrowing was, nevertheless, not the occasion of the loss of the volume; not only is the entry deleted (normally, as already stated, a sign of the return of a loan) but there was also another borrowing of the volume in 1621, this time by Lord Treasurer Montagu.[169]

APPENDIX

In the Cottonian catalogue in Harl. MS. 6018 each entry is allocated a number; these numbers are frequently written towards the top of a flyleaf or at the head of the contents table or of the first page of text in the appropriate manuscript (an example can be seen in fig. 4). The list that follows is of numbered entries in Harl. 6018 that have yet to be identified.

13   Thomas Becket, *miracula*, etc. (marked as lent to Sir Richard St George)

28   *De Dominio Politico et Regale*, etc. (lent to John Selden or 'My lord privy seal')

30, 83, 98, 115, 153, 177, entered merely as 'Saxon'

37   No entry

40   'Tenentes de abbate Certesey...per feoda militum' and 'In quibus casibus prohibitio regia non habet locum', removed from beginning of Chertsey cartulary now in Vitellius A. XIII

78   Heraldic miscellanea (lent to the earl of Arundel; see also note 67)

90   'Psalmi et preces...in grene velvett' (lent to Thomas Reid, Latin secretary to James I; possibly an octavo volume)

102   'Fragmentum vitae Will*elmi* I'

131   'Liber Chartarum'

137   'Collectiones...de chartis'

147   *Modus tenendi Parliamentum: officium senescalli* et *mariscalli*; etc.

221, 229, entered merely as 'Irishe'

228 'Homelia Alfrici saxonice'

230 'Irishe physique'

231 Register of Bermondsey Abbey (probably lent to John Selden)

232 'Vitae sanctorum'

234 'Titulus domini Richardi ducis Eboracensis...ad regem Castellae', etc. (once owned by Savile: see Watson, *Savile of Banke*, no. 12)

259 *Polychronicon*

271 'Historia Eliensis', Etheldreda – Edward I, arranged in the usual three books (lent to 'Doctor Lindsey', perhaps Augustine Lindsell, later bishop of Peterborough)

272 Pontifical

287 Gervase of Tilbury; *Historia Brittonum*; etc. (lent to Augustine Vincent or his son)

300 Patents of nobility, xvi cent. (lent to Sir John Borough)

324 *Registrum brevium* (see CUL, MS. Ff.1.32, discussed in section X)

364 'Liber Astrologiae iudiciariae Gall:'

370 'Sermones quedam'

371 'Stephanus Langton ut videtur'

380 'Charta...1255. tempore...Gulielmi Abbatis...de Waverleya'

384 *Calendarium*

Some of the manuscripts to which these inventory numbers relate may, of course, have been destroyed; others may still remain in the Cotton library, though with opening leaves damaged or removed and numbers therefore lost. Occasionally, users of the library (James Ussher is one example) referred to the books they were consulting by their inventory numbers.

I am grateful to James Carley, Nigel Ramsay and Andrew Watson, who kindly read a draft of this paper and made a number of valuable comments.

1 Cotton's own writings are excluded from this survey. These exist in many copies and in many locations, and I have not seen them all. Very few, however, appear to exhibit signs of his ownership (as opposed to his authorship), despite claims to the contrary. One example of such a claim will suffice: BL, Harl. MS. 2245 is a copy of Cotton's 'Life of Henry III' (bound with 'Leicester's Commonwealth'). The volume has been assigned to Cotton's ownership on the strength of its marginalia, but these are not, in my opinion, in his hand: cf. C. E. Wright, *Fontes Harleiani* (London, 1972), p. 113.

2 Conveniently printed in *A Summary Catalogue of Western Manuscripts in the Bodleian Library at Oxford*, 7 vols. in 8 (Oxford, 1895–1953) (henceforth *SC*), vol. i, pp. 76–122. The gift from Cotton is on pp. 86–7.

3 The style and design of the inscription were doubtless influenced by Cotton's studies during his visit to the area around Hadrian's Wall in 1600 when, with William Camden, he spent time making drawings and collections of this type of monument. (See also his design for a monument to Robert Cecil: BL, Cotton Fragments XXV, f. 25v. As this makes no reference to Cecil's elevation in 1604 to the earldom of Salisbury, it probably dates from much the same period as the inscriptions in the gifts to the Bodleian.) The letters 'LL.M.DD.' (which also appear in the Cecil inscription) are an abbreviation for 'Laetus Libens Merito Dono Dedit', a common dedicatory inscription; 'HAC' (which has sometimes been read as 'HIC') is probably being used adverbially. The inscription might therefore be paraphrased: 'For the public good, Robert Cotton of Conington, happily, freely and justly made this thank-offering to the spirit of the library restored by Bodley'. I am much indebted to Scot McKendrick of the Department of Manuscripts, the British Library, for explaining the inscription to me and for confirming my interpretation of the meaning of the word *restituo*

on which I rely below. (For illustrations of the inscription and of the monument to Cecil, see David Howarth, 'Sir Robert Cotton and the commemoration of famous men', *British Library Journal*, xviii (1992), p. 2, and above, p. 41.)

4 Cotton already owned an Anglo-Saxon copy of this, now largely in Otho B. II: N. R. Ker, *Catalogue of Manuscripts containing Anglo-Saxon* (Oxford, 1957), no. 175. Whether by the date of his gift to Bodley he owned other copies of some of these works is unknown.

5 For the identification of these volumes as part of the gift, see *SC*, vol. i, pp. 86–7, and (for Bodl. 343) see Humfrey Wanley, *Catalogus Librorum veterum septentrionalium...* in G. Hickes, *Linguarum veterum septentrionalium Thesaurus*, vol. ii (Oxford, 1705), p. 25, and Ker, *Cat. Anglo-Saxon MSS*, no. 310.

6 The correspondence between Wanley and Hearne is printed in D. W. Rannie (ed.), *Remarks and Collections of Thomas Hearne*, vol. iv (Oxford, 1898), pp. 416, 421, and H. Ellis, *Original Letters of Eminent Literary Men* (Camden Society Old Series, xxiii (1843)), p. 356. See also W. D. Macray, *Annals of the Bodleian Library* (2nd edn, Oxford, 1890), p. 9, and P. L. Heyworth (ed.), *Letters of Humfrey Wanley* (Oxford, 1989), nos. 146, 147. Wanley, who was well aware of the wording of the inscription, did not interpret it as Macray later did.

7 See R. W. Hunt's statement (*SC*, i, p. 76) that the Register is far from complete and that Bodley would only have considerable gifts entered. For single volumes, Bodley normally regarded it as sufficient if the donor's name was written in the book itself.

8 Rannie, *Hearne*, vol. iv, p. 416; C. E. and Ruth C. Wright (eds.), *The Diary of Humfrey Wanley 1715–1726*, 2 vols. (London, 1966), vol. i, p. xix. A note in a hand of *c.* 1700 on f. 1*v of the manuscript reads: 'Mr Cobs saith y^t this tractatus erat ad Bodleum Colledge et est in Cantica Canticorum incerti autem authoris est pretium 1^l.5^s.0'. The number '236' (or perhaps '238'), possibly an inventory number, is written below.

9 The modern spelling has no double 'n'.

10 It must, however, be safe to say that he would not have used 'Bruceus' *before* 1603, so that signatures incorporating it and with a date preceding this must have been backdated (see,

for example, Bodl. MS. Rawlinson C. 208 and Cotton Titus E. V, sections IV and X below). For a discussion of the dating of Cotton's signatures from their form, see C. E. Wright, 'The Elizabethan Society of Antiquaries and the formation of the Cottonian library', in Francis Wormald and C. E. Wright (eds.), *The English Library before 1700. Studies in its History* (London, 1958), pp. 192, 200.

11 However, the first mention of a book bound with Sir Robert Cotton's arms occurs in a loan of 1608: Harl. MS. 6018, f. 153r.

12 There is nothing in any of the volumes to indicate when or from whom Cotton may have acquired them. Auct. F. 2.27 has the signature of 'Ro Shirbourn' (presumably the bishop of Chichester who died in 1536) on f. 252r. Or. 135 was once owned by John Grandisson, bishop of Exeter (d. 1369).

13 Cotton Julius C. III, f. 332r.

14 The date of the gift is discussed in the entry for the manuscript in *SC*. The *ex dono* inscription, in Bodley's hand, is on f. 1r. Treswell had been appointed Somerset Herald in 1597.

15 I owe this information about the uniqueness of the binding to Dr Bruce Barker-Benfield of the Bodleian Library. The binding is described and reproduced in W. Salt Brassington, *Historic Bindings in the Bodleian Library, Oxford* (London, 1891), pl. 4.

16 For Butler, see *D.N.B.* (which says that his books went to Clare College, Cambridge) and John and J. A. Venn, *Alumni Cantabrigienses. Part I: From the earliest times to 1751*, 4 vols. (Cambridge, 1922–7). For Cotton's illness, see London, Inner Temple, MS. Petyt 537/18, ff. 50r + v, and W. Notestein, F. H. Relf and H. Simpson (eds.), *Commons Debates 1621*, 7 vols. (New Haven, 1935), vol. vii, p. 644. Anne Sadler was the daughter of Sir Edward Coke: Venn (under Ralph Sadler); Catherine Drinker Bowen, *The Lion and the Throne. The Life and Times of Sir Edward Coke 1552–1634* (London, 1957), pp. 100, 145. I am grateful to the Librarian of the Inner Temple for permission to consult the manuscripts in his care.

17 Ker, *Cat. Anglo-Saxon MSS*, no. 344. The contents list on f. iv is in a well-known, though unidentified, Cottonian hand; Cotton's binding instructions are still partly legible on f. ivv.

18 The dating of this dismemberment is arrived at as follows: Cotton's signature, followed by

'Bruceus', is found twice in Vespasian D. XXI, on f. 1r ('Nennius') and on f. 18r (the start of Guthlac). It is unlikely that Cotton would have signed the manuscript in both places after he had brought the component parts together and as he uses Bruceus he is equally unlikely to have attached his signature before 1603. The new manuscript ('Nennius and vita Sancti Guthlaci 8[o]') features (possibly as an addition) in a list of books on loan to Camden at 20 Dec. 1606: Harl. MS. 6018, f. 154r.

19 Ker, *Cat. Anglo-Saxon MSS*, no. 344.

20 Lisle's loan at April 1621 is entered in Harl. MS. 6018, f. 148v; in a letter of March 1631 to Cotton (Julius C. III, f. 242r), he acknowledges still having on loan a manuscript that must be either Laud Misc. 509 or Cotton Claudius B. IV. James's extracts (in Bodl. MS. James 18 (*SC* 3855), p. 66) are in the context of notes from other Cottonian manuscripts. For his career see *D.N.B.* As late as 1624 his uncle, Thomas James, Bodley's Librarian, was recommending Archbishop Ussher to engage him: R. Parr (ed.), *The Life of ...James Usher...* (London, 1686), p. 310 (letter of 27 July 1624).

21 Julian Roberts and Andrew G. Watson (eds.), *John Dee's Library Catalogue*, Bibliographical Society (London, 1990), M181 and DM 113. There are no recorded loans to Digby although correspondence survives from him to Cotton. For one such letter, see Andrew G. Watson, 'Thomas Allen of Oxford and his manuscripts', in M. B. Parkes and Andrew G. Watson (eds.), *Medieval Scribes, Manuscripts and Libraries: Essays presented to N. R. Ker* (London, 1978), pp. 302–3.

22 In his forthcoming revision of the catalogue of the Digby manuscripts, Andrew Watson will correct his statement in 'Allen of Oxford', pp. 290 and 311 n. 109, that this manuscript once belonged to Allen.

23 For the complex reconstruction which makes possible this bald statement, see A. G. Watson, 'A Merton College manuscript reconstructed', *Bodleian Library Record*, ix (1976), pp. 207–17.

24 Roberts and Watson, *John Dee's Library Catalogue*, M29, M95; Watson, 'Allen of Oxford', p. 290.

25 The transaction is recorded in lists in Harl. MS. 6018, f. 159v, and BL, Add. MS. 35213, ff. 34v + r (leaf reversed in binding). The lists overlap to a considerable extent, although

problems of reconciliation exist. The dating to *c*. 1616 is suggested by an entry in the Harlean list: see n. 31, below. The descriptions quoted below are taken from the Add. MS. list unless otherwise stated. The identifications follow those made by G. F. Warner and J. P. Gilson in the *Catalogue of Western Manuscripts in the Old Royal and King's Collections* (London, 1921).

26 Two versions of Cotton's signature, with and without the 'Bruceus', are to be found on f. 4r. This is probably the manuscript of Horace that Cotton acquired from a Mr Higgins, no doubt the John Higgins who was an antiquary, historian and classicist in the last decades of Elizabeth's reign: Harl. MS. 6018, f. 162v; *D.N.B.*

27 'Ro: Cotton' is on f. 4r. It is probable that the manuscript was owned by Sir Walter Cope before Cotton acquired it: see Andrew G. Watson, 'The manuscript collection of Sir Walter Cope (d. 1614)', *Bodleian Library Record*, xii (1987), p. 289. Cotton's copies of these works in Vitellius E. II were destroyed in the fire of 1731 and it is not known whether he owned them at the time of the exchange with Young.

28 Add. MS. 35213, f. 34 + Harl. MS. 6018, f. 159v. This identification of Thomson differs from that proposed in the first edition of this article (see no. 161, below). Cotton had probably owned the Philostratus manuscript for some years: his signature 'Ro: Cotton Bruceus' on f. 1r is in a rather formal, Elizabethan style. This manuscript also appears in another Cotton memorandum (Add. MS. 35213, f. 43r) whose status and date have, however, yet to be determined.

29 The only other copy of Caesar's 'Commentaries' now in the Royal library is 16 G. VIII. As this was at Richmond Palace in 1535 and as there is nothing in the Cotton memoranda to indicate that the manuscript listed there was being returned rather than given, 16 G. VIII can reasonably be ruled out of consideration.

30 In the list in Harl. MS. 6018, f. 159v.

31 The entry for this manuscript part way through the Harleian list suggests the dating for the whole Cotton–Young transaction: 'Item the 22 July 1616 a grecke Manuscript in paper foll of de Anonia [*sic*]. [and] divers tracts to be exchanged for som other books. Foll.'

32 Andrew G. Watson (ed.), *Supplement* (London, 1987) to N. R. Ker (ed.), *Medieval Libraries of Great Britain* (2nd edn, London, 1964) (henceforth *MLGB*); James P. Carley, 'John Leland

and the contents of the English pre-dissolution libraries: Lincolnshire', *Transactions of the Cambridge Bibliographical Society*, ix (1989), p. 339 n. 13, and his forthcoming edition of the 1542 inventory of the Royal library at Westminster.

33 Royal 13 A. XXI was rebound in 1969; its previous covers do not survive.

34 Which of his other copies of *Imago Mundi* Cotton owned by this time is uncertain but those in Vespasian E. III and E. IV are possible: he undoubtedly had both in time to enter them in the catalogue of his manuscripts that he began in 1621: Harl. MS. 6018, ff. 48r, 115v, 141v.

35 In an intricate and complex argument, Watson has identified and reconstructed the Kirkham manuscript which, apart from the sections mentioned, also included what is now Arundel 36: Andrew G. Watson, *The Manuscripts of Henry Savile of Banke* (London, 1969), pp. 74–7.

36 Watson argued convincingly (*Savile of Banke*, pp. 74–7) that the manuscript was divided before Savile's time and that Savile acquired only the Arundel section, probably in loose-leaf form, but his conclusion is not incompatible with my suggestion that the Vespasian and Royal sections remained together until Cotton separated them. (There is no evidence that Cotton ever owned Arundel 36.) The dating of Cotton's division of the Kirkham volume to much the same time as the exchange of manuscripts with Young (*c.* 1616) can be confirmed by another route: ff. 62r–71v of Vespasian B. XI is 'A book contayning the Genelogy of the Hows of Luxembrough', a manuscript which Cotton acquired some time after the death of William Dethick, Garter, which occurred in 1612: Add. MS. 35213, f. 33r.

37 Cotton already had one copy of Jerome's lives (in Caligula A. XV, acquired in or by 1602) and possibly by this time another (in Vespasian A. XIII). The Kirkham leaves added to Royal 13 A. XXI (ff. 151r–192v) must occupy precisely the position from which Cotton abstracted the Hagnaby chronicle and the existence, on f. 14r, of the original volume's Westminster inventory number must indicate that the present art. 1 (ff. 2r–11v), a Bible paraphrase in French verse, is another addition, possibly also by Cotton.

The implication of Cotton's well-known habit of providing his manuscripts with fragments, taken from other volumes and often then used as binding material, should be noted here, for such activity is *prima facie* evidence that he had access, in some way, to the donor volumes: see James P. Carley and Colin G. C. Tite, 'Sir Robert Cotton as collector of manuscripts and the question of dismemberment: British Library, MSS Royal 13 D. I and Cotton Otho D. VIII', *The Library*, 6th Series, xiv (1992), pp. 94–9, where we argue, *inter alia*, that the psalter leaves, now Royal 13 D. I*, must have passed through Cotton's hands or those of his binder; see also Otto Pächt, *The Master of Mary of Burgundy* (London, 1948), pp. 64, 69, and D. H. Wright (ed.), *The Vespasian Psalter* (Copenhagen, 1967), pp. 33–4, for the breviary, now Cambridge, St John's College, MS. H.13, where at present the evidence that Cotton handled this volume seems less clear-cut. I owe this second example to Nigel Ramsay and I am grateful to the Assistant Librarian, Special Collections, at St John's College for allowing me to examine their manuscript.

38 I am much indebted to Jayne Ringrose of Cambridge University Library for drawing my attention to this manuscript, the earliest extant copy of Fortescue's work, and to CUL, MSS. Ee.1.1, Ff.1.32, Hh.4.6 and Mm.5.14, discussed later in this paper. Miss Ringrose has also informed me that all five manuscripts belonged to John Moore, bishop of Ely (d. 1714), whose books were bought and presented to the University Library by George I in 1715, and who owned a number of manuscripts, including CUL, Ee.1.1, formerly belonging to Cotton's friend, Francis Tate.

39 Harl. MS. 6018, ff. 112v (no. 282), 148v, 162r, 165r. The Christ Church manuscript had previously belonged to Sir Walter Cope: Watson, 'The manuscript collection of Sir Walter Cope', p. 290 (no. 200). Salter's suggestion that it was not bound before Cotton's time is incorrect. In the loan to Agarde, Cotton describes it as 'old bound', evidence which, as he provided it with his own binding, may also indicate that it had only recently come into his hands: H. E. Salter (ed.), *Cartulary of Osney Abbey*, Oxford Historical Society, lxxxix etc. (1929–36), iv, p. vii. My suggestion that the exchange occurred closer to 1621 than 1612 derives from a letter (Cotton Julius C. III, f. 274r) from Montague to Cotton in which he asks to borrow the Burton annals. The letter is undated but must clearly have

prompted the loan to him that was extant in 1621. Montague says that he had entreated an intermediary, Sir Henry Savile, 'to borrow of Mr Th. Allen his Annales Burtonenses. His answer was you had them in exchange'. This interesting phraseology not only suggests that the exchange was recent but that Allen had played some part in it. I have not been able to date precisely Philip King's tenure of the Christ Church position, although Anthony Wood says he was appointed in 1608 and he was still holding it in 1638: P. Bliss (ed.), *Athenae Oxonienses*, vol. iv (London, 1820), col. 195 and (second numbering) col. 89. The Oxford scholar, Brian Twyne, made extracts 'ex libro Osney, apud M. Philip Kinge' (Bodl. MS. Twyne XXII at p. 362). Twyne's notebook is probably the work of some years but one of his other entries (at p. 162) is dated 1617. Cotton's signature ('Ro: Cotton. Bruceus') is on f. 1r of the Christ Church manuscript and his is the hand responsible for the title on the same leaf. His instructions to his binder are on f. 339r, his signature is repeated on f. 362r, and, as Salter says (iv, p. viii), the disordering of the final leaves must have occurred during his rebinding. I am indebted to the Assistant Archivist at Christ Church for allowing me to examine this manuscript.

40 The signature, 'Ro: Cotton Bruceus', survives on ff. 1r and 3r. Cotton's ownership is not recorded in G. R. C. Davis, *Medieval Cartularies* (London, 1958), no. 635. For Tate (d. 1616), see *D.N.B.*

41 See W. O'Sullivan, 'Ussher as a collector of manuscripts', *Hermathena*, lxxxviii (1956), pp. 34–58.

42 Bodl. MS. Selden Supra 64 (*SC* 3452), f. 267r. I am indebted to Prof. Anne Hudson for this reference.

43 R. L. Poole and M. Bateson (eds.), *Index Britanniae Scriptorum* (Oxford, 1902), p. xvii and n. 1, and p. xxxii (under Russell) of Caroline Brett's and James P. Carley's Introduction to the reissue of this work (Cambridge, 1990).

44 Thomas Smith, *Gulielmi Camdeni et Illustrium Virorum ad G. Camdenum Epistolae* (London, 1691), p. 86.

45 Harl. 6018, ff. 148v, 154v, 158r.

46 The late-sixteenth-century ownership of Harl. 6613 is, to some extent, established: Wright, *Fontes Harleiani*. Harl. 2324 has an erased inscription, possibly a signature, at the foot of f. 1r. This does not respond to ultra-violet light but it can be seen to be neither Cotton's nor Beale's signature. I am grateful to Patricia Basing of the Department of Manuscripts, the British Library, for guidance on Beale and to Anne Hudson for advice on the surviving manuscripts of the 'Lanterne'.

47 I am grateful to Anne Hudson for pointing out the rarity of the Rawlinson text to me. As already mentioned, unless Cotton was employing the name 'Bruceus' before 1603, which seems most improbable, this signature must have been backdated. Of Cotton's other Wycliffite texts, those in Titus D. I and D. XIX were in his hands by the early 1620s: Harl. MS. 6018, ff. 58r (no. 105), 112r (no. 278). See also Pepys Library MS. 2073 and Norwich Castle Museum MS. 158.926/4g3, discussed below in section XII.

48 Watson, *Savile of Banke*, no. 100; Marvin L. Colker, *Trinity College Library Dublin. Descriptive Catalogue of the Mediaeval and Renaissance Latin Manuscripts*, 2 vols. (Aldershot, 1991), which establishes that Ussher had the manuscript by 1631. I am grateful to Dr Bernard Meehan, Keeper of Manuscripts at Trinity College, for permitting me to consult the typescript of this catalogue before publication, for granting me access to the manuscripts in his care and for answering my questions.

49 Watson, *Savile of Banke*, no. 34; Colker, *Catalogue*.

50 Watson, *Savile of Banke*, nos. 127, 176; Colker, *Catalogue*. For these descriptions of Cleopatra B. VI, see Margaret T. Gibson and Nigel F. Palmer, 'Manuscripts of Alan of Lille, "Anticlaudianus" in the British Isles', *Studi Medievali*, 3rd series, xxviii (1987), pp. 965–7.

51 For another example of Cotton's activities in this direction, see Carley and Tite, 'Cotton as collector of manuscripts', pp. 94–9.

52 J. T. Gilbert (ed.), *Chartularies of St Mary's Abbey, Dublin*, 2 vols. (Rolls Series, 1884), vol. ii, p. cxi. Of Cotton's other copies of Martinus Polonus, that in Faustina B. II was certainly in his hands by 1615 and probably three years earlier: Carley and Tite, 'Cotton as collector of manuscripts', p. 97 n. 14.

53 The position may be even more complicated, as there can be no doubt that a manuscript sent to Selden by Ussher two years previously, in 1625, is ff. 1r–13v of TCD 175: C. R. Elrington, *The*

Whole Works of the Most Rev. James Ussher, 17 vols. (Dublin, 1847), vol. xv, p. 303; Gilbert, *Chartularies of St Mary's Abbey*, ii, p. cxiii; Cotton Julius C. III, ff. 386r, 388r; Colker, *Catalogue*. Ware acted as go-between for Ussher and Cotton: Cotton Julius C. III, f. 384r. His extracts from the 'Annals' in Add. MS. 4787 are on ff. 29r–33v. Although they are undated, others in the volume bear dates between 1623 and 1633; as the Cotton library was closed in 1629 and access to it remained difficult until after Robert Cotton's death in 1631, Ware's extracts are likely to have pre-dated this period.

54 Another FitzRalph manuscript should be noted here. Oxford, St John's College, MS. 65, a volume of his sermons, is almost certainly one of the items listed in a catalogue of manuscripts belonging to Henry Savile of Banke. Against the entry is written 'My lord Carew had this book. lost.' This note, which is in Cotton's hand, points to his interest in the manuscript and may also indicate that he handled or owned it, although there are no marks in the volume itself to connect it with him: Watson, *Savile of Banke*, no. 23. I am grateful to the Assistant Librarian of St John's College for permitting me to examine this manuscript.

55 Harl. MS. 6018, f. 77r (no. 163). The note of gift, in Cotton's hand, is on f. 1r of TCD 497.

56 O'Sullivan, 'Ussher as a collector of manuscripts', p. 36 n. 10; Colker, *Catalogue*, p. 21. I am grateful to James Carley and Nigel Ramsay for examining this manuscript on my behalf.

57 Harl. MS. 6018, f. 168r; A. G. Watson, 'Sir Robert Cotton and Sir Simonds D'Ewes: an exchange of manuscripts', *British Museum Quarterly*, xxv (1962), pp. 19–24; Andrew G. Watson, *The Library of Sir Simonds D'Ewes* (London, 1966), pp. 22–4 and A.167. Watson suggests that Cotton may have acquired the manuscript from William Crashaw: *D'Ewes*, pp. 221–2 n. 21.

58 Watson, *D'Ewes*, C.205, E.18.

59 Ibid., A.592, A.890. For Malynes see *D.N.B.*

60 Harl. 513 has 'Ro: Cotton. Bruceus' with flourishes above and below. Harl. 525 has 'Ro: Cotton' with flourishes below. Harl. 547 has 'Rob Cotton', without flourishes.

61 The possible exception is Harl. MS. 547 which bears two unexplained numbers, perhaps from an inventory of some type. The number '55' on f. 1r is not Cottonian; the '37' on f. 8r is also unlikely to be – its form and position are wrong – but the entry for no. 37 has been omitted from the catalogue in Harl. MS. 6018. It is possible that Harl. MS. 525 is the volume intended by the entry 'Diverse Poems in old English' in Add. MS. 36789, f. 34r, a catalogue of the Cotton library which I have elsewhere dated to 1631–2: see Colin G. C. Tite, 'The early catalogues of the Cottonian library', *British Library Journal*, vi (1980), pp. 144–57. See also the interesting re-examination of the dating of this Cotton catalogue (and others) by E. C. Teviotdale, 'Some classified catalogues of the Cottonian library', *British Library Journal*, xviii (1992), pp. 74–87, and reprinted above, pp. 194–207.

62 As Watson has pointed out (*D'Ewes*, p. 24), Cotton already owned another copy of Goscelin, in Vespasian B. XX (listed in Harl. MS. 6018, f. 31r, no. 45). He had, of course, finer copies of the gospels and psalter.

63 Harl. MS. 6018, f. 148r; Kevin Sharpe, *Sir Robert Cotton 1586–1631. History and Politics in Early Modern England* (Oxford, 1979), pp. 129, 136, 176, 184.

64 Harl. MS. 6018, ff. 178v–179r. I am indebted to Dr Koert van der Horst for permitting me to examine the Utrecht Psalter (Utrecht University Library MS. 32). Sir Frederic Madden, Keeper of Manuscripts at the British Museum from 1837 to 1866, probably recognized the link between Cotton and the Lovel Lectionary if the pencil note 'Now MS. Harl.' in the margin of Harl. MS. 6018 is in his hand, but the connection seems not to have been made since his time (see, for example, Wright, *Diary of Humfrey Wanley*, vol. i, p. 115 and n. 6, and Wright, *Fontes Harleiani*). For the recovery of the Genesis, see my edition of Thomas Smith's *Catalogue of the Manuscripts in the Cottonian Library 1696* (Cambridge, 1984), p. 24.

65 Add. MSS. 36789 and 36682. See my article, 'Early catalogues', p. 148.

66 W. de Gray Birch, *The History, Art and Palaeography of the Manuscript styled the Utrecht Psalter* (London, 1876), pp. 107–8; Koert van der Horst and Jacobus H. A. Engelbregt, *Utrecht-Psalter. Vollständige Faksimile-Ausgabe im Originalformat der Handschrift 32 aus dem Besitz der Bibliotheek der Rijksuniversiteit te Utrecht: Kommentar* (Graz, 1984), pp. 59–60. I thank Kathleen Tite for translating the technical German in this volume.

67 Harl. 6018, ff. 178v–179r. An earlier version of the memorandum (ibid., f. 163r) lists the 'divers other tracts' in the second volume, establishing the identification given here. It also supplements the descriptions of the first and third items; the third item is also entered at ff. 51r–52r (no. 78) in the catalogue of manuscripts that precedes the memoranda. The only surviving copy (see Conyers Read, *Lord Burghley and Queen Elizabeth* (London, 1965), pp. 508, 587 n. 106) of Burghley's 'Meditations' (P.R.O., SP 12/255 no. 84 (ff. 185r–208v)) is not in his autograph. I am grateful to David Carlson for advice on the volume by Francis Thynne.

68 Cotton owned another copy of Osbern's life, in Vitellius D. XV, by 1612 and possibly by 1602: Harl. 6018, f. 165r; Titus C. I, ff. 140r + v.

69 The connection between the catalogue entry and Arundel 20 is noted in manuscript in the working copy of the *Catalogue of Manuscripts in the British Museum. New Series. Vol. 1, part I. The Arundel Manuscripts* (London, 1834) in the Department of Manuscripts, the British Library.

70 Watson, *Savile of Banke*, no. 232 and n. 232.2. It is interesting to note that both manuscripts are associated with early-sixteenth-century heralds, Carlisle in the case of Julius E. VI and the Windsor Herald, Thomas Wall, in the case of Arundel 59. Wall's arms are emblazoned on the first leaf while his record of purchase in 1525 is on f. 130v. The connection with Wall could explain the earl of Arundel's interest in the manuscript: Arundel became Earl Marshal in 1621.

71 The record of Fowler's borrowing (Harl. MS. 6018, f. 173v) has not been crossed through. The octavo volume is now in an Arundel binding and exhibits no marks of Cotton's ownership. I am indebted to Fr Albert Loomie for identifying Fowler and to Linda Peck for recognizing the manuscript to which this loan relates. For Cotton's contacts with Gondomar and his efforts to secure Arundel's patronage, see Sharpe, *Cotton*, pp. 131–7.

72 Add. MS. 5161, ff. 9v, 10r (where Madden annotates the loan with his identification); Cotton Appendix XLV, art. 13, f. 2r.

73 Bodl. MS. Add. C. 301 (*SC* 30283), f. 40r. Preceding and following this folio are Ussher's notes on the proofs of Spelman's *Concilia*, which the latter received on 20 Dec. 1638 (see f. 46r). Ussher assigns the Arundel manuscript to St Augustine's, Canterbury, but this must be an error.

74 Thomas Howard, first Viscount Bindon: Davis, *Medieval Cartularies*, no. 435 and p. 174. Bindon (d. 1582), who was Arundel's great-great-uncle, was succeeded, in turn, by his two surviving sons, the younger dying in 1611.

75 *D.N.B.* under Lord William Howard; G. B. Parks (ed.), *Gregory Martin 'Roma Sancta'* (Rome, 1969), pp. xiii, xvii, xviii, xxii, xxiv. The manuscript was bought by the National Library of Australia in 1964.

76 Harl. MS. 6018, ff. 149r, 176r. Other entries, undated, are on ff. 155v and 162v, and in Add. MS. 35213, f. 38v.

77 Pits notes (*De Rebus Anglicis*, p. 990) the date of completion of his book.

78 In the two further undated lists in Harl. 6018 (on ff. 155v and 162v), Lord William is joined as borrower of *Roma Sancta* by Nicholas Roscarrock (who entered his household in 1607). Three other items in the same lists were the subject of a specific request from Roscarrock in August 1607 that he be permitted to take them with him to Naworth, Lord William's seat. The Gregory Martin manuscript is not one of those mentioned by Roscarrock and is probably an addition to both lists. (For Roscarrock's request, see Smith, *Camdeni Epistolae*, p. 92.)

79 The script, an unexceptional secretary, is certainly not unlike Roscarrock's but, as few examples of his hand are known, the scope for comparison is limited. It is also unfortunate that nothing resembling this manuscript features in the various (and somewhat contradictory) lists of Lord William Howard's manuscripts. I am grateful to Andrew Watson for advice on both these points, and to Ian Doyle and Nicholas Orme for guidance on Roscarrock's hand.

80 See, for example, Harl. MS. 6018, ff. 181r + v (where Howard's identity, by virtue of his description as 'brother' [i.e. brother-in-law] to Thomas Cotton, is made clear).

81 The manuscript is discussed by J. B. Trapp, 'Notes on MSS written by Peter Meghen', *The Book Collector*, xxiv (1975), pp. 80–96. On its final flyleaf, f. 116v, is an *ex libris* of one John Russell, dated 8 Mar. 1589. Another copy of the *Speculum*, in Cleopatra D. IX, had been in the library for some years: Harl. MS. 6018, f. 13r, no. 16.

82 Janet Backhouse of the Department of Manu-

scripts, the British Library, recognized James's hand and kindly brought this manuscript to my attention.

83 Cotton Appendix XLV, art. 13, f. 6v.

84 The record of loan confirms this. A Cottonian pressmark (Claudius A. VIII) is given only for the other volume borrowed by Howard.

85 For Smith, King and Morgan see *D.N.B.* Two possible Roger Nortons are listed by H. R. Plomer, *A Dictionary of the Booksellers and Printers...1641 to 1667*, Bibliographical Society (London, 1907). 'Ro: Cotton Bruceus' is to be found on the title page of the manuscript.

86 Seymour de Ricci, *Census of Medieval and Renaissance Manuscripts in the United States and Canada*, 3 vols. (New York, 1935–40), vol. i, p. 385. De Ricci suggests a date of *c.* 1610 for the manuscript but Le Neve says that the work was dedicated to Lord Burghley. William Cecil, Lord Burghley, died in 1598; his son Thomas who inherited the title was created earl of Exeter in 1605. A date earlier than 1610 is also suggested by the inclusion at f. 11r of an account of the funeral of Sir John Savage in January 1597/8. Smith himself died in 1618.

87 The work of this scribe, who writes an unmistakable italic hand, is to be found in many of the Cotton state paper volumes and in Holkham MS. 677 (see section X, below). For examples in Add. MS. 4712, see ff. 23r, 28r, 38r–46v, etc.

88 Earlier loans, also to St George, of this same volume make it clear that 'velom' refers to the binding and not to the leaves and that the 'Court' is that of Henry VII, whose articles of 1493 these are: Harl. MS. 6018, ff. 149r, 155r, 160r.

89 It may have been an Office of Arms book, abstracted by Dethick. For the record of Cotton's purchase (noted on f. 1r) see also Add. MS. 35213, f. 33r, a list of books handled by Chaloner. Add. MS. 6113 is the volume there described as 'An other old book in paper contayning som nots of Christing and Creation gathered by a Herald for his privat use'. For Colbarne and Chaloner, see L. Campbell and F. Steer, *A Catalogue of Manuscripts in the College of Arms. Collections*, vol. i (London, 1988), pp. 474–5.

90 Harl. 6018, f. 152v: 'A Book in Foll of Creations of Noblemen and other Ceremonis it was on[e] of Sʳ William Dethiks Books'.

91 Harl. 6018, f. 161v. The same book, similarly described, had been lent earlier: ibid., f. 160v. For the history of Add. MS. 12530 after the mid-eighteenth century, see David Carlson, 'The writings and manuscript collections of the Elizabethan alchemist, antiquary and herald Francis Thynne', *Huntington Library Quarterly*, lii (1989), p. 244, no. 41. I am grateful to David Carlson for suggesting this identification.

92 Linda Levy Peck, *Northampton. Patronage and Policy at the Court of James I* (London, 1982), p. 12.

93 There is little doubt that the heavily deleted words in the inscription are 'Robert Cotton Bruceus' while the inscription itself, though formally written, could well be in Cotton's hand. The manuscript is listed as belonging to Queen Elizabeth and to Cotton by Wright, *Fontes Harleiani*, but Elizabeth's ownership should be treated with caution. F. 1v of the volume carries a curious illustration of a rose surmounted by a royal crown, with below it a lion and the words 'Quid ultra', possibly a motto. The significance of this has yet to be established but it is probably indicative of the intended recipient of the manuscript. Linda Peck has kindly given me the benefit of her knowledge of the manuscripts of Howard's work and Ann Payne has advised me on the illustration.

94 Harl. MS. 6018, f. 150r: 'Defenc of womens government. Lord of Northampton. Mr Starky'.

95 Bodl. MS. Ashmole 1141, art. II, p. 1. Herbert's account is in the form of a letter.

96 Joseph Planta was Keeper of Manuscripts from 1776 to 1799, Robert Nares from 1799 to 1807. The note is probably by Sir Frederic Madden: its tone would certainly be in character. It is to be found in the archive known as the Cotton Catalogue Box. For other examples of confusion between the Cotton and Harleian libraries, see Watson, *D'Ewes*, p. 36.

97 There seems to be no justification for the title found on the spine, 'Collections from records public & private by Sir Robert Cotton': presumably it was prompted by the signature 'Ro: Cotton. Bruceus' on f. 1r. The claim in *A Catalogue of the Harleian Collection of Manuscripts...preserved in the British Museum*, 4 vols. (London, 1808–12), vol. ii, p. 564, that the manuscript contains material in Cotton's hand is also, I believe, unwarranted.

98 Bodl. MS. Smith 140 at the Julius B. X

pressmark. For the checklist of volumes missing in 1657, see Add. MS. 36682, f. 1r.

99 C. Davenport, *English Heraldic Book Stamps* (London, 1909), p. 127. The *SC* entry questioning Cotton's ownership has been corrected in the working copy in the Bodleian Library. The manuscript bears other annotations, *passim*, in hands of the sixteenth, and seventeenth centuries, and on f. 154r 'Henric*us* de la Wade d*ominus* de Stant*on* iuxta Wodstok... . According to a note by Francis Douce, written on the front pastedown, the volume once 'contained some Coventry charters which I gave to Mr Sharpe of Coventry'. This is the antiquary, Thomas Sharpe (d. 1841: see *D.N.B.*), who was a friend of Douce. The charters appear to have been removed from the very front of the manuscript and it is obviously likely that they, too, were once owned by Cotton. Unfortunately, many of Sharpe's manuscripts were destroyed by fire at Birmingham Reference Library in 1879, a point I owe to Nigel Ramsay.

100 I am particularly indebted to Jayne Ringrose for assistance with details of this volume which bears a number of scribbled names: 'Thome Smyth pertinet' (xv or xvi cent., f. 270v), 'Thomas Bury Smyth' (?) (xvi. cent., f. 168v), 'Rychard Smyth' (xvi cent., f. 168v).

101 Seymour de Ricci, *A Handlist of Manuscripts in the Library of the Earl of Leicester at Holkham Hall* (Oxford, 1932), p. 63, says that the manuscript belonged to Cotton, presumably on the basis of the evidence here discussed. I am indebted to Lord Coke for permitting me to examine this and other manuscripts in his possession. I am also very grateful to Mr Fred Jolly and Dr Bryan Ward-Perkins, respectively Administrator and past Librarian at Holkham Hall, for their advice on Coke's hand. Sir Edward Coke was one of the users of the Cotton library but none of his borrowings seems to resemble MS. 752. The name, 'Mr Pagitts', on f. 3r of the manuscript, may be an *ex libris*: Cotton had a cousin 'James Pagett' from whom he hoped to obtain a register of Cirencester Abbey: Harl. MS. 6018, f. 150v.

It is worth here drawing attention to Holkham MS. 677, article 50 (ff. 253r–257r), although as a tract composed by Cotton it is strictly outside the scope of this article. It is a copy of a paper written for the earl of Northampton in 1604 on 'Reasons to maintain the Navigation of the English Merchants into the East and West Indians [*sic*]'. It bears Cotton's signature and annotations, and the text is in the familiar italic hand of one of Cotton's scribes (see the discussion of Add. MS. 4712 in section VIII, above). Another copy, in the same hand, is Cotton Vespasian C. XIII, ff. 47r–50v. The paper and the use Cotton made of it are discussed by Peck, *Northampton*, pp. 106–9.

102 On ff. 1v–174v. The remainder of the volume, ff. 175r–205v, is a collection of medieval statutes. The two sections have their own contemporary quiring and are in different hands, although the presentation is similar and both parts are in Law-French. Cotton's ownership may or may not have extended to the second part.

103 There has been some debate over the degree of Cotton's involvement in the campaign: see Sharpe, *Cotton*, p. 42 and n. 155. The Cotton copies of the parliament rolls, together with a volume of abridgements in Titus E. I, are in Titus E. II–XIV, F. I and F. II. They are not a wholly homogeneous set (some contain original documents interspersed among the transcripts) and one at least was in Cotton's possession at an earlier date than the campaign: Titus E. V, the rolls of 1–16 Henry VI, has 'Ro: Cotton Bruceus 1600', presumably another example of backdating, on f. 1r. Another manuscript, Add. MS. 34811, is a copy, apparently made for John Williams, bishop of Lincoln from 1621 to 1624, of Titus E. V: Cotton's signature is reproduced by the scribe but there is no evidence that Williams's manuscript is a Cotton stray.

104 I am indebted to Mr Daniel Huws, Keeper of Manuscripts and Records, the National Library of Wales, for drawing my attention to the second of these manuscripts.

105 The volume has Sir Robert Cotton's name on the spine but the binding is, of course, modern. The many annotations are not by him in spite of the statement to the contrary in the *Catalogue of Additions to the Manuscripts*.

106 Cotton Appendix XLV, art. 13, f. 9r. This loan memorandum could also fit Titus E. I, a manuscript which Selden certainly borrowed some years later: ibid., f. 14v. Titus E. I has

the same design of engraved title page as Add. MS. 33216.

107 The signature, on f. 8r which is now the first folio in the manuscript, is more stylized than normal and may date from the earlier years of James I's reign. My thanks are due to the Assistant Librarian of the College for allowing me to examine this volume and for answering my questions.

108 Harl. MS. 6018, f. 159r. The entry has not been deleted.

109 *D.N.B.* under Lambe; J. D. Martin, *The Cartularies and Registers of Peterborough Abbey*, Northamptonshire Record Society, xxviii (1978), p. 46.

110 '[B]egin uppon a new pag': f. 63r; 'another pag': f. 82r, etc. Cotton's signature, 'Robertus Cotton Bruceus', is on f. 3r.

111 Harl. MS. 6018, f. 149v.

112 Cotton Appendix XLV, art. 13, f. 8v. This loan memorandum is not deleted as was the usual custom when a book was returned. A previous loan of the volume, to Sir John Borough on 11 June 1640, gives the pressmark: ibid., f. 7v. The pressmark is still to be seen on f. ii^v of the manuscript.

113 Add. MS. 36682, ff. 73r, 100r. The Pentateuch had been a gift from Archbishop James Ussher in 1629. Extracts from Add. MS. 46410, found in BL, Hargrave MS. 219, are preceded on f. 2 by a note, *c.* 1700, stating that the original was 'wanting at the library' and was in the hands of 'Mr Grimes the late Usher of the Rolls'.

114 Crown Office Miscellaneous Books; P.R.O., C 193/2. I owe this reference to departmental records maintained by the Department of Manuscripts, the British Library.

115 For Oseley see, for example, *Calendar of State Papers Domestic, Addenda, 1547–65*, pp. 492, 576; *Addenda, 1580–1625*, p. 18; *CSP Dom. 1598–1601*, pp. 371, 492, 510. Oseley does not identify the Lord Treasurer, but as he says that he had received his commission approximately six years previously and as he seems not to have been active into James I's reign, the probability is that this was William Cecil.

116 Bernard noted the gift at the start of the index which he added to the volume.

117 Sharpe, *Cotton*, p. 65; Harl. MS. 6018, f. 160v. The entry is not deleted. An alternative identification for the loan may be Vespasian B. XXII, a volume in large quarto; however,

118 the Tanner manuscript is bound in white vellum.

118 Roger B. Manning, 'Antiquarianism and the seigneurial reaction: Sir Robert and Sir Thomas Cotton and their tenants', *Historical Research*, lxiii (1990), pp. 277–88, especially p. 283.

119 Sir John Cotton, third baronet, succeeded to the title in 1662 and died in 1702. The fourth and sixth baronets, also called John, succeeded in 1702 and 1749, the latter dying without issue in 1752. Castle's son was still championing the cause of the Cotton tenants as late as 1651: Manning, 'Antiquarianism and the seigneurial reaction', p. 288. At the end of the manuscript are a few separately foliated pages which include notes by Cotton of rents due at Lady Day 1613.

120 I acknowledge with gratitude my debt to Mr William Proby for granting me access to manuscripts in the Elton Hall Collection, and for his kindness during my visits to Elton. The Cotton volumes (and many others) at Elton Hall were carefully calendared by Mr Granville Proby earlier in this century.

121 The Cotton interest in Elton nevertheless predated the marriage: the manor was conveyed to Sir Thomas Cotton in 1633. Elton Hall Collection, Miscellaneous, II (modern transcript), pp. 46–51.

122 The trade price in 1619 for such a binding was between 4s and 5s 6d. I am indebted to Mirjam Foot for advice on this point. There is a brief note by Cotton, recording some book binding commissions, on the final flyleaf of Titus A. XV. Most of the Emperor volumes were rebound by the British Museum in the nineteenth century and their previous bindings were discarded: Cleopatra B. VI, discussed in this article (section IV), is an exception, still possessing Cotton's covers and the remains of their clasps.

123 These have been taken from a so far unidentified manuscript of musical notation. Below the binding instructions is a date, 'Monday 23 June quarto caroli'.

124 For example, in Nero B. II, Galba B. VII *et seq.*, Vitellius E. XI. See also (section X, above) the discussion of Add. MS. 33216, whose title page, however, differs from that of the Elton volume. These title pages require classification and analysis. Volume I of the

Elton Hall manuscripts chiefly relates to Normancross and the honour of Gloucester fee, Huntingdonshire, together with some material concerning Falkworth. It also includes various Cotton family pedigrees.

125 The Emperor arrangement was in place by the late 1630s, well before these volumes left for Elton: Tite, 'Early catalogues', p. 148.

126 Two further pieces of evidence bearing upon this should be mentioned. Firstly, despite appearances to the contrary, the Cotton Appendix manuscripts probably did not escape the Emperor classification. The history of the group is complex but, for those volumes which existed in their present form in the seventeenth century, there is some evidence of a location under the Augustus pressmark. See Colin G. C. Tite, 'The Cotton Appendix and the Cotton Fragments', *The Library*, 6th Series, xv (1993), pp. 52–5'. Secondly, none of the library's main administrative tools (catalogues, loan lists, memoranda) received an Emperor pressmark. (By contrast, Thomas James's annual record of accessions at the Bodleian Library, MS. Bodl. 510 (*SC* 2569), had a pressmark by about 1650, although his register of reader admissions did not: Ian Philip, *The Bodleian Library in the Seventeenth and Eighteenth Centuries* (Oxford, 1983), pp. 14, 20, 117 n. 60, 118 n. 88; *SC*.) Such manuscripts are clearly a special category, of course, but one of the consequences of their omission from the Emperor system is that there are gaps in, and different patterns to, their subsequent history, which are worth noting briefly here. For example, did Harl. MS. 6018 remain with the Cottonian library and then get mixed up with the Harleian library after the latter's arrival at the British Museum in the 1750s? If Add. MS. 36789, the next catalogue, was owned by the Cottons (rather than being an official document, a product of the library's closure in 1629 by order of the government), it left their possession at an unknown date and was bought by the Museum in 1903. On the other hand, the first Emperor catalogue, Add. MS. 36682, undoubtedly the most useful of the three, stayed with the Cotton family after 1702 and, according to a note on f. 3r, narrowly escaped destruction: 'When Stretton Estate [Sir John Cotton's estate in Bedfordshire] was sold in the year 1764, the family left in the

house there some MSS as rubbish to be thrown away, & not worth preserving. These I sent for, being unwilling they should be destroyed, & among them was a catalogue of the Cotton library in 2 vol⁵ folio...'.

127 'Su*m* Guiliel. Bowyer. 1566': ff. 3r, 5r; Stow's annotations occur, for example, on ff. 66v, 67r and 78r.

128 The manuscript is assigned to Cotton's ownership in *A Catalogue of the Lansdowne Manuscripts in the British Museum* (London, 1819). The Macclesfield arms are on f. iv.

129 This has been worked out by David Dumville and will be discussed in detail in the forthcoming volume dealing with the 'Gildasian recension' in his edition of the *Historia Brittonum*, 10 vols. (Cambridge, 1985–). For a summary of his argument see Carley, 'John Leland and the contents of the English predissolution libraries: Lincolnshire', pp. 346–7.

130 C. E. Wright, 'Sir Edward Dering: a seventeenth-century antiquary and his "Saxon" charters', in C. Fox and B. Dickins (eds.), *The Early Cultures of North-West Europe* (Cambridge, 1950), pp. 369–93. Llanstephan 175 came to the National Library of Wales from the library of Sir John Williams who, interestingly, also owned Cotton's copy of Humphrey Lhuyd, *Commentarioli Britannicae Descriptionis Fragmentum* (Cologne, 1572), now National Library of Wales pressmark Wa.11 (identified by Richard L. DeMolen, 'The library of William Camden', *Proceedings of the American Philosophical Society*, cxxviii (1984), p. 382). Cotton, of course, owned other copies of the *Historia Brittonum*.

131 For this identification compare, for example, the references to Pope Joan and Archbishop Thomas Arundel in article 5 of the entry in Harl. MS. 6018 (ff. 141v, 143r) with the similar references on pp. 53 and 60 of the Cambridge manuscript, the mention of the fable of Albina in article 6 (and on p. 61 of the manuscript) and the reference to the prioress strangled in her bed (article 7 and p. 78). The order of items in the manuscript remains as in the Harl. MS. 6018 entry. No marks of Cotton's ownership survive in the volume.

132 I am grateful to Ann Hutchison for carrying out a preliminary inspection of this manuscript and to Jayne Ringrose of Cambridge University Library for providing me with a photocopy of

the draft catalogue entry. The volume was owned by John Twyne of Canterbury in 1578 and it may be the 'Sprott and Thorne of Canterbury' that Cotton acquired from Lord William Howard (Harl. MS. 6018, f. 149v), although Tiberius A. IX, ff. 107r–180v, is an alternative candidate. (Vespasian B. XIX, the *Chronicon* of Gervase of Canterbury, demonstrates that such a pattern of ownership is possible. This manuscript passed from Twyne to Lord William, who gave it to Cotton: Andrew G. Watson, 'John Twyne of Canterbury (d. 1581) as a collector of medieval manuscripts: a preliminary investigation', *The Library*, 6th Series, viii (1986), p. 147 no. 7.) The entry at no. 396 in Harl. MS. 6018 lists both a 'Chronica Tho: Sprott...' and a 'Chronica. Ja: [*sic*] Thorne Ab. A° 778 ad Annu*m* 1356'. The latter is no longer in the Cambridge manuscript and may have become Tiberius B. VII, a volume missing since the mid-seventeenth century: Add. MS. 36682, ff. 1r, 77v; Harl. MS. 6018, f. 187r. Much of CUL, Add. MS. 3578 was edited by Thomas Hearne in his *Thomas Sprotti Chronica* (Oxford, 1719), an attribution now, of course, rejected.

133 On f. 1r is written 'Arth*ur* Maynwaring is my name A° 1567', possibly an indication of former ownership. Several other names, in sixteenth-century hands, are scribbled on the final flyleaves.

134 These annotations are found, respectively, on ff. 351v, 337v and 338r. M. R. James, *Bibliotheca Pepysiana. A descriptive Catalogue of the Library of Samuel Pepys. Part III: Mediaeval manuscripts* (London, 1923). For Weston, see *D.N.B.* There is no firm identification for Herendon or Bache, although a Thomas Bache who died *c.* 1632 was a canon of Hereford: J. Foster, *Alumni Oxonienses 1500–1714*, 4 vols. (Oxford, 1888). A 'Mr Randall' is listed as a borrower from Cotton (Harl. MS. 6018, f. 156v) but of books unrelated in subject matter to this manuscript. I am indebted to the Pepys Librarian for the opportunity to see this volume.

135 N. R. Ker, *Medieval Manuscripts in British Libraries*, vol. iii (Oxford, 1983) (henceforth *MMBL*). I am grateful to Andrew Watson for drawing this manuscript to my attention.

136 Either 'the positions of Wicklife in 8[°]' to 'my lord of London after Archbisshop...it was sent by Mr Doctor Pasfeild', a form of words that must indicate a borrowing by George Abbot in 1611 (Harl. MS. 6018, f. 157v and cf. f. 153r), or 'A Book of Wicklife...' which was lent to the preacher, William Crashaw, according to a memorandum which can be dated from its context to no later than 1614–15 (ibid., f. 158v and cf. f. 156r).

137 It was owned by W. F. Patteson in 1818 and was presented to Norwich Castle Museum by Mrs J. Perowne in 1961: *MMBL*, vol. iii.

138 *MLGB*; *MMBL*, vol. ii, p. 347; HMC, *Various Collections*, ii (London, 1903), pp. 24–7. The signature, 'Ro. Cotton', was read in 1903 with the assistance of a reagent. It is just possible that Cotton did not own the second part of the present manuscript (although the annotation on f. 81r is likely to be his). However, the fact that the binding of the manuscript is of the sixteenth or seventeenth century and that the sixteenth-century foliation of the first manuscript is not continued into the second points to Cotton or a contemporary as the agent in the creation of the combined volume.

139 *MMBL*, vol. ii, p. 347, records the twentieth-century provenance of the manuscript but does not mention Greene.

140 There is an entry for 'S[t] Augustine against the Pelagians etc' in Add. MS. 36789 (f. 169v), the catalogue of 1631–2, but Cotton Appendix LVI art. 2 is a possible alternative identification for this.

141 According to a note on f. 1r.

142 Quoted in A. Clark (ed.), *The Life and Times of Anthony Wood, antiquary of Oxford, 1632–1695, described by himself*, vol. ii (Oxford Historical Society, xxi, 1892), p. 174 n. 10. After Prideaux's death in 1650, the manuscript was bought at Worcester by Dr Thomas Barlow, from whom it reached the Bodleian in 1693. For Dee's ownership, see Roberts and Watson, *John Dee's Library Catalogue*, M110. Other copies of the Grosseteste material in Nero D. II and Otho C. XIV were in the library by the early 1620s, though the latter manuscript was out on long-term loan: Harl. MS. 6018, ff. 92v, 114r (nos. 197, 295); Teviotdale, 'Classified catalogues', p. 81 (reprinted above, p. 201) and nn. 51, 52.

143 The Pontefract cartulary was owned in 1620 by Francis Bunney of Newland: MS. Dodsworth 116, f. 39r.

144 Another of Barlow's manuscripts, Bodl. MS. Barlow 13 (*SC* 6421), a composite volume in part connected with James Ussher, has at f. 342 a single leaf with Cotton's signature at the head. The leaf is damaged and the text has yet to be identified, but the opening words of chapter ten of a treatise on presbyterianism can be read.

145 Davis, *Medieval Cartularies*, no. 722; Warner and Gilson, *Old Royal Catalogue*.

146 Warner and Gilson, *Old Royal Catalogue*. The survey of the library was conducted by three commissioners, of whom Humfrey Wanley was the most important. Their report was appended to several copies of Smith's *Catalogue*.

147 'Robertus Cotton Bruceus' is on f. 3r.

148 According to Sir Frederic Madden, the arms on f. 1r are those of Louis Malet, Sire de Graville and Admiral of France, who had died in 1516: cf. *Dictionnaire de la Noblesse de la France* (Paris, 1868). For Peiresc's connections with Cotton, see Sharpe, *Cotton*, especially pp. 95–8. The date of Cotton's acquisition of the Oleron material in Nero A. VI is unknown; that in Julius E. I seems to have been procured by Richard James: Harl. 7002, f. 122r.

149 Sloane MS. 3677, f. 157v.

150 Harl. MS. 6018, f. 150r; Bodl. MS. Dugdale 48 (*SC* 6536), f. 63v. MS. Dodsworth 76 (*SC* 5018), ff. 56r–64v, 121r–123v, are fragments of a St Mary's register. The first group of leaves is quarto in size, the second folio, and either or both could fit the description 'unbound' in the loan to Dodsworth. All these pages have been assigned to the ownership of Christopher Hatton (see, for example, Davis, *Medieval Cartularies*, nos. 1098, 1099, 1105). As far as concerns ff. 56r–64v this is undoubtedly correct: William Dugdale, *Monasticon Anglicanum*, vol. i (London, 1655), pp. 393–4, prints material which is to be found in these folios and says that it is 'Ex fragmento Registri S. Mariae Ebor. in bibl. Hattoniana' (wording which, however, echoes the description of the unbound Cottonian manuscript and may therefore indicate what had become of it). While there seems not to be the same authority for the provenance of ff. 121r–123v the probability must also favour Hatton, although it is possible that these leaves could have reached Dodsworth by some other route, even maybe as a consequence of the loan of 1621.

151 MS. Dugdale 48, f. 61v; Harl. MS. 6018,

f. 104r, no. 231; MS. Selden supra 111 (*SC* 52557), f. 7r; Davis, *Medieval Cartularies*, no. 45.

152 Harl. MS. 6018, f. 113r, no. 287.

153 This transaction was carefully investigated by Alistair Campbell, *Encomium Emmae Reginae*, Camden Society, 3rd Series, lxxii (1949), pp. xii–xiv.

154 College of Arms, London, Vincent MS. 6, p. 227; MS. Dugdale 48, f. 56v; Davis, *Medieval Cartularies*, no. 1039.

155 MS. Dugdale 48, ff. 55r, 58v. In a book of extracts devoted to Cottonian manuscripts, Dodsworth made notes 'ex Registro de Belvoir penes Comitem Rutlandiae', probably in 1639: MS. Dodsworth 78 (*SC* 5019), f. 70r.

156 Cf. Sharpe's comment that the 'list of those borrowing…reads like a *Who's Who* of the Jacobean administration': *Cotton*, p. 78.

157 Some of the losses must also, of course, be blamed on the borrowers. Smith comments on this in his address 'To the Reader': 'You will share my regret and be both amazed and distressed to find, as is easily apparent from gaps in the catalogue, that many books today are missing, but frequent precedent shows that even literary treasure is vulnerable to theft …The eminent kindness of the Cottons…little deserved to suffer treatment conflicting so shamefully with right and justice. If only the borrowers or their heirs into whose hands the books came had the honesty to make amends!': *Catalogue*, p. 24.

158 Julius C. III, ff. 29r, 30r. The grant of monopolies, damaging to both trade and the consumer, was a major political issue in early-seventeenth-century England.

159 K. Tsantsanoglou, *To Lexiko tou Photiou Chronologese-Cheirographe Paradose. Ellenika*, Occasional Paper 17 (Thessalonika, 1967), pp. 40–3, 116. Later owners were John Owen, Thomas Gale and his son, Roger, who gave the manuscript to Trinity College in 1738 (p. 116). For Thomson see *D.N.B.*

160 Harl. MS. 6018, f. 159v. I owe the identification of Cotton's loans record to Scot McKendrick who also told me of Tsantsanoglou's work and very generously provided me with a paraphrase of its Modern Greek text.

161 Because Richard Thomson is thus firmly established as the source from whom Cotton acquired the Photius manuscript, he must also

have provided Cotton with the manuscript of Philostratus, discussed in Section II above: an entry for the Philostratus manuscript immediately follows that for the Photius manuscript in one of the lists of exchanges with Young and 'Mr Tompson' is named as the source (Harl. MS. 6018, f. 159v). This identification of the previous ownership of the Philostratus manuscript therefore supersedes that given in the first edition of this article where I suggested that the man in question might have been Paul Thomson, chaplain to James I. Paul Thomson remains a member of Cotton's circle, however: it is he, not Richard, who is noted as a borrower in, for example, the list of printed books in Add. MS. 35213: see Colin G. C. Tite, 'A catalogue of Sir Robert Cotton's printed books?', *British Library Journal*, xvii (1991), p. 7 (reprinted above, p. 189) and n. 24.

162 An unnumbered flyleaf at the beginning of the manuscript and f. 152 at the end have been so treated; a stub from the same psalter is also visible between f. 148 and f. 149. I am very grateful to Dr David McKitterick for a valuable description of the present appearance of the manuscript and for allowing me to examine it.

163 For the psalter see Carley and Tite, 'Cotton as collector of manuscripts', especially pp. 96–7 and nn. 10, 14.

164 Nicholas Pronay and John Taylor, *Parliamentary Texts of the Later Middle Ages* (Oxford, 1980), pp. 117–18. See also John Taylor, 'The manuscripts of the *Modus Tenendi Parliamentum*', *English Historical Review*, lxxxiii (1968), pp. 673–4.

165 Harl. MS. 6018, f. 161r. The Great Seal of Ireland is still attached to MS. EL 1699, information I owe to the kindness of Mary L. Robertson, Curator of Manuscripts at the Huntington Library.

166 Harl. MS. 6018, f. 154v.

167 On 9 Oct. 1612, in preparation for the new Irish parliament, the clerk of its Lower House was ordered to go to England to familiarize himself with procedures: *Calendar of the State Papers relating to Ireland. 1611–14* (1877), p. 291. There are copies of the *Modus* in the following Cottonian manuscripts: Jul. B. IV, Tib. E. VIII, Nero C. I, D. VI, Vit. C. IV, Vesp. B. VII and Dom. XVIII. A further copy has yet to be identified: see no. 147 in Appendix, above.

168 Harl. MS. 6018, f. 159r. I am very grateful to Ceridwen Lloyd-Morgan of the National Library of Wales for a detailed description of the appearance of the manuscript.

169 'Parlament Book of Ed: 3 time in velome. Foll': Harl. MS. 6018, f. 148r.

306

BRITISH POST-MEDIAEVAL VERSE
IN THE COTTON COLLECTION:
A SURVEY AND HANDLIST

HILTON KELLIHER

THE Cotton collection has long been recognized as one of the richest sources for Latin and vernacular writings of the Anglo-Saxon period; while from the mediaeval holdings alone, it has been said, 'the history of Middle English literature might be largely written'.[1] In particular, the poetry of these ages constitutes one of its greatest strengths, masterpieces like *Beowulf* and *Sir Gawain and the Green Knight* being merely the pick of a flourishing crop. That such a large and important body of creative writing should survive here may seem surprising when we consider that Cotton's concerns were in general quite other than aesthetic ones. Nothing that is known about him suggests any very pronounced or sophisticated literary tastes. Yet, with his broad interest in British antiquities and English history in all their diverse aspects, he clearly thought it appropriate to seek out records of former ages regardless of the medium in which they were framed. In this respect literature, which fleshes out the bones of history and offers contemporary commentary on events and attitudes of the past, would fall quite naturally within his province.

Among the post-mediaeval manuscripts in Cotton's library poetry as such is rather less readily definable as a separate sub-division.[2] Verse accessions from the period after 1500 may be divided into five categories, mirroring the whole range of his intellectual interests and professional concerns. In literary terms, pride of place must go to the small number of verse miscellanies and other items primarily of aesthetic interest. Next come collections of epitaphs and inscriptions, not infrequently unknown from any other source, that survive among the papers that accrued to Cotton from fellow members of the Elizabethan Society of Antiquaries – most notably from William Camden (d. 1623).[3] Thirdly, there are the many scattered items of verse preserved among official and quasi-official papers on English history, politics and diplomacy during the sixteenth century, such as those found in the archive of materials relating to Mary, Queen of Scots. The fourth category comprises a small but not insignificant section of verse relating to persons and events of the reign of James I: in particular, the papers of Cotton's patron the Catholic Henry Howard (d. 1614), Earl of Northampton, preserve several interesting items. The final class is entirely haphazard, consisting of chance survivals of verse in marginal and fly-leaf jottings.

Taken altogether, in view of the miscellaneous nature of the sources and the fact that, unlike the Harleian and Royal libraries, Cotton's collection includes only two or three verse miscellanies of the post-mediaeval period, the corpus of almost four hundred and fifty texts identified below is no mean showing. The great bulk of the verse, however, derives from the English State Papers and the antiquarian collections, where it figures mostly as a species of political or personal history. Yet the very fact of its random distribution throughout Cotton's 'modern' political papers affords a powerful testimony to the part that it played in the social, cultural and political life of the time. Men of affairs turned naturally to verse on many occasions; and, given the nature of the prevailing literary culture, individual poems tend to be occasional in character and fairly limited in genre. Inevitably, much that is found here will be of more immediate interest to the antiquary and historian than to the general reader of poetry or the literary critic. If the Latin pieces outnumber the English by a factor of five to four, that is not merely because so many happen to be memorial inscriptions but rather because, in literature as in diplomacy, Latin was still the *lingua franca* of educated Europeans.[4] Item for item they are little inferior to the English verse in subject-matter or style, and at their best, in the work of Lily or Buchanan for instance, they are true poetry.

Though Cotton was brought up at a time when the social accomplishments of the well-bred gentleman included the making of music and verses there is no reason to suppose that he had any very strong inclination to either, let alone to poetry for poetry's sake. The only specimen of contemporary verse to survive in his own hand is his jotting, on the last page of one of the strays from his collection (Add. MS. 4712), of a brief lyric on the death of Elizabeth I.[5] Yet this may be no more than a testimony to the ever-present political dimension in his collecting interests; and it would be merely fanciful to suppose, in view of the vogue enjoyed by this particular piece at the time, that it was of his own composition.[6] What is more, even though he lived two centuries before the great age of autograph-hunting it still strikes one as remarkable that, for a man of his period, his collection includes no significant holograph poem. He seems never to have taken advantage of his personal contacts with contemporary poets: the most famous of them all, Donne and Jonson, are represented solely by letters in which they sought the loan of manuscripts.[7]

For present purposes it would serve little purpose to trace the sequence of Cotton's acquisition of those manuscripts that happen to incorporate verse, even if that were feasible.[8] Some information might perhaps be gleaned from the various extant manuscript catalogues, but the codices themselves seldom offer much help.[9] Only Caligula B. X and Vespasian E. VII carry specific dates, of 1603 and 1604 respectively, in conjunction with a signature. The addition of 'Bruceus' after Cotton's name in ownership inscriptions, made in assertion of his Scots ancestry, seems to have begun with the accession of James I.[10] Four other volumes that are prefaced by contents lists written out in the bold hand of his librarian Richard James may perhaps have been acquired during the last half-dozen years of Cotton's life.[11] But the fact that at least four include lists drawn up by Sir Thomas Cotton (1594–1662), the second baronet, shows that this is mere supposition.[12]

Another case in which we seem initially to be on firm ground proves to be a disappointing one. One of the few verse manuscripts that can be claimed as primarily literary, as opposed to political or historical, is the miscellany of early to mid sixteenth-century songs and ballads that survives in Vespasian A. XXV, where it is interspersed with other items.[13] Though part at least of this volume belonged to Cotton's contemporary, Henry Savile of Banke (d. 1617), its absence from Smith's catalogue of 1696 and the inscription 'Ex dono Joha*nn*is Anstis Arm*igeri*' (f. 2) imply that it came into the collection only about 1706–18 and cannot therefore have been one of Sir Robert's own acquisitions.[14] On the other hand, even where collective volumes incorporate an item that is clearly later than 1631 this does not necessarily imply that the bulk of the tracts entered the collection after its founder's death. Most of Titus A. XXIV, for example, probably belonged to Cotton even though at least one of the tracts included here is datable to no earlier than 1634.[15]

Titus A. XXIV affords an appropriate starting-point for a survey of the post-mediaeval verse in the collection. Among the separate tracts that it comprises is a miscellany of verse (ff. 79–102) that in the table added by Sir Thomas Cotton is characterized as 'verses on seuerall subiects about queen marys time'. It consists of English and Latin pieces by the poet and playwright Richard Edwards and several of his contemporaries at Christ Church, Oxford. Although Edwards's own work has been the subject of scholarly commentary the remaining contents seem never to have been fully explored.[16] Some of the more familiar English poems may possibly predate their inclusion in Surrey's *Songes and Sonettes*, 1557, while the Latin are mostly loyal effusions on the accession of Queen Mary in July 1553 (ff. 79, 79v) and her marriage to Philip II of Spain in the following July (ff. 92v–95). It is easy enough to see why a friendly exchange of verses (f. 95), unpublished until 1576, between the Dean of Christ Church, Richard Cox, and the Cambridge Latinist Walter Haddon is found here. Three further Latin epigrams (f. 96v) are connected with Thomas Palmer, a fellow of the then recent foundation of St John's, Oxford, two of them being translations of verses in his unprinted 'Two hundred poosees', the earliest known English emblem book.[17]

The only other major gathering of pre-Elizabethan verse in the collection forms part of one of the manuscripts that Cotton inherited from Camden. Julius F. VI, ff. 69–73v, preserves thirty-one Latin epigrams by William Lily (d. 1522), the grammarian and first High Master of St Paul's School, copied in a single scribal hand. This near-contemporary source has been strangely neglected by scholars in favour of the partial copy of it by John Stow in Harley MS. 540. Although eight of the pieces were published in *Epigrammata Guil. Lilii Angli* (1521) the majority never reached print in their author's lifetime. Some hendecasyllables written in reply to Skelton's now lost verses in the 'grammarians' war' of 1519 with Robert Whittington survive here alongside Lily's brief epitaph on Elizabeth of York. On the earlier occasion, at least, Skelton appears to have

309

got the better of his rival, for it was his Latin elegiacs on Elizabeth, and his English Eulogy of Henry VII (d. 1509), that were inscribed '*In tabula pensili*' over their joint tomb in Westminster Abbey.[18] Three or four other pieces relate to members of the leading humanist circle of the day, notably some lines on the double portrait that Erasmus and Peter Gillis presented to Sir Thomas More in 1517, and on which More himself wrote a poem.[19] Six further epigrams (ff. 73–73v) were composed for the pageants that greeted Charles V on his entry into London on 6 June 1522, displayed as inscriptions on structures set up over the conduits.[20] The present texts seem to represent an early attempt, for the title (f. 73) of the first one implies that they were to be spoken by London schoolboys on the royal barge in the Thames.

The bulk of the post-mediaeval verse in the Cotton collection comes from Elizabeth's reign, and here the only two works of any length by well-known writers are both political in inspiration. Thomas Churchyard's poem *The scole of warre callid the sege of Lethe* describes the surrender of some French partisans of Mary, Queen of Scots, to an English force under Lord Grey in 1560. A version differing in some respects from that first printed in 1575 is preserved as a self-contained item in Caligula B. V (ff. 365–382v) where it is signed by the scribe 'Finis W Pentney'.[21] The statement that it was 'made by Mr Churcheyarde at his beinge ther:' has been added after the title (f. 365) in an unidentified hand that was responsible for annotations throughout this composite volume. The second work is a series of poems entitled 'Partheniades' (Vespasian E. VIII, ff. 169–178), composed between about 1579 and 1582 and presented as a New Year's gift to Queen Elizabeth I. The attribution to George Puttenham, a writer not given to self-advertisement, rests on the appearance of manifestly authorial quotations from them in his putative *Arte of English Poesie* (1589). 'Partheniades' was first printed in Nichols's *Progresses...of Queen Elizabeth* as long ago as 1788, and has twice been edited since.[22] This unique copy seems fairly certain to be in one of the several hands practised by William Camden, the manuscript of which it forms part having perhaps been among those that he bequeathed to Cotton in 1623. Though the second half (ff. 75–183v) of this composite volume is copied throughout on a single stock of French paper dated by Briquet to 1564 the contents are clearly rather later in date.[23] They include a draft (ff. 75–96v, 161–167) of Camden's famous Westminster Greek Grammar, the *Institutio Graecae grammatices compendaria* (printed in 1597), an Old English-Latin word-list (ff. 132–155v) and brief onomasticon (ff. 156–159).

Camden's manuscripts form probably the most important single element among Cotton's historiographic collections. The vast majority are working papers surviving from all phases and aspects of his career, from Oxford undergraduate to Headmaster of Westminster School, and from antiquary to herald. Among notes and drafts of passages for the *Britannia*, sometimes jotted on the back of Latin themes written by his pupils, occur scattered verses of his own composition. These include sections of *De Connubio Tamæ et Isis*, a poem that he is not known to have brought to completion and that survives solely in a number of extracts incorporated in the editions of his great work that were published between 1586 and 1607.[24] This poem, which takes its inspiration from

Leland's *Cygnea cantio* (1545) and its title from Camden's imaginative etymology for the name *Thamesis*, is said to have originated in a survey made in his youth of the whole course of the river.[25] Nevertheless, some caution must be exercised over the attribution to him of verses that happen to survive in his hand, as many turn out to be merely transcripts made during wide reading in British and continental Latin poetry. A single page of Julius F. X (f. 105v) comprises Latin extracts relating to Britain that are evidently all the work of other writers. This seems likely to be the case also with the extract from an unidentified poem on the reign of the legendary Brutus (ff. 66v, 67).[26]

Camden's greatest contribution to Cotton's verse acquisitions lies in his collections of inscriptions and epigrams. A short paper on 'Epitaphes' that he read before the Elizabethan Society of Antiquaries in November 1600 (Faustina E. V, ff. 162, 162v) was later expanded into the essay published in the first edition of *Remaines of Britain* (1605). Besides borrowing freely from contributions made by others to the Antiquaries' debate, Camden collected many of the English and Latin verse epitaphs in Julius F. XI. Perhaps the sturdy epitaph of John Bell 'Brokenbrow' (f. 165v) that he added in his own hand to this paper had been gleaned earlier that very year, during his visit to Hadrian's Wall with Cotton, and possibly, as the alleged place of origin may suggest, while they were staying with Lord William Howard at Naworth.

A notebook (Appendix LXII) kept while Camden was at Christ Church between about 1568 and 1570 has much to tell us about his friendships and intellectual interests during that early period. Into it he entered fair copies of some of his Latin academic exercises and private letters. The former include (f. 9v) '*Virtutis descriptio ex Anglico*', two renderings into elegiac couplets of some verses of Nicholas Grimald that were printed in *Tottel's Miscellany* (1557) and again in Kendall's *Flowers of Epigrams* (1577).[27] We need not suppose that Camden was unaware of the original epigram by Beza of which Grimald's was, in turn, a translation.[28] Other pieces are of a more personal nature, such as the series of verses (ff. 2, 2v) addressed to senior members of the college and headed '*Xenia, Calendis Juniis* 1569'. Most interesting of all are the two elegiac couplets headed '*Ad P S. cum Horat.*' (f. 4v), for these seem likely to have been addressed to Philip Sidney who was an undergraduate there between about February 1568 and April 1571. No direct relationship between the poet and the antiquary has been known, but if this identification is correct it would seem to have been fairly close.[29] This wish for Sidney's future happiness, written to accompany the gift of a volume of Horace's poetry, is expressed in a repetitive format that subtly varies its praise of the author's work as both sublime and learned. As at various other points in the manuscript the ink has faded, so that most of the line-endings have to be supplied conjecturally.

Ad P S. cum Horat.
Quot sunt hoc compto sublimia metra libello:
Tot sint in vita tempora laeta tibi.
Innumeris doctis metris scatet iste libellus:
Innumeris faelix sit tua vita bonis.[30]

311

Several other sets of verse written in commemoration of Camden's famous contemporary are preserved among the various collections of epitaphs on which he drew when compiling the *Remaines*. Titus B. VIII includes two threnodies in elegiac couplets on Sidney (d. 1586) and on his father-in-law Sir Francis Walsingham (d. 1590). These are, in fact, straightforward versifications, apparently intended as inscriptions for memorial tablets in St Paul's Cathedral, of some biographical notes drawn up in English 'In the person of S[r] Phillipp Sidney [*and of* Mr Secretarie] for the epitaphe to be considered' that survive in a different hand on the preceding leaf (f. 291). Both the writer of these *schemas* and the poet remain unidentified, although drafts of the prose notes found in Vespasian C. XIV (ff. 214–215v) are presumably autograph originals. Furthermore, in the Vespasian manuscript these drafts are in turn accompanied (f. 206) by copies, in yet another hand, of two biographical accounts in Latin prose. That commemorating Walsingham was actually painted or carved in wood, along with some acrostic English verses by 'E. W.', on a tablet standing in the north aisle of the Cathedral, adjoining the choir. It survived long enough to be printed by Dugdale in 1658.[31] The transience of such artefacts is apparent from the fate, not only of Skelton's epitaph for Henry VII and his Queen, but also of the lengthy memorial to John Redman (d. 1551), preserved in Cleopatra C. III, which as early as 1631 was no longer to be seen in Westminster Abbey.

All this suggests that the accompanying tablet to Sidney, now lost, would have included a set of English acrostics rather than, for example, the well-known elegy beginning 'England, Netherland, the heavens and the arts' that was circulating as early as 1593.[32] The loss of this tablet and its inscription was the direct outcome of a greater omission by Sidney's contemporaries. By 1598 Thomas Bastard was lamenting that 'Philip and Francis have no tomb', complaining that the enormous monument to Sir Christopher Hatton (for which see Julius F. XI, f. 88v), who died in 1591, 'hath all the room'.[33] Perhaps as a result of the wider currency given to this complaint in 1614 by Henry Holland, in September of the following year Fulke Greville proposed to remedy the deficiency by building a tomb for Sidney and himself; but though he is known to have been working on a verse epitaph, nothing came of this scheme.[34] At all events two further, anonymous, laments for Sidney were considered by the poet Sir John Davies to be of particularly high quality, and are copied (Faustina E. V, f. 170v) in his own hand in the paper on epitaphs that he read before the Society of Antiquaries on 3 November 1600. Incidentally, yet another, entitled '*Georgii B—— Carmen epicedium*' (Julius F. XI, f. 93v), may be the work of George Benedicti Werteloos of Haarlem – though not found in the commemorative volume issued by him – but can hardly have been written by George Buchanan, who had died in 1582.[35]

The great Scots humanist poet and historian is represented by some interesting texts of familiar poems, as well as by a number of unpublished but apparently authentic ones. The three fire-damaged Cotton manuscripts in which they are found have been briefly described by Buchanan's biographer and bibliographer, I. D. McFarlane.[36] Several uncollected Latin pieces survive in Caligula B. V, a manuscript annotated throughout in a hand that has not been identified: a pasquil and two other epigrams occurring on ff. 325v, 332v are probably not his, but of continental origin. Vitellius E. X includes two moral epigrams in Latin, with English versions that may be Buchanan's own: all are attributed to him in the later index (f. 1).[37] Again, Caligula D. I, which carries some complimentary verses that he wrote on members of Lord Burghley's family, includes three hexameters and an elegiac distich in parallel Latin and English versions that seem to have been intended for inscription on a cup. It is perhaps worth remarking also that a French translation of Buchanan's verses (f. 36) on a device cut in a ring sent by Mary Queen of Scots to Elizabeth in 1564 – beginning '*Superbe ne me faict d'estre du fer uainqueur*' – is preserved elsewhere (Caligula B. IX, pt. ii, f. 284) on a leaf bearing the date 1565. This gains considerable interest from the fact of its being docketed in the hand of Thomas, fourth Duke of Norfolk, who in 1568 presented himself as Mary's suitor and was subsequently executed for his part in the Ridolfi plot. Finally, in addition to Cotton's three main collections of Buchanan's poems two single pieces are preserved in the seventeenth-century abstract (Caligula B. X, pt. ii, ff. 259v, 260) of a letter of Thomas Randolph to Burghley, the original of which has never been traced.

Among the papers that Cotton acquired from Mary's learned co-religionist, Henry Howard, Earl of Northampton, there survives an autograph draft (Titus C. VI, ff. 207–209v) of the Latin epitaph that he wrote for the fine tomb erected in Westminster Abbey by her son James I in September 1612. An earlier version of this memorial (Caligula C. IX, pt. ii, ff. 626v, 627), subscribed '*H. N. gemens*', was rejected by James because of some provocative allusions to Elizabeth I's treatment of his mother.[38] One wonders whether the inscription was thrown open to public competition, for a further epitaph that survives in the same manuscript is evidently by Camden himself (f. 629), while the removal of Mary's body from Peterborough to Westminster was celebrated by the Catholic historian and poet Edmund Bolton (Titus A. XIII, ff. 178–184). In literary terms, however, pride of place among the poems surviving in the large volume of Northampton's largely autograph theological papers that is Titus C. VII must go to a previously unrecorded scribal copy of Robert Southwell's poem 'Of the blessed Sacrament of the alter' (ff. 535–536v), erroneously subscribed 'W: S'.

Mary is obliquely brought to mind by a letter addressed to Cotton in Julius C. III (ff. 164, 164v). Writing from Wensley in Yorkshire in 1603 or 1604 Oswald Dykes reported that he had been 'a while agoe at S* An of Buxton in Darbyshire wher I fond in sondrie places about the howse and well these verses…'. The 'house' was the structure built for the reception of visitors in this, even then, popular place of resort by the local landowner, the sixth Earl of Shrewsbury, and his second wife Bess of Hardwicke. A contemporary description says 'Ioyning to the cheefe spring, betwene the riuer, and the Bathe, is a very goodly house, foure square, foure stories hye…'.[39] Evidently, like other buildings of the period, it boasted verse inscriptions on its walls. Camden, to whom the information was passed by Cotton, seems to have found the first set inelegant, for although he used it in his next edition of *Britannia* (1607) he took the liberty of recasting the lines. The connection with Mary comes from the fact that she allegedly inscribed a distich in the window of her lodging at Buxton when she visited the spa for the last time in the summer of 1584, at the end of her confinement in the Shrewsbury houses in the North Midlands. The probable reason for its omission by Dykes is that it had already figured in the *Britannia* of 1590, where the identity of the author was discreetly hidden under the formula '*quaedam magni ingenii, sed multo maioris prosapiae*'.[40]

The same collection of letters includes an autograph epigram by Cotton's first librarian, Richard James, that was first printed by Grosart.[41] Uncollected but possibly also by James is the epigram headed '*Sibylla Hippocratis*' that he entered into Claudius C. II: this relates to Edward Cecil, Viscount Wimbledon, who commanded the disastrous Spanish expedition of 1625. From the equally well-known volume of letters addressed to Camden comes a leaf (Julius C. V, f. 393) carrying two sets of Latin verses by Edward, Lord Herbert of Cherbury, copied in a scribal hand not unlike his own. The first is Herbert's reply to an epigram of François Guiet in praise of Joan of Arc, a copy of which, entitled *Joanna Virgo Aureliana* ('*Rustica sum sed plena deo sed pectore forti*'), precedes Herbert's epigram. Herbert's '*Desine Galle tuam tandem jactare Bubulcam*' was included in the posthumous edition of his *Occasional Verses* (1665), but the present manuscript was unknown to previous editors, as too was the full text of Guiet's epigram. Its recovery confirms Percy Simpson's guess that the first distich of Herbert's reply was complete in itself: in the manuscript it follows the other set, from which it is distinguished by the heading *Anglus*.[42]

In any collection of late Tudor or early Stuart epigrams or epitaphs – such as Camden's gatherings in Faustina E. V and Julius F. XI – the name of John Hoskins, the witty sergeant-at-law, is likely to figure fairly prominently. Not all the pieces that bear his name are verifiably authentic, but one of these is the series of ten linked elegiac poems (Julius F. X, ff. 115, 115v) commemorating the virtues of Anne Cecil, daughter of Lord Burghley and first wife of Edward de Vere, seventeenth Earl of Oxford.[43] She died at Court in Greenwich on 5 June 1588 and was buried in Westminster Abbey on 25 June, her estranged husband being absent from the ceremony. This revised fair copy concludes merely with the motto '*Vni M. Pergama*', but another, transcribed in the same formal italic and carrying an attribution to Hoskins, occurs among Burghley's papers in Lansdowne MS. 104, ff. 195–198v. The individual sets of verse that make up the whole constitute an expanded commentary on the various elements of the long inscription or title. Interestingly enough, some English verses sent by one Wilfred Samonde to Burghley on the same occasion and now among the Cecil papers at Hatfield House, are ordered according to much the same *schema*.[44]

Several other items in the collection deserve notice. A series of parodies – in the wholly serious sense now obsolete – of odes by Horace (Titus A. XIII, ff. 166–177) was dedicated to James I by Thomas Goad of King's College, Cambridge, following the frustration of the Gunpowder Plot. For generations this anniversary was observed almost as an Anglican holy day in schools and universities, an annual Gunpowder Plot sermon and oration having been decreed at Cambridge as early as 20 October 1606. Goad's offering appeared well ahead of all competitors: the first version of it was entered in the

Stationers' Register on 11 December 1605. The fact that the present manuscript is dated 22 November but corresponds with the second edition, entered on 18 February 1605/6, implies that the first printed version was out within seven weeks of the event.[45]

Not all the verses in Cotton's library are solemn exercises. While travelling through France on an embassy from Henry VIII in 1526 Dr John Taylor and his nephew felt moved to answer an anti-English satire that they found written with a piece of charcoal on the wall of an inn in Châteauneuf (Titus B. VI, f. 13). After this, the parting comment '*malum hospicium invenimus*' was perhaps inevitable. Easily the most eccentric item in the collection is a series of verses displaying much loyalty but little literary merit that was composed in 1618 and 1619 by Sir Edward Fox of 'Steventon by Ludlow'. The writer was, like Camden, an alumnus of Christ Church and had been knighted at Newark Castle in April 1603 by James I during his journey southward to the English throne. In letters that Fox addressed to Camden and to Daniel Featley (Julius C. V, ff. 290, 327) he incorporated a series of patterned verses, arranged, for example, in the form of a portcullis, or of '*versus reciproci*' consisting of a fixed number of letters each. Those sent to Camden were accompanied by a manuscript of verses, now either lost or unidentified, that Fox requested him to forward to King James.

The concluding word in this survey has been reserved for pageantry and drama. The former is represented by some verses written for the arrival in London of Catharine of Aragon and her marriage to Prince Arthur in November 1501 (Vitellius A. XVI), though they are not, as was once thought, by William Dunbar.[46] This seems a suitable place to mention Thomas More's little tract of Latin verses (Titus D. IV) celebrating the coronation of Catharine and Henry VIII who thus became Arthur's successor in two roles. The sole specimen of drama consists of an unrecorded verse translation into Latin of Sophocles's *Ajax*, formerly numbered as Appendix XLV (art. 7, ff. 22–28), and now as Cotton Fragment 32. This translation, which is copied in one variable hand, occupies thirteen pages of a notebook that includes observations on the West Saxon Kings, a list of English commentators on the Bible and extracts from Holinshed's *Chronicle* (1578). The text is imperfect at the beginning owing to the loss of a preliminary leaf, and breaks off abruptly: it now comprises ll. 65–812 only of the original. The version is not that of either Johann Lonicer (Basle, 1533) or the younger Scaliger (Paris, 1573). Possibly it is to be identified with the lost Latin tragedy *Ajax Flagellifer* that was made ready for performance before Elizabeth I at Cambridge University on 9 August 1564, but cancelled following her sudden indisposition.[47]

HANDLIST OF BRITISH POST-MEDIAEVAL VERSE IN ENGLISH AND LATIN
IN THE COTTON COLLECTION

All pre-1500 vernacular texts surviving in the Cotton collection were included in Carleton Brown's and Rossell Hope Robbins's alphabetical first-line *Index of Middle English Verse* (1943), though the lack of any separate index of manuscript sources has until recently rendered them virtually impossible to isolate.[48] A considerable portion of the pre-Elizabethan material has recently been catalogued in the splendidly compendious *Bibliography and Index of English Verse in Manuscript 1501–1558*, devised and carried through almost to publication by the late William A. Ringler Jr. In due course English verse of the Elizabethan period, both manuscript and printed, will be covered in a further extension of this *Index* that is now being prepared by Ringler's one-time pupil, Steven W. May. Meanwhile, the present handlist is intended to supply a provisional list of the English and Britanno-Latin verse composed after 1500.

For the purposes of the present handlist leaf-by-leaf examination of the whole Cotton collection has not been attempted, even though in volumes so miscellaneous and so rich in marginalia this means that the current tally of over four hundred poems is most unlikely to be exhaustive. Selection of items has, therefore, been based principally on a reading of Planta's *Catalogue of the Manuscripts in the Cottonian Library* (1802) and of the handwritten Index of Poetry in the Manuscripts Students' Room, supplemented by a first-hand if rather hasty search of the shelves.[49] As with the Bodleian *First-Line Index*, which has been taken as the model for the format adopted here, the lower date-limit has to a large extent been predetermined by the scope and contents of the other great index by Brown and Robbins. The arrangement of entries is, however, modelled on Brown's earlier two-volume *Register of Middle English Religious Verse* (1920), where individual items are listed serially in manuscript and folio order, with an index of first lines at the end. This work has one notable advantage over the expanded *Index* of 1943: it automatically incorporates a key to the manuscripts consulted. Moreover, it gives a clearer picture of the disposition of verses within each source and of their relationship to each other.

In the list that follows, a simple alphabetical ordering of manuscripts has been preferred to Planta's chronological sequence of Emperors, the Cotton Appendix and Fragments being kept to the end. Each manuscript is introduced by a brief statement of its character and overall dates, though as this description is generally extrapolated from the 1802 Catalogue it must not be regarded as definitive. Each entry is intended to cover the salient features of each poem in the following order: first and last line; author; title; manuscript reference; metre or verse form; status of witness; relevant information from elsewhere in the source; cross-reference to standard works (listed under 'Abbreviations' below); bibliographical details; genre; and subject. All texts are, unless otherwise stated, scribal copies. First and last lines are quoted in the form in which they appear in the manuscripts, though variant wordings in the (usually) contemporary printed texts cited in the entries are noted, and any significant variant forms of the first line are given cross-references in the first-line index at the end. Where individual pieces are extracts from longer poems the first line of the whole poem, if known, is also given a cross-reference in the index. This means that those using the list side by side with a particular manuscript should be in no doubt about the identity of the poem before them, while those working from a printed text should be able readily to identify the poem in question. In identifying metres, which were at first intended to be confined to simple descriptions such as 'Hexameters' or 'Rhyme Royal', it has sometimes seemed necessary to adapt (though not simply to adopt) the exhaustive format devised by Ringler.

Otherwise the editorial conventions adopted, though visually intrusive perhaps, should give little trouble. Dots placed before a first or after a last line indicate that this is not the actual first or last line of the poem: where known, this is supplied within pointed brackets from a source identified in the entry. Readings supported by editorial conjecture alone are reckoned to be relatively secure unless set within square brackets also. Long dashes within pointed brackets indicate that a word or phrase is either wanting or has so far defied decipherment. 'Titles' enclosed in square brackets are drawn from dockets or adjacent descriptions – for example, from an accompanying letter or other text – that afford a handy description of the content.

A word of explanation may be offered for some of the more obvious omissions and inclusions. First of all, only those manuscripts still known by their Cotton pressmarks are covered here: strays now incorporated in other collections have not been included. The adoption of an arbitrary lower limit of 1500 for manuscript material, whether based on the presumed date of composition or on that of transcription, is bound to involve some difficult decisions. (This is no less true of Ringler's *Index*, which sets out to include all English verse judged to have been copied, rather than merely composed, in the period concerned.) Fascinating as it is, the manuscript of Skelton's *Garland of Laurel* (Vitellius E. X, ff. 208–225v) is omitted on the grounds of an apparent composition date for the poem of about 1492–97.[50] Other cases are more debatable. With the epitaphs collected by Camden, Thynne and Stowe much research has been necessary to ensure that their subjects died after this lower limit. Two lyrics jotted in an early sixteenth-century hand on the back flyleaves of Lydgate's *Pilgrimage of the Life of Man* (Vitellius C. XIII, ff. 310, 311) have not been listed here, on the grounds that their composition almost certainly belongs to the late fifteenth century. The first of them is also found in manuscript in a copy of Caxton's *Boethius* (1478) now in the Pierpont Morgan Library, from which it was recorded in Robbins's and Cutler's *Supplement* to Brown and Robbins (no. 2013): the present texts are listed in Ringler's *Index* alone.[51] The same is apparently true of John Lacy's 'As I stode in a park streght bi a tre' (Julius A. V, f. 131v). On the other hand, the inclusion of some other items is at least questionable. Robert Fabyan's *New cronycles of Englande and of Fraunce* (Nero C. IX, pts. i & ii), which end with the death of Richard III, was apparently completed by 1504, though it did not see print until 1516, three years after the death of its author. While it is possible and perhaps even likely that the translations of mediaeval Latin elegies on English kings were made before 1501, the element of doubt, no less than their omission by Brown and Robbins, has encouraged their listing here.

The very latest verse item in point of copying did not, in all probability, form part of Sir Robert's own collections. Thirty-nine rhymed couplets found in Titus B. VIII were copied from the originals in the stained glass of nine windows in the cloister of Peterborough Abbey by a certain George Rainer, probably not long before their destruction in 1644.[52] The Abbey itself was dissolved in 1539, and neither the date at which the windows were glazed nor the precise period at which the verses were originally written is now known. Their inclusion here, prompted by uncertainty about the precise date of the originals, will at the worst supply an omission by Brown and Robbins.[53]

In addition to this, the Latin poems offer a further problem. The close links with continental neighbours at this period sometimes make it difficult to be certain precisely which of them are the work of Britons. Although in the interests of space individual rejections have not been noted, barring editorial oversight the omission of any neo-Latin poem that figures in a manuscript may be put down to the existence of evidence for, or at least a strong presumption of, continental origin. A few pieces so far unattributable (e.g. Julius F. X, f. 105v, and F. XI, ff. 86v, 134) have been given the benefit of the doubt, though the Sidney elegy mentioned above as apparently by Benedicti has been omitted. Nine alliterative lines headed '[Thomas] Nortonus in Reginam' (Caligula D. I, f. 32v; see also Add. MS. 48029, f. 69) are rejected on the grounds that their metrical status is uncertain.

Finally, some statistics may be useful. The handlist comprises 442 entries representing 431 distinct poems, 189 of which are in English and 242 in Latin. Fifty-five of the English pieces are included by Ringler in his index of pre-Elizabethan manuscript verse, twenty-nine of these being also recorded by him from early printed versions in the *Bibliography and Index of English Verse Printed 1476–1558*. In addition, thirty-four of the poems are traceable in the Bodleian *First-Line Index*; while a further three that were certainly composed after 1500 nevertheless found their way into Brown and Robbins. Thereafter the individual pieces are listed folio by folio in order of appearance.

HANDLIST OF VERSE

Manuscripts are listed by pressmark arranged, not chronologically by Emperor as in the published Cotton catalogues, but in alphabetical and numerical order. Their overall character is briefly defined in a general heading, with sub-headings for individual articles or sections. Poems are listed folio by folio in order of appearance.

Key to Abbreviated Titles of Reference Works

BR	Carleton Brown and Rossell Hope Robbins, The *Index of Middle English Verse*, New York, 1943; with *Supplement* by Robbins and John L. Cutler, Lexington, Kentucky, 1965. (BR is the abbreviation adopted by Ringler: some other authorities refer to it as IMEV.)
Crum	Margaret Crum (ed.), *First-Line Index of English Poetry in Manuscripts of the Bodleian Library, Oxford*, Oxford, 1969.
Ringler TM	William A. Ringler, Jr., *Bibliography and Index of English Verse in Manuscript 1501–1558*, prepared and completed by Michael Rudick and Susan J. Ringler, London, 1992.
Ringler TP	William A. Ringler, Jr., *Bibliography and Index of English Verse Printed 1476–1558*, London, 1988.

Caligula A. XI

Religious poems in Latin and English, including Layamon's Brut and (ff. 170–286) the B-text of Piers Ploughman; circa 14th–15th cent. Contents list (f. 1) by unidentified Cotton scribe.

f. 286v. Verses jotted as pen-trials in early to late 16th cent. hands.

When raginge loue withe extreme payne
Serving a worthier wight than she.
    Howard, Henry, Earl of Surrey.
    Caligula A. XI, f. 286v.
First 2 verses only of 4 octosyllabic stanzas rhyming ababcc. *Imperfect*, wanting all after l. 2, 'moste krule can plei ther parte'. First verse recopied above in hand of later 16th cent. Ringler TM 1887, TP 2184. Pr., with variants, in *Tottel's Miscellany*, 1557 (no. 16 in the edition of H. E. Rollins, Cambridge, Mass., 1928–9). Love song.

Caligula B. IV

Papers relating chiefly to Mary, Queen of Scots; circa 1559–1600.

A dolefull time of wepinge teares
But whatsoever they thinke or saye...
    Singleton, —.
        'The Copie of a ryme made by one Singleton a gent of Lancashire now Prisoner at York for religion'.
    Caligula B. IV, ff. 247, 247v.
51 octosyllables in undifferentiated 12-verse stanzas rhyming ababccdedeff. *Imperfect*, stanza 5 wanting all but the first 3 verses. Followed by an anecdote concerning the subject of this lament, Thomas Percy, 11th Earl of Northumberland, executed at York on 22 August 1572.

Caligula B. V

State papers relating to transactions, circa 1174–1604, between England and Scotland; copied temp. Henry VIII–1604. Included at various points are verses in the unidentified scribal hand that was also responsible for Buchanan's poems in Caligula D. I, ff. 31v–36; as follows:

Gallia dum passim ciuilibus occidit armis
Bis rex qui fuerat, fit modo Grammaticus.
    'Du changement de la france | Epig.'.
    Caligula B. V, f. 41.
3 elegiac couplets. Preceded by some French verses headed 'Le ieu de la Prime de L'estat de la France | Sonnet'. On James I of England.

ff. 267v–271, 320–321. Latin poems chiefly by George Buchanan, several of them included, with variants, in printed editions of his *Epigrammatum Libri*, etc. The eight pieces on ff. 268, 268v are headed 'Carmina. G. Buconano autore', titles being given in the left-hand margin. Copied immediately after the first set of verses (f. 267v), and in the same hand, is a list of 'Libri scripti per Georgium Bocananum Scotum'. Some of the pieces (ff. 268v, 320v) have titles, etc., added in an unidentified Italic hand that appears in annotations throughout the composite MS. For description of contents see I. D. McFarlane, 'George Buchanan's Latin Poems from Script to Print: a preliminary survey', *The Library*, 5th ser., vol. xxiv, no. 4 (Dec. 1969), pp. 318–19.

Quanquam flere nefas te cælo Jacobe
           receptum
Tam genitum gaudet, quam periisse
           debet.
    Buchanan, George.
    'Epitaphium Ja. St Proregis Scotiæ'.
    Caligula B. V, f. 267v.
4 elegiac couplets. Pr. in Buchanan's *Epigrammatum Liber II*, 1584, p. 176, beg. 'Quamvis flere...'. On James Stewart, Earl of Moray, Regent of Scotland 1567–1570.

Illa procax Mori lingua irreuerenter in
           omnes
Quorum habet & gladios muta fauilla
           suos.
    Buchanan, George.
    'Morus'.
    Caligula B. V, f. 268.
3 elegiac couplets. On Sir Thomas More (d. 1535).

Sum marie malegrata patri malegrata
           marito
Fida pudicitiæ forma maligna meæ.
    Buchanan, George.
    'Maria R A'.
    Caligula B. V, f. 268.
2 elegiac couplets. Pr. in Buchanan's *Epigrammatum*

Liber II, 1584, p. 183. On Mary I, Queen of England (1553–1558).

Formosam, uiduam, ditemque in flore iuuentæ
Non oculis tantum captus opinor, erat.
    Buchanan, George.
    'Penelope'.
    Caligula B. V, f. 268.
2 elegiac couplets. Pr. in Buchanan's *Epigrammatum Liber II*, 1584, p. 181.

Quod præter patrias iuga fers muliebria leges
Et uerte in Thuscam regia Sceptra colum.
    Buchanan, George.
    'R Galliæ'.
    Caligula B. V, f. 268.
2 elegiac couplets. Pr. in I. D. McFarlane, *Buchanan*, 1981, p. 353. Satirical epigram on Catherine de Medici.

Casta decens, generosa animi Phænisa peregi
Conaris, famæ non sine labe tuæ.
    Buchanan, George.
    'Dido'.
    Caligula B. V, f. 268.
2 elegiac couplets. Followed by mottoes 'Ius inarmatum est' and 'Pietas sine vindice luget'. Pr. in Buchanan's *Epigrammatum Liber II*, 1584, p. 181.

Mille petita procis totidem repetita carinis
Laus est matronæ prima latere probæ.
    Buchanan, George.
    'Helina'.
    Caligula B. V, f. 268v.
2 elegiac couplets. Pr. in Buchanan's *Epigrammatum Liber II*, 1584, p. 180, with the last verse reading 'Maxima matronæ est laus latuisse probæ'. On Helen of Troy.

Vt Mariam finxit Natura, ars pinxit utrunque
Vt natura rudis, ars uideatur iners.
    Buchanan, George.
    'Picta imago mariæ R. S.'.
    Caligula B. V, f. 268v.

2 elegiac couplets. In margin: 'Ma Reg. Scotiæ dum erat'. Pr. in Buchanan's *Epigrammatum Liber II*, 1584, p. 182. On a portrait of Mary, Queen of Scots, as a girl.

Et decor et facies cum simplicitate modesta
Hec faciet, Superi sint tibi pene pares.
    Buchanan, George.
    'Ad nobilissimam quandam verginem omnibus vertutibus præclaram præterque quod dubitatur an sit constans'.
    Caligula B. V, f. 268v.
3 elegiac couplets. Note in margin in the annotator's hand: 'Ad Catherinam Cocum nunc nobilissimi Viri Henrici Kyllegrewe Vxorem'. Pr. in Buchanan's *Epigrammatum Liber I*, 1584, pp. 163–4, with 'venusta' for 'modesta' in the first verse and the last verse reading 'Efficiet superos haec tibi pæne pares'. On Catherine Cooke, later (1565–1583) wife of Sir Henry Killegrew (knighted 1591).

To shyne in silke to glitter all in gold
Which losing had a rushe for all the rest.
    [Buchanan, George].
    'Verses Upon a good Conscience in English & Latyne'.
    Caligula B. V, f. 271.
21 decasyllables in 3 stanzas rhyming ababbcc. Note at foot of f. 271: 'These are sayd to haue been giuen to the L. Burghley, L Thresorer by a disguised Petitioner, in forme of a Letter closed, departing thence after he had delyvered it ryding toward Westminster hall. So the same in Latyne on the other syd hereof'. Copy of English version in Lansdowne MS. 98, ff. 204, 204v, concludes with initials 'H K' in form of notarial mark. See also below, Vitellius E. X, f. 78. On a clear conscience.

Bissina quod vestis multo tibi splendeat auro
Deliciis, solida hæc nimirum et Gloria sola est.
    [Buchanan, George].
    Caligula B. V, f. 271v.
21 hexameters. Latin version of preceding verses. On a clear conscience.

Calta velut flores tenebris sub noctis
opacæ
Sic nunque pietas interitura tua est.
> Constantine, Patrick.
> 'Epitaphium. Episcopi Salisburiensis'.
> Caligula B. V, f. 320.

6 elegiac couplets. Marginal attribution: 'per Patricium Constantinum Scotum'. On John Jewel (d. 1571), Bishop of Salisbury.

Quum tormenta olim Siculis sudaret in
antris
Pacata irati numinis ira fuit.
> Constantine, Patrick.
> 'Ducis Guisii Epitaphium.'.
> Caligula B. V, f. 320.

4 elegiac couplets. Title in margin, with attribution 'per eundem Constantinum' added later. On (?) François de Lorraine, 2nd Duc de Guise, assassinated 1563.

Reginæ geminæ pari labore
famæ in tempora cuncta comparasti.
> Buchanan, George.
> 'Epitaph. Jo. Juelli Episcopi Salisburiensis. per G. Bocananum Scottum'.
> Caligula B. V, f. 320v.

17 Phalaecian hendecasyllables. 'Scottum' in title added in the annotator's hand. Pr. in Buchanan's *Epigrammatum Liber II*, 1584, pp. 177–8. On John Jewel (d. 1571), Bishop of Salisbury.

Juelle mater quem tulit Deuonia,
Quam parua tellus nomen ingens occulit.
> Buchanan, George.
> 'Alias. per eundem'.
> Caligula B. V, f. 320v.

7 iambic trimeters. Attribution added and text corrected in the annotator's hand. Pr. in Buchanan's *Epigrammatum Liber II*, 1584, p. 178. On John Jewel (d. 1571), Bishop of Salisbury.

Regis auus, regis pater, alto è sanguine
regum
Fortuna attingas cætera dignus auo.
> Buchanan, George
> 'Epitaphium Mathæi Comitis Leuiniæ, [cum comentarium G. Bocana *deleted*] cum explanatione per Georgium Bocan-

anum Scottum omnium Poetarum prestantissimum'.
> Caligula B. V, f. 321.

5 elegiac couplets. All in title after square brackets added in the annotator's hand. Followed by an 'Expositio Epitaphii' in Latin prose notes. Pr., without notes, in Buchanan's *Poemata*, Edinburgh, 1615, as no. 26 in the *Miscellaneorum Liber*, with 'Attingas fato' as the first two words of the last verse. On Matthew Stewart, Earl of Lennox, Regent of Scotland 1570 (d. 4 Sept. 1571).

ff. 365–382. Churchyard, Thomas: 'The scole of warre callid the sege of Lethe'; *circa* 1560. Single gathering comprising scribal copy signed 'Finis W Pentney' (and see f. 382v, where signature occurs along with, vol. rev., 'Thomas Forster'). Note after title on f. 365, in the hand of the annotator (see headnote to ff. 267v–271, 320–321, above): 'made by Mr Churcheyarde at his beinge ther:'. Watermark of crowned crescent over letters 'PM': similar to C. M. Briquet, *Les Filigranes*, ed. Alan Stevenson, Amsterdam, 1968, no. 5323 (dated 1558).

As marche did ende so mars begane his
rayne
And but shorte tyme I hadd to vse my
penne.
> Churchyard, Thomas.
> 'The scole of warre callid the sege of Lethe'.
> Caligula B. V, ff. 365–382v.

665 decasyllables in 95 stanzas rhyming ababbcc. Pr., with variants, in *The first parte of Churchyardes chippes*, 1575. On the siege of Leith, 1560.

Caligula B. X (pt. ii)

State papers relating to transactions between England and Scotland; 1562–1567. Ownership-inscription (pt. i, f. 2) of 'Ro: Cotton Bruceus', with inscription beneath it in contemporary hand '1603 | Ro: Cotton Bruceus | Thomas Ctt'.

ff. 259v, 260. Letter of Thomas Randolph to William Cecil, later Lord Burghley, quoting verses in Italian and Latin spoken in honour of Elizabeth I at a 'great feast' during the Shrovetide festivities of the Scottish Court in Edinburgh; 27 Feb. 1563/4. Abstract, early 17th cent. Pr. in Robert Keith, *History of the Affairs of Church and State in Scotland*, ed. J. P. Lawson, Spottiswoode Society, Edinburgh, vol. II, 1845, pp. 219, 220.

Castitas blandi domitrix amoris
Reddita vitæ.
Buchanan, George.
Caligula B. X (pt. ii), f. 259v.

4 Sapphic stanzas. Headed by: 'The second service a fayer young maid'. Pr. in Buchanan's *Poemata*, Edinburgh, 1615, as no. 2 ('In Castitatem') in the *Miscellaneorum Liber*. In celebration of chastity.

Armata telis dexteram,
Anglam Angla Scotam diliget.
Buchanan, George.
Caligula B. X (pt. ii), f. 260.

20 iambic dimeters. Headed by: 'This last was a younge Childe set furth like vnto tyme[.] These verses were sung by the wayters'. Pr. in Buchanan's *Poemata*, Edinburgh, 1615, as no. 16 ('Mutuus Amor') in the *Miscellaneorum Liber*. On the friendly relations between Elizabeth I and Mary, Queen of Scots.

Caligula C. I

Papers relating to Mary, Queen of Scots, including (ff. 364–365v) verses attacking James Stewart, Earl of Moray, Regent of Scotland 1567–1570.

If Momus children seke to knowe my
name and where I dwell
and holde themselues herewith content
till further prouf be made.
'Tom Truth', *pseud.*
'A Rhyme in defence of the Q. of Scotts against the Earle of Murray... Tom Troath, to the Envious'.
Caligula C. I, f. 364.

2 fourteener couplets. Prefaced to verses immediately following.

If tongue would tell or you could write, the
craftie cloaked case
No more such Chordes and tawnes to give
least he be caught in snare.
'Tom Truth', *pseud.*
'A Rhyme in defence of the Q. of Scotts against the Earle of Murray... The double dealinge of the Rebells in Scotland'.
Caligula C. I, ff. 364–365v.

92 fourteener couplets. Concludes: 'Finis q^d Tom

Trowth'. Dated by head, in margin, '1568 ix° Decembris'.

Caligula C. IX (pt. i)

State papers relating to transactions between England and Scotland; 1581–1587.

To Jesabell that Englishe heure
For murthering of oure quene.
'fruere pro funere fune'.
Caligula C. IX (pt. i), f. 226.

4 verses in common measure. Copy, in hand of Robert Carlyle of Berwick, enclosed in his letter (f. 227) to Burghley, as one of two 'sett upp att my Lodginge, very odiouse & detestable ageynst the Quenes majestie' on 4 March 1586/7. Marginal date, in Cotton's hand, of '6. Martii 1586[/7]'. On the execution of Mary, Queen of Scots, 8 Feb. 1586/7.

Caligula C. IX (pt. ii)

State papers relating to transactions between England and Scotland; 1581–1587.

ff. 626–629. Two proposed inscriptions for the tomb erected by James I in Westminster Abbey for his mother, Mary, Queen of Scots, *circa* Sept. 1612, composed by:-

(1) Henry Howard, Earl of Northampton: *Autograph fair copies*. Concludes (f. 627) 'Finis. H. N. gemens'. The final version, comprising 11 elegiac couplets beg. 'Obruta frugifero sensim sic cespite surgunt', is pr. in Camden's *Remaines concerning Britain*, 1623. See also below, Titus C. VI, ff. 207–209v, and Additional MS. 40629, ff. 126–127.

Si generis splendor, raræ si gratia formæ,
æternos videant hinc sine nube dies.
Howard, Henry, Earl of Northampton.
['D. O. M. Bonæ memoriæ et Spei æternæ'].
Caligula C. IX (pt. ii), ff. 626v, 627.

21 elegiac couplets, disposed in three sections of 5, 5 and 11 couplets respectively. Title (f. 626) taken from prefatory Latin prose introduction. Docketed (f. 627v) 'Inscriptions upon the Queene of Scotts tombe'. Pr. from this text in *Calendar of State Papers relating to Scotland*, vol. ix (1585–1588), pp. 314–15.

(2) William Camden: *Autograph fair copies*, with revisions.

> **Magna ortu, maior virtutis honore Maria**
> **Maior & invidiâ regna beata tenet.**
> > ['Bonæ memoriæ, & Spei æternæ. D. O. M.'].
> > Camden, William.
> > Caligula C. IX (pt. ii), f. 629.

5 elegiac couplets. Last three words of first line copied above first version reading 'sponsa, sed maxima partu'. Title from heading (f. 628) of inscription, which begins and ends with Latin prose (ff. 628, 630).

> **Me natam coluit Reginam Scotia, Regi**
> **Et serie æterna succrescere laude perenni.**
> > ['Bonæ memoriæ, & Spei æternæ. D. O. M.'].
> > Camden, William.
> > Caligula C. IX (pt. ii), f. 629.

7 hexameters. Final word of last line replaces original reading 'nepotes'.

Caligula D. I

State papers relating to transactions between England and Scotland; 1587–1589.

ff. 31v–36. Latin and English poems of George Buchanan, several of them included, often with variants, in printed editions of his *Epigrammatum Libri*. The same scribe was also responsible for Buchanan's poems in Caligula B. V, ff. 267v–271, 320–321, above. For description of contents see I. D. McFarlane, *loc. cit.*

> **…Cor pueri figit Prexasp⟨—⟩**
> **Clitus Alexandri furioso tollit ⟨—⟩.**
> > Buchanan, George.
> > Caligula D. I, f. 31v.

2 (of 3 or 4) hexameters. *Imperfect*, first verse missing, owing to mutilation of leaf (but cf. English version below). This and the Latin verses immediately following appear to be inscriptions for a cup.

> **Vt fidei Charites æternæ vincula nec⟨tunt⟩**
> **Pocula sic veri testes amoris erunt.**
> > Buchanan, George.
> > Caligula D. I, f. 31v.

Elegiac distich. Inscription for a cup.

> **Of everlastinge faithe looke howe the**
> > **Gracies three**
> **Do knite the knotte so of my loue this**
> > **Cupe a proofe shalbe.**
> > [Buchanan, George?].
> > Caligula D. I, f. 31v.

Rhymed couplet in poulter's measure. Translation of Latin hexameters immediately above.

> **The Lacedemonian Kinge by drinkinge**
> > **was vndon.**
> **Greate Alexander with his Sworde through**
> > **Clitus ribbes d⟨id [run]⟩.**
> > Buchanan, George.
> > Caligula D. I, f. 31v.

Fourteener triplet. *Imperfect* by loss of endings in ll. 2 and 3, owing to mutilation of leaf. Translation of Latin hexameters '…Cor pueri…' above.

> **Quam tibi notum erat viuens Randolphe**
> > **Iuell⟨us⟩**
> **tam rare, et fidei tessera nulla, pie.**
> > [Garbrand, John].
> > 'Garbrandus De Juello et Randolpho'.
> > Caligula D. I, f. 31v.

6 elegiac couplets. To Thomas Randolph (1523–1590), on the death of John Jewel (d. 1571), Bishop of Salisbury.

> **Sæpe tibi Randolphe iubes me pingere**
> > **Regem**
> **In tabula nostram qui mihi pingis hæram.**
> > Buchanan, George.
> > 'Ad Thomam Randulfu*m*'.
> > Caligula D. I, f. 32.

10 elegiac couplets. Prefaced by some lines of Latin prose, *imperfect* from mutilation of leaf. Pr., in a version of nine couplets, in Buchanan's *Epigrammatum Liber II*, 1584, pp. 183–4. To Thomas Randolph (1523–1590).

> **Hunc Ransforte tuo cineri Bucananus**
> > **honorem**
> **Non metus exitii, sed fuga seruitii.**
> > Buchanan, George.
> > 'Epitaphiu*m* Ranfforti Equitis Aurati Angli q⟨ui⟩ Multa beneficia contulit in G. Bochanan⟨um⟩ cum exul esset è Scotia'.
> > Caligula D. I, f. 32v.

5 elegiac couplets. Preceded by some lines (illegible) of Latin prose, subscribed 'Tuus G. ⟨Buchananus⟩'. Pr. in Buchanan's *Epigrammatum Liber II*, 1584, pp. 174–5, the final verse reading 'Iam pulso exitii, seruitiique metu'. To Sir Thomas Rainsforde.

⟨—⟩ defunctus posses Iacobe reduci
In numero quorum mors pietosa Deo.
    [Buchanan, George].
    Caligula D. I, f. 33.
7 elegiac couplets. *Imperfect*, opening word(s) of first verse missing owing to mutilation of leaf. On the death of James Stewart, Earl of Moray and Regent of Scotland, 21 Jan. 1569/70.

Quanquam flere nefas te cælo Jacobe receptum
Tam genitum gaudet, quam periisse dolet.
    Buchanan, George.
    Caligula D. I, f. 33.
4 elegiac couplets. Pr. in Buchanan's *Epigrammatum Liber II*, 1584, p. 176, beg. 'Quamvis flere…'. On the death of James Stewart, Earl of Moray and Regent of Scotland, 21 Jan. 1569/70.

Qui nuper Scotos iustèque pièque regebas
Nunc speculum cunctis triste Jacobe iaces.
    [Buchanan, George].
    Caligula D. I, f. 33
2 elegiac couplets. On the death of James Stewart, Earl of Moray and Regent of Scotland, 21 Jan. 1569/70.

⟨Amplector, Rogere, tuum vehementer amorem⟩
Errorem de me dulcis amice tuum.
    Buchanan, George.
    Caligula D. I, f. 33v.
5 elegiac couplets. *Imperfect*, first verse largely missing owing to mutilation of leaf: supplied from pr. versions in Buchanan's *Epigrammatum Liber I*, 1584, pp. 157–8. Thanks to Roger Ascham for the gift of a book.

Iane pater solus partes qui uersus in omnes
Et mea uota ratam iussit habere fidem.
    Buchanan, George.
    'Dialogus Buchanani & Iani de xeniis ad Reginam Angl: mittendis'.
    Caligula D. I, f. 34.
16 elegiac couplets. Pr. in Buchanan's *Epigrammatum Liber III*, 1584, pp. 189–190, with 'dicta' for 'uota' in last verse. New Year's verses, in form of a dialogue, addressed to Elizabeth I on the tenth anniversary of her reign, 1568/9.

Munera quæ tibi dem Jani Mildreda Calendis
Quodcunque optaris tu mihi, id opto tibi.
    Buchanan, George.
    'Ad Mildredam Cæcilii'.
    Caligula D. I, f. 34.
10 elegiac couplets. Pr. in Buchanan's *Epigrammatum Liber III*, 1584, pp. 191–2, with 'do' for 'dem' in first verse. To Mildred, wife of William Cecil, later Lord Burghley.

Ni Mildreda tui viri patrisque
Vicino admonitus velit periclo.
    Buchanan, George.
    'Ad eandem'.
    Caligula D. I, ff. 34, 34v.
23 Phalæcian hendecasyllables. Pr. in Buchanan's *Epigrammatum Liber III*, 1584, pp. 192–3, with 'monitus' for 'admonitus' in last verse. To Mildred, wife of William Cecil, later Lord Burghley.

Quod tibi vis tacito uoto, quod mater aperto
Hoc tibi sors cito det filia Cæcilii.
    Buchanan, George.
    'Ad Agnetam Cæcilii filia*m*'.
    Caligula D. I, f. 34v.
Elegiac distich. Pr. in Buchanan's *Epigrammatum Liber III*, 1584, p. 194, with 'fors' for 'sors' in last verse. To Agnes, daughter of Mildred and William Cecil, later Lord Burghley.

Si nisi pro genere & meritis Hauerta dabuntur
Seruiet obsequio nostra thalia tuo.
    Buchanan, George.
    'Ad Hauertam'.
    Caligula D. I, ff. 34v, 35.

8 elegiac couplets. Pr. in Buchanan's *Epigrammatum Liber III*, 1584, pp. 190–91, as 'Ad Joannam Havartam', with last verse reading 'Promta erit obsequio nostra Thalia tuo'.

⟨Cum mihi quod⟩ donem nil sit, tibi
          resque supersit
Munus erit medicis aptius illa tuis.
    Buchanan, George.
    Caligula D. I, f. 35.
3 elegiac couplets. *Imperfect*, opening three words of first line lost owing to mutilation of manuscript. Pr. in Buchanan's *Epigrammatum Liber III*, 1584, p. 195, with 'suis' for 'tuis' of last verse. To Matthew Stewart, Earl of Lennox, Regent of Scotland 1570 (d. 4 Sept. 1571).

Quod præter patrias iuga fers muliebria
          leges
Et verte in Thuscam regia Sceptra colum.
    Buchanan, George.
    'Ad galliam'.
    Caligula D. I, f. 35.
2 elegiac couplets. Pr. in I. D. McFarlane, *Buchanan*, 1981, p. 353. Satirical epigram on Catherine de Medici.

Innuba quæ fueras papistica, iuncta mar-
          ito
Hoc quoque mobilior tu Catharina fores.
    Buchanan, George.
    'Ad Cath. Medicæam'.
    Caligula D. I, f. 35.
2 elegiac couplets. Satirical epigram on Catherine de Medici.

Regia flaminia iamdudum sceptra ten-
          eres,
Virtutem erranti credo fuisse ducem.
    Buchanan, George.
    'Carmina in Honorem Mariæ Beton G. Boca'.
    Caligula D. I, f. 35.
6 elegiac couplets. Pr. in Buchanan's *Epigrammatum Liber III*, 1584, p. 204, as 'Ad Mariam Flaminiam forte Reginam', with 'cæcæ' for 'erranti' in last verse. On Mary Beton, maid of honour to Mary, Queen of Scots.

Qui te videt beatus est
Qui te potitur est Deus.
    Buchanan, George.
    Caligula D. I, f. 35.
4 iambic dimeters. Jotting at the foot of the page. Pr. in Buchanan's *Epigrammatum Liber I*, 1584, p. 155, as 'E. Græco Rufini'.

⟨Regno animus tibi dignus erat tibi regia
          virtus⟩
Gauderet Sceptro læta subesse tuo.
    Buchanan, George.
    Caligula D. I, f. 35v.
4 elegiac couplets. *Imperfect*: first verse, lost owing to mutilation of leaf, supplied from Buchanan's *Epigrammatum Liber III*, 1584, p. 205, where the poem is pr. as 'Ad Mariam Betonam pridie regalium Reginam forte ductam', with 'regno' for 'Sceptro' in last verse. Followed immediately by two paraphrases in French verse. To Mary Beton.

⟨Non me materies facit superbum⟩
Quam sim durior omnibus lapillis.
    Buchanan, George.
    Caligula D. I, f. 36.
26 Phalæcian hendecasyllables. *Imperfect*: first verse, lost owing to mutilation of leaf, supplied from Buchanan's *Hendecasyllabon Liber*, Paris, 1567, where the poem is pr. as 'Adamas in cordis effigiem sculptus, annuloque insertus, quem Maria Scotorum Regina ad Elizabetham Anglorum Reginam misit, anno M. D. LXIV', with 'sum' for 'sim' in last verse. Composed for an exchange of rings between Mary, Queen of Scots and Elizabeth I, 1564.

Hoc tibi quæ misit cor, nil quod posset
          habebat
Charius esse sibi quam fuit ante tibi.
    Buchanan, George.
    Caligula D. I, f. 36.
2 elegiac couplets. Pr. in Buchanan's *Epigrammatum Liber I*, 1584, pp. 165–6, as 'De Adamante misso a Regina Scotiæ ad Reginam Angliæ', and with the second hemiepes of the pentameter reading 'gratius esse tibi'. Composed to accompany the gift by Mary, Queen of Scots to Elizabeth I of a diamond ring fashioned like a heart.

Caligula D. II

State papers relating to transactions between England and Scotland; 1590–1603.

Wyll Watsons wordes or Bruces boist availl
prescribinge pointes as Scribes in euery thing.

['Libellous verses cast into the pulpit in the great church, against the ministers of Edinburgh. Oct. 24, 1592'].
Caligula D. II, f. 50v.

28 decasyllables in 2 stanzas rhyming abab-bcbccdcdee. Title, lost by mutilation, supplied from Planta's *Catalogue* (1802). Satire on various complaints made by the ministers of the kirk to James VI.

Claudius C. II

Collections relating to the nobility and to heraldry, temp. Henry III-Henry VI, assembled by William Camden; circa late 16th cent. Contents list (f. 1) in hand of Dugdale. Ownership inscription of 'Ro: Cotton Bruceus' (f. 2).

Consuluit Phæbum nuper Cecilius Heros,
Fiet et exhaustis gens tua læta Cadis.

[James, Richard].
'Sibylla Hippocratis'.
Claudius C. II, f. 339.

6 elegiac couplets. Apparently *autograph fair copy*. Dialogue, comprising 'Petitio' and Sibyl's 'Responsio'. Not included in *The Poems of Richard James*, ed. by A. B. Grosart, 1880. On Edward Cecil, Viscount Wimbledon, commander of the disastrous Spanish expedition of 1625.

Cleopatra A. IV

William Camden's collections for Britannia.

My prime of youth is but a frost of care
And now I live and now my life is done.

Tichborne, Chidiock.
Cleopatra A. IV, f. 11.

11 decasyllables in 2 stanzas rhyming ababcc. *Imperfect*, ending at stanza 2, l. 5, 'My thride is cute and yet it is not spune'. Crum M863. Pr., with variants, in *Verses of Prayse and Joye...upon her Majesties preservation*, 1586. Verses allegedly written by Tichborne before his execution (1586).

Cleopatra C. III

Miscellaneous collections assembled circa *1581–1583 by Francis Thynne (d. 1608), Lancaster Herald, including material in the hand of John Stowe, etc.; 15th–16th cent. Mostly* autograph. *Signatures on f. 3 of Thynne and 'Robert Cotton Bruceus'. Instructions to binder on f. 1, apparently* temp. *Cotton. Modern foliation (followed below) in pencil at the foot of the leaves.*

ff. 1–209v. Thynne's *autograph* notebook of monuments and inscriptions in various churches; etc.; 22 September 1582–23 August 1583. Including (ff. 12v–19) inscriptions 'taken 5 November 1582 Westminster Churche'. In the 1720 edition of Stow's *Survey of London*, Bk. VI, p. 22, the Redman and Brigham memorials are noted as among the 'Monuments gone'.

No tyme that stintethe teares and weares out woo
from whiche mey weyne & bring me to thy rest.

Morgan, —.
Cleopatra C. III, ff. 10v–11v.

7 stanzas in rhyme royal. Opening lines of first stanza defective in rhyme and metre: first line begins 'No tyme dothe st that stintethe...'. Preceded by Latin prose epitaph attributing verses to brother of deceased. Concluding 'these verses are covered with glasse', and followed by family arms in trick. Epitaph of George Morgan (d. 8 July 1581), son of William Morgan of Monmouthshire and his wife Elizabeth.

Hic sita Redmanni sunt ossa ô candide lector
Precones populis da precor usque tuis.

Cleopatra C. III, f. 12v.

14 elegiac couplets. This and the two sets of verse following form part of a long inscription (ff. 12v–13v) described as 'hanging on the piller next to the graue'. Concludes: 'Requiescat in pace ecclesie Amen'. See translation into English verse below, ff. 13, 13v. This and the three sets of Latin and English verse following form the epitaph of John Redman, D.D. (d. 4 Nov. 1551).

Hospes siste gradum hos et numeros lege hunc planctum neque opis sed neque lachrimis.

Cleopatra C. III, f. 13.

4 lesser Asclepiads.

His bones here rest shall in a chest whome
Redman men did call
graunt him that peace to reste [at least]
that to thy flocke thow giues.
Cleopatra C. III, ff. 13, 13v.

14 fourteener couplets. *Imperfect*, scribal omission of
words in last verse signalled by blank space.
Translation of Latin elegiacs above, f. 12v.

Johannes Redmannus humo tumulatus in
ista
Ast eius nihil est igitur bene vale valeque.
Cleopatra C. III, f. 13v.

11 hexameters. Preceded by: 'vppon his [tombe
deleted] graue stone is this wrytten'; and concluding
with 'vixit annos 43. decessit anno domini 1551
nouemb. [14 *deleted*] 4. Requiescat in pace ecclesie'.

Vnica quae fueram proles spesque alma
parentum
Hoc rachel Brigham condita sum tumulo.
Cleopatra C. III, f. 14.

Elegiac distich. Headed 'M[emoriae]. P[iae].', and
concluding with '22 die Junii 1557 Vix annis 4 [3
deleted]. mensibus .3. Diebus .4. horis .15. nascentes
morimur'. John Weever, *Ancient Funerall Monuments*, 1631, p. 488, notes that Chaucer's monument
was erected by Nicholas Brigham, 'who buried his
daughter *Rachell*...neare to the Tombe of this old
Poet...such was his loue to the Muses'. Epitaph of
Rachel Brigham (d. 22 June 1557) aged 4.

Nil decus aut splendor nil regia nomina
prosunt
Funere nunc valeas consociata deo.
'In clariss. domine francisce Suffolcie
quondam ducisse epicedion'.
Cleopatra C. III, f. 18.

3 elegiac couplets. Pr. in Camden's *Reges, reginæ,
nobiles in Ecclesia Collegiata ... sepulti*, 1600, sig. [F3]ʳ,
and in *Survey*, 1633, p. 515a. Epitaph of Frances,
Duchess of Suffolk (d. 1563).

ff. 31v–34. Inscriptions copied '7 Sept. 1583 Welles'
[i.e. Wells Cathedral].

Sic jacet ecce Thomas obscuro haud
sanguine natus
in ceterum famulum suscipe queso tuum.
Fitzjames, or Fitzwilliams, —.

'Epitaphium thome fitzJames per filium
editum'.
Cleopatra C. III, f. 33.

17 elegiac couplets. Not recorded in Arthur A.
Jewers, *Wells Cathedral: its monumental inscriptions
and heraldry*, 1892. Epitaph of William, later
Thomas, Fitzjames *al*. Fitzwilliams, Dean of Wells
1540–1548.

ff. 50, 50v. Inscriptions copied '9 Novemb 1582.
Ictham [i.e. Igtham] in Kent'.

Dei ouis placida, parentum agna
In puluere prestolatur aduentum.
[?Lambard, William].
'Jane the wyfe of Williame lambarde of
lincolns Inne gent daughter of george
molton of Itham esquier & of Agnes
polhill his wyfe'.
Cleopatra C. III, f. 50v.

5 verses in unidentified metre. Preceded by description: 'in a marbell stone erected in the wall is
this sett in brasse a trumpett comynge out of the
clowdes vnder whiche is written ecce venio volonter'.
For tentative attribution see entry in Lambarde's
diary, quoted in *Archaeologia Cantiana*, vol. V (1863),
p. 251. Epitaph of Jane Lambard (d. 21 Sept. 1573)
in Igtham Church, Kent. See also below Faustina E.
V, f. 180v.

Faustina E. V

*Collection of antiquarian papers used by Camden in the
compilation of the* Remaines; *1590–1605. Included
are several discourses (ff. 162v–182v) on epitaphs that
were read before the Society of Antiquaries on 3
November 1600 by Camden, Arnold Oldisworth,
Francis Tate, Sir John Davies, Arthur Agarde, Francis
Thynne, Joseph Holand or Holland and John Stow.
Described in the mid 17th cent. contents list (f. 1) as
'Miscellanies, by the Heralds'. Pr. in Thomas Hearne,
A Collection of Curious Discourses, 2nd edn., ed. J.
Ayloffe, 1771, vol. i, pp. 228–60; and see C. E.
Wright, 'The Elizabethan Society of Antiquaries and
the Formation of the Cottonian Library', in Wormald
and Wright*, The English Library before 1700, *1958,
pp. 176–212.*

ff. 162, 162v, 165v. Verses added in Camden's
current hand to a fairly-copied paper headed '3.
Nou: 1600 Epitaphes Camd:', and docketed 'Mr
Clarencieux | Epitaphes' (f. 165v). The text was

revised and expanded for *Remaines*, 1605. Partly pr. in Hearne, *op. cit.*, pp. 228–32; and see 310–54.

Here lies lord haue mercy vpon her!
She dide a mayde the more's the pittie.
> [?Hoskins, John].
> 'Vpon one Margarett Radcliffe I found theise Verses'.
> Faustina E. V, f. 162v.

4 verses of varying lengths, in rhymed couplets. Attributed to 'Ser*jeant* Hoskins' in Bodleian MS. Ashmole 38, p. 181. Crum H956. Pr., with variants, in *Remaines*, 1623, p. 349, and, from Ashmole MS. 38, in L. B. Osborn, *Life, letters and writings of John Hoskins* (Yale Studies in English, vol. 87), New Haven, 1930, p. 170. The verse inscription on her memorial tablet in St Margaret's, Westminster, beg. 'Here underneath entomb'd a Dazie lies', pr. in Stow's *Survey*, 1633, p. 812. On Margaret, dau. of Sir John Radcliffe, who d. 10 Nov. 1599. See also below, f. 171.

Here under this S⟨tone⟩
of this c⟨hurch Peti-canon⟩.
> 'A ridiculous Epita⟨ph⟩ in Norwich Cha⟨pter House⟩'.
> Faustina E. V, f. 162v.

6 doggerel verses in rhymed couplets. *Imperfect*, line-endings wanting owing to mutilation of leaf. Crum U33. Pr. in *Remaines*, 1605, Certaine Poemes, p. 57, beg 'Under this S⟨tone⟩'. Epitaph of John Knapton (d. 28 Aug. 1590) in Norwich Cathedral.

Digna hæc luce diuturniore
Nisi quòd luce meliore digna.
> 'Margareta Sands'.
> Faustina E. V, f. 162v.

2 verses in unidentified metre. On Margaret Sandys.

John Bell Brokenbrow liggs vnder this
stean
I liued on my owne lond, but with mickle
strife.
> Faustina E. V, f. 165v.

4 verses of varying lengths, in rhymed couplets. Crum J114. Pr. in *Remaines*, 1605, Certaine Poemes, p. 59, as 'At *Farlham* on the west marches neare *Naworth* Castle', co. Cumberland. A copy in Nottingham University Library, Portland MSS., Pw 2V 43, dates it to 1506. A variant version beg. 'I Jocky Bell o' Braikenbrow' is pr. in T. J. Pettigrew,

Chronicles of the Tombs, 1857, p. 217, as in Annandale Church.

ff. 166–167. Paper docketed (f. 167v) 'Mr [Arnold] Oldsworth'.

Par iacet hoc tumulo sociale uxore mari-
tus
Plurima, nunc regnat iunctus uterque
Deo.
> 'In S[t]. Warborowghes church. \ on a monum*ent.* / in Bristoll'.
> Faustina E. V, f. 167.

3 elegiac couplets. Dated at foot '1556'. Epitaph of John Smyth (d. 1 Sept. 1555), Mayor of Bristol, and his wife Joan, in St Werburgh's Church.

ff. 168–171v. Paper docketed (f. 171v) 'Epitaphs M[r] Davies'. Pr. in Hearne, *op. cit.*, pp. 238–45; and see *The Poems of Sir John Davies*, ed. Robert Kreuger, Oxford, 1975, pp. xli–xliii.

Conditur in tumulo gratis qui nil dedit
unquam
nunc quod gratis perlegis ista dolet.
> 'as of a Covetous person'.
> Faustina E. V, f. 170.

Elegiac distich. This and the four pieces following introduced by: 'But in this later refined Age there haue been many Epitaphes of excellent composition; both serious, & rediculos'.

Promus eram non Condus opum, diuesque
videbar
non Capiendo alijs, non Cupiendo mihi.
> 'of a moderate contented person'.
> Faustina E. V, f. 170.

Elegiac distich.

Calculus exesit mihi vivo in Corpore renes
Quis poterit tumuli non meminisse sui.
> 'Of one that died of the Stone'.
> Faustina E. V, f. 170.

2 elegiac couplets.

Qui Jacet hic non ille Jacet, sed ad astra
volauit
Vt neque totus abis, sic neque totus obis.
> 'of Sr Phil. Sidney. among many this was very excellent'.
> Faustina E. V, f. 170v.

2 elegiac couplets. Epitaph for Sir Philip Sidney (d. 1586).

Ecce arcto terræ in tumulo, exiguique Sepulchri
Et vixit vivitque dêum genus et mixtus dijs.

> 'but [of Sʳ Phil. Sidney] another there is of more State & more magniloquent'.
> Faustina E. V, f. 170v.

10 hexameters. Epitaph for Sir Philip Sidney (d. 1586).

Ho who lies heere
What we lent we lost.

> Faustina E. V, f. 170v.

6 verses rhyming aaabb. This and the five pieces following introduced by: 'of the ridiculous Epitaphs the best that I have noted are these'. Sixteenth-century epitaph on the monument of Edward Courtenay, 3rd Earl of Devon (d. 1419), at Tiverton: pr. in G.E.C., *Complete Peerage*, vol. IV, 1916, p. 326, note (a), as 'Ho, ho, who lies here?'. Its basis is some early 15th-cent. Latin lines, 'Ecce quod expedi habui...'. A variant version was transcribed by Francis Thynne (Sloane MS. 3836, f. 30v) from the tomb of Robert and Margaret Byrkes (d. 1579) in Doncaster Church.

Ho who lies heer for a groate
for he died against his will.

> 'another of the Same Kind is at Southampton'.
> Faustina E. V, f. 170v.

4 verses of varying length, in rhymed couplets. On Roger Wilmot of Southampton.

Who would trust to others breath
Sands I was but now am dust.

> 'another of one \ Mr / Sands'.
> Faustina E. V, f. 171.

Heptasyllabic quatrain rhyming abab. Pr. in *Remaines*, 1605, Certaine Poems, p. 53, as 'Who would live in others breath?'. Punning epitaph for — Sandys.

O mors crudelis fecisti plurima damna
dum legitur talis daret tibi scamna sedere.

> 'another of one Elis that Setts the formes before the Crosse at the Sermons'.
> Faustina E. V, f. 171.

4 hexameters. Epitaph for — Ellis, officer of St Paul's Cathedral.

Here lies old Craker a Maker of Bellowes
he that made bellowes Could not make breath.

> [Hoskins, John; or Davies, Sir John, *attribs.*].
> 'The epitaph of the bellowes maker is in every mans mouth'.
> Faustina E. V, f. 171.

4 verses of varying length, in rhymed couplets. Crum H848. Pr. in *Poems of Sir John Davies*, ed. Robert Kreuger, Oxford, 1975, p. 303, among 'Poems possibly by Davies', as 'Here lies Kit Craker, the kinge of good fellowes'. On Christopher Craker or Croker (*al.* Cooker and Brooker) see Edward Doughtie, *Liber Lilliati*, Newark (Delaware), 1985, pp. 147–149.

Here lies Lord haue mercy vppon her
that died a maid the more the pitty.

> [?Hoskins, John].
> 'but the newest pleasant Epitaph that I know; is that of Mʳˢ Ratclif the maide of honor to her Maiestie that died lately'.
> Faustina E. V, f. 171.

4 verses of varying lengths, in rhymed couplets. On Margaret, dau. of Sir John Radcliffe, who d. 10 Nov. 1599. See also above, f. 162v.

He that lies heer was borne & cried
told threescore yeare, fell sick & died.

> [?Hoskins, John].
> Faustina E. V, f. 171v.

Octosyllabic couplet. Crum H1011. Attributed to John Hoskins in Chetham Library MS. 8012, p. 158, and included in L. B. Osborn, *Life, letters and writings of John Hoskins* (Yale Studies in English, vol. 87), New Haven, 1930, p. 171, beg. 'Here lyes the man was borne and cryed'. Pr., with variants, in *Remaines*, 1605, Certaine Poems, p. 58.

ff. 172–175. Paper signed 'Arthure Agarde'. Pr. in Hearne, *op. cit.*, pp. 246–51.

Vaillant Duke Rollo stout & fierce
and clappinge of handes with strikinge
noice.

[?Agarde, Arthur].
Faustina E. V, f. 174.

6 verses of varying length, in rhymed couplets. Translation of preceding Latin verse epitaph of Rollo, first Duke of Normandy (d. 932).

ff. 176v–180v. Paper docketed (f. 176v) 'Epitaphes Mr Thinne', Lancaster Herald. Pr., with omissions, in Hearne, *op. cit.*, pp. 251–6.

Conde tibi tumulum. nec fide heredis
amori
mortuus est, nec emit libris haec verba
ducentis.

Faustina E. V, f. 176v.

2 hexameters, interspersed with three non-scanning lines. Last verse in MS, 'Mortuus est, nec libris emit verba ducentis', corrected from Julius F. XI, f. 88, below. On Peter Woodgate, chaplain of New College Oxford, buried in the cloisters there, 4 Nov. 1590.

De semisse, tricente annos, quadranteque
subduc
Cum quadrante tridus sesquipla quinque
vivat.

Leeche, James.
Faustina E. V, f. 178v.

5 elegiac couplets. Prefatory note: 'Vppone the deathe of a noble Inglishmann whose name I cannott fynde Mr Jeames leche of Oxforde a lerned gentle-mann being then at paris composed this epitaphe conteynyng his age [*first couplet quoted*] adding this further [*remaining couplets quoted*] conteynynge the yere the monthe and daye of his deathe'. (James Leeche was a fellow of Merton 1557–1567.) Epitaph in the form of a chronogram.

O sic o Iuncti tumulo maneamus in vno
Quos semper viuos iunxerat unus amor.

'In the churche of Grenwiche is this epitaphe of Susanne the wyfe of Robert Wisemane esquier'.
Faustina E. V, f. 178v.

Elegiac couplet, introducing epitaph that follows. Inscription for grave of Robert and Susan Wiseman.

Que pia que prudens, que docta pudica
modesta
Putre cadauer humo, spiritus ipse polo.

Faustina E. V, ff. 178v, 180.

6 elegiac couplets, the first standing alone. Introduced by: 'First these two verses alone [*introductory couplet quoted*] then followe these verses by them selues [*remaining five couplets quoted*]'. Epitaph of Susan, wife of Robert Wiseman, Gentleman Pensioner.

SpIrItVs erVpto saLVVs GILberte No-
VeMbre
CaRCere TrIstIs In hoc Æthere BarCLe
Crepat.

'In the churche of Welles is this epitaphe of Barkley bishoppe of that see in w*hi*che verses the number signyficant great letters do shewe the yere of our lord wherin he dyed'.
Faustina E. V, f. 180.

Elegiac distich. Followed by: 'Annum dant ista salutis 83'. Pr., with additions, in Arthur A. Jewers, *Wells Cathedral: its monumental inscriptions and heraldry*, 1892, p. 110. Chronogrammatic epitaph of Gilbert Berkeley, Bishop of Bath and Wells (d. 2 Nov. 1581).

Vixi videtis premium
Septem per annos triplices.

Faustina E. V, f. 180.

4 iambic dimeters. Pr. in Arthur A. Jewers, *Wells Cathedral: its monumental inscriptions and heraldry*, 1892, p. 110. Second part of epitaph of Gilbert Berkeley.

Vita quid est? fumus, quid census? res
peritura
Solus adest Christus vita salusque mihi.

'In the same churche of Welles is one other epitaphe of Sydname'.
Faustina E. V, f. 180v.

2 elegiac couplets. Second couplet introduced by 'whereunto the dede dothe answere'. Epitaph, in dialogue form, of — Sydname.

Dei ouis placida, parentum agna
In puluere prestolatur aduentum.

[?Lambard, William].
'In the churche of Itham in Kent is this epitaphe of Jane daughter of george

multon esquier & wyfe of william lambarde esquier'.
Faustina E. V, f. 180v.
5 verses in unidentified metre. Epitaph of Jane Lambard (d. 1573) in Igtham Church, Kent. See also above, Cleopatra C. III, f. 50v.

ff. 182–183v. Paper, copied in two scribal hands, of Joseph Holand or Holland, describing himself (f. 183) as 'the last, that was admitted into this Societe'. Pr. in Hearne, *op. cit.*, pp. 258–60.

Totum terra tegit, qui Totus Terra Vocatur
Hollandus iacet hac contumulatus humo.
　　Holand, *al.* Holland, Joseph.
　　Faustina E. V, f. 182.
Elegiac distich. Added later, at foot of page, below signature 'Joseph Holand'. Punning epitaph for himself.

Agnes Tidenham married first to Thomas Marshall, then
Of our Lord as by the Date here written may appere.
　　'The ridiculouse [epitaphe] is in Lambehith Churche, grauen in a wall there; and ronneth forsooth in Ryme as extraordinarie, as euer I heard any...'.
　　Faustina E. V, f. 183v.
3 fourteener couplets. Pr. in *History and antiquities of...Lambeth* included in J. Nichols' *Bibliographia Topographica Britannica*, vol. II, 1786, no. 39, p. 36, preceded by the statement 'Ad sumptum Thomae Folkis, Anno Domini 1583'. Epitaph of Agnes Tidenham (d. *circa* 1583).

ff. 185–188v. Paper docketed (f. 188v) 'Epitaphs Mr Stowe'.

Like as the day his course dothe consume so full of change, is of this world the glorye.
　　'Robert fabian later aldarman buried s. michaell vpon Cornhill. his Epitaphe [1511.]'.
　　Faustina E. V, f. 186.

7 verses of varying length, rhyming ababbcc. Dates given in square brackets in this and the three entries following are copied in the left-hand margin of the MS. Pr. in Weever's *Funerall Monuments*, 1631, p. 416. Epitaph of Robert Fabyan, the chronicler (d. 1511).

Here Thomas Tusser, clad in earth doth lye
Who reads his bokes, shall fynd his faythe was soo.
　　'In s. mildreds churche in the Pultry. T. Tusser his epitaphe [1580.]'.
　　Faustina E. V, f. 187.
6 decasyllabic couplets. Pr. in Stow's *Survey*, 1633, p. 274. Epitaph of Thomas Tusser, writer on husbandry (d. 1580).

No welthe, no prayse, no bright renowne, no skill,
his fame yet lives, his sowl in heven doth rest.
　　'Ser John Leigh. s. margarets lothbere his epitaphe [1564.]'.
　　Faustina E. V, ff. 187–187v.
12 decasyllabic couplets. Pr. in Stow's *Survey*, 1633, p. 292. Epitaph of Sir John Leigh (d. 1564), of London and Lambeth.

When the bells be meryly ronge
For their soulys say a Pater Noster and an Aue.
　　'Traps. 1526. his Epitaphe'.
　　Faustina E. V, f. 188.
8 verses of varying length, in 4 rhymed couplets. *Imperfect*, concluding with the verse: 'Then shall Robart Traps, his wyves, and children be forgotten'. Pr., in longer version of 5 rhymed couplets, in Weever's *Funerall Monuments*, 1631, p. 392. Epitaph on memorial brass to Robert Trapp (d. 1526), goldsmith, in St Leonard's, Foster Lane.

Galba E. IV

Register of Christ Church, Canterbury, etc.; early 14th cent. Contents list (f. 1a) in hand of Richard James.

f. 182v. Verses by William Greshop jotted in the margin, *circa* 1558.

> **Venit vt æthereas Edwardus sextus ad**
> **ædes:**
> **Heu male sanguineis cædimur ambo feris.**
>> Greshop, William.
>> Galba E. IV, f. 182v.

5 elegiac couplets. Apparently *autograph*, and *signed* 'Gul. Greshop' (Fellow of Corpus Christi College, Oxford, 1558; d. at Rome, 1569). Political satire, alluding to a rumour that Edward VI (d. 6 July 1558) had been poisoned by John Dudley, Duke of Northumberland.

Julius C. II

Miscellaneous chronicles and extracts from registers, etc.; 16th cent.

ff. 97–263. John Herd, M.D.: Verse-chronicle of the reigns of Edward IV–Henry VII; *circa* 1560–1562. *Autograph fair copy* with extensive revisions, the final five pages (ff. 261–263) copied in another hand. Dedicated in prose (ff. 98–100v) to Sir William Cecil, later Lord Burghley. Edited, from another manuscript, by Thomas Purnell, Roxburghe Club, 1868.

> **Edwardi quarti Cano multa et lubrica**
> **bella**
> **Henricus celo qui nunc reqiescit in alto.**
>> Herd, John.
>> '[Historia Anglicana heroico carmine conscripta authore Joanne Herdo medicinæ doctore]. Historia Edwardi quarti'.
>> Julius C. II, ff. 105v–263.
>> Four books, in hexameters.

Julius C. III

Letters, etc., addressed to Sir Robert Cotton; circa 1595–1630, n.d.

ff. 164, 164v. Letter of Oswald Dykes, from Wensley, '5. of ma⟨–⟩ Aᵒ domini– 1603', that is, either 5 May 1603 or 5 March 1603/4. Dykes had been 'a while agoe at Sᵗ An of Buxtons in Darbyeshire wher I fond in sondrie places about the howse and well these verses'.

> **Monstra Peco tria sunt alto, Barathrum,**
> **specus, anthrum**
> **Mille sed occurrunt his inimica locis.**
>> Julius C. III, f. 164.

2 elegiac couplets. Introduced by: 'This topographic

discription pleased me well, wᶜʰ if you Like well of yow may make Mr Camden acquanted therwᵗ ...'. Followed by an interpretation of the verses. See also Camden's reworking below, Julius F. VI, f. 311. On the wonders of the peak.

> **Pulchrius hoc nihil est, nil turpius at-**
> **tamen ex⟨[tat]⟩**
> **Ut sit supremo gloria tota deo.**
>> Julius C. III, f. 164.

4 elegiac couplets. Introduced by: 'And in an other chamber of the same place were fare wr⟨rit⟩ten these verses'.

> **Hunc fontem domini concessione sacrauit**
> **Quæ peperit Christum virginis anna**
> **mater.**
>> Julius C. III, f. 164v.

Elegiac distich. This and the set immediately following introduced by: 'In other places about the howse where the well is were written these *verses*'.

> **Si dedit Anna tibi virtutem Buxtona,**
> **serues,**
> **Hoc dedit omnipotens, seruat cum ille**
> **tibi.**
>> Julius C. III, f. 164v.

2 elegiac couplets.

> **Balnea, Vina, Venus, corrumpunt corpora**
> **nostra**
> **At tibi si indulges singula damna ferent.**
>> Julius C. III, f. 164v.

2 elegiac couplets. Introduced by: 'Item in an other place'. Copied below the last verse is apparently an alternative reading for the first hemiepes, 'in his si pecces'.

f. 214. Letter of Richard James, 25 October [*circa* 1629–1630].

> **Det Deus auspiciis propriis vt vivere**
> **possim**
> **Ferre animo et cælum suspicere vt patri-**
> **am.**
>> James, Richard.
>> Julius C. III, f. 214.

4 elegiac couplets. Introduced by: 'by our niew Masters wicked pride and practise forc't I am to take

somme favour abroade, and at leasure to contriue my discontent into this Epigramme'. Letter and verses pr. in *The Poems of Richard James*, ed. by A. B. Grosart, 1880, pp. xxxiii, xxxiv.

ff. 352–353. Congratulatory letter of Thomas Sparrow to Cotton; n.d., *circa* 1609 (?).

Scribentem inuitat Pietas, et gratia vultus,
Pocula Pegaseâ plæna ministret acquâ.

> Sparrow, Thomas.
> '[Ornatissimo, Doctissimoque viro, Domino Roberto Cotton equiti Aurato suo*que* Patrono plurimum colendo 'ενδαιμονειν]'.
> Julius C. III, f. 352v.

12 elegiac couplets. *Autograph.* Title from covering letter (f. 352), *signed* 'Thomas Sparreus'. Four Greek elegiac couplets following (f. 353) may also be Sparrow's. Congratulatory verses, extolling Cotton's library.

f. 385. Verses of Joseph Walter to Cotton; n.d., *circa* 1606–31.

Cur Meleager aprum neglecta vulpe fati-
gas?
Relliquias vafri vulpis, sævique Renaldi.

> Walter, Joseph.
> 'Emeriti poetæ nugæ'.
> Julius C. III, f. 385.

19 hexameters. *Autograph.* Concludes: 'Tuæ Dignitatis studioss. Joseph Walter' (Vicar, 1606–1631, of Alconbury Weston, near Cotton's family seat at Conington). Conjecturally dated in modern pencil hand on the guard '1611?'.

Julius C. V

Letters, etc., addressed to William Camden; circa *1578–1623, n.d.*

Jana reciprocicornis, origo mensis, et anni
Cum premit obiectam torridas igne pla-
gam.

> Alabaster, William.
> Julius C. V, f. 23.

7 elegiac couplets. Probably *autograph.* Subscribed 'Guilielmus Allib⟨aster⟩', and dated '1583' at head in another hand. (Alabaster was a pupil at West-

minster School until Easter 1584.) Pr. in Camden's *Epistolae*, ed. Thomas Smith, 1691, p. 389. Congratulatory verses to Camden.

Te Noua Villa fremens, odioso murmure
Nympha
Iste redit. Sic liuor inest et pugna perennis.

> Stradling, Sir John.
> Julius C. V, f. 56.

10 hexameters. *Autograph.* Incorporated in a letter of Stradling, from St Donats, 14 November 1594. Pr. in Camden's *Britannia*, 1600, p. 575, and, with text of the letter, in Camden's *Epistolae*, ed. Thomas Smith, 1691, pp. 54–8. On the spring at Newtown, Glamorganshire.

Romanæ huic aquilæ sanctus nunc insidet
Agnus;
Qui fuerit famulus, Justiniane, tuus.

> Harris, Nathan, LL. D.
> Julius C. V, f. 127.

7 elegiac couplets. *Autograph, signed* 'Nathan Harris Legum Dr Anno 1612°'. On a royal device incorporating a Roman eagle and paschal lamb.

f. 290. Letter of Sir Edward Fox, 20 December 1618.

Vnum deprecor hoc: libros des supplico
Regi
Sola mihi spes es: valeas mi Candide
Cambden.

> Fox, Sir Edward.
> Julius C. V, f. 290.

6 hexameters. *Autograph.* Marginal note: 'Literarum his singulis sunt 36'. Request to Camden to present a MS. of Fox's own verses to the King.

Concidit Henricus flos famæ, gloria Gen-
tis.
Gentis ocellus, Amator Honoris, Vive
Perenne.

> Fox, Sir Edward.
> 'In Obitum illustrissimi Henrici Magnæ Britanniæ Principis in versibus bipartite dispositis'.
> Julius C. V, f. 290.

6 hexameters. *Autograph.* Verses arranged in rows, reading the same downwards as across. Prefatory note states that these verses 'I meant to have

indorsed on the back of the Princes Epitaphe I sent you; which I made after booth the Universities made thers'. On the death of Henry Frederick, Prince of Wales, 1613.

Ne peto condoleas, rex o rex comprime luctus
Sara quasi Sobolum sis pia progenitrix.
    Fox, Sir Edward.
    'Ad Regem Carmen consolatorium in Hex: et Pent reciproci⟨s⟩'.
    Julius C. V, f. 290.
11 elegiac couplets. *Autograph*. Note beside the eighth couplet, 'hoc distichon est in Libro', refers to the MS. that Fox in a marginal note hopes will be reserved for King James's private use.

ff. 327, 327v. Letter of Sir Edward Fox to Dr Daniel Featley, from 'Steventon by Ludlowe', 4 Dec. 1619, incorporating further elaborately contrived Latin verses, with notes on their format.

Anna fuit Phænix mundi; coniux Jovis Anna
Anna nitet cælo personas tres colit Anna.
    Fox, Sir Edward.
    Julius C. V, f. 327.
4 hexameters. *Autograph*. Each verse in this and the following two sets, which are each encompassed within the bars of a portcullis, consists of 34 letters. All are epitaphs for the Queen, Anne of Denmark (d. 1619).

Anna beat numen votis; dominum canit Anna
Anna manet Jesu; ter fælix iam micat Anna.
    Fox, Sir Edward.
    Julius C. V, f. 327.
4 hexameters. *Autograph*. Each verse consists of 34 letters.

Anna rex regnat, regitabat Anna
Anna cælestis celebrabit Anna…
    Fox, Sir Edward.
    Julius C. V, f. 327.
2 sets of 4 Sapphics, each followed by an adonean. *Autograph*. *Imperfect*, last verse lost owing to wear at foot of leaf. Sapphics consist of 26 letters each and adoneans of 14.

O pater clemens misere fontis
Perpetuumque.
    Fox, Sir Edward.
    Julius C. V, f. 327v.
12 Sapphic stanzas. *Autograph*. First three verses of each stanza consist of 25 letters each and the final ones of 12. A prayer to God.

Iesus Soter Salvat Servat Sacrat Iesus
Iesus ⟨-⟩at crimen clarat curat Iesus.
    Fox, Sir Edward.
    Julius C. V, f. 327v.
4 hexameters. *Autograph*. Verses of 33 letters each, words of each line having same initial letter (as noted in margin). With addition before and after of name 'Iesus' middle verses may also be read downwards to make four hexameters. Verses copied within an elaborate rectangle.

Metra retro recte cev tessellaria versant
Apta reor numeris aptis et versibus extant.
    Fox, Sir Edward.
    Julius C. V, f. 327v.
2 hexameters. *Autograph*. Each verse in this and the two sets following consists of 36 letters.

Sæpe scio summo Steuarto sancio sacre
Sacra sacro senis sacrate sumite Seni.
    Fox, Sir Edward.
    Julius C. V, f. 327v.
2 hexameters. *Autograph*. Each word in this and the following verses begins with same letter; and both sets are recopied immediately below within a ruled square.

Dona dabo Dominis divinis Dædala Dono
Dedo Dico Daniæ Dynastis dedico divis.
    Fox, Sir Edward.
    Julius C. V, f. 327v.
2 hexameters. *Autograph*.

f. 393. Verses by Edward, Lord Herbert of Cherbury, written in reply to a Latin epigram by François Guiet in praise of Joan of Arc, a copy of which, entitled 'Joanna Virgo Aureliana', and beg. 'Rustica sum sed plena deo, sed pectore forti', immediately precedes these verses. This MS., and the text of Guiet's epigram, not recorded in *The*

Poems…of Edward, Lord Herbert of Cherbury, ed. by G. C. Moore Smith, Oxford, 1923, pp. 89–90.

Desine Galle tuam tandem jactare Bubul-
cam

Numine, sit Virgo quam licet illa minus.

    Herbert, Edward, Lord Herbert of Cherbury.

    'Respons. Gallo supradicto qui Joanna*m* Aurelian*am* Virginem et plenam Deo fuisse contendit'.

    Julius C. V, f. 393.

6 elegiac couplets. Subscribed 'E: Herb.'. Pr. posthumously, with variants, in Herbert's *Occasional Verses*, 1665, and in G. C. Moore Smith, *ed. cit.*, pp. 89–90.

Quod nequiêre viri potuit si foemina, quid
ni

Galle fores tandem Tu muliere minor?

    Herbert, Edward, Lord Herbert of Cherbury.

    'Anglus'.

    Julius C. V, f. 393.

Elegiac distich. Subscribed 'E: Herb.'. Pr. posthumously, without title, in Herbert's *Occasional Verses*, 1665, and in G. C. Moore Smith, *ed. cit.*, p. 89.

Julius F. VI

William Camden's collections, partly relating to Mary, Queen of Scots, and partly for his Britannia. *The material includes communications from antiquaries working in various parts of the country. Camden has added an index of contents at the back (ff. 466–467v). The name 'George Toker' is jotted at foot of first page (f. 1) of the vellum bifolium bound in at the front.*

Cur iam cognatas acies & prælia pandis

Bellipotens Anglus…

    Camden, William.

    Julius F. VI, f. 4.

2 elegiac couplets. *Autograph draft. Imperfect*, wanting all after beginning of l. 4. One of a number of drafts, which includes a version beginning 'Cognatas acies & tela minantia telis', incorporated in a page of pen-trials, along with the distich following. Apparently on an English military commander.

Est tua penna quidem gratissima, penna
vide⟨[tur]⟩

Hæc tamen Edmundi gratior esse mihi.

    Camden, William.

    Julius F. VI, f. 4.

Elegiac distich. *Autograph draft*. Jotting on penmanship.

Mira alto Pecco tria sunt, barathrum,
specus, antrum

Plura sed occurrunt quæ spetiosa minus.

    Camden, William.

    Julius F. VI, f. 311.

2 elegiac couplets. *Autograph draft*. Camden's reworking of some verses (see above, Julius C. III, f. 164) inscribed at St Ann's Well in Buxton, as sent to Cotton by Oswald Dykes, 5 May 1603 or 5 March 1603/4. Pr. in *Britannia*, 1607, p. 421; and in G. B. Johnston, 'Poems by William Camden', *Studies in Philology, Texts and Studies*, 1975, p. 110. On the wonders of the peak.

This seate and soyle from Saxon Bade a
man of honest fame,

as god shall please, who is the king, and
lord, and god of all.

    Ferrers, Henry.

    Julius F. VI, f. 312.

20 fourteener couplets. *Autograph*. Crum T2041. Metrical history of Baddesley Clinton, co. Warwick.

ff. 377–412v. Collections of the antiquary William Darell or Dorell (see f. 411) relating to Dorset and Somerset; 1579. Apparently *autograph*.

Aspice (quisquis ades) Reginæ insignia
pulchra,

Disce (puer) Regem: disce timere deum.

    'The verses which are written in bruton Schole'.

    Julius F. VI, f. 379.

8 elegiac couplets. Subscribed in the same hand 'Johan*ne*s Alsappus', probably John Alsopp, Vicar of Chilton upon Polden, co. Somerset, 1600–1605 (who like Darell was a member of Corpus Christi College, Cambridge). The rest of the bifolium is taken up with Darell's notes on the history of the school, 1579. Inscription set up in the grammar school at Bruton, co. Somerset, *temp.* Elizabeth I, commemorating its founder Edward VI.

Julius F. X

William Camden's collections for Britannia *and* Remaines. *Contents list (f. 3) in hand of Sir Thomas Cotton.*

ff. 53–66v. Jest-book of 'Witty answeres & saienges of Englishmen', and 'Witty sayenges of English woemen', mainly up to the time of Henry VIII. Pr. as 'Grave speeches, and witty apothegmes of woorthie Personages of this Realme in former times', in *Remaines*, 1605.

A famous Isle, of riches great, while Priamus Kingedome stoode, nowe nothinge but a baggage baye, & harbrough nothinge good.
    [Camden, William].
    Julius F. X, f. 61v.
Fourteener couplet. The Latin original of these lines was quoted by Cardinal Pole to Jacopo Sadoleto in a letter dated Venice, 27 Oct. 1532: see Pole's *Epistolarum...Pars I*, Brescia, 1744, p. 400. Translation of *Aeneid*, II, ll. 21–23, as quoted immediately above in MS., comparing the study of philosophy to Virgil's description of the island of Tenedos.

I there were men which then did say that hores brought men unto decay.
    Julius F. X, f. 67v.
Octosyllabic couplet, jotted at head of final blank leaf. On whores.

ff. 69–73v. William Lily: Latin epigrams and epitaphs; copied *circa* early- to mid-16th cent. Described in Sir Thomas Cotton's table of contents (f. 3) as 'Carmina in laudem Mariæ, Epitaphia'. Eight of the pieces were collected in *Epigrammata Guil. Lilii Angli*, 1521. The MS. shows evidence of careless copying. The poems on ff. 70–72, from the Atwater epitaph to that on the King of Spain's voyage, but without the ode on fortune (f. 71v), are also transcribed in the same order in Harley MS. 540, ff. 57–59, in Stow's hand.

Aggredior matrem summi celebrare Tonantis Cederet et flagrans ignibus athna suis.
    Lily, William.
    'In laudem virginis Marie'.
    Julius F. X, ff. 69, 69v.
43 elegiac couplets. In praise of the Virgin Mary.

Hec tibi clare Pater posuerunt marmora Cives Hæc tua, sed pietas & benefacta manent.
    Lily, William.
    'Gulielmi Londinensis episcopi primum diuo Edwardo rege ac postea sub Gulielmo Normanno claruit et plurima Londinensium priveligia impetravit Epitaphium'.
    Julius F. X, f. 70.
Single elegiac couplet (of 4). *Imperfect*, ending at l. 2 of epitaph, space being left by scribe for subsequent verses. Note below: 'obiit anno a christo nato 1070 | Sedit episcopus annis 20'. Pr. in Dugdale's *History of St Paul's*, 1658, p. 51, as the opening couplet of a set of five. Epitaph of William, Bishop of London (d. 1075).

Huius percelebris decus et spes vnica sedis Criste precor famulum transfer in astra tuum.
    Lily, William.
    'Gulielmi cognomento Atwater [Lond *deleted*] Lincolnensis episcopi Epitaphium'.
    Julius F. X, f. 70.
4 elegiac couplets. Note below: 'Obiit anno ætatis 81 | Consecrationis sexto 1520'. Pr., as 'Upon his grey marble', in Peck's *Desiderata curiosa*, 1779, p. 307. Epitaph of William Atwater, Bishop of Lincoln (d. 4 Feb. 1520/1).

Inclita Johannes Londine gloria gentis Hac dormit tectus membra coletus humo.
    Lily, William.
    'Johannis Coleti insignis theologi ad diuum paulum londini Decani Epitaphium'.
    Julius F. X, f. 70.
4 elegiac couplets. Note below: 'obiit anno domini 1519'. First verse in MS. has 'Londine' for 'Londini' and final verse 'caletus' for 'Coletus'. Pr. in Henry Holland, *Monumenta sepulchraria Sancti Pauli...*, 1614, sig. Dv, from inscription on monument in old St Paul's. Epitaph of John Colet (d. 1519).

Iusticia insignes tres olim nomine reges Cacus et minos et Radamanthus erant.
    Lily, William.
    Julius F. X, f. 70.
Elegiac distich. Epigram on the judges of the underworld.

336

Carole Germanie gentis decus Hesperi-
eque
Turcarum illuuies te duce victa cadit.
    Lily, William.
    'Ad Carolum 5 Germanie Imperatorem'.
    Julius F. X, f. 70v.
6 elegiac couplets. Pr., with variants, in Lily's
Epigrammata, 1521, sigs. Aiii–Aiii^v. To the Holy
Roman Emperor Charles V.

Extinctum iacet hic genus a Plantagine
ductum
Et regem hic annos viuere nestoreos.
    Lily, William.
    'Elizabethe regine henrici 7^{mi} coniugis et
    Edwardi 4^{ti} filie Epitaphium'.
    Julius F. X, f. 70v.
5 elegiac couplets. Pr. in Weever's *Funerall Monuments*, 1631, p. 476, as 'transcribed out of a
Manuscript in Sir *Robert Cotton's* Library'. On
Elizabeth of York (d. 1503), consort of Henry VII.

Quid me Scheltone fronte sic aperta
Doctrinam nec habes nec es poeta.
    Lily, William.
    'Lilii Endecasillabi in Scheltonum eius
    carmina calumniantem'.
    Julius F. X, f. 70v.
7 Phalæcian hendecasyllables. Pr. in Weever's *Funer-
all Monuments*, 1631, p. 498, from 'the collections of
Master *Camden*'. Reply to Skelton in the quarrel over
Robert Whittinton's *Vulgaria*, 1520.

Vir pius et simplex tum vita et morte
beatus
Hac Lupsetus iit qua ibis et ipse via.
    Lily, William.
    'Epitaphium'.
    Julius F. X, f. 70v.
Elegiac distich. Epitaph for Thomas Lupset (d.
1530).

Sunt tria que cunctis iter ad penetralia
mortis
accelerant semper balnea vina venus.
    Lily, William.
    Julius F. X, f. 70v.
Elegiac distich. Epigram on fatal indulgences.

Pictam morus habet Quintino authore
tabellam
Quilibet effigiem viuere utranque putet.
    Lily, William.
    'Gulielmi Lilii in mori tabullam conti-
    nentem effigies erasmi et egidii'.
    Julius F. X, ff. 70v, 71.
4 elegiac couplets. Pr., from MS. Harley 540, ff.
223v–224, in *Complete Works of Sir Thomas More*,
vol. III, pt. 2, *Latin Poems*, ed. Clarence H. Miller *et
al.*, p. 422. On the diptych by Quentin Massys
portraying Erasmus and Peter Gillis that was
presented by them to More, *circa* May–Oct. 1517.

En tibi cum Christo Jani rediere calende
ut tibi cum Christo faustior annus eat.
    Lily, William.
    'Ad Polidorum vergilium urbinatem G
    L'.
    Julius F. X, f. 71.
3 elegiac couplets. To Polydore Vergil, with a New
Year's gift.

Quos dederas nuper pisces Polidore di-
serte
Carpio natus aquis o Polidore tuis.
    Lily, William.
    'Polidoro vergilio G L'.
    Julius F. X, f. 71.
5 elegiac couplets. To Polydore Vergil, thanking him
for a gift.

Dicuntur numero septem sapientia quorum
Et milite suo vestit honore Thales.
    Lily, William.
    Julius F. X, f. 71.
4 elegiac couplets. Attrib. at head to 'G L.'. On the
seven wise men of Greece.

Est omnis mulier fallax malaque inquit
Homerus
Causa at odisse stat proba Penelope.
    Lily, William.
    Julius F. X, f. 71.
3 elegiac couplets. Epigram on women in Homer's
Iliad.

**Pro flamina quondam fuit a Iove femina
missa**
Extingui aut tangi sed truculenta fuit.
    Lily, William.
    Julius F. X, f. 71v.
5 elegiac couplets. Satirical epigram on women.

**Hagnes hic iaceo coniux olim Gulielmi
Authorem lucis supplice mente roga.**
    [Lily, William, or Lily, George].
    'Epitaphium Hagnetis Liliæ G Lilie con-
    iugis [defunc *deleted*]'.
    Julius F. X, f. 71v.
5 elegiac couplets. Pr. in Weever's *Funerall Monuments*, 1631, pp. 369–370, 'as I found it in the
Collections of Master *Camden*'. Epitaph of Agnes (d.
11 Aug. n.y.), wife of William Lily, as inscribed on
monument in old St Paul's, erected by their son
George.

**Fortune dubio non ego turbine
nec me cura metus nec labor anxius…**
    Lily, William.
    'Guilielmi Lilii humane fortune insta-
    bilitatem detestantis Ode dicolos tetra-
    st[ro]phos'.
    Julius F. X, f. 71v.
9 ll. of third Asclepiad. *Imperfect*, wanting all after
first verse of third stanza. In title MS. reads
'tetrastaphos'. On the fickleness of fortune.

**Quid possit virtus docte o pater inclite
Thoma**
Et romæ expectat te diadema triplex.
    Lily, William.
    'Ad Reverendum in Christo prelatum
    Thomam Cardinalem Eboracens*em* Archi-
    episcopum Angliæ primatem et Apostolice
    sedis Legatum'.
    Julius F. X, ff. 71v, 72.
15 elegiac couplets. A faint rule appears at the foot of
f. 71v, after the third couplet. Congratulatory verses
to Cardinal Wolsey, *circa* 1518.

**Dum parat Hesperiam volucri rex classe
Philippus**
Dicere et in tuto regis adesse rates.
    Lily, William.
    'De rege Castellæ Philippo naviganti in

hispaniam et vi tempestatis ad anglicum
littus appulso'.
    Julius F. X, f. 72.
8 elegiac couplets. Pr., with additional couplet, in
Lily's *Epigrammata*, 1521, sig. [Aiiii^v]. On Philip the
Fair, of Burgundy and Castile; 1506.

**Ornarat patriam Nestor Pilon inclitus
heros**
Livi [Antenoreos] verba diserta lares.
    Lily, William.
    Julius F. X, f. 72v.
2 elegiac couplets. This and three pieces following
attrib. at head to 'G L.'. Second word in last verse
above supplied conjecturally for MS. reading 'athno-
kias'. On classical writers famous for their eloquence.

**Sustulit e terris elementum Cinthius ignis
Sed Labor ægideum reddidit herculeus.**
    Lily, William.
    Julius F. X, f. 72v.
3 elegiac couplets. Attrib. at head to 'G L.'. Epigram
on mythological subject.

**Qui cupit ex factis sinceræ præmia laudis
Militie exemplum nobile cæsar erit.**
    Lily, William.
    Julius F. X, f. 72v.
3 elegiac couplets. Attrib. at head to 'G L.'. Epigram
on classical subject.

**Lucifer in cælo stella fulgentior omni
Est urbes inter nobile roma caput.**
    Lily, William.
    Julius F. X, f. 72v.
3 elegiac couplets. Attrib. at head to 'G L.'. In praise
of Rome.

**Johannes cubat hic Sextinus marmore
clausus**
Hunc precor admittas in tua regna virum.
    Lily, William.
    'Johannis Sextini Jurisconsulti Epita-
    phium'.
    Julius F. X, f. 72v.
4 elegiac couplets. Concludes: 'obiit a*n*no d*o*mini
1519'. Epitaph for John Sextun (d. 1519), a lawyer
and friend of Erasmus. A. B. Emden, *Biographical
Register of the University of Oxford to 1500*, III, 1675,
records that Sextun's will requested burial in St
Paul's churchyard.

338

Carole qui fulges sceptro et diademate
sacro
Miscens hispano sanguine uterque genus.

   Lily, William.
   'Ad carolum 5 caesar*em* Londini urbem
   una cum Henrico octavo rege intra*ntem*
   et eiusde*m* Henrici hospicio magnificen-
   tiss[imo] apparatu acceptu*m* Pan[e]girica
   carina pube londini p*r*onunciata'.
   Julius F. X, f. 73.

2 elegiac couplets. Scribal errors 'eiusdu*m*' and
'Pandgirica carin*n*a pube*m*' emended in title above.
Pr., with additional final couplet, in Lily's *Epig-
rammata*, 1521, sig. Aiiii^v, with heading 'Divo Carolo
semper Augusto et Henr. Prin. opt. G. L.'. These,
and the five related sets of verse that follow, pr. in
Edward Hall's *Chronicle*, 1548. On the entry of the
Emperor Charles V into London, 6 June 1522.

Leticiæ quantum miniis præbebat Iason
Intrans henrici principis hospicium.

   Lily, William.
   'Aliud'.
   Julius F. X, f. 73.

3 elegiac couplets. Pr. in Lily's *Epigrammata*, 1521,
sig. Aiii^v.

Carole christigenum decus et quem scripta loquuntur
Vectos huc fausto sidere gestat ovans.

   Lily, William.
   'Aliud'.
   Julius F. X, f. 73.

3 elegiac couplets. Pr. in Lily's *Epigrammata*, 1521,
sig. Aiii^v.

Laudat magnanimos urbs inclita roma
catones
Regnet ut in terris pacis amica quies.

   Lily, William.
   'Aliud'.
   Julius F. X, f. 73.

4 elegiac couplets. Pr. in Lily's *Epigrammata*, 1521,
sigs. Aiii^v–Aiiii^r.

Quanto amplexetur populus te cesar
amore
O decus o rerum gloria cæsar ave.

   Lily, William.

'Aliud'.
Julius F. X, f. 73.

3 elegiac couplets. Pr. in Lily's *Epigrammata*, 1521,
sigs. Aiiii^r, ^v.

Ob quorum adventum toties gens ipsa
britanna
Exhilarant nostros numina vestra lares.

   Lily, William.
   'Aliud'.
   Julius F. X, f. 73v.

4 elegiac couplets. Pr. in Lily's *Epigrammata*, 1521,
sig. Aiiii^v.

Laurencius adest ille dum Campegius
Quid prestat ubi mors venerit.

   Lily, William.
   'In Gerardium Molsam Italum Reveren-
   diss⟨imi⟩ Cardinalis campegii familiarem
   Londini defunctum Epitaphium'.
   Julius F. X, f. 73v.

18 iambics, trimeters alternating with dimeters. On
Girardo Molza, servant to Cardinal Lorenzo Campeg-
gio.

f. 105v. Page of Latin extracts described in Sir
Thomas Cotton's table of contents (f. 3) as 'Notæ in
Britania': copied in Camden's hand, but mostly,
and perhaps wholly, by foreign writers.

⟨————————⟩ Gemini qua ianua ponti
Gallorum Anglorumque uetat concurrere
terras.

   Julius F. X, f. 105v.

3 hexameters. Pr. in *Britannia*, 1590, p. 257, under
Kent, as 'ut inquit nostri temporis Poeta'; and in
G. B. Johnston, 'Poems by William Camden', *Studies
in Philology, Texts and Studies*, 1975, p. 108, among
the 'Poems of Doubtful Authorship', with facing
translation by Philemon Holland from the English
edition of 1610. On 'The strait of Calleis'.

ff. 114–115v. Bifolium comprising *imperfect* text of
elaborate epitaph or funerary inscription for Anne
Cecil, 1st wife of Edward de Vere, 17th Earl of
Oxford, who died 5 and was buried 25 June 1588 in
Westminster Abbey. Leaves bound in wrong order:
text should run ff. 115, 115v, 114, 114v. Described

in Sir Thomas Cotton's table of contents (f. 3) as 'Carmina de Anna Comittissa Oxoniæ'.

Anna soror soror Anna suæ charissima Elisæ
Condidimus vitiis carmina flenda suis.

[Hoskins, John].

'Anna Vera vxor Eduardi Veri Comitis Oxoniæ, filia Guil*ielmi* Burghlei summi Angliæ Quæstoris, mulier pietate, prudentia, patientia, pudicitia, & in Coniugem amore singulari, tres filias superstites reliquit, Principi parentibus, fratribus, & vniuersæ Aulæ regiæ admodum chara. Obiit in Aula regia Greenvvici'.
Julius F. X, ff. 115, 115v.

101 verses in mixed metres, mainly elegiac couplets. *Fair copy*, with revisions. Disposed in ten sets of verse forming an expanded commentary on the various elements of the inscription or title. Subscribed: 'Vni M. Pergama'. Pr. by Louise Brown Osborn, *Life, Letters, and Writings of John Hoskins*, New Haven (Yale Studies in English, vol. 87), 1930, pp. 184–188, from another MS. in the same hand, with attribution to Hoskins, in Lansdowne MS. 104, ff. 195–198.

Julius F. XI

William Camden's collections for Britannia *and* Remaines. *Contents list (ff. 1v, 1) in hand of Sir Thomas Cotton.*

An yll yeare of a Goodyer us bereft
Wise, comely, Learned, eloquent, and kynde.

'To the honour of Sir Henrye Goodyer of Polesworth a knight [honourable *deleted*] memorable for his virtues an affectionat freend of his framed this tetrastich'.
Julius F. XI, f. 85.

4 decasyllables in rhymed couplets. Pr. in *Remaines*, 1605, Certaine Poemes, p. 55. Crum A1215. On Sir Henry Goodyer, the elder (d. 1595).

Septimus hic situs est Henricus gloria regum
Henricum quibus octauum terra Anglia debes.

[Skelton, John, *attrib.*].

'Happye \ and prudent / Henry 7 who stopped the streames of ciuyll bloude which so longe overflowed England, and left a most peaceable state to his posterity, hath his magnifical monument att Westminster inscribed thus'.
Julius F. XI, f. 86.

8 hexameters. Followed by biographical details in Latin prose. Pr. in Camden's *Reges, reginæ, nobiles in Ecclesia Collegiata…sepulti*, 1600, sigs. [C4]ᵛ-Dʳ, and in *Remaines*, 1605, Certaine Poemes, p. 48; and, with attribution to Skelton, in Weever's *Funerall Monuments*, 1631, p. 476. For the actual epitaph inscribed on the tomb of Henry VII (d. 1509) in Westminster Abbey, beg. 'Septimus Henricus tumulo requiescat in ipso', see E. W. Brayley, *History and Antiquities of the Abbey Church of St Peter, Westminster*, 1818, I, Appendix, p. 60.

Looke man before thee how thy death hasteth
Looke man benethe thee the paynes without reste.

'An other likewise [In the Cathedrall church of S. Paule] suppressing his name, for his Epitaphe did sett downe this goodly admonition'.
Julius F. XI, f. 86.

6 verses of 4 stresses each, in rhymed couplets. Crum L576.

Phænix Jana iacet nato Phænice, dolendum
Secula Phænices nulla tulisse duos.

'Queen Jane who died in Childbirth of King Edward the 6. which used for hir deuice a Phænix, had this therunto alluding. for Epitaph conteyning'.
Julius F. XI, f. 86v.

Elegiac distich. Pr. in Camden's *Remaines*, 1605, Certaine Poemes, p. 50. On Jane Seymour (d. 1537), consort of Henry VIII.

Vna fides viuos coniunxit, relligio vna
Vna vrna, ac mentes vnus Olympus habet.

'The Duke of Suffolk and his Brother \ sonnes of Charles Brandon / which died of the sweat at Bugden were buried together with this'.
Julius F. XI, f. 86v.

2 elegiac couplets. Pr. in *Remaines*, 1605, Certaine Poemes, p. 50. On Henry and Charles Brandon, 2nd and 3rd Dukes of Suffolk (d. 1551).

This worldes worshippe
And help us now in our most need.
> 'In St Albanes churche in London this is
> read uppon a gravestone'.
> Julius F. XI, f. 86v.

10 verses of varying length, rhyming irregularly. Apparently of early 16th-cent. composition. (St Alban's, Wood Street, was pulled down in 1632 and rebuilt two years later.)

Anglia quem genuit, fueratque habitura
patronum
Ex æquo iuuenes præcipitatque senes.
> 'The last Earle of Devonshyre Edwarde
> Courteney honorably descended from the
> fourth daughter of K. Edward 4. is buried
> att S. Anthonies in Padua with this'.
> Julius F. XI, f. 86v.

9 elegiac couplets. Pr. in *Remaines*, 1605, Certaine Poemes, p. 51. On Edward Courtenay, Earl of Devonshire (d. 1556). Possibly of continental authorship.

...Proh dolor ergo homini quænam fiducia
Martis
Si iugulant etiam quos putat ille iocos?
> Julius F. XI, f. 87.

Final elegiac couplet of epitaph. *Imperfect*, incipit lost owing to mutilation of leaf.

Hic Nicolaum ne Baconum conditum
Ara dicata sempiternæ memoriæ.
> 'This ensuing \ for Sir N Bacon Keeper
> of the great seal / is worthy to be read
> both for the honour of the person…and
> the rarenes of Iambique verses in Epi-
> taphes (albeit this oure age doth delight
> 'ιαμβιζειν)…'
> Julius F. XI, f. 87.

12 iambic trimeters, arranged in groups of three. Pr. in *Remaines*, 1605, Certaine Poemes, pp. 52–3, and in Henry Holland, *Monumenta sepulchraria Sancti Pauli…*, 1614, sig. D2. Epitaph on Sir Nicholas Bacon (d. 1579) in old St Paul's.

Hic Dick Nowell ego
pueris, ad cœlum contendo.
> 'And yf it please you, take here also a
> Childish Epitaph of Dic Nowell buried at
> Yorke:'.
> Julius F. XI, f. 88.

2 rhymed couplets in Latin doggerel verse.

Digna hæc luce diuturniore
Nisi quòd luce meliore digna.
> 'Margareta Sandes'.
> Julius F. XI, f. 88.

2 verses in unidentified metre. On Margaret Sandys. Preceded by: 'Shorte and yet a sufficient commendation of M. Sandes was this'.

Conde tibi tumulum, nec fide hæredis
amori
Mortuus est, nec emit libris haec verba
ducentis.
> Julius F. XI, f. 88.

2 hexameters, interspersed with three irregular lines. The full text runs: l. 1 'Heus Peripatetice'; l. 3 'Epitaphiumque compara'; and l. 5 'WOODGATVS HIC SEPVLTVS EST'. Prefatory note: 'In the Cloyster of New college in Oxford this following is written with a coale for one Woodgate who bequeathed 200^li to one, who would nott bestowe a plate for his memoriall'. Pr., with additions and variants, in Camden, *Remaines*, 1605, Certaine Poemes, p. 54. On Peter Woodgate, chaplain of New College, Oxford, buried in the cloisters there, 4 Nov. 1590.

Quæ verò, quæ digna tuis virtutibus Heros
Ipsa tuos caperat vix tota Britannia
Manes.
> 'The magnificall monument erected in S.
> Paules for Sir Christopher Hatton late
> Lord Chancellour of England hath vppon
> the one syde [*verses quoted*]'.
> Julius F. XI, f. 88v.

10 hexameters. Pr. in Henry Holland, *Monumenta sepulchraria Sancti Pauli…*, 1614, sig. D2v. Epitaph of Sir Christopher Hatton (d. 1591) in old St Paul's.

Short was thy life
Yet diest thou never.
> 'Uppon Thomas Owen Bachelour of Arts
> in Christchurch Oxon, a youngman of
> great hope a Student of that place made
> this'.
> Julius F. XI, f. 88v.

Quatrain rhyming x⁴a⁵x⁴a⁵. Crum S426. Pr. in *Remaines*, 1605, Certaine Poemes, p. 55. According to Foster's *Alumni Oxonienses* two Thomas Owens graduated from Christ Church in 1591 and 1604.

Hic situs est cuius vox, vultus, actio possit
Ex Heraclito reddere Democritum.
> 'That which a learned gentleman made
> for merye Tarlton the [Roscius *deleted*]
> Sestrius of our time, shall make vp [the
> Century *deleted*] this matter'.
> Julius F. XI, f. 90v.

Elegiac distich. A copy in C.U.L. Add. MS. 42, f.
143, has 'gestio' for 'actio' in l. 1. On Richard
Tarlton, the actor (d. 1588). See also below, f. 92.

Cum patre Radulpho Babthorp iacet ecce
                                    Radulphus
Det deus his lucem, det sine nocte diem.
> 'In templo S. Petri. St Alban'.
> Julius F. XI, f. 91v.

4 elegiac couplets. Incorporates a chronogram of 22
May 1455, the date of the subject's death at the first
Battle of St Albans. Pr. in Sir Henry Chauncy,
Historical Antiquities of Hertfordshire, 1826, II, 332.
On Ralph Babthorp of Yorkshire (d. 1455).

Iunior ense rui, fueram tunc ensifer virj
Ipse Thomas dictus Packinton eramque
                                    vocatus.
> Julius F. XI, f. 91v.

5 hexameters. Pr. in Sir Henry Chauncy, *Historical
Antiquities of Hertfordshire*, 1826, II, 332. On
Thomas Packington (d. *temp.* Henry VII), servant to
a Percy Earl of Northumberland.

Hic situs est cuius vox, vultus, actio, possit
Ex Heraclito reddere Democritum.
> 'That which a learned gentleman made
> for merrye Tarleton the Sestrius of our
> time, shall make upp this matter'.
> Julius F. XI, f. 92.

Elegiac distich. *Fair copy* of *draft* above, f. 90. On
Richard Tarlton, the actor (d. 1588).

It is not pride I lie so high
So it be out of the way for stumbling.
> Challenor, John.
> 'Upon Mr [John] Chaloner clarke of the
> counsayle for Ireland. made by him self in
> his death bed. upon this that they told him
> he should be buryed in the highest place
> of the cathedrall church of Devilin'.
> Julius F. XI, f. 93.

4 verses rhyming $a^8b^{10}a^8b^{10}$. Extempore epitaph for
himself by John Challenor (d. 7 Sept. 1580).

Aureus ille leo (reliqui trepidate leones)
quem modò terra tulit nunc paradisus
                                    habet.
> 'Of y^e Lion of Henry Fitz Alan late Erle
> of Arundell'.
> Julius F. XI, f. 94.

3 elegiac couplets. Note added later: 'Vppon the
golden Lion rampant in Gueles of the house of
Albenye which that Earle bare in his Armes as
receaving the Earldome of Arundell from the house
of Albigny one composed this Epitaph'. Pr. in
Remaines, 1605, Certaine Poemes, p. 54. On Henry
Fitzalan, 12th Earl of Arundel (d. 1580).

Non nostra impietas, aut actæ crimina
                                    vitæ
Quæ vitæ causa est, est mihi causa necis.
> 'of Mr Walter Milles, martyred'.
> Julius F. XI, f. 94v.

2 elegiac couplets. Pr. in Foxe's *Acts and Monuments*,
1563, as 'Non prava impietas, aut actæ crimina vitæ'.
On Walter Mylne or Miln (d. 1558), last protestant
martyr of Scotland.

My frend iudg not mee
mercy I askd mercy I found.
> 'Upon one that brake his neck with a fall
> from his horse so that he dyed in a
> moment without speech:'.
> Julius F. XI, f. 95.

4 doggerel verses in rhymed couplets. Crum M674.
Pr. in *Remaines*, 1605, Certaine Poemes, p. 55.

Here Edward Cordell's body lies
which gone all flesh thus sleeps.
> 'Upon the grave of Mr Cordell one of the
> six clarkes of the Chauncerey'.
> Julius F. XI, f. 95v.

3 stanzas in common measure. Pr., with variants, in
Stow's *Survey of London*, 1633, p. 432. Engraved on
the monument to Edward Cordell (d. 8 Dec. 1590) in
St Dunstan's in the West.

Heer lyeth Menalcas as dead as a logg
without either book candell or bell.
> 'Of one Menalcas buryed in the night
> without ceremony'.
> Julius F. XI, f. 95v.

6 verses of 4 stresses in rhymed couplets. Crum
H1030. Pr., with variants, in *Remaines*, 1605, Certaine
Poemes, p. 51.

Heer lyeth old Henry
no frend to mischevous envy.
> Stanyhurst, Richard.
> 'thus translated by Ri. Stanyhurst'.
> Julius F. XI, f. 96.

Rhymed distich, in dogerell verse. Possibly *imperfect*. Translation of first verse of preceding Latin epitaph of Henry Abingdon, where he is described as 'sometime a singing man of Welles in the b's chaple…'. Crum H1037, incorporating translation of 2nd verse also. On Henry Abingdon (d. 1497), Master of the Choristers of the Chapel Royal.

Cales cælestis pars terræ reddita terra,
Est mausoleum spiritus ipse polus.
> 'upon Sr Jon Bourgh Knight'.
> Julius F. XI, f. 96v.

2 elegiac couplets. Followed by the text of a Latin prose inscription. Apparently on Sir John Burgh (d. 1594), whose 'true' monument, according to Stow's *Survey*, 1720, Bk. 6, p. 21, formerly stood in St Andrew's Chapel, Westminster Abbey.

Robertum Buccus patrio Suffolcius ortu,
Vir pius et prudens hic peregrinus obit.
> Blaxton, Henry.
> 'Vpon Rob. Buck esquire buryed in the south isle of the great church in Chichester'.
> Julius F. XI, f. 97.

2 elegiac couplets. Prefaced by a biographical note in Latin prose signed 'Hen. Blaxtonus S. Theol. D. Testam. Proc. M. P.'. On Robert Buck of Suffolk (d. 1581).

O Lord my Savior, & hevenly maker
Haue mercy on Elizabeth Graistock &
Daker.
> 'Upon the \ tombe / of Lady Elizabeth Nevill wif to S. Tho. Nevil. & daughter to the L. Dakers and Dam⟨e⟩ A. Graistock. in Merewood church in Kent'.
> Julius F. XI, f. 97v.

Rhymed couplet in doggerel verse. Pr. in Weever's *Funerall Monuments*, 1631, p. 291, as epitaph of Lady Elizabeth Neville at Narden, co. Kent. Epitaph of Catherine (d. before 1532), dau. of Humphrey, 1st Lord Dacre of Gilsland, and first wife of Sir Thomas Neville, M.P., in Mereworth Church, co. Kent.

Heer lyeth John Croker a maker of bellowes
He that made bellowes, could not make breath.
> [Hoskins, John; or Davies, Sir John, *attribs*.].
> 'the bellowes maker of Oxford'.
> Julius F. XI, f. 98.

2 rhymed couplets. Crum H1019, with attribution to Hoskins. Pr. in *Poems of Sir John Davies*, ed. Robert Kreuger, Oxford, 1975, p. 303, among 'Poems possibly by Davies', as 'Here lies Kit Craker, the kinge of good fellowes'. On Christopher Craker or Croker.

Hic situs est sitiens, atque Ebrius Eldertonus
Quid dico his situs est? hic potius sitis est.
> [Hoskins, John, *attrib*.].
> 'Eldertonus'.
> Julius F. XI, f. 98.

Elegiac distich. Prefatory note: 'Thomas Elderton the Ballad maker who did arme himself with ale (as Ennius did with wine) when he ballated had this in that respect made to his memorie'. Pr. in *Remaines*, 1605, Certaine Poemes, p. 56. On William Elderton (d. *circa* 1592).

Heer is Elderton lyeng in dust
For who knew him standing all his life long.
> [Hoskins, John, *attrib*.].
> Julius F. XI, f. 98.

4 verses of 4 stresses each, in rhymed couplets. Crum H713. Pr. in *Remaines*, 1605, Certaine Poemes, p. 56. On William Elderton (d. *circa* 1592).

Here lieth Thom Nickes body
Whether fooles soules goe to heauen or to hell.
> 'Some wise man was he; and so reputed for whom this was composed'.
> Julius F. XI, f. 98.

4 doggerel verses in rhymed couplets. Crum H1056 (and see H983). Pr. in *Remaines*, 1605, Certaine Poemes, p. 56.

Here lyeth father Spargis
That died to saue charges.
> Julius F. XI, f. 98.

Rhymed hexasyllabic couplet. Crum H807a. On — Spargis.

Who would lyve in others breath
Sands I was, but now am dust.
> 'Sandes'.
> Julius F. XI, f. 99.

Heptasyllabic quatrain rhyming abab. Crum W2204.
This version pr. in *Remaines*, 1605, Certaine Poemes,
p. 53. Punning epitaph for — Sandys.

Here lies the man whos horse did gayne
You or that horse rather to read it.
> Julius F. XI, f. 99.

4 verses rhyming aa^{8}bb^9. Numbered '2' in sequence
on the page. Crum H961. Pr., with variants, in
Remaines, 1605, Certaine Poemes, p. 58, and by L. B.
Osborn, *Life, Letters and Writings of John Hoskins*
(Yale Studies in English, vol. 87), New Haven, 1930,
p. 189, from Chetham Library MS. 8012, where they
are attributed to Hoskins. Possibly on Henry Herbert,
2nd Earl of Pembroke (d. 1601).

Here lieth the stark theefe J a Drones
That the dogges may the sonne scrap vp
> his bones.
> Julius F. XI, f. 99.

Rhymed couplet in doggerel verse, each line followed
by refrain 'Sit tibi terra levis'. Added in margin and
numbered '3' in sequence.

Here lyes the man that madly slayne
On lyfe to lose, another to lyue.
> Julius F. XI, f. 99.

2 octosyllabic couplets. Numbered '4' in sequence.
Crum H958. Pr. in *Remaines*, 1605, Certaine Poemes,
p. 58.

I was the first mad christendom see
I cryed out I die and so I did.
> [Hoskins, John, *attrib.*]
> Julius F. XI, f. 99.

4 verses of varying length, in rhymed couplets. Crum
I567. Pr. in L. B. Osborn, *ed. cit.*, p. 189, from
Chetham Library MS. 8012, p. 157, where they are
attributed to Hoskins. Satirical epitaph for Richard
Fletcher, Bishop of London (d. 1596).

Here lieth C. under grownd
Drinck was his lyfe, & drynke was his end.
> Julius F. XI, f. 99.

2 rhymed couplets in doggerel verse. Numbered '5'
in the sequence on the page. Crum H1002. Pr. in
Remaines, 1605, Certaine Poemes, p. 59.

Here lyeth Rich[ard] a Green
And he that will die after him may.
> Julius F. XI, f. 99.

2 rhymed couplets in doggerel verse. Dated 1589 in
l. 2. Cf. Crum H906 (and see H1044, 'Here lyeth
Richard a Preen'). On Richard a Green.

The Tomb of good ale lyeth in this tomb
Now the wormes are dronk with the
> marrow of his bones.
> Julius F. XI, f. 99.

4 couplets in doggerel verse. Epitaph for 'Altitonant
Ned', a drunken lawyer.

Here lyethe Richard Hill
Who died full sore against his will.
> Julius F. XI, f. 100.

Rhymed couplet in doggerel verse. Humorous
epitaph for Richard Hill.

Here lieth Willinge Wills
With his head full of Windmills.
> Julius F. XI, f. 100.

Rhymed distich in doggerel verse. Notes: 'Mr Wills
Doctor of Physick who died at Vienna would often
say that he would haue this verse onlye for his
epitaphe: [*l. 1. quoted*] But a frend of his that knew
him to be Caprichious, wished him to adde one verse
more to make vpp rime after the English manner, but
when he sayd he had nothing he might adde more,
one extempore sayd it might be well mayd vp thus [*l.
2 quoted*]'. Pr. in *Remaines*, 1605, Certaine Poemes, p.
57. Crum H1060. On (?) Richard Wills, M.D., of
Cambridge (d. *circa* 1630).

Here lyeth he
Which with himself could never agree.
> Julius F. XI, f. 100.

Rhymed couplet in doggerel verse. Crum H1009. Pr.
in *Remaines*, 1605, Certaine Poemes, p. 57.

Here he lieth who was borne and cried
Tould threescore yeares, fell syck and
> died.
> Julius F. XI, f. 100.

Rhymed octosyllabic couplet. Crum H1011. 'Sandes'
written in right-hand margin. Pr. in *Remaines*, 1605,
Certaine Poemes, p. 58, beg. 'Here lieth he, who was
borne and cried', and in L. B. Osborn, *ed. cit.*, p. 171,
from Chetham Library MS. 8012, where it is

attributed to Hoskins, beg. 'Here lyes the man was borne and cryed'.

Here lieth the B[ishop] whom the World did see
First for to marye a Lady-Lady.
Julius F. XI, f. 100.

Rhymed decasyllabic couplet. Satirical epitaph for Richard Fletcher (d. 1596), Bishop of London.

Here lieth bald Dobson on the mould
That grubd upp the heare and droue away lice.
[Davies, Sir John. *attrib*.].
Julius F. XI, f. 100.

4 verses rhyming aa^{9}bb^{10}. Crum H1003 (and see H855, H881). Pr. in *Poems of Sir John Davies*, ed. Robert Kreuger, Oxford, 1975, p. 304, among 'Poems possibly by Davies'. On — Dobson (*al.* Hobson), elsewhere described as the cook of Christ Church, Oxford, see Edward Doughtie, *Liber Lilliati*, Newark (Delaware), 1985, p. 149.

Ut vultu roseo rubicundo fulget in ortu
Ignis quod gelido ferveat amne stupet.
Julius F. XI, f. 106v.

4 elegiac couplets. This and the two epigrams immediately following, not certainly of British origin, jotted on verso of Latin prose theme on the topic 'Confessio peccati satis est' by Anthony Fixer, Queen's Scholar at Westminster School, who matric. Christ Church, Oxford, Dec. 1595.

Mars Venerem secum deprensam fraude maritj
Signat, habet maculas utraque Luna suas.
Julius F. XI, f. 106v.

3 elegiac couplets. On the adultery of Mars with Venus.

Qualiter Anglorum possum describere gentem
Summa petit liuor...
Julius F. XI, f. 106v.

16 hexameters. Final verse concludes with initial letters only. On the English character.

Dii summi quibus est sali solique
Cedant Dardanidæ trophæa metris.
[?Camden, William].
'Carminibus cædant reges regumq; triumphi'.
Julius F. XI, f. 134.

15 Phalæcian hendecasyllables. Copied, and perhaps composed, by Camden, seemingly as an example of the metre. Title from Ovid's *Amores*, Bk. I, xv, v. 53. This and the following set celebrate the power of verse.

Fælices homines queis Polyhimnia
Cedant perpetuò doctiloquis metris.
[?Camden, William].
'Ascle:'.
Julius F. XI, f. 134.

8 lesser Asclepiads. Copied and perhaps composed by Camden, seemingly as an example of the metre.

Ius summum sæuum est, ius summum iniuria summa
Non tangit, qui omnes plectere morte solet.
Downton, Paul.
'Summu*m* ius summa iniuria'.
Julius F. XI, f. 135v.

4 elegiac couplets. *Autograph*. Followed by 4 Greek hexameters. Downton was Queen's Scholar at Westminster School, 1596. Theme on a proverb.

When the bells be merrylie runge
A Pater noster & an Aue Maria.
Julius F. XI, f. 190.

5 rhymed couplets, in verses of varying length. Copied in unidentified hand on surviving fragment of page ruled with borders. Pr. in Weever's *Funerall Monuments*, 1631, p. 392. Crum W1502. Inscription on memorial brass to Robert Trapp (d. 1526), goldsmith, in St Leonard's, Foster Lane.

A Christo virtus virtutis et optima merces
Istaque dat Christus quod dedit illa prius.
Julius F. XI, f. 202v.

2 elegiac couplets. Epigram on Christ.

Quid queris? non est hostis quærendus in agris
Tu si te possis viuere victor eris.
Julius F. XI, f. 202v.

2 elegiac couplets. Moral epigram.

345

Lanigeros quâ lata greges Cottswoldia
pascit
Qua Scotis dat f⟨ren⟩a feris, et calcat
Hibernos...
>   Camden, William.
>   Julius F. XI, f. 208.

18 hexameters. *Autograph* extract from *De Connubio Tamæ et Isis*. Verso of leaf later used for notes from Camden's reading. Pr., without final verse, in *Britannia*, 1590, p. 282; and in G. B. Johnston, 'Poems by William Camden', *Studies in Philology, Texts and Studies*, 1975, p. 88, with facing English translation (1610) by Philemon Holland. The present MS. has not been used by editors. On the watersmeet of Thames and Isis in Gloucestershire. See also below f. 219v.

Nulla fides terris, fraus improba regnat
ubique
Communisque fid[es]....
>   Harborne, Symon.
>   'Nulla fides terris'.
>   Julius F. XI, f. 219.

2 elegiac couplets. *Autograph*. *Imperfect*, wanting all after beginning of l. 4. Symon Harborne, whose signature appears at the foot, though not recorded by G. F. R. Barker and A. H. Stenning, *The Records of Old Westminsters*, 1928, was probably a pupil there under Camden. School theme.

Vndoso hic solio residet regnator aquarum
Et salientis aque prorumpit vndique venæ.
>   Camden, William.
>   Julius F. XI, f. 219v.

7 hexameters. *Autograph draft*, with revisions, of passage for *De Connubio Tamæ et Isis* (cf. above, f. 208). Pr. in *Britannia*, 1590, p. 282; and in G. B. Johnston, *ed. cit.*, p. 88, with facing translation (1610) by Philemon Holland. On the watersmeet of Thames and Isis in Gloucestershire.

Pro strenis librum, pro donis accipe
Votum
Qui velit ille nequit, det Deus ille valet.
>   Camden, William.
>   Julius F. XI, f. 244v.

4 elegiac couplets. *Autograph*. Presentation verses accompanying gift of a book.

f. 307. Extracts from Sir John Harington's translation of Ariosto's *Orlando Furioso*, 1591 (beg. 'Of Dames, of Knights, of armes, of loves delight').

Follows Camden's draft (ff. 306, 306v) of a discourse on 'Artillerie', published, without these verses on the culverin, in *Remaines*, 2nd edn., 1614.

For first he is of limbs and bodie strong
Deuised it to do man kind a spite.
>   Harington, Sir John.
>   'Ariosto. Cant. 9'.
>   Julius F. XI, f. 307.

2 ottava rima stanzas. Pr. in Harington's *Orlando Furioso*, Book IX, sts. 24, 25.

But now a while of him I speake no more
To be tormented ay with Core & Dathan.
>   Harington, Sir John.
>   '[Ariosto]. Cant. 11. de bomabarda'.
>   Julius F. XI, f. 307.

6 ottava rima stanzas. Pr. in Harington's *Orlando Furioso*, Book XI, sts. 19–24.

Nero C. XI (pts. i & ii)

Robert Fabyan's New Cronycles of Englande and of Fraunce; *after 1506. The work was begun circa 1485: the edition printed in 1516 was completed in 1504, and that of 1533 incorporated a continuation to the year 1509.*

Now wold I ffayn
As yt hath hidyr tyll.
>   Fabyan, Robert.
>   Nero C. XI (pt. i), ff. 30v–31v.

96 verses of varying length in 12 stanzas rhyming aaabcccb. Ringler TM 1121, TP 1245. Pr. in *Cronycles*, 1516, as prologue to vol. II. In praise of London.

Who soo hym lykyth, these verses to Rede
As yt shuld duely, aske of Rygth.
>   Fabyan, Robert.
>   Nero C. XI (pt. i), f. 31v.

2 stanzas in rhyme royal. Ringler TM 1971. Apology for his 'Ryme Dogerell'.

Cryste of the theeff, whych on thy Rygth
hand was
Was, and of Grace, ffound lyke to hym
noon.
>   Fabyan, Robert.
>   Nero C. XI (pt. i), f. 47v.

3 stanzas in rhyme royal. Ringler TM 308, TP 307. Pr. in *Cronycles*, 1516. Translation of Latin epitaph of Richard I, *circa* 1200.

The kynge of kynges, that lord, that Rulyth
All
And vyce before vsyd vttyrly Renye.
Fabyan, Robert.
Nero C. XI (pt. i), f. 52.
1 rhyme royal stanza. Ringler TM 1544, TP 1762. Pr. in *Cronycles*, 1516. Paraphrase of Latin hexameters, *circa* 1204.

Iff Excellence of wytt, or Grace of good
vertu
Noble & Ignoble, ther is noo thyng may
lett.
Fabyan, Robert.
Nero C. XI (pt. i), ff. 76v–77.
1 rhyme royal stanza. Ringler TM 716, TP 830. Pr. in *Cronycles*, 1516. Translation of Latin verses on Frederick II, Holy Roman Emperor, *circa* 1247.

ffre ffretith this world, and de confoundeth
alle
And thus ys ffrederyk, all devoyd of Grace.
Fabyan, Robert.
Nero C. XI (pt. i), f. 77.
1 rhyme royal stanza. Ringler TM 442, TP 438. Pr. in *Cronycles*, 1516. Translation of Latin verses on Frederick II, Holy Roman Emperor, *circa* 1247.

The ffrende of pyte, and of almesse dede
That as oon God, Regnyth in personys
thre.
Fabyan, Robert.
Nero C. XI (pt. i), f. 117.
1 rhyme royal stanza. Ringler TM 1522, TP 1727. Pr. in *Cronycles*, 1516. Translation of Latin epitaph of Henry III, *circa* 1272.

Of Inglish men the scourge, of walsh the
protector
here in this Grave, of people lyeth the
lygth.
Fabyan, Robert.
Nero C. XI (pt. i), f. 140v.
1 rhyme royal stanza. Ringler TM 1265, TP 1407. Pr. in *Cronycles*, 1516. Translation of Latin verses on Llywelyn ap Gruffydd, Prince of Wales, *circa* 1283.

Here lyeth of Errour, the prynce yf ye wyll
ken
A Rote of ffalshode, and cawse of many yll
dede.
Fabyan, Robert.
Nero C. XI (pt. i), f. 140v.
8 verses of 4 stresses each in rhymed couplets. Ringler TM 583, TP 613. Pr. in *Cronycles*, 1516. Translation of Latin verses on Llywelyn ap Gruffydd, Prince of Wales, *circa* 1283.

The morow ffolowyng, Tiburce and Val-
erian
Of that wynde cam, the while that yt dydd
last.
Fabyan, Robert.
Nero C. XI (pt. i), f. 147v.
8 verses of 4 stresses each, rhyming ababcdcd. Ringler TM 1569, TP 1804. Pr. in *Cronycles*, 1516. Translation of Latin verses on the great snow of 1294.

Whyle lyvyd this kyng
And honeste hadd mygth.
Fabyan, Robert.
Nero C. XI (pt. i), f. 161v.
6 verses of 2 stresses each, rhyming aabccb. Ringler TM 1934, TP 2221. Pr. in *Cronycles*, 1516. Translation of Latin couplet on the death of Edward I, 1307.

This Sorowfull deth, which bryngith grete
full lowe
Graunte hym Sorowlees, Evermore to
taste.
Fabyan, Robert.
Nero C. XI (pt. i), ff. 162–164.
6 rhyme royal stanzas. Ringler TM 1672, TP 1917. Pr. in *Cronycles*, 1516. Translation of Latin epitaph of Edward I, 1307.

Wyth Ropes were thow bounde, and on the
Galow hong
ffrom the wrecchid hugth, all worldly
welth was take.
Fabyan, Robert.
Nero C. XI (pt. i), f. 190v.
1 rhyme royal stanza. Ringler TM 2007, TP 2303. Pr. in *Cronycles*, 1516. Translation of Latin verses by 'Hugh the vercyfyer' on the execution of Sir Hugh Le Despencer the younger, 1326.

Whan Satorn, wyth his cold Isy fface
It in rest and peace.
    Fabyan, Robert.
    Nero C. XI (pt. i), ff. 191v–192v.
58 verses in 5 sections of varying metres, viz.: (1) Monk's Tale stanza; (2) 28 decasyllabic couplets; (3) 8 varying verses, aaabcccb; (4) 7 decasyllabic verses, aaabcccb; and (5) 8 verses as (3). Ringler TM 1890 and TP 2185. Pr. in *Cronycles*, 1516. Translation of Latin lament of Edward II, 1326.

Of Inglysh kynges, here lyeth the bew-
                  tevous ffloure
To worthy machobe, in vertv peregall.
    Fabyan, Robert.
    Nero C. XI (pt. i), f. 255v.
1 rhyme royal stanza. Ringler TM 1264, TP 1406. Pr. in *Cronycles*, 1516. Translation of Latin epitaph of Edward III, 1377.

Whan that this Cokk, loo here doth synge
Than shall this newe ffond kyng, his hoost
                  in brynge.
    Fabyan, Robert.
    Nero C. XI (pt. ii), f. 257.
Rhymed accentual couplet. Ringler TM 1905, TP 2189. Pr. in *Cronycles*, 1516. Translation of French verses of *circa* 1477.

Parffygth & prudent, Richarde by Rigth
                  the secvnd
Theyr lyvis to excercise, in vertuous
                  constancy.
    Fabyan, Robert.
    Nero C. XI (pt. ii), f. 350v.
2 rhyme royal stanzas. Ringler TM 1323, TP 1463. Pr. in *Cronycles*, 1516. Translation of Latin epitaph of Richard II, 1400, in St Edmund's Chapel, Westminster Abbey.

The perverse heretyke, thouth that he doo
                  brenne
Do hym Reward, syne he wyll not Refreyn.
    Fabyan, Robert.
    Nero C. XI (pt. ii), f. 357.
1 rhyme royal stanza. Ringler TM 1579, TP 1814. Pr. in *Cronycles*, 1516. Translation of Latin verses of 1410.

loo here is notyd, and putt in memory
That was on erth, kyng of kynges callid.
    Fabyan, Robert.
    Nero C. XI (pt. ii), ff. 373–374.
4 rhyme royal stanzas. Ringler TM 910, TP 1056. Pr. in *Cronycles*, 1516. Translation of Latin verses of 1422.

lygth into the world, now doth spryng &
                  shyne
ffelix vnto Nicholas, alle ffrely doth Re-
                  syne.
    Fabyan, Robert.
    Nero C. XI (pt. ii), f. 405.
Couplet, in poulter's measure. Ringler TM 892, TP 1038. Pr. in *Cronycles*, 1516. Translation of Latin verses on the Papal succession, 1448.

An ende of this book, or of this Rude werk
And Requyre of ⟨God⟩ he may have his
                  mede.
    Fabyan, Robert.
    'Lenvoy'.
    Nero C. XI (pt. ii), f. 462.
4 rhyme royal stanzas. Ringler TM 148, TP 143. Pr. in *Cronycles*, 1533. Translation of Fabyan's Latin envoy to his *Cronycles* ('Limas adest, præcessit opus, ne lividus assis').

That mannys lyffe, is ffull vnstable
Naturally, and myend well...
    Fabyan, Robert.
    'Tragedia'.
    Nero C. XI (pt. ii), f. 462v.
4 rhyme royal stanzas. *Imperfect*, wanting last three and a half verses of stanza 4 owing to mutilation of leaf. Ringler TM 148, as part of 'Lenvoy' above, and Ringler TP 143, as separate poem. Envoy.

Titus A. XIII

Composite collection of English chronicles, etc.; 15th cent.–1605. Ownership inscriptions of 'Robertus Cotton Bruceus' (ff. 2, 42) and 'Ro: Cotton' (f. 42).

ff. 166–177. Thomas Goad's 'Lyra Decachorda, plectro pulsata Horatiano, psalmum nouum concinens Britannicæ Liberationis'; dated from King's College, Cambridge, 22 November 1605. Unsigned calligraphic MS. of a series of parodies of odes of

Horace, celebrating the failure of the Gunpowder Plot. This version largely agrees with that published as *Cithara octochorda pectine pulsata Horatiano cantionem concinens novam, triumphum Britannicum*, 1605 (dated 15 Nov. and entd. in S.R. 11 Dec.). An enlarged and annotated edition, dedicated to Henry Howard, Earl of Northampton, was issued as *Proditoris prodidor*, 1606 (entd. 18 Feb.).

Eheu recenti mens trepidat metu
Demetuit rapuitque florem.
> Goad, Thomas.
> 'Chorda 1ª. quæ tremulum, & querulum sonat. Siue Ode 1ª. In qua ex nuperrimo, & quasi adhuc calentj periculo animorum perturbatio'.
> Titus A. XIII, f. 166v.

5 Alcaic stanzas.

Fæcunda culpæ sæcula! Quod scelus,
Colchus Hyperboreiue campi.
> Goad, Thomas.
> 'Chorda 2ª. quæ stridulum, & clamosum. Siue Ode 2ª. In qua horrendæ proditionis detestatio'.
> Titus A. XIII, f. 167.

6 Alcaic stanzas.

O patre divo Dæmone divior
Consiliis, & Apostolorum.
> Goad, Thomas.
> 'Chorda 3ª. quæ canorum, & frendens. Siue Ode 3ª. In qua parricidarum indagatio. Exinde Romanensium quorundam criminatio'.
> Titus A. XIII, ff. 167v–168v.

16 Alcaic stanzas.

Consortium audax omnia perpetj
Fulmineo lacerandus ictu.
> Goad, Thomas.
> 'Chorda 4ª. quæ submissum, & immurmurans. Siue Ode 4ª. In qua conjuratio, insidiarum destinatio, delecto sceleris capitalis ministro monstro quodam hominis Guidone Fausio'.
> Titus A. XIII, ff. 168v–170.

16 Alcaic stanzas. This and the ode immediately following pr. in *Cithara octochorda*, 1605, as a single poem.

Fornix stat amplus, qui Superae Domus
Quintus erit celebris ruinâ.
> Goad, Thomas.
> 'Chorda 5ª. quæ cauernosum, & ambiguum. Siue Ode 5ª. In qua insidiarum locus, integumentum fraudis, & in ipsum crastinum apparatus'.
> Titus A. XIII, ff. 170–171.

15 Alcaic stanzas.

Ah sic peribit immiserabilis
Dente Lupi excutiuntur agris.
> Goad, Thomas.
> 'Chorda 6ª. quæ blandum & vndosum. Siue Ode 6ª. In qua Diuinæ misericordiæ imploratio, & opportunè succurrentis agnitio'.
> Titus A. XIII, ff. 171v, 172.

9 Alcaic stanzas.

Cælo minax vis mole ruit sua,
Dante Deo Dominoque nostro.
> Goad, Thomas.
> 'Chorda 7ª. quæ penetrans & fragosum. Siue Ode 7ª. In qua modus retegendi Sceleris, & Guidonis invicta pertinacia'.
> Titus A. XIII, ff. 172v–173v.

14 Alcaic stanzas.

Fidi, sagaces Consiliarii,
Tela suis fabricata dextris.
> Goad, Thomas.
> 'Chorda 8ª. quæ flexum, & humile. Siue Ode 8ª. In qua ad Proceres honoratissimos, qui Serenissimæ Regiæ Maiestati a secretoribus sunt consiliis, alloquium officiosum'.
> Titus A. XIII, ff. 173v–174v.

14 Alcaic stanzas. Not included in *Cithara octochorda*, 1605.

Guido bibendum nunc tibi liberè
Vix fuerit satis Orcus Orcj.
> Goad, Thomas.
> 'Chorda 9ª. quæ asperum, & imperiosum. Siue Ode 9ª. In qua Proditoris ad iustum supplicium raptatio'.
> Titus A. XIII, ff. 174v–175v.

10 Alcaic stanzas.

Quæ cura Patrum, quiuè fidelium
Dum lauat Oceanus Britannos.

Goad, Thomas.

'Chorda 10ᵃ. quæ rotundu*m*, clangidu*m*, & triu*m*phale quasi Disdiapason sub extrema*m* clausula*m* reboat. Siue Ode vltima. In qua ad ara*m* Cælestis Tutelæ gratia*rum* oblatio, pro futura incolumitate obtestatio, metus deniq*ue* omnis in triu*m*phu*m* conu*er*sus'.

Titus A. XIII, ff. 176–177.

12 Alcaic stanzas (but see next).

Non hæc minorj conueniunt Lyræ
Magna modis tenuare paruis.

Goad, Thomas.

Titus A. XIII, f. 177.

Alcaic stanza. Followed by motto 'Deo Liberatorj gloria'. This stanza marked off here by rules but pr. in *Cithara octochorda*, 1605, as final stanza of the preceding ode.

ff. 178–184. Edmund Bolton: Congratulatory verses to James I on the removal of the body of the King's mother, Mary, Queen of Scots, to a tomb in Westminster Abbey; *circa* September 1612. *Autograph* calligraphic MS. The full title (f. 178) runs: 'Carmen Personatum. In quo, Maria, Regina Scotorum, gratulatur sibi de corpore suo, ab obscurâ, et deuiâ urbeculâ, Petriburgo, filii sui Iacobi Regis pietate, ad lucem Wesmonasterii, Proauum suorum sepulchreti, officiosissimè traducto. A.D.MDCXII. Tabulæ ad monimentum eiusdem Reginæ ab authore destinatum'.

Non de plebe aliquis Reginæ hos consecro
uersus
Maiestas alias pellit de carmine uoces.

Bolton, Edmund.

'*Edmundus Bolton Anglus* Lectori'.

Titus A. XIII, f. 179.

16 hexameters. Prefatory verses addressed to the reader.

Sera decennalis, sub rege hærede Iacobo
Optima, maxima tum, Regina MARIA
STVARTA.

Bolton, Edmund.

'Prosopopoea Basilica. Loquitur Maria Regina Scotorum sola'.

Titus A. XIII, ff. 180–184.

95 hexameters. Text on rectos only, with part of running-title and catchwords repeated on blank versos. Concludes: 'Finis. Deo Gratias'. Imaginary soliloquy of Mary, Queen of Scots.

Titus A. XXIV

Composite collection of theological tracts, etc.; 15th–2nd quarter of 17th cent. Contents list (f. 1) in hand of Sir Thomas Cotton.

ff. 79–102v. Miscellany of English and Latin verses by members of Christ Church, Oxford; *temp.* Philip and Mary. Five of the pieces are pr. by Leicester Bradner, *Life and poems of Richard Edwards*, New Haven (Yale Studies in English, no. LXXIV), 1927, pp. 102–109. Some theological and other notes in English and Latin prose on ff. 145–168v seem also to have formed part of the same notebook.

O rightefull rule and lyghte of lyghtes
whose beams bene fulgent brighte
longe lyfe to rayne and rule in rest her
subiectes all and one.

Pigot, Valentine.

Titus A. XXIV, ff. 79, 79v.

8 fourteener couplets. Subscribed 'Va. Pig.' (member of Christ Church, 1552–*circa* 1558). Final stanza recopied in later hand. Ringler TM 1231. Prayer for Queen Mary I on her accession, July 1553.

Stay gentel frend that passest by
thus marke my words and fare thow well.

[Norton, Thomas. *attrib*.].

Titus A. XXIV, f. 79v.

20 octosyllables in 5 undifferentiated quatrains rhyming abab. Concludes: 'Finis. norton'. Ringler TM 1461, TP 1633. Pr. in Surrey's *Songes and Sonettes*, 1557, as 'An other of the same' by 'Vncertain auctor'. On Henry Williams (d. 1551).

My frende the thinges that do attayne
not wishinge deathe, nor dread his
myghte.

Howard, Henry, Earl of Surrey.

Titus A. XXIV, f. 80.

4 octosyllabic quatrains rhyming abab. Subscribed 'Finis. Surre:'. Described by later hand in margin as 'Martialis lib. 9' and in Sir Thomas Cotton's contents list (f. 1) as 'translation of an epigram in martial: lib: 10'. Ringler TM 1036, TP 1116. This version pr. in William Baldwin's *A treatise of moral philosophy*,

1547; another, beg. 'Martiall, the thinges that do attayn', in Surrey's *Songes and Sonettes*, 1557. Translation of Martial, *Epigrams*, X, 47.

Who iustely may reioyce in owghte vnder the skye
hathe broughte him heauen: thoughe somwhat sonne whiche life cold neuer giue.

[Harington, John, the elder].
Titus A. XXIV, ff. 80, 80v.
13 rhymed couplets in poulter's measure. *Imperfect*. Concludes: 'Finis'. Ringler TM 1941, TP 2232. Pr., with variants and an additional final couplet, in Surrey's *Songes and Sonettes*, 1557, as 'Of the death of master [Richard] Deuerox the lord Ferres sonne (d. 1547)'.

A man may liue thris Nestors lyfe
to kepe me fre from ether yll.

Norton, [Thomas].
Titus A. XXIV, f. 80v.
14 octosyllables rhyming ababcdcdefefgg. Concludes: 'Finis Norton'. Ringler TM 26, TP 30. Pr. in Surrey's *Songes and Sonettes*, 1557, as 'Against women either good or badde'. Satire on women.

Who liste to liue upryghte and holde him selfe content
thy enemis shall waste the same that never swett therefore.

Titus A. XXIV, ff. 81, 81v.
8 rhymed couplets in poulter's measure. Concludes: 'Finis'. Ringler TM 1945, TP 2234. Pr., with variants, in Surrey's *Songes and Sonettes*, 1557, as 'Of the wretchednes in this world'.

The winter withe his ougly storms no lenger dare abyde
nor theseus cowlde not call to life his frinde perithous.

Titus A. XXIV, ff. 81v–82v.
15 fourteener couplets. Described in margin in later hand as 'horatius li: 4: od. 7.', and in Sir Thomas Cotton's contents list (f. 1) as 'A translation of Horace lib. od: 4. ode 7'. Ringler TM 1610, TP 1858. Pr., with variants, in Surrey's *Songes and Sonettes*, 1557, beg. 'The winter with his griesly stormes no lenger dare abyde'. Translation of Horace, *Odes*, IV, vii.

Layde in my quiet bed in studye as hit were
from boy to manne from manne to boy wolde choppe and chawnge degry.

Titus A. XXIV, f. 83.
6 rhymed couplets in poulter's measure. *Imperfect*. This and the section of verses following (ff. 83–96v) are described in Sir Thomas Cotton's contents list (f. 1) as 'verses of seuerall subiects about queen marys time'. Ringler TM 876. Pr., with variants and eight concluding couplets, in Surrey's *Songes and Sonnets*, 1557. On the ages of man.

My fance fanned onne me somwhat of y[e] to see
for bewtise prayse and vertues sake eche one a Quene showld be.

Edwards, Richard.
Titus A. XXIV, f. 83v.
10 rhymed couplets in poulter's measure. Subscribed 'finis. R. E.'. Ringler TM 1033. Pr. by Harington, *Nugae Antiquae*, London, 1804, pp. 392–4; Bradner, *op. cit.*, p. 102; and David Loades, *The Tudor Court*, 2nd edn., Bangor, 1992, pp. 211, 213. In praise of eight ladies-in-waiting (named) to Queen Mary I, the reference (ll. 17–18) to Katharine Brydges dating the composition to before 1555.

Truthe withe the towche stoune triethe
is only cause of this.

Edwards, Richard.
Titus A. XXIV, ff. 83v–85.
16 rhymed couplets in poulter's measure. Subscribed 'finis. R. E.'. Ringler TM 1777. Pr. in Bradner, *op. cit.*, pp. 102–4. In defence of women.

When wemen firste dame nature wrowghte
ha, ha, me thinkes I make a lye.

[Edwards, Richard; or Case, William].
Titus A. XXIV, ff. 85, 85v.
20 octosyllabic couplets in 5 stanzas. Subscribed 'finis. R. E.'. Ringler TM 1919; and Crum W1633 (version beg. 'When woman first dame nature wrought', with attribution to William Case). Pr., with omission of stanza 4, by G. Ellis, *Specimens of the Early English Poets*, London, 1790, vol. II, p. 109; and Bradner, *op. cit.*, pp. 104–5. Satire on women.

O lorde that ruleste bothe lande [and] sea
even by thy hevenly povre
O christe o christe take thow my sprite
that trowstethe in thy bloodd.
Edwards, Richard.
Titus A. XXIV, ff. 85v–87v.
26 rhymed couplets in poulter's measure. Subscribed
'finis. R. E.'. Ringler TM 1186. Pr. in Bradner, *op. cit.*, pp. 105–8. Prayer.

O catife corps that long hast felt the
present panges of death
Therefore my last and gasping hest[t] to
honor the shall serue.
Edwards, Richard.
Titus A. XXIV, f. 91v.
9 rhymed couplets in poulter's measure. Possibly
autograph. Headed 'Mr Wylson' and subscribed
'finis per me. R. E.'. Ringler TM 1134. Pr. in
Bradner, *op. cit.*, pp. 108–9. Love poem.

Iam satis terræ sua ferit Angliæ
Ut videamur.
M[arbeck], R[oger].
Titus A. XXIV, f. 92.
4 Sapphic stanzas. Alternative readings added in
same hand. Subscribed: 'Finis [Ex Ecclesia Christi
Rogerus Marbeccus *deleted*] R M' (Student of Christ
Church, 1552–1567). Parody of Horace, *Odes*, I, ii, in
praise of Queen Mary I, *circa* July 1553–July 1554.

Anglia quæ nuper sævis quassata procellis
Sed Mariam firmo semper amore coles.
Allen, Richard.
Titus A. XXIV, f. 92v.
13 elegiac couplets. Subscribed 'Ri. Alen'. (Richard
Allen was a member of Christ Church, 1552–1558.)
This and the following seven sets of verse celebrate
the marriage of Mary I and Philip II of Spain, July
1554.

Tristi Britannos genitor cum mente
uideret
Hæc tua nota fient.
Titus A. XXIV, f. 93.
36 first Archilocheans.

Anglica lætetur pubes, lætare Maria
Quod regina tibi quod pia virgo data est.
Titus A. XXIV, f. 93v.

2 elegiac couplets. This and the three sets of verses
following, all apparently by the same author, appear
to have formed part of a single tribute.

Anglorum teneat quæ regia sceptra poten-
tem
Cuius ad astra decus fortia facta ferant.
'Vt stirpem suum sobolemque propaget
Regina deum imploremus'.
Titus A. XXIV, f. 93v.
2 elegiac couplets.

Viuat ametque suum felix regina maritum
Et peragant longos sic tua fata dies.
'bene precemur reginæ ac regi nostro'.
Titus A. XXIV, f. 93v.
2 elegiac couplets.

Seperet hispanos discordia nulla Britannis
An ne potest notum plenius esse meum.
'Optemus ut concordes cum hispanis et
una mente britannos cernamus'.
Titus A. XXIV, f. 93v.
2 elegiac couplets.

Anglia quæ multo fueras suppressa dolore
fædere iunguntur lumina sacra sacro.
Carr, Thomas.
Titus A. XXIV, f. 94.
7 elegiac couplets. Subscribed 'Thomas Carrus'
(member of Christ Church, 1553–1556).

Læta quid gestis populi britanni
Carmina læti.
Titus A. XXIV, ff. 94v, 95.
Sapphic ode of 9 stanzas. The word 'finis', faintly
added after stanza 6 at the foot of f. 94v, apparently
in error, is repeated after stanza 9.

Vix caput attolens e lecto scribere carmen
Qui potuit is noluit scribere plura uale.
Haddon, Walter.
Titus A. XXIV, f. 95.
Elegiac distich. Subscribed 'Hadd'. Pr. in *Poematum
Gualteri Haddoni…libri duo*, 1576, sig. H1^r, as 'Ad
D. Coxum'. This and the following formed an
exchange between Haddon and Richard Cox, Bishop
of Ely.

Te magis optarem saluum sine carmine
sibi
Quoniam sine te saluo carmina plura uale.

> Cox, Richard.
> Titus A. XXIV, f. 95.

Elegiac distich. Subscribed 'Cox'. Pr. in *Poematum Gualteri Haddoni…libri duo*, 1576, sig. H1ᵛ, as 'Resp. Coxi ad Haddonum'.

When that I call to memori what learned
men do shoo
as writers have aproved still more worthie
prese the men.

> Titus A. XXIV, ff. 95v, 96.

22 fourteener couplets. Ringler TM 1900. On women's love.

When words of witt [will] not prevaile
to chastice those which reacthlese are.

> Titus A. XXIV, f. 96.

6 octosyllables rhyming ababcc. Ringler TM 1920. Moral precepts.

Quid vitrum est? hominis corpus, quid
membra? vita
qua cito arena cadit, tam cito vita ruit.

> Titus A. XXIV, f. 96v.

6 elegiac couplets. Latin version of emblem 11 in Thomas Palmer's unpublished 'Two hundred poosees' (Sloane MS. 3794: composed *circa* 1562–1565), where the illustration depicts an hour-glass.

Si vitrum vertas, cursus nouus incipit
alter
exemplar vitæ, mortis imago. Vale.

> Titus A. XXIV, f. 96v.

6 elegiac couplets. Latin version of emblem 12 in Palmer's 'Two hundred poosees', where the illustration depicts an hour-glass.

Palma aurem claudens palmorum signat
at ecce
Augeat et spicam palma triumphis opes.

> [? Marbeck, Roger].
> Titus A. XXIV, f. 96v.

4 elegiac couplets. Concludes: 'Finis'. English verses of a similar kind by 'R.M.' were prefixed to Palmer's 'Two hundred poosees', the initials probably standing for Roger Marbeck of Christ Church, who may

also have been the author of the present Latin elegiacs. Verses punning on Palmer's name.

As frendes to frendes, so greteng we yow
sende
Nomore in ryme but all the reste in prose.

> [Cr—, —].
> Titus A. XXIV, ff. 98v, 99.

7 stanzas in rhyme royal. Subscribed 'finis. Cr.'. Ringler TM 176. Acknowledgement for verses received and commiseration for the writer's 'dolefull drerye case'.

I Liue that dieth everey houre
low how I were and waste.

> Titus A. XXIV, ff. 99, 99v.

12 stanzas in common measure, numbered in margin. Ringler TM 658. On mortality.

Titus B. VI

Miscellaneous historical and political collections, British and foreign; copied circa *16th cent.–1612. Ownership-inscription of 'Robertus Cotton Bruceus' on free-standing leaf (f. 2).*

ff. 8–18. Verses recorded in the diary and letters of Dr. John Taylor, Master of the Rolls, while Resident Ambassador to France; 3 January–18 April 1526. Partly pr. in *Letters and Papers of Henry VIII*, vol. IV, pt. 1, 1870, pp. 858–59.

Immiti a domino Maurus tractatus in igne
Ne nimis in seruis seviat ullus herus.

> Taylor, Dr. John.
> 'Epigramma de Mauro seruo a domino
> crudeliter tractato'.
> Titus B. VI, f. 10v.

22 elegiac couplets. Followed (ff. 11, 11v) by *drafts* of these verses. On a master's cruelty to his Moorish servant.

Semper lingua mali poltroni pessima pars
est
peius (non dubitas) de Joue forte loqui.

> Taylor, Dr. John.
> Titus B. VI, f. 13.

2 elegiac couplets. Introduced by: 'addidi hos versus'. Dated at end '2° Marcij 1526'. Pr. *loc. cit.*, p. 859. Reply to a pasquil (quoted) against the

English 'in hospicio in muro carbone scriptum' at Châteauneuf.

Quisquis eris non nota tibi satis anglica gens est
Sed male de superis vult mala lingua loqui.

Dacre, Robert.

Titus B. VI, f. 13v.

Elegiac distich. Introduced as 'In eundem nepos meus Robertus Dacrus Juuenis non ingenii spernendi ceu doctrine', and followed by several suggested improvements by Taylor. Pr. *loc. cit.*, p. 859. Reply to pasquil (as above).

f. 249v. Jotting, on otherwise blank leaf, of distich attributed to Hugh Holland (d. 1633), a former pupil of Camden's at Westminster School.

Magne minorque dei quanquam mihi magnus uterque
Magne pater solo sed patre nate minor.

Holland, Hugh.

Titus B. VI, f. 249v.

Elegiac distich. Name 'hugo Holland' bracketed on right side.

Titus B. VIII

State papers, circa 1484–1618, n.d.; copied temp. *Elizabeth I and James I.*

f. 291. Verse epitaphs for Sir Francis Walsingham and his son-in-law Sir Philip Sidney, who shared a tomb in old St Paul's Cathedral. Preceded (f. 289) by two lists, copied in a different hand, of biographical points headed 'In the person of Mr Secretarie [*and* Sr Phillipp Sidney] for the epitaphe to be considered'. Seemingly *autograph drafts* of these lists survive in Vespasian C. XIV (ff. 214–215v), where they are preceded (f. 206) by texts, copied in another hand, of two epitaphs in Latin prose, of which that for Walsingham was pr., from the wooden tablet in St Paul's, in Dugdale's *History of St Paul's*, 1658, p. 99, along with some English verses there, subscribed 'E. W.'. Presumably the text of Sidney's epitaph was also the one formerly to be found there.

Gloria Franciscus generis præclara uetusti
Duxit, Sydnæo quum viduata foret.

Titus B. VIII, f. 291.

7 elegiac couplets. Epitaph of Sir Francis Walsingham (d. 6 April 1590).

Musarum soboles, decus immortale parentis
Chara patris soboles, Elizabetha sui.

Titus B. VIII, f. 291.

7 elegiac couplets. Epitaph of Sir Philip Sidney (d. 17 Oct. 1586: bur. 16 Feb. 1586/7).

f. 227. Latin verses by Edmund Bolton in commendation of Mary, Queen of Scots, and condemnation of Buchanan's *De Iure Regni* (1579). Copied on two sheets of paper pasted at the foot of a third that comprises *drafts* of proposed headings.

Cælitus hoc, Regina, parens augusta Jacobi,
Bassilicamque tibi tumuli pro munere ponet.

Bolton, Edmund.

'Ad gloriossissimos Regem Iacobum filivm, Annam…Carmen Votivum…Edmundus Maria B. Anglo-Britannus…adversus superbissimos Anactomastygas G. Buchananum, cæterosque sui similes… huic nostræ Mariae et cunctis principibus capitaliter, atque sacrilige iniurios, vindex paratissimus'.

Titus B. VIII, f. 227.

38 hexameters. *Autograph* fair copy. Title given above abbreviated from original.

ff. 323–324. Couplets on the foundation of Peterborough Abbey, formerly inscribed in the nine windows of the South Cloister that were destroyed in 1644. The verses are of uncertain date, but possibly after 1500, the present copy belonging to the 2nd quarter of the 17th cent. Pr. in Simon Gunton, *The History of the Church of Peterborough*, 1686, pp. 104–113, and in Dugdale's *Monasticon Anglicanum*, 2nd edn., 1817, I, 377. For their subject-matter see *VCH Northants.*, II, p. 84.

King Penda a paynym as writinge sayth
God saue and keepe it euer for his Grace.

'These verses were transcribed out of the cloyster windowes of peterborough church by George Rainer'.

Titus B. VIII, ff. 323–324.
39 rhymed couplets, in varying metre. Heading added in a second hand. In margin beside first couplet, in a third hand, 'Historicall Fragmentes'. George Rainer may be the Rayner (*circa* 1615–1681) who is listed in the Venns' *Alumni Cantabrigienses*, pt. i, vol. III, p. 430.

Titus C. VI

Correspondence and papers of Henry Howard, Earl of Northampton; circa *1568–1614, n.d. Mostly* autograph. *Contents list (f. 2) in mid 17th cent. hand.*

Good fortune is th'Horizon of thine ey; Yet darck my fortunes, who haue long been thine.

'The Earl of Northamptons SPHEAR'.
Titus C. VI, f. 183.
Shakespearian sonnet. Complimentary verses to Northampton, *circa* 1605–1614.

ff. 207–209v. Three *autograph drafts* by Northampton for the inscription on the tomb erected by James I in Westminster Abbey for his mother, Mary, Queen of Scots, *circa* Sept. 1612. All begin with a similar passage of varying length that was later rejected. The final version, comprising 11 elegiac couplets beg. 'Obruta frugifero sensim sic cespite surgunt' and ending as below, ff. 207, 207v, was pr. in Camden's *Remaines*, 1623. See also above, Caligula C. IX, pt. ii, ff. 626v, 627, from which the text is printed in *Calendar of State Papers relating to Scotland*, vol. IX (1585–1588), pp. 314–15.

Si generis splendor raræ si gratia formæ Æternos videant hinc sine nube dies.

Howard, Henry, Earl of Northampton.
'In obitum potentissimæ principis D. Mariæ Stuartæ Scoto[r]um Reginæ Franciæ Dotariæ et coronæ Anglicanæ hæredis indubitatæ atque proximæ Henricus Northampt[oniæ] comes memoriæ suæ celebritati devotissimus carmen lugubre posuit'.
Titus C. VI, ff. 207, 207v.
21 elegiac couplets.

Si generis splendor raræ si gratia formæ conditur hic Regum filia sponsa parens.

Howard, Henry, Earl of Northampton.

'In obitum piissimæ potentissimæque principis D Mariæ Stuartæ Scotoru*m* Reginæ Franciæ Dotariæ et iure successionis Anglicani regni hæredis proximæ Henr[icus] Howardus Comes Northamptoniæ carmen lugubre posuit'.
Titus C. VI, ff. 208, 208v.
21 elegiac couplets.

Si generis splendor raræ si gratia formæ Tempora læta deos tempora dura dedit.

Howard, Henry, Earl of Northampton.
'In obitum potentissimæ principis Mariæ Stuartæ Scotoru*m* Reginæ Franciæ Dotoriæ et iure successionis Angliæ hæredis indubitatæ atque proximæ'.
Titus C. VI, ff. 209, 209v.
19 elegiac couplets.

ff. 535–536v. Scribal *fair copy* of verses occupying four sides of a single bifolium.

In Paschall feast the ende of auncient right The water wyne, a snake of Moyses wande.

Southwell, Robert.
'Of the blessed Sacram*ent* of the alter:'.
Titus C. VI, ff. 535–536v.
90 decasyllables in 15 stanzas rhyming ababcc. Subscribed 'W: S.'. First pr. in *S. Peters Complaint and St Mary Magdalens Funerall Teares*, [St Omer], 1616, as 'The Christian's Manna'.

Titus C. VII

Collections assembled by William Camden; circa *1554–1618. Contents list (ff. 1, 1v) in Camden's hand.*

ff. 21–30. Papers relating to Sir Edward Coke, Lord Chief Justice.

In extremity and when Swelling with too stiff a gale.

Titus C. VII, f. 26.
2 heptasyllabic couplets. Quoted, with original, in an anonymous letter addressed to Coke, headed 'An aduertisment to L. Cooke' and undated but of *circa* 21 Dec. 1616. Letter summarized in *Calendar of State Papers 1611–1618*, p. 415. Crum I1308. Translation of Horace, *Odes*, II, x, 21–24.

ff. 85–98. Papers relating to Sir Walter Ralegh and his execution, 1618.

Of Raleighs life and death
He hath deceaud the Diuill.
    Titus C. VII, f. 93.
8 verses of 3-stress verses in 2 quatrains rhyming xaxa bcbc. Satirical epigram jotted at foot of list of charges brought against Ralegh.

Viderat Acephalos nulla ceruice Raleighus
Sed captum gemino lumine pectus erat.
    Titus C. VII, f. 93v.
3 elegiac couplets. Transcribed, possibly by William Camden, on verso of list of charges (f. 93). Satirical verses playing on Ralegh's claim to have encountered a race of men with heads below their shoulders.

Raleigh, in this thy selfe thy selfe trans-
                        cends
As well to those that doe as suffer ill.
    Scory, Sylvanus.
    'The aduise of Sylvanus Scory to Sr Walter Raleigh preparing for Guaiana 1617'.
    Titus C. VII, f. 94.
3 heroic quatrains. Title added in hand of William Camden. Crum R4. On Ralegh's voyage to Guiana, 1617.

Great heart whoe taught thee thus to die
Wee died thou only liued'st that daye.
    'Vpon the Death of Sr W. Raleigh'.
    Titus C. VII, f. 95.
7 octosyllabic couplets. Crum G504. Pr. in *Wits Recreations*, 1641, sig. S1.

Sir this my little Mistris here
But sure this is Pope Innocent, or none.
    'Of the Ladye Popes Daughter presented to the King att Halsteed 25 Junii *1618*'.
    Titus C. VII, f. 97v.
15 verses of varying lengths and rhyme-scheme. On verso of transcript headed in Camden's hand 'Out of the Apologie of Sr Walter Ralegh after his infortunate successe in Guaiana. 1618'. Crum S751. Pr. in *Cheerfull Ayres or Ballads*, 1660, p. 82, and in Nichols, *Progresses of…James I*, 1828, I, 529, and, from the present MS., III, 483. According to Nichols, the subject is Anne, dau. of Sir William Pope and his wife Elizabeth, dau. of Sir Thomas Watson of Halstead, co. Kent.

Titus D. IV

Miscellaneous historical and cosmological tracts; circa late 13th–early 16th centt.

ff. 1–14v. Sir Thomas More: Tract comprising five congratulatory epigrams on the coronation, etc., of King Henry VIII and Catharine of Aragon on 23 and 24 June 1509. Prefaced by an address in Latin prose (ff. 2–3v) headed 'Thomas Morus Potentissimo Britanniæ Galliæque Regi Henrico VIII° foelicissimo S. D.'. Scribal fair copy, on vellum, with illuminations and rubricated titles, etc. The second (f. 1) of two front fly-leaves, formerly blank, carries a contents-list for the whole composite volume in the hand of Richard James. Text pr., with minor variants and an additional epigram at the end, in *Epigrammata…Thomae Mori Britanni…*, to follow the *Utopia*, 3rd edn., Basle, March 1518.

Si qua dies unquam, si quod fuit Anglia
                        tempus
Et gnatus, gnati gestet et inde nepos.
    More, Sir Thomas.
    'In suscepti Diadematis diem Henrici Octaui Britanniarum Galliarumque Regis augustissimi faustissimi. Ac Catherinæ Reginæ eius foelicissimæ Carmen gratulatorium Thomæ Mori Londinensis'.
    Titus D. IV, ff. 4–11v.
95 elegiac couplets. First page has rubricated title within a Flemish-style decorative border: last carries illumination of a double rose of red enclosing white. Rubricated marginal section-headings.

Dum peterent sacras Rex et Regina
                        coronas
& Phoebus radiis & Iouis uxor aquis.
    More, Sir Thomas.
    'Eiusdem in subitum Imbrem qui in pompa Regis ac Reginæ largiter obortus nec Solem abstulit: nec durauit'.
    Titus D. IV, ff. 12, 12v.
6 elegiac couplets. Concludes with illumination of Tudor roses and pomegranates entwined, surmounted by fleur-de-lis, crown and portcullis. On the rainstorm during the procession of 23 June.

356

Cuncta Plato cecinit, tempus quae pro-
                        ferat ullum
O possit uates hactenus esse Plato.
  More, Sir Thomas.
  'Eiusdem ad Regem De aureo sæclo per
  eum redeunte Epigramma'.
  Titus D. IV, f. 13.
5 elegiac couplets.

Quaecunque reges ediderunt hactenus
Insignit innocentia.
  More, Sir Thomas.
  'Eiusdem ad Regem de spectaculis eques-
  tribus per eum editis Epigramma Iam-
  bico Carmine'.
  Titus D. IV, ff. 13v, 14.
16 verses, in iambic strophe.

Purpureæ uicina fuit Rosa candida utran-
                        que
Nempe etiam spinas flos habet iste suas.
  More, Sir Thomas.
  'Eiusdem De Rosa utraque in unum florem
  coalita Epigramma'.
  Titus D. IV, ff. 14, 14v.
6 elegiac couplets.

Titus D. XI

Letters of Thomas Becket (ff. 3–41v), with Tractatus
De Imagine Peccati *(ff. 42–55), attributed here to
Walter Hilton; late 14th cent. Inscribed in early 16th-
cent. hand 'liber Gulielmi Skypton teste Rychardo
Atkynsono' (f. 3), and, by a Cotton librarian, 'Ex dono
Iohannis Seldeni' (f. 2).*

ff. 55v, 56v. Vocal music jotted on blank fly leaves
in hand of the early 16th cent, with incipits only
of 'O lux beata Trinitas' and two secular songs.

Coll standyth...
  Titus D. XI, f. 56v.
Fragment: incipit only surviving from otherwise
unrecorded text. Ringler TM 318. Song.

Ravyshyd was I⟨, that well was me,⟩
⟨To be Englandes righte heire.⟩
  Titus D. XI, f. 56v.
Fragment: three-word incipit only, from song of 6
stanzas in common measure. BR 2794.2. Ringler TM
1349. Crum R15. Pr., from MS. Ashmole 176, f.

100v, in T. Wright and J. O. Halliwell, *Reliquiae
Antiquae*, 1841, I, 258. Ballad on Henry VIII's
dancing with his daughter Mary, composed *circa*
1516–1527.

Titus D. XII

*Chronicles of England and France, with prophetic
verses attributed to John of Bridlington; 14th–15th
centt. Contents list (f. 1) in hand of Richard James.*

Twoe men came riding ouer Hackney hay
Loe yonder stood Reuess that faire Abbay.
  Titus D. XII, f. 93v.
4 verses of varying lengths in monorhyme. Note
below in early-mid 17th cent. hand: 'Henry Cawton
a monke som times of Reves Abbay in Yorkshire
affermed that he had often read this in a M.S.
belonging to y^t Abbay contayning many prophesies
and was extant there before y^e time of y^e dissolution.
but when \ he / or any other of his fellowes redde it;
they used to throw, y^e book, away in anger as
thinking it impossible euer to come to passe. E. B.'
Beneath this, vol. rev., is jotted 'Jo: Andrewes'. BR
3815.8. Ringler TM 1778. Pr. in T. Wright and J. O.
Halliwell, *Reliquiae Antiquae*, 1841, I, p. 205, and in
Dugdale's *Monasticon*, 1825, V, p. 280. Prophecy
concerning Rievaulx Abbey, North Yorkshire.

Titus F. VII

William Camden's collections for Britannia.

Mira canam, soles quot continet arvus, in
                        vna
Res mira at vera res celebrata fide.
  Rogers, Daniel.
  Titus F. VII, f. 26.
6 elegiac couplets. Prefaced by: 'De quo ornatiss. vir
Daniel Rogerius amicus nobis singularis, et maxi-
marum artium disciplinis imprimis excultus præclare
cecinit'. Pr. *Britannia*, 1586, p. 118. On the columns
in Salisbury Cathedral.

Thamisis, et subito placide ridentibus
                        undis
Urbs pietate potens, numeroso ciue su-
                        perba.
  Camden, William.
  Titus F. VII, ff. 47v, 48v.
9 hexameters. Extract from *De Connubio Tamæ et*

Isis, concluding 'Et cæt.'. Prefaced by: 'His vero priusquam Londinio valedicam libet versiculos quosdam de Londino attexere quos mihi valde iuveni dum Thamesim a fontibus ad Oceanum deducem, patriæ quodamodo charitas extorserit'. Pr., in an 8-line version beg. 'Londinum gemino procurrit litore longe', in *Britannia*, 1590, p. 336; and in G. B. Johnston, 'Poems by William Camden', *Studies in Philology, Texts and Studies*, 1975, pp. 102, 103, with facing English translation (1610) by Philemon Holland. This MS. and its readings not recorded by Johnston. On the watersmeet of Thames and Isis in Gloucestershire.

Vespasian A. XXV

Composite volume of tracts, in prose and verse, partly of a religious nature; early 15th to mid 16th cent. Signature of 'Henry Sauill' (d. 1617) of Banke, and inscription 'Ex dono Johannis Anstis Armigeri' (d. 1745), Garter King of Arms, on f. 2. Contents list (f. 1v) in hand of late 17th cent. In the margins of the first of two vellum singletons (ff. 204, 205) at the end of the volume is written in a hand or hands of late 16th–early 17th cent. 'This is master Jac his booke', along with the names 'Edward', 'William' and 'R. Rouland (?)'.

ff. 37–40v, 125–163, 178–179. The verses on ff. 37–40v are jotted at the end of a calendar (ff. 28–37) of events in the reigns of Henry VII and VIII, from 1501 to 8 Nov. 1545. Those on ff. 125, 126v survive on two vellum leaves at the end of a 15th-cent. tract (ff. 66–126) of mixed verse and prose. At the head of f. 125 is inscribed 'per me Willia*m* (?) Colsu*m*', while on f. 126 occurs the incipit of a deed dateable to between 1547 and 1553. Thereafter the manuscript comprises songs and ballads, copied *circa* 1555–1606, in a notebook apparently of Yorkshire provenance (for details of which see individual entries below). Several of these belong to the first half of the 16th cent., and many of the ballads are to be traced in the Stationers' Register between 1561 and 1606. Most of the pieces were edited, and the whole manuscript described in detail, by Peter J. Seng, *Tudor songs and ballads from MS. Cotton Vespasian A-25*, Cambridge, Mass., 1978.

Fyll the cuppe Phylyppe & let vs drynke a drame
Yf yow will pledge me the same.
Vespasian A. XXV, f. 37.
6 verses in poulter's measure. Among jottings on the blank half-page immediately following an account of

events in the reigns of Henry VII and VIII, 1501–8 Nov. 1545. Ringler TM 410. Pr. by Seng, *ed. cit.*, p. 1. Drinking song.

Whan all this ssowghte that may be fownde
Neither wysche it for mysery, or for feare it flye.
Vespasian A. XXV, f. 39v.
28 verses of 4 stresses each in rhymed couplets. Ringler TM 1849. Pr. by Seng, *ed. cit.*, pp. 1–2. Translation of Martial, *Epigrams*, X, 47.

Lerne this lesson in welthe and woo
To doo as he woolde be doone vnto.
Vespasian A. XXV, ff. 39v–40v.
54 verses of 4 stresses each in 13 stanzas of rhymed couplets, with prefatory couplet. Ringler TM 880. Pr. by Seng, *ed. cit.*, pp. 2–3. Moral instruction.

So longe may a droppe fall
I truste we shall it haue.
Vespasian A. XXV, f. 40v.
40 verses of 3 stresses each in 10 quatrains rhyming abab. Ringler TM 1434. Pr. by Seng, *ed. cit.*, pp. 4–5. On truth, error and God's mercy.

After droght commythe rayne
and Joye afte[r] payne and woo.
Vespasian A. XXV, f. 125.
5 verses of varying lengths, rhyming aabab. Ringler TM 72. Pr. by Seng, *ed. cit.*, p. 6. Proverbial verses.

A⟨s I sat⟩ vpon astrawe
our cate lyet syke and takyte gret sorow.
Vespasian A. XXV, f. 126v.
7 stanzas in common measure, nos. 1 and 6 *imperfect*. Preceded by burden 'Newes newes newes newes | ye never herd so many newes' repeated also after each stanza. Lacuna in first verse supplied by conjecture of Hyder Rollins in transcript now Harvard MS. 25254.24.14F*. Ringler TM 196. Pr. by Seng, *ed. cit.*, pp. 6–7. Nonsense carol.

To hurt the widowe in distresse
⟨—⟩ to apprehend.
Vespasian A. XXV, f. 127.
29 verses in 5 stanzas of rime couée, rhyming aabccb: stanza 5 internally *imperfect*. Possibly the ballad

358

'Herodes persecution &c'. entd. in S.R. for Thomas Colwell, 1562–63. Pr. by Seng, *ed. cit.*, p. 8. Moral precept.

Who trusts Christs in Carnatyone
Where ever shalbe mirth.

'A Carroll'.
Vespasian A. XXV, ff. 127v, 128.
42 verses in 7 stanzas of rime couée, rhyming aabccb. Preceded by couplet. Pr. by Seng, *ed. cit.*, pp. 9–10. On the paradoxes of Christianity.

As said the prophet a bacuce
in mydst of them Dothe site.

[Masson, —].
Vespasian A. XXV, ff. 129, 129v.
36 verses in 6 stanzas of rime couée, rhyming aabccb. Subscribed 'Finis Masson'. Pr. by Seng, *ed. cit.*, p. 11. On Christ.

There was no deathe nor worldly Ioie
and for geve all our fosse.

'A caroll of sainct stephen | Chorus'
Vespasian A. XXV, f. 129v.
46 verses in 7 stanzas of rime couée, rhyming aabccb. Pr. by Seng, *ed. cit.*, pp. 12–14. On St Stephen.

Man to redeme & not angell
In charitie.

M[?asson, —].
Vespasian A. XXV, ff. 130v, 131.
36 verses of varying length in 6 stanzas rhyming aabccb, with internal rhyme in third verse. Preceded by a 'chorus' or burden 'Then may we Ioie in vnitie | & thanke the holie trinitie' repeated at the end of each stanza. Concludes: 'above the fiere | I you desyre' and 'Finis M[?asson]'. Pr. by Seng, *ed. cit.*, pp. 14–15. Religious carol.

By reason of two & poore of one
And at the last ende the great ioyes endles.

Vespasian A. XXV, ff. 131v–132v.
65 verses of varying length in 7 stanzas rhyming ababbccbb; with prefatory couplet. Pr. by Seng, *ed. cit.*, pp. 16–18. On God and man.

Longe haue I bene a singinge man
the meane of meanes that dothe excell.

[Heywood, John; or Redford, John].
Vespasian A. XXV, ff. 132v–133.
48 octosyllables in 8 stanzas rhyming ababcc. Concludes: 'Finis Mr haywood'. In Add. MS. 15233, ff. 45, 45v, these verses are attributed to John Redford. Pr. in Heywood's *'Works' and miscellaneous short poems*, ed. Burton A. Milligan, Illinois Studies in Language and Literature, Urbana, 1941, pp. 275–77; and by Seng, *ed. cit.*, pp. 19–20. On singing.

There is no tre that growe
vinum letificat cor hominis.

Vespasian A. XXV, ff. 133v–135.
112 verses in 14 stanzas rhyming aaa^{6}b^{4}ccc^{6}b^4. Alternate stanzas have refrain of 4 verses beg. 'Then put aside all wrathe'. Pr. by Seng, *ed. cit.*, pp. 23–25. Carol in praise of wine.

Awak ye wofull wightes
Damon my frend ys Iudged to dye.

Edwards, Richard.
'A balet'.
Vespasian A. XXV, ff. 135, 135v.
4 stanzas in short metre. For musical setting see Add. MS. 15117, f. 3. Pr. in Richard Edwards' *Damon and Pithias*, 1571 (play composed *circa* 1564–8); and by Seng, *ed. cit.*, pp. 26–27. Song of Pithias lamenting the sentence of death passed on her lover Damon.

Of lingeringe love mysliking growes
Who lokes to sayle must wache a tydde.

Vespasian A. XXV, ff. 135v–136v.
48 verses in 6 stanzas rhyming aabb^{8}c^{4}c^{8}d^{4}d^8. 'A ballett intituled of lyngerynge Love' entd. in S.R. for William Griffith, 1563–4. Pr. by Seng, *ed. cit.*, pp. 30–31. On the dangers of loving.

Where griping greues the hart wold wound
what beste ys he wull the disprove.

[Edwards, Richard, *attrib*.].
'A songe to the Lute of musicke'.
Vespasian A. XXV, f. 137.
24 octosyllables in 4 stanzas rhyming ababcc. For musical setting see Add. MS. 30513, f. 108v. Pr. in Richard Edwards' *Paradise of Dainty Devices*, 1576, with attribution to 'Master Edwards' (not found in

359

later edns.); and by Seng, *ed. cit.*, pp. 32–33. In praise of music.

**The man ys blest that lyves in rest
that haith so evell A name.**
　　'A Ballet'.
　　Vespasian A. XXV, ff. 137v, 138.
6 stanzas in common measure. Pr. by Seng, *ed. cit.*, p. 35. Satire on female dominance.

**Wyll ye complayne without a cavsse
they shalbe sure to have my praysse.**
　　'A ballet'.
　　Vespasian A. XXV, ff. 138–139.
12 octosyllabic quatrains rhyming abab. Pr. by Seng, *ed. cit.*, pp. 36–38. In defence of women.

**God helpe vs all god helpe vs all
And in the works of faith ys very slow.**
　　Vespasian A. XXV, ff. 139, 139v.
28 octosyllables in 7 stanzas of triplets + first verse (above), as refrain. Pr. by Seng, *ed. cit.*, pp. 39–40. On the sin of blasphemy.

**A horse chuying on the brydle
for my Idle besynes.**
　　'A Ballyt'.
　　Vespasian A. XXV, f. 140.
50 octosyllables in 5 stanzas of rhymed couplets, the last line a refrain beg. 'ys love this Idle busynes'. Possibly the ballad 'loue' entd. in S.R. by Thomas Colwell, 1562–63. Pr. by Seng, *ed. cit.*, pp. 40–41. On inert lovers.

**By west off late as I dyd walke in the
　　　　pryme tyme of the day
grant vs all pray both night & day that god
　　　　such grace may sende.**
　　'Ballet'.
　　Vespasian A. XXV, ff. 140v–142.
55 fourteener couplets in 11 stanzas, of which nos. 1–6 are numbered. This and most of the pieces copied on ff. 140v–163v below carry stanza-numbering in the left-hand margin. Possibly the ballad 'A merye ieste of a wife that threst her husband with a Flealle', entd. in S.R. for Thomas Scarlet, 15 August 1590. Pr. by Seng, *ed. cit.*, pp. 42–44. On a brawling married couple.

**What tyme that god his holy hande
with swete of thi browes shalt eat thi
　　　　breade.**
　　'A Ballett of Adame & Eve'.
　　Vespasian A. XXV, f. 142v.
30 octosyllables with variable rhyme, in 5 stanzas, all numbered. *Imperfect*, the rest of the page being left blank. Probably the ballad entd. in S.R. for Thomas Colwell in 1564–65. Pr. by Seng, *ed. cit.*, pp. 46–47. On Adam and Eve.

**Now lesten a whyle & let hus singe
then man shall graunt his wyffe to haite.**
　　'A mery ballett'.
　　Vespasian A. XXV, ff. 143, 143v.
40 octosyllables in 5 stanzas rhyming ababcdcd, all numbered. Late entry in S.R. to Simon Stafford, 28 June 1606. Pr. by Seng, *ed. cit.*, pp. 47–48. On marital discord.

**O heavenly god o father dere cast downe
　　　　your tender eye
that after deathe my soule may haue in
　　　　heaven a dwelling place.**
　　[Kinwelmersh, Francis].
　　'A prayer of earle of essex deathe'.
　　Vespasian A. XXV, ff. 143v, 144.
12 fourteener couplets in 6 stanzas of four verses each, nos. 1–5 numbered. Crum O485. Title refers to Walter Devereux, 1st Earl of Essex (d. 1576). Attrib. to F[rancis] K[inwelmersh] in *The Paradyse of Daynty Devises*, 1576, where it is pr. as 'O Heavenly God, O Father dere, cast doun thy tender eye': see edn. of H. E. Rollins, Cambridge, Mass., 1927, pp. 95, 351. The copy made by William Cole from a MS. seen in 1773, now in Add. MS. 5845, ff. 171–176v, is signed 'E. L.'. Pr. by Seng, *ed. cit.*, p. 49. Deathbed plea for god's mercy.

**As I lay musing all alone
even in the twinkling of an eye.**
　　'A ballet of the Judgment day'.
　　Vespasian A. XXV, ff. 144, 144v.
13 octosyllabic quatrains rhyming abab, all numbered. Concludes: 'now let us pray for christ his sake'. Possibly the ballad 'the twyntlynge of an ee' entd. in S.R. for John Alde, 1561–2. Pr. by Seng, *ed. cit.*, pp. 52–54. On the Day of Judgement.

**I am a poore sheperd yet borne of hye
　　　　blode**

a sheperd ys better then any riche kyng.
'A Ballett of a sheperd'.
Vespasian A. XXV, f. 145.
30 hendecasyllables in 5 stanzas of rhymed couplets, all numbered. Pr. by Seng, *ed. cit.*, pp. 55–56. In praise of the shepherd's life.

Geve eare my children to my wordes
whom god haith dearly bought
that I may have you in the heavens where
I do hoppe to rest.
Smith, Robert, *alias* Rogers, Mathew.
'A Ballet of A father warning his children to feare god & kepe his commaundements'.
Vespasian A. XXV, ff. 145v–147v.
92 fourteener couplets in 23 stanzas, all numbered. Final 10 couplets copied, vol. rev., on f. 147v. Concludes: 'Finis quod Mathew Rogers'. Ringler TM 464, TP 458. Pr. in John Bradford, *The complaynt of Veritie*, [?1558], sigs. A4ᵛ–A8; and by Seng, *ed. cit.*, pp. 56–61. On Robert Smith of Windsor, martyred at Uxbridge, 1555. Religious instruction.

Lycke as the Towche doowyth trewly trey
no great deversytte.
Vespasian A. XXV, f. 148v.
6 verses of varying lengths. Possibly *imperfect*. Pr. by Seng, *ed. cit.*, p. 63. Moral proverbs.

Who wislye wyll with gostlye eye
Defferr not Lorde thie Judgment day.
'A Ballet of the Last dayes'.
Vespasian A. XXV, ff. 149–150.
96 verses, arranged in 6 stanzas rhyming aa⁸b⁷cc⁸b⁷ddeeffgghh⁸, all numbered. Pr. by Seng, *ed. cit.*, pp. 64–66. Religious instruction.

Marche out godes soldiours
come Reigne with me in heaven for aye.
'A ballet declaring how everye christian ought to prepaire them selffe to warre & for to fighte valiantly vnder the banner of his capton christ; – to be Songe after Rowe well you maryners'.
Vespasian A. XXV, ff. 150v, 151.
108 verses of varying lengths in 9 stanzas rhyming ababccddeeff, all numbered. Apparently either the ballad 'howe every christian souldiour shulde fyghte vnder his captayne Christ', entd. in S.R. for John

Cherlewood, 1569–70; or 'A faythfull and vnfayned incouragement to all true christian Souldiers to perseuer in the loue and loyaltie of their Christe &c'. entd. to Richard Jones, 29 July 1583. Pr. by Seng, *ed. cit.*, pp. 67–69. Religious instruction.

Hardnes ys headstrong, and will not be
hampered
haite overthawrte wrangling lest truth be
maide blind.
'Another ballet of this present tyme or worlde'.
Vespasian A. XXV, ff. 151, 151v.
28 verses of 4 stresses each in 7 stanzas of rhymed couplets, all numbered in the margin. Pr. by Seng, *ed. cit.*, p. 71. Moral commentary.

The golden tyme ys nowe at hande
Reioyce therefore bothe more & lesse.
'A carroll of the birthe of christ'.
Vespasian A. XXV, ff. 151v–152v.
77 verses in 11 stanzas rhyming ababccb, all numbered. Possibly the carol 'The byrthe of Christe' entd. in S.R. for Richard Jones, 1569–70. Pr. by Seng, *ed. cit.*, pp. 72–74. On the birth of Christ.

Would god that deth with cruell darte
vnto my latter ende.
'Ellin thorne songe'.
Vespasian A. XXV, ff. 152v, 153.
6 stanzas in common measure, all numbered. Pr. by Seng, *ed. cit.*, p. 75. Lover's complaint.

Ego ros campi in the feld
are compast all in the.
Harforth, Peter.
'A Songe of Ladie Sion the churche | A Balet of Sir peter hartforthe making | vpon the [87th *vacat*] spalme vicare of hoveden departed'.
Vespasian A. XXV, f. 153.
9 stanzas in common measure, all numbered. Pr. by Seng, *ed. cit.*, pp. 76–77. In praise of Mother Church.

The fragraunt flowers most freshe to vewe
to his eternitie.
[Pearson, T[?homas]].
'Another ballett T peirson doing 1578 {maid in [?may] at yorke}'.
Vespasian A. XXV, f. 153v.
5 stanzas of common measure doubled, rhyming

ababcdcd, all numbered. Possibly the ballad 'a mery milde may wherin is vnsiphored how all thynges Decaye' entd. in S.R. to Thomas Colwell, 1569–70. Pr. by Seng, *ed. cit.*, pp. 78–79. On the fragility of life.

O man Refraine thie vile desyre
god graunt to hus that plaice eternall.
[Pearson, T[?homas]].
'Another songe of T person doing'.
Vespasian A. XXV, f. 154.
36 verses of mixed metre in 9 quatrains rhyming abab, all numbered. Probably the ballad 'Remember the poore' entd. in S.R. for Richard Jones, 9 September 1578. Pr. by Seng, *ed. cit.*, pp. 80, 81. Moral instruction.

It was a maide of my countre
to talke againe of the hathorne grene.
[Peele, George, *attrib.*].
'A mery Ballet of the Hathorne tre to be songe after donkine dargeson'.
Vespasian A. XXV, ff. 154v, 155.
52 octosyllabic couplets in 13 stanzas, all numbered. In title 'dargeson' corrected from 'darkeson'. Attribution at end in different ink to 'G. Peele'. See also musical setting in C.U.L. MS. Dd. 2. 11, f. 8. Pr. by Seng, *ed. cit.*, pp. 82–83. Moral precept.

The happiest man that nowe dost lyve
thie will be done we do praie all.
Richardson, Thomas.
'To the toune of the Raire and greatest gift'.
Vespasian A. XXV, ff. 155, 155v.
48 octosyllables, in 6 stanzas rhyming ababcc + refrain 'Yet hap what hap fall what may fall | alyff content exceedeth all' (varying in stanza 6). Concludes: 'Fi⟨ni⟩s T Richeson'. Possibly the ballad 'the plesure of Content preferred before all other estates' entd. in S.R. to John Cherlewood, 22 Sept. 1592. Pr. by Seng, *ed. cit.*, pp. 84–85. On content.

Whoso in wedloke doth intend
& eche from other never starte.
'A ballet of mariag'.
Vespasian A. XXV, f. 156.
8 octosyllabic couplets in 2 stanzas. *Imperfect.* Possibly the ballad ascribed by Herbert-Ames to

[William] Elderton in 1573. Pr. by Seng, *ed. cit.*, p. 87. On the benefits of marriage.

Yf musing thos that do behould my woe, &
rufull staite
And to be myndfull of that price which
once he paide for synne.
'A notable Instrucyon for all men to bewaire the abuses of dycce wynne & women'.
Vespasian A. XXV, ff. 157v, 157, 156v.
32 fourteener couplets. Copied at right angles to rest. Epigraph at head: 'dives eram dudum, sed tria me fecerunt nudum | alia vina venus, tribus his sum factus egenus'. This ballad entd. in S.R. for William Griffith, 1565–66, and, with shortened title, for Abraham Newman, 17 Sept. 1578. Pr. by Seng, *ed. cit.*, pp. 88–90. Moral admonition.

Behould as rewfull ratlyffe died
lett thes my verse be founde.
'A Ballett of the deathe of Ratlyffe which rosse with the earle of northumberlande lord pearse whiche he maide a lytle spaice before he was handged | 1570'.
Vespasian A. XXV, f. 158v.
22 stanzas in common measure, all but last numbered in margin. Title refers to Egremont Radcliffe who, however, after the failure of the Northern Rebellion under Thomas Percy, 7th Earl of Northumberland (beheaded in 1572), escaped and was executed at Namur in 1578. Pr. by Seng, *ed. cit.*, pp. 93–96.

I selly crosse that here do stande
which spoyle me standing here.
'The lamentacion of the crosse'.
Vespasian A. XXV, f. 159.
18 stanzas in ballad metre. In margin at head 'St Augustin'. Pr. by Seng, *ed. cit.*, pp. 96–98, and in a longer version from Harvard MS. Eng. 749, pp. 100–109. On the banishment of the cross from religious worship.

A bonne god wote
tyll I have dronken onc.
'A Cristenmus carroll'.
Vespasian A. XXV, f. 159v.
36 verses in 6 stanzas rhyming $aa^4b^6cc^4b^6$, nos. 1–5 only numbered. Verse 19 includes a reference to

'master wortley' of Wortley Hall, co. W.R. Yorks: cf. ff. 172–177v for verses by Lydgate recited 'in the cappell of wortley of wortley hall'. Pr. by Seng, *ed. cit.*, p. 110. Drinking song.

Whye dothe the vaine fantasie dust in thy faice
in tyme to follow yt thus endyth my songe.
'A Ballet'.
Vespasian A. XXV, ff. 160, 160v.
108 2-stress verses in 9 stanzas rhyming ababcccdeeed, all numbered. Concludes: 'Finis | Experto crede Roberto'. Pr. by Seng, *ed. cit.*, pp. 111–13. On the trials of marriage.

Who sekes to tame the bustering winde
a dewe Reward for all our paine.
'A dyttie to hey downe'.
Vespasian A. XXV, f. 161.
30 octosyllables in 5 stanzas rhyming ababcc, all numbered. Pr. by Seng, *ed. cit.*, pp. 114–15. On vain labours.

In sommer tyme I dyd prepaire
which makes our harttes so merye.
'Another ballet'.
Vespasian A. XXV, ff. 161v, 162.
32 octosyllables in 8 stanzas rhyming aaab (b-rhyme invariable), nos. 1–6 numbered. Possibly ballad 'in prayse of the grene fylde' entd. in S.R. for Alexander Lacy, 1569–70. Pr. by Seng, *ed. cit.*, pp. 115–16. Description of a summer's day.

Drawe nere good frendes & list awhile
apply we to this end.
'A true Balett of Deniing a poore man a Loffe of brede which he paid for 1577'.
Vespasian A. XXV, ff. 162, 162v.
38 stanzas in ballad metre. Pr. by Seng, *ed. cit.*, pp. 117–21. A warning to evil doers.

The second person in trenitie
our lord to [lo]ve let hus be fain.
'A carroll'.
Vespasian A. XXV, f. 163.
24 octosyllabic couplets in 6 stanzas, with prefatory couplet 'Praisse we the lord that haith no peare |

And thanke we hym for this new yere'. *Imperfect* at various points. Lacuna in last verse supplied by conjecture. Pr. by Seng, *ed. cit.*, pp. 122–23. On Christ's sacrifice.

God ys the cheffest vnizon
& so to thend may Ronne our Raysse.
Harforth, Peter.
Vespasian A. XXV, f. 163v.
5 octosyllabic quatrains rhyming abab, middle stanzas numbered as 1–3. Concludes: 'Finis Sʳ peter h⟨-⟩ harfurthe Doing 1576 | curat of hoveden & died 1577 att lamas'. Four bars possibly of musical setting jotted along inner margin. Pr. by Seng, *ed. cit.*, pp. 123–24. On concord under God and the Queen.

It befell at martynmas
All & my Louesome wyffe.
[Assheton, William].
Vespasian A. XXV, ff. 178–179.
30 stanzas of 8 verses incorporating 4-line refrain beg. 'Syck sicke & totowe sike'; both parts of stanza in ballad metre. Concludes: 'finis per me Willielmum Asheton clericum'. Possibly the ballad 'sick sick &c'. entd. in S.R. to Richard Jones, 24 March 1579. Pr. in Percy's *Reliques*, 1765, vol. I, 99, as 'Edom Gordon'; and in Francis J. Child, *English and Scottish popular ballads*, vol. III, 430ff.; and by Seng, *ed. cit.*, pp. 128–32. Folk ballad.

Vespasian D. IX

Composite collection of tracts, in prose and verse, relating to religion, etc.; circa 14th cent.–1606. Contents list (f. 1) in hand of Richard James.

ff. 169–176v. John Johnston's 'Vrbes Britanniæ'; 1606. Latin epigrams on English and Scottish towns and cities, with *autograph* dedication (f. 169v) 'Clarissimo & doctissimo viro D. Guil. Camdeno amoris pignus Johan. Jonstonus'. A covering letter, dated 11 August 1606, is pr. in Camden's *Epistolae*, ed. Thomas Smith, 1691, pp. 75–6 (and see pp. 95–6). Most of these epigrams were included in the 1607 edition of *Britannia*. A further manuscript is preserved among Camden's books in Westminster Chapter Library: see Richard L. DeMolen, 'The Library of William Camden', *Proceedings of the American Philosophical Society*, vol. 128 (Dec. 1984), p. 377.

Urbs Augusta, cui cælum tellusque, fre-
tumque,
Auctior hoc se nunc, maior ut anté aliis.
    Johnston, John.
    'Londinum'.
    Vespasian D. IX, f. 170.
7 elegiac couplets. On London.

Præsidet extremis Arctoæ finibus oræ
Huic satis a prima proxima jura dare.
    Johnston, John.
    'Eboracum'.
    Vespasian D. IX, ff. 170, 170v.
5 elegiac couplets. On York.

Vos ego vos veneror, cælestia pignora,
Divæ
Aut Cælum ducis Sedibus ætheriis.
    Johnston, John.
    'Oxonia et Cantabrigia'.
    Vespasian D. IX, f. 170v.
6 elegiac couplets. On Oxford and Cambridge.

Quæ minima in parvo regno pars anté
fuisti;
Non iterum huic par sit reddere velle
suos?
    Johnston, John.
    'Cantuaria'.
    Vespasian D. IX, ff. 170v, 172.
7 elegiac couplets. On Canterbury.

Sub vario Natura diu certamine ludens
Sol novus inlustrans lumine cuncta suo.
    Johnston, John.
    'Sarisburia'.
    Vespasian D. IX, f. 171.
7 elegiac couplets. *Autograph* revisions. Copied on an
inserted slip, with the *autograph* direction 'Ponatur
[post *deleted*] ante Nordovic'. On Salisbury.

Urbs speciosa situ, nitidis pulcherrima
tectis:
Fors regno desit, hæc Caput esse queat.
    Johnston, John.
    'Nordovicus'.
    Vespasian D. IX, f. 172.
5 elegiac couplets. On Norwich.

Cernis uti Oceanus prono ruit obvius æstu,
Æqua animi est, docilis quæ ratione regi.
    Johnston, John.
    'Bristolia'.
    Vespasian D. IX, ff. 172, 172v.
6 elegiac couplets. On Bristol.

Vedra ruens rapidis modo cursibus,
agmine leni,
Hæc armis cluit, hæc Religione potens.
    Johnston, John.
    'Dunelmum'.
    Vespasian D. IX, f. 172v.
5 elegiac couplets. On Durham.

Rupe sedens celsa, rerum aut miracula
spectat
Hæc quot alit? quot alit Scotia nostra
Deos?
    Johnston, John.
    'Novum Castrum'.
    Vespasian D. IX, f. 172v.
6 elegiac couplets. On Newcastle-upon-Tyne.

Mænia tuta loco fertur posuisse Gradivus.
Aut genuit, faciles aut genuere Deæ.
    Johnston, John.
    'Coventria'.
    Vespasian D. IX, f. 173.
3 elegiac couplets. On Coventry.

Romanis quondam statio tutissima signis,
Immensis animis hic posuisse modum.
    Johnston, John.
    'Carleolum'.
    Vespasian D. IX, f. 173.
6 elegiac couplets. On Carlisle.

Monte sub acclini Zephyri procurrit in
auras
Hæc cernens, oculis credis an ipse tuis?
    Johnston, John.
    'Edinburgum'.
    Vespasian D. IX, ff. 173, 173v.
7 elegiac couplets. On Edinburgh.

Ad Boream porrecta, jugis obsessa super-
                bis,
Pingere non ulla Ars, ingeniumvè valet.
    Johnston, John.
    'Abredonia'.
    Vespasian D. IX, f. 173v.
7 elegiac couplets. On Aberdeen.

Propter aquas Tai liquidas, et amæna
                vireta,
Perge recens, priscum, perpetuare decus.
    Johnston, John.
    'Perthum'.
    Vespasian D. IX, f. 174.
6 elegiac couplets, with *autograph* corrections. On
Perth.

Qua Notus argutis adspirat molliter auris,
Cætera dic Patriæ dona beata tuæ.
    Johnston, John.
    'Taodunum sive Deidonum'.
    Vespasian D. IX, f. 174.
6 elegiac couplets, with *autograph* corrections. On
Dundee.

Imminet Oceano, paribus descripta vi-
                arum
Alme Deus. Coeant Pax Pietasque simul.
    Johnston, John.
    'Fanum Reguli, sive Andreapolis'.
    Vespasian D. IX, f. 174v.
7 elegiac couplets. Carries *autograph* corrections. On
St Andrews.

Non te Pontificum luxus, non Insula
                tantum
Glascua fæcundat flumine cuncta suo.
    Johnston, John.
    'Glascua'.
    Vespasian D. IX, f. 174v.
4 elegiac couplets. On Glasgow.

Regia sublimis celsâ despectat ab arce
Lætior aut Cæli frons, geniusvé soli.
    Johnston, John.
    'Sterlinum'.
    Vespasian D. IX, ff. 174v, 175.
5 elegiac couplets. On Stirling.

Aureolis Urbs picta rosis: mons molliter
                Urbi
Pollice Melvini se velit una cani.
    Johnston, John.
    'Celurca sive Mons Rosarum'.
    Vespasian D. IX, f. 175.
5 elegiac couplets, with *autograph* corrections and
marginal note, now trimmed: 'ponatur ⟨[post]⟩
Bervicu⟨m⟩'. On Montrose.

Scotorum extremo sub limite, meta fu-
                roris
Excelsum tollit libera in astra Caput.
    Johnston, John.
    'Bervicum'.
    Vespasian D. IX, ff. 175, 175v.
7 elegiac couplets. On Berwick.

Parva Urbs, ast ingens animis in fortibus
                hæret.
Aurea fors dici debuit illa prius.
    Johnston, John.
    'Æra sive Æria'.
    Vespasian D. IX, f. 175v.
4 elegiac couplets. On Ayr.

Planities prætensa jacet prope flumina
                Tinæ;
Præsidio gaudet jam potiore Poli.
    Johnston, John.
    'Hadina'.
    Vespasian D. IX, f. 175v.
4 elegiac couplets. On Haddington.

Imperii veteris duo propugnacula quon-
                dam,
Corpora, cum videas oppida, regna mori?
    Johnston, John.
    'Ennernessus & Ennerlothea'.
    Vespasian D. IX, f. 176.
7 elegiac couplets. *Autograph* corrections. On Inver-
ness and Innerleithen.

Oppida sic toto sunt sparsa in littore, ut
                unum
Magnanimos acuunt damna, pericla,
                labor.
    Johnston, John.
    'Oppida ad Fortham'.

Vespasian D. IX, ff. 176, 176v.
7 elegiac couplets, with *autograph* revisions. On the towns of Fifeshire.

Vespasian E. VII

Composite collection of tracts, in Latin and English, partly relating to astronomy, history and prophecies; 15th–16th cent. Ownership inscription (f. 4) of 'Robertus Cotton Bruceus 1604'.

ff. 133–134. Verse prophecies jotted on final blank leaves at end of 'Prophecia Aquile…super muros ciuitatis Wynton*iae* (ff. 132–133)…' in hands of early 16th cent. to *circa* 1688.

> **The hinde shall hunte the harte to deathe,**
> **Tyll he him selfe hath lost his breathe.**
> Vespasian E. VII, f. 133.
> Rhymed octosyllabic couplet. This and the verses immediately following copied in early- to mid-16th cent. hand. Ringler TM 1539. Prophecy.

> **When the beare ys musselyd & cann nott**
>   **byte,**
> **then shall ye spley foote into Englande**
>   **wyne.**
> Vespasian E. VII, f. 133.
> 2 decasyllabic couplets. Ringler TM 1906. Prophecy.

> **When fowre lightes begynne to shyne**
> **none knowst but god therfore adew.**
> Vespasian E. VII, f. 134.
> 13 octosyllables rhyming ababccddeefff. Copied in late 16th or early 17th cent. hand. Prophecy.

> **When dearth decreasis & treason begynne**
> **no chaunge wilbe till comes the Dome.**
> Vespasian E. VII, f. 134.
> 6 verses of 4 stresses each, in rhymed couplets. Followed by: '{1666 / gods Angells} | {7000 / knowes} | 1573 / many a toy y^t time wilbe | god shild vs from bane & bring vs to blithe / happy is he y^t is on live. wth godes'. Copied in late 16th or early 17th cent. hand. Prophecy.

Vespasian E. VIII

Composite collection of tracts partly by William Camden; circa 14th–16th cent. Included are a draft (ff. 75–96v, 161–167) of his Institutio Graecae *grammatices compendaria (pr. in 1597), an Old English-Latin word-list (ff. 132–155v) and brief onomasticon (ff. 156–159). The Camden portion (ff. 75–183v) is copied throughout on a single stock of French paper dated by Briquet to 1564. Contents list (f. 1) in hand of Sir Thomas Cotton.*

ff. 169–178. George Puttenham: 'Parthenaides', comprising nineteen poems composed as New Year's gifts for Queen Elizabeth I, *circa* 1579–1582, in a copy apparently in Camden's hand. Described in Sir Thomas Cotton's contents list on f. 1 as 'Verses to Queen Eliz:'. General heading 'Parthenaides' and poem-numbering copied throughout in the left-hand margins. Pr. by John Nichols, *Progresses…of Queen Elizabeth*, vol. II, 1788; by Joseph Haslewood, with Puttenham's *Arte of English Poesie*, 1811; and by W. R. Morfill, *Ballads from MSS* (Ballad Society Publications), 1873, vol. II, pp. 72–91. For discussion of authorship see Puttenham's *Arte of English Poesie* (1589), ed. Gladys D. Willcock and Alice Walker, Cambridge, 1936, p. xxxi, n. 1.

> **Gracious Princesse, Where princes are in**
>   **place**
> **Vttringe your honours, to hyde her owners**
>   **name.**
> Puttenham, George.
> 'Parthe[naides] 1: Thaleia. The principall address in nature of a new yeares gifte, seeminge therebye the Author intended not to have his name knowne'.
> Vespasian E. VIII, f. 169.
> 12 decasyllables rhyming abbaacddccee. vv.28–29 pr. in *Arte of English Poesie*, 1589, p. 151, introduced by: 'as we said in one of our *Parthenaides*'.

> **Greeke Achilles, and his peeres did enioye**
> **Whose woorthes surmount them all that**
>   **they reherse.**
> Puttenham, George.
> 'Parthe[naides] 2: Clio. The author choosinge by his verse to honour the Queenes Matie of England Ladye Elizabeth, bodily preferreth his choise & the excellencye of the subiect before all others of anye Poet auncient or moderne'.
> Vespasian E. VIII, ff. 169, 169v.
> 30 decasyllables in 3 stanzas rhyming abbabccb + 1 rhyming ababcc.

Youthfull bewtye, in body well disposed
What lackt her highnes them to all erthly
blisse.
> Puttenham, George.
> 'Parthe[naides] 3 Erato. That her Ma*jest*ie
> (two thinges except) hath all partes that
> iustly make to be sayd a most happy
> creature in this world'.
> Vespasian E. VIII, f. 169v.

16 decasyllables rhyming ababcdcdeeefgfgf.

Whome princes serve and Realmes obay
To serpentes hedd and angells face.
> Puttenham, George.
> 'Parthe[naides] 4: Thalia. That her
> Ma*jest*ie surmounteth all the Princesses of
> our tyme in wisedome bewtye and mag-
> nanimitye and ys a thynge very admirable
> in nature'.
> Vespasian E. VIII, f. 170.

18 octosyllables, in 3 stanzas rhyming ababcc. vv. 1–4
pr. in *Arte of English Poesie*, p. 161, introduced by:
'as we our selues wrote of our Soueraigne Lady
thus'.

The Phrigian youth full ill advised
So as thy raigne can no tyme cease.
> Puttenham, George.
> 'Parthe[naides] 5 Melpomene. That wise-
> dome in a princesse is to be preferred
> before bewtye riches honour or puis-
> saunce: but where all the partes concure
> in one *per*son as they doe moste evidently
> in hir Majestie the same is not to be
> reputed an humane, but rather a diuine
> *per*fection'.
> Vespasian E. VIII, ff. 170, 170v.

18 octosyllables in 3 stanzas rhyming ababcc.

Princesse ye haue the doome that I can
giue
T'addore all three godheads in your owne
starre.
> Puttenham, George.
> '[Parthenaides]. The addresse'.
> Vespasian E. VIII, f. 170v.

Heroic quatrain.

Fayre Britton may[d]e
Of youre bountee.
> Puttenham, George.
> 'Parthe[naides] 6 Melpomene. That virtue
> ys always suiect to envy and many times
> to perill and yf her Ma*jest*ies most notable
> prosperities haue ever beene maligned the
> same hath beene for her only vertues
> sake'.
> Vespasian E. VIII, ff. 170v, 171.

30 verses of varying lengths in 5 stanzas rhyming
abccba. Final stanza, vv. 25–30, pr. in *Arte of English
Poesie*, p. 181, introduced by: 'as we in a
Partheniade...closed it vp with this *Epiphoneme*'.

I saw marche in a meadowe greene
What iolly dame this ladye is.
> Puttenham, George.
> 'Parthe[naides] 7 Euterpe. A ryddle of the
> princesse Paragon'.
> Vespasian E. VIII, ff. 171–172.

26 octosyllabic couplets. vv. 5–8, 13–16, 9–12, 25–28
pr. in *Arte of English Poesie*, pp. 204–5; and vv. 47–50
ibid., p. 180, introduced by: 'These are our verses in
the end of the seuenth *Partheniade*', and 'Thus in the
latter end of a *Partheniade*'.

This fleshe and bloode this head members
and harte
Hye and beholde a while the mayden
Queene.
> Puttenham, George.
> 'The assoile'.
> Vespasian E. VIII, f. 172.

6 decasyllables rhyming ababab.

A hed harbroughe of all counsayle & witt
And bidd repulse of the great Britton
Mayde.
> Puttenham, George.
> 'Parthe[naides] 8 Thalia. The assoile at
> large moralized in three Dizaynes'.
> Vespasian E. VIII, ff. 172, 172v.

30 decasyllables in 3 stanzas rhyming (1)
ababcbbcdd; (2) abbaabcdcd; and (3) abaabccbdd.
vv. 5–6 pr. in *Arte of English Poesie*, p. 217.

In fruitfull soyle beholde a flower sproonge
Why fades this flower, and leaues noe fruit
nor seede.
Puttenham, George.
'[Parthenaides 9]. A verye strange and
rufull vision presented to the authore, the
interpretation wherof was left to her Matie
till by the purpose discovered'.
Vespasian E. VIII, ff. 172v, 173.
15 decasyllables rhyming ababbcbcddedfef.

A royall shippe I sawe by tyde and by
winde
Thow strike mizzen and anker in his porte.
Puttenham, George.
'Parthe[naides] 10 Calliope. Another
vision happned to the same authore as
Comfortable & recreatyve as the former
was dolorous'.
Vespasian E. VIII, f. 173.
16 decasyllables rhyming ababacacdccedffd.

Oh mightye Muse
Which cannot dye.
Puttenham, George.
'Parthe[naides] 11 Urania. That her
Majesties most woorthye renowne can not
perishe, while the worlde shall laste, with
certayne philosophicall opinions touchinge the begininge and durabilitye of the
worlde'.
Vespasian E. VIII, ff. 173–174.
60 verses of varying lengths in 7 stanzas of 8 ll. + 1
stanza of 4 ll.

Not youre bewty, most gratious soveraigne
To conquer all, and be conquerd by none.
Puttenham, George.
'Parthe[naides] 12 Urania. What causes
mooved so many forreinge Princes to bee
sutours to her Majestie for marriage, and
what by coniecture hath hitherto, mooved
her to refuse them all'.
Vespasian E. VIII, ff. 174–175.
40 decasyllables in 4 stanzas of varying rhyme-
scheme. This and the following five pieces all
preceded by statement of 'Purpose' and prose
headnote. vv. 1–30 pr. in *Arte of English Poesie*,
pp. 186–7; and vv. 37–40 in p. 180.

Princesse my Muse thought not amys
Confoundinge all to make a Chaos quite.
Puttenham, George.
'Parthe[naides] 13 Thalia. What thinges
in nature, common reason and cyvill
pollicye goe so faste linked together as
they maye not esilye bee soonedred
without preiudice to the politike bodye
whatsoever evill or absurditye seeme in
them'.
Vespasian E. VIII, ff. 175, 175v.
24 octosyllabic couplets.

Deny honoure to dignitye
Greene wooddes from forrests, and sunne
shine from the daye.
Puttenham, George.
'Parthe[naides] 14 Calliope. That amonge
men many thinges be allowed of neces-
sitye, many for ornament which cannot be
misliked nor well spared without blemishe
to the cyvile life'.
Vespasian E. VIII, f. 176.
12 mainly octosyllabic couplets.

Builde me of bowghes a little bower
In myne from everye other Queene.
Puttenham, George.
'Parthe[naides] 15. That her Matie is the
onlye paragon of princes in this oure age'.
Vespasian E. VIII, ff. 176, 176v.
10 octosyllabic couplets. vv. 9–14, 19, 20 pr. in *Arte
of English Poesie*, p. 196, as 'in the eighteene
Partheniade'.

As faulcon fares to bussardes flighte
The famoust Queene that ever was.
Puttenham, George.
'Parthe[naides] 16 Euterpe. A comparison
shewinge her Majesties superexcellency in
all regal vertues'.
Vespasian E. VIII, f. 176v.
4 octosyllabic couplets. vv. 1–8 pr. in *Arte of English
Poesie*, p. 196, introduced by: 'as when we sang
of our Soueraigne Lady thus, in the twentieth
Partheniade'.

O Pallas. Goddesse soverayne
Takinge for one thys hymne of myne.
>Puttenham, George.
>'[Parthenaides]. An hymne or divine prayse under the title of the goddesse Palas settinge foorthe hir majesties commendation for her wisedome & glorious governement in the single lief'.
>Vespasian E. VIII, ff. 177–178.

55 octosyllabic couplets.

Vitellius A. XVI

Anonymous chronicle of London; 1509. Pr. as The Great Chronicle of London, *ed. A. H. Thomas…and I. D. Thornley, 1938. Ownership inscription (f. 2) of 'Robertus Cotton Bruceus'. Contents list (f. 1) in hand of unidentified Cotton scribe.*

I katerynn of the Court Celestyall
that one for your noble Spouse & that
other for you.
>'The speche of Saynt Katerynn'.
>Vitellius A. XVI, ff. 184v–195.

378 verses in 54 rhyme royal stanzas. BR 1322.8. Ringler TM 652. Title on f. 184 followed by a Latin elegiac couplet. Entertainment in verse, recited at reception of Catharine of Aragon in London, 12 Nov. 1501. Pr. *ed. cit.*, pp. 297–305. On the marriage of Prince Arthur and Catharine of Aragon, 14 Nov. 1501.

London thou art, of Townes A per se
London thou art the Flower of Cities all.
>Vitellius A. XVI, ff. 200–201.

56 verses in 7 Monk's Tale stanzas. BR 1933.5. Ringler TM 922. Spoken at a royal banquet in Westminster Hall, 19 Nov. 1501, when 'one of the said Scottes giuyng attendaunce upon a Bisshop …made the Balade folowyng'. Formerly attrib. to William Dunbar, but rejected by J. W. Baxter, *William Dunbar*, 1952, p. 225, and in Dunbar's *Poems*, ed. James Kinsley, Oxford, 1979. Pr. *ed. cit.*, pp. 316–317. In praise of London.

Vitellius C. IX

Composite collection of historical tracts; circa 1559–1575. Contents list (f. 1) in hand of Richard James.

ff. 63v–128. Christopher Watson's ecclesiastical history of Durham, 1575.

Ass Thebe to Amphion yealdes, Immortall
lawde & praysse
⟨Of all that haue⟩ that dothe or shall, ther
lyve he merytes beste.
>Richard Cavendish.
>'Ri: Cauend: to the contye of Duresme'.
>Vitellius C. IX, f. 63v.

23 fourteener couplets. *Fair copy*, apparently in hand of Christopher Watson, with revisions. Final 3 verses added in different ink, and further verses, copied sideways in the margin, subsequently deleted. Dated 'finis 20 Januarii Anno 1574[/5]'. Commendatory verses on Watson's history.

While pagan poets seacke the prayse of
foolishe fitings strange
And florishinge all figures trye; to furnishe
out ther forgerye.
>[Watson, Christopher].
>['Geta…of whome Sedulius that excellent and Christian poett (in paschali carmine) hath these wordes in sence and substance'].
>Vitellius C. IX, f. 106.

4 verses rhyming aa^{14}bb^{8}. Precis of Sedulius, *Carmen Paschale*, I, ll. 1–6. On the Roman Emperor Geta (189–212).

Asse Thebæ to Amphion yealdes, Immortall lawde & praisse
Of all that haue, that do, or shall, ther
lyve, he meryttes beste.
>Richard Cavendish.
>'Th'istorye of Duresme, longe drow⟨ned in the voradge⟩ of obliuion; nowe first recouerid out ⟨of⟩ the soylle of sacrid Antyquitye, bye the travell and charges of Christopher Wats⟨on⟩ Deiragrantus 1574. Ætat sue .29.'.
>Vitellius C. IX, ff. 127, 127v.

23 fourteener couplets. *Fair copy*, apparently in the hand of Christopher Watson. Subscribed 'Carolus Constance' (f. 127v); but see attribution on f. 63v. Missing words in title supplied from f. 128. Commendatory verses on Watson's history.

Aurea nunc tandem leguntur scripta Deiræ;
Cuius te nunquam penituisse potest.
    Brandol⟨?⟩, Gabriel.
    Vitellius C. IX, f. 127v.
9 elegiac couplets. Subscribed 'Gabriel Brandol:'. Commendatory verses on Watson's history.

ff. 188v–199. Latin verses by John Harpsfield (d. 1578), described in Planta's Catalogue (1802) as 'Versus elegiaci, ex centuriis summatim comprehensi, de Historia Ecclesiastica Anglorum'.

⟨-⟩ Ioseph
Dum fuerit monachus, condidit historiam.
    Harpsfield, John.
    Vitellius C. IX, ff. 188v–199.
Approx. 457 elegiac couplets. *Autograph. Imperfect*, title and all but final word of first verse missing owing to charring of leaf. Lines authorially numbered, each page separately. On the history of the church in England, in fifteen sections ('*Secuta*'), carried up to Wolsey's foundation of Christ Church, Oxford, in 1525.

Vitellius C. XVII

Miscellaneous state papers; circa *early 16th cent.–1623.*

O heauenly god and father dere cast downe thy tender eye
That after deathe my soule maye haue in heauen a dwelling place.
    [Kinwelmersh, Francis].
    Vitellius C. XVII, f. 380.
12 fourteener couplets. *Imperfect*, first and last two words of first verse missing owing to mutilation: supplied from Vespasian A. XXV, ff. 143v, 144, above. Follows 'The discowrse of the Earle of Essex on his death 1576' (ff. 367–376: title given in docket, by different hand, on f. 381v). Crum O485. Pr., with attrib. to F[rancis] K[inwelmersh], in *The Paradyse of Daynty Devises*, 1576, where it is pr. as 'O Heavenly God, O Father dere, cast doun thy tender eye': see edn. of H. E. Rollins, Cambridge, Mass., 1927, pp. 95, 351. The copy made by William Cole from a MS. seen in 1773, now in Add. MS. 5845, ff. 171–176v, is signed 'E.L.'. Pr. by Seng, *ed. cit.*, p. 49. Deathbed plea for god's mercy.

Vitellius E. X

Miscellaneous collection of tracts, in prose and verse; circa 15th–16th cent. Contents list (f. 1) in hand of unidentified Cotton scribe.

ff. 76v–78. Latin and English poems attributed to George Buchanan in the later index (f. 1), as 'Carmina aliquot Buchanani, et Latinè, et Anglicè'. The Latin verses are copied in Italic and the English in Secretary script. For description of contents see I. D. McFarlane, *loc. cit.*

Aulæ eadem est omnino ⟨fides, quæ nobilis auræ⟩
Zenones fatui sunt atque Thrasones in Aula.
    Buchanan, George.
    Vitellius E. X, ff. 76v, 77.
23 hexameters. *Imperfect*: first verse, in which all but first four words are missing owing to mutilation, supplied from Corpus Christi College, Oxford, MS. CCLVII, f. 55v. Verses 8–9 added in margin of f. 77, beside ll. 7–8 of the English version that follows. Subscribed 'G. Buchanon'. See McFarlane, p. 316, where the verses are described as 'alphabetum aulicum'. Satire on court life.

As winde which constant never bides, such fayth in Courte is founde
Zeno the wise, and Terence knyght in Court both fools a like.
    Buchanan, George.
    'G. B. Court. A. B. C. English'.
    Vitellius E. X, ff. 76v–77v.
11 fourteener couplets. English version of above (ff. 76v, 77). In the Corpus MS. the first line runs 'As winde that never constant is, such faith in courte we find'. Alphabetical verses. Satire on court life.

Bissina quod vestis multo tibi splendeat auro
Delitiis solida hæc nimirum et gloria sola est.
    Buchanan, George.
    'Alia carmina latina'.
    Vitellius E. X, f. 77v.
21 hexameters. *Imperfect*, all but first three words of final verse missing owing to mutilation of leaf: supplied from text in Caligula B. V, f. 271v, above. On a clear conscience.

To shin in silke and glitter all in goulde
Which beinge had a rush for all the rest.
> Buchanan, George.
> Vitellius E. X, f. 78.

21 decasyllables in 3 stanzas rhyming ababccdd. See
Caligula B. V, f. 271, above. On a clear conscience.

Appendix L

Miscellaneous state letters and papers; circa
1524–1637.

Immodest death, that wouldst not once
Conferre,
Was faine to yeald to death, good Lord
twas so.
> '1608 An Epitaph one the death of
> Thomas Sackuile Lord Buckhurst Earle of
> Dorset & Lord Treasurar of England who
> died Suddainly at the Counsell table at
> whitehall 19ᵗʰ. Aprilis 1608 as he was
> Speaking in his owne Cause against Sir
> John Lawson Knight'.
> Appendix L, f. 169.

5 decasyllabic couplets. Concludes: 'Finis'. Crum
I1182. Satirical verses on Thomas Sackville, 1st Earl
of Dorset.

Appendix LVIII

*Letters to Sir Thomas Cotton and Sir John Cotton,
2nd and 3rd Barts., 1630–1684, n.d.*

Gratia pro tanto reddatur munere magno
Si mihi condones gratia major erit.
> [? Cotton, William].
> Appendix LVIII, f. 68.

Elegiac couplet. Concludes a letter to his father
apparently written from Winchester College, *circa*
1660–1663. Not certainly of his own composition.
Address of gratitude to Sir Thomas Cotton, 2nd
Bart.

Appendix LXII

*William Camden's notebook of forty-six (numbered)
compositions in Latin verse and prose, incorporating
letters and themes written while at Christ Church,
Oxford; circa 1569–1571.* Autograph. *The collection
begins (ff. 2, 2v) with 'Xenia, Calendis Januar. 1569',*

*that is, New Year's verses addressed to various Masters
of Arts of Christ Church on 1 Jan. 1569/70.*

Accipe pro dono votum, mentemque fide-
lem
Qui cupio nequeo, det deus, ille potest.
> Camden, William.
> 'Mʳᵒ Jameso'.
> Appendix LXII, f. 2.

2 elegiac couplets. To William James.

Omnia quæ dantur pro donis carmina,
Ioui
Quot voluere breues, singula metra, dies.
> Camden, William.
> 'Mʳᵒ Dorsetto'.
> Appendix LXII, f. 2.

2 elegiac couplets. To Robert Dorsett.

Thus, mirrha, ac aurum qui donabatur ab
illo
Vita, salus, cælum, sint data, dona ⟨tibi⟩.
> Camden, William.
> 'Mʳᵒ Busto'.
> Appendix LXII, f. 2.

Elegiac distich. Followed immediately by two illegible lines, not certainly verse. To John Bust.

⟨——⟩ mihi nil, sed totum me
tibi dono
Mortuus atque tuus si modo possis, ero.
> Camden, William.
> 'Mʳᵒ Thorntono'.
> Appendix LXII, f. 2v.

2 elegiac couplets. To Thomas Thornton.

⟨Sit⟩ tibi vita diu, sit semper blanda
salusque
Et celso cælo, post moriere, locus.
> Camden, William.
> 'Mʳᵒ Turnero'.
> Appendix LXII, f. 2v.

Elegiac distich. First word of first verse supplied
conjecturally. To William Turner.

Quot tibi non nolim, tot felix sæcula viuas:
Tot valeasque veni, quot velis ipse dies.
> Camden, William.
> 'Mʳᵒ Dew'.
> Appendix LXII, f. 2v.

Elegiac distich. To Richard Dew.

Si velis, & cupias tibi vitæ tempora longa
Viuas mille tuis, millia multa deo.
    Camden, William.
    'Eidem [i.e. M^{ro} Dew]'.
    Appendix LXII, f. 2v.
Elegiac distich. To Richard Dew.

Est tibi musæum latum, facies quoque
                    lata,
Os tutum lato nam cupit esse lato.
    Camden, William.
    'J Wordæo'.
    Appendix LXII, f. 3v.
Elegiac distich. To Isaac Worde (B.A. 15 Jan.
1570/1).

Discere Grammaticam, si uis, ne discito
                  Græce
Ad summam, graculis debentur nulla
                Pelasgis.
    Camden, William.
    'Ad Græcæ linguæ studiosum'.
    Appendix LXII, ff. 3v, 4.
17 hexameters. Admonition against the learning of
Greek.

Quot sunt hoc compto sublimia metra
                 lib⟨ello⟩
Innumeris fælix sit tua vita bonis.
    Camden, William.
    'Ad P S. cum Horat.'.
    Appendix LXII, f. 4v.
2 elegiac couplets. Composed to accompany the gift
of a volume of Horace's poems, probably to Sir Philip
Sidney who was an undergraduate at Christ Church
circa Feb. 1568–April 1571.

Quis fuit, ille tibi fidus amicus erit
⟨————————————————⟩
    Camden, William.
    'N C.'.
    Appendix LXII, f. 4v.
Elegiac distich: pentameter largely illegible.
Imperfect, owing to mutilation of leaf.

⟨Cum⟩ tibi tot versus, & hunc pro munere
                 librum
Est memor ille tui, tu memor esto sui.
    Camden, William.
    'Jacobo Lantdspergero Germ. ⟨-⟩'.
    Appendix LXII, f. 5.
Elegiac distich.

Pastor egenus habet telum, sed vendidit
                  agrum
Pastor egenus miles, miles arator ⟨erit⟩.
    William Camden.
    Appendix LXII, f. 5v.
2 elegiac couplets. Final word of last line supplied
conjecturally.

Quis tu? non nosti, sum præclarissima
                  virtus
Vixero sed semper, tu moriere cito.
    Camden, William.
    'Virtutis discriptio ex Anglico'.
    Appendix LXII, f. 9v.
4 elegiac couplets. This and the verses immediately
following are translations of an English poem by
Grimald pr. in *Tottel's Miscellany*, 1557 (no. 149 in
the edition of H. E. Rollins, Cambridge, Mass.,
1928–9), and in Kendall's *Flowers of Epigrams*, 1577.
Grimald's English was in turn a rendering of an
epigram of Theodore Beza (*Poemata*, 1548, p. 68).

Quis tu tam pauper, sic pannis obsita,
                 quis tu
Non ego sum mortis, cætera mortis erunt.
    Camden, William.
    'Aliter'.
    Appendix LXII, f. 9v.
6 elegiac couplets.

Ver spargit flores, Autumnus pomifer uvas
Dat segetes Æstas, frigora tristis hiems.
    Camden, William.
    Appendix LXII, f. 9v.
Elegiac distich. On the seasons of the year.

Qui scribunt vitam, diuino numine pleni,
Postremum librum scripsit ut ipse viuit.
    Camden, William.
    Appendix LXII, ff. 10v, 11.
19 elegiac couplets. On the Acts of the Apostles.

Fragments XXXII

*Miscellaneous fragments, incorporating items formerly
in Appendix XLV.*

Et Domi vinctos flagris cedet
Qui servare cupimus ad mortem festin-
                  antem virum.
    Fragments XXXII, ff. 22–28.

749 verses. *Imperfect* at beginning owing to loss of leaf, and at end where they conclude abruptly; with loss of text at foot of all leaves from fire. Text, copied in one variable hand, occupies thirteen pages of a notebook that includes extracts from Holinshed's *Chronicle* (1578). Anonymous translation of Sophocles' *Ajax*, ll. 64–812, possibly to be identified with Latin tragedy *Ajax Flagellifer* intended to be staged at Cambridge University before Elizabeth I on 9 August 1564, but never performed: see *Records of Early English Drama: Cambridge*, ed. Alan H. Nelson, 2 vols., Toronto, 1989, pp. 231, 235, 238, etc. Described in Planta's Catalogue (1802), Appendix XLV, art.7, as 'Opusculi dramatici fragmentum'.

Mishap doth hold the helme, the sens mi
                ship doth shake
I will not long be from her sight, on whom
                mi hart is sett.
[Herthe, William].
Fragments XXXII: unfoliated, item i in folder labelled 7(a–i).

16 rhymed couplets in poulter's measure. Copied on both sides of the leaf in a Secretary hand, with subscription in Italic script 'Alpha & omega. Quod W. Herthe. R.'. Followed by Latin prose, beg. 'Maior sum quam Cui fortuna nocere potest...'. Complaint couched as the allegory of a stormy sea-voyage.

INDICES TO HANDLIST OF POST-MEDIAEVAL COTTON VERSE

(1) Index of First Lines and Refrains

In the 'Index of First Lines and Refrains' the orthography of the manuscript is retained but the arrangement, alphabetical by word, runs according to modern spelling. Thus, 'Yf' occurs in the sequence as 'If', 'Syke' as 'Sick' and 'Whan' as 'When'. Standard practice is followed with regard to Latin, 'Quum' being rendered as 'Cum', 'Faecunda' as 'Fecunda', 'Hec' as 'Haec' and 'Maenia' as 'Moenia'. Again, where the first word begins with an 'I' having the modern value of 'J' it will be listed under 'J'. English and Latin vocative 'A' is indexed as 'Ah' to distinguish it from the indefinite article, with 'O' treated as 'Oh'. Acephalous verses are listed alphabetically by first or only surviving word in a separate section at the end. Refrains are signalled as such in brackets after each entry.

A bonne god wote	Vespasian A. XXV, f. 159v.
A Christo virtus virtutis et optima merces	Julius F. XI, f. 202v.
A dolefull time of wepinge teares	Caligula B. IV, ff. 247, 247v.
A famous Isle, of riches great, while Priamus Kingedome stoode,	Julius F. X, f. 61v.
A hed harbroughe of all counsayle & witt	Vespasian E. VIII, ff. 172, 172v.
A horse chuying on the brydle	Vespasian A. XXV, f. 140.
A man may liue thris Nestors lyfe	Titus A. XXIV, f. 80v.
A royall shippe I sawe by tyde and by winde	Vepasian E. VIII, f. 173.
Above the fiere	
v. Man to redeme & not angell	
Accipe pro dono votum, mentemque fidelem	Appendix LXII, f. 2.
Ad Boream porrecta, jugis obsessa superbis	Vespasian D. IX, f. 173v.
After droght commythe rayne	Vespasian A. XXV, f. 125.
Aggredior matrem summi celebrare Tonantis	Julius F. X, ff. 69, 69v.
Hagnes hic iaceo coniux olim Gulielmi	Julius F. X, f. 71v.

373

Agnes Tidenham married first to Thomas Marshall, then	Faustina E. V, f. 183v.
Ah sic peribit immiserabilis	Titus A. XIII, ff. 171v, 172.
Amplector, Rogere, tuum vehementer amorem	Caligula D. I, f. 33v.
An ende of this book, or of this Rude werk	Nero C. XI, f. 462.
An yll yeare of a Goodyer us bereft	Julius F. XI, f. 85.
Anglia quæ multo fueras suppressa dolore	Titus A. XXIV, f. 94.
Anglia quæ nuper sævis quassata procellis	Titus A. XXIV, f. 92v.
Anglia quem genuit, fueratque habitura patronum	Julius F. XI, f. 86v.
Anglica lætetur pubes, lætare Maria	Titus A. XXIV, f. 93v.
Anglorum teneat quæ regia sceptra potentem	Titus A. XXIV, f. 93v.
Anna beat numen votis; dominum canit Anna	Julius C. V, f. 327.
Anna fuit Phænix mundi; coniux Jovis Anna	Julius C. V, f. 327.
Anna rex regnat, regitabat Anna	Julius C. V, f. 327.
Anna soror soror Anna suæ charissima Elisæ	Julius F. X, ff. 115, 115v.
Armata telis dexteram,	Caligula B. X (pt. ii), f. 260.
As faulcon fares to bussardes flighte	Vespasian E. VIII, f. 176v.
As frendes to frendes, so greteng we yow sende	Titus A. XXIV, ff. 98v, 99.
As I lay musing all alone	Vespasian A. XXV, ff. 144, 144v.
A⟨s I sat⟩ vpon astrawe	Vespasian A. XXV, f. 126v.
As marche did ende so mars begane his rayne	Caligula B. V, ff. 365–382v.
As said the prophet a bacuce	Vespasian A. XXV, ff. 129, 129v.
Ass Thebe to Amphion yealdes, Immortall lawde & praysse	
	Vitellius C. IX, ff. 63v; 127, 127v.
As winde that never constant is, such faith in courte we find	
v. As winde which constant never bides, such fayth in Courte is founde	
	Vitellius E. X, ff. 76v–77v.
Aspice (quisquis ades) Reginæ insignia pulchra	Julius F. VI, f. 379.
Aulæ eadem est omnino fides, quæ nobilis auræ	Vitellius E. X, f. 76v.
Aurea nunc tandem leguntur scripta Deiræ	Vitellius C. IX, f. 127v.
Aureolis Urbs picta rosis: mons molliter Urbi	Vespasian D. IX, f. 175.
Aureus ille leo (reliqui trepidate leones)	Julius F. XI, f. 94.
Awak ye wofull wightes	Vespasian A. XXV, ff. 135, 135v.
I there were men which then did say	Julius F. X, f. 67v.
Balnea, Vina, Venus, corrumpunt corpora nostra	Julius C. III, f. 164v.
Behould as rewfull ratlyffe died	Vespasian A. XXV, f. 158v.
Bissina quod vestis multo tibi splendeat auro	Caligula B. V, f. 271v;
	Vitellius E. X, f. 77v.
Builde me of bowghes a little bower	Vespasian E. VIII, ff. 176, 176v.
But now a while of him I speake no more	Julius F. XI, f. 307.
By reason of two & poore of one	Vespasian A. XXV, ff. 131v–132v.
By west off late as I dyd walke in the pryme tyme of the day	
	Vespasian A. XXV, ff. 140v–142.
Cælitus hoc, Regina, parens augusta Jacobi	Titus B. VIII, f. 227.

Cælo minax vis mole ruit sua,	Titus A. XIII, ff. 172v–173v.
Calculus exesit mihi vivo in Corpore renes	Faustina E. V, f. 170.
Cales cælestis pars terræ reddita terra	Julius F. XI, f. 96v.
Calta velut flores tenebris sub noctis opacæ	Caligula B. V, f. 320.
Carole christigenum decus et quem scripta loquuntur	Julius F. X, f. 73.
Carole Germanie gentis decus Hesperieque	Julius F. X, f. 70v.
Carole qui fulges sceptro et diademate sacro	Julius F. X, f. 73.
Casta decens, generosa animi Phænisa peregi	Caligula B. V, f. 268.
Castitas blandi domitrix amoris	Caligula B. X (pt. ii), f. 259v.
Cernis uti Oceanus prono ruit obvius æstu,	Vespasian D. IX, ff. 172, 172v.
Cryste of the theeff, whych on thy Rygth hand was	Nero C. XI, f. 47v.
Cognatas acies & tela minantia telis	
v. Cur iam cognatas acies & prælia pandis	
Coll standyth...	Titus D. XI, f. 56v.
Concidit Henricus flos famæ, gloria Gentis.	Julius C. V, f. 290.
Conde tibi tumulum. nec fide heredis amori	Faustina E. V, f. 176v;
	Julius F. XI, f. 88.
Conditur in tumulo gratis qui nil dedit unquam	Faustina E. V, f. 170.
Consortium audax omnia perpetj	Titus A. XIII, ff. 168v–170.
Consuluit Phæbum nuper Cecilius Heros	Claudius C. II, f. 339.
Cum mihi quod donem nil sit, tibi resque supersit	Caligula D. I, f. 35.
Cum patre Radulpho Babthorp iacet ecce Radulphus	Julius F. XI, f. 91v.
⟨Cum⟩ tibi tot versus, & hunc pro munere librum	Appendix LXII, f. 5.
Quum tormenta olim Siculis sudaret in antris	Caligula B. V, f. 320.
Cuncta Plato cecinit, tempus quae proferat ullum	Titus D. IV, f. 13
Cur iam cognatas acies & prælia pandis	Julius F. VI, f. 4.
Cur Meleager aprum neglecta vulpe fatigas	Julius C. III, f. 385.
De semisse, tricente annos, quadrantaque subduc	Faustina E. V, f. 178v.
Dei ouis placida, parentum agna	Cleopatra C. III, f. 50v;
	Faustina E. V, f. 180v.
Deny honoure to dignitye	Vespasian E. VIII, f. 176.
Desine Galle tuam tandem jactare Bubulcam	Julius C. V, f. 393.
Det Deus auspiciis propriis vt vivere possim	Julius C. III, f. 214.
Dicuntur numero septem sapientia quorum	Julius F. X, f. 71.
Digna hæc luce diuturniore	Faustina E. V, f. 162v;
	Julius F. XI, f. 88.
Dii summi quibus est sali solique	Julius F. XI, f. 134.
Discere Grammaticam, si uis, ne discito Græce	Appendix LXII, ff. 3v, 4.
Dona dabo Dominis divinis Dædala Dono	Julius C. V, f. 327v.
Drawe nere good frendes & list awhile	Vespasian A. XXV, ff. 162, 162v.
Dum parat Hesperiam volucri rex classe Philippus	Julius F. X, f. 72.
Dum peterent sacras Rex et Regina coronas	Titus D. IV, ff. 12, 12v.

Ecce arcto terræ in tumulo, exiguique Sepulchri   Faustina E. V, f. 170v.
Edwardi quarti Cano multa et lubrica bella   Julius C. II, ff. 106–263.
Ego ros campi in the feld   Vespasian A. XXV, f. 153.
Eheu recenti mens trepidat metu   Titus A. XIII, f. 166v.
En tibi cum Christo Jani rediere calende   Julius F. X, f. 71.
Est omnis mulier fallax malaque inquit Homerus   Julius F. X, f. 71.
Est tibi musæum latum, facies quoque lata   Appendix LXII, f. 3v.
Est tua penna quidem gratissima, penna videtur   Julius F. VI, f. 4.
Et decor et facies cum simplicitate modesta   Caligula B. V, f. 268v.
Et decor et facies cum simplicitate venusta
     v. Et decor et facies cum simplicitate modesta
Et Domi vinctos flagris cedet   Fragments XXXII, ff. 22–28.
Extinctum iacet hic genus a Plantagine ductum   Julius F. X, f. 70v.

Fayre Britton may[d]e   Vespasian E. VIII, ff. 170v, 171.
Fæcunda culpæ sæcula! Quod scelus   Titus A. XIII, f. 167.
Fælices homines queis Polyhimnia   Julius F. XI, f. 134.
Fidi, sagaces Consiliarii   Titus A. XIII, ff. 173v–174v.
Fyll the cuppe Phylyppe & let vs drynke a drame   Vespasian A. XXV, f. 37.
For first he is of limbs and bodie strong   Julius F. XI, f. 307.
Formosam, uiduam, ditemque in flore iuuentæ   Caligula B. V, f. 268.
Fornix stat amplus, qui Superae Domus   Titus A. XIII, ff. 170–171.
Fortune dubio non ego turbine   Julius F. X, f. 71v.
ffre ffretith this world, and de confoundeth alle   Nero C. XI, f. 77.

Gallia dum passim ciuilibus occidit armis   Caligula B. V, f. 41.
Geve eare my children to my wordes whom god haith dearly bought
     Vespasian A. XXV, ff. 145v–147v.
Gloria Franciscus generis præclara uetusti   Titus B. VIII, f. 291.
God helpe vs all god helpe vs all   Vespasian A. XXV, ff. 139, 139v.
God ys the cheffest vnizon   Vespasian A. XXV, f. 163v.
God shild vs from bane & bring vs to blithe
     v. When dearth decreasis & treason begynne
Good fortune is th'Horizon of thine ey   Titus C. VI, f. 183.
Gracious Princesse, Where princes are in place   Vespasian E. VIII, f. 169.
Gratia pro tanto reddatur munere magno   Appendix LVIII, f. 68.
Great heart whoe taught thee thus to die   Titus C. VII, f. 95.
Greeke Achilles, and his peeres did enioye   Vespasian E. VIII, ff. 169, 169v.
Guido bibendum nunc tibi liberè   Titus A. XIII, ff. 174v–175v.

Hec tibi clare Pater posuerunt marmora Cives   Julius F. X, f. 70.
Hagnes hic iaceo coniux olim Gulielmi
     v. above, as 'Agnes...'

376

Hardnes ys headstrong, and will not be hampered	Vespasian A. XXV, ff. 151, 151v.
He that lies heer was borne & cried	
v. Here lieth he, who was borne and cried	
Here Edward Cordell's body lies	Julius F. XI, f. 95v.
Here he lieth who was borne and cried	
v. Here lieth he, who was borne and cried	
Heer is Elderton lyeng in dust	Julius F. XI, f. 98.
Here lies Kit Craker, the kinge of good fellowes	
v. Here lyeth John Cruker a maker of Bellowes	
Here lies lord haue mercy vpon her	Faustina E. V, ff. 162v, 171.
Here lies old Craker a Maker of Bellowes	
v. Here lyeth John Cruker a maker of Bellowes	
Here lyes the man that madly slayne	Julius F. XI, f. 99.
Here lyes the man was borne and cried	
v. Here lieth he, who was borne and cried	
Here lies the man whos horse did gayne	Julius F. XI, f. 99.
Here lieth bald Dobson on the mould	Julius F. XI, f. 100.
Here lieth C under grownd	Julius F. XI, f. 99.
Here lyeth father Spargis	Julius F. XI, f. 98.
Here lyeth he	Julius F. XI, f. 100.
Here lieth he, who was borne and cried	Faustina E. V, f. 171v;
	Julius F. XI, f. 100.
Heer lyeth John Croker a maker of bellowes	
v. Here lyeth John Cruker a maker of Bellowes	
Here lyeth John Cruker a maker of Bellowes	Faustina E. V, f. 171;
	Julius F. XI, f. 98.
Heer lyeth Menalcas as dead as a logg	Julius F. XI, f. 95v.
Here lyeth of Errour, the prynce yf ye wyll ken	Nero C. XI, f. 140v.
Heer lyeth old Henry	Julius F. XI, f. 96.
Here lyeth Richard a Green	Julius F. XI, f. 99.
Here lyethe Richard Hill	Julius F. XI, f. 100.
Here lieth the B[ishop] whom the World did see	Julius F. XI, f. 100.
Here lieth the stark theefe J a Drones	Julius F. XI, f. 99.
Here lieth Thom Nickes body	Julius F. XI, f. 98.
Here lieth Willinge Wills	Julius F. XI, f. 100.
Here Thomas Tusser, clad in earth doth lye	Faustina E. V, f. 187.
Here under this Stone	Faustina E. V, f. 162v.
Here underneath entomb'd a Dazie lies	
v. Here lies lord haue mercy vpon her	
Heus Peripatetice	
v. Conde tibi tumulum. nec fide heredis amori	
Hic Dick Nowell ego	Julius F. XI, f. 88.
Hic Nicolaum ne Baconum conditum	Julius F. XI, f. 87.

Hic sita Redmanni sunt ossa ô candide lector	Cleopatra C. III, f. 12v.
Hic situs est cuius vox, vultus, actio possit	Julius F. XI, f. 92.
Hic situs est sitiens, atque Ebrius Eldertonus	Julius F. XI, f. 98.
His bones here rest shall in a chest whome Redman men did call	
	Cleopatra C. III, ff. 13, 13v.
Ho who lies heere	Faustina E. V, f. 170v.
Ho who lies heer for a groate	Faustina E. V, f. 170v.
Hoc tibi quæ misit cor, nil quod posset habebat	Caligula D. I, f. 36.
Hospes siste gradum hos et numeros lege	Cleopatra C. III, f. 13.
Huius percelebris decus et spes vnica sedis	Julius F. X, f. 70.
Hunc fontem domini concessione sacrauit	Julius C. III, f. 164v.
Hunc Ransforte tuo cineri Bucananus honorem	Caligula D. I, f. 32v.
I am a poore sheperd yet borne of hye blode	Vespasian A. XXV, f. 145.
I katerynn of the Court Celestyall	Vitellius A. XVI, ff. 184v–195.
I Liue that dieth everey houre	Titus A. XXIV, ff. 99, 99v.
I saw marche in a meadowe greene	Vespasian E. VIII, ff. 171–172.
I selly crosse that here do stande	Vespasian A. XXV, f. 159.
I there were men which then did say	
v. above, as if 'Aye...'	
I was the first mad christendom see	Julius F. XI, f. 99.
Iff Excellence of wytt, or Grace of good vertu	Nero C. XI, ff. 76v–77.
If Momus children seke to knowe my name and where I dwell	Caligula C. I, f. 364.
Yf musing thos that do behould my woe, & rufull staite	
	Vespasian A. XXV, ff. 157v, 157, 156v.
If tongue would tell or you could write, the craftie cloaked case	
	Caligula C. I, ff. 364–365v.
Illa procax Mori lingua irreuerenter in omnes	Caligula B. V, f. 268.
Imminet Oceano, paribus descripta viarum	Vespasian D. IX, f. 174v.
Immiti a domino Maurus tractatus in igne	Titus B. VI, f. 10v.
Immodest death, that wouldst not once Conferre	Appendix L, f. 169.
Imperii veteris duo propugnacula quondam,	Vespasian D. IX, f. 176.
In extremity and when	Titus C. VII, f. 26.
In fruitfull soyle beholde a flower sproonge	Vespasian E. VIII, ff. 172v, 173.
In Paschall feast the ende of auncient right	Titus C. VI, ff. 535–536v.
In sommer tyme I dyd prepare	Vespasian A. XXV, ff. 161v, 162.
Inclita Johannes Londine gloria gentis	Julius F. X, f. 70.
Innuba quæ fueras papistica, iuncta marito	Caligula D. I, f. 35.
Ys love this Idle busynes (refrain)	
v. A horse chuying on the brydle	
It befell at martynmas	Vespasian A. XXV, ff. 178–179.
It is not pride I lie so high	Julius F. XI, f. 93.
It was a maide of my countre	Vespasian A. XXV, ff. 154v, 155.
Iam satis terræ sua ferit Angliæ	Titus A. XXIV, f. 92.

Jana reciprocicornis, origo mensis, et anni	Julius C. V, f. 23.
Iane pater solus partes qui uersus in omnes	Caligula D. I, f. 34.
Iesus Soter Salvat Servat Sacrat Iesus	Julius C. V, f. 327v.
Johannes cubat hic Sextinus marmore clausus	Julius F. X, f. 72v.
Johannes Redmannus humo tumulatus in ista	Cleopatra C. III, f. 13v.
John Bell Brokenbrow liggs vnder this stean	Faustina E. V, f. 165v.
Juelle mater quem tulit Deuonia	Caligula B. V, f. 320v.
Iunior ense rui, fueram tunc ensifer virj	Julius F. XI, f. 91v.
Iure Scotos, thalamo Francos, spe possidet Anglos	
v. Obruta frugifero sensim sic cespite surgunt	
Ius summum sæuum est, ius summum iniuria summa	Julius F. XI, f. 135v.
Iusticia insignes tres olim nomine reges	Julius F. X, f. 70.
King Penda a paynym as writinge sayth	Titus B. VIII, ff. 323–324.
Læta quid gestis populi britanni	Titus A. XXIV, ff. 94v, 95.
Leticiæ quantum miniis præbebat Iason	Julius F. X, f. 73.
Layde in my quiet bed in studye as hit were	Titus A. XXIV, f. 83.
Lanigeros quâ lata greges Cottswoldia pascit	Julius F. XI, f. 208.
Laudat magnanimos urbs inclita roma catones	Julius F. X, f. 73.
Laurencius adest ille dum Campegius	Julius F. X, f. 73v.
Lerne this lesson in welthe and woo	Vespasian A. XXV, ff. 39v–40v.
Let come good Lord what pleasse the shall	
v. The happiest man that nowe dost lyve	
Lygth into the world, now doth spryng & shyne	Nero C. XI, f. 405.
Like as the day his course dothe consume	Faustina E. V, f. 186.
Lycke as the Towche doowyth trewly trey	Vespasian A. XXV, ff. 148v.
Loo here is notyd, and putt in memory	Nero C. XI, ff. 373–374.
Londinum gemino procurrit litore longe	
v. Thamisis, et subito placide ridentibus undis	
London thou art, of Townes A per se	Vitellius A. XVI, ff. 200–201.
Longe haue I bene a singinge man	Vespasian A. XXV, ff. 132v–133.
Looke man before thee how thy death hasteth	Julius F. XI, f. 86.
Lucifer in cælo stella fulgentior omni	Julius F. X, f. 72v.
Magna ortu, maior sponsa, sed maxima partu	
v. Magna ortu, maior virtutis honore Maria	
Magna ortu, maior virtutis honore Maria	Caligula C. IX (pt. ii), f. 629.
Magne minorque dei quanquam mihi magnus uterque	Titus B. VI, f. 249v.
Man to redeme & not angell	Vespasian A. XXV, ff. 130v, 131.
Marche out godes soldiours	Vespasian A. XXV, ff. 150v, 151.
Mars Venerem secum deprensam fraude maritj	Julius F. XI, f. 106v.
Martiall, the thinges that do attayn	
v. My frende the thinges that do attayne	

Me natam coluit Reginam Scotia, Regi   Caligula C. IX (pt. ii), f. 629.
Metra retro recte cev tessellaria versant   Julius C. V, f. 327v.
Mille petita procis totidem repetita carinis   Caligula B. V, f. 268v.
Mira alto Pecco tria sunt, barathrum, specus, antrum   Julius F. VI, f. 311.
Mira canam, soles quot continet arvus, in vna   Titus F. VII, f. 26.
Mishap doth hold the helme, the sens mi ship doth shake

                               Fragments XXXII, folder 7(i).

Mænia tuta loco fertur posuisse Gradivus   Vespasian D. IX, f. 173.
Monstra Peco tria sunt alto, Barathrum, specus, anthrum   Julius C. III, f. 164.
Monte sub acclini Zephyri procurrit in auras   Vespasian D. IX, ff. 173, 173v.
Munera quæ tibi dem Jani Mildreda Calendis   Caligula D. I, f. 34.
Munera quæ tibi do Jani Mildreda Calendis
    v. Munera quæ tibi dem Jani Mildreda Calendis
Musarum soboles, decus immortale parentis   Titus B. VIII, f. 291.
My fance fanned onne me somwhat of ye to see   Titus A. XXIV, f. 83v.
My frend iudg not mee   Julius F. XI, f. 95.
My frende the thinges that do attayne   Titus A. XXIV, f. 80.
My prime of youth is but a frost of care   Cleopatra A. IV, f. 11.

Ne peto condoleas, rex o rex comprime luctus   Julius C. V, f. 290.
Newes newes newes newes (burden)
    v. A⟨s I sat⟩ vpon astrawe
Ni Mildreda tui viri patrisque   Caligula D. I, ff. 34, 34v.
Nil decus aut splendor nil regia nomina prosunt   Cleopatra C. III, f. 18.
No tyme dothe that stintethe teares and weares out woo
    v. No tyme that stintethe teares and weares out woo
No tyme that stintethe teares and weares out woo   Cleopatra C. III, ff. 10v–11v.
No welthe, no prayse, no bright renowne, no skill   Faustina E. V, f. 187–187v.
Non de plebe aliquis Reginæ hos consecro uersus   Titus A. XIII, f. 179.
Non hæc minorj conueniunt Lyræ   Titus A. XIII, f. 177.
Non me materies facit superbum   Caligula D. I, f. 36.
Non nostra impietas, aut actæ crimina vitæ   Julius F. XI, f. 94v.
Non te Pontificum luxus, non Insula tantum   Vespasian D. IX, f. 174v.
Not youre bewty, most gratious soveraigne   Vespasian E. VIII, ff. 174–175.
Now lesten a whyle & let hus singe   Vespasian A. XXV, ff. 143, 143v.
Now wold I ffayn   Nero C. XI, ff. 30v–31v.
Nulla fides terris, fraus improba regnat ubique   Julius F. XI, f. 219.

Ob quorum adventum toties gens ipsa britanna   Julius F. X, f. 73v.
Obruta frugifero sensim sic cespite surgunt   Caligula C. IX (pt. ii), ff. 626v, 627;
                                  Titus C. VI, ff. 207–209v.

Of Dames, of Knights, of armes, of loves delight
    v. But now a while of him I speake no more
        For first he is of limbs and bodie strong

Of Inglysh kynges, here lyeth the bewtevous ffloure	Nero C. XI, f. 255v.
Of Inglish men the scourge, of walsh the protector	Nero C. XI, f. 140v.
Of everlastinge faithe looke howe the Gracies three	Caligula D. I, f. 31v.
Of lingeringe love mysliking growes	Vespasian A. XXV, ff. 135v–136v.
Of Raleighs life and death	Titus C. VII, f. 93.
O catife corps that long hast felt the present panges of death	Titus A. XXIV, f. 91v.
O heauenly god and father dere cast downe thy tender eye	
v. O Heauenly God, O Father dere, cast doun thy tender eye	
O Heauenly God, O Father dere, cast doun thy tender eye	
Vespasian A. XXV, ff. 143v, 144; Vitellius C. XVII, f. 380.	
O heavenly god o father dere cast down your tender eye	
v. O Heauenly God, O Father dere, cast doun thy tender eye	
O Lord my Savior, & hevenly maker	Julius F. XI, f. 97v.
O lorde that ruleste bothe lande [and] sea even by thy hevenly povre	
Titus A. XXIV, ff. 85v–87v.	
O man Refraine thie vile desyre	Vespasian A. XXV, f. 154.
Oh mightye Muse	Vespasian E. VIII, ff. 173–174.
O mors crudelis fecisti plurima damna	Faustina E. V, f. 171.
O Pallas. Goddesse soverayne	Vespasian E. VIII, ff. 177–178.
O pater clemens misere fontis	Julius C. V, f. 327v.
O patre divo Dæmone divior	Titus A. XIII, ff. 167v–168v.
O rightefull rule and lyghte of lyghtes whose beams bene fulgent brighte	
Titus A. XXIV, ff. 79, 79v.	
O sic o Iuncti tumulo maneamus in vno	Faustina E. V, f. 178v.
Omnia quæ dantur pro donis carmina, Ioui	Appendix LXII, f. 2.
Oppida sic toto sunt sparsa in littore, ut unum	Vespasian D. IX, ff. 176, 176v.
Ornarat patriam Nestor Pilon inclitus heros	Julius F. X, f. 72v.
Palma aurem claudens palmorum signat at ecce	Titus A. XXIV, f. 96v.
Par iacet hoc tumulo sociale uxore maritus	Faustina E. V, f. 167.
Parva Urbs, ast ingens animis in fortibus hæret	Vespasian D. IX, f. 175v.
Pastor egenus habet telum, sed vendidit agrum	Appendix LXII, f. 5v.
Parffygth & prudent, Rycharde by Rigth the secvnd	Nero C. XI, f. 350v.
Phænix Jana iacet nato Phænice, dolendum	Julius F. XI, f. 86v.
Pictam morus habet Quintino authore tabellam	Julius F. X, ff. 70v, 71.
Planities prætensa jacet prope flumina Tinæ	Vespasian D. IX, f. 175v.
Præsidet extremis Arctoæ finibus oræ	Vespasian D. IX, ff. 170, 170v.
Praisse we the lord that haith no peare	
v. The second person in trenitie	
Princesse my Muse thought not amys	Vespasian E. VIII, ff. 175, 175v.
Princesse ye haue the doome that I can giue	Vespasian E. VIII, f. 170v.
Pro flamina quondam fuit a Iove femina missa	Julius F. X, f. 71v.
Pro strenis librum, pro donis accipe Votum	Julius F. XI, f. 244v.

Promus eram non Condus opum, diuesque videbar	Faustina E. V, f. 170.
Propter aquas Tai liquidas, et amæna vireta	Vespasian D. IX, f. 174.
Pulchrius hoc nihil est, nil turpius attamen extat	Julius C. III, f. 164.
Purpureæ uicina fuit Rosa candida utranque	Titus D. IV, ff. 14, 14v.

Qua Notus argutis adspirat molliter auris	Vespasian D. IX, f. 174.
Quæ cura Patrum, quiuè fidelium	Titus A. XIII, ff. 176–177.
Quæ minima in parvo regno pars antè fuisti	Vespasian D. IX, ff. 170v, 172.
Que pia que prudens, que docta pudica modesta	Faustina E. V, ff. 178v, 180.
Quæ verò, quæ digna tuis virtutibus Heros	Julius F. XI, f. 88v.
Quaecunque reges ediderunt hactenus	Titus D. IV, ff. 13v, 14.
Qualiter Anglorum possum describere gentem	Julius F. XI, f. 106v.
Quam tibi notum erat viuens Randolphe Iuellus	Caligula D. I, f. 31v.
Quanquam flere nefas te cælo Jacobe receptum	Caligula B. V, f. 267v; Caligula D. I, f. 33.

Quamvis flere nefas te cælo Jacobe receptum	
v. Quanquam flere nefas te cælo Jacobe receptum	
Quanto amplexetur populus te cesar amore	Julius F. X, f. 73.
Qui cupit ex factis sinceræ præmia laudis	Julius F. X, f. 72v.
Qui Jacet hic non ille Jacet, sed ad astra volavit	Faustina E. V, f. 170v.
Qui nuper Scotos iustèque pièque regebas	Caligula D. I, f. 33.
Qui scribunt vitam, diuino numine pleni	Appendix LXII, ff. 10v, 11.
Qui te videt beatus est	Caligula D. I, f. 35.
Quid me Scheltone fronte sic aperta	Julius F. X, f. 70v.
Quid possit virtus docte o pater inclite Thoma	Julius F. X, ff. 71v, 72.
Quid queris? non est hostis quærendus in agris	Julius F. XI, f. 202v.
Quid vitrum est? hominis corpus, quid membra? vita	Titus A. XXIV, f. 96v.
Quis fuit, ille tibi fidus amicus erit	Appendix LXII, f. 4v.
Quis tu? non nosti, sum præclarissima virtus	Appendix LXII, f. 9v.
Quis tu tam pauper, sic pannis obsita, quis tu	Appendix LXII, f. 9v.
Quisquis eris non nota tibi satis anglica gens est	Titus B. VI, f. 13v.
Quod nequiêre viri potuit si foemina, quid ni	Julius C. V, f. 393.
Quod præter patrias iuga fers muliebria leges	Caligula B. V, f. 268; Caligula D. I, f. 35.

Quod tibi vis tacito uoto, quod mater aperto	Caligula D. I, f. 34v.
Quos dederas nuper pisces Polidore diserte	Julius F. X, f. 71.
Quot sunt hoc compto sublimia metra libello	Appendix LXII, f. 4v.
Quot tibi non nolim, tot felix sæcula viuas	Appendix LXII, f. 2v.

Raleigh, in this thy selfe thy selfe transcends	Titus C. VII, f. 94.
Ravyshyd was I⟨, that well was me,⟩	Titus D. XI, f. 56v.
Regia flaminia iamdudum sceptra teneres	Caligula D. I, f. 35.
Regia sublimis celsâ despectat ab arce	Vespasian D. IX, ff. 174v, 175.

Reginæ geminæ pari labore	Caligula B. V, f. 320v.
Regis auus, regis pater, alto è sanguine regum	Caligula B. V, f. 321.
Regno animus tibi dignus erat tibi regia virtus	Caligula D. I, f. 35v.
Robertum Buccus patrio Suffolcius ortu	Julius F. XI, f. 97.
Romanæ huic aquilæ sanctus nunc insidet Agnus	Julius C. V, f. 127.
Romanis quondam statio tutissima signis	Vespasian D. IX, f. 173.
Rupe sedens celsa, rerum aut miracula spectat	Vespasian D. IX, f. 172v.
Sæpe scio summo Steuarto sancio sacre	Julius C. V, f. 327v.
Sæpe tibi Randolphe iubes me pingere Regem	Caligula D. I, f. 32.
Scotorum extremo sub limite, meta furoris	Vespasian D. IX, ff. 175, 175v.
Scribentem inuitat Pietas, et gratia vultus	Julius C. III, f. 352v.
Semper lingua mali poltroni pessima pars est	Titus B. VI, f. 13.
Seperet hispanos discordia nulla Britannis	Titus A. XXIV, f. 93v.
Septimus hic situs est Henricus gloria regum	Julius F. XI, f. 86.
Sera decennalis sub rege hærede Iacobo	Titus A. XIII, ff. 180–184.
Short was thy life	Julius F. XI, f. 88v.
Si dedit Anna tibi virtutem Buxtona, serues	Julius C. III, f. 164v.
Si generis splendor, raræ si gratia formæ	
v. Obruta frugifero sensim sic cespite surgunt	
Si nisi pro genere & meritis Hauerta dabuntur	Caligula D. I, ff. 34v, 35.
Si qua dies unquam. si quod fuit Anglia tempus	Titus D. IV, ff. 4–11v.
Si velis, & cupias tibi vitæ tempora longa	Appendix LXII, f. 2v.
Si vitrum vertas, cursus nouus incipit alter	Titus A. XXIV, f. 96v.
Sic jacet ecce Thomas obscuro haud sanguine natus	Cleopatra C. III, f. 33.
Syck sicke & totowe sike (refrain)	
v. It befell at martynmas	
Sir this my little Mistris here	Titus C. VII, f. 97v.
Sit tibi terra levis (refrain)	
v. Here lieth the stark theefe J a Drones	
⟨Sit⟩ tibi vita diu, sit semper blanda salusque	Appendix LXII, f. 2v.
So longe may a droppe fall	Vespasian A. XXV, f. 40v.
SpIrItVs erVpto saLVVs GILberte NoVeMbre	Faustina E. V, f. 180.
Stay gentel frend that passest by	Titus A. XXIV, f. 79v.
Sub vario Natura diu certamine ludens	Vespasian D. IX, f. 171.
Sum marie malegrata patri malegrata marito	Caligula B. V, f. 268.
Sunt tria que cunctis iter ad penetralia mortis	Julius F. X, f. 70v.
Sustulit e terris elementum Cinthius ignis	Julius F. X, f. 72v.
Te magis optarem saluum sine carmine sibi	Titus A. XXIV, f. 95.
Te Noua Villa fremens, odioso murmure Nympha	Julius C. V, f. 56.
Thamisis, et subito placide ridentibus undis	Titus F. VII, ff. 47v, 48v.
That mannys lyffe, is ffull vnstable	Nero C. XI, f. 462v.

The fragraunt flowers most freshe to vewe	Vespasian A. XXV, f. 153v.
The ffrende of pyte, and of almesse dede	Nero C. XI, f. 117.
The golden tyme ys nowe at hande	Vespasian A. XXV, ff. 151v–152v.
The happiest man that nowe dost lyve	Vespasian A. XXV, ff. 155, 155v.
The hinde shall hunte the harte to deathe,	Vespasian E. VII, f. 133.
The kynge of kynges, that lord, that Rulyth All	Nero C. XI, f. 52.
The Lacedemonian Kinge by drinkinge was vndon	Caligula D. I, f. 31v.
The man ys blest that lyves in rest	Vespasian A. XXV, ff. 137v, 138.
The morow ffolowyng, Tiburce and Valerian	Nero C. XI, f. 147v.
The perverse heretyke, thouth that he doo brenne	Nero C. XI, f. 357.
The Phrigian youth full ill advised	Vespasian E. VIII, ff. 170, 170v.
The second person in trenitie	Vespasian A. XXV, f. 163.
The Tomb of good ale lyeth in this tomb	Julius F. XI, f. 99.
The winter with his griesly stormes no lenger dare abyde	
v. The winter withe his ougly storms no lenger dare abyde	
	Titus A. XXIV, ff. 81v–82v.
Then may we Ioie in vnitie (burden)	
v. Man to redeme & not angell	
Then put aside all wrathe (burden)	
v. There is no tre that growe	
There is no tre that growe	Vespasian A. XXV, ff. 133v–135.
There was no deathe nor worldlie Ioie	Vespasian A. XXV, f. 129v.
This fleshe and bloode this head members and harte	Vespasian E. VIII, f. 172.
This seate and soyle from Saxon Bade a man of honest fame	Julius F. VI, f. 312.
This Sorowfull deth, which bryngith grete full lowe	Nero C. XI, ff. 162–164.
This worldes worshippe	Julius F. XI, f. 86v.
Thus, mirrha, ac aurum qui donabatur ab illo	Appendix LXII, f. 2.
To hurt the widowe in distresse	Vespasian A. XXV, f. 127.
To Jesabell that Englishe heure	Caligula C. IX (pt. ii), f. 226.
To shin in silke [and/to] glitter all in gold	Caligula B. V, f. 271;
	Vitellius E. X, f. 78.
Totum terra tegit, qui Totus Terra Vocatur	Faustina E. V, f. 182.
Tristi Britannos genitor cum mente uideret	Titus A. XXIV, f. 93.
Truthe withe the towche stoune triethe	Titus A. XXIV, ff. 83v–85.
Twoe men came riding ouer Hackney hay	Titus D. XII, f. 93v.
Vna fides viuos coniunxit, relligio vna	Julius F. XI, f. 86v.
Under this Stone	
v. Here under this Stone	
Vndoso hic solio residet regnator aquarum	Julius F. XI, f. 219v.
Vnica quae fueram proles spesque alma parentum	Cleopatra C. III, f. 14.
Vnum deprecor hoc: libros des supplico Regi	Julius C. V, f. 290.
Urbs Augusta, cui cælum tellusque, fretumque	Vespasian D. IX, f. 170.

Urbs speciosa situ, nitidis pulcherrima tectis	Vespasian D. IX, f. 172.
Vt fidei Charites æternæ vincula nectunt	Caligula D. I, f. 31v.
Vt Mariam finxit Natura, ars pinxit utrunque	Caligula B. V, f. 268v.
Ut vultu roseo rubicundo fulget in ortu	Julius F. XI, f. 106v.
Vaillant Duke Rollo stout & fierce	Faustina E. V, f. 174.
Vedra ruens rapidis modo cursibus, agmine leni	Vespasian D. IX, f. 172v.
Venit vt æthereas Edwardus sextus ad ædes	Galba E. IV, f. 182v.
Ver spargit flores, Autumnus pomifer uvas	Appendix LXII, f. 9v.
Viderat Acephalos nulla ceruice Raleighus	Titus C. VII, f. 93v.
Vir pius et simplex tum vita et morte beatus	Julius F. X, f. 70v.
Vita quid est? fumus, quid census? res peritura	Faustina E. V, f. 180v.
Viuat ametque suum felix regina maritum	Titus A. XXIV, f. 93v.
Vix caput attolens e lecto scribere carmen	Titus A. XXIV, f. 95.
Vixi videtis premium	Faustina E. V, f. 180.
Vos ego vos veneror, cælestia pignora, Divæ	Vespasian D. IX, f. 170v.
What tyme that god his holy hande	Vespasian A. XXV, f. 142v.
Whan all this ssowghte that may be fownde	Vespasian A. XXV, f. 39v.
When dearth decreases and treason begin	Vespasian E. VII, f. 134.
When four lightes begin to shine	Vespasian E. VII, f. 134.
When raginge loue withe extreme payne	Caligula A. XI, f. 286v.
Whan Satorn, wyth his cold Isy fface	Nero C. XI, f. 191v.
When that I call to memori what learned men do shoo	Titus A. XXIV, ff. 95v, 96.
Whan that this Cokk, loo here doth synge	Nero C. XI, f. 257.
When the beare ys musselyd & cann nott byte	Vespasian E. VII, f. 133.
When the bells be meryly ronge	Faustina E. V, f. 188; Julius F. XI, f. 190.
When woman first dame nature wrought	
v. When wemen firste dame nature wrowghte	
When wemen firste dame nature wrowghte	Titus A. XXIV, ff. 85, 85v.
When words of witt will not prevaile	Titus A. XXIV, f. 96.
Where gripinge greues the hart wold wound	Vespasian A. XXV, f. 137.
Whyle lyvyd this kyng	Nero C. XI, f. 161v.
While pagan poets seacke the prayse of foolishe fitings strange	Vitellius C. IX, f. 106.
Who iustely may reioyce in owghte vnder the skye	Titus A. XXIV, ff. 80, 80v.
Who liste to liue upryghte and holde him selfe content	Titus A. XXIV, ff. 81, 81v.
Who sekes to tame the bustering winde	Vespasian A. XXV, f. 161.
Who trusts Christs in Carnatyone	Vespasian A. XXV, ff. 127v, 128.
Who wislye wyll with gostlye eye	Vespasian A. XXV, ff. 149–150.
Who would lyve in others breath	Faustina E. V, f. 171; Julius F. XI, f. 99.
Who would trust to others breath	

v. Who would lyve in others breath

Whome princes serve and Realmes obay	Vespasian E. VIII, f. 170.
Who soo hym lykyth, these verses to Rede	Nero C. XI, f. 31v.
Whoso in wedloke doth intend	Vespasian A. XXV, f. 156.
Whye dothe the vaine fantasie dust in thy faice	Vespasian A. XXV, ff. 160, 160v.
Wyll Watsons wordes or Bruces boist availl	Caligula D. II, f. 50v.
Wyll ye complayne without a cavsse	Vespasian A. XXV, ff. 138–139.
Wyth Ropes were thow bounde, and on the Galow hong	Nero C. XI, f. 190v.
Would god that deth with cruell darte	Vespasian A. XXV, ff. 152v, 153.

Yet hap what hap fall what may fall
   v. The happiest man that nowe dost lyve

Youthfull bewtye, in body well disposed	Vespasian E. VIII, f. 169v.

Acephalous verses

…Cor pueri figit Prexasp⟨—⟩	Caligula D. I, f. 31v.
⟨—⟩ defunctus posses Iacobe reduci	Caligula D. I, f. 33.
⟨—⟩ Gemini qua ianua ponti	Julius F. X, f. 105v.
⟨—⟩ Ioseph	Vitellius C. IX, ff. 188v–199.
…Proh dolor ergo homini quænam fiducia Martis	Julius F. XI, f. 87.
⟨—⟩ mihi nil, sed totum me tibi dono	Appendix LXII, f. 2v.

(2) Index of Authors and Attributed Authors

Agarde, Arthur	Faustina E. V, f. 174.
Alabaster, William	Julius C. V, f. 23.
Allen, Richard	Titus A. XXIV, f. 92v.
Assheton, William	Vespasian A. XXV, ff. 178–179.
Blaxton, Henry	Julius F. XI, f. 97.
Bolton, Edmund	Titus A. XIII, ff. 178–184;
	Titus B. VIII, f. 227.
Brandol⟨?⟩, Gabriel	Vitellius C. IX, f. 127v.
Buchanan, George	Caligula B. V, ff. 267v–271, 320v, 321;
	Caligula B. X (pt. ii), ff. 259v, 260;
	Caligula D. I, ff. 31v–36 *passim*;
	Vitellius E. X, ff. 76v–78.
Camden, William	Caligula C. IX (pt. ii), f. 629;
	Julius F. VI, ff. 4, 311;
	Julius F. X, f. 67v;
	Julius F. XI, ff. 134, 208, 219v, 244v;
	Titus F. VII, ff. 47v, 48;
	Appendix LXII, *passim*.
Carr, Thomas	Titus A. XXIV, f. 94.
Case, William	Titus A. XXIV, ff. 85, 85v.

Cavendish, Richard	Vitellius C. IX, ff. 127, 127v.
Challenor, John	Julius F. XI, f. 93.
Churchyard, Thomas	Caligula B. V, ff. 365–382.
Constantine, Patrick	Caligula B. V, f. 320.
Cotton, William	Appendix LVIII, f. 68.
Cox, Richard	Titus A. XXIV, f. 95.
Cr—, —	Titus A. XXIV, ff. 98v, 99.
Dacre, Robert	Titus B. VI, f. 13v.
Davies, Sir John	Faustina E. V, f. 170;
	Julius F. XI, ff. 98, 100.
Downton, Paul	Julius F. XI, f. 135v.
Edwards, Richard	Titus A. XXIV, ff. 83v–91v.
	Vespasian A. XXV, ff. 135, 135v, 137.
Fabyan, Robert	Nero C. XI, ff. 30v–462v *passim*.
Ferrers, Henry	Julius F. VI, f. 312.
Fitzjames, or Fitzwilliams, —	Cleopatra C. III, f. 33.
Fitzwilliams *v.* Fitzjames	
Fox, Sir Edward	Julius C. V, ff. 290, 327, 327v.
Garbrand, John	Caligula D. I, f. 31v.
Goad, Thomas	Titus A. XXIV, ff. 166–177.
Greshop, William	Galba E. IV, f. 182v.
Haddon, Walter	Titus A. XXIV, f. 95.
Harborne, Symon	Julius F. XI, f. 219.
Harforth, Peter	Vespasian A. XXV, ff. 153, 163v.
Harington, John, the elder	Titus A. XXIV, ff. 80, 80v.
Harington, Sir John	Julius F. XI, f. 307.
Harpsfield, John	Vitellius C. IX, ff. 188v–199.
Harris, Nathan	Julius C. V, f. 127.
Herbert, Edward, Lord Herbert of Cherbury	Julius C. V, f. 393.
Herd, John	Julius C. II, ff. 106–263.
Herthe, William	Fragments XXXII.
Heywood, John	Vespasian A. XXV, ff. 132v–133.
Holand, Joseph	Faustina E. V, f. 182.
Holland, Hugh	Titus B. VI, f. 249v.
Hoskins, John	Faustina E. V, ff. 162v, 170, 171v;
	Julius F. X, ff. 115, 115v;
	Julius F. XI, f. 98.
Howard, Henry, Earl of Northampton	Caligula C. IX (pt. ii), ff. 626v–627;
	Titus C. VI, ff. 207–209v.
Howard, Henry, Earl of Surrey	Caligula A. XI, f. 286v;
	Titus A. XXIV, f. 80.
James, Richard	Claudius C. II, f. 339;
	Julius C. III, f. 214.

Johnston, John	Vespasian D. IX, ff. 169–176v.
Kinwelmershe, Francis	Vespasian A. XXV, ff. 143v, 144;
	Vitellius C. XVII, f. 380.
Lambard, William	Cleopatra C. III, f. 50v;
	Faustina E. V, f. 180v.
Leeche, James	Faustina E. V, f. 178v.
Lily, George	Julius F. X, f. 71v.
Lily, William	Julius F. X, ff. 69–73v.
Marbeck, Roger	Titus A. XXIV, ff. 92, 96v.
Masson, —	Vespasian A. XXV, ff. 129, 129v, 130v, 131.
More, Sir Thomas	Titus D. IV, ff. 1–14v.
Morgan, —	Cleopatra C. III, ff. 10v–11v.
Norton, Thomas	Titus A. XXIV, ff. 79v, 80v.
Pearson, Thomas	Vespasian A. XXV, ff. 153v, 154.
Peele, George	Vespasian A. XXV, ff. 154v, 155.
Pigot, Valentine	Titus A. XXIV, ff. 79, 79v.
Puttenham, George	Vespasian E. VIII, ff. 169–178.
Redford, John	Vespasian A. XXV, ff. 132v–133.
Richardson, Thomas	Vespasian A. XXV, ff. 155, 155v.
Rogers, Daniel	Titus F. VII, f. 26.
Rogers, Mathew v. Smith, Robert	
Scory, Sylvanus	Titus C. VII, f. 94.
Singleton, —	Caligula B. IV, ff. 247, 247v.
Skelton, John	Julius F. XI, f. 86.
Smith, Robert *al.* Rogers, Mathew	Vespasian A. XXV, ff. 145v–147v.
Southwell, Robert	Titus C. VI, ff. 535–536v.
Sparrow, Thomas	Julius C. III, f. 352v.
Stanyhurst, Richard	Julius F. XI, f. 96.
Stradling, Sir John	Julius C. V, f. 56.
Taylor, John	Titus B. VI, ff. 10v, 13.
Tichborne, Chidiock	Cleopatra A. IV, f. 11.
'Tom Truth'	Caligula C. I, ff. 364–365v.
Walter, Joseph	Julius C. III, f. 385.
Watson, Christopher	Vitellius C. IX, ff. 63v, 106.

1 C. E. Wright, 'The Elizabethan Society of Antiquaries and the Formation of the Cottonian Library', in Francis Wormald and C. E. Wright (eds.), *The English Library before 1700* (London, 1958), p. 194. The article includes a useful overall view of the character of the collection (see pp. 192–208). See also Kevin Sharpe, *Sir Robert Cotton 1586–1631: History and Politics in Early Modern England* (Oxford, 1979), pp. 48–83.

2 Grateful thanks are owed to a fellow worker in the field, Steven W. May of Georgetown College, Kentucky, and to my colleagues T. S. Pattie and Nigel Ramsay for their kind assistance during preparation of the handlist.

3 Richard L. DeMolen, 'The Library of William Camden', *Proceedings of the American Philosophical Society*, cxxviii (1984), p. 332.

4 J. W. Binns, *Intellectual Culture in Elizabethan*

and *Jacobean England: the Latin Writings of the Age* (Leeds, 1990); and see Wolfgang Mann, *Lateinische Dichtung in England vom Ausgang des Frühhumanismus bis zum Regierungsantritt Elisabeths* (Halle, 1939).

5 BL, Additional (i.e. Birch) MS. 4712, f. 94v.

6 For example, BL, Add. MSS. 29921, f. 38, and 33998, f. 89; Egerton MS. 923, f. 8v; Harley MSS. 293, f. 94, and 3511, f. 72; and three Bodleian MSS. recorded by Margaret Crum, *First-line Index of English Poetry in Manuscripts of the Bodleian Library, Oxford* (Oxford, 1969), S389, W187 and W189.

7 Cotton MS. Julius C. III, ff. 153 and 222.

8 The origin and sources of Cotton's collections were explored in the first of Colin G. C. Tite's British Library Panizzi Lectures for 1993, published as *The Manuscript Library of Sir Robert Cotton* (London, 1994), pp. 1–39.

9 Colin G. C. Tite, 'The Early Catalogues of the Cottonian Library', *British Library Journal*, vi (1980), pp. 144–57.

10 See Caligula B. X (pt. ii), Claudius C. II, and Cleopatra C. III.

11 Galba E. IV, Titus D. XII, Vespasian D. IX and Vitellius C. IX.

12 Julius F. X and XI, Titus A. XXIV and Vespasian E. VIII.

13 *Tudor Songs and Ballads from MS Cotton Vespasian a-25* (Cambridge, Mass., 1978). Reviewed by P. J. Croft in *Notes & Queries*, ccxxv (Apr. 1980), pp. 187–9.

14 *Tudor Songs*, pp. xi–xiii; and A. G. Watson, *The Manuscripts of Henry Savile of Banke* (London, 1969), p. 70, no. 283.

15 See ff. 103–115v: Urban VIII's 'Modus præficiendi sive Ordinandi Militem Inclyti ac Heroici Ordinis Equitum Immaculatæ Virginis', 5 July [1634].

16 Leicester Bradner, *The Life and Poems of Richard Edwards*, Yale Studies in English, no. lxxiv (New Haven, Conn., 1927).

17 Now Sloane MS. 3794: see John Manning (ed.), *The Emblems of Thomas Palmer: 'Two Hundred Poosees'* (New York, 1988).

18 *Reges, reginae, nobiles, et alii in Ecclesia Collegiata B. Petri Westmonasterii sepulti* (London, 1610), pp. 21–2; and see Philip Henderson (ed.), *Complete Poems of John Skelton*, 2nd edn. (London, 1948), pp. 434–6; and H. L. R. Edwards, *Skelton* (London, 1949), p. 136.

19 For More's own lines on the portrait see the collected Latin Poems in his *Complete Works*, vol. iii, pt. 2, ed. Clarence H. Miller *et al.* (New Haven, 1984), p. 298.

20 C. R. Baskervill, 'William Lily's Verse for the Entry of Charles V into London', *Huntington Library Bulletin*, ix (1936), pp. 1–14.

21 *The first parte of Churchyardes Chippes* (London, 1575).

22 Ed. by Joseph Haslewood (with the *Arte*) in 1811 and by W. R. Morfill, *Ballads from MSS*, Ballad Society Publications (London, 1873), vol. ii, pp. 72–91. See also Gladys D. Willcock and Alice Walker (eds.), *Arte of English Poesie* (Cambridge, 1936), p. xxxi, n. 1.

23 C. M. Briquet, *Les Filigranes*, ed. Alan Stevenson (Amsterdam, 1968), no. 4433.

24 George Burke Johnston, 'Poems by William Camden', *Studies in Philology*, lxxii, no. 5 (Dec. 1975), *Texts and Studies, 1975*, p. 21.

25 Prefatory note to extract given in Titus F. VII, ff. 47v, 48v, printed in handlist below, pp. 357–8.

26 The fragment beginning 'Gemini qua ianua ponti' on f. 105v, credited to Camden with some reservations in Johnston, op. cit., pp. 108 and 133, has been included in the handlist as of unspecified authorship.

27 H. E. Rollins (ed.), *Tottel's Miscellany, 1557–1587* (Cambridge, Mass., 1928–9), no. 149.

28 Théodore Bèze, *Poemata* (Paris, 1548), p. 68.

29 Katherine Duncan-Jones, *Sir Philip Sidney: Courtier Poet* (London, 1991), p. 40.

30 [1] 'May there be as many happy times in your life as there are fine poems in this book'. [2] 'This book bristles with many learned poems: may your life be blessed with endless good things'.

31 Sir William Dugdale, *The History of St Pauls Cathedral in London* (London, 1658), p. 99: twenty verses beg. 'Shall Honour, Fame, and Titles of Renown'.

32 John Eliot, *Ortho-epia Gallica* (London, 1593), p. 163; and see Camden's *Remaines*, ed. R. D. Dunn (Toronto, 1984), p. 478.

33 *Chrestoleros*, Bk. 4, epigram 31; also printed in Stow's *Survey* (London, 1598), p. 263: for an answer see Crum S704.

34 Henry Holland, *Monumenta sepulchraria Sancti Pauli* (London, 1614), sig. C[4]; and the exchange of letters between Greville and Sir

John Coke in Add. MS. 64875, ff. 166–171v.

35 *Epitaphia in mortem nobilissimi et fortissimi viri D. Philippi Sidneii Equitis...* (Lyons, 1587).

36 'George Buchanan's Latin Poems from Script to Print: a preliminary survey', *The Library*, 5th ser., xxiv (1969), p. 319.

37 However, the English verses beginning here as 'As winde which constant never bides, such fayth in Courte is founde' occur in the Corpus Christi MS. as 'As winde that never constant is, such faith in courte we find'. (I am indebted to Christopher Butler, assistant archivist of the College, for the reading of the Latin original.)

38 Another, apparently contemporary, copy occurs in BL, Add. MS. 40629, ff. 126–127.

39 John Jones, M.D., *The Benefit of the auncient Bathes of Buckstones* (London, 1572), ff. 2v–3. See further Stephen Glover, *History and gazeteer of the county of Derby*, ed. Thomas Noble (Derby, 1833), vol. ii, pp. 203–4.

40 The text as given by Camden reads:
Buxtona, quae calidae celebrabare nomine lymphae
Forte mihi posthac non adeunda, vale.

41 A. B. Grosart (ed.), *The Poems of Richard James, B.D.* (London, 1880), pp. xxxiii, xxxiv.

42 G. C. Moore Smith (ed.), *The Poems of Edward Lord Herbert of Cherbury* (Oxford, 1923), pp. 89–90 and 163.

43 Louise Brown Osborn, *Life, Letters, and Writings of John Hoskins*, Yale Studies in English, vol. lxxxvii (New Haven, Conn., 1930), pp. 184–8.

44 H.M.C,, *9th Report, Salisbury MSS.*, vol. xiii (London, 1915), p. 362: ref. Hatfield MS. 277.8.

45 In the British Library Catalogue of Printed Books these editions are listed under, respectively, 'ENGLAND. MISCELLANEOUS PUBLIC DOCUMENTS, ETC. III. CHRONOLOGICAL SERIES. – JAMES I', and 'G., T. Collegii Regalis Cantabrig. Socius'.

46 For manuscript and printed accounts of this event see Kate Harris, 'Richard Pynson's *Remembraunce for the Traduction of the Princesse Kateryne*: the Printer's Contribution to the Reception of Catharine of Aragon', *The Library*, 6th Ser., xii (1990), pp. 91–109.

47 Alan H. Nelson (ed.), *Records of Early English Drama: Cambridge*, 2 vols. (Toronto, 1989), pp. 231, 235, 238, etc.

48 Carleton Brown and R. H. Robbins, *The Index of Middle English Verse* (New York, 1943); with the *Supplement* by Robbins and John L. Cutler (Lexington, Kentucky, 1965). See also Richard Hamar, *A Manuscript Index to the Index of Middle English Verse* (London, 1995).

49 *A catalogue of the Manuscripts in the Cottonian Library deposited in the British Museum* (London, 1802). The Cotton entries in the seventeen handwritten volumes of the Index of English Poetry in the MSS. Students' Room of the British Library run to some hundred and thirty items only, many of them mediaeval.

50 It is described and collated as *The Book of the Laurel*, ed. F. W. Brownlow (Newark, Delaware, 1990).

51 William A. Ringler Jr., *Bibliography and Index of English Verse in Manuscript, 1501–1558* (London, 1992), TM 397, 951.

52 For Rainer or Rayner (*c.* 1615–81) see perhaps the Venns' *Alumni Cantabrigienses*, Part i.

53 They were printed in Simon Gunton, *History of the Church of Peterburgh* (London, 1686), pp. 104–13, and in Dugdale's *Monasticon Anglicanum*, ed. J. Caley, H. Ellis and B. Bandinel (London, 1817), vol. i, p. 377. The events of which they treat are outlined in *V.C.H. Northants.*, vol. ii, p. 84.

'THEIR PRESENT MISERABLE STATE OF CREMATION': THE RESTORATION OF THE COTTON LIBRARY

ANDREW PRESCOTT

The aged overseer paused. 'Well, I doubt if you'd even understand it. I don't. He seems to have found a method for restoring missing words and phrases to some of the old fragments of original text in the Memorabilia. Perhaps the left-hand side of a half-burned book is legible, but the right-hand page is burned, with a few words missing at the end of each line. He's worked out a mathematical method for finding the missing words. It's not foolproof, but it works to some degree'.*

W. M. Miller, Jr, *A Canticle for Leibowitz* (1959)

THE October 1731 number of the newly-established *Gentleman's Magazine* included the following notice in its reports of 'Casualties' for the month:

23 [Oct.]. A Fire broke out in the House of Mr *Bently*, adjoining to the King's School near *Westminster Abbey*, which burnt down that part of the House that contained the *King's* and *Cottonian* Libraries. Almost all the printed Books were consumed and part of the Manuscripts. Amongst the latter, those which Dr *Bentley* had been collecting for his *Greek Testament*, for these last ten Years, valued at 2000 l.[1]

This short note, tucked away between reports of the discovery of a disfigured corpse near Bath and an accidental shooting at Hackney, records what was perhaps the greatest bibliographical disaster of modern times in Britain. It is difficult to quantify the scale of the losses to the Cotton library as a result of the fire at Bentley's residence, Ashburnham House. A number of letters preserve colourful anecdotes about the fire, such as the famous story of Dr Bentley escaping from the flames in nightgown and wig with Codex Alexandrinus under his arms,[2] but the most detailed source of information about the fire and the damage inflicted by it is the report of a parliamentary committee established to investigate the incident, which was published in 1732.[3] This contained two valuable appendices. The first was 'A Narrative of the Fire…and of the Methods used for preserving and recovering the Manuscripts of the Royal and Cottonian libraries',[4] compiled by the Rev. William Whiston the younger, the clerk in charge of the records kept in the Chapter House at Westminster, another notorious firetrap.[5] The second was a list of lost and damaged manuscripts, prepared by David Casley, the deputy librarian of both the Royal and Cotton libraries, with the assistance of Whiston.[6] Casley's list was afterwards reprinted in summary form, with a few amendments, in his 1734 catalogue of the Royal Library.[7]

Whiston stated that the Cotton library contained before the fire 958 manuscript volumes, of which 114 were 'lost, burnt or intirely spoiled' and another ninety-eight so damaged as to be defective.[8] These figures have invariably been cited in accounts of the Cotton fire. They are, however, misleading. In one sense, they overstate the amount of damage. Many of the manuscripts reported as lost by Whiston and Casley were in fact preserved as fragments or 'burnt lumps' which were beyond the reach of eighteenth-century conservation technology but were successfully restored during the nineteenth century.[9] Consequently, the majority of manuscripts reported as lost in 1732 are available for consultation today. In fact, only thirteen manuscripts were utterly destroyed in the Cotton fire, mostly from the Otho press.[10]

Although relatively few complete volumes were destroyed, many manuscripts lost important articles or survive only as charred fragments. In this sense, the details given by Whiston and Casley underestimate the damage. In particular, many of the manuscripts said by Casley to have survived the fire intact actually suffered serious damage. One of the most famous victims of the fire was the manuscript containing the unique exemplar of *Beowulf*, Vitellius A. XV.[11] The edges of this manuscript were badly scorched and the vellum left very brittle. Its subsequent handling caused serious textual loss. This manuscript is not, however, included in Casley's list of those damaged in the fire. Tiberius A. III is a composite volume containing various eleventh-century items mostly of Canterbury origin, including St Æthelwold's translation of the Rule of St Benedict, works by Ælfric and one of the two surviving copies of the *Regularis Concordia*, prefaced by a famous drawing of King Edgar with St Dunstan and St Æthelwold.[12] This volume was also said by Casley to have survived the fire unharmed, but again there was damage to the edges of the folios and the water used to put out the fire caused staining. The drawing of King Edgar had become warped and buckled.

In the absence of any meaningful statistics, the best way of conveying the catastrophic nature of the losses in the Ashburnham House fire is by a random roll-call of some of the victims.[13] Cotton's pride and joy, the fifth-century Greek Genesis (Otho B. VI), one of the earliest illustrated Christian manuscripts in existence, was reduced to a pile of cinder-like fragments.[14] Cotton possessed two of the four surviving letters patent of King John recording the grant of Magna Carta. One of these, now Cotton Charter XIII. 31a, was the only one with the Great Seal still attached. In the heat, not only was the text damaged but the seal was left a shapeless blob.[15] The Bull of Pope Leo X conferring the title 'Defender of the Faith' on Henry VIII (now Vitellius B. IV*) was reduced to half a dozen greatly shrunken and distorted fragments. Otho A. XII contained unique exemplars of two key texts for the Anglo-Saxon period, Asser's *Life of Alfred* and *The Battle of Maldon*, together with other Old English material.[16] Although 40 folios of the original 155 were eventually recovered, both Asser and Maldon perished completely. Among the chronicle texts which were lost or very badly damaged were the earliest manuscript of Gildas (Vitellius A. VI),[17] the 'G' manuscript of the Anglo-Saxon Chronicle in Otho B. XI,[18] and the only extant manuscript of Æthelweard's Chronicle (Otho A. X).[19] Cartularies from such houses as Lenton (Otho B. XIV),[20] St Albans (Otho D. III) and St Augustine, Canterbury (Otho B. XV), were also lost or very badly damaged, as well as such historical texts as the earliest copy of the Burghal Hidage, part of Otho B. XI.[21] Among the illuminated manuscripts ruined in the fire might be singled out a portion of an early eighth-century gospel book from Northumbria, Otho C. V, if only because another fragment of this manuscript survives intact in Cambridge, Corpus Christi College, MS. 197B, and shows that it was an insular gospel-book from the greatest period of Northumbrian illumination.[22] These are mostly medieval examples. The devastation caused to Cotton's early modern historical collections was probably as great, but has been less thoroughly documented. It is a measure of the richness of Cotton's library that, despite such losses, it still remains an incomparable source for the history, literature and art of medieval and Tudor England.

II

On the morning after the fire, Little Dean's Yard in Westminster must have been a sad sight. Ashburnham House was a smouldering ruin. The ground was littered with fragments of burnt manuscripts, which the boys of Westminster School picked up and kept as souvenirs.[23] As the manuscripts had been rescued from the flames, they had been taken to various rooms in Westminster School. When the fire had finally been put out, they were assembled in the great boarding house of the school, opposite Ashburnham House. Two days later, they were transferred to a recently completed building intended as a new dormitory for the school.[24] These operations were supervised by the Speaker, Arthur Onslow, a Cotton trustee, who on hearing of the fire had rushed from his house nearby to help save the manuscripts. Onslow summoned together a group of experts, including not only Bentley and Casley, but also keepers of such other record repositories as the Chapter House at Westminster, the Tower of London and the Exchequer, to consider how the damaged manuscripts could be conserved.[25] The deliberations of this group and the work subsequently undertaken were recorded by William Whiston in his appendix to the 1732 parliamentary report.[26] Although Whiston's report is well known, little notice has been taken in descriptions of individual Cotton Manuscripts of the impact of the emergency conservation work undertaken immediately after the fire, when a number of manuscripts were broken up and rebound. It seems likely that, in the process, leaves were not reassembled in the correct order and the collation of some volumes was permanently disrupted. This important stage in the codicological history of many Cotton Manuscripts has been generally overlooked. It is therefore worth describing in some detail the procedures adopted by Whiston and his colleagues.

It is difficult nowadays, looking at the collection after more than two hundred years of conservation work, to imagine the scale of the problem confronting Speaker Onslow's panel of experts. The picture which comes to mind is of a huge collection of loose charred fragments, but the pattern of damage caused by the fire and 'engine-water' was more complex.[27] The vellum manuscripts had frequently stayed together as a single unit, but had warped and shrunk in the heat, each codex rolling up into a misshappen ball. Animal fat had been drawn out from the vellum by the heat and then congealed, turning the manuscript into a glutinous mass, blackened around the edges. As it cooled, the manuscript became very brittle. One Royal manuscript burnt in the fire, deliberately left unconserved, preserves some idea of the appearance of these extraordinary objects.[28] It looks like an irradiated armadillo. Moreover, as is still the case with library fires, the water used to extinguish the blaze had caused as much damage as the flames.[29] The paper manuscripts in particular were sodden and urgently needed drying, as there was a risk of mould.[30] Initial conservation work began on 1 November 1731, just over a week after the fire.[31] The stained and damp paper manuscripts, mostly sixteenth-century State Papers, were disbound, and a bookbinder employed to clean the leaves and wash them in an alum solution. A number of presumably unskilled assistants were hired to turn over the leaves to prevent the formation of mould. The leaves were hung on lines to dry and afterwards bound up again. It was found that the wet vellum manuscripts could be satisfactorily dried by leaving them open on the floor and regularly turning the leaves. The worst affected were dried in front of a fire. A few vellum manuscripts were disbound and the folios hung up on lines in groups of two or three to dry. Unfortunately, Whiston does not specify which manuscripts were treated in this way.

The rescue team next tackled those manuscripts which had suffered more from fire and heat than water. Where possible, the burnt vellum manuscripts were opened up leaf by leaf and 'the glutinous Matter, that had been forced out upon the Edges of the Vellum and Parchment by the Heat of the Fire, was carefully taken off by the Fingers...'.[32] Despite Whiston's claim that, except for a few of minor value, all the damaged vellum manuscripts had been treated in this way, it seems that little progress was made. Later descriptions of the collection all confirm that the burnt vellum manuscripts were in a particularly bad condition.[33] In any case, the treatment described by Whiston would hardly have left these manuscripts in a fit condition for use.

The burnt paper manuscripts were an easier proposition. The individual leaves were washed, cleaned and hung up to dry. Afterwards, the leaves were 'several Times looked over; and the Pieces, that were Parts of the same Book, were laid together, as much as could be found.'[34] Whiston stated that, from the surviving paper fragments, 'several large Portions of Books, and some entire Books have been made up out of them'.[35] He does not identify these eighteenth-century reconstructions of Cotton Manuscripts. He urged that, when a volume had been recovered in this way, 'each Book or Portion of Book, so collected together, should be carefully collated, and the Leaves placed, as near as possible, in the same Order, that they were in before the Fire'.[36]

Despite these efforts, a large number of 'single Leaves, or Pieces of Leaves' remained unidentified, and were put into drawers. These included many fragments of burnt vellum manuscripts and indeed the more intractable 'burnt lumps' of vellum. Whiston proposed that these fragments be arranged 'into Covers or Drawers, according to the

394

respective Subjects they treat of, that so the least Fragment may not be lost'.[37] It does not seem that this far-sighted proposal was implemented.

The initial rescue work was conducted at enormous speed. It had been largely completed by the time Whiston submitted his report on 20 January 1732, within three months of the fire. Inevitably there must be doubts about the accuracy of work undertaken with great haste, partly by unskilled assistants, in primitive conditions and without the aid of modern bibliographical tools. Later workers on the collection commented that it had suffered 'by the carelessness of those that have been the first employed in preserving them'.[38] Whiston does not specify how individual manuscripts were treated, but the general figures he provides indicate that about a third of the volumes in the collection were subjected to this rough and ready conservation work.[39]

The labours of Whiston and his colleagues already place a very great gulf between the modern user of the Cotton library and the library as it existed before the fire. In discussing the collation of any Cotton manuscript which shows signs of severe damage from damp, it is worth remembering that in 1731 the manuscript may have been taken apart and the leaves hung up on washing lines by an illiterate artisan. Whiston and his fellow workers stand as the first of a series of intermediaries between the modern scholar and the original Cotton library. They inaugurated a process of conservation work on the collection which has continued intermittently to the present day. Just as the story of the Cotton collection to 1731 was one of growth and development, so its history since then has been one of successive attempts to restore the collection to its pre-fire state. Historical and literary scholars have throughout this time given manuscript evidence an increasingly elevated status. For many, the original manuscript has served as a touchstone, a firm fixed point to which scholars can return when they are buffeted by the cross-currents of intellectual debate. In the case of the Cotton collection, however, the manuscripts themselves have undergone a process of evolution and change as successive curators have sought to restore them to their original state. In a number of cases, a particular manuscript is little more than an intelligent reconstruction of the original, comparable to, and just as open to doubt and challenge as, say, an archaeological reconstruction.[40]

III

Whiston's concern that each manuscript fragment from the Cotton library should be carefully preserved was echoed in more elevated language by the Rev. Thomas Fitzgerald, the Usher of Westminster School, in his lines *Upon the Burning of the Cottonian Manuscripts at Ashburnham House*.[41] Fitzgerald reflects on how these 'learned Spoils of twice a thousand years' had survived Goths, Vandals and, even more dangerous in Fitzgerald's view, 'reforming Zeal', only to perish in a fire. In the climax of the poem, Fitzgerald called for each fragment to be treated as if it were a holy relic:

> Whate'er the Fury of the Flames has spar'd
> With zealous Care, with awful Rev'rence guard ...
> Each Code, each Volume, ev'ry Fragment Prize:

395

As Rome her Relicks sav'd from Times of Old:
With Gems profusely decks, and shrines in Gold;
Tho' none like these, with all her Pomp and Cost,
Or Rome, or all her Vatican can boast.

Despite these poetic injunctions, nothing was done for the further preservation of the Cotton library following the publication of the parliamentary report in 1732. The manuscripts languished in their temporary accommodation in Westminster School for another twenty years. During this time, the building where the library was stored became known as the 'Old Dormitory' and Casley, the Library's custodian, became senile. The only immediate effect of the catastrophe at Ashburnham House appears to have been to encourage the first moves in 1751 for the publication of Domesday Book, then kept in the Westminster Chapter House and also at great risk from fire.[42] In 1743, Major Arthur Edwards, a Fellow of the Society of Antiquaries and enthusiastic amateur archaeologist,[43] left seven thousand pounds 'to erect a house in which to preserve the Cotton Library, or should such a house have meantime been provided, to purchase manuscripts, books of antiquities, ancient coins, medals and other curiosities to come to the Library.'[44] Edwards's bequest was, however, subject to a life interest and did not become available until 1769.[45] Edwards also left his books and pictures as additions to the library.[46] It was through the intervention of another Edwards, Vigerus Edwards, that the collections of the record scholar and historian of the Exchequer, Thomas Madox, were also deposited with the Cotton library.[47] The Edwards and Madox deposits represent perhaps the last vestiges of the idea that the Cotton library might form the nucleus of a national historical archive.[48]

The future of the Cotton library was finally secured in 1753 by the establishment of the British Museum as a result of Sir Hans Sloane's bequest. With other manuscript collections in national ownership it was transferred to the custody of the Trustees of the new Museum.[49] One of their first actions was to inspect the collections placed in their charge. On 2 February 1754 a committee of the Trustees visited the Old Dormitory to examine the Cotton Library.[50] They found that Casley was by now 'disabled by age and infirmity from executing the duty of his post in his own person' and his responsibilities were discharged by his wife, who showed the library to visitors. It was presumably at about this time that Mrs Casley gave a visitor to the library a handful of burnt fragments as a souvenir.[51] Casley was also assisted by Richard Widmore, the Keeper of the library of Westminster Abbey, who undertook detailed work on the charters, probably the most confused part of the collection. Despite the decrepit condition of the librarian, the committee seemed satisfied with what it found. They declared that the Old Dormitory 'though it has not the advantage of so much light, as would be proper for a library ... is dry and secured from the weather. The MSS. as well as the books [presumably Major Edwards's legacy together with the remnants of Cotton's own printed books] appear to have sustained no injury from damp since the depositing them there, but they are in general so dusty that a speedy care of them is necessary in that respect.' Indeed, the committee felt that the Old Dormitory would provide suitable temporary accommodation for the Harley manuscripts, 'if a proper person were appointed for the custody and care of that collection'.

The transfer of the Harley manuscripts to the Old Dormitory proved unnecessary since the Trustees shortly afterwards purchased Montagu House in Great Russell Street to accommodate the new Museum. The work necessary to prepare Montagu House to receive the Museum's collections proved protracted, and it was not until 1756, immediately before the removal of the Cotton collection to Great Russell Street, that a more systematic examination was made of the Cotton library.

In July 1756, two Museum officers, Matthew Maty, the first Keeper of Printed Books and from 1772 to 1776 Principal Librarian, and Henry Rimius, submitted two reports on the Cotton library to the Trustees. The first was published in an abridged form in Samuel Hooper's 1777 catalogue of the collection,[52] but the second has never been printed.[53] Both are therefore printed in full in Appendix I below. Maty and Rimius checked the collection against Smith's 1696 catalogue and Casley's list of manuscripts damaged in the fire, counting the volumes and comparing the contents of a sample from each press against the catalogue entries. They declared that the manuscripts in ten of the presses (Julius, Augustus, Claudius, Nero, Vespasian, Titus, Domitian, Cleopatra, Faustina and the Appendix) 'have suffered nothing by the fire, and have been found to agree with Mr Smith's catalogue. Yet several of these being placed in presses much exposed to dampness in a cold and shady place, could hardly notwithstanding Mr Widmore's endeavours (which he has assured us have been very assiduous) be preserved from must and mouldiness and will want to be aired and carefully dried up before they are placed in the Museum.'

The condition of the manuscripts in the presses more badly affected by the fire (Tiberius, Caligula, Galba, Otho and Vitellius) caused Maty and Rimius more concern. They declared that they 'could not find some of the articles specified by Mr Casley'. Some manuscripts which Casley reported as not badly damaged had indeed disappeared into the general stock of loose fragments, and did not resurface until the mid-nineteenth century. For example, Maty and Rimius were unable to find Tiberius D. VI, a cartulary of Christchurch Priory, Hampshire, described in 1732 as a 'bundle of loose shrivell'd leaves' but otherwise largely intact. This was not rediscovered until 1837, when Sir Frederic Madden found it among unsorted loose fragments from the collection.[54] On the other hand, they identified some manuscripts which Casley had been unable to trace, stating that 'several of those which he [Casley] declares to be entirely destroyed, may still be of some use in careful hands'.

These discrepancies were worrying enough, but an even greater cause for concern was the environmental condition of some of the presses, particularly the Vitellius press. 'Besides the damage done by the fire to the manuscripts in this press,' Maty and Rimius reported, 'it has suffered no less by the carelessness of those that have been the first employed in preserving them, as well as by the extraordinary moistness of the place. The great humidity, together with the extension of that hue, which the fire extracted from the volumes wrote on vellum, having rolled the edges of most of them, defaced the marks [presumably the pressmarks] and afforded both lodging and food to numberless shoals of worms and other insects.'

The second report dealt with the surviving 'charters, curiosities & co.' Maty and Rimius complained that 'The charters, warrants, deeds and other records contained in the last press of the Cottonian cabinet might have been examined with more ease and in less time had we found them disposed in any order, properly endorsed, or at least regularly numbered and sufficiently described.' This necessitated an examination of each item and a preliminary numeration of every one 'by which they could more easily be found out'. They were assisted in this by a draft catalogue prepared by Widmore.[55] The unnamed press containing the charters was divided into two parts. Sixteen drawers in the top section and seven in the lower were stuffed with paper and parchment including several 'entirely relative to the Cotton family' which Maty and Rimius felt were 'of little use to the public'. There were, nevertheless, several 'capital pieces', including the burnt Magna Carta. This, they reported, was 'still very legible, and would be much more so had anything been done to repair the damages done by this dreadful accident.' It was placed by itself 'in a separate drawer, viz. no. 16 at the bottom'. This press also contained a further three or four drawers filled with antiquities and 'other trinkets neither remarkable for their rareness or workmanship'.

The most interesting part of this second report is, however, the statement that some charters had been lost 'amidst the rubbish of bits of parchment or of paper, scorched by the fire, or consumed by old age, which Mr Widmore thought too much destroyed to be either used or described'. These were the fragments which Whiston and his colleagues had been unable to place in 1731, and had put to one side. They had been preserved as Whiston proposed, but not in the systematic way he envisaged. Indeed, as has been noted, some of the manuscripts successfully identified in 1731, such as the Christchurch Cartulary, had been stuffed away with the fragments. Widmore apparently thought the fragments should be disposed of, but Maty and Rimius wisely urged 'a more particular examination' before any further action, 'as it is not impossible but some things may still be retrieved'.

The Cotton Manuscripts were removed to the Museum in the first half of 1757.[56] Unlike the Sloane or Harley Manuscripts which were shelved according to subject classifications, they were arranged on shelves there by the existing 'emperor' pressmark system.[57] The Museum officers were unhappy about this arrangement, which they regarded as inelegant and unscientific. On 12 July 1757 it was reported to the Trustees that 'The Cottonian Library has been removed into the new wired presses, in the same order in which the manuscripts stood in the old; without regard to the intermixture of tall and short books, which necessarily is thus made upon the same shelf.' It was suggested it would be better to 'range them all anew'. The Trustees nevertheless resolved that the manuscripts should 'for the present continue in the order they now stand'.[58] As for the burnt manuscripts, it was reported that those 'which have been ascertained by the Catalogue, stand likewise in their order', suggesting that most of the items noted as usable by Casley were put in their appropriate places in the emperor sequence.[59] The 'other crusts and loose leaves' were, however, kept in the old presses, presumably the drawers formerly containing the charters which had been brought to the Museum. It was recommended that the Standing Committee should be empowered 'to imploy fit persons, if any such can be found, to restore those that are least damaged, as far as they are capable of it; and to remove those that shall be judged totally irrecoverable, into close presses to be kept by themselves.' Approving this proposal, the Trustees ordered that any material found to be beyond repair 'be for the present placed in the closet of the room where the Harleian Carts. now stand'.[60] The loose Cotton fragments remained associated with the Harley Charters and in 1775 the Trustees ordered that these latter 'be removed in their presses as they now stand into one of the front garrets'. The fragments remained with these charters in Garret no. 8, which became known as the charter garret.[61]

In July 1757 a Mr Mores, perhaps the typographical historian Edward Rowe Mores, wrote to the Principal Librarian claiming to have developed a method of restoring the leaves of vellum books damaged by fire. Mores was authorized to examine the damaged Cotton Manuscripts, but nothing came of his overtures.[62] In February 1758, Maty showed the Standing Committee a specimen of some loose sheets of fire damaged parchment restored by Mr Padeloup, a French bookbinder.[63] Impressed, the Committee ordered the Keeper of Manuscripts, Charles Morton, to give Padeloup one of the burnt Cotton Manuscripts. A month later Padeloup returned the manuscript duly repaired. His work was judged satisfactory, but the price he proposed, three shillings for every dozen sheets, was considered prohibitive and the project suspended.[64]

Thus matters were left for another forty years. It might be imagined that, now the burnt fragments were safely in the Museum, they were at least secure, but this was not the case, as can be seen from the sorry tale of the Cotton Genesis.[65] Casley reported that, after the fire, 'Of this valuable Monument of Antiquity, about 60 pieces of Leaves remain.' In 1743, George Vertue had borrowed some to make water-colour drawings of them to be shown at the Society of Antiquaries. Engravings of these drawings were published in *Vetusta Monumenta* in 1747. These fragments then disappeared from sight. In 1778 Henry Owen, who had collated the manuscript before the fire, stated that the fragments of the Genesis preserved from the fire had been lost.[66] At the end of the eighteenth century, Joseph Planta could only find eighteen, none of which were among those copied by Vertue. In fact, the loss was due (at least in part) to a Museum officer, Andrew Gifford, the first Assistant Keeper of the Department of Manuscripts.[67] On his death in 1784, Gifford, a Baptist minister, left his collections to the Bristol Baptist College. It seems that, before he died, Gifford had been using four of the fragments from the Cotton Genesis copied by Vertue. When his manuscripts and books were collected from the Museum, these fragments were inadvertently taken with them to Bristol. There they remained, unidentified and forgotten. In a 1795 catalogue of the Bristol library they were described as 'some pieces of an old copy of the Septuagint said to have been found in the ruins of the city of Herculaneum'. They were only finally reidentified in 1834 by

399

Frederic Gotch, who wrote to Hartwell Horne, an Under-Librarian at the Museum, pointing out their survival. Horne amended a footnote in one of his publications referring to the Cotton Genesis, but the Museum authorities took no further action.[68] Gotch's discoveries remained virtually unknown until 1881 when he published a transcription of the Bristol fragments as a supplement to Tischendorf's edition of the text of the fragments left in the Museum.[69] Five other fragments used by Vertue have never been traced.[70] In his diary for 13 March 1856,[71] the redoubtable Keeper of Manuscripts Sir Frederic Madden speculated that the lost fragments might also have been taken to Bristol with Gifford's books. However, they have never been identified there. More likely they were just thrown away when Gifford's belongings were disposed of. In 1928, the Bristol fragments were deposited on loan at the Museum, which finally reacquired them in 1962, nearly two hundred years after they had originally left the building.[72]

IV

In 1792, Thomas Astle, Keeper of Records at the Tower of London, urged the Trustees to authorize the compilation of a new catalogue of the Cotton library.[73] Users of the Cotton collection were at this time still chiefly reliant on Smith's 1696 catalogue. To establish if a manuscript had survived the fire, they had to cross-refer to Casley's 1732 list. In 1777 Samuel Hooper had produced a subject catalogue of the Cotton collection,[74] but, although he published the corrections of Maty and Rimius to Casley's schedule of damaged manuscripts,[75] his work was of limited assistance to readers grappling with Smith and Casley. Accordingly, the Standing Committee of the Trustees ordered the Keeper of Manuscripts, Joseph Planta, to investigate the matter. In his report, dated 14 December 1793,[76] Planta declared that most of the volumes contained a great number of articles 'bound up with very little attention to any arrangement either as to authors, matter or date'. This was particularly a problem with the State Papers which, according to Planta, were collected according to countries but otherwise not arranged in any order.[77] He considered Smith's catalogue wholly deficient, both in its arrangement and in the lack of detailed descriptions of individual State Papers. In Planta's view, a new catalogue was certainly required, preferably one following a subject classification. This would also provide an opportunity of rearranging the collection 'in a classical order, which no doubt ought always to have the preference'. Alternatively, the new catalogue should have a detailed index.

Luckily, the Trustees were unwilling to see the collection rearranged. Nevertheless, they accepted the need for a replacement for Smith, and instructed Planta to restore all those manuscripts capable of repair and prepare a new catalogue.[78] The descriptive section of the catalogue was completed by November 1796.[79] The index was compiled between 1796 and 1802,[80] and the whole catalogue finally published by the Record Commission in 1802.[81] The section of the published preface describing the procedures adopted by Planta in conserving and cataloguing the manuscripts is copied almost word for word from a report submitted by him to the Trustees on 4 November 1796.[82] In this,

Planta gives a detailed account of the second phase of major restoration work on the Cotton collection.

Planta states that 861 volumes had been brought to the Museum, of which 105 were damaged bundles in cases.[83] This indicates that he concentrated on those burnt manuscripts whose identity was readily ascertainable and which had been placed on their arrival in the Museum in the main emperor sequence. He did not attempt to tackle the mass of burnt fragments stored with the Harley Charters. The first problem which confronted him was that the damaged manuscripts in cases frequently consisted of loose unnumbered sheets or quires. The order of these sheets – already disrupted as a result of the fire and the hasty rescue work in 1731 – had been further confused by their use in the Reading Room. Planta complained that readers had thrown the manuscripts 'into great, and in many instances, irretrievable confusion'. Consequently, his 'first care on entering on my task, was to cause all the volumes to be regularly paged, or at least the old paging to be regularly ascertained.' This ink foliation can still be seen on many of the manuscripts.[84] The foliations are in a variety of different hands, and were probably made for Planta by various attendants in the Department.[85] Damage to the manuscript margins made it difficult to position the numbers and occasionally the foliators were forced to write them in the middle of the page.[86] Ink foliation notes are given at the end of the volumes, using the characteristic early Museum formula 'Constat fol.'

Planta then 'proceeded to examine the bundles in cases, and found means, after many repeated and not a few unsuccessful attempts, to arrange several volumes and parts of volumes of State Papers. Some of the shrivelled MSS. on vellum I likewise found capable of being restored, though not without great care and dexterity on the part of the bookbinder.' In his original report he identifies the binder as C. Elliot, the Museum binder from 1773 to 1815. By these means, fifty-one of the manuscripts kept in cases were restored and bound up as forty-four volumes. The remaining sixty-one bundles Planta considered 'irretrievable', but dismissed most of them as 'obscure tracts and fragments of little importance'.

Planta's report gives an unduly rosy picture of the condition of the Cotton collection at the conclusion of his work. Little progress had been made with the damaged vellum manuscripts.[87] A number of important manuscripts were left as loose sheets in cases, including, for example, one of the earliest manuscripts of Bede (Tiberius A. XIV). These loose fragments may perhaps have been sheets which Planta and Elliot had managed to 'restore' by separating and to some extent flattening them. Many other manuscripts were left simply as 'crusts' in cases. Far from being 'obscure tracts and fragments of little importance', they included cartularies of St Albans (Tiberius E. VI, Otho D. III), St James, Northampton (Tiberius E. V), the Annals of Dunstable (Tiberius A. X), and the eleventh-century Vitellius Psalter (Vitellius E. XVIII).

Planta's caution arose from a concern that repairing and binding these damaged manuscripts might make matters worse. This is borne out by comments by two later Keepers of Manuscripts. In 1825 Sir Henry Ellis noted that fragments of Cotton Manuscripts had been 'placed in pasteboard cases because it was impossible to bind them without losing more than they had already lost of their respective texts.'[88] Similarly, in 1835 Josiah Forshall reminded a parliamentary Select Committee investigating the Museum that 'In many cases there is a great risk of doing more injury by any attempt to repair a manuscript that has been damaged by the fire than if it is left in its damaged state.'[89]

Like his predecessors in 1731, Planta concentrated on the paper manuscripts. Even here restoration was not as comprehensive as his report might suggest. Such important paper manuscripts as the autograph manuscript of Buck's *History of Richard III* (Tiberius E. X), a volume of Joscelin's collections (Vitellius D. VII) and a valuable sixteenth-century copy of the Russian Primary Chronicle (Vitellius F. X)[90] were left as loose sheets in cases, as were some volumes of the early State Papers such as Caligula D. IV, V, X and XI.[91] Planta's success in identifying and reconstituting the paper manuscripts is difficult to establish. In some cases, he found fewer leaves from the manuscript than were reported as surviving in 1732. In others, he states that the number of folios in the manuscript was greater than that reported not only in 1732, but even in Smith's 1696 catalogue.[92] These discrepancies may be partly due to the rearrangement of papers, but may also suggest that Planta's methods for identifying loose papers and reuniting them with their parent volumes were less rigorous than might be hoped.

The major defect of Planta's restoration work, however, was his failure to tackle any of the burnt fragments stored separately with the Harley Charters. Large portions of many of the numerous manuscripts marked 'deest' or 'desideratur' by him were in fact sitting in a garret not far from his study. Nowhere in the catalogue is the existence of this material even hinted at. Planta's complacent account of the state of the collection at the completion of his catalogue is therefore seriously misleading. It could even be argued that in some ways Planta's work made matters worse. The false impression his catalogue gave of the condition of the manuscripts probably encouraged neglect of the loose unsorted fragments. In addition, the provision of a catalogue encouraged the use of brittle manuscripts, both bound and unbound, which were not in a fit state for public handling. The vulnerable edges of the manuscripts were completely unprotected, and pieces of text broke off as they were used by readers. Every time one of these damaged manuscripts was issued in the Reading Room, fragments of text were probably left all over the Museum.

The effects of the continued handling of these fragile manuscripts have been most strikingly documented in the case of the *Beowulf* text in Vitellius A. XV. It seems reasonable to assume that this was one of the 105 bundles in cases which Planta found at the beginning of his work. The state of the manuscript in the 1780s is recorded in the two transcripts associated with the Danish antiquary Grímur Jónsson Thorkelin,[93] which record over 1,900 letters which afterwards disappeared as a result of the crumbling of the edges of the manuscript.[94] Apparently, fragments of text were being lost even as the transcripts were being prepared. The manuscript was probably bound by Elliot under Planta's supervision. Planta's catalogue entries usually indicated if a particular volume was kept in a case, and there is no such reference in his description of Vitellius

A. XV.[95] Given the testimony of Ellis, Forshall and Planta himself as to the hazards of binding brittle vellum manuscripts, it seems likely that further damage to the *Beowulf* text occurred in the process of binding the manuscript in the 1790s. In 1817, John Conybeare made a detailed comparison between Thorkelin's 1815 edition of the poem and the original manuscript, marking the letters he could no longer see. According to Conybeare, over 900 letters had vanished by 1817.[96] A more accurate collation made by Sir Frederic Madden in 1824 shows even greater loss than that noted by Conybeare.[97] Much of the damage to the manuscript in the early nineteenth century was due to unrestricted handling of it by readers. Ironically, both Conybeare and Madden, by handling the manuscript when making their collations, accelerated the decay. The erosion of the *Beowulf* text continued until 1845, when the manuscript was inlaid, at last providing the fragile edges of the manuscript with some protection and preventing further loss. Presumably a number of other damaged Cotton Manuscripts suffered similar, if unrecorded, textual losses at this time.[98]

Planta's successors as Keepers of Manuscripts, Robert Nares and Francis Douce, did not undertake any further work on the Cotton Manuscripts. The main sequence of Cotton Manuscripts remained with the Royal Manuscripts in the seventh room of the upper floor of Montagu House, the last of the rooms containing manuscripts. Both collections remained in their original order, the 1808 synopsis of the Museum noting apologetically that 'These two libraries are not classed in a strict scientific order.'[99] At this time, the Cotton Manuscripts occupied twenty-one presses, six more than those allowed for by the Emperor system (including the Appendix as a separate case). The use of boxes to house some burnt manuscripts presumably made it difficult to follow the system of one press per emperor.[100] This perhaps prompted the decision to write numerical pressmarks, consisting of a roman numeral for the press and a letter for the shelf, in pencil on the flyleaf of the manuscripts. Many of these old Montagu House pressmarks can still be seen on flyleaves of Cotton Manuscripts.[101]

As long as manuscripts continued to be stored as loose vellum sheets in flimsy boxes, there were endless possibilities for loss and confusion. In June 1825 Sir Henry Ellis, who succeeded Douce as Keeper of Manuscripts in 1812, reported to the Trustees a misfortune with the autograph manuscript of Sir George Buck's *History of Richard III* (Tiberius E. X).[102] A reader called Yarnold had collated the Cotton manuscript with another in his possession. 'Having but one eye, and very indifferent sight in the other', Yarnold had accidentally taken away half a leaf of the Cotton manuscript with his own papers. On discovering his mistake, he had returned the fragment. Sometime later, Yarnold's books were sold. One lot was described as a manuscript of Buck. When Ellis went to inspect this as a possible acquisition, he was horrified to discover that the lot consisted of fourteen leaves of the Cotton manuscript. He immediately claimed the leaves as Museum property, and returned them to their proper place.

Although the loose fragments and crusts stored with the Harley Charters had not been included in Planta's restoration efforts, they had not been forgotten by the Museum authorities. On 14 May 1825, the Standing Committee of the Trustees agreed that a small bundle of cinders and other fragments of Cotton Manuscripts should be sent to William Hyde Wollaston so that he could undertake experiments on them.[103] Wollaston was distinguished as a physiologist, chemist and physicist, who even anticipated some of Faraday's discoveries about electricity. Indeed, it was said that each of Wollaston's fifty-six papers in many different fields marked 'a distinct advance in the particular science concerned'.[104] The reasons for Wollaston's interest in the Cotton fragments are unclear. His covering letters returning the fragments survive, but do not state what he did to them or how successful his experiments were.[105] In fact, whatever his experiments, the results were disastrous. The state of the leaves treated by Wollaston was described in his diary by Sir Frederic Madden thirty years later: 'these leaves are almost like *biscuit*, and contracted to one third of their original size! Simply soaking them in water would have been much more effectual. Of these leaves sent to Dr. W. sixteen prove to be part of Grosthead's Works in Otho D. X, and *complete the volume*; while eleven others belong to the Higden, Otho D. I, and one to Vitellius E. IX.'[106] Madden later reported that he was able to counteract the effects of Wollaston's process by soaking the leaves in water, so that they expanded again to 'one half of their original size'.[107]

Despite the unpromising results of Wollaston's first experiments, Ellis proposed in June 1825 that he be sent some fragments from the Cotton Genesis.[108] Ellis felt that these leaves would be particularly suitable for experiment, since this manuscript had not been as badly shrunken by the fire as others. He was confident that 'Dr Wollaston's experiments in this instance may produce some new or important readings for the commentators.' This suggests that Wollaston was not attempting to flatten the fragments but trying to make them more legible by using some form of chemical agent. The results of his experiments on the Cotton Genesis are not known. Perhaps the most revealing aspect of the affair is Ellis's statement to the Trustees that the Cotton fragments 'do not form a Part of the Collection of Manuscripts at the present time but are kept in a garret at the top of the House, perfectly useless to the Museum in every sense of the word.'[109] Ellis was shortly to be proved quite wrong.

V

In January 1826, a few months after Wollaston had finished his further shrivelling of Cotton fragments, Henry Petrie, Keeper of Records at the Tower, wrote to the Standing Committee of the Trustees, 'expressing a hope that some mode might be devised by which certain masses of the Fragments of the Cotton Library, ... which are at present preserved in cases, may be rendered readable without the risk of losing portions of their leaves from their adhesion and brittleness whenever an attempt is made to ascertain their contents.'[110] The Committee asked Sir Humphry Davy, a Trustee, to talk to Petrie about the problem.[111] A month later the Standing Committee 'Resolved that the plan proposed by Sir Humphry Davy of submerging the burnt manuscripts on vellum belonging to the Cottonian collection which were injured in the fire of 1731 be adopted, from time to time, upon such MSS. as it may be desirable to examine: also that the edges of such manuscripts may be cut, where there is no writing, for the sake of separating the leaves.'[112] On 12 May 1826 the Assistant Keeper of Manuscripts, Josiah Forshall, informed the Trustees that 'The means recommended by the President of the Royal Society for the restoration of these MSS. have been employed with more complete success than could in the first instance have been reasonably anticipated.'[113] Tiberius D. III, a collection of saints' lives in which Petrie had expressed a particular interest, 'was first carefully divided into convenient portions, and these were severally immersed for a longer or shorter time as they appeared more or less scorched. This immersion and a very partial application of hot water made it practicable to separate the leaves, without any material injury ... By making incisions between the columns and lines of writing, thus making room for an expansion of the parts most shrivelled and contracted by the fire, and by subsequently applying a gentle pressure until the moisture was evaporated, the leaves have been rendered sufficiently flat and smooth to admit of the contents being read for the most part with great facility.'[114] The process recommended by Davy was therefore to soak the manuscript to make it more pliable and then cut it open. The exact nature of the solution used to soften the manuscript is not known; Madden reported that it consisted of a solution of spirits of zinc and water.[115]

Encouraged by their success with Tiberius D. III, Ellis and Forshall were keen to try and restore some of the fragments stored in the charter garret. Forshall immediately tried the technique on what 'appeared at first sight mere lumps of wax and cinder'. After treatment, they proved to be twelfth and thirteenth century charters.[116] During June 1826, Ellis and Forshall sorted through the material in the garret to establish which fragments were worth treating. Ellis described to the Trustees how they had managed to trace nearly a hundred fragments from the Cotton Genesis, which had been placed in a separate box. Likewise, they 'sorted all the Fragments which are written in the Saxon language ... ; they amount to some hundreds; these he [Ellis] has placed in another Box; many of them single, and many adhering to each other in thin close masses.'[117]

Forshall bore the brunt of this difficult work,[118] which continued after he became Keeper in 1827.[119] About forty manuscripts were treated in this way.[120] The leaves were separated, partially flattened and stored loose in solander cases. Even after treatment the leaves remained brittle, and were clearly still at great risk from careless handling in the Reading Room. Madden afterwards described Forshall's efforts as only a 'very partial' attempt at restoration,[121] and this seems to have been a justified criticism. Nevertheless, substantial progress was made.[122]

Forshall's work led to the recovery of a number of important Anglo-Saxon manuscripts which were described by Planta as being either lost or unusable. Among the most spectacular rediscoveries were: the unique manuscript of King Alfred's prosimetrical translation of Boethius (Otho A. VI);[123] 131 leaves from the Old English translation of the Pastoral Care (Tiberius B. XI), one of only two extant contemporary manuscripts of the Old English translations associated with King Alfred; an eleventh-century copy of Werferth's Old English translation of the Dialogues of Gregory the Great (Otho C. I, vol. 2); the Vitellius Psalter (Vitellius E. XVIII), complete except for eleven leaves, ten of which were afterwards found by Madden; fragments of the insular Gospels in Otho C. V; two eleventh-century manuscripts of Ælfric's Homilies (Vitellius C. V and D. XVII); and a large part of Tiberius A. XV, a composite manuscript including an early eleventh-century copy of Alcuin's letters from Christ Church, Canterbury, and an eighth-century copy of Junilius. Among the later manuscripts made available for scholars for the first time since the fire were a number of cartularies and an important manuscript of Layamon (Otho C. XIII).[124] Forshall also located extra leaves of manuscripts probably partly restored by Planta, such as the early Bede (Tiberius A. XIV) to which he added five leaves, and the Worcester cartulary (Tiberius A. XIII). Most notable of all was the work on the Cotton Genesis. Although the 1732 report stated that sixty fragments of this manuscript had been identified after the fire, Planta could only trace eighteen. In July 1826, Forshall reported that 110 fragments of the volume, previously among the loose fragments in the charter garret, had been identified, unrolled and cleaned, '88 of which it had been found possible to appropriate to their respective places.' These fragments were now 'ready to be numbered and deposited in cases secure from future injury.'[125] Madden was afterwards to increase the number of fragments preserved to 147.[126] Madden's work in identifying and preserving this manuscript has long been recognized, but Forshall's major role has not been noted.

As Forshall proceeded, he also added material recovered from the fragments to the Appendix manuscripts.[127] Above all, however, he also prepared detailed descriptions of the restored volumes, and proposed printing these in a supplement to Planta's catalogue.[128] A few of these survive, still unpublished, in copies made for Sir Frederic Madden and inserted in an annotated copy of Planta, preserved in the reference library of the Manuscripts Department.[129]

Forshall is a forgotten pioneer in the restoration of the Cotton Manuscripts. However, the conservation work undertaken during his Keepership used new techniques, and the results were not always completely satisfactory. Not only was the restoration incomplete, resulting in a pile of loose brittle leaves in a box, but some unnecessary damage was caused. In particular, vellum leaves were cut at the edge both to allow the fat-covered crusts to be opened and individual leaves to be flattened. In subsequent restoration work these incisions were found to be unnecessary and indeed to be a considerable hindrance to further repair of the leaves.[130] The incisions that Forshall had made account for the serrated appearance of the leaves in many burnt Cotton Manuscripts, and are particularly visible in, for example, Otho B. II, a copy of Alfred's translation of the Pastoral Care,[131] Otho C. XIII, an early copy of Layamon, and Otho C. I, volume one, an Anglo-Saxon translation of the Gospels.

The greatest blot on Forshall's record in the conservation of the Cotton Manuscripts is the work on the burnt Magna Carta, Cotton Charter xiii. 31a. In May 1834, he drew the Trustees' attention to the condition of 'Magna Carta and the ancient and otherwise valuable charters in the Cottonian MS. Augustus A.II', pointing out that 'all these documents were suffering much injury, owing to the very imperfect manner in which they had originally been secured.'[132] It is clear from a later report that Forshall was referring to the burnt Magna Carta rather than the other exemplar (Augustus II. 106).[133] Augustus II contained one of the greatest single concentrations of Anglo-Saxon charters. Forshall's minute implies that the 136 varied documents with this pressmark were still bound as a single volume, which would inevitably have caused damage to them. Forshall recommended that Hogarth, the restorer who had been used in unrolling and fixing the Egyptian papyri (then kept in the Manuscripts Department), should repair and secure the charters.[134] A month later, he reported that this work had been satisfactorily accomplished.[135] In fact, the results as far as the Magna Carta was concerned seem to have been far from satisfactory. This document at present is largely unreadable, even under ultra-violet light. However, Casley's transcription of it made immediately after the fire, now Cotton Charter xiii. 31b, gives a virtually complete text.[136] Similarly, in 1733 John Pine published an engraving of the burnt Magna Carta which showed the damage caused by the fire as limited chiefly to the melting of the seal.[137] Moreover, Maty and Rimius reported in 1756 that the document was still 'very legible'.[138] This certainly could not be said of its present condition. Most of the damage to this document was, therefore, probably due to the repair work of 1834 rather than the fire, a conclusion supported by Madden's comment that this copy of Magna Carta was 'Injured in the fire of 1731 (and still more by the injudicious treatment it received from Mr Hogarth)'.[139]

Forshall's restoration work received some public attention during the proceedings of a parliamentary Select Committee into the administration of the Museum in 1835–6. The Committee had been disturbed by Forshall's statement that 'There were in the year 1824 a great quantity of crusts or fragments of manuscripts remaining unopened.'[140] Pressed by the Committee, Forshall explained that he referred only to 'the fragments and relics left by the fire, namely, the remnants of about 130 volumes, which were damaged to a considerable extent, and perhaps much more than one half of them, being those manuscripts that were very much damaged, remained in the same condition until the year 1824 … I thought them, when I came to the Museum, of so much value, that I spent a great deal of pains in washing and opening them. The operation took up much time, and occasioned some expense.'[141] Questioned as to how he knew that there were not other Cotton Manuscripts worth unrolling, Forshall emphasized that such a judgement depended on the description in Smith's catalogue, claiming that the value of a burnt crust could be 'ascertained in most cases from bare inspection', and that the crusts left unconserved were not worth the expense of unrolling.[142] By this time, Forshall felt, like Planta before him, that he had completed the restoration of the Cotton library and that everything worth saving was available for scholars to consult. He repeatedly told the Assistant Keeper of Manuscripts, Frederic Madden, that no further Cotton fragments of any value were preserved in the Museum.[143]

During the Easter week of 1827, the Manuscript collections of the Museum were transferred from Montagu House to the accommodation in the new Museum building which (until the opening of the St Pancras building) they still occupy.[144] It was at this point that use of the emperor pressmarks for shelving the Cotton Manuscripts finally ceased. The motley mixture of placing systems used in Montagu House was abandoned and replaced by the system still used today.[145] The manuscripts were ranked on the shelf according to size, regardless of previous numeration or subject content. They were then given a separate pressmark. At first, this consisted of a roman numeral for the press and a letter for the shelf; from the mid-nineteenth century, arabic numerals were used for the press. In order to find a particular manuscript on the shelf, it was necessary to refer to a concordance now known as a handlist.[146] These pressmarks were pencilled on the flyleaf. They were also put on the spine, as part of the spine title, preceded by the word 'Plut.' for *Pluteus* or shelf.[147] Later in the nineteenth century, the modern procedure of using printed labels on the spine for the pressmark was introduced.[148]

VI

One of the 1835–6 Select Committee's principal recommendations was that the office of Secretary of the Museum should no longer be combined with one of the Keeperships, and, by April 1837, Forshall had confided to his assistant, Sir Frederic Madden, his intention to retain the office of Secretary and resign as Keeper of Manuscripts.[149] On 17 April Madden asked Forshall if they could inspect the old charter garret. Madden's diary records what they found:[150]

Mr Forshall ... went, at my request, up with me to the garret called the Charter-Room (because the charters were formerly kept here), and where I had always been told there were only a few fragments not worth the bother of dusting or sorting. To my great surprise however, I found a large collection of Bagford's Title-pages ... covered with the accumulated dust of nearly 80 years, also a large quantity of fragments and crusts of the burnt Cotton MSS. many of which appeared to me well worth the process of restoration. Mr F. had always assured me he had selected from them every thing worth preserving, but I saw enough before me to doubt the accuracy of his statement, and going on with my searches, I discovered in an old cupboard the identical *Cartulary of Christ Church Twinham* in Hampshire [Tiberius D. VI], which I have so often and so fruitlessly inquired after, and very little the worse for the fire, except being wrinkled up! Is not this very disgraceful of the Keepers of MSS. from the middle of the last century to the present day? ... I saw enough to make me resolve in my own mind, to have the entire room cleared out, whenever it should be my lot to be Keeper of the MSS. and I resolved at once to bring down into my own room the two large bundles which formed the Christ Church Cartulary, and a third bundle which apparently contains an English Chronicle. I left up in the garret fragments of crusts of vellum enough to fill several bushel baskets, likewise a box full of receipts of Sir Robert Cotton's, and three boxes said to contain the refuse of the Hargrave collection. It is very much to the discredit of Mr F that affairs should have remained thus, and so I believe he felt, when I produced to him the long lost Christ Church Cartulary, which he had declared to me over and over again could not by any possibility exist!

Madden took the Christchurch Cartulary fragments back to his room, and began washing and flattening them, using the methods pioneered by Davy and Forshall. His personal diary for 26 April 1837 notes:

Continued the washing & pressing of the burnt Cartulary of Ch. Ch. Twinham, Hants., which

I am happy to find, will be perfectly legible, after it has undergone the process. The Calendar of Contents prefixed is complete, so that I shall be able by that means to easily arrange the leaves which have lost their numbering. The account given of this Priory in the New Editn. of the Monasticon is very trifling, and, Ellis declares, without any reason, that the Cartulary was lost in the Cotton fire![151]

In July 1837 Madden was appointed Keeper of Manuscripts. On 16 August he began to 'make a list of all the Cotton MSS. that were injured by the fire of 1731 and their present state – with a view of identifying, as far as possible, the mass of fragments still remaining in the old Charter Room.'[152] On his return from holiday in October 1837, Madden badgered Forshall into handing over the keys of the charter room,[153] and immediately made a further examination of its contents. He gave a detailed account of the material stored there in his work diary for 31 October 1837 (afterwards adding notes on further investigations undertaken during November):

Went up in the old Charter Room & looked out Bagford's long neglected loose collections – also the remainder of the Cartulary of Ch[rist] Ch[urch] Twinham, Hants and many other valuable fragments which I propose to have restored. The contents of this room are at present as follows.
1. A very large box filled with fragments of burnt vellum Cotton MSS. the greater part broken and single leaves. In a dreadful state of dirt and confusion. (lock)
2. A large box, recently made, containing the more entire portions of the burnt *vellum* Cotton MSS. (lock)
3. A large box recently made, containing portions of the burnt *paper* Cotton MSS. and also bundles of Cotton bills & Accounts &c. (lock)
4. A box, locked, but found to be empty, when forced open on 23d Nov.
5. A larger box, containing Hargrave law papers (opened 23 Nov.)
6. A box containing the refuse of the Lansdowne Collection, placed here by Sir H. Ellis (Nailed down)[154]
7. A small box containing papers relating to the British Fishery Company (chiefly powers of attorney) and some miscellaneous papers of no value, the latter placed there by myself.[155]

As Madden's annotations indicate, these precious boxes of Cotton fragments were locked up again after he had examined them, but he removed some of the larger vellum fragments and on 2 November again spent most of the day personally washing and flattening the further fragments of the cartulary of Christchurch Priory he had found.[156] Madden was a native of Hampshire and planned to write a history of the county.[157] The rediscovery of the Christchurch Cartulary was an achievement of which he was particularly proud.[158]

The fact that Madden himself made the first attempts at restoring the Christchurch Cartulary indicates the limited resources for major conservation work at his disposal. He doubted whether the Museum's binder, Charles Tuckett, was equal to the intricate task of dealing with the brittle vellum fragments. Forshall had preferred to use Hogarth on more delicate work, such as unrolling the Egyptian papyri, and even he had caused great damage when working on the burnt Magna Carta. On 11 January 1838 Madden reported to the Trustees:

that he has received from Dr [Bulkeley] Bandinel, chief librarian of the Bodleian Library, and Dr [Philip] Bliss, Registrar, very strong testimonials in favour of a person named [Henry] Gough, who has been extensively employed to repair, inlay, and restore damaged manuscripts in the Bodleian and several of the College Libraries at Oxford ... [He] recommends most seriously, that he should be permitted to have a trial, in the restoration of the burnt Cotton charters (now from the state in which they are in, impossible to be used), and also on a few of the most valuable MSS. such as the Greek psalter on papyrus, purchased of Dr Hogg;[159] the fragments of the burnt Cotton Genesis; the remains of the Saxon Boethius, and other Saxon fragments, which cannot at present [be] consulted without injury to them, and which require a very practiced hand to restore them.
Dr Bandinel assures Sir F.M. that the terms of Gough are very moderate. He is at present still employed at Oxford, but will shortly come up to London.[160]

It is evident that Madden did not at this stage envisage using Gough for a full-scale restoration of the Cotton Manuscripts. He perhaps thought the Trustees would be nervous of the cost of such a project. Instead, he seems to have intended employing him to protect those manuscripts of which large sections had been recovered by Forshall and which were in danger of damage as a result of the handling of loose unprotected leaves in the Reading Room. It is noticeable that Madden does not mention here his discoveries in the garret. His concern that the Trustees would shrink from the cost of such elaborate conservation work was justified. On 26 May they refused Gough's services.[161] Madden noted in his diary: 'I am of opinion they neglect the interests of this Department by such a step.'[162] He continued working himself on some of the newly recovered fragments. In his personal diary for 17 July 1838, he wrote: 'Went up in the Old Charter Room and finished looking over the larger box containing the burnt Cotton fragments, and selecting the best portion. Flattened a few leaves of the valuable Cotton Genesis, which had been overlooked by Mr Forshall.'[163] On the following day, he 'Flattened some fragments of Saxon MSS. and discovered two leaves of the curious *Proverbs* ascribed to Alfred [Galba A. XIX], supposed to have been totally destroyed in the fire.'[164]

The impetus for the full restoration of the Cotton collection came not from Madden, but from that ubiquitous figure in nineteenth-century manuscript studies, Sir Thomas Phillipps. On 10 October 1838 Phillipps wrote to William Richard Hamilton, a Museum Trustee, expressing his concern about the condition of the damaged Cotton Manuscripts and suggesting that the most valuable should be transcribed before they were sent for binding.[165] The Trustees were at last persuaded of the need for action and instructed Madden to prepare a report on the damaged Cotton Manuscripts, indicating which were sufficiently important to be worth the expense of transcription.

Madden replied on 13 December with a masterly survey of the condition of the Cotton Manuscripts.[166] This was more comprehensive than any previous survey of the condition of the manuscripts, since he described all the volumes damaged in the fire, not just those worst affected. He divided the damaged manuscripts (as distinct from the fragments) into three classes. The first comprised 'Those MSS. which by the agency of heat have been compressed and corrugated, with the edges burnt, and in many cases, broken, torn, and dirtied. These are in number 35, all of which, if skilfully flattened, inlaid and repaired, might be protected from further injury, and rendered in a comparatively good condition for general use.'[167] Madden pointed out that 'Many of these MSS. are among the most valuable of those possessed by the Museum, such for instance, as the unique Saxon poem of Beowulf [Vitellius A. XV], the Saxon Grammar of Ælfric [Julius A. II], a copy of the Saxon Chronicle [Tiberius B. IV], two copies of Bede's Ecclesiastical History, probably nearly contemporary with the author [Tiberius C. II, and presumably Tiberius A. XIV, although this was in fact stored as loose leaves at this time, and was elsewhere correctly assigned by Madden to the third class]; two exceedingly curious copies of Aratus &c., with illuminations, of the tenth and eleventh centuries [Tiberius B. V and C. I], a Psalter with a Saxon Gloss [Tiberius C. VI]; the Cartulary of Worcester with the Saxon Charters &c. [Tiberius A. XIII].' He observed that 'None of these MSS. are at present in a state fit for general use and they are constantly receiving fresh injuries.' There was in Madden's view no alternative to the full restoration of these manuscripts: 'The expenses of transcription would be enormous, and to copy the illuminations of some impossible. Sir F.M. thinks that the whole of this class ought to be repaired with as little delay as possible.' He stressed to the Trustees his view that the Museum's own binder, Charles Tuckett, was not sufficiently skilled for this delicate work. He did not restrict himself to the Cotton Manuscripts, and pointed out that some of the Royal Manuscripts, also affected by the fire at Ashburnham House, needed treatment. Madden drew the Trustees' attention in particular to Royal MS. 15 C. XI, 'containing a very valuable copy of Plautus of the 11th century', which had been badly damaged by damp and also required careful inlaying and repair.

Madden's second class of damaged manuscripts consisted of 'those MSS. (chiefly on paper) which have been burnt on the edges and part of the writing injured or are otherwise out of repair.' These manuscripts were no less valuable than those in the first class, since they 'comprehend a very large portion of the original State Correspondence between England and other countries from the reign of Henry the Eighth to the reign of James the First.' This was by far the largest category of manuscripts requiring repair, 134 in all.[168] Unlike the manuscripts of the first class, Madden felt that all were 'capable of being inlaid or bound by Tuckett.' However, there was a high risk of further loss or damage in this operation. Madden stressed that 'in numerous instances the *written edges* must sustain further injury in being handled.' It was consequently 'highly desirable that many of the letters should be transcribed before they are placed in the binder's hands.'

The third class of damaged manuscripts consisted of those loose leaves in solander cases, chiefly the manuscripts reclaimed by Forshall but also including a number which Planta had been reluctant to have bound up. Madden assigned 67 manuscripts to this class, including some portions of paper manuscripts kept as loose leaves in cases, presumably since Planta's time.[169] He recommended that these manuscripts should also be inlaid and bound, and the most vulnerable parts transcribed. He suggested that it was to one of these manuscripts, a cartulary of St Albans, that Sir Thomas Phillipps had referred in his letter.[170] Madden pointed out that the edges of this manuscript had been '*greatly injured* and broken by readers'. This was certainly a manuscript worthy of full transcription.

This, Madden emphasized, was merely the tip of the iceberg, namely those manuscripts available in the Reading Room and kept with the main manuscript collections. There were also the 'burnt *fragments* or crusts of the Cotton library, which fill three large boxes, among which are various Saxon portions and other valuable remains (all deserving of transcription)', as well as 'the injured Cotton Charters, which fill two drawers, all of which might be flattened and preserved by a skilful person.' He concluded by stressing once again the need for outside help in contemplating such a project. He sought to 'press on the attention of the Trustees...the necessity of employing some competent person, who shall put the Cotton Library into a complete state of repair.' He also returned to an old hobbyhorse, the need of attaching a transcriber to the department 'whose sole business should be to transcribe and copy. The utility of such a measure must soon become apparent, for many of the Royal and other autographs are wearing out from constant use, and the same is the case in regard to the Indexes to the Heraldic Visitations and collections of pedigrees.'

Madden's report provided a blueprint for the restoration of the Cotton Manuscripts. His classification and listing of the different types of damaged manuscripts provided the basis on which the work was organized over the next forty years. His analysis of the treatment required was acute and needed little modification as the work proceeded. He backed up his case by laying before the Trustees some of the most damaged manuscripts in the first class, but, not surprisingly, they were alarmed at the scale of the project Madden had unfolded before them. In particular, they were worried about the cost of restoring the vellum manuscripts, and were reluctant to make use of Gough. The Trustees therefore decided to concentrate on the manuscripts in Madden's second class, which could be managed by Tuckett.

They ordered that the damaged paper manuscripts should be repaired, and on 10 January 1839 Madden presented them with a detailed list of these manuscripts.[171] Twenty-five of these were marked by him as at risk of serious textual loss in the course of binding. He described these as consisting largely 'of Original State Correspondence and Papers between England and France, 1577–1620, between England and Belgium, 1516–1586, and between England and Rome, 1509–1529'. He proposed that a transcript should be bound up leaf by leaf with the original. The remaining manuscripts in this list only required careful repairing and rebinding, so that the labour of transcribing their contents before binding was not justifiable. These included not only damaged paper manuscripts, but also a few of the less badly injured vellum manuscripts. In order to reduce the cost of the proposed transcriptions, Madden suggested 'the plan not of copying these papers *in intire*, but only the marginal words, which run the risk of being broken off in the hands of the reader or binder (indeed[172] several of this class of scorched

MSS. have already materially so suffered), and after the transcript is made, to bind it up leaf by leaf with the original.'[173]

Madden describes the Trustees' reactions to his proposals: 'although they saw with their own eyes & confessed the necessity, yet the *expense* (about 300£) seemed such a bugbear in their eyes, that they would only authorise me to have one volume done in the manner I proposed.'[174] It was agreed to prepare a transcript of Caligula E. VII as a trial.[175] The experiment proved unsuccessful. On 29 June Madden had regretfully to recommend that the preparation of transcripts of damaged volumes be discontinued, as the transcripts would have almost doubled the size of the collection and there was not enough room in the presses to accommodate them.[176] It was therefore agreed that 'all of this class should be inlaid and rebound forthwith by Tuckett.'[177] On 11 July 1839 work finally began in earnest. Madden 'gave Tuckett the binder Caligula E. VII, as well as one of the injured Saxon charters.'[178] Once started, the restoration of the paper manuscripts proceeded quickly. By the end of 1841 the bulk of the manuscripts in this category had been successfully repaired.[179]

Madden had not forgotten the damaged vellum manuscripts. His reaction to the Trustees' decision to concentrate on the paper manuscripts was to urge on them 'the propriety of placing certain restrictions on the use of the damaged Cotton MSS. until they shall have been secured against further injury.'[180] He gave a characteristically vivid description of the danger facing these manuscripts: 'At present every person who receives a ticket to the Reading Room, has thereby a sanction to send for every MS. in the collection, without regard to its condition or value, and it may be adviseable, without placing any check to the researches of persons properly qualified to examine MSS. to put these arrangements on a somewhat different footing.' Manuscripts were at this time read in the general Reading Room.[181] Asked to outline what changes he would make, he proposed issuing 'a distinct ticket for readers wishing to use MSS'.[182] This proposal did not find favour and Madden's later attempts to ensure that the more valuable manuscripts did not leave his department caused great antagonism.[183]

During 1840, although much preoccupied with the repair of the paper manuscripts, Madden nevertheless found time to make some preliminary notes on the contents of the boxes of burnt fragments and to prepare a further detailed schedule of the current condition of the damaged manuscripts.[184] He had also given to Tuckett for inlaying a few of the damaged vellum manuscripts of the first class which he felt Tuckett could be trusted with.[185]

The continued threat to the vellum manuscripts that resulted from allowing them to remain as loose leaves is illustrated by an incident involving Forshall. Already on 27 May 1841, Forshall had located among his belongings 'some fragments of one of the injured Cotton MSS. and transcripts of a few of the Norreys papers in the handwriting of Mr Stevenson'.[186] On 3 April 1843, Madden was checking a transcription of Tiberius A. X and found ff. 141–172 missing.[187] He ordered an immediate search. Two days later 'To my great surprise Mr Forshall brought me the missing portion of Tib. A X, ff. 141–172 together with some other fragments of vellum Cotton MSS. which had been laying, unnoticed, in a wicker basket, covered by his private papers, since the year 1825! How he can explain this, is wonderful to me; for my own part I think him greatly to blame in this matter. Among the fragments in this basket I found portions of the 2d text of Layamon, which I am vexed at, as I have been prevented from including the lines in my edition.'[188]

In 1841 Madden returned to the offensive on behalf of the vellum manuscripts, and on 5 May he again drew the Trustees' attention to 'the deplorable condition of the valuable Cottonian MSS. on *vellum*' and 'the injuries to which they are now daily subject. He therefore urgently[189] recommends[190] that Mr Gough, the person employed formerly to repair MSS. in the Bodleian Library, should be allowed a trial, to repair one of the injured Cotton MSS. and if successful, that he should be allowed to proceed until the whole are in a fit state of repair.'[191] The timing of this report was perfect. Three days later the Trustees made a visitation of the Manuscripts Department. Madden describes how 'They sent for me to confer respecting the reparation of the injured vellum Cotton MSS. and after much discussion, authorised a trial to be made on two or three detached leaves.'[192] With an evident sense of relief, Madden noted that 'The address of H. Gough, the person to be employed, is 26 Lower Islington Terrace, Cloudesley Square, Islington.'[193] Gough called on Madden and Sir Frederic 'placed in his hands three vellum leaves much injured, to flatten and inlay.'[194]

On 29 May, Gough returned to Madden the three trial leaves. As a further test, Madden gave him three more 'of a better description'.[195] On 3 June, Madden wrote in his personal diary 'In the evening received from Gough the additional fragments of injured Cotton MSS. that I placed in his hands...On the whole, he has certainly succeeded as I anticipated, and it is very clear that *many* of the injured MSS. may be carefully inlaid & rendered fit for use.'[196] On 9 June, Madden submitted the fragments flattened and inlaid by Gough to the Trustees and reported:[197] 'Mr Gough would be willing to employ his time in this description of work at the rate of 12s. per diem, from 9 in the morning till 4 in the afternoon. He estimates the time and labor expended on the six fragments placed in his hands to be about a day's work, but he states that if regularly employed, a much greater number of leaves, say from 10 to 16 might be taken in hand at the same time, & consequently greater progress made.[198] Sir F.M. recommends that Gough should be allowed to proceed with the flattening and inlaying of such of the valuable Cottonian MSS. as are at present in *loose leaves*, such as the Saxon Boethius, Otho A. VI, the interlineary Saxon Psalter, Vitell. E. XVIII, the Saxon Gospels and Gregory's Dialogues, Otho C. I, Alcuin's Letters, Tib. A. XV, the Cartulary of Christchurch Twinham, Tib. D. VI. etc. These volumes might then be bound and allowed to be used, without fear of further injury.' Thus Madden's first priority was to inlay the manuscripts separated by Forshall and preserved as loose leaves, with the addition of the Christchurch Cartulary, treated by Madden himself in the same way. Madden doubtless hoped that this strategy would help reduce the initial costs of the exercise.

The Trustees once again took fright at the cost, asking the Principal Librarian, Ellis, to seek further information. Madden was furious. 'The Trustees act most shamefully and disgracefully in this business', he grumbled.[199] His exasperation is evident in his reply of 1 July to Ellis.[200] 'In reply to your note of 16 June on the subject of the injured Cotton MSS. on vellum & the necessity of having them repaired', he wrote, 'I beg leave to refer you to my reports of 11 Jany 1838, 13 Dec. 1838, 3 Jan. 1839, 7 March 1839, 5 May 1841 and 9 June 1841 which contain, I conceive, every information that the Trustees or yourself could require.' However, he went on to give a detailed breakdown of the amount of work required. The number of cases containing loose leaves was, Madden reckoned, altogether seventy-one, amounting altogether to about 7,300 leaves. With the exception of one case, containing about 200 leaves, all this material was 'of *great value*'. In the drawers in his own room, there were a further 450 leaves, and additionally about 1,000 leaves had recently been extracted from the boxes in the garret as suitable for treatment. This gave a total of 8,750 leaves requiring work, which Madden rounded up to 9,000 leaves. He guessed that, of these, about 2,900 leaves were from Anglo-Saxon manuscripts. Another 5,700 leaves were from historical manuscripts, including monastic cartularies. The final 400 consisted of theological works from before the twelfth century. Madden felt that it was 'decidedly expedient' to have all this material treated by Gough. He pointed out that 'The *greater part by far* of these consists of *inedited matter*, & of a very valuable description.' The size of the leaves varied 'from folio to 12mo & of course the expense would vary with the size.'

Despite these detailed figures, it was still difficult to produce an accurate costing of the work, and Madden urged that, to establish this, Gough should be allowed 'to flatten and inlay *three* of these MSS. *simultaneously*'. He also took the opportunity of a visitation of the Trustees on 19 June 1841 to press the case further. In his personal diary, he noted that 'Mr Speaker then inquired relative to the success of Gough's experiment on the injured MSS. and came into my private room, accompanied by the Archbishop, Lord Ashburton, and others, and I shewed them and urged the necessity of repairing the Cotton vellum MSS. seriatim. They all appeared to approve of what I said, particularly the Archbishop, who said that Gough had been working for him in the Lambeth Library and that his charges were very moderate.'[201] Eventually, on 15 July, the Trustees authorized Madden to employ Gough to flatten and inlay three of the damaged vellum manuscripts stored as loose leaves, namely the Vitellius Psalter (Vitellius E. XVIII), the Christchurch Cartulary (Tiberius D. VI) and the volume containing a copy of Alcuin's letters (Tiberius A. XV). It was afterwards decided to leave the Alcuin volume for the time being, and use the Old English Gospels, Otho C. I, volume one, for the trial instead.[202]

It was some time before Gough was able to start work. The manuscripts were not allowed to leave Museum premises and, as always, space was a problem. In his work diary for 19 November 1841, Madden noted showing Gough the rooms beneath the Manuscripts Department and elsewhere, and discussing the subject with Ellis. 'The only room he can possibly use (before Hogarth finishes his work) is the small room underneath my own, which is very badly lighted and very damp. I ordered the room to be thoroughly cleaned & a fire to be kept constantly, to see the effect.'[203] Gough eventually started work, beginning with the Vitellius Psalter. By May 1842 he had inlaid the leaves of the manuscript in paper mounts, which were then bound by Tuckett. By November 1842, he had also inlaid Otho C. I and Tiberius D. VI, which were similarly bound up by Tuckett.[204] On 10 November 1842 Madden laid the results of Gough's work before the Trustees:

For nearly a century none of these MSS. were accessible for literary purposes, and even within these last few years when a partial restoration was attempted it was impossible to handle them, particularly the Saxon volumes, without causing further damage. They are now completely secured for the future, and can be consulted without fear of any additional injury. In regard to the expense, the great value of the MSS. of this class, in Sir F.M.'s opinion, sufficiently authorise it and he begs leave to remark, that in the payments made to Gough, no charge is made by him for the tracing paper at 12s. per quire or isinglass at 14s per lb.; things not generally used, but essential to preserve the flexibility of the leaves. Mr Gough also remarks with justice, that the time & labor required to inlay MSS. that have previously been flattened by incisions (as is the case with those now completed) is far greater than if the leaves had remained *intact*. The great proportion however of the MSS. proposed to be restored and inlaid, are of the *latter class*. Sir F.M. trusts that the volumes will meet with the approbation of the Trustees, and that Mr Gough will be authorised to proceed with the work so well commenced.[205]

Despite Madden's reassurances, the Trustees, worried at the expense, would agree to Gough's working only on 'four or five of the more valuable MSS. which Sir F.M. is to select'.[206] Madden chose Tiberius B. V, Tiberius C. VI, Otho A. VI and 'one without a number', a household book of Edward I. Gough completed these by April 1843, then delivered what must have been a body-blow to Madden, by writing on 19 April to say that 'having made his mind to reside at Oxford, he should resign his employment at the Museum.'[207] Madden's comment in his work diary, 'This really is vexatious', sounds an understatement.[208]

Two days later, when Gough brought up to Madden the inlaid leaves of Tiberius C. VI and Otho A. VI, Madden tried to persuade him to change his mind. Madden recorded that 'He will discontinue his work here for the present, but I am in hopes that he will be able to give 3 months of his time yearly to the Museum, after he is settled in Oxford.'[209] Gough's departure put paid to further work on the vellum manuscripts in 1843, and Madden had to report to the Trustees that 'no person could be found to supply Gough's place, and until he resumes and proceeds with the work undertaken by him, Sir F.M. feels himself under the necessity of withholding from the readers several valuable MSS. too much injured to be handled.'[210]

In January 1844 Gough was able to resume the work for three months,[211] but it was not until 1845 that Madden was able finally to settle this problem. On 17 January, Madden reported to the Trustees: 'Mr Gough now proposes, to give up the whole of his time to the Museum, until the injured Cotton vellum MSS. are entirely restored; and to facilitate this, he begs to be allowed an assistant at the rate of 5d per diem.'[212] The assistant Gough had in mind was his son Philip, who started work at the Museum in March 1845, and continued until November 1849.[213] The Trustees' minute of 18 March 1845 approving this also gave Madden permission to 'proceed with the reparation of the burnt vellum MSS. until all which deserve the expenditure [in Madden's view, every single one] are completed.'[214]

For nearly seven years Madden had been seeking authorization from the Trustees for a full programme for the restoration of the damaged Cotton Manuscripts. At last he had secured it. He interpreted the Trustees' instructions as widely as possible. Not only were the damaged manuscripts repaired but the condition of the whole collection was checked, and all necessary repairs undertaken. Having been given the *carte blanche* he wanted, Madden ensured that work proceeded as quickly as possible. 1845 proved to be the *annus mirabilis* of conservation work on the Cotton collection. Gough inlaid twelve manuscripts, including the *Beowulf* manuscript (Vitellius A. XV), the early Bede (Tiberius A. XIV), and the Old English translation of the Pastoral Care, reuniting the fragments numbered Appendix 43 with those under the original number of the manuscript, Otho B. II, as well as cartularies from Chertsey and Winchcombe.[215] In 1846, Gough dealt with a further eleven manuscripts, including the autograph manuscript of Knighton's Chronicle, Tiberius C. VII, and Otho B. XI, a tenth-century compilation of Old English historical works.[216]

In the meantime, Tuckett had continued with the paper manuscripts and some of the less badly damaged vellum material. Indeed, Madden's confidence in Tuckett's ability to deal with damaged vellum manuscripts increased, and from 1847 Tuckett was allowed to inlay the leaves of some of the older vellum manuscripts.[217] Eventually, his work in this respect began to equal if not surpass that of Gough. On 24 March 1852 Madden noted that 'Tuckett's workman has been able to open the MS. of Capgrave [Otho D. IX] which Gough injured so much. I shall put the worst in his hands. Gough's work could draw to a close in another twelvemonth or so.'[218]

By 1852, the Trustees were growing anxious about the length of time the restoration was taking, and asked Madden to indicate 'which of these MSS. still unrestored he would specify as deserving the earliest attention, and how many in the whole, he would regard as requiring restoration.'[219] This was a difficult question to answer. At the beginning of his work on the Cotton Manuscripts, Madden had been able to find manuscripts from the loose fragments which were still largely intact and could be readily identified. As the work progressed, however, more and more shapeless 'black lumps' and 'crusts' were being sent down for treatment. These could not be identified until they were opened up and flattened. Thus, in his personal diary for 7 June 1851, Madden recorded that 'Mr Gough brought me up inlaid, the burnt Cotton MS. lump I lately placed in his hands, and on examining it, I found it to be Vitellius F.III, which is stated to be totally lost both by Casley and Planta. It contains the Lives of several saints &c. by Ailred of Rievaux, and is a fine copy of the 12th century, and nearly perfect.'[220]

Madden therefore laid before the Trustees a selection of the burnt lumps and crusts to show them the impossibility of ascertaining their contents 'in their present miserable

417

state of cremation, dirt and neglect'.[221] However, he also proposed an important change in procedure to speed up the work.[222] He suggested 'that instead of taking each single lump, and fragment, and after flattening it, proceeding to *inlay* it, as at present, that for the present Mr Gough should be directed to confine his operations wholly to the task of cleaning, separating and flattening, until the whole have been done. By this means, very great progress could be made, and Sir F.M. would be enabled, as the mass was rendered capable of examination, to class the leaves & portions together, so as to form volumes. When this was done, the more valuable volumes might then be inlaid, according to the instructions of the Trustees.' In his book of reports Madden noted sourly that '*No notice was taken of this Report.*'[223] He nevertheless took this as assent to his proposal for a preliminary flattening of the burnt crusts, and from July 1852 Gough concentrated on separating and flattening loose leaves.[224] During 1852, not only were Tiberius B. VI, Otho A. VII, Otho C. XI, part of Otho D. X, Otho E. XII and XIII, and Vitellius F. VII – all supposed to have been lost in the fire – identified, flattened, inlaid, collated and bound, but also 4,939 loose leaves were flattened, 2,894 identified and 1,375 inlaid.[225] By 1854, Madden was able to report that 'the entire mass of the burnt vellum fragments of the Cottonian Collection (which originally in bulk would have filled a small cart) have now been *flattened* & not a scrap remains *unexamined.*'[226] Two years later, on 30 October 1856 Madden was finally able to report that Gough would within a few days complete his 'long and arduous work' in inlaying the fragments.[227]

Madden lost no opportunity to publicize these achievements. In 1848–9, a Royal Commission investigated the Museum. Madden proudly laid before them some examples of restored Cotton Manuscripts, including the Christchurch Cartulary, and described how two hundred of the damaged manuscripts had been inlaid.[228] The centrepiece of the first public exhibition of manuscripts at the Museum in 1851, arranged on the occasion of the Great Exhibition, was a drawing commissioned by Gough from the miniaturist and accomplished imitator of medieval manuscripts, Caleb W. Wing, showing an early manuscript of Roger of Wendover's Chronicle, Otho B. V, before and after its restoration by Gough.[229] This remarkable drawing dramatically illustrates the extent and skill of Gough's work. Indeed, this was more like resurrection than restoration.[230] To emphasize the point, the exhibition also included an example of a burnt manuscript from the Royal Library, Royal MS. 9 C. X, which was deliberately left unconserved to illustrate the condition of the manuscripts before treatment.[231]

The departure of Gough did not mark the end of the work on the Cotton Manuscripts. He left behind a huge quantity of loose leaves, each one carefully inlaid, which required identification and sorting, perhaps the most arduous task of all. In the early 1860s, Madden enlisted the help of a number of his brightest assistants, including the young Edward Maunde Thompson, in a final assault on the fragments.[232] It was largely as a result of this concentration on the Cotton material that the cataloguing backlog for which Madden was afterwards criticized built up.[233] By 1864, this last work on the fragments was well advanced. Madden could afford to feel, if not complacent, then at least pleased with himself for having pushed to the verge of completion one of the largest programmes of manuscript conservation ever undertaken, even if the Trustees failed to recognize its importance. On 10 March 1864, Madden recorded in his personal diary:

Gave into the hands of Mr Thompson, one of my assistants, the whole of the remaining vellum fragments of the Cottonian Collection, not yet bound, or not identified, with instructions for him and Mr Scott [Edward Scott, afterwards Keeper of Manuscripts], to go carefully over them, and arrange such as are identified, and then identify, as far as possible, the rest. I have long had this work at heart, as, when it is done, I shall be able finally to bind up in boards the whole of what now remains of the loose 'refuse' of the Cotton MSS. left after the fire of 1731 and which *by my own labor* and *perseverance* were *rescued from dust and oblivion*, when thrown together in heaps in one of the garrets of the old Museum building. I shall be truly glad to get this completed before I quit the Museum. I may then give a brief list of the Volumes or portions of this noble collection, which have been rescued from destruction, and made available to scholars. I have received no thanks from the Trustees, nor indeed from the Public, for the pains I have taken since 1844 to restore these missing portions of the Cottonian Collection, but I have the satisfaction of my own conscience in having undertaken and carried out a task so onerous and difficult, that I do not believe any other man living would have attempted it.[234]

When he wrote these words, Madden was unaware that the work on the restoration of the Cotton Manuscripts was about to receive its greatest setback.

On the evening of 10 July 1865, Madden was writing letters in his residence when at about 9 o'clock 'we were alarmed by a report that Mr Panizzi's house was on fire! It was the work of a few moments to fly downstairs, put on my boots and overcoat, get out the Museum keys, and rush into the Court. The first thing I saw was an immense column of black smoke, followed by flames, rising apparently out of the corridor leading to Mr. P's house, but on approaching closer, I perceived that the fire was not in the corridor but in Tuckett's the binder's work shops! The sight was terrible, for I knew that many MSS. of value had lately been sent down to him!'[235] The Museum's fire drill did not prove very effective. Policemen with vital keys could not be found; the fireman was on leave, and no trained replacements were available, so that on the first attempt to use the fire hydrants, the hose burst; Panizzi was (as usual, comments Madden) dining out, and did not return until midnight; when the fire brigade, summoned by telegram, arrived after half an hour with two fire engines, only one could be used. 'Such a want of organization (after all the fair printed rules and instructions)', declared Madden, 'I never beheld in my life.'

The fire raged for over an hour. By 10.15 pm it had been put out, and Madden sent one of his attendants, George Gatfield, to try and find out which manuscripts had been damaged. Fortunately most of them had been placed in an iron safe in the stone-vaulted room where the Duke of Bedford's muniments were formerly deposited and had escaped injury. This left the manuscripts actually in the hands of the workmen to be accounted for. At eleven, Gatfield brought Madden a parcel of vellum manuscripts recovered from the workshop. It was burnt on the outside and saturated with water. 'I could not tell what they were, but put them away to dry. I was very weary and vexed beyond measure at so unfortunate an occurrence, although I had *always feared it*!'

419

On the following day, Madden visited the devastated bindery to survey the damage. It appeared that the cause of the fire was a charcoal brazier in the finishing room, and the manuscripts left overnight in this room had been destroyed and damaged. Madden ordered one of the assistants, Richard Sims, to make a complete list of manuscripts sent down to the binder, and check it by those returned so as to ascertain the extent of the loss. 'The MSS. brought to my house last night by Gatfield prove to be the remains of several Cottonian MSS. which after having had so much labor & time expended on them, in flattening, inlaying, identifying, collating & arranging, had been finally described and sent down to be bound. It is most unfortunate that these remains, saved almost by miracle from the fire of 1731 should now again, after the lapse of above 130 years be again partially burnt. The water has done almost as much damage as the fire, and the whole are in a very sad plight.'

Madden gave his deputy, Edward Augustus Bond, instructions as to the salvage work to be undertaken and went to acquaint some of the Trustees with the bad news. He returned to the scene of the disaster in the afternoon. 'Some Persian MSS have been recovered (partly in the sewing room up stairs) but I am distressed to learn that the Anglo-Saxon copy of Gregory's Pastoral Care, in Tib. B. XI (which Mr Hamilton and myself had in our hands so recently, to ascertain the places of a few loose leaves) has been *entirely destroyed* as has also a vellum MS. of the Arundel Collection, No. 243.' The techniques used by Madden and his staff in trying to rescue the damaged manuscripts were much the same as those employed in 1731: 'All my Assistants, aided by Mr Bond and myself, were at work to separate the burnt & soaked leaves of vellum and paper, and then, with the help of one of C. Tuckett's men, to wash them, and hang them on lines to dry.' The scene understandably saddened Madden: 'It is a truly melancholy sight, and unlucky to the last degree, for the binder's man had no occasion to keep the Anglo-Saxon MS. out all night. It ought to have been restored to the iron safe. I met Mr. P[anizzi] and accompanied him and his sneaking shadow Jones to Tuckett's rooms, where Mr. P. behaved like a brute!'

The 1865 bindery fire is arguably the greatest single disaster to have struck the collections since the establishment of the Museum in 1753. In terms of the quality and importance of material destroyed, the loss was greater than the destruction of a large number of printed books by enemy action during World War II. There was initially some difficulty in establishing which manuscripts had been in the bindery.[236] One at least (Arundel MS. 152) had been taken down as a pattern without Madden's knowledge. Others, at first thought lost, were afterwards found,[237] whereas other volumes thought only to have been damaged had been completely destroyed. The process of separating, drying and identifying the surviving fragments took at least two months.[238]

The most notable loss was Tiberius B. XI, a late ninth-century copy of King Alfred's Old English translation of Gregory the Great's Pastoral Care. Madden described the circumstances of its destruction: 'it lay on a board immediately above the bin of charcoal, and a slate slab was placed above it. The slate flew into fragments from the heat, and the MS. (a good thick folio written on vellum, bound in russia) must have fallen into the midst of the burning charcoal.'[239] Eight tiny fragments from Tiberius B. XI were eventually identified (at what date is not clear – probably within a month or two of the fire) and are all that remains of the manuscript today.[240]

In the event, three Cotton Manuscripts were completely destroyed in the fire: Galba A. I, II and III. Galba A. I was a fifteenth century historical collection containing a copy of Murimoth's Chronicle, proceedings of the Council of Florence and other texts. Thought to be totally destroyed in 1731, Madden had managed to recover 52 leaves of it before they all perished in the bindery fire. Galba A. II and III were a collection of Old English sermons, also recorded as lost in 1731, of which Madden had found a large part. In addition to Tiberius B. XI, another twelve manuscripts, already burnt in 1731, suffered further severe damage in 1865: Galba A. XIX, Otho A. I, IX-XII, XIV, Otho B. III-IV, IX, XII and Tiberius E. XI. Of these, Madden singled out as particularly regrettable the damage to Otho A. X, containing the unique text of Æthelweard's Chronicle, and Otho A. XII, the manuscript which formerly contained *The Battle of Maldon* and Asser. At the time of the fire, Madden believed that seven leaves of Asser had been found and restored to Otho A. XII. In fact, these leaves were from the text of Æthelweard in Otho A. X.[241]

Apart from the Cotton Manuscripts, which bore the brunt of the effects of the fire, Arundel MS. 343 and Egerton MSS. 1961 and 1962 were completely destroyed. Arundel MS. 152 and Additional MSS. 25686 and 25805 were severely damaged. A final blow was the loss of the complete impression of the third volume of Madden's long-standing bugbear, the *Catalogue of Maps and Topographical Drawings*, on which Madden's former Assistant Keeper, John Holmes, had, to Madden's great annoyance, laboured for many years, which Madden himself had spent a great amount of time finally preparing for the press after Holmes's death, and for which Madden had prepared an important appendix of corrections and additions, only to see it suppressed by Panizzi and the Trustees. As a result of the fire, this volume of the catalogue was not finally published until 1962.[242]

The undoing of so much of his recent work on the Cotton Manuscripts devastated Madden. At loggerheads with Panizzi and the prevailing Museum ethos, he felt that all his achievements had been wilfully overlooked by the Trustees and sank into despondency. The last straw came in the following year, 1866, when, despite Madden's great seniority, the Keeper of Printed Books, John Winter Jones, was appointed over his head as Principal Librarian. He decided to retire. On 12 July 1866, he submitted a last memorial to the Trustees reminding them how, in the twenty-nine years since he had been appointed Keeper, the collections had doubled in size, accurate registers and inventories of the manuscripts been prepared, and many catalogues produced.[243] He then went on to describe his work on the Cotton Manuscripts: 'it is not too much for me to say, that, after the lapse of more than twenty years, I may claim, without egotism, the title of the Restorer of the Cottonian Library, for out of the number of volumes supposed to be lost or destroyed, above one hundred under my direction and superintendence have been in great measure recovered, and the whole of the damaged volumes have been repaired, and rendered accessible.'

421

He retired on 29 September 1866. His official diary for the previous Saturday, 22 September, describes how he took his leave of the Cotton Manuscripts:

Completed notes of Cotton MSS. and placed in Mr Thompson's hands the whole of the remaining fragments on vellum & paper of the Cotton MSS. to be prepared for the binder. I now say *Finis* to my long and arduous labors on this Collection during so many years, by means of which *upwards of 100 volumes have been restored for use* supposed to be lost or totally useless! The schedule of injured MSS. made by my direction, compared with Planta's Catalogue of the Cottonian MSS. in 1802 will prove the extent of what I have done, *but for which I have neither received recompense nor thanks*!![244]

VII

The story of Madden's forty-year struggle to restore fully the Cotton Manuscripts is a heroic one, with, perhaps, a hint of tragedy in its conclusion. The scale of the achievement of Madden and his colleagues is even more apparent when the techniques used in recovering these burnt manuscripts are considered. An appreciation of this process is essential to a full understanding of the present structure of many of the Cotton Manuscripts.

The records of Madden's work on the Cotton Manuscripts are voluminous. His massive personal diaries, forty-three large foolscap volumes covering the period 1819 to 1872, contain much information about the Cotton library. However, as Madden himself makes clear,[245] his personal diary was not the main record of his day-to-day work in the Manuscripts Department. He kept a more detailed record of his work as Keeper in his official diaries.[246] In these 'memoranda of business', every action of Madden as Keeper – whether letter, conversation, meeting, cataloguing, binding order or recommendation for purchase – is carefully recorded. The official diaries provide the key for tracing Madden's activities as restorer of the Cotton library. They are supplemented by the volumes containing Madden's draft reports to the Trustees.[247] These contain not only such major reports as Madden's memorandum of 13 December 1838 giving his plan for the restoration of the Cotton collection, but also his monthly reports to the Trustees giving precise details of the gradual progress of the work. Some assistance in tracing the main reports relating to the Cotton collection is provided by three notebooks compiled by Madden containing digests of key information from his reports and elsewhere arranged alphabetically by subject.[248] These notebooks were intended to assist him in giving evidence to the Royal Commission on the Museum in 1848 and 1849.

The Trustees' constant anxiety about the cost of the work on the Cotton Manuscripts has been noted. In July 1849, Madden 'Began to make a complete list of the Cotton MSS. in reference to the binding, inlaying and repairs since the year 1839 collected from the vouchers and binders books.'[249] This notebook was kept up until 1866 and provides perhaps the best survey of the work on individual manuscripts.[250] Details are given in manuscript order of the exact treatment each volume received, the date when it was done, the number of folios in the volume, and the binder responsible for the work (either

422

'T', Tuckett, or 'G', Gough).[251] In 1845, Madden purchased a copy of the 1732 report on the fire which he had interleaved and which he also used to help keep track of the restoration work.[252] These records presumably provided the basis for the detailed description of the current condition of the Cotton Manuscripts prepared for Madden in 1866. This exists in three versions, namely a draft corrected by Madden,[253] and two fair copies, which are in the form of interleaved copies of the 1732 report.[254]

A number of Madden's working lists and notes on damaged Cotton Manuscripts also survive, but are difficult to use because they have been bound up in the wrong order.[255] The most important was probably that prepared by Madden in 1837, which he described as 'a list of the whole of the MSS. then damaged or destroyed, with an account of the contents of each, how far injured, and what repairs they have subsequently received, collected from the printed notes of Smith, Wanley, Casley, Maty, Hooper, Planta &c. and the MS. notes of Mr Forshall and himself.' Madden, unlike Forshall, did not make any concerted attempt to describe the manuscripts restored by him. The only exceptions were some of the State Papers, for which Madden and his Assistant Keeper, Bond, prepared detailed lists of the articles not noted in Planta. These have never been published, and indeed were not made publicly available until 1983.[256]

Of great value are the numerous annotations by Madden in the copy of Planta formerly kept in the Keeper's Room and now preserved in the Departmental Reference Library. This volume summarizes much of the information about the structure of the Cotton library gleaned in the process of restoration. Nevertheless, it is a bewildering and patchy compilation. The rearrangement, reidentification and recovery of masses of material is recorded in a very piecemeal fashion, through a mass of scribbled notes, many of them by Madden and sometimes vitriolic in their denunciation of earlier workers on the collection. Another valuable source for the history of the restoration under Madden is the printed annual returns of progress in the British Museum, which list each of the Cotton Manuscripts restored year by year.[257] Finally, Madden's own annotations on the manuscripts themselves often contain valuable information. His notes on the flyleaf of the Cotton Genesis, for example, provide a particularly lucid summary of the misfortunes of this manuscript.

Much of this material lay hidden from public view until recently. Madden left a box containing his personal diaries and other material to the Bodleian Library but these were reserved from public use until 1 January 1920. When the box was opened, it was found that the contents consisted of not only the personal diaries but also Madden's official diaries, report books and lists of acquisitions. Recognizing that these belonged more properly to the Museum's archives, the Curators of the Bodleian Library offered them to the Trustees.[258] The then Keeper of Manuscripts, Julius Gilson, reported that these volumes 'are almost wholly concerned with the business of the Department of MSS. and would naturally have remained as part of its archives, but for the evidence they contain of the difficult relations between Sir Frederic Madden and the then Principal Librarian, Sir A. Panizzi.' Gilson therefore recommended that this material should be accepted as a gift to the Museum, but proposed that 'they remain part of the archives of the department instead of being placed with collections open to the public, to whom they would be of little use.'[259] These vital records of the restoration process consequently remained in the departmental archives, virtually unknown, until they were incorporated as Additional Manuscripts in 1981. Similarly, Madden's notes on his restoration work, including the ledger recording the work on each manuscript, were kept in the Departmental Archives until 1983, when they were also made Additional Manuscripts.

Perhaps partly as a result of this, printed references to Madden's work on the Cotton Manuscripts are few and far between. In 1854, Gustav Waagen, in his guide to *Treasures of Art in Great Britain*, described how in 1835, on his first visit to the British Museum, the leaves of the Cotton Genesis were 'still quite crumpled up with the effects of the fire.' By 1854, 'they had been successfully smoothed out, and mounted on separate sheets of paper, so as to admit a due estimate being formed of their style of art.'[260] Julius Zupitza in his 1882 facsimile of *Beowulf* noted how further textual losses to the manuscript had been stopped by a new binding. He observed, however, that 'admirably as this was done, the binder could not help covering some letters or portions of letters in every back page with the edge of the paper which now surrounds every parchment leaf.'[261] Zupitza does not mention Madden's name, neither does he indicate that the work on Vitellius A. XV was part of a general restoration of the Cotton Manuscripts. A few other editions of texts rescued by Madden also mentioned his work.[262] More detailed accounts of the restoration process were given in two nineteenth-century guides to the Museum Library. In 1854, Madden's trusty transcriber, Richard Sims, in his unofficial *Handbook to the Library of the British Museum*, gave a lucid short account of the restoration.[263] The work of Madden and Forshall was also briefly noted by Edward Edwards in his 1859 *Memoirs of Libraries*.[264] Of recent histories of the Museum, Esdaile gives Madden's work the briefest passing mention,[265] while Miller refers only to the discovery of material in the garret in 1837.[266]

It was not until 1981 that the procedures adopted by Madden and his binders in restoring the Cotton Manuscripts were first described in detail, by Professor Kevin S. Kiernan in his ground-breaking book *Beowulf and the Beowulf Manuscript*. Kiernan describes how, in inlaying the individual leaves of the *Beowulf* manuscript, 'The binder first made pencil tracings of the separate folio leaves on sheets of heavy construction paper. These tracings are usually quite visible in the MS ... the binder then cut out the center of the paper, following the outline, but leaving from 1 to 2 mm. of paper within the traced line, so that the frame would be slightly smaller than the vellum leaf it was designed to hold. Paste was then applied to this marginal retaining space, and the folio was pressed into place. Finally, transparent paper strips were pasted on like Scotch tape along the edge of the vellum on the recto, thus to secure the mounted leaf from both sides.'[267]

Kiernan points out the advantages of this procedure. It saves having to touch the vellum while consulting the manuscript. Moreover, it avoids the risk of confusion inherent in handling the loose leaves. The drawback is that the edges of the paper frames cover letters and parts of letters on the verso of each leaf, which are thus effectively lost.

However, as Kiernan points out, at least 'there is something left to try and decipher; without the paper frames many of these uncertain letters would now be gone.'[268] In 1983, Kiernan triumphantly vindicated this conservation strategy. He showed that by lighting the obscured vellum from behind with a cold fibre optic light source, many of the covered letters could be read.[269] Recently, Kiernan has used a digital camera to record images of the obscured letters and demonstrated the use of computer imaging to restore the hidden letters to their place in the manuscript.[270] Thus, by stabilizing the condition of the vellum, Madden and Gough had allowed future scholars, using technological aids undreamt of in the mid-nineteenth century, to read letters which would otherwise have disappeared in the British Museum Reading Room in the nineteenth century.

Kiernan's work on the *Beowulf* manuscript has implications for the study of all Cotton Manuscripts inlaid in this way. Wherever the text on the verso of an inlaid leaf runs up to the edge of the paper frame, there is likely to be text concealed beneath the edge of the mount, which may be read with the aid of fibre optic backlighting. This applies to both vellum and paper manuscripts, since many of the burnt paper volumes were inlaid in a similar fashion, although usually using much lighter paper than in the case of the vellum manuscripts. Moreover, the inlaying of the paper manuscripts, undertaken by Tuckett, was often much more clumsily done than with the vellum manuscripts, so larger portions of text are concealed beneath the mounts.

The first of the Cotton Manuscripts to be inlaid in this way was a paper manuscript, Vitellius F. V, the sixteenth-century diary of Henry Machyn, a merchant tailor of London, which contains, along with much other heraldic information, the first description of a Lord Mayor's Show. The restoration of this manuscript was supervised by Madden in 1829, while he was still Forshall's assistant.[271] Madden noted that 'The fragments forming the present Volume were formerly kept in a case, without any regard to order, and are thus described by Dr Smith[272] in his Catalogue. "Cod. chartac. in fol. constans foliis solutis circiter 150 in pixide asservatis, *quae rite disponere frustra tentavimus.*"'[273] The paper leaves were badly singed around the edges by the fire, but none were lost.[274] The pages were inlaid by Tuckett using exactly the same technique as the later restorations.[275] Much lighter paper was used for the frames of Vitellius F. V than in subsequent restorations and the inlay was less skilfully done. Nevertheless, the result is an impressive first attempt. Just as in the *Beowulf* manuscript, the paper mounts conceal odd letters and words around the edges of the leaves on the verso which can now be read by the use of a fibre optic light.[276]

Madden took the inlaid leaves of Vitellius F. V and compared them with Strype, who, in Madden's words, 'made use of the MS. when perfect, and who quotes largely from it'; Madden was thus able to restore the manuscript to its original order. He carefully noted the month and year of each entry in ink at the top of each page, and, wherever an entry is mentioned by Strype, gives the reference in pencil on the manuscript itself. His comment on the work might serve as a motto for the whole restoration process: 'The curiosity and value of these fragments seemed a sufficient warrant for the labor and time consumed in arranging them in their present form.'[277] As a result of Madden's work, John Gough Nichols was able to produce the first full edition of Machyn's diary in 1848.[278]

Madden was sufficiently pleased with the results of this first experiment to have two further burnt paper manuscripts in the Vitellius press, Vitellius F. IV and VIII (which afterwards turned out, in fact, to be ff. 1–95 of Otho D. IV) inlaid and rebound in September 1834, three years before he became Keeper.[279] These early prototypes show that the credit for devising the techniques used in restoring the Cotton Manuscripts belongs to Madden, though he may have been inspired by examples of Gough's work he had seen in Oxford. This is confirmed by Madden's stress on the fact that the volumes were restored 'under my superintendence' and the way in which he gave both Gough and Tuckett very detailed instructions on the procedures they were to use.

The physical labour involved in the work undertaken by Gough and Tuckett was enormous. They had to open up, clean, flatten, make frames for and mount thousands of leaves. Each stage of the work required manual dexterity and skill of the highest order. Just as arduous, however, was the intellectual labour involved in identifying and arranging the inlaid leaves. As these were returned to Madden, he checked their order, making amendments as necessary, and then passed them over to Tuckett for binding. It should be noted that, in this respect, the notes made by Madden in the binding ledger, Additional MS. 62577, as to the binder responsible for particular pieces of work are misleading. Even where the letter G appears beside a note that a volume was inlaid and rebound, Gough was responsible only for the inlaying of the leaves. The inlaid folios arranged by Madden were actually bound up by Tuckett. Gough's time was too valuable to be spent on such routine tasks.[280]

Madden provides little information in his diaries and elsewhere as to the precise method adopted by him in sorting and arranging the inlaid leaves.[281] References to work on individual manuscripts are usually frustratingly vague, but it is clear that, in establishing the order of the leaves, he relied heavily on early catalogues such as Smith and Wanley. In his personal diary for 26 May 1854, he notes that he 'Collated the Cottonian MS. Otho D. X (now inlaid) with Smith's list of contents. Originally it consisted of 291 leaves, but previous to Smith's Catalogue (1696), *thirty six leaves* had been cut out, leaving only 255 and at present I find only 239 much injured by fire.'[282] By 1865, Madden had traced the remaining leaves and placed them in the appropriate places in the volume.[283] In other cases, the process of arrangement was more complex. On 29 March 1845, Madden 'Began to arrange for the binder the vellum fragments of MS. Cotton Otho B. II containing Alfred's Saxon version of Gregory de Cura Pastorale. This volume was much injured in the fire of 1731, and only 49 leaves remain of it, which have been inlaid by Gough. I am enabled to place them in order by comparing each leaf with the printed Latin text of Gregory's work, a tedious and rather difficult task.'[284] Madden was still engaged on this work four months later.[285] The reconstructed Otho B. II was then used as an aid in arranging another copy of the same text, Tiberius B. XI.[286]

The complexity of the task confronting Madden and the care with which he carried

426

it out is evident, to take a random example, from a collection of twelfth-century historical works, Otho D. VII. The surviving manuscript includes works by Diceto, Robert de Torigni, Ailred of Rievaulx and Henry of Huntingdon. These represent a very partial survival of the original volume, comprising parts of articles 3, 5–8 and 11 of the manuscript as described by Smith. In the first of them, Diceto's *Abbreviationes Chronicorum*, the order of the leaves has been determined by reference to two different manuscripts (Royal MS. 13 E. VI and Cotton MS. Claudius E. III) together with Twysden's printed edition. Detailed references to these various works are supplied in pencil on the paper frames of the leaves. On f. 10 a reference to the Royal MS. has been replaced with one from Claudius E. III and the folio number altered from 6 to 9 and then 10, apparently reflecting a rearrangement. Between ff. 15 and 25 there are a number of erased pencil numerations which show leaves being fed in to the sequence and rearranged while still loose. After f. 14, where two leaves are noted as missing, blank paper leaves, already ruled with ink borders, have been provided to receive the missing leaves if found. On ff. 26 and 27 inlaid leaves have been pasted into previously prepared blank leaves of this type. Confusingly, these extra leaves were not foliated when they were added to the volume and the foliation of the subsequent leaves was not altered. Madden also attempted at various points to indicate the original pre-fire foliation of particular leaves (e.g. ff. 62–65). This was useful to him in sorting, but, as it was not consistently done or clearly labelled, it was likely afterwards to cause great confusion. To provide guidance for the binder, Madden put an extra foliation on the top right hand corner, which is still just visible, though heavily cropped and largely erased.

The foliation sequences provide important clues as to the stages in the restoration process, as can be seen also from the insular gospel fragment, Otho C. V.[287] Casley reported that 'some pieces of leaves' of this manuscript had survived the fire and indeed illustrates one of them.[288] Nevertheless, the manuscript is described as wanting by Planta. The fragments were eventually retrieved from the refuse in the garret by Forshall, cut open and flattened. The manuscript consisted in 1841 of sixty loose leaves.[289] However, six of the fragments thought by Forshall to belong to Otho C. V were in fact from Otho A. I.[290] Moreover, some of the fragments now joined together to form a single folio were probably separate in Forshall's time.[291] Nevertheless, it is clear that the bulk of the manuscript was recovered by Forshall, and that the additions made by Madden from the loose material in the garret were relatively few. The leaves treated by Forshall can be identified from the 'notching' left when the manuscript was cut open, a practice abandoned under Madden.[292] The volume, including the six leaves from Otho A. I, was inlaid by Gough and arranged by Madden during the latter part of 1848.[293] A much heavier grade paper than usual was used for the inlay, perhaps in order more effectively to protect the fragments, which are particularly brittle. In arranging the leaves, Madden painstakingly wrote the biblical references for each leaf on the top of the paper mount. Some of the points at which identification proved particularly difficult are evident from the occasional erasure and correction of these references.[294] During the course of the arrangement, Madden established that some fragments belonged to the same folio and could be joined together, so he returned them to Gough to be inlaid again.[295] The old foliation in the top right hand corner of the ink border framing the inlaid leaf was made by Madden shortly before he sent the leaves to Tuckett to be bound. Four leaves were added to the sequence after Madden had completed this foliation[296] and were given starred folio numbers. In 1855, seven years after the manuscript was bound, six of the leaves which Madden's assistant Hamilton[297] realized in fact came from Otho A. I[298] were removed.[299] There is no disruption in the sequence of Madden's foliation and his binding ledger does not show that the manuscript was rebound after 1848. The most reasonable inference from this is that the leaves from Otho A. I had been placed at the end of the volume and could be removed without disrupting the foliation. At the same time as the leaves from Otho A. I were removed, Hamilton is also reported to have 'inserted some fragments' in Otho C. V.[300] Since the only indication of any disruption in the foliation are the four starred folios, the most likely explanation is that these are the fragments identified by Hamilton, which were presumably tipped in to the old binding. Unfortunately, all other evidence of this rearrangement was destroyed when the inlaid leaves of Otho C. V were mounted on guards and rebound in 1963.[301]

Although the various foliations are vital evidence of the restoration process, one of the weaknesses of Madden's work was the confusion he left in the referencing system of particular manuscripts. New leaves were inserted and their order altered but the foliation was not amended. Occasionally, asterisks were used to indicate additional folios, but this was not done consistently. Thus, in Vitellius C. VIII, Madden inserted new material after Planta's f. 139. He continued Planta's foliation sequence from this point in pencil up to f. 153, then used starred foliation for some further added leaves. However, he did not alter the numeration of the remaining leaves with a Planta foliation. As a result, before 1875, the manuscript contained *two* sets of ff. 148–153. Such a situation was clearly unsatisfactory, and was one of the reasons for the refoliation of all the Cotton Manuscripts in the 1870s and 1880s, when Madden's successors, Bond and Thompson, introduced the system of foliation still used in the Department of Manuscripts.[302]

The work performed by Madden and his team on the arrangement of the restored leaves was a bibliographical and palaeographical *tour de force*. Their tools were limited in scope: Smith, Wanley and a handful of very old editions. Many of the fragments were scorched and shrunk beyond recognition. Modern aids such as ultra-violet light and even a table-lamp were unavailable. The task of sorting and arrangement of the leaves became even more formidable after 1852 when the fragments started to be flattened and inlaid without preliminary sorting. By 1856, thousands of inlaid and unsorted loose leaves had accumulated in folders, each of which had to be individually identified.

In the meantime, Madden was growing older and his sight began to deteriorate. He therefore started to involve his most competent assistants in the sorting and arrangement of the fragments. The first to be recruited in this way was his Assistant Keeper, Edward Augustus Bond, who was to succeed him as Keeper and afterwards rose to be Principal Librarian. In 1850, Madden noted that he 'Gave Tiberius A. XV into Mr Bond's hands to arrange.'[303] Bond was also extensively involved in work on the State Papers. Some of

Madden's assistants were unequal to the task. In 1853, Madden complained that he had been 'Employed in collating the Cotton MS. Otho D. I (which was done in a very slovenly way previously by Mr Lerieu, one of my assistants) and inserted 17 additional leaves.' Three years later, 'Mr Lerieu brought me the remains of MS. Cott. Calig. D. X, XI, E. I and E. II which have been in his hands ever since 1852.'[304]

More enthusiastic about the work was N. E. S. A. Hamilton, who in 1876 published the *Inquisitio Comitatus Cantabrigiensis*,[305] a text which came to his attention as a result of his work with the Cotton Manuscripts. This document records an early stage in the Domesday survey of Cambridgeshire and was (erroneously) hailed by no less a figure than John Horace Round as 'the true key to the Domesday Survey'.[306] In Galbraith's view, Round's misinterpretation of the function of this document, compounded by Maitland's acceptance of Round's position, fundamentally distorted Domesday studies until very recently.[307] Hamilton's edition of the *Inquisitio* was dedicated to the memory of Madden, 'the greatest palaeographer of the age', and in his introduction Hamilton described how he had been asked by Madden 'to arrange and where possible to restore to their proper places a considerable number of separate and damaged leaves, which were known to belong to manuscripts in the Cotton collection; and it was while thus employed that he made the discovery of the important nature of the Domesday portion of the manuscript [Tiberius A. VI].'[308] Madden urged Hamilton to publish the text, which had been omitted from Henry Ellis's edition of Domesday-related material even though it was in the same manuscript as another text, the *Inquisitio Eliensis*, which had been included.[309]

Hamilton did a great deal of work on the Cotton fragments, but was not wholly reliable. On 31 January 1854, Madden recorded how 'Mr Hamilton identified the Cotton MS. Append. XXXI to be Vitellius F.VI said by Planta to be *lost*';[310] on closer examination three months later Madden felt some doubts about the identification, observing that 'It does not correspond satisfactorily with Smith, but it maybe.'[311] In the 1860s Hamilton was assigned the arrangement of the remaining Old English fragments, most of which are now in Otho A. VIII, Otho B. X and Otho B. XI.[312] These three volumes are among those where recent work has revealed serious deficiencies in the arrangement, with leaves inserted upside down and assigned to the wrong manuscripts.[313] It seems that these volumes were in an even worse state when they left Hamilton's hands and were sent to Madden for checking. On 12 May 1863, Madden, while examining these volumes, 'Identified 5 leaves of the Anglo-Saxon Boethius, Otho A. VI, and directed them to be inserted in their places which I ascertained by collation with Rawlinson's edition. Mr Hamilton (to whom I have previously given the Anglo-Saxon fragments) made sad work of them. Five leaves of Boethius he notes as "Colloquy. Description of Britain"!!'[314] Even so, when Madden sent the checked volumes to the binder, very obvious errors in the reconstruction remained, evidence perhaps of his own failing powers.[315]

Madden's most important associate in the task of identifying and arranging the fragments was the young Edward Maunde Thompson. Thompson had been a clerk in

Panizzi's office, and was transferred, at Panizzi's insistence, to Manuscripts in 1862.[316] Despite this unpromising start, he soon distinguished himself. In May 1863, Thompson identified article 3 of Vitellius A. III,[317] located a number of fragments from Otho A. III and rearranged Vitellius A. VII.[318] On 1 June, he found the last eleven leaves of the Chronicle of Roger of Wendover, Otho B. V.[319] 'This is important', Madden declared.[320] On the following day, 'Mr Thompson identified the leaves of the commencement of Tib. A. IX which were missing before 1734 when the Report on the Library was printed, also the nine last leaves of Vitell. A. VIII.'[321] Madden was delighted: 'Mr Thompson is a most useful assistant & his services more valuable than several of the older ones.'[322] However, even Thompson was not above making mistakes. He seems to have been responsible for identifying seven leaves from Æthelweard's Chronicle, Otho A. X, as part of the unique manuscript of Asser, the first article of Otho A. XII,[323] a mistake which seriously misled Henry Bradshaw in his account of the placenames in Asser[324] and was only rectified by Sir George Warner some years later.[325] These leaves, further damaged in the bindery fire, still form the first seven folios of Otho A. XII. It is perhaps only when mistakes like this come to light that the modern reader becomes conscious that many of the Cotton Manuscripts are in a way replicas or reconstitutions, made from the original materials by Madden and his colleagues. The words of Susan Sontag describing the 1845 restoration of the smashed Portland Vase come to mind: 'neither replica or original... A perfect job of reconstruction, for the time.'[326]

Madden's great enterprise has been exhaustively described here, but there are still many other aspects of the work which would be worth further investigation. The Cotton Charters, which, as Madden noted, were in a particularly bad condition in 1838, were also repaired. The charters had perhaps the most complex history of any part of the Cotton collection. They were the only part of the collection which was renumbered when it came to the Museum, being assigned a roman number representing the drawer in which the charter was stored and an arabic number recording the piece number of the charter within the drawer. The original Cotton Charters only extend as far as XVI.3. The numbers from this point onwards were assigned by Samuel Ayscough to various unnumbered charters and seal impressions while he was compiling his catalogue of charters in the 1790s.[327] These included a number of Harleian charters.[328] Madden was afterwards to lament the 'sad confusion' that Ayscough had caused in the charter numeration.[329] In Madden's time, these later additions to the charters were distinguished, following Ayscough's usage, as 'Cartae Miscellaneae Addendae' or 'Various Collections'. During Bond's Keepership (1866–78), the use of a separate designation for these charters ceased, and they have since always been referred to as Cotton Charters and Rolls. This has led to the confusing situation whereby the item known nowadays as Cotton Charter XXIV.17 was in fact presented to the Museum by Mr Leake of Middlewich in 1788.[330] Madden not only restored damaged charters but also recovered many charters from the damaged fragments in the garret.[331] The numeration assigned to these charters presumably reflects Madden's view of their likely provenance.

Hand in hand with the restoration of the Cotton Manuscripts went a closer investigation of the history of the collection, leading to the rediscovery of much lost and stray material. Madden compiled a detailed list of lost or strayed Cotton Manuscripts.[332] He persuaded Sir Thomas Phillipps to sell a stray Cotton manuscript in his possession, Vitellius D. IX, to the Museum at a special price.[333] Perhaps the most exciting rediscovery was that of the Utrecht Psalter. On 1 December 1856, Madden 'Received a letter from Mr D. Laing giving me a description of a MS. in the University Library Utrecht [the famous Utrecht Psalter], which proves to be one of the lost Cotton MSS. Claudius C.VII which is marked *Deest* in Smith's Catalogue of 1696 ... Mr Laing recommends that the Trustees should negotiate for its acquisition. *I think so too.*'[334]

The second half of the nineteenth century saw a great leap forward in critical and editorial standards. Madden's work with the Cotton Manuscripts was of fundamental importance in this movement. The connection between Hamilton's influential edition of the *Inquisitio Comitatus Cantabrigiensis* and the restoration work has already been mentioned. Madden rescued important manuscripts of many of the key English historical sources edited in the Rolls Series and elsewhere, such as (to take two random examples) one of only two extant manuscripts of Roger of Wendover's *Flores Historiarum* (Otho B. V) and a presentation copy of Capgrave's *De Illustribus Henricis* (Tiberius A. VIII). Moreover, the work on the restoration of the Cotton Manuscripts, by establishing the exact extent of the survival of particular manuscripts, helped clear the ground for new editions of texts whose chief witnesses had been destroyed or reduced to a few fragments, such as Gildas and Asser. Madden's achievements as 'Restorer of the Cotton library' may not have received much public recognition, but they can be seen as underpinning the emergence of modern historical technique in Britain. This is reflected in the prominence of those most closely associated with the work on the Cotton Manuscripts – Thompson, Hamilton, Bond and Madden himself – in the editing of the Rolls Series.

VIII

The two main published catalogues of the Cotton Library, those of Thomas Smith, published in 1696, and Joseph Planta, published in 1802, had both, within fifty years of their publication, ceased to be accurate guides to the collection they describe. The 1731 fire reduced Smith's catalogue overnight to the status of a historical document: an indispensable guide to the contents of the collection before the fire but no longer an up-to-date working catalogue. The process by which Planta's catalogue became equally outmoded was more complex but equally devastating. Criticisms of it had begun to be widely voiced as early as the 1830s. Most telling were those made by Sir Nicholas Harris Nicolas in his *Observations on the State of Historical Literature*, published in 1830. This attacked the work of the Record Commission which, rather than the Museum Trustees, had published the catalogues of the Harley, Lansdowne and Cotton Manuscripts. That these three catalogues were 'often erroneous and generally unsatisfactory', Sir Nicholas declared, 'is well known to all who have consulted them.'[335] He complained that the

Cotton catalogue, like the third volume of the Harley catalogue, was full of short and vague descriptions of complex manuscripts.[336] He also attacked the accuracy of the catalogue: 'The descriptions of the manuscripts are not unfrequently erroneous, and what is equally material, the general index at the end of the volume is extremely incomplete. For example, the Cottonian collection contains the highly valuable Chronicle of Lanercost, but no special *reference* is to be found to it in the general index; and other omissions of equal consequence might easily be cited.'[337]

In giving evidence to the 1836 Select Committee on the Museum, Nicolas not only repeated the criticisms in his earlier work, but also drew attention to the problem of the burnt manuscripts. He noted that Planta did not give any indication as to the contents of manuscripts thought to be completely lost, and offered no hint that any further fragments might still be surviving in the Museum.[338] Forshall's initial restoration work had, of course, already rendered Planta seriously out of date in this respect and it was no longer an accurate statement of those Cotton Manuscripts which were available for consultation in the Reading Room. Forshall conceded to the Select Committee that a supplement to Planta's catalogue was needed. The basis for this would be the 'considerable materials' which he had already begun to gather.[339]

Planta's inadequate treatment of the burnt and missing manuscripts was a glaring deficiency in his catalogue. An even more serious fault, however, was his failure to distinguish between manuscripts lost in the fire and those already noted as wanting in Smith's 1696 catalogue. Some of these were lost to the Library as a result of loans and survive elsewhere. Others may simply have been phantoms which never existed.[340]

As Madden's restoration work proceeded, the refrain of 'deest' and 'desideratur' which echoes through Planta's catalogue became more and more misleading. Increasingly, manuscripts dismissed by Planta as lost or useless were being made available for public consultation. Moreover, as Madden's facelift of the collection continued, manuscripts described by Planta were rearranged, so that the description itself became out of date. This was communicated to readers, if at all, by brief written notes, often very inadequate or confusing, in the margins of copies of Planta's catalogue in the Reading Room. Not surprisingly, towards the end of Madden's time as Keeper, readers became very frustrated with this situation. Madden's personal diary for 6 December 1861 contains the following entry:

Saw Mr Panizzi in his room, who shewed me a printed sheet sent to him by the post, anonymously, in which some person bearing no good will to the Dept. of MSS. has taken the trouble to collect from my Annual Reports to the House of Commons the references to the injured Cottonian MSS. which have been restored by my direction and under my superintendence, and then by way of a grievance, asking why a copy of Smith's Catalogue of 1696 has not been placed in the Reading Room, with an account of those MSS. which had been restored. My answer is thus, to this anonymous piece of spite.

1. There *is* a copy of Smith's Catalogue in the Reading Room & always has been.

2. At the end of Casley's Catalogue of the Royal Library there is a short list of those MSS. damaged or lost by fire in 1731.

3. A great part of the MSS. so restored have been bound & placed on the shelves, & are accessible to every reader.

4. Practically the whole are easily accessible, for every reader who wishes to know if any remains of a MS. (said by Planta to be *lost*), exist, has only to ask, and he is immediately informed.

5. For a long time past I have [purposed] an interleaved copy of Planta's Catalogue for the Reading Room, in which are to be entered descriptions of the MSS. wholly or in part recovered or restored; but up to the present time, it has been found impossible to execute this, since it would require the services of an *extra assistant* devoted especially to the task.[341]

Despite his dusty reply to this anonymous criticism, Madden was conscious of the need to provide better information about the availability of particular Cotton Manuscripts. In June 1861, he had pointed out to the Trustees that all the restored manuscripts needed to be described, and that Planta's catalogue 'requires careful revision, and additions to be made; to do which would require a good palaeographer & one well versed in English History and Middle Age literature.'[342]

As Madden approached the end of his work on the manuscripts, he had prepared a detailed account of the current condition of those reported by the parliamentary committee of 1732 as lost or injured.[343] This information was inserted in two interleaved copies of the committee's report. One was retained for internal Departmental use. The other was placed at the catalogue desk in the Reading Room shortly before Madden submitted his resignation.[344] This provided an authoritative account of the restoration work, but unfortunately it did not stay in the Reading Room for very long. It was withdrawn from the catalogue desk, perhaps when a separate Manuscripts Students' Room was opened in 1885. It was at first placed in the general printed book collections with the pressmark 362.b.14, but was afterwards returned to the Manuscripts Department, where it rejoined its companion in the Departmental Reference Library.[345] The two volumes remained there until 1983, when the copy originally intended for the Reading Room was incorporated in the Manuscript collections as Additional MS. 62573. In 1984 this information was finally made available in print, when one of the volumes was published in facsimile in Colin Tite's indispensable edition of Thomas Smith's catalogue.[346]

The interleaved copy of the parliamentary report is the only convenient statement available of the work done by Madden on the Cotton Manuscripts but is nevertheless unsatisfactory in a number of ways. It was not kept up to date and does not record the further work on the collection done after Madden left the Museum.[347] Moreover, Madden's notes are restricted to the manuscripts listed by Casley as lost or effectively destroyed but his work was far more wide-ranging than this. Many leaves were added to manuscripts described by Casley as damaged but usable, and there are only indirect references to the extensive work undertaken in rearranging and sorting the manuscripts in the Appendix. Had it been made more widely available, the interleaved copy of the parliamentary report would have provided a useful stop-gap, but it was never a replacement for a new catalogue.

The preparation of a new catalogue was a constant aspiration of successive Keepers

433

of Manuscripts, rather as the restoration of the fragments had been up to Madden's time. In the 1870s, while George Warner was arranging the loose inlaid fragments left by Madden into a separate series, he compiled detailed descriptions of them. Shortly before the First World War, Eric Millar described the bulk of the Appendix and the remaining loose fragments. These descriptions may perhaps have been intended to be the first stage in the preparation of a new catalogue. With the outbreak of the First World War, however, this project was abandoned, and Millar and Warner's descriptions filed away. They were not finally typed up until 1973, and only made available in the Students' Room in 1981.[348]

In 1931, the tercentenary of Cotton's death, a special exhibition of his finest manuscripts was held in the King's Library. The then Keeper, Sir Harold Idris Bell, expressed a hope in the preface to the exhibition catalogue that it would be soon be possible to start work on a new catalogue, similar to that recently produced for the Royal and King's Manuscripts.[349] Shortly afterwards, the Trustees gave permission for this work to begin.[350] Manuscripts in the Julius, Tiberius and Caligula groups were assigned for description to various officers including Bell himself, Robin Flower, Francis Wormald, Eric Millar, and Theodore Skeat. The rules drawn up for the new catalogue still survive. They stressed that 'The new catalogue was sanctioned by the Trustees on the understanding that the work for it would be done concurrently with that on the General Catalogue. It is important that it should not interfere too much with the latter, the arrears in which, though reduced, are as yet by no means overtaken. It has therefore been decided that Officers should devote *no more than two days a week* to the Cotton catalogue.' It was proposed to issue the catalogue in a series of fascicules, with the descriptions arranged in Emperor order. It was hoped to draw on the expertise of readers and an appeal for information on the manuscripts was to be circulated among them. F. M. Powicke and V. H. Galbraith were to be consulted on the treatment of chronicles and F. M. Stenton was to act as advisor on the cartularies. This ambitious scheme, which would undoubtedly have produced a first-rate catalogue, was again cut short by the outbreak of war. The dispersal of staff and collections during the war, as well as such vicissitudes as the destruction during the Blitz of the printer's stock of the descriptions of the *Catalogue of Additions to the Manuscripts* for 1921–1925 and part of 1926–1930, meant that delays arose in publication which are only just being eradicated.[351]

IX

The retirement of Madden did not mark the conclusion of work on the restoration of the Cotton Manuscripts. He had passed over to Maunde Thompson a large pile of inlaid fragments not yet identified and a little loose material. The annual reports of the Museum for 1867 and 1868 indicate that work continued on these fragments,[352] but it was soon abandoned as Madden's successor, Bond, began to concentrate on his pet project, the creation of the Class Catalogue. When Maunde Thompson himself became Keeper in 1878, the decision seems to have been taken to bind up the remaining inlaid fragments in separate volumes. Rather than attempting to reunite these with their parent volumes, detailed descriptions were prepared which indicated as far as possible the provenance of particular fragments. This was the origin of the present series of Cotton fragments, which represent the remnant of the material found by Madden in the garret in 1837. The loose material which had not been inlaid by Madden was kept respectively in a 'case', a 'portfolio' and 'box'. Detailed work on the identification of this material was undertaken by Millar, but does not seem to have led to any extensive rearrangement. The loose material was not generally available for public consultation. Eventually in 1990 the decision was taken to sew the loose material into inert transparent plastic sleeves to facilitate its use in the Students' Room. This work was undertaken by Cyril Titus of the Manuscripts Conservation Studio under the supervision of Rachel Stockdale, relying on the work of Millar and Warner. The material from the former 'case' is now available as Fragments XXX. It is intended that the contents of the 'box' and 'portfolio' will also be bound up in this fashion.

The story of the restoration is not yet ended. Indeed, it may be beginning afresh. Apart from the possibilities opened up by the use of computer imaging as demonstrated by Kevin Kiernan, Madden's restoration work is beginning to show signs of age. Vellum behaves in a different way from paper. As the vellum moves in one direction, the paper pulls in another. Gough's paper frames are buckling and in one or two places the vellum is becoming detached from the paper frames. Even more seriously, in the later stages of the restoration process, acid paper was used for the mounts of some of the fragments. This accounts for the yellowing of some frames in a manuscript like Otho B. X.[353] In order to stabilize the situation, some of the burnt Cotton Manuscripts have been recently encapsulated in plastic[354] but, as David Dumville has observed,[355] this makes study of the manuscripts difficult. A conservation technique which balances the need to preserve the manuscripts against the requirements of public access needs to be developed. In some respects, we are back in the time of Ellis and Forshall. Again the words of Susan Sontag in respect of the Portland Vase seem apposite: 'A perfect job of reconstruction, for its time. Until time wears it out. Transparent glue yellows and bulges, making seamless joints visible ... Can something shattered, then expertly repaired, be the same, the same as it was? Yes, to the eye, yes, if one doesn't look too closely. No, to the mind.'[356]

APPENDIX I

Reports of Matthew Maty and Henry Rimius on the condition of the Cotton Library, July 1756: Printed from the Minutes of the Standing Committee of the Museum Trustees, vol. 1, 1754–1757 (British Museum, Central Archives: CE 3/1), 102–106, 110–114.

435

The report of Dr Maty and Mr Rimius concerning the state in which they have found the manuscripts and medals in the Cottonian collection. According to the order given us by the Honourable Committee of the Trustees of the British Museum, Friday July 16th, 1756, we waited upon Mr Widmore at the Cottonian Repository, and examined the manuscripts, by comparing them both with the catalogue, composed by Mr Smith and printed in 1695, and with the account which was given by Mr Casley in 1732 of the state of the manuscripts after the fire. For this purpose we opened the several presses distinguished by the names of the twelve Caesars, those of Cleopatra and Faustina, and the Appendix; and having counted the number of volumes under every division, we took one or two of each and compared them with the catalogues, to be satisfied they answered to the accounts given of them. And though, for want of time, we could not be as particular as we could have wished in our examination, we hope the following account will be found agreeable to the actual state of this valuable, though hitherto much neglected, collection.

The manuscripts contained in the presses called Julius, Augustus, Claudius, Nero, Vespasianus, Titus, Domitianus, Cleopatra, Faustina, and those of the Appendix, have suffered nothing by the fire, and have been found to agree with Mr Smith's catalogue. Yet several of these being placed in presses much exposed to dampness in a cold and shady place, could hardly notwithstanding Mr Widmore's endeavours (which he has assured us to have been very assiduous) be preserved from must and mouldiness and will want to be aired and carefully dried up before they are placed in the Museum.

The condition of the manuscripts contained in the presses called Tiberius, Caligula, Galba, Otho and Vitellius, obliges us to be a little more particular, as we could not find some of the articles specified by Mr Casley, and as several of those which he declares to be entirely destroyed, may still be of some use in careful hands.

Beginning therefore with Tiberius we find the division
A. Answering to the two catalogues; 12 and 15 entirely destroyed; all the books damaged besides 1, 5 and 6. Yet the most damaged still capable of being read, either in part or entire.
B. 1, 2, 3, 4, 5 and 8 still subsisting; 9, though said to be burnt to a crust, very legible in the inside.
C. Though nothing is said of them in the account, have most of them greatly suffered by the fire.
D. 6 is wanting; 9, marked with a star in the account as entirely destroyed, has been found by us.
E. Answers to the catalogue compared with the report.

Caligula
A, B, C. Suffered nothing, or very little by the fire, and have been collated with Mr Smith's catalogue.
D & E. Answers to Mr Casley's account of the effect of the fire upon them.

Galba
A. 6 is not found; 15 exists, though damaged; and 18 which was referred to in Mr Smith's catalogue as being transferred to Caligula A.14 was reported to be lost by Mr Casley.
B, C, D, E. Answer to the catalogues compared one with the other.

Otho

A. According to the report consists of 18 numbers all destroyed; yet we discovered the first part of number XII being the Life of Alfred by Asser Menevensis.

B. Wants no. 9.

C. 1, 4 and 13, said to be destroyed, are in part legible. The other numbers answer to the catalogue as well as

D & E. Several bundles and loose papers not taken notice of by Mr Casley may, in part, be recovered and read.

Vitellius

Besides the damage done by the fire to the manuscripts in this press, it has suffered no less by the carelessness of those that have been the first employed in preserving them, as well as by the extraordinary moistness of the place. The great humidity, together with the extension of that hue, which the fire extracted from the volumes wrote on vellum, having rolled the edges of most of them, defaced the marks and afforded both lodging and food to numberless shoals of worms and other insects. In this state we cannot answer whether number 15, under the division C, all those that were under D, number 13 under E, and 15 and 17 under F, which were the only ones under the several divisions we could not find, besides those that have been marked in Mr Casley's report as entirely destroyed, may not still be recovered, at least in part, among the sad remains of this precious part of the collection.

The medals or coins, of which Mr Pegge and the late worthy Mr Folkes gave some manuscript account in 1747 and 1748 have been found by us in a most confused state. The Reverend Mr Widmore has never examined them according to these accounts, and answers only to the number, which we found to be as follows:

Pope's Heads, Seals & co	197
Medals or English coins	352
In all	549

The account of the charters, curiosities & co. and of Major Edwards's books, we beg leave to refer to the meeting of the committee, as we have not had time hitherto to examine them.

London. July 22 1756.

[*The further report*]

The charters, warrants, deeds and other records contained in the last press of the Cottonian cabinet might have been examined with more ease and in less time had we found them disposed in any order, properly endorsed, or at least regularly numbered and sufficiently described. But as nothing of all this has to our knowledge hitherto been done, and as no other assistance could be procured but the rough draft of a catalogue, which the Reverend Mr Widmore has made of them for his own use, we were obliged to look them over one by one, to pick up the late learned Keeper's loose sheets, and to affix to every one of them a number by which they could more easily be found out.

We cannot and indeed we ought not to be very particular in our account of these precious relics, as such an account would not only be dry and tedious, but also in a manner useless, since

Mr Widmore has promised to lend his notes. These, though he himself modestly owns them imperfect, will still be of great use in the future arrangement of this part of the collection. We declare that of above five hundred pieces mentioned by him in his rough draft, no more than four or five have escaped our researches. These few appeared to us to be of little consequence, to lose more time than we could spare in looking for them amidst the rubbish of bits of parchment or of paper, scorched by the fire, or consumed by old age, which Mr Widmore thought too much destroyed to be either used or described. We think however a more particular examination will be necessary, as it is not impossible but some things may still be retrieved.

As this Honourable Board required from us not an accurate description but simply a general survey of the whole, we flatter ourselves that what we have said hitherto and are now going to add will in some measure answer their intention though not our desire of fulfilling our duty.

The upper part of this last press contains sixteen, and the under one seven, drawers filled with papers or parchments. Several of them being entirely relative to the Cotton family seem to be of little use to the public, and the same may be said of many more, which only serve to swell but in our opinion by no means to enrich this collection.

Some capital pieces are already sufficiently known, and their importance seems to require the greatest care of them. Among them deserves the first rank, King John's famous grant of privileges, which though one of the sufferers by the fire, is still very legible, and would be much more so had anything been done to repair the damages done by this dreadful accident. We have put this piece by itself in a separate drawer, viz. no. 16 at bottom. The explanations of Magna Carta and of that of the Forests by Edward the First are likewise subsisting, and ought we think to be brought nearer than they now are to the preceding piece.

Amongst the public records preserved in our collection, we beg leave to mention Pope Innocent's Bull containing the cession of the weak king [John], Robert de Bruce's claim to the crown of Scotland as laid before Edward I in French in 1297, the Scotch Barons' submission to the English King's determination, the declaration of John, King of France, about the quarrel between the Dukes of Lancaster and Brunswick in 1352, the Archbishop of Canterbury and of York's letter to Henry VIII containing their synod's compliance with his desires in the affair of the divorce with Ann of Cleves, an instrument of the Dutch commissioners in 1585 confirming the cautionary cession of some of their towns. Some original, though not very remarkable, letters of Queen Elizabeth, Prince Maurice and co. are likewise found there.

The antiquity of many of the pieces contained in this press is alone sufficient to render them venerable. Several of them are of the ancient Saxon and Danish kings, viz. Ethelbert, Edred, Kinewolf, Canut, Alfred and co. and must be very near a thousand years old.

Historical, chronological and genealogical rolls, drawn up by monks, in the ages of ignorance and darkness, may still afford some satisfaction. Inventories of the books and effects of the several monasteries, expenses for the table of their abbots, and orders for the table of some princes, will probably likewise be examined and compared.

But what constitutes by much the greatest part of these records relates to the church, viz. Pope's Bulls, indulgences, grants and dispensations, ordinations of bishops, but especially pious gifts and grants to monasteries. Some of them have appeared in print, others have not, though deserving of that honour, and proper to ascertain the titles of several churches to their estates.

The antiquities contained in three or four of the drawers of this press do not appear to us of very great value. Some ancient little brass statues of Egyptian or other heathen gods or heroes, a few scales, instruments, and other trinkets neither remarkable for their rareness or workmanship do not deserve, at least at present, a more particular description, and we already too much fear to have abused the patience of this learned assembly by our hasty and very imperfect account.

London. July 30th 1756.

APPENDIX II

Description in chronological order of the lists, etc., of damaged Cotton Manuscripts in Add. MS. 62576

(1) Labels from boxes containing loose fragments of Caligula D. V (f. 11) and Vitellius E. IX (f. 15).

(2) Notes of lost Cotton and Royal MSS., early 19th cent.(?). ff. 59–60.

(3) List by Forshall of 'Saxon MSS. wanting', *circa* 1827. ff. 52–52v.

(4) List of injured Cotton MSS., *circa* 1830. ff. 2–7.

(5) Comparative table of descriptions in Casley, Planta and annotated catalogues in the Manuscripts Department of damaged MSS. in the Tiberius press, with notes of restoration undertaken by Forshall. Afterwards dated by Madden 'about 1836'. ff. 57v–58, 55v–56, 53v–54.

(6) List of injured Cotton MSS. compiled by Madden from Smith, Casley, Maty, Hooper, Planta, etc., August 1837 (cf. Add. MS. 62001, ff. 7v–8). As follows:-
    (a) Tiberius A. VIII – Caligula E. IV. ff. 36–38v;
    (b) Caligula E. V – Otho D. VI. ff. 27–32v;
    (c) Otho D. VII – Vitellius E. XII, arts. 1–4. ff. 21–26v;
    (d) Vitellius E. XII, arts. 5–35 – Appendix XLV (additional later notes on the Appendix are inserted at ff. 18–19). ff. 16–20v.

(7) 'Damaged Cotton MSS. on paper and vellum inspected and to be given to Mr Tucket, 1838', annotated with details of the conservation work undertaken by Madden. ff. 46, 39–41.

(8) Preliminary notes by Madden on burnt Cotton vellum remains in the boxes in the charter garret and drawers in the Keeper's Room, 1840. ff. 49–49v.

(9) Table by Madden of the injured Cotton Manuscripts on vellum, showing their condition in 1841. ff. 61–62v, 47.

(10) List by Madden of volumes of loose or injured state papers, *circa* 1844. ff. 12–14.

(11) List in manuscript order of paper manuscripts inlaid and rebound by Tuckett. f. 41v.

(12) List in chronological order of vellum Cotton MSS. inlaid by Gough, viz:- (a) Work undertaken between 1842 and 1848. ff. 42–42v;- (b) Work undertaken between 1849–1850. f. 34.

(13) List in chronological order of vellum Cotton MSS. inlaid by Tuckett, 1849–1851. f. 35.

(14) List in manuscript order of vellum MSS. inlaid or rebound by Tuckett. ff. 33–33v.

439

(15) List of injured Royal MSS., *circa* 1851. ff. 48–48v.

(16) List in chronological order of manuscripts inlaid by Gough and Tuckett, 1854–1856. f. 35v.

(17) Lists by Madden of Saxon MSS. injured in the fire and other Saxon MSS. in the Cotton Library, n.d. ff. 51, 43.

(18) Notes by Madden on paper MSS. preserved in cases. ff. 10, 44–45v.

(19) Notes by Madden on contents of Appendix XL and XXIX. ff. 8–8v.

(20) Rough notes of apparently missing MSS. f. 50.

* See M. Teresa Tavormina, 'Order, liturgy and laughter in *A Canticle for Leibowitz*', in B. Rosenthal and P. E. Szarmach (eds.), *Medievalism in American Culture* (Binghamton, 1987), pp. 45–64.

1 *Gentleman's Magazine*, i (1731), p. 451. I am grateful to Robin Alston, Janet Backhouse, Carl T. Berkhout, Michael Borrie, Michelle Brown, Tim Graham, J. R. Hall, Philip Harris, Simon Keynes, Phillip Pulsiano, Nigel Ramsay, Colin Tite and Elaine Treharne for many valuable discussions about the history of the Cotton library. They have saved me from many blunders. Above all, however, I am deeply indebted to Kevin S. Kiernan, whose spellbinding scholarship on the *Beowulf* manuscript first drew attention to many of the issues associated with the post-fire history of the Cotton collection and showed their importance for its modern users.

2 Cf. E. Miller, *That Noble Cabinet: A History of the British Museum* (London, 1973), pp. 34–5, and S. Keynes, 'The reconstruction of a burnt Cottonian manuscript: the case of Cotton MS. Otho. A. I', *British Library Journal*, xxii (1996), pp. 113–14. I am grateful to Dr Keynes for showing me a draft of his article.

3 *A Report from the Committee Appointed to View the Cottonian Library, and such of the Publick Records of this Kingdom, as they think proper ...* (London, 1732), hereafter cited as *1732 Report*. This report was reprinted in *Reports from the Committees of the House of Commons ...* (London, 1803), vol. i, pp. 443–535. It was reproduced in facsimile from an annotated copy in the British Library (not Add. MS. 62573 as stated by Tite in his introduction: see n. 254 below) by C. G. C. Tite in his edition of Thomas Smith, *Catalogue of the Manuscripts in the Cottonian Library 1696* (Cambridge, 1984), hereafter cited as *Smith* (1984 ed.). Other copies are Add. MSS. 24932 and 62572.

4 *1732 Report*, pp. 11–15.

5 Ibid., p. 5.

6 Ibid., pp. 15–139.

7 D. Casley, *A Catalogue of the Manuscripts of the King's Library* (London, 1734), pp. 313–45. Sir F. Madden, *Layamon's Brut* (London, 1847), vol. i, p. xxxvii, states that the original draft of Casley's report was preserved in the Museum in 1846. I have not been able to trace it.

8 *1732 Report*, p. 15.

9 See further below, pp. 404–22. Madden notes with regard to these figures that 'a distinction was not made between those MSS. *lost* and *burnt*, and those stated to be *intirely spoilt*. Most, if not the whole, of the latter class are capable of being restored.': Add. MS. 62572, f. 9v.

10 The manuscripts listed in the departmental handlists as completely burnt in 1731 are: Galba A. VIII, Otho A. XV–XVII, Otho B. I, VIII, XV, Otho C. VI, Otho E. II, V, Vitellius D. XIV, Vitellius F. XIV. In addition, a cartulary of Lenton Priory which Smith had numbered Otho B. XIV was also destroyed. This pressmark had previously been assigned to a manuscript containing records of Sheen Priory and other houses which strayed from the Cotton library sometime between *circa* 1639 and 1696. The Sheen manuscript was rediscovered in 1787, purchased by the British Museum, and restored to its former pressmark in place of the lost Lenton cartulary. Planta incorrectly speculated that Otho B. I, returned as destroyed, may in fact have been the Sheen manuscript: see further G. R. C. Davis, *Medieval Cartularies of Great Britain* (London, 1958), nos. 551, 891, and the nineteenth-century note on this manuscript in the annotated Casley reprinted in *Smith* (1984 ed.).

11 See further Kevin S. Kiernan, *Beowulf and the Beowulf Manuscript* (New Brunswick, 1981) [hereafter cited as Kiernan, *Beowulf*], pp. 67–8.

12 N. R. Ker, *Catalogue of Manuscripts Containing Anglo-Saxon* (Oxford, 1957), nos. 155, 185–8; Elżbieta Temple, *Anglo-Saxon Manuscripts, 900–1066* (London, 1976), no. 100; J. Backhouse, D. H. Turner and L. Webster (eds.), *The Golden Age of Anglo-Saxon Art* (London, 1984), pp. 47, 49.

13 Cf. also the account of damaged manuscripts in the Otho press in Keynes, art. cit.

14 K. Weitzmann and H. L. Kessler, *The Cotton Genesis* (Princeton, 1986).

15 But see further pp. 406–7 below.

16 Ker, op. cit., nos. 171–2; H. Gneuss, 'Die Handschrift Cotton Otho A.XII', *Anglia*, xciv (1976), pp. 289–318; D. G. Scragg (ed.), *The Battle of Maldon* (Manchester, 1981), pp. 1–4; H. L. Rogers, '*The Battle of Maldon*: David Casley's transcript', *Notes and Queries*, ccxxx (1985), pp. 147–55; D. G. Scragg (ed.), *The Battle of Maldon, AD 991* (Oxford, 1991), pp. 15–16; Leslie Webster and Janet Backhouse (eds.), *The Making of England: Anglo-Saxon Art and Culture AD 600–900* (London, 1991) [hereafter cited as *The Making of England*], no. 234, and works cited there. The first seven folios in the restored Otho A. XII are, in fact, part of Æthelweard's Chronicle from Otho A. X, which were misidentified in 1864 as being from Asser: see further below, p. 430 and E. Barker, 'The Cottonian Fragments of Æthelweard's Chronicle', *Bulletin of the Institute of Historical Research*, xxiv (1951), pp. 46–62. I will deal with this incident at greater length in a forthcoming note, 'The Ghost of Asser'.

17 A. Gransden, *Historical Writing in England c. 550–c. 1307* (London, 1974), p. 2, n. 4.

18 Ker, op. cit., no. 180; R. J. S. Grant, 'Laurence Nowell's Transcript of BM Cotton Otho B.XI', *Anglo-Saxon England*, iii (1974), p. 115; A. Lutz, *Die Version G der Angelsächsisen Chronik: Rekonstruktion und Edition* (Munich, 1981).

19 Gransden, op. cit., p. 43, n. 13.

20 See n. 4 above.

21 *The Making of England*, no. 241, and works cited there.

22 Ibid., no. 83, where an eighteenth-century facsimile of a page from Otho C. V made for Edward Harley, Earl of Oxford, now Stowe MS.

1061, f. 36, showing the appearance of the manuscript before the fire, is also reproduced. A full study of this manuscript is forthcoming: M. Budny, R. Page and C. D. Verey (eds.), *The Cambridge-London Gospels: An Eighth-Century Insular Gospel-Book from Northumbria*.

23 In April 1766, some fragments of letters burnt in the fire were presented to the British Museum by Charles Grey. They had been given to Grey by Sir Roger Newdigate whose brother, then at Westminster School, had picked them up after the fire: British Library, Manuscripts Department Archives, Acquisitions 1759–1836, ff. 3–4. Madden sought in vain to identify these fragments. Presumably they were added to the general stock of burnt fragments and other 'refuse' without any indication of their provenance. A fragment from Otho B. X, presumably also picked up as a keepsake, was given to Thomas Hearne by Browne Willis on 15 Nov. 1731 and is now Bodleian Library, MS. Rawlinson Q.e.20: Ker, op. cit., no. 177.

24 *1732 Report*, pp. 11–12.

25 Ibid., p. 12.

26 Ibid., pp. 12–15.

27 Ibid., pp. 12–14; cf. the remarks of Forshall to the parliamentary Select Committee investigating the Museum in 1835: *Report from the Select Committee on the Condition, Management and Affairs of the British Museum* (1835) (hereafter cited as *1835 Select Committee Report*), no. 1108.

28 Royal MS. 9 C. X. See also the 'before' and 'after' drawing of Otho B. V made for Henry Gough by Caleb W. Wing, now Add. MS. 18457, described further on p. 418 below.

29 Thomas Hearne commented that 'what the fire did not entirely destroy suffer'd very much by water, both very dangerous elements to MSS': H. E. Salter (ed.), *Hearne's Collections*, Oxford Historical Society, xi (1921), p. 8.

30 *1732 Report*, pp. 12–13.

31 For all the following, see *1732 Report*, pp. 13–15.

32 Ibid., pp. 13–14.

33 Cf. pp. 397–8, 401, 410–11 below. In his copy of the *1732 Report*, Madden wrote 'Not True' beside Whiston's comment that only a few vellum manuscripts of little value had been left untreated: Add. MS. 62572, f. 8v.

34 *1732 Report*, p. 14.

35 Ibid.

36 Ibid., pp. 14–15.

37 Ibid.
38 See the report of Maty and Rimius, p. 437 below.
39 *1732 Report*, p. 15.
40 I owe this point to Kevin Kiernan.
41 *Poems on Several Occasions* (Oxford, 1781), pp. 71–4.
42 Elizabeth M. Hallam, *Domesday Book through Nine Centuries* (London, 1986), pp. 135–6.
43 *D.N.B.*
44 A. Esdaile, *The British Museum Library* (London, 1946), p. 17.
45 Ibid., p. 352.
46 Ibid. On Edwards's library, which contained about four thousand volumes, see further F. J. Hill, 'The Shelving and Classification of Printed Books' in P. Harris (ed.), *The Library of the British Museum* (London, 1991), pp. 3–4. According to the *D.N.B.*, he left 'pictures of King George 1st, the Czar Peter, Oliver Cromwell, and Cosimo de Medici the 1st, with his secretary Bartolomeo Concini' to be placed in the Cotton library. These are presumably items 3, 6, 46 and 88 in the list of portraits in the Mineral gallery of the British Museum in the *Synopsis of the Contents of the British Museum* (London, 1838), pp. 132–5, where they are misleadingly described as having 'belonged to the old Cottonian Library'. I owe the reference to the list of pictures to Dr Colin Tite. The picture of Peter the Great was presumably that on the wall of the sitting room in the residence of the Director of the British Museum in 1992.
47 Hargrave MS. 304, a catalogue of the Madox collection, contains on f. 1 the following note by E. Umfreville, dated 1760: 'From the collections of Vigerus Edwards Esq. whose sister married Mr Madox … The MSS. were not sold, but Lodg'd by Mr Edwards in the Cotton Library for public use – whence with the Cotton Library they were removed to the British Museum at Montague House in Gt Russell Street Bloomsbury.' The transfer of the Madox collections to the Museum was formalized by their bequest to the Museum by Catherine Madox in 1756: see *Catalogue of Additions to the Manuscripts 1756–1782* (London, 1977), p. 181. According to the *Synopsis of the Contents of the British Museum* (London, 1808), p. 14, she stated that these volumes should be treated as an addition to the Cotton library, and, while they were in Montagu House, they were kept in the same room as the Cotton

MSS., under press XIX of Room VII. They are now Add. MSS. 4479–4572.
48 Colin Tite, *The Manuscript Library of Sir Robert Cotton* (London, 1994), p. 33, notes that in the mid-1730s, Gilbert Burnet the younger considered depositing in the library the original manuscript of his father's *History of His Own Time.*
49 Esdaile, op. cit., pp. 17–18.
50 British Museum, Central Archives (hereafter BM, CA:), CE 1/1, 25 (13 Feb. 1754). The following classes of material in the British Museum Archives have been used: CE 1 (Minutes of the Trustees' General Meetings); CE 3 (Minutes of the standing committee); CE 4 (Original papers); CE 5 (Officers' reports). Some of these volumes are foliated and others paginated. References are to folio or page. I am very grateful to Miss Janet Wallace for her assistance and advice in making available material from the Museum Archives. Extracts are printed by kind permission of the Trustees of the British Museum. A draft of these minutes is Add. MS. 4450, ff. 43–44. See also Miller, op. cit., p. 49.
51 The catalogue of the sale of the library of Joseph Ames, the bibliographer and antiquary, on 5 May 1760 included the following as part of lot 166: 'Two Bundles of MSS. presented to Mr. Ames by Mrs. Casley, being part of the Cottonian [*sic*] damaged by the Fire.' In the copy of the Ames sale catalogue in the BL, Manuscripts Department library, this entry has been marked with a large 'N.B.', apparently by Sir Frederic Madden. Madden declared in 1847 that he would 'like much to know the name of the purchaser & what these MSS. were.': Add. MS. 62006, f. 11.
52 S. Hooper, *A Catalogue of the Manuscripts in the Cottonian Library* (London, 1777), pp. xii–xiv.
53 These reports are also briefly noted in E. Miller, op. cit., pp. 60–1. They are BM, CA: CE 3/1, 102–106 (23 July 1756) and 110–114 (30 July 1756), and are printed in Appendix I below.
54 See below, p. 408.
55 A copy of this catalogue is now Harl. MS. 7647, ff. 13–52. This volume also contains (ff. 2–12v) a copy of the list of charters and other items drawn up by Humfrey Wanley in 1703, on which see further *Smith* (1984 ed.), pp. 10–12. The transcripts in Harley 7647 were both made for Charles Morton, the first Keeper of Manuscripts. Further details are given in the following

minute of the Standing Committee meeting on 5 Nov. 1756 (BM, CA: CE 3/1, 144–145): 'Dr Morton delivered in two catalogues of the carts contained in the Cotton Library which he had transcribed. The first of these was made by Mr Matthew Hutton, Mr John Anstis and Mr Humphrey Wanley; and transcribed from the original in Mr Wanley's handwriting, annexed to a copy of Dr Smith's catalogue of the Cottonian Library, belonging to the Lord Chancellor [Lord Hardwicke], and lent by his Lordship to the trustees for their use [the copy used by Morton is possibly that formerly owned by Sir Nathan Wright, Lord Keeper of the Great Seal 1700–5, now Printed Books, 125.l.11, which may have passed to Hardwicke with other official papers]. The other catalogue was transcribed from one drawn up by the Reverend Mr Widmore. The Committee upon inspection of the Lord Chancellor's copy, having observed a report prefixed, and marginal notes throughout the book, all in the handwriting of Mr Wanley; ordered that the said report and notes be transcribed into another of Dr Smith's catalogues, as soon as a good one be procured.' These transcripts are not in Morton's hand, but were checked and corrected by him (e.g. ff. 19v–21). They were incorporated as Add. MS. 4998, but, because of the reference to Wanley, they were mistakenly renumbered as Harl. MS. 7647 some time between the publication of the catalogue of Harleian manuscripts, 1808–12, and the appointment of Madden as Keeper in 1837. The 'loculi' of Widmore's list are the sixteen drawers referred to by Maty and Rimius. The numeration given here was altered when the charters were moved into new drawers at the Museum in 1758: see further p. 430 below. The notes by Morton in the Harley copy of Widmore's catalogue altering the numeration of the charters (e.g. ff. 45v, 46v) were presumably made in the course of this rearrangement.

56 The Trustees had ordered that the Sloane and Cotton collections be moved to Montagu House 'with all convenient speed' on 19 June 1756: BM, CA: CE 1/1, 119. However, the move of the Sloane collections seems to have been undertaken first, and the completion of the move of the Cotton library was not reported to the Trustees until 12 July 1757: ibid., 185–6.

57 On the classifications adopted for the Sloane and Harley collections, see e.g. Add. MSS. 4450, f.

106; 45871, ff. 14v–15, 49, 54v, and the description of these collections in the *Synopsis of the Contents of the British Museum* (London, 1808), pp. 7–13; cf. Hill, art. cit., p. 4.

58 BM, CA: CE 1/1, 185–186.

59 These burnt crusts were made available in the Reading Room in the normal way: e.g. Add. MS. 46508, f. 88v (recording issue of the crust of Tiberius A. X to John Bacon, July 1764); Add. MS. 46509, f. 31v (recording issue of Vitellius E. XVIII to Richard Gough, April 1768); Kevin S. Kiernan, *The Thorkelin Transcripts of Beowulf*, *Anglistica*, xxv (1986), p. 25 (recording issue of Tiberius E. I, V and VII). The reaction of readers to being presented with these charred, fat-encrusted manuscripts is not recorded; but Bacon kept Tiberius A. X out until April 1765.

60 BM, CA: CE 1/1, 185–186.

61 BM, CA: CE 1/3, 743; CE 3/6, 1491.

62 BM, CA: CE 3/2, 338 (22 July 1757).

63 Ibid., 415 (18 Feb. 1758).

64 Ibid., 418–9 (3 Mar. 1758).

65 See Weitzmann and Kessler, op. cit, pp. 6–7, from which, unless otherwise stated, all the following is drawn.

66 'Schedas quasdam flammis misere vitiatas, nunc vero deperditas': cited in F. W. Gotch, *A Supplement to Tischendorf's Reliquae ex Incendio Ereptae Codicis Celeberrimi Cottoniani* (Leipzig, 1881), p. v.

67 On Gifford, see further Miller, op. cit., p. 100, and Esdaile, op. cit., pp. 45–6.

68 Gotch, op. cit., p. vi. In 1847, Madden gave a detailed report of the circumstances of the loss of the Bristol fragments to the Trustees and urged that action should be taken for their recovery, but nothing was done: Add. MS. 62028, ff. 48v–51.

69 Gotch, op. cit.

70 *Vetusta Monumenta* (London, 1747), pl. I, nos. i, ii, iii, v, vi, vii and x.

71 Madden's personal diary is Bodleian Library, MS. Eng. hist. c. 140–182. Extracts are printed by kind permission of the Bodleian Library. A copy is in the British Library: MS. Facs. *1012. It is hereafter cited as MJ.

72 The Tyndale Bible purchased by the British Library from the Baptist College in 1994 also came from Gifford's collection.

73 BM, CA: CE 3/8, 2080. Samuel Hooper states in the dedication of his subject catalogue of the Cotton Manuscripts, op. cit., that Astle had

provided him with the manuscripts from which the catalogue was compiled. The precise meaning of this is unclear; perhaps Astle gave Hooper access to material in his collections, such as the seventeenth-century catalogue of cartularies, now Add. MS. 5161.

74 Hooper, op. cit.

75 Ibid., pp. xii–xiv.

76 BM, CA: CE 4/2, 691.

77 But see Tite, *The Manuscript Library of Sir Robert Cotton*, pp. 51–7.

78 BM, CA: CE 1/2, 708–711.

79 Ibid.

80 The indexes were still in the process of completion in 1800: *Reports from the Select Committee ... into the State of the Public Records* (London, 1800), p. 391.

81 J. Planta, *A Catalogue of the Manuscripts in the Cottonian Library, deposited in the British Museum* (London, 1802), hereafter cited as Planta. It is interesting to note, in view of some of the later criticisms of Planta's catalogue, that it is described in the 1812 report of the Record Commission as a corrected version of Smith, 'The Catalogue of the Cotton Library ... corrected by Joseph Planta, Esq.': *First General Report from the Commission on Public Records* (London, 1812), p. 231.

82 BM, CA: CE 4/2, 708–711. The published version is pp. xiv–xv of Planta's catalogue.

83 This figure differs from that given by Planta in his 1793 report to the Trustees, in which he states that the Library had been reduced by the fire to 880 volumes, about 100 of which were at that time too much damaged to be bound and were therefore preserved in cases.

84 It was first correctly identified, as far as I am aware, by Kiernan, *Beowulf*, pp. 99–103.

85 None of the foliations or foliation notes appear to be by Planta. For an example of his hand, see Add. MS. 5015, ff. 123–145. Presumably the practice of foliation was the same in Planta's time as later: the foliation was entered by an attendant, and then checked by another attendant, who entered the foliation note.

86 E.g. Vitellius C. III, ff. 60, 61; Vitellius C. XII, ff. 159–160. Since the Planta foliation was written on the unprotected vellum leaves, the numbers occasionally crumbled away from use in the Reading Room and were replaced by new pencil numbers, written at some time before the inlaying of the leaves under Madden, most likely

during the keepership of Forshall, who seems to have been responsible for introducing the use of pencil for writing folio numbers: e.g. Tiberius A. III, ff. 21, 24–26, 57, 93; Vitellius C. III, f. 33.

87 The condition of the MSS. at the end of the conservation work is described by Planta himself in his descriptions of the manuscripts.

88 BM, CA: CE 5/8, 1895–8.

89 *1835 Select Committee Report*, no. 1105.

90 On this MS., see further R. Cleminson, *The Anne Pennington Catalogue: A Union Catalogue of Cyrillic Manuscripts in British and Irish Collections* (London, 1988), no. 96. A description in Russian of its condition in 1818, including a crude diagram showing the shape of the loose burnt leaves, is Add. MS. 47289 B, ff. 1–4v.

91 A slip apparently kept with Caligula D. V when it was stored loose in a case is now Add. MS. 62576, f. 11.

92 These details are conveniently summarized in Madden's notes: Add. MS. 62576, ff. 12–14.

93 Kevin S. Kiernan, *The Thorkelin Transcripts of Beowulf*; K. Malone (ed.), *The Thorkelin Transcripts of Beowulf, Early English Manuscripts in Facsimile*, i (Copenhagen, 1951).

94 Ibid., p. 34.

95 This is confirmed by Madden's 1841 list of injured vellum Cotton MSS.: Add. MS. 62576, ff. 61–62v, 47. This lists all the loose and most badly damaged material, but has no entry for Vitellius A. XV. Presumably this first post-fire binding of Vitellius A. XV was similar to other Elliot-Planta bindings, of which an example is Vespasian B. XXVI, a full binding in brown calf, with gold letters 'M.B.' on the front cover, and gold tooling on the spine.

96 Kiernan, op. cit., p. 150, n. 46; W. F. Bolton, 'The Conybeare Copy of Thorkelin', *English Studies*, lv (1974), pp. 97–107. In 1994, Prof. Bolton most generously donated the Conybeare collation to the British Library to facilitate the scanning of the collation as part of the Electronic Beowulf project.

97 Kiernan, op. cit., p. 150, n. 46; idem, 'Madden, Thorkelin and MS. Vitellius/Vespasian A XV', *The Library*, viii (1986), pp. 127–32; J. R. Hall, 'Some Additional Books at Harvard Annotated by Sir Frederic Madden', *Notes and Queries*, ccxxx (1985), p. 315.

98 Analogous losses also occurred in Otho C. XIII, an early manuscript of Layamon. They are noted

in Madden, op. cit., p. xxxviii, n. 1. cf also G. L. Brook and R. F. Leslie (eds.), *Layamon: Brut*, E.E.T.S., O.S., ccl, cclxxvii (1963, 1978), vol. i, p. x. Some of these 'M' readings could perhaps now be recovered with the aid of fibre optic backlighting.

99 *Synopsis of the Contents of the British Museum* (London, 1808), pp. 13–14.

100 This may perhaps partly account for the ambiguities in references by Thorkelin and Madden to the pressmark of the Beowulf manuscript: Kiernan, 'Madden, Thorkelin and MS. Vitellius/Vespasian A XV', pp. 127–32.

101 The majority of the Cotton MSS. have always, since being moved from Montagu House, been kept in roughly the same presses, namely those numbered from 16 to 27 in the Manuscript Saloon: see the various descriptions of the distribution of MSS. in the presses in the volume of papers from Madden's keepership labelled *Miscellanea* in the Manuscripts Department Archives. References to press numbers lower than sixteen on the flyleaves of Cotton MSS. are therefore Montagu House press-marks: e.g. Julius D. II has a Montagu House pressmark of I A on f. iv; Julius D. V a pressmark of III A on f. 1; Nero C. IX a pressmark of VI D on a flyleaf; and Tiberius C. VI a pressmark of XII F on the flyleaf. Some of these pressmarks are in ink and others in pencil.

102 BM, CA: CE 5/8, 1895–8.

103 BM, CA: CE 3/10, 2915. The story of Wollaston's experiments was drawn to my attention by Philip Harris and Nigel Ramsay.

104 *D.N.B.*

105 Manuscripts Department Archives, Acquisitions 1759–1836, ff. 35*, 36*.

106 MJ, 6 June 1854; cf. also Add. MS. 62010, ff. 32v–33.

107 Add. MS. 62035, f. 3.

108 BM, CA: CE 3/10, 2921; CE 5/8, 1895–8.

109 BM, CA: CE 5/8, 1880.

110 BM, CA: CE 3/10, 2945; CE 4/6, 2119.

111 Ibid.

112 BM, CA: CE 3/10, 2951.

113 BM, CA: CE 5/9, 2020.

114 Ibid.

115 Add. MS. 62022, f. 65v.

116 BM, CA: CE 5/9, 2020.

117 BM, CA: CE 5/9, 2027.

118 The progress of the work is described in BM, CA: CE 5/9, 2040, 2046, 2057, 2076–2076b, and CE 5/10, 2102b–2103, 2122, 2141.

119 This is evident from a list of missing and damaged MSS. apparently compiled for Forshall, Add. MS. 62576, ff. 2–7. This shows a number of the manuscripts recovered by Forshall as still missing or in the process of restoration, e.g. Otho A. III, Otho B. II, Otho C. V, Vitellius D. XVII, Vitellius F. XI. This list dates from 1830 at the earliest, since it states that John Holmes, who did not join the Department until that year, was working on Otho A. VI. Holmes's name was afterwards crossed out and 'Sir F. Madden' inserted in its place. Madden was knighted in 1832. All this suggests that this list must be dated 1830–2, and restoration work was still in progress at that time.

120 The fullest guide to the MSS. on which Forshall worked is Madden's table of the condition of the damaged vellum MSS. in 1841, Add. MS. 62576, ff. 61–62v, 47. The MSS. restored by Forshall are, with the exception of the Christchurch cartulary (Tiberius D. VI), those noted in Madden's table as having been described by Planta as missing or a crust but preserved in a case in 1841. This suggests that the following MSS. were 'restored' under Forshall: Galba A. V; Otho A. II, VI; B. II; C. I, V, XIII; D. III, VII, VIII; E. I; Tiberius A. XII, XV; B. IX, XI; D. III, IV, V, VII; E. I, II, IV-VII, XIII; Vitellius A. IX; C. V; D. XVII; E. IX, XIII, XV, XVIII; F. XI, XVI, XVII. In addition, some leaves were recovered but misidentified: e.g. six leaves of Otho A. I were mistakenly placed with Otho C. V (see below, p. 428). Further information about the restoration work is given in Ellis's and Forshall's reports for 1826–7 in the Officers' Reports for those years in BM, CA: CE 5/9–10. These are very patchy in details of work on individual MSS., but give explicit references to treatment of the following: Otho B. VI; C. XIII; Tiberius A. V, XV; D. III, IV; E. I, II (all the preceding are identified as having been treated by Forshall in Madden's 1841 list, whereas the work on the following is not evident from Madden's list); Caligula D. X, XI; Galba A. IX, X, XV; Tiberius A. IX, X; E. III, IX. The paper slip apparently kept with Vitellius E. IX

when it was stored loose in a box is Add. MS. 62576, f. 15.

121 In Madden's resignation memorial, MJ 12 July 1866.

122 Ellis still hankered after something more dramatic than the results achieved as a result of Davy's sensible advice. On 10 Feb. 1827, he suggested that leaves from the restored Tiberius A. XV be sent to William Wollaston for further experiments. He advised the Trustees that 'all that can be done for it in the MS. Department has already been done, but Dr Wollaston thinks that by chemical applications he may be able to do something more for it.' The leaves to be sent to Wollaston would contain the text of letters known from other copies 'so that even if experiment was to destroy them, their contents will not have been lost': BM, CA: CE 5/10, 2102b–2103.

123 The description of this MS. in F. Robinson and E. Stanley, *Old English Verse Texts from Many Sources: A Comprehensive Collection, Early English Manuscripts in Facsimile*, xxiii (Copenhagen, 1991), 5.6.1.1, refers to the inlaying of this MS. by Gough in 1844, but not to its earlier rediscovery. A list of missing and damaged Cotton MSS. compiled for Forshall and dating perhaps from about 1830–2 states that this manuscript was 'Much damaged, but now being restored by [Mr Holmes deleted] Sir F. Madden': Add. MS. 62576, f. 4.

124 Edited by Madden, op. cit., and by G. Brook and R. Leslie, ed. cit. Madden notes Forshall's initial restoration of the MS. in 'about 1827' and describes how this led to part being printed by Benjamin Thorpe, who called it 'only a bundle of fragments': op. cit., p. xxxvii. The facsimile of this manuscript in Madden's edition illustrates f. 92 *before* it was inlaid in 1846. It shows the top part of the initial and the pricking on the top half of the leaf, which are now largely concealed by repair. The facsimile gives a very good idea of the appearance of the MSS. restored by Forshall, with their characteristic incisions, where the crust was cut open.

125 BM, CA: CE 5/9, 2020.

126 Add. MS. 62573, f. 57.

127 Details of this can be most easily reconstructed from Madden's notes in Add. MS. 62577. On f. 45, Madden notes the following as '*Cottonian Papers* bound by Mr Forshall before 1832 with *temporary numbers* now altered. Append. xlvi. Miscell. Papers. xlvii. Do. (part of Cal. D.VIII). xlviii. do. (…Wolsey &c.). xlix. Journal to Greenland 1605. l. Camdens Pedigrees. The papers in xlvii and xlviii have been distributed in other vols. FM. Jan. 1859.' On f. 46, Madden further notes that 'Mr Forshall bound up some miscellaneous Papers and marked them Append. xlvi. Many of them were taken out and placed among charters.' The use of the Appendix as a means of temporarily numbering loose papers while they were being sorted continued under Madden. In Add. MS. 62577, f. 42, he notes that the numbers xlix to lv in the Appendix were reserved for 'MSS or Papers not identified'. On all this, see further C. Tite, 'The Cotton Appendix and the Fragments', *The Library*, xv (1993), pp. 52–5.

128 *1836 Select Committee Report*, nos. 4389, 4397.

129 Descriptions are preserved of Galba A. V; Otho A. VI; B. II, VI; Vitellius D. XVII; E. XVIII; F. XI. Phillip Pulsiano and I hope to publish samples of these.

130 See below, p. 416.

131 Cf. illustration in Temple, op. cit., fig. 57.

132 BM, CA: CE 3/13, 3807.

133 BM, CA: CE 3/13, 3827.

134 BM, CA: CE 3/13, 3807.

135 BM, CA: CE 3/13, 3827.

136 According to a note by Casley on the dorse and also the *1732 Report*, p. 14, words and letters completely destroyed by the fire were supplied in red. Just a few letters are given in red and the only words marked as completely destroyed are the words 'De forestis' and the first part of 'afforestandis' in the last line of the transcript (presumably endorsements on the original).

137 A copy of this engraving is Stowe MS. 1060, f. 55. In the legend, Casley attests that in his transcript only nineteen letters are supplied from other sources. Pine shows the damaged Magna Carta surrounded by the arms of the barons, presumably because, as Casley states, the sides of the document were the parts worst affected by the fire. Posters showing representations of Magna Carta in this way are still on sale in souvenir shops; it would be interesting to establish how far they are descendants of Pine's engraving.

138 See below, p. 438.

139 MJ, 7 Dec. 1858.

140 *1835 Select Committee Report*, no. 1108.

141 Ibid., no. 1112.

142 Ibid., nos. 1117–1118.

143 See below, p. 408.

144 Details are given in Ellis's report on the move: BM, CA: CE 5/10, 2141. See also P. Harris, 'The Move of Printed Books from Montagu House, 1838–1842', in P. Harris (ed.), *The Library of the British Museum*, p. 76.

145 Ellis's report states that 'The marks of Reference to the Presses and shelves in the new Room have been inserted by the Officers in the inside of every volume, and the larger portion marked in a corresponding manner upon the outside by the Book Binder.' F. J. Hill, art. cit., p. 4, was unaware that the emperor pressmark system was abandoned, and states wrongly that 'the Old Royal and Cotton Manuscripts are still shelved by the pressmarks which they already had when received in the Museum'.

146 The clearest description of the modern placing system of the Manuscripts Department is in a draft paper by Maunde Thompson preserved in a volume of loose papers dating from Bond's keepership in the Manuscripts Department Archives, 'Memorandum of the system of Registering, Cataloguing and Labelling of MSS. in the Dept. of MSS. in the British Museum', which provides a succinct summary of the housekeeping practices of the Department, much of which is still valid today. Under 'Labelling and Pressmarking', Bond writes as follows: 'Each MS. (in addition to its own individual number) has small printed labels attached to the back, one placed at the top and the other at the bottom of the volume. The first bears the number of the press, the second the letter-mark of the shelf and the number of the volume in its order on the shelf. e.g. the Additional MS. 28816 bears the labels marked 176 and G.5., indicating that it is the fifth book on the G shelf in Press 176. The Handlists contain lists of the MSS. with their pressmarks. The Shelf-lists contain lists of the presses and shelves with the number of volumes which they contain.'

147 This can be seen on the spines of many Cotton MSS. e.g. Tiberius A. IX; Galba C. VIII, X; D. III, IV. The use of roman numerals for the press numbers was found to be cumbersome and from the mid-nineteenth century arabic numbers started to be used, to denote pressmarks, as can be seen on the spines of Egerton MSS. 873, 1172, 1870. In some cases the word 'Plut.' has been put on the spine by the binder, but no pressmark has been added. Sometimes, this may indicate that the MS. was regarded as Select and kept separately in a locked cupboard, e.g. Harley MS. 2278, Royal MS. 12 C. XIX and Cotton MS. Nero D. VII. In others, the lack of a pressmark may mean that, owing to space problems as a result of Madden's failure to secure storage in the room containing the Grenville Library, the MS. never received a final placing. The practice of incorporating the pressmark in the spine title was apparently introduced at the time of the move from Montagu House: see n. 141 above. In recent years, when MSS. have been rebound, the new title on the spine has (quite correctly) retained the old pressmark information, so that, oddly, the new binding can preserve shelving information that is a hundred years out of date, e.g. Tiberius E. V. Madden experimented with a system whereby 'each row of volumes, as they stand in order on the shelves, should be marked with a large number in white, black or red paint, from no. 1 to the highest number on the shelf, as by this means, if a volume were missing or out of place, it could immediately be detected…': Add. MS. 62022, ff. 17–17v. Many MSS. were numbered in this way, but the experiment was unsuccessful and the painted numbers afterwards washed off.

148 Apparently by Bond. Madden had objected to the Printed Books practice on the grounds that the printed labels easily fell off the spine: Add. MS. 62022, ff. 17v–18.

149 Miller, op. cit., p. 148.

150 MJ, 17 Apr. 1837.

151 MJ, 26 Apr. 1837.

152 Add. MS. 62001, ff. 7v–8. This list, bound up in the wrong order, is now Add. MS. 62576, ff. 36–38v, 27–32v, 21–26v, 16–20v. The notes on the Appendix inserted at ff. 18–19 are apparently later additions.

153 Add. MS. 62001, f. 11.

154 This turned out to contain all the charters from the Lansdowne collection, 658 in number. The Lansdowne Charters were arranged and incorporated in their present form by Madden in 1839: Add. MS. 62072, f. 20. Madden raged against the negligent treatment of this material: 'The then Keeper of Manuscripts [Nares] presuming that it would give him *some trouble*

to catalogue these charters *wisely* determined to NAIL them up ... So much for the zeal of Messrs. Douce, Ellis and Forshall! For my part, I am determined not to suffer a scrap to be put away which I have not thoroughly examined and I am resolved to rescue from oblivion every paper of the least value.': MJ, 24 Nov. 1837, cited by Miller, op. cit., p. 151.

155 Add. MS. 62001, ff. 11v–12v.

156 Ibid., f. 12v; Add. MS. 62072, f. 21. In February 1838, Madden reported that the cartulary had been washed and flattened and placed in a solander case: Add. MS. 62072, f. 20.

157 Madden's collections on the history of Hampshire are Add. MSS. 33278–33285 and Bodleian Library, MSS. Top. Hants. e. 1–7.

158 This was one of the restored Cotton volumes which Madden showed to the Royal Commission on the Museum in 1848, declaring that 'I myself discovered [this MS.] in 1837 in the old Charter Garret as refuse, which had never been seen from the year 1731, when the fire took place, until the time I found it.': *Report from the Commissioners Appointed to Inquire into ... the British Museum* (London, 1850) [hereafter cited as *1850 Royal Commission Report*], no. 3691.

159 Papyrus 37 (1–32). This papyrus was afterwards inlaid and the fragments placed between sheets of glass, although it is not known if Gough was responsible for the inlay. The surviving inlay probably dates from Madden's time; the present glass frames probably date from the late nineteenth century.

160 Madden had met Gough for the first time on 3 Nov. 1837: 'Saw Mr Gough the binder, recommended by Dr Bliss to restore our burnt MSS.': Add. MS. 62001, f. 13.

161 Ibid., f. 38v.

162 Ibid. A despairing letter of 10 Aug. 1839 from Gough to Philip Bliss, thanking Bliss for his help in trying to secure him work, lamenting his failure to obtain it from the British Museum and Record Commission, explaining that it was proving impossible to meet the 'daily wants' of his family, so that he had even been forced to sell his 'own little stock of books', and asking for Bliss's help in obtaining employment as an attendant or messenger in any public office, is Add. MS. 34573, ff. 113–114.

163 MJ, 17 July 1838.

164 MJ, 18 July 1838.

165 Add. MS. 62001, f. 56v.

166 The draft of the report is Add. MS. 62022, ff. 64–66v.

167 Madden listed the thirty-five manuscripts of the first class in his work diary, Add. MS. 62001, f. 59v, as follows: Julius A. I, II; Tiberius A. II, III, IV, VI, VII, XIII; B. III, IV, V, XIII; C. I, II, VI, VII, VIII, IX, X, XI, XII; F. XII; Vitellius A. X, XI, XII, XIII, XV, XVII; C. VI, VIII, XII, XIII; F. XII; Galba E. VIII; and Royal MS. 15 C. XI.

168 In his work diary, Add. MS. 62001, ff. 59v–60, he identified them as follows: Julius B. VI, XIII; C. II, V, IX; D. XI; E. IV, VII; F. VI, VII; Claudius A. I, IV, V, VIII, XII; B. IV, V, VI, VII, IX; C. I, II, III, IX, XI; D. II, VI, VII, VIII, X, XI, XII, XIII; Caligula B. II, III, V, VI, VII, VIII, IX, X; C. I, II, III, IV, VI, VIII, IX; E. VII, IX, X, XI, XII; Tiberius A. V, VI; B. I; D. II, IX; Vitellius A. IV, XVI; B. II, III, IV, V, VII, VIII, XI; C. XI; F. XVIII; Galba B. I, II, IV, V, IX, X, XII; C. V, VI (two parts), IX, X; D. V, VIII; E. VI, X; Nero A. VIII, XII; B. V, VI; C. VIII, XII; D. VI; E. VII; Otho E. II; Vespasian A. V; B. VII; C. XIII, XIV, XVI; E. XVII, XVIII; F. I, III, IV, V, IX, XIII; Titus B. I, II, IV, V, VII, XI; C. II, IV, VI, VIII, IX; Domitian I, VII; Faustina E. I, II, V, VI; Cleopatra E. I, II, III, IV, VI; F. III, V, VI; Appendix XXVII.

169 These were listed by Madden in his work diary, Add. MS. 62001, f. 60, as follows: Tiberius A. IX, X, XI, XIII, XIV, XV; B. IX, XI; D. III, IV, V, VI, X; E. I, II, III, IV, V, VI, VII, IX, X; Otho A. II, VI; B. III, VI; C. I, XIII; D. III, VIII; E. VI; Vitellius A. VIII, IX; C. V; D. II, VII, XVII; E. IX, XIII, XV, XVII, XVIII; F. II, X, XVI, XVII; Galba A. V, X, XV; E. XIII; Caligula D. IV, V, X; Appendix XXX, XXXIII, XXXIV, XXXV, XXXVII, XXXIX, XLI, XLII, XLIII, XLIV, XLV, XLVI; together with four cases containing portions of unidentified MSS. on both paper and vellum. The Royal MSS. 9 B. X, 9 C. IX, X and XI were in a similar condition.

170 Madden identifies this in his draft report as Tiberius A. VI, but this is an Ely cartulary and in any case was placed by Madden in the first class of damaged MSS. Probably Madden meant to write Tiberius E. VI, which is a fourteenth-fifteenth century St Albans register.

171 Add. MS. 62022, ff. 79–79v.
172 The words 'very shamefully some' have been deleted in the draft.
173 Add. MS. 62022, ff. 75–76.
174 MJ, 2 Feb. 1839.
175 Ibid.; Add. MS. 62001, f. 67v.
176 Add. MS. 62023, ff. 9–9v.
177 Add. MS. 62001, f. 91v. Madden noted in his work diary for 10 July 1839 'Also received from the Secretary a Minute of Committee 6 July ordering that the Volumes of State Papers in the Cotton Collection, consisting of about 25 in number, and the other volumes requiring careful binding, to the number of about 100, should without delay, be inlaid, bound and repaired, in the manner recommended by me, and *the progress made reported to the monthly meetings of the Trustees*': Add. MS. 62001, ff. 94–94v.
178 Ibid., ff. 95–95v. The MS. was returned on 5 September.
179 Ibid., ff. 59v–60.
180 Add. MS. 62022, ff. 77v–78 (7 Feb. 1839).
181 Cf. Esdaile, op. cit., p. 83.
182 Add. MS. 62022, ff. 89v–90 (11 Apr. 1839).
183 E.g. see Add. MS. 62013, ff. 60–60v.
184 Add. MS. 62576, ff. 49–49v, and 61–62v, 47.
185 E.g. Tiberius A. VI: Add. MS. 62023, f. 38.
186 Add. MS. 62002, ff. 84–84v.
187 MJ, 3 Apr. 1843.
188 MJ, 5 Apr. 1843. The folios from Otho C. XIII which were found in Forshall's wicker basket can be identified from Madden's annotated copy of his edition of Layamon, now in the Houghton Library, Harvard University, as the bottom corner of f. 135 and the whole of f. 146: E. J. Bryan, 'Sir Frederic Madden's annotations on Layamon's *Brut*', in H. Pilch (ed.), *Orality and Literacy in Early Middle English* (Tübingen, 1996), pp. 21–69. I owe this reference to Prof. J. Roberts.
189 The word 'strongly' has been deleted in the draft.
190 The words 'with the strongest' have been deleted in the draft.
191 Add. MS. 62024, ff. 12v–13.
192 Add. MS. 62002, f. 82.
193 Ibid.
194 Ibid., f. 83.
195 Ibid., ff. 84v–85.
196 MJ, 3 June 1841. Gough's letter accompanying the restored fragments is Eg. MS. 2842, ff. 338–339. Gough writes from Oxford, indicating that the work was done there. Gough notes that 'The Gellatine in those I have had being effectively destroy'd renders it utterly impossible to bring them to their original size and form. Those leaves of greater substance, as the one inlaid is literally baked & reduced to a horny substance. Had I been able to have kept them a little longer, to have given them a longer pressing, they would have had an improved appearance. They will however convey an idea (capable of improvement).'
197 Add. MS. 62024, ff. 20–21.
198 Gough gave this information to Madden in a letter of 8 June: Eg. MS. 2842, f. 340.
199 Add. MS. 62002, f. 87.
200 Ibid., ff. 89v–90.
201 MJ, 19 June 1841.
202 Add. MS. 62003, f. 3.
203 Ibid., ff. 19–19v. Madden's room was probably the former Manuscripts Interview Room, in the angle between the Middle Room and the corridor leading to the eastern block of official residences. Gough was in the basement area reached by the staircase leading from the northeast corner of the Middle Room: cf. Madden's complaints about Gough's accommodation, Add. MS. 62032, ff. 6–7. To make matters worse, despite Madden's entreaties, the Trustees refused to allow Gough a house key: ibid.
204 Add. MS. 62003, ff. 19–19v.
205 Add. MS. 62024, ff. 85–86.
206 Add. MS. 62003, f. 67.
207 Ibid., f. 90.
208 Ibid.
209 Ibid., f. 90v.
210 Add. MS. 62025, ff. 24v–25v.
211 Ibid., ff. 52v, 65v. Gough returned again in November 1844: ibid., f. 88.
212 Add. MS. 62026, f. 14.
213 Add. MSS. 62004, ff. 62, 71; 62007, ff. 50v, 87.
214 Ibid., f. 62.
215 Add. MS. 62576, f. 42.
216 Ibid., f. 42v; cf. n. 18 above.
217 E.g. Julius A. II (Add. MS. 62028, f. 21v), Tiberius C. I, X (ibid., f. 62v), Vitellius A. XII (Add. MS. 62029, f. 36v), Vitellius A. XVIII, XX (ibid., f. 72v).
218 Add. MS. 62009, f. 65v.
219 Add. MS. 62033, f. 56v.
220 MJ, 7 June 1851.

449

221 Add. MS. 62033, ff. 56v–61v.

222 Ibid.

223 Ibid.

224 Cf. Add. MS. 62034, ff. 70v, 78.

225 Ibid., ff. 85v–86.

226 Add. MS. 62035, ff. 3v–4.

227 Add. MS. 62036, f. 46.

228 *1850 Royal Commission Report*, nos. 3690–3692.

229 Add. MS. 18457; *British Museum: List of Autograph Letters, Original Charters, Great Seals and Manuscripts exhibited to the Public in the Department of Manuscripts* (London, 1851), p. 22.

230 The phrase used by Roger Ellis to describe the conservation work of the twentieth-century Keeper of Public Records, Hilary Jenkinson.

231 *British Museum: List of Autograph Letters …* p. 22.

232 See further below, pp. 428–30.

233 Cf. Richard Garnett's comments in his article on Madden in the *D.N.B.*

234 MJ, 10 Mar. 1864.

235 The following is based, unless otherwise stated, on MJ, 10–12 July 1865. Extracts from this account of the bindery fire have been printed from a transcription by Michael Borrie in the journal of the Madden Society, *The Staircase*, ii (Feb. 1992), pp. 1–5.

236 The precise extent of the damage is recorded by Madden in three places: MJ, particularly entries for 11 and 12 July 1865; Add. MSS. 62016, ff. 68–68v; 62041, ff. 36–38v. The returns of Madden's assistants as to which MSS. were in the bindery at the time are also preserved in the Manuscripts Department Archives.

237 E.g. Add. MSS. 25786, 25804, 26106.

238 Add. MS. 62041, ff. 68–68v.

239 MJ, 12 July 1865.

240 A stray leaf, found in a binding at Kassel in 1853, is Kassel, Landesbibliothek, Anhang 19: Ker, op. cit., no. 195.

241 See below, p. 430.

242 M. Borrie, 'Panizzi and Madden', *British Library Journal*, v (1979), p. 33.

243 The resignation memorial is cited from the fair copy in the personal diary, MJ, 12 July 1866.

244 Add. MS. 62017, f. 28v.

245 Madden wrote in his personal diary for 1 Nov. 1837 'Occupied with Mr Holmes arranging about the List of Additions for 1836 but for this and other occupations connected with the

Department of MSS I must refer once for all to a *Notebook* of *business of the Department* I have kept since my appointment as Keeper', presumably directing the reader to his official diaries.

246 Add. MSS. 62001–62017. On the circumstances of the transfer to the British Library of these and other departmental records kept by Madden, now Add. MSS. 62001–62078, see pp. 422–4 below.

247 Add. MSS. 62022–62041.

248 Add. MSS. 62072 ('Memoranda relating to the Department of MSS Brit. Musm. to be used in evidence before the Commrs. of Inquiry 1847'), ff. 21–22; 62075, compiled by Madden in 1847 (f. 1), but relating to the 1830s, so that the material relating to the Cotton MSS. on f. 7 mainly consists of a summary of Forshall's evidence to the 1835–6 Select Committee (Forshall's claim that 'The contents [of the burnt crusts are] of no great value, not worth the expense of unrolling' is marked '*Not true*' by Madden); 62076, ff. 13–14, also apparently compiled *circa* 1847.

249 MJ, 24 July 1849; cf. Add. MS. 62007, f. 36.

250 Add. MS. 62577.

251 Although note that where Gough inlaid a volume, he was not generally responsible for binding it up: see p. 426 below.

252 Add. MS. 62572.

253 Add. MS. 62578.

254 One was compiled for internal departmental use, and remains in the Departmental Reference library. The other was intended for the Reading Rooms and is now Add. MS. 62573. The facsimile in *Smith* (1984 ed.) is said (p. 12) to have been taken from Add. MS. 62573, but in fact it is a reproduction of the volume in the Departmental Library, as can be seen from the pencil annotation in the entry for Otho A. XII, which does not appear in Add. MS. 62573. On the circumstances of the compilation of these volumes, see further p. 433 below.

255 Add. MS. 62576. A description of this volume in chronological order is Appendix II.

256 Add. MS. 62575.

257 Copies are preserved in the Manuscripts Department Archives.

258 M. Clapinson and T. D. Rogers, *Summary Catalogue of post-Medieval Western Manuscripts in the Bodleian Library, Oxford* (Oxford, 1991), nos. 39761–39807.

259 Manuscripts Department Archives, Minutes of Acquisitions 1914–1930, f. 160.

260 G. F. Waagen, *Treasures of Art in Great Britain*, 4 vols. (London, 1854–7), vol. i, p. 97.

261 J. Zupitza (ed.), *Beowulf*, E.E.T.S., O.S., lxxvii (1882), p. vi.

262 E.g. J. G. Nichols (ed.), *The Diary of Henry Machyn*, Camden Society, xlii (1848), pp. xii–xiii; H. G. Hewlett (ed.), *The Flowers of History by Roger Wendover*, Rolls Series (1886), vol. i, p. viii.

263 Richard Sims, *Handbook to the Library of the British Museum* (London, 1854), pp. 26–7.

264 Edward Edwards, *Memoirs of Libraries including a Handbook of Library Economy* (London, 1859), vol. i, p. 433.

265 Esdaile, op. cit., p. 230.

266 Miller, op. cit., p. 151.

267 Kiernan, *Beowulf*, p. 69.

268 Ibid., p. 70.

269 Kevin S. Kiernan, 'The State of the *Beowulf* manuscript 1882–1983', *Anglo-Saxon England*, xiii (1984), pp. 23–42; idem, *The Thorkelin Transcripts of Beowulf*, ed. cit., pp. 45–6.

270 Kevin S. Kiernan, 'The Digital Preservation, Restoration and Dissemination of Medieval Manuscripts' in A. Okersen (ed.), *Scholarly Publishing on the Electronic Networks* (Washington, D.C., 1994). This paper is also available in electronic form, with colour illustrations, for Internet users with a World Wide Web client at the following U.R.L.: http://www.uky.edu/~kiernan/BL/kportico.html

271 Add. MS. 62577, ff. 24v–25, and Madden's account of the restoration of the manuscript on the flyleaf.

272 The description is actually by Planta. Madden was misled by an ambiguous turn of phrase in Planta's description of the MS. There is no indication in Smith that the MS. was kept loose before the fire.

273 Vitellius F. V, flyleaf.

274 *The Diary of Henry Machyn*, ed. cit., p. xii.

275 The MS. was unfortunately rebound in 1958, but the inlays are still Tuckett's original work.

276 Many of these readings can be inferred from the main text, but they nevertheless illustrate the way in which fibre optic light can be used to read concealed text. For example, on f. 102v, in the description of the funeral of Sir Anthony St Leger, in the first line the word 'day' can be made out at the beginning, while in the second line 'of the' can be read before 'garter'. In the next line, 'of' can be read before Kent, and the 'C' of Crest can be clearly seen.

277 Vitellius F. V, flyleaf.

278 Ed. cit.

279 Add. MS. 62577, ff. 24v–25. Neither of these early Madden restorations survive intact, although the inlay in both cases is the original 1834 work. Vitellius F. IV was rebound in May 1914, and the work on the so-called Vitellius E. VIII was destroyed when the leaves were moved to Otho D. IV in 1865.

280 Thus, Tiberius B. V was 'inlaid by Gough and bound by Tuckett': Add. MS. 62025, f. 13v. A similar division of labour was noted for Tiberius C. VI (Add. MS. 62025, f. 24v), while Madden notes that Tiberius A. XI, E. IV, Vitellius A. XIII and D. XVII were 'inlaid by Gough and three of the number bound by Tuckett' (Add. MS. 62026, f. 80). See also Add. MS. 62006, ff. 10–10v, 34, 54–54v, 72. Kiernan, *Beowulf*, p. 69, attributes the binding of Vitellius A. XV to Gough, but presumably the leaves, reported as inlaid by Gough in August 1845, were also subsequently bound up by Tuckett after rearrangement of their order by Madden: Add. MSS. 62026, f. 71v; 62027, f. 2v; MJ, 7 Aug. 1845 ('Gough is getting on nicely with the restoration of the injured *vellum* Cotton MSS. and brought me up today the Bede of the 8th century, Tib. A. XIV, and the Beowulf and other Saxon treatises, Vitell. A. XV. both inlaid and perfectly repaired and preserved').

281 For example, on 28 Jan. 1844, Madden 'found several portions of Tiberius E. IX and gave the whole in Tuckett's hands' (Add. MS. 62004, f. 27). The leaves came back in April, and Madden spent three days arranging them, but his official diary merely states that he was 'Employed in arranging Tiberius E. IX'. His personal diary is equally uninformative.

282 MJ, 26 May 1854.

283 Add. MS. 62573, f. 81.

284 MJ, 29 Mar. 1845; cf. Add. MS. 62004, f. 71v.

285 Add. MS. 62026, f. 66v.

286 Add. MS. 62004, f. 82.

287 A full study of this MS. is forthcoming: Budny, Page and Verey, op. cit. Much of the following is based on Timothy R. Graham's account of the restoration of this MS. in the forthcoming volume. I am grateful to Mr Graham and Dr

Simon Keynes for valuable discussions on the nineteenth-century history of this manuscript.

288 Casley, op. cit., pl. xii, no. 4.

289 Add. MS. 62576, f. 62. A question mark after this figure has been deleted, suggesting the leaves were in such a bad condition that it was difficult to establish how many there were.

290 MJ, 3 Jan. 1855; Keynes, art. cit.

291 See n. 299 below.

292 E.g. ff. 16, 20, 24, 26, 28, 29, 31, 37, 39, 43, 55, 56, 59, 60, 64.

293 Add. MSS. 62577, ff. 19v–20; 62006, ff. 83–83v; 62572, f. 63.

294 E.g. ff. 37, 39, 43, 54, 55.

295 Add. MS. 62006, f. 83v; cf. the adjustments of the number of folios in the volume given by Madden in Add. MS. 62572, f. 63.

296 Ff. 3, 5, 14, 36. These were given by Madden the starred numbers 2*, 3*, 11*, 32* respectively.

297 On whom, see further below, p. 429.

298 See n. 219 above.

299 Otho A. I was further damaged in the bindery fire, but it nevertheless seems likely that the six leaves placed by Forshall with Otho C. V were the present ff. 1–4 and 6–7. They all show evidence of Forshallian 'notching'.

300 Add. MS. 62035, f. 48. I owe this reference to Simon Keynes and Timothy Graham.

301 It is also possible that the starred folios were late additions made in the course of Madden's initial arrangement in 1848, and that the fragments identified by Hamilton were small pieces inserted in the existing inlays. The 1963 rebinding makes it impossible to establish the exact character of the 1855 rearrangement.

302 The refoliation of the Cotton MSS. was part of a general refoliation of all MSS. in the British Museum at this time, apparently prompted by the theft of an unfoliated leaf from a MS.: see further Bond's *Memoranda* in the Departmental Archives. This refoliation has caused endless confusion ever since, but was essential to fulfil the fundamental requirements that foliation should ensure the security of all leaves in a MS. and provide a simple means of denoting each leaf. One refoliation that has caused particular confusion is that of Vitellius A. XV, since Zupitza's facsimile was produced before the MS. was refoliated, and the old foliation has continued to be used: see further Kiernan, *Beowulf*, pp. 85–110. In this case, matters were

further confused by the removal of f. 1 from Vitellius A. XV to Royal MS. 13 D. I* in 1913. Kiernan argues for the reinstatement of an amended form of the earlier foliation, but does not take account of the fact that the refoliation was not intended to represent an official view of the structure of the MS., but formed part of a completely new system of foliation for the entire collection, designed to improve the security of the MSS. In view of the interest that the refoliation of Vitellius A. XV has aroused, it is perhaps worth noting that foliation was at this time undertaken by the attendants who then performed low grade clerical duties (cf. Kiernan, *Beowulf*, p. 71, n. 9). The attendants who refoliated the Beowulf MS. in June 1884 can easily be identified from the annual return of progress for that year in the Departmental Archives. The actual foliation was done by Frederick John Mackney, the attendant who had special responsibility for keeping the register of artists copying miniatures and superintended the use of select and other MSS. The foliation was checked by George Gatfield. These two were responsible for refoliating many of the Cotton MSS.

303 Add. MS. 62007, f. 81v.

304 Add. MS. 62011, f. 14.

305 N. E. S. A. Hamilton, *Inquisitio Comitatus Cantabrigiensis* (London, 1876). The MS. is Tiberius A. VI, ff. 71–98v. Hamilton was perhaps involved in arranging the MS. when it was rebound by Tuckett in March 1862: Add. MS. 62577, ff. 6v–7.

306 J. H. Round, *Feudal England* (1964 ed.), p. 17. Round showed that this document was known to Philip Carteret Webb, but nevertheless praised Hamilton's 'noble edition' which in his view represented 'an extraordinary amount of minute wearisome labour': ibid., pp. 17–18.

307 V. H. Galbraith, *Domesday Book: its Place in Administrative History* (Oxford, 1974), *passim*.

308 Hamilton, op. cit., pp. x–xi.

309 Ibid. Hamilton notes that he 'had the advantage of discussing the matter with Sir Henry Ellis himself, and was informed that the only explanation was then possible for him to give was this:- that he (Ellis) had directed an amanuensis to transcribe for him whatever related to the Domesday Survey from MS. Tiberius A. vi., and that the transcriber, by some strange oversight, having omitted the

most important portion, Ellis must have supposed that the MS itself had by that time ceased to contain it, and deferred further inquiry into the matter to a future occasion, which, owing to accident or forgetfulness, never arrived.': ibid., p. x. One of Madden's motives in encouraging Hamilton to print the newly-identified text may have been the hope that it would embarrass Ellis.

310 Add. MS. 62010, f. 60v.

311 Ibid., f. 68v.

312 Add. MS. 62015, f. 42v: 'Mr Hamilton returned to me the injured leaves of the Saxon MSS. Otho A. VIII, Otho B. X, Otho B. XI arranged as far as possible' [11 Feb. 1863]. Note, however, that the final responsibility for the arrangement of the volumes was Madden's: 'Prepared Otho B.X, Otho B. XI & the Saxon fragments for the binder' [13 May 1863]: Add. MS. 62015, f. 60. .

313 Ker, op. cit., nos. 168 (where the leaves of the Life of St Machutus in Otho A. VIII are described as 'quite out of order'), 175, 177, 178, 180, 181; D. Yerkes, *The Old English life of St Machutus*, Toronto Old English Series, ix (Toronto, 1984).

314 MJ, 12 May 1863. The five leaves of Boethius misidentified by Hamilton are probably the present Otho A. VI, ff. 63–67, which were inlaid with paper from a different stock to the rest of the Boethius. The paper used to inlay these additional leaves was more acid than the older stock and is now discoloured. In Hamilton's favour, it should be noted that he corrected the error of Madden and Forshall in placing leaves from Otho A. I with Otho C. V. Moreover, the quality of the arrangement of the burnt leaves, even those undertaken by Madden, was often very uneven. Francis Hingeston in his edition of Capgrave's *De Illustribus Henricis*, Rolls Series (London, 1858), p. l, n. 1, notes that in Tiberius A. VIII, Capgrave's presentation copy to Henry VI, 'The binder has unfortunately misplaced many of the leaves, so as to render it no easy matter for a reader to hunt his way through the MS.' The MS. was inlaid by Gough in 1848, but responsibility for the arrangement probably rests with Madden.

315 E.g. Otho B. X, ff. 26–27, where the leaves are very obviously upside down, even under ordinary daylight. Hamilton also worked on Otho D. VII (Add. MS. 62009, f. 89v) and

Vitellius A. VII (MJ, 3 Apr. 1854). Vitellius A. VII was, however, reworked by Maunde Thompson nine years later: Add. MS. 62015, ff. 62–62v.

316 Add. MS. 62014, f. 83v.

317 Add. MS. 62015, f. 59v.

318 Ibid., f. 62.

319 Ibid., f. 62v; MJ, 1 June 1863.

320 MJ, 1 June 1863.

321 MJ, 2 June 1863.

322 Ibid.

323 MJ, 30 Sept. 1864. The misidentification is not explicitly attributed to Thompson, but the diary entry makes it evident that Madden was at that time discussing the Cotton materials with Thompson.

324 Henry Bradshaw, *Collected Papers* (Cambridge, 1889), p. 467.

325 The note correcting the identification in the interleaved copy of Smith in the Manuscripts Department Reference Library, reproduced in *Smith* (1984 ed.), pointing out the misidentification is apparently in Warner's hand.

326 Susan Sontag, *The Volcano Lover* (London, 1993), p. 347.

327 Add. MS. 43502, ff. 210v, 217.

328 In Ayscough's charter catalogue (Add. MS. 43502), Madden notes the following as Harleian: XVI. 11–16, XXIV. 25, XXIV. 28, XXVI. 1–16. XXVI. 29 is also possibly Harleian. Ayscough also managed to put Cottonian material in the Harley collection. On 23 Apr. 1855, Madden 'carried into execution what I have long contemplated, viz. the remarking of the rolls numbered by Ayscough as Harleian, EE from 1 to 21 inclusive. The whole of these are Cottonian, with the exception of three and I have had these remarked as follows: Harl. EE 1–5 made Cott. XIII. 31–35. Harl. EE. 6 made Harl. DD. 3. Harl. EE 7–19 made Cott. XIII. 36–48. Harl. EE 20, 21 made Harl. DD 4, 5.': Add. MS. 62010, f. 69v.

329 MJ, 7 Apr. 1852. Attempts were made by Madden to improve the situation. Some charters were removed from the Cartae Miscellaneae Addendae to the main Cotton charter sequence, so that Cotton Charter XVII. 33 was renumbered XI. 63. Other renumberings correct duplication of numbers by Ayscough, e.g. IV. 20, now XXIX. 41, and X. 10, now XXV. 13.

330 Add. MS. 43502, f. 243. On the confusion

between the Cotton and Harley Charters, see
further A. G. Watson, 'Sir Simonds D'Ewes's
collection of charters, and a note on the charters
of Sir Robert Cotton', *Journal of the Society of
Archivists*, ii (1962), pp. 247–54.

331 On 28 May 1855, Madden inserted in the
charter catalogue notes of the following Cotton
charters which had apparently been restored:
X. 18–21; XV. 27–52; XVI. 30–74; and XVIII.
49, 50: Add. MS. 62010, f. 74.

332 MJ, 13 Sept. 1859.

333 A. N. L. Munby, *Portrait of an Obsession* (New
York, 1967), p. 190.

334 Add. MS. 62011, ff. 60–60v; cf. MJ, 6 Nov.
1856. On 22 Jan. 1857, Madden noted that he
had 'Received a minute 10 Jan. to say that the
Minister at the Hague had been instructed to
endeavour to recover the Cotton MSS. at
Utrecht.': Add. MS. 62011, f. 74.

335 Nicholas Harris Nicolas, *Observations on the
State of Historical Literature* (London, 1830),
p. 75.

336 Ibid.

337 Ibid., pp. 76–7.

338 *1836 Select Committee Report*, nos. 3675–80.

339 Ibid., nos. 4389, 4397.

340 The limitations of Planta are succinctly described in C. G. C. Tite, 'The Cotton Appendix and the Cotton Fragments', *The Library*,
xv (1993), p. 52.

341 MJ, 6 Dec. 1861.

342 MJ, 5 June 1861. Madden records that, once
again, 'No notice was taken by the Trustees.'

343 The draft corrected by Madden and with an
imposing calligraphic title page is Add. MS.
62578.

344 Add. MS. 62573, f. 1 and facing page.

345 Ibid., page facing f. 1.

346 Note, however, that the volume reproduced in
Smith (1984 ed.) is that in the Manuscripts
Department Reference Library, not, as stated

in the introduction, Add. MS. 62573: see n. 254
above. There is another copy of this description
of the state of the Cotton Library in the
Reference Library, apparently dating from the
1880s.

347 For example, it does not record the rearrangement of some volumes of State Papers in the
early part of this century.

348 See further Tite, art. cit., pp. 52–5.

349 *A Guide to a Select Exhibition of Cottonian
Manuscripts in celebration of the Tercentenary of
the Death of Sir Robert Cotton, 6 May 1931*
(British Museum, 1931), p. 10.

350 All the following is based on some loose typed
sheets in the Manuscripts Department Reference Library, 'Rules for Cotton Catalogue'
and 'Provisional List of Assignments for Cotton
Catalogue. Julius-Caligula'.

351 *Catalogue of Additions ... 1921–1925*, p. xii, and
Catalogue of Additions ... 1926–1930, p. xiii; see
further Nigel Ramsay, 'Towards a New Catalogue of the Cotton Manuscripts', *Historical
Research* (forthcoming).

352 The printed parliamentary returns of progress
are in the Manuscripts Department Archives.
According to these, during 1866 the leaves of
Tiberius A. VI, Otho B. III, IX and C. XI
were arranged. In 1867, the leaves of Otho B.
IV, Tiberius B. XI, Galba A. XIX, Otho A.
IX, XI, XII were arranged. Much of the work
was therefore concerned with remedying damage caused by the 1865 bindery fire.

353 E.g. ff. 46, 47, 49. Other folios, e.g. ff. 33–36,
are inlaid in paper from a different stock, and
show no discoloration.

354 E.g. Otho A. XII, Vitellius A. VII.

355 David Dumville, *Liturgy and the Ecclesiastical
History of late Anglo-Saxon England* (Woodbridge, 1992), p. 79.

356 Sontag, op. cit., p. 347.

INDEX

Illustrations are cited in italic

460